MAKING CONTEMPORARY ART

HOW TODAY'S ARTISTS THINK AND WORK

Thames & Hudson

MAKING CONTEMPORARY ART

HOW TODAY'S ARTISTS THINK AND WORK

Linda Weintraub

TABLE OF CONTENTS

* These chapters include an interview with the artist

Why am I an artist?

Who is my audience?

How can I communicate with this audience?

What is art's function in society?

Never in all the history of art-making have these questions been greeted with so many credible answers. Today's artists typically meet in cafes and then return to their studios where one may plug into a bank of computers while the other sorts scavenged debris and a third sketches the origins of the universe. The work of one may ponder eternity, the other may instigate political protest, and the third may conjure futuristic fantasies. Art-making has become so inclusive that even the manners of being innovative have proliferated. Only some precedent-defying artists expel cherished traditions. Others may innovate by rejecting the assumption that originality is a hallmark of great art. This assumption is so widespread that artists who preserve historic styles can also be labeled as rebels. Thus, contemporary art embraces the maverick and the traditionalist. No topic, no medium, no process, no intention, no professional protocols, and no aesthetic principles are exempt from the field of art. Also missing are preexisting standards, predetermined measures of success, and ready-made definitions of art. Such artistic license grants to artists an exceptional opportunity. They are free to originate new cultural possibilities. Indeed, they are uniquely unencumbered by methods, rules, and requirements. As such, they are our culture's "free radicals," constitutionally primed to disrupt states of equilibrium and initiate change. *In the Making: Creative Options for Contemporary Art* addresses six crucial aspects of this vast and relentlessly expanding domain of artistic freedom: scoping an audience, sourcing inspiration, crafting an artistic "self," expressing an artistic attitude, choosing a mission, and measuring success.

This expanded domain of art production can be traced to a broader cultural circumstance. Local customs of all kinds are being pummeled by the incursions of competing traditions from around the globe and across the spans of time. Imported cultures pervade books, television, exhibitions, music, home furnishings, cuisines, advertisements, health care, college curricula, religious practices, and the Internet. Each augments the stockpile of artistic prototypes. Some local artistic traditions are malleable and accommodate new influences. Others become hopeless misfits and succumb to obsolescence. Artistic responses to this mixing and matching of cultural traditions range from decrying the contamination of cultural pedigrees to welcoming the rich diversity they afford. Both responses demonstrate that the artistic models are no longer limited to artists' ancestors and their places of birth. Being a "traditional" artist now requires choosing from a profusion of cultural options, all available for adoption in part, in combination, or in their entirety.

It seems that contemporary culture is ripe for rapid and drastic change. Free radicals are reproducing in the arts as they are in physical matter. Because artists are uniquely capable of both initiating and adapting to change, art forms are mutating all around us. As in biochemistry, evolutionary development depends on free radicals. But evolutionary development also entails a disruption of the status quo. Progressive art can be unsettling. It can be threatening. Its long-term affects can be gradual or precipitous, superficial or dramatic. Selection rules in culture, as in the biological realm. Some artworks pass on without effect, while others produce a temporary deviation from a norm, and a few cause irreversible mutations in the DNA of an entire culture. Art can have profound consequence.

The preceding paragraphs address the potential impact of artistic freedom upon a society. But how does this freedom impact the artists themselves? *In the Making* presents forty remarkable responses to this question. Amid the clamor of their discordant voices, two general truths can be heard: free radical status escalates artistic responsibility and artistic challenge. Current possibilities far exceed any single artist's capacity to engage them. Indeed, every known way of making art ever undertaken in all of history is included in today's inventory of creative options. Thus, choices must be made. This has had a profound effect upon the quantity and diversity of skills needed to become an artist today. In addition to such conventional forms of artistic talent as visual acuity, manual dexterity, sensitivity, intelligence, ingenuity, and perseverance, contemporary artists must also be able to make judicious choices from a limitless inventory of alternatives. A decisive aspect of the creative act involves choosing a place amid possibilities that are as bountiful as they are eclectic and chaotic. Even this process entails choices. In staking the territory they wish to occupy, artists may be gluttons or ascetics, connoisseurs or commoners. Furthermore, no decision demands a lifelong commitment. Relationships between artists and their career choices may be lifelong and monogamous, or sequentially monogamous, polygamous, or promiscuous. But artists' options even exceed selecting precedents. Free access to the past is amplified by freedom to augment the catalogue of creative options by contributing something new.

Boundless artistic possibility is a modern phenomenon, but its inception can be traced to the progressive decline of a powerful, historic, international institution. In Italy, this institution was terminated by a papal decree issued in the year 1539. In England it disappeared in the seventeenth century. In France it concluded with the Revolution in 1791. In Japan it met its demise in 1868. In India it dissolved after British rule was established. German and Austrian versions were abolished in the nineteenth century. In China and in the Muslim Middle East it persisted until the early decades of the twentieth century. Each of these dates marks the dissolution of the medieval guild system.

Typically, each guild monopolized the production of a specific form of art or craft. Membership was compulsory for anyone carrying out this calling. Those members whose work attained standards stipulated by the guild were designated as masters. In order to enter the profession it was mandatory to serve as an apprentice to a master. The sum paid by apprentices to masters for their training was stipulated. The duration of this training was delineated. The conditions of work were regulated. Rules even governed working processes. Those who had completed their training but had not attained master status were employed by masters and classified as journeymen. Raw materials were either bought by a delegated purchaser or purchased under the supervision of overseers. Tools were subjected to the approval of quality testers and then distributed equally to all masters. Use of special tools was prohibited. Conspicuous self-promotion was banned. Output was limited. How strictly were these rules enforced? A "Statute of the White Tawyers" that was issued in London in the year 1346 provides one example: "If any member disobeys these statutes and is convicted by his fellows, he is to be fined 2 shillings the first time, 3 shillings and 4 pence the second, 6 shillings and 8 pence the third, and 10 shillings the fourth. For the fourth offense he shall be excluded from the trade."

In addition to regulating production, guilds also guarded their monopolies by governing the sale and distribution of the products created by their members. Consumers had no choice but to purchase standardized goods at preset prices. Only items that passed guild inspection were permitted to enter the market. Prices were set at a uniform sum.

Security and confidence were the twin advantages of guild regulation. Guild members benefited because they were able to anticipate both the desires of their patrons and the principles of excellence by which their work would be judged. Skill became the defining collective social principle. Competence was certain to be rewarded. Guilds glorified workers who demonstrated compliance and diligence. Furthermore, because guilds limited entry into each profession, artists and artisans were protected from the pressures of competition. Guilds also offered security and confidence to consumers. The strict rules established by each guild simplified the consumers' task of discriminating between products and determining a fair price. Buyers knew they would receive quality for their money because all objects on the market honored the standards of the guild.

Guilds collapsed one by one, at different times in each geographical location. Typically their demise coincided with the improvement of communications, the expansion of trade, the influx of foreign-made goods. The guilds, with their rigorous controls and emphasis on stability and quality, were not equipped to cope with diversification of products available for sale and expanding methods of production. The collapse of the tidy guild system gave rise to the messy, diffuse scenario that characterizes today's art scene. This convoluted evolution can be summarized as follows:

PRODUCTION: Once a single regulating institution ceases to monopolize art production, entry into the art profession is no longer dependent upon the judgment of experts. Instead, becoming an artist is simply a matter of self-declaration. Artists forfeit guild protection as they gain freedom from guild regulation. Likewise, they sacrifice identifiable goals as they acquire opportunities to experiment. Self-appointed artists are free to invent their own artistic standards, their own technical means of production, their own manners of expression, and their own entrepreneurial strategies for distributing their creations. Meanwhile, there are two less favorable byproducts of free entry: the population of artists increases and competition becomes an unavoidable component of the art profession.

CONSUMPTION: When the guilds collapsed, the aristocracy, the monarchy, and the church ceased being the exclusive consumers of art. The emergence of the bourgeois class added a new sector to the art market since the middle class, too, desired an artistically adorned mode of life. It delighted in worldly values that never appeared among the artistic virtues sponsored by the guilds. As a result, consumer taste for art shifted from monolithic to pluralistic and from predictable to erratic.

THE ARTIST: Artists had no choice but to participate in an open market, creating works of art that were not commissioned prior to their production. They speculated on their own fortunes by creating work knowing neither who would become the owner, nor the physical setting in which their work would be installed, nor the price it might fetch, nor even if it would ever be sold. At the same time, they discovered that compliance with respected conventions no longer assured success. In fact, nonconformity often inspired the greatest degree of admiration. Furthermore, delays between production and success often meant that artists died in obscurity and then earned post-mortem fame. A great chasm separated the most successful artists from the majority of their colleagues. Artists faced uncertain fates.

THE MARKET: Works of art that earned the admiration of influential people did not merely maintain their value; these works increased in value. Buying and selling art provided opportunities for financial gain. Furthermore, collecting attracted those who used art as a status symbol, proclaiming their wealth and social prestige and personal taste. A new profession, the art dealer, came into existence to service this commercial potential. In addition, a new institution, the art gallery, was established to formalize this function. Commerce became integral to art production. As a commodity, marketability was added to aesthetic merit, technique, and thematic relevance as components of art.

CONCLUSION: The dissolution of the guild system is commonly credited with catapulting artistic freedom. But even this powerful narrative cannot encapsulate today's vast inventory of creative options. Artists are also propelled to optimize their free radical status by the accelerated pace of new technologies, fluctuations in economic or political or spiritual tempers of society, and personal experiences. Border crossings remain a primary stimulus to artistic change, but even artists who never leave home experience culture shifts due to the bustle of immigrations and emigrations of people, goods, and ideas. Artistic stimuli dart across continents and ricochet across oceans, setting the conditions for, and accelerating the tempo of, artistic reform.

Every option presented in this book is operational because, long ago, art ceased being a foreordained effort yielding a predetermined result. The fallout from the collapse of the guild system remains in evidence today. Risk, sacrifice, and improbability are fixtures of the art profession in the current era. Art is such an unregulated field of endeavor that any disposition within the catalogue of human conceptual and emotional responses can be released into art. The gates of entry are flung wide open. No theme is disallowed because it is too sentimental, too vulgar, or too sacred. Even neglected possibilities are not discarded. They are simply relegated to a holding pen awaiting reactivation by future generations of artists. Art seems to glory in the flush. This book is dedicated to each individual who participates in these accountings. Whether you are among the observers or the producers of art, you have selected to engage in an activity that offers neither guarantees, nor defined measures of value, nor supervision, nor even a definition of itself. Yet compensation is granted. It comes in the form of unfettered freedom and the opportunity to enrich human experience through your efforts.

SCOPING AN AUDIENCE

Eve Andrée Laramée, *Secret History: Yves Fissi-ault, Artist of the Cold War Era* (1997),
installation view, ink and gouache on paper,
collage, ink on varnished linen, oil on
canvas, found and constructed devices,
photographs, suitcases, clothing, artifacts
and objects, and text. Courtesy of the artist.

Production and consumption comprise complementary aspects of art's cultural course. On the production side, artists transform the private zones of their imaginations, insights, knowledge, emotions, and intuitions into forms that are transmittable to others. On the consumption side, viewers not only have the option of purchasing works of art, they also consume art each time they delight in it, learn from it, and identify with it, or reject it, criticize it, and condemn it. Without the crucial linkage between the creator and recipient, art is stuck in a state of pure potential, like a battery that is fully charged but not in service. As a result, the artistic process really doesn't culminate until a recipient tunes in to a work's power source and receives its charge. By devoting the first chapter to audiences, this book honors the fact that viewers are as essential to art's consequence as are artists and works of art. Furthermore, it proposes that the audience's expectations, values, tastes, and concerns are not necessarily after-effects or postscripts. They can affect artists' conceptual initiation of works and their subsequent fabrication of them.

Textbooks examining the history of art, like the living room walls on which paintings are hung, provide innumerable examples of two equally effective approaches to the relationship between artists and their audiences. One might be known as "populism," which typically refers to a common majority. Its antithesis is "exclusivism," a privileged minority. Majority and minority are quantitative designations, but they are not necessarily indicators of an artist's impact. Since influencing a few young artists can have the same resonance on the future of culture as brisk sales to the mass market, artists representing both camps are eligible for acclaim. Furthermore, "privileged" is a qualitative word that does not belong solely to exclusive audiences. Although unsophisticated viewers may not comprehend fine-art precedents and intellectual theories, sophisticated viewers may lack the necessary background to recognize an artist's references to ghetto experiences and popular culture. Today's artists dip into such a well-stocked storehouse of artistic themes and styles that most art viewers take turns being knowing recipients or baffled outsiders. As a result, many works of art provoke contradictory responses. A style may constitute beauty to some viewers and ugliness to others. Topics may seem suitable or offensive. Imagery may be exciting or banal. Manners of expression may be familiar or exotic. Such audience heterogeneity is not unique to art. Indeed, it is an abiding characteristic of contemporary culture where the technological sophistication of cable networking, satellite transmissions, and the Internet has made it possible to multiply and divide audiences. "Consumers" of art are being treated to the same abundance of choices available to consumers of coffee, aspirin, and sneakers—contemporary artworks can be plain and fancy, cheap and expensive, conventional and unusual.

The reception of a work of art is not only subject to the particular values and expectations of individual viewers. The artist's task is further complicated by the need to contend with expectations that derive from shared cultural experiences. For example, entertainment, sports, fashion, and politics have progressively amplified the aesthetics of the visual and aural environment. More, louder, faster, brighter, and bigger are guiding principles for the designers of today's media-dominated environment. As a result, contemporary artists are challenged to attract the interest of a population that is bombarded by powerful stimuli throughout the waking hours of every day. Capturing the attention of the viewer is the initial challenge for the artist. But a successful linkage merely enables passage into the next zone of interaction—a multifarious and unpredictable response triggered by the artwork. Audience response is hardly exhausted by the refrains "I like it" and "I don't like it." This bilateral opposition suggests that an art response is as simple as an on/off switch. Responses to art seem more accurately compared to a cockpit control panel with its elaborate array of devices monitoring numerous simultaneous variables. A Direction Dial might point to the location of a response, revealing if it is emotional, intellectual, intuitive, sensual, or neutral. A Pleasure/Pain Indicator might register enthusiasm or abhorrence. A Comprehensibility Dial might specify instantaneous recognition, eventual comprehension after prolonged analysis, or permanent confusion. A Temporal Dial might compute how long the memory of the work of art survived. Each and every one of these dials could be accompanied by an Intensity Dial to measure the gradations of response from disinterested, to mild, to extreme.

Decisions regarding whom to affect, how to affect, and where this affecting transpires can occur at any juncture within the creative process. Some artists consciously design both the artwork and the means by which it interacts with an audience. In these cases, genius, innovation, insight, vision, perseverance, and sensitivity are applied to determining an artwork's consumption as well as its production. Other artists postpone these concerns until the work of art has been completed. A third group ignores this entire discussion and surrenders the authority position. No rule is violated when they allocate the public presentation of their work to a representative or even to happenstance. Thus marketing, promotion, and advertising can either be instigated by the artist or the artist's representative. In either case, they can reflect exclusivist or populist motives. Furthermore, they can serve the egotistical desire to bolster personal fame, or an altruistic desire to advance social awareness of a worthy cause. But no matter how the process of linking an artwork and an audience is conducted, exhibiting successfully usually means that the artwork and the audience are tuned and synchronized.

One-for-All

Thomas Kinkade

Born 1958 Placerville, California
1976–1978 University of California, Berkeley, fine art
1976–1978 Center College of Design, Pasadena, fine art
Lives and works in Los Gatos, California

Thomas Kinkade is an artist who, instead of working in isolation, is associated with a corporate empire that facilitates the accomplishment of his goal—to spread his vision of peace and harmony throughout the culture. Kinkade is devoted to creating art that appeals to the majority. But even more attention is directed to creating distribution outlets to realize this ambition. His work not only satisfies popular tastes and expectations, it employs marketing channels beyond the confines of the art world, occupying popular sites that promote mass-produced housewares, collectibles, and books. Accountants, marketers, manufacturers, publicists, distributors, and lawyers contribute to realizing Kinkade's mission.

It is no exaggeration to report that the painter Thomas Kinkade is dedicated to making his art a presence in every American household. Indeed, he has almost succeeded. He claims that one in every twenty American homes has a Kinkade work displayed in it. By aspiring to become "a leading art-based brand," he epitomizes the artist for whom popular approval is the all-abiding principle. Kinkade is the self-proclaimed "Painter of Light." But he might also be called the Sun King of Art since throngs of people are captivated by the otherworldly glow that suffuses his favorite subjects: cozy cottages, blossom-bursting gardens, picturesque waterfalls, quaint arched bridges, and distant mountain vistas. The incandescent radiance of his paintings is formidable, amplified to spill beyond their frames and into the living and working environments of their owners, who are thereby infused by a perpetual state of rapture. This at least is the assertion made in his promotional material; it declares that Kinkade's work appeals to an all-pervasive impulse, the "nesting" instinct.

Having created several hundred hand-painted images, Kinkade's output is measurable according to standards set by industry and commerce, not art. Still, he cannot produce enough originals to satisfy his evangelical ambition. He explains his mission: "I represent the forefront of an entirely new trend, a populist movement that takes images people understand and creates an iconography for our era.... *We* are creating an avalanche of imagery that is impacting the world."[1] The use of the word "we" is significant. Paintings are usually one-of-a-kind artworks painted one-at-a-time by a single creator. Kinkade's paintings, however, form the basis of multitudes of multiples—proofs, editions, and "collections" spawn an array of subcategories. Proofs are categorized by the following designations: Artist, Exhibitor, Gallery, Publisher, International Publisher, and Studio proofs. Editions are identified by another set of defining terms: Portfolio, Renaissance, Studio Proof Paper, and Master editions. Collections are listed as Plein Air, Studio Impressionism, French Impressionism, Brushwork, Classics, Accessories, Magnet, Media, Nightlight, and Photo Frame collections. In addition, Kinkade productions include "Inspirational" and "Collectors" prints.

This array of products is marketed to the public via an extensive network of over 300 independently owned Thomas Kinkade stores, known as the Signature Thomas Kinkade Galleries.

SCOPING AN AUDIENCE

Thomas Kinkade, *Everett's Cottage* (1998), dimensions variable, canvas lithograph. ©2002 Thomas Kinkade, Media Arts Group, Inc., Morgan Hill, CA.

His dissemination strategies also include *Light Posts for Living*, a book illustrated with Kinkade paintings that celebrates, according to its promotional literature, "American pastimes and values." *A Child's Garden of Verses* proffers this inspirational message to the youngest members of the public. These titles are just two (of 127) books illustrated and/or written by Kinkade. But Kinkade does not limit opportunities of engaging with his work to viewing and reading. It is possible to sit on a Kinkade, sleep on a Kinkade, and eat on a Kinkade. A licensing agreement with La-Z-Boy Furniture resulted in the production of upholstered and wood furniture decorated with Kinkade images; similar arrangments are in place for the manufacture of home decorative accessories; and Goodwin Weavers is licensed to create a full line of Thomas Kinkade pillows, placemats, table runners, wall tapestries, and bell pulls. Items emblazoned with his images also include vases, trays, mugs, and ornaments that are distributed through gift shops, department stores, and catalog retailers. Furthermore, relationships have been formed with Hallmark for Kinkade-branded stationery items, Avon for gift products, and QVC for unlimited-edition paper lithographs. A Kinkade Museum and Cultural Center has been established in Monterey, California, and internet opportunities for disseminating spiritual light have not been neglected: a Kinkade screen saver is also available. Still in the planning stage are craft and activity kits for the "do-the-Kinkade-yourself" market and a series of novels based on his paintings.[2]

Plentiful inducements exist to make purchasing his work a frequently recurring practice. For example, by creating works in series, Kincade encourages consumers to become collectors. Collectors are afforded the opportunity to strengthen their commitment by joining the Thomas Kinkade Collectors' Society (with over 20,000 members, the society is as "exclusive" as Kinkade gets). Serious admirers graduate from collector rank to investor status when they become shareholders in Media Arts Group, Inc., a publicly traded company dedicated to producing and circulating the works of Thomas Kinkade. The financial status of the company can be researched by ordering its Annual Report on Earnings, but information can also be acquired through the Securities and Exchange Commission. Shares are traded on the Nasdaq National Market, and Kinkade is the only painter whose work is traded on the New York Stock Exchange. In 1999, Media Arts Group, Inc. posted $126 million in revenues and $84 million in profits. The complicated agreement between Kinkade and the company that markets his work can be summarized as follows: the artist receives five percent of net sales. He is a wealthy man.

The fact that this agreement has made Kinkade a wealthy man testifies to the fact that Kinkade is inspired by the same aesthetic that emerges from market surveys of public taste. He apparently concurs with the popular assumption that "pretty" is a component of art, and that definitions of "pretty" conform to a predictable cluster of visual qualities that include colors that are rich but not garish and compositions that are orderly but not rigid. Kinkade earnestly declares his desire to apply these insights to achieve humanity's well-being when he states that his mission is "to provide hope to people in despair, provide a reminder of the beauty of God's creation despite the darkness surrounding our lives."[3] The titles of his works confirm these sentiments: *Home is Where the Heart Is*, *The Blessings of Loved Ones*, *The Garden of Prayer*, *Grandmother's Memories to Her Grandchild*.

Not everyone is enchanted. Proponents of the avant-garde tend to dismiss Kinkade as sentimental, not to mention irrelevant to the serious world of art. These sophisticated viewers comprise a minority, who tend to accept sentimentality and prettiness only when it is introduced by artists intent on interrogating the effects of lowbrow tastes, not condoning them. These artists and their audience operate in the elite territories that lie outside mainstream culture. They approach popular taste analytically, critically, and ironically. Other detractors espouse the postmodernist principle that discredits the concept of universality that was once claimed by Europeans who believed that their religious, cultural, social, and political approaches were applicable to all people. To them, it is presumptuous for Kinkade to aspire to mass appeal. Humans are not generic; they represent a multiplicity of variables. The popularity of Kinkade's creations, however, seems to indicate the need to reconsider the validity of this discarded concept. The broad appeal of Kinkade's aesthetic confirms the existence of a near universal set of values that exemplify righteous behavior and emotional fulfillment. Kinkade depicts them in his art and enacts them in his life: he married his childhood sweetheart, who is the mother of his four daughters, all of whom share the middle name Christian, a redundancy that affirms their father's religious devotion.

Unlike the many artists who contrive a personal style, theme, or technique, Kinkade presents the politics, religion, and family values of the mainstream. If he is exceptional, it is because he represents the values that many people share. He is a romantic idealist who prefers the homey to the sublime, the past to the present, the rural to the urban, the sensual to the intellectual, the cheerful to the sorrowful. Sales reports are not the only measure of Kinkade's success. He also summons a more poignant standard of success when he says, "I own the hearts of the people."[4] Kinkade has earned the public's hearts by reiterating their definitions of art and delight. This harmonious relationship contrasts dramatically with vanguard artists' interactions with the public. Shock and distress are frequently summoned as strategies to break conventions or provoke debate. But Kinkade has no need to make converts. His audience requires no convincing because he offers them the opportunity to remain complacent as they escape into a perfect dreamworld. In the presence of his paintings they revel in the status quo of their desires.

Kinkade's works are not only accessible in terms of their pictorial qualities; they are also user-friendly. While many forms of contemporary art are unwieldy in scale, utilize complex technologies, are high maintenance, intrude on living space, or are devoid of decorative value, Kinkade's works are amenable to apartment walls, office hallways, and suburban interiors. They are offered in several sizes, and can be selected to hang attractively in rooms of varying size.

Kinkade's work appeals to markets comprising a broad range of purchasing powers, marketing affordable items as well as high-end products. Nor is anyone excluded on the basis of age, geographical region, race, or sexual preference. The work's visual appeal and emotional satisfaction transcends these human differences. Even education is not a limiting factor. Ph.D.s, CEOs, mayors, and army generals are as likely as waiters and truck drivers to enjoy the soothing harmonies of a Kinkade image.

Because these lush and luxuriant paintings are mostly devoid of human inhabitants, they function like empty stages beckoning viewers to imagine themselves strolling or relaxing within the painted vistas. Unobstructed visual pathways invite viewers to enter. Once within, they are greeted by sensual enticements unmarred by reality's flaws. Smoke curls from the chimneys—it is warm inside. Candlelight glows in the windows—it is bright. Snow has been removed from the pathways—walking is comfortable. The bridge across the stream is in good repair—there is no danger. The rain has stopped—you won't get wet. Meanwhile, the entire catalogue of modern annoyances is absent: computer viruses, cell phones, insurance rate increases, traffic jams, and the incessant beeps, sirens, screeches, and poundings of modern machinery. But most significantly, rural annoyances in his pastoral settings—insects, poison ivy, mud, bitter winds, and searing sun—are also deleted.

Thomas Kinkade, *The Sea of Tranquility*, *Seaside Memories V* (1998), dimensions variable, canvas lithograph. ©2002 Thomas Kinkade, Media Arts Group, Inc., Morgan Hill, CA.

But creating art that pleases the eye and satisfies the soul is not sufficient to earn mass appeal. The artwork must also provide evidence that it has earned the status of a masterpiece. People demand the authentic mark of the artist's brushstroke and signature. Kinkade's lithographs may not be originals, but that does not interfere with their having the aura of an original bestowed upon them. Not only do collectors receive certificates of authenticity, each work bears the signature of Thomas Kinkade applied in DNA-infused ink, thus assuring double authentication of the signing process. According to the literature that accompanies each purchase, the canvas versions of the lithographs are hand-highlighted to create the appearance of original paintings. The value of the altered lithograph varies depending on who performs the operation. "Highlighters," as they are called, range from dozens of workers who each contribute some detail to a single image, to "master highlighters" who have been trained by Kinkade himself. But the works that are most coveted carry the mark of the master. They have been highlighted by Kinkade's very own hand. As an added bonus to consumers, this factory-produced art can be further personalized: at openings, anyone purchasing a work is entitled to become Kinkade's collaborator by "dabbing" their own lithograph for an extra fee. Because the editions are extensive, but not unlimited, collectors are urged to order before they sell out, a real and frequent occurrence.

Perhaps the ultimate Kinkade experience is now available. In 2001, the first of 101 Kinkade-inspired homes—set on narrow streets with picket fences—became available for sale in Vallejo, California, with prices starting at $425,000. "The Village" promises life in a setting of wholesome faith and tranquility, and the models are furnished exclusively with Kinkade products. The artist explains, "They beckon you into this world that provides an alternative to your nightly news broadcast. It's compelling to people. People are reminded that it's not all ugliness in the world."[5] If the reader is interested, complete information is available by dialing Kinkade Headquarters at (800) 366-3733.

[1] Tessa DeCarlo, "Landscapes by the Carload: Art or Kitsch?," *New York Times*, 7 November 1999, Living Arts section, 51.

[2] John Leland, "Subdivided and Licensed, There's No Place Like Art," *New York Times*, 4 October 2001, House and Home section, 1.

[3] DeCarlo.

[4] ibid.

[5] Leland.

CHOOSING A CONSTITUENCY

One-for-Some

Isaac Julien
Born 1960 London, England
1980–1984 St Martin's School of Art, First Class Honors Degree, fine art film
Lives and works in London

Isaac Julien's films, film installations, and photographs present evidence of his physical characteristics, his lifestyle decisions, and his sexual preferences. Many of his behaviors are only practiced by a minority of minorities. The majority of majorities classify them as taboos. Such deviations from social and sexual norms are typically confined to underground networks and classified as pornography. But Julien presents them in refined art galleries and museums where they are welcomed because of his high standards of craftsmanship and erudite conceptualizations. His choice of venue not only dignifies material that is often categorized as deviant, it channels his presentations to sophisticated and liberal-minded audiences that are not likely to take offense. In this way Julien mitigates the controversy that often erupts around art that violates social mores. His goal is to encourage tolerance, not provoke antagonism.

It takes exactly seven minutes and fifty-five seconds for Isaac Julien to disclose that he is a man who exists on the outermost fringes of society's norms. These seven minutes comprise the duration of his 1993 film installation, *The Attendant*[1]. The film compiles evidence of the inaccuracies of assigning stereotypes to people. Specifically, it enumerates the cluster of characteristics that describe the filmmaker himself. These characteristics either contradict or are omitted from standard stereotypes. As a result, Julien himself is beset with people's false assumptions and unwarranted expectations. This vexing circumstance has led Julien to direct his work to a specific audience—those who have been guilty of imposing false stereotypes upon him.

Because Julien himself doesn't conform to the stereotype of the non-conforming artist, he has discovered that all kinds of people are capable of inaccurate typecasting. In fact, outcasts can also be guilty of it. They, too, are capable of degrading people who abide by different rules of conduct or distrusting those who uphold a different heritage. When Julien's films shatter the superficial labels people adopt in order to simplify the process of navigating through a complex world, he is addressing a massive number of people. But instead of satisfying existing values in the manner of Kinkade, he challenges them to dislodge these values. Julien's art is confrontational, not escapist.

In order to accomplish this goal, Julien creates fictional narratives that expose the vagaries of his real life experience. He prowls clubs, bars, highways, and backyard pools, exposing the closeted taboos and unmentionable sexual acts that transpire in these places. Most viewers condemn these kinds of acts as shameful and offensive, preferring to avoid contact with them. But Julien, instead of assuming an apologetic or self-recriminating posture, inserts them boldly into the dignified context of sophisticated artistry and broadcasts their existence in vivid color on the big screen. In this unlikely context, people are likely to pay attention to material they would normally avoid. They are prodded to take the first step toward accepting taboo behaviors. This is a difficult assignment. Julien entices viewers to undertake rigorous analysis of their habitual judgments, to revise entrenched sensibilities and replace them with a more compassionate set. Reform is an arduous process that counters the effortless delight that Kinkade cultivates by drawing on

Isaac Julien, *The Attendant* (1993), single screen projection (still), 35 mm color film. Courtesy the artist and Victoria Miro Gallery.

nostalgic idealizations of bygone days of innocence and rendering them according to existing definitions of prettiness, quaintness, and sweetness. Kinkade's intent to include as much of humanity as can fit within an artist's embrace is diametrically opposed to Julien's efforts to dismantle the assumption that humanity conforms to one-size-fits-all generalities. Thinking in bulk comes at the price of disrespect for those who deviate from the average. In order to counter the standardization of humanity, Julien divides, subdivides, and then subdivides the subdivisions of his lifestyle taxonomies. This essay, like his films, tracks these departures from social norms. *The Attendant*, one of Julien's major films, dramatizes one lifestyle within the catalogue of human variability. Each entry articulates the repressive power of stereotypes.

To begin with, Julien is male and British. These designations support ground rules that claim the authority to pursue privileges and demand rights. Julien, however, doesn't fit this stereotype. In order to create an accurate self-portrait, he whittles away at the assumptions associated with the image of the British male, removing the many areas of non-compliance that apply to him. Some of these shards represent physical characteristics. Others represent cultural experiences. Still others identify behaviors and desires. Julien directs his camera at the remains, an alternative to the mainstream cultural image of the British male that is typically recorded on film. In this way he features a life experience that is neglected in mainstream communication networks. Julien asserts the right to register his objection to the prevailing stereotype that he identifies as "disturbing, masculinist in a phallocentric-sort-of-way." He is explicit about his goal: "I want to undermine it."[2]

The first sentence of the definitive catalogue on Julien's films and photographs, *The Film Art of Isaac Julien*, identifies him as "an internationally recognized writer/teacher/and scholar."[3] Despite the fact that there is no spoken dialogue in Julien's films, his intellectual's reliance on language is evident in the extensive texts that he both writes and cites. Since 1988 examples of his erudition have appeared regularly in publications devoted to those versed in cultural and political commentary and social reform, as well as the historic, critical, and theoretical discourse that supports cinema studies. The intellectual foundation of his work is buttressed by scholars who analyze popular culture and the politics of representation, avant-contemporary art, postcolonial studies, historiography, identity studies, the history of black cinema, the history of queer cinema, and so forth. But his intellectual stature is most apparent in the citations that support these texts. One nine-page essay authored by Julien, "Introduction: De Margin and De Centre," which appeared in *Screen* magazine, contains thirty-five footnotes and over sixty references. The extensive network of cultural producers that he acknowledges in his writings include theorists Ngugi wa Thiong'o, Raja Rao, Langston Hughes, Henry Louis Gates, Jr., bell hooks, Gayatri Spivak, Homi K. Bhabha, Cornel West, Kwame Anthony Appiah, Chris Marker, and Edward Said; the filmmakers Charles Burnett, Derek Jarman, Kenneth Anger, Julie Dash, Djibril Diop Mambéty, Andy Warhol, Terence Davies, Mohsen Makhmalbaf, and Abel Gance; and contemporary artists Douglas Gordon, Tony Oursler, Bill Viola, Doug Aitken, and David Hockney. Julien's films appeal to the brains of the tutored few, not the hearts of the majority, reversing Thomas Kinkade's formula. Scholarship, however, does not suffice as the sole qualifier for audience membership. Julien is not a disinterested intellectual committed to quotations, footnotes, and analyses. He is an artist whose films augment the contributions among this impressive roster of people. He explains, "By destabilizing signs of race, gender, and sexuality, these artists draw critical attention to the cultural constructedness, the artifice, of the sexual roles and identities we inhabit."[4]

His sophisticated approach to film suits cultured viewers. The typical member of his audience is a white, educated museum-goer with a taste for contemporary art. His relationship to this audience is bellicose. He seeks to disrupt their habits of thought by insinuating a tabooed lifestyle into the cultural mainstream that they occupy. His challenge is to promote cultural change despite the work's hurdles. Julien has raised the difficulty level so high that only people who are willing to accept intellectual challenges, dislodge entrenched attitudes, endure emotional disruptions, and accommodate seismic shifts in their value systems are eligible. The few who fulfill this requirement honor his achievement.

Julien's own life supplies the basis of "race, gender, and sexuality" that prevail in his films. Each undermines the scripted image of a British, male intellectual. Isaac Julien is black, and being black in an Anglo society subjects him to unequal status and inclines him to an adversary relationship with England's colonial past. Blacks remain marginalized in many areas of British society. According to Julien, there are only two categories of black males in the collective thought of most British people: the self-effacing, castrated "Uncle Tom" and the boastful, aggressive "superspade."[5] Furthermore, Julien explains, "blacks fit into this terrain by being confined to a narrow repertoire of types—the super-sexual stud and the sexual savage on one hand, or the delicate, fragile, and exotic oriental on the other. These are the lenses through which black men become visible in the urban gay subculture."[6]

Because Julien does not conform to either of these standard behaviors, he can attest that blackness is neither politically fixed nor culturally definable. He champions all forms of difference, saying, "It's not as if we could strip away the negative images of black masculinity created by Western patriarchy and discover some natural black male identity which is good, pure, and wholesome."[7] He goes on to explain, "Social definitions of what it is to be a man, about what constitutes manliness, are not natural but are historically constructed and this construction is culturally variable."[8]

But viable options for black males are further constrained by stereotypical roles assigned within the black community itself. Black leaders typically view toughness as a demonstration of defiance against oppressive racist tactics. They are contemptuous of homosexuality because it compromises the black struggle. As a result, gay black men, like Julien, are subject to the double jeopardy of being ostracized by white racists and black homophobes. In fact, his jeopardy is quadrupled because he also fails to measure up to the physical specifications of the idealized black male. Julien is not youthful, not lean, and not muscular; the star in his film is played by someone of similar body type who exposes the existence of censored and disputed black behaviors. In this way he campaigns to reverse the wrongs imposed by the majority against the rights of his minority.

Whereas Thomas Kinkade reinforces mainstream ideas of romance, Julien's version of sexuality is scandalous. He is not merely "out," meaning that he is a publicly declared homosexual; he is "out there," an extremist among homosexuals. For example, Julien locates his sexual desires on the periphery of black homosexuality by referring to himself as a "snow queen," a term for gay black men who desire white men. Julien breaks another gay stereotype by preferring older men to younger. Mark, Julien's partner, is white and twelve years his senior. Another trio of tabooed sexual behaviors accompanies this list of deviations from the approved homosexual "norms": fetishism, sado-masochism, and voyeurism.

In *The Attendant*, Julien assigns his own physical traits, psychological desires, and sexual practices to a uniformed guard in a British art museum. It is the first in a trilogy of films that also includes *Trussed* (1996) and *Three (The Conservator's Dream)* (1996-1999). The attendant for whom the film is titled is middle-aged, stocky, black, gay, a "snow queen," and a willing participant in aberrant sexual practices. These traits become apparent early in the narrative when a white male visitor to the museum becomes the recipient of the attendant's lusty gaze. As the film progresses, his fantasies of sadomasochistic pleasures, complete with whippings and groanings, fill the screen. But the theme of perversity is not confined to sexuality. It also applies to the perversion of the museum as the setting for a seduction of a white person instigated by a black person. This museum, like many others, glorifies and preserves the achievements of European culture. Julien describes the values it perpetuates as a "colonial fantasy" about "cultural legacies of slavery, empire and imperialism."[9] These legacies are replete with racial prejudice against blacks. Yet the black museum attendant accepts the responsibility of protecting the artifacts of white culture, perhaps in the same manner that he desires a white lover. Reading Julien's own text about his film is necessary to mitigate this clash of cultural histories. In it he reveals that even common stereotypes about museums can be flawed. In this instance as in so many others, assumptions lead to misunderstandings. *The Attendant* is set in an atypical art institution, the Wilberforce House Museum in Hull, an antislavery museum established by a white abolitionist.

The intent to confuse suppositions and challenge assumptions is further conveyed by the museum's prized possession, a nineteenth-century painting by Francois-Auguste Biard entitled *Slaves on the West Coast of Africa*. The painting provides the film's central motif. Julien describes it in the following manner: It "incorporates several tableaux which visually narrate the history of slavery: the buying and selling of black slaves; black men being whipped by black men under orders from the white master; bartering over black bodies."[10]

There is an area of stillness in the midst of Biard's painted depiction of the bustle and commotion caused by the imminent departure of the slave ship. A prone black man occupies the area. He is motionless because a rope restrains him. An inspector forces the man's mouth wide open and peers inside to determine his value as a slave. A bid is offered to a group of black men. The gazes of sailors, slave owners, and slaves all converge in this scene, the painting's compositional and narrative center. Julien expands the sequence of gazes to include the examination of the painted slave by the visitors to the museum. In the film, as in most museums, the visitors are white. Their admiring demeanors reveal that they have ignored the odious implications of the event depicted. The gaze is then transferred to the museum guard who is shown looking intently at the central motif of the painting—with pleasure! Instead of identifying with the plight of the black slave, the black attendant appears to relish the erotic implications of the scene. Costumed actors enact the contents of his lusty imagination. In his mind, Biard's vivid representation of a restrained black man in the foreground and slaves being whipped by white men in the background, morphs into fantasies of gay, sadomasochistic, mixed-race eroticisms. Sympathy for the victim of the brutal lashing is replaced by the pleasures of arousal. Instead of decrying the brutal politics of race, the painting ignites politically incorrect desires. Julien explains that the Biard painting becomes "tantalized by his closeted queer desire."[11] This perversion is confirmed by Biard's obvious fascination with black bodies that compromises his avowed intention to condemn the use of these black bodies as slaves. Both the artist and the guard seem titillated by the scene despite the reprehensible implications of slavery.

Actual museum visitors observing the installation of *The Attendant* are also gazers upon this scene. The responses transpiring in their heads may be out of the range of Julien's

Francois Auguste Biard (1798-1882), *Slaves on the West Coast of Africa* (c.1833), 25 x 90 inches, oil on canvas. Courtesy the Bridgeman Art Library. Collection Wilberforce House, Hull City Museums and Art Galleries, UK.

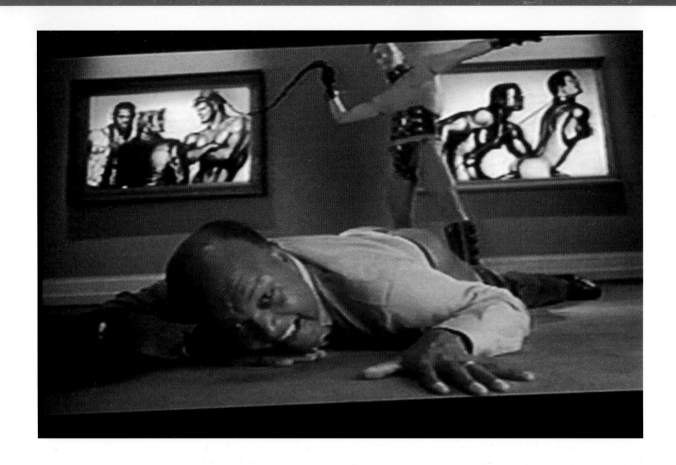

Isaac Julien, *The Attendant* (1993), single screen projection (still), 35 mm color film. Courtesy the artist and Victoria Miro Gallery.

camera, but they comprise the most crucial aspects of this essay about an artist and his audience. Viewers must confront their own biases and identify an allegiance from among the multiple choices provided in this short film. They can identify with the black victim (the slave), the white master (the slave owner), the painter (white male master), the museum visitor (white observer/voyeur), or the black museum guard (black, gay, sadist/masochist). Each option carries socially inscribed roles and moral codes. This painting is framed in gilt and guilt. Viewers pity the victim or admire his physique, associate enslavement with misery or bliss, abuse power or relinquish control. In all these ways the film hovers uncomfortably between pornography and fine art, a zone of discomfort few people seek in an art experience.

Julien introduces a third hurdle to accessibility by overlaying a "camp" aesthetic upon this hard-hitting narrative. Camp is a style identified as a humorous parody of popular taste. It exaggerates such lowbrow qualities as cute, gaudy, banal, and trite. These qualities are as alien to pornography as they are to fine art. In *The Attendant*, for example, the seduction of the visitor by the attendant is so overstated and the drama is so contrived, it resembles daytime television soap operas. Likewise the attendant's imagined erotic adventures are surrounded by so much extravagance and pretension, they are staged like early Hollywood musicals. The guard does not merely insert himself and the object of his lust into the painting. He replaces the actual onlookers with actors who sprout wings, take up bows and arrows, and assume the poses of cupids costumed in gold lamé loincloths, sparkling glass-beaded vests, and filigree wigs. Through trick photography, they are greatly reduced in scale. Thus miniaturized to the size of knick-knacks, they rotate in the mechanical manner of figurines inside a music box. Like ridiculous haloes on unlikely saints, they circle the heads of the leather-clad sadistic characters. The visitor who is the object of the attendant's seduction undergoes a transformation into the opposite style of expression. Instead of cuteness, he morphs into a menacing sadist lashing the bare bottom of the attendant. The lasher is literally "dressed to kill" in studded black leather gloves, belt, boots, and codpiece. Pornographic deviance coincides with kitsch innocence. These disparate life and fashion styles are not only forced into partnership, they exchange behaviors. In another scene, the onlookers assume the guise of leather-clad white hunks. They, too, disrupt stereotypes of both masculinity and homosexuality by gazing lustfully at the pudgy, middle-aged, black, male attendant. Camp exaggeration strips pornographic depictions of their perversity. By creating a parody of his own deviance, Julien defuses the condemnation, scandal, and scorn his sexual behavior typically ignites. At the same time, camp spoofs the pretensions of high art, robbing it of its power to support conventional attitudes about morality and decorum. Excavating the significance of these stylistic discrepancies is demanding. Admirers of Julien's films must enjoy being put to the test.

The Attendant twists tidy assumptions that slavery only refers to black people being subjugated to physical punishment and restraint. These assumptions are undermined by the black attendant's *desire* to be placed in bondage and whipped. This conflation of opposites is made apparent by the double use of neck rings. When they encircle the necks of enslaved Africans in the painting, they represent physical restraint. However, when they encircle the neck of the white visitor in the whipping scene, they enhance his menacing demeanor. Julien explains his intent: "Could not the fetish slave-band in the film, mimicking the metal collars worn by black slaves—which, for some readers, enacts this colonial memory—be read as something else: namely, the unspeakable masochistic desire for sexual domination? Surely, in this postcolonial moment, black queers should have the choice of acting out the roles of slaves or masters in the realm of desire and sexual fantasy."[12] For most people, removing the trappings of slavery from their pigeonhole in the catalogue of human misfortunes and recasting them as desirable eroticisms is too disgraceful to consider.

The third primary character in the film introduces yet another taboo behavior. She is the female museum conservator who eavesdrops on the attendant's sexual cavortings. Like the guard, she is black and middle aged. Since her job entails cleaning and restoring works of art, she functions, as the guard does, to protect the cultural artifacts of her oppressors. Julien explains her character: "As a conservator in the museum, she too has an ambivalent but intimate relationship to the construction of whiteness and high art in modernist culture. She knows she is ironically placed, given her relationship to the history of Western art...sometimes she caresses the figure-heads of white dead kings; high culture is the living-dead of whiteness."[13] In one scene she hears the sound of moaning and lashing coming from behind the painting she is cleaning. She presses her ear against the wall and listens with pleasure to the erotic sadomasochistic encounter between the guard and the visitor. Then the scene changes abruptly, and the conservator's listening ceases to be surreptitious. She is seated in the public space of a concert hall where the attendant, who has traded in his museum uniform for formal wear, stands alone on a grand stage. He sings an aria from the end of Henry Purcell's *Dido and Aeneas*. The opera is set on the coast of Africa, the same coast depicted in the Biard painting. Dido is the mythical Queen of Carthage who has fallen in love with the Trojan Aeneas. Julien has selected the climactic moment in the opera, when the African queen mounts a funeral pyre and is about to plunge a knife in her breast. She sings of her grief in being abandoned by a white, male lover. The black guard shares the African queen's lament. Comprehending this operatic contribution to the film's racist, sexist themes depends on knowledge that only a few people have, and even fewer are willing to acquire.

In this scene, the conservator applauds from the balcony, her hands coming together with the same ominous clap, clap, clap of the whip searing human flesh, whether it is to punish or arouse. Julien explains that she is "a kind of dominatrix figure. As she responds to the attendant's singing, one might read revenge and pathos projected back onto her husband's fate—her resentment at being used as an alibi for his closeted identity. The rhythm of the whiplash is heard forlornly in the rhythm of her clap. Where there is a closet, there will always be bitterness and abjectness, due to the desire repressed by black conservative family values, which must produce silence at any cost."[14]

Films, like concert halls, are designed to accommodate large audiences. It seems that the filmmaker, like the singer, wishes to share his lament. Yet they both perform for small, elite audiences. Except for a few musicians and the conservator, the concert hall is empty. Julien says he chose film as his medium because of the mind-controlling and trendsetting powers of cinema. But cinema only activates these powers when it is seen by the masses. Films with this kind of mass appeal have played a profound role in establishing the standards of masculinity and the attitudes toward race that affect human interactions today. The camera has validated certain values, and systematically excluded others. Julien actively seeks ways to record those that were excluded. *The Attendant* promotes acceptance for middle-aged, black snow queens. But the opinions it actively manipulates belong to the few, not the masses.

1. Super 16 mm color film and stereo sound transferred to DVD, front-projected.

2. Philip Martin, "LONESOME Cowboy," conversation with Isaac Julien, Ten by Ten (February 2001).

3. Amada Cruz, introduction to *The Film Art of Isaac Julien* by Isaac Julien (New York: Center for Curatorial Studies, Bard College, 2000), vi.

4. Isaac Julien and Kobena Mercer "True Confession," in *The Film Art of Isaac Julien* by Isaac Julien (New York: Center for Curatorial Studies, Bard College, 2000), 61.

5. ibid., 60.

6. ibid., 57.

7. Thelma Golden, *Black Male: Representations of Masculinity in Contemporary American Art* (New York: Whitney Museum of American Art, 1994), 59.

8. Martin.

9. Julien and Mercer.

10. Isaac Julien, "Confessions of a Snow Queen: Notes on the Making of The Attendant," *Cineaction!*, Fall 1993, <www.cineaction.org>.

11. ibid.

12. ibid.

13. ibid.

14. ibid.

One-on-One

Skip Schukmann

Born 1945 Colorado
1967 Colorado State University, BS
1972 University of Massachusetts, MA, technical biological education, forestry service
and wildlife management
Lives and works in California and upstate New York

Skip Schuckmann establishes a third artist/audience outpost. Unlike Kinkade, his tactics of dissemination are remote from those typically used for non-art commodities. Unlike Julien, his manner of interacting with his audience diverges from the cultural mainstream. Schuckmann exempts himself from all mass-media tactics by initiating and formulating his work around the desires of each client, one at a time, accommodating his or her particular location and life circumstance. In creating his artwork, Schuckmann honors each client's desires. At the same time, he seeks opportunities to integrate his own abiding commitment to the health of the planet, the vitality of its life forms, and the spiritual rewards of pursuing these principles. Instead of buying his art, Schuckmann's clients buy into a personal relationship with the artist.

Whereas the effects of much contemporary art rely on bombast and theatrics, Skip Schuckmann attempts to enrich the ongoing, ordinary moments in each of his client's lives. He explains, "Since people vary tremendously in their capabilities to perceive and in the concerns that distract them, it seems to me that a generalized approach can create tremendous misconceptions. For this reason, although I sometimes entertain an offering for broader audiences, at this point I've decided it doesn't serve me or my public."[1] The approach he is referring to requires the reinvention of all aspects of art production and presentation. "When I chose not to do a gallery gig or the museum scene, I had to decide what to call the people with whom I work. The word 'audience' implies multiplicity. I work with individuals. Some artists have patrons, but patrons patronize and that is condescending. Another choice was 'customer.' But, 'customer' is the term for people who buy goods and services. 'Brother and sister' sounded wishy-washy. I've also considered 'coach and trainer,' but the word 'client' seems to best describe the relationship I want—as a mentor and orchestrator in the development of people's physical and mental properties. My teaching technique is not institutional, but a one-on-one tutoring. I am working for them by guiding them toward an understanding of their immediate surroundings and helping them to articulate their desires. In the process we create form." Thus Schuckmann is a site-specific artist who responds to the site-specific personalities of his clients. He replaces professional neutrality with personal engagement.

Skip Schuckmann orders the same meal every day at the same café. You can confirm this by asking Clarissa, the waitress at Antonio's Mexican Café in Ojai, California. Schuckmann explains, "We are operating in a dream made manifest by television and money, engineering and computers. We have had enough rapture for a while. What we need now is plainness. We need to start responding to the world without emotional attachments and simplistic enchantments and the belief that buying things is the only way to get satisfaction. We must learn how to be satisfied." How does he propose to accomplish this? He suggests, "Move a rock. Sit awhile. Dirt is always under your feet." Schuckmann revives ancient and neglected forms of ordinariness. "Micro-climate sculpting" is the term he invented for his

Skip Schuckmann, *Turkey Nest Kiva* (1998), interior of two-room subterranean pit house. Natural stone, carved earth, wood weaving, two-liter plastic bottles. Courtesy of the artist. Photograph: Adam L. Weintraub.

One-on-One: **Skip Schukmann**

artistic process. His studio is anywhere he can nudge stones from their ancient lodgings, coax dirt to hold its form by applying pressure and heat, prepare a bed to lay a fire, weave supportive structures of vines, twigs, and tree limbs, create a rock shadow on a stump to accelerate its transformation into soil, or divert a stream to create a musical symphony of water flows and falls. In all these ways, he beckons the earth to yield its forms and resources. The process is respectful, the response graceful. The activities he cultivates present an alternative to what he calls the "military/Mattel attitudes which treat life like war or a trading table." Evidence to support this thesis, he says, is even apparent in our language. Schuckmann thinks it is significant that "convulsion" and "revulsion" are common words in our vocabulary, and therefore our thoughts, while "provulsion" does not exist. Provulsion suggests affirming, favoring, supporting, whereas convulsion is a violent disturbance and revulsion indicates repugnance. They reflect a commandeering approach to the environment, a cultural attitude that Skip identifies as "hacking our way out of the wilderness or the mountaineering mode of approaching nature as a challenge that requires a competitive drive. We are not here for the sporting-ness of it. We must learn to go into the wild with the delicacy of the zephyr creating playful eddies of wind. I want to include compassion within my working process." The sculpting part of his micro-climate sculpting is enacted directly upon the land, utilizing a shovel, pruning shears, a rake, and two of our most basic tools: fire and water. He harvests their elemental energies. Fire cleanses, releases, and fractures. Water softens, displaces, and anneals. With these simple means of crafting form, humble demeanors are reintroduced into human interactions with the environment. The "micro" part of his endeavor means he prefers to reintroduce techniques not dependent upon bulldozers, cranes, backhoes, and fossil fuels. Likewise, his artistic interactions conform to this micro principle. They are scaled to avoid the broadcasting approach to art production and display—no advertising, no institutional presentations, no mass audience. People learn about his work through observing it, knowing a mutual acquaintance, or meeting him.

This personalization of art commenced in 1978, the year Schuckmann decided to apply his academic training as an ecological resource planner to environmental art. Most people with his training work for corporations, universities, or governments. He decided to conduct resource planning on a micro level by helping individuals understand how to develop their land holdings thoughtfully. Perhaps it would be more accurate to say "thought fully" since Schuckmann's contemplations of suburban backyards and narrow creek beds are vast and embracing. These contemplations cultivate an interplay between the plants, trees, land contours, shadow patterns, rock formations, and all the other parts of the environment that are visible as well as those that are hidden under the earth, in the shadows, or perceived by sensory apparatus primed to detect minute fluctuations in moisture, air flow, temperature, and light. To these he adds agriculture, architecture, and the present inhabitants of the land, along with the lifestyles and histories of genera-tions of people who formerly occupied the site, and the myths that once guided its inhabitants, and the values that have come to replace them.

In designating his activities "art," Schuckmann retained his engagement with his scientific knowledge base but dispensed with the necessity to conform to regimented procedures, predetermined hypotheses, standardized preconceptions, and the sanitized environments of laboratories. These were replaced with spontaneity, aesthetic delight, social responsi-bility, and metaphysical investigation. He offers this entire catalogue of creative insights to each client, one by one. The process commences with an evaluation of the present resource base of the client's land, not galleries and museums. Schuckmann then proposes ways to utilize local materials in accord with the client's thoughts about development. Garden? Studio? Walkway? Pond? Amphitheater? Stone, plants, soil, water, and animal products are all eligible for crafting. Rarely are materials imported, but when they are, the first option of this last resort is to utilize someone else's discards.

Case in point: there is a pasture on which one of Schuckmann's clients was constructing a home. Unsightly mounds of soil were left from the previous excavation. An enormous pile of brush lay nearby. The ground had been shorn of its topsoil by the bulldozers. Schuckmann's reasons for beginning his work at this location were twofold. The first was to heal the land of the damage it had sustained. But the second was the delight it offered. He did not perceive the massive amounts of disheveled material that lay upon it as a blight. To him they were an enticing inventory of materials available for forming. Yet Schuckmann approached this massive disturbance of the landscape delicately, with the simple act of leaning eight-foot logs vertically against facing edges of two of the largest mounds of earth. He then perched a single horizontal log on top of them. There appeared an elemental doorway to nowhere. It transformed the site. It provided focus for the dispersed materials, directing attention away from the ungainly piles and toward a form that suggested the habitat of ancient peoples.

During the weeks that followed Schuckmann carved into the heaped dirt and sorted through the brush pile. The large limbs were set aside for future projects, while the unusable twigs were burned. Smoke rose from the site all day and well into the night. The fire was continuous, but its function varied. It produced light in the evening. It provided warmth when it was cool. It drove away the mosquitoes when it was hot. Always, it assisted the artist in the sculpting process by loosening the soil. Schuckmann dug down deep into the earth. The soil he removed became the medium for walls that gradually rose around the depression. He carved the soil mounds and stacked stone from the surrounding fields to form these walls. Gradually, a semi-subterranean circular space began to form on the land. Low platforms became seating. The deepest hole became the fire pit. A lined cavity collected water for bathing. An earthen ledge supported a sleeping area. Spaces in the stone walls were filled with empty two-liter soda bottles to provide interior light. Large limbs were woven across the top of the walls and juniper branches were shingled on top of them to form a roof that was removed on sunny days to welcome in the sunshine and replaced when it rained. At the end of the summer the structure was named "The Turkey Nest Story-Telling Kiva" to honor the abandoned wild turkey's nest with a dozen eggs that was discovered amid the brush. The kiva was used by his client as a guesthouse and the site for fireside gatherings with friends.

The next spring one of the bottle-windows was dismantled to make another doorway and a second room was constructed. By the end of the second summer, the pile of brush had been fully utilized, the mounds of dirt had been reformed, and aspen trees and day lilies were growing all around. During the second winter a guest at one of the client's gatherings accidentally knocked a timber that was supporting the roof. Gradually, the roof collapsed under the weight of the snow, assuming, as if by design, the concave shape of a turkey's nest. The form was beautiful on the land and so it remained for several months. Then, on a lovely autumn day, Schuckmann began to work on its next manifestation. Instead of repairing it, he removed much of the material to a different part of the property, and the structure took the form of a picturesque ruin on the landscape. Then the reworking began anew: A new fire pit was dug. Stone tiers were constructed. The earth reformed. A small chamber was erected. An asymmetrical sixty-seat amphitheater with multiple performance spaces and a dressing room emerged on the landscape.

Schuckmann explains, "As I introduce my cosmology onto my client's land, I make evident the stones, sticks, zephyrs, and rills that have always existed there. I contrive ways to develop their joy in these ordinary things. Most people aren't aware of the effects of these general principles, so when I apply them specifically to their habitats they perceive what I've done as magical. But it's really only sleight of shovel or pruning shears. To bring the unseen resources of a locale into evidence and demonstrate their utilization on a personal human scale is what I delight in. Often, my clients don't get most of the ephemeral minutiae. They get some of it, but they don't get what I get because I experience the intricacy of the design as it develops at my fingertips, the subtle changes of the flow of silt in a newly disturbed rill, a zephyr that grabs the ashes of the fire as I stir it. That is why I encourage my clients to mess with stuff so that they can have the same delight. Sometimes they do. They climb into their ponds and grab algae and throw it on the banks, and build fires, and retrieve stones from their streams. This helps them to create an intimate and sensual relationship with their land."

Nature determines the temporal aspects of Schuckmann's workday. He is paid by the day (the diurnal cycle of the sun), not the hour (the dials on a clock). He never has a contract. At the end of each day, he and his client decide if they should continue the relationship and when the next meeting might be—next week or next year, every week or every year. Thus, although Schuckmann engages his clients individually, the relationships are often sustained for decades. The nature of work expands when it is based upon an "until death do us part" commitment. For one thing, the artist/client relationship can evolve into a long-term investment for both parties. Certain kinds of dividends are not immediate. Unless time is allotted for the payoffs to accrue naturally, they become lost opportunities. Soils change under cultivation. Water accumulates or dissipates or relocates. Trees and shrubs mature. Stumps decay. But even these time frames lengthen when activities that occur in a client's backyard can be designed within the context of sunspot activity, glacial cycles, and fossil evidence of evolutionary change, as well as medicine wheels and vision quests.

Schuckmann is not hired to do a job. Each day's activities are determined by his client's disposition and the opportunities afforded by that day's moisture, temperature, light, and wind. Constructing an embankment of dry-stacked fieldstone is as likely to occupy his day's employment as discussing the child-rearing practices of the first inhabitants of this continent, or demonstrating how the disposition of garbage can be a spiritual practice. Schuckmann is an artist who sculpts the value systems of his clients as well as their land. One value system that inevitably gets challenged is the expectation that a job can be completed and anticipated results will be accomplished. Because Schuckmann is nature's partner, not its warden, his manner of working evolves in the same way that life and the universe evolve. Thus, even an elaborate configuration that he has just constructed, and that his clients have just paid him for, always remains catalogued as raw material for succeeding manifestations.

Schuckmann provides an alternative to the conventional view that art and architecture should remain forever in the condition in which it exists the last time the artist touched it. A vast system of museums, conservators, framers, insurance policies, security systems, climate-control devices, and archival materials support this notion. Schuckmann's work originates within the life stream and remains forever responsive to the ongoing effects of climate, weather, and human interactions, including his own. He reports that people's initial response when they encounter him at work is to say, "It looks like a big sewer problem." This is because they fail to consider the possibility that someone might dig

Skip Schuckmann, *Turkey Nest Kiva* (1998), exterior showing brush pile that was found on site beside the pit house constructed of dry stacked stone, roof of laminated carpet and plastic with earthen covering. Courtesy of the artist. Photograph: Adam L. Weintraub.

Skip Schuckmann, *Turkey Nest Kiva* (2002), natural rail fence and gravity-fed stream leading to sweat lodge to the left of the amphitheater.

Courtesy of the artist. Photograph: Adam L. Weintraub.

SCOPING AN AUDIENCE

and pile rocks without an immediate functional motivation. Eventually, after observing that these efforts continue at the same location for weeks, months, and years, they become curious. "People cannot help but wonder why this guy is forever digging. This moment is my challenge as a poet/artist/teacher/scientist to somehow translate and communicate a disparate value system." Schuckmann waits for the optimal moment. These moments depend upon eye-to-eye contact and handshake proximity. They occur one person at a time.

"One at a time" mirrors the intricacies of the evolutionary process that occurs one molecule at a time. Environmental and cultural change doesn't happen to everything all at once. Schuckmann observes that backyards are part of the universe. "Water falls on your roof. If you create a gutter that leads to a pool, the flow patterns of the hydrologic cycle of the earth are altered. In some small way, people affect evolutionary change. Each decision has enormous consequence when placed within a context that exceeds our property lines and ordinary perceptions." As a result, Schuckmann prefers to engage actual evolution rather than virtual evolution. He explains, "Actual evolution occurs through the actions of one thing on another. I craft the physical world directly by cutting, digging, planting for its own sake, not to make it an image of something else. I'm working on actual scale in an actual world. Most other artists craft images or convey ideas."

 The one-at-a-time approach to art making has multiple consequences that alter the entire cycle of art production and dissemination. Mutual exchange with people, as with plants and earth and water, cannot be contained in a finite art object. Interactive exchanges disqualify it for static museum display. The determining influence of each encounter with individuals makes it impossible to document an end product. Schuckmann's one-at-a-time predilection is suited to conversation, not lectures. The effect of unmediated discourse is unpredictable because human behavior is idiosyncratic. He notes, "We become unintegrated when we are pushed around by a talker, and we are not really listening so no one disagrees. We are only integrated when we are both encoding and decoding. Then communication can occur."

As part of the continual evolution of his work, Schuckmann has augmented the language that surrounds it with words that represent life-affirming concepts missing from common discourse. They are also absent from approaches to problem solving and possibilities for delight. He offers this idiosyncratic lexicon to his clients, a shared private language that deepens their connections and intensifies the intimacy of their communications. Thus, he plants words like others plant watermelons, surrounding them with his fertile discourse. Some examples of his attempt to "create defined opinions to give ideas a place to grow" follow:

Primordial waste: The process of taking command of our own feces, urine, and other by-products, bypassing public health management and centralized treatment systems, and returning them to usefulness in our resource base.

Wilding: Gardening that returns land to its natural aesthetics, i.e. fallen branches are reinstalled and rocks are rescattered.

Unlaxing: The design of a lifestyle in which work is so satisfying that vacations and retirement become undesirable. "The lilies of the field don't take vacations."

Carrion artists: Artists who consume life and its resources rather than enhance them.

Cleverage: Ideas and images that distract people from developing behaviors that integrate art and education and healing.

Bulldozer consistency: The holding pattern within which many people live even if it does not provide gladness or satisfaction.

Materiality: An erotically charged compound that incorporates earthly matter and spiritual energy.

Emotional velcro: The greed and laziness that make us stick to our ideas about ourselves.

Protocolic: The discomfort that ensues from excessive politeness.

Schuckmann supplies his own best concluding definition. It consists of a single word—atonement. Though the word has journeyed through the ages to come to mean "reconciliation," Shuckmann, by separating this compound word into its parts, allows its original meaning, a meaning he has applied to the "oneness" of his artistic practice, to take precedence:

At-onement: The physical and mystical interconnectedness of all things.

Schuckmann applies this principle to his audience of one.

[1.] All quotes from an interview with the artist, September 2002.

Implicit Meanings—Metaphor and Symbol

Michal Rovner

Born 1975 Tel Aviv, Israel
1979–1981 Tel Aviv University, studied philosophy, cinema, and television
1985 Bezalel Academy of Art and Design, Jerusalem, BFA
Moved to New York in 1987
Lives and works in New York City

Michal Rovner has an aversion to stating an opinion because opinions are based on single points of view. As a native of Israel, she is keenly aware of conflicting outlooks. Rovner believes that accurate portrayals of history involve straddling both sides of political, mythic, and psychological borders. She utilizes metaphors and symbols to accomplish the task of communicating complex, interwoven perspectives. These devices function in her photo-graphic murals and video installations as they do in literature—to expand significance, augment meaning, and embody opposing truths. But metaphors and symbols only accomplish these tasks when members of the audience interpret them. Rovner offers her audience opportunities to go beyond first impressions and undertake an active search for meaning.

If language was a machine, then the prefix "re" would be the lever that drives a concept backward in time or makes an action happen again. The words return, recall, reverse, remind, rearrange, redo, and reconnect exhibit the normal meaning of the prefix. But when this prefix is attached to the verb "present" or the noun "presentation," these two letters generate a multiplicity of meanings, directions, and dimensions. Something that is presented is displayed for viewing. But something that is "represented" by an artist is much more than a mere duplication of the original. It indicates that the subject has been created in a new form. Similarities between the object and its representation are apparent, but so are the differences. One of the remarkable attributes of artistic representation is that the subject of the work of art may be different from the subject of the representation. It is this rich, expressive zone of differentiation that has long been contemplated by art historians and explored by artists. But this essay deals with its impact on art observers. It explores how audiences discern meanings that are obscured by metaphors and camou-flaged as symbols. This imposes a responsibility upon viewers. They must recognize this difference, deduce its relationship with the subject, and interpret the manner in which it enriches the work's significance. This essay provides three examples of this fertile category of artistic expression and the special demands it imposes on viewers. In the first instance, the represented object expresses the emotional state of the artist. In the second, it conveys a political circumstance. In the third, it transcends these specific references to address a universal condition. This triumvirate of representational strategies coalesces within *Mutual Interest*, a film installation by Michal Rovner.

The first sign of distress that the visitor encounters upon entering the pitch-black room in which *Mutual Interest* is installed, is the foreboding drone of helicopter engines reverber-ating throughout the gallery. The visual field is occupied floor to ceiling and corner to corner on three walls by the continuous projections of masses of surging birds. The birds seem warped and distorted beyond their skeletal and muscular limits, their formations unraveling as they traverse the skies. They charge in a specific trajectory as if driven by some fearsome force, then abruptly halt their momentum and hover in eerie suspension. Suddenly they explode into chaos and lunge in the opposite direction. A frenzy of wings

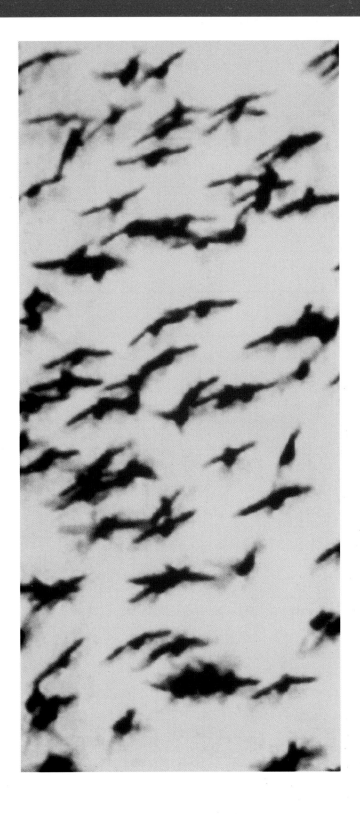

Michal Rovner, *Mutual Interest #1* (1997), 50 x 96 inches, c-print. Collection of the artist.

Michal Rovner, *Mutual Interest #2* (1998), 34 x 49 inches, c-print. Collection of the artist.

flaps against the horizonless abyss, accompanied by the relentless and anxiety-producing rat-tat-tat-tat-tat of the helicopter engines. Collisions never occur, but they are perpetually and terrifyingly imminent. Assaulted on all sides by this visual and aural drama, references to its actual museum setting in midday vanish along with the comforting distance normally provided by the frame of photography, the proscenium of theater, the screen of film. *Mutual Interest* offers no such escape. Viewers and birds are fellow voyagers groping for spatial markers and orienting clues.

Rovner refers to her films as "icons" and "metaphors for emotions."[1] Ornithological classifications and avian physiology are not her concerns; she cannot even identify the species of birds she filmed. Instead of using the camera for journalistic or scientific reporting, she reassigns its function. It becomes an expressionistic device that responds to her impulses and registers her activities like clay in the hands of a sculptor. "I altered the speed. Made quick cuts. Changed directions. Stopped action. Blurred images. Brought them back in focus. Played light against a dark sky, light against the dark mass of earth. The camera rose and fell like explosions." The emotional maelstrom is further intensified because Rovner carefully orchestrates the timing of the projections so that the films, shown simultaneously on three walls, slide discordantly in and out of synch. She describes the effect upon the viewer: "The birds swirl around you until you are dizzy. I use four microphones. You become obliterated."

Through an elaborate processing technique, Rovner further expands the expressive potential of film by continually transferring the image from one medium to another: printing it again and again, adding paint and ink, manipulating it on a computer, intermixing still and video shots. At each juncture, some distinguishing characteristic of the original image falls away. Focus blurs, details become obscured, facts become mere impressions. Rovner states that processing proceeds until she discovers "resemblances among mutual parts, what things have in common that make their identity ambiguous." In this manner, ravens, magpies, jays, starlings, and finches merge into a composite image of all migrating avians—birds, swarming bees, charging helicopters, or even rioting mobs viewed from above. Meanings and interpretations proliferate. Through these means, Rovner explores three functions of representation, offering her audience different opportunities to relate to the work. By crossing the boundaries of visual truth she first gains entry into a vast emotional repository. Because response at this stage is automatic, it is not demanding upon the audience. But subsequent stages that lead into an extended territory of metaphor and that open into an expansive domain of symbol both depend upon the willful investment of time, effort, analysis, and reflection.

Rovner's initiation into the field of photography introduced her to the medium's enormous expressive properties. "The first time I took pictures for a class I was shocked that the objects didn't look the way they did in reality, but like my feelings."[2] *Mutual Interest* is an expressionistic work of art. The theme, as described by Rovner, "is not about birds. Birds are the vehicle, the material, the point of departure. This film is a comment on my feelings. Things are unstable, in flux. They go from good to bad to good." The artist amasses anxiety-inducing aesthetic ingredients: the visually overwhelming scale of the piece (wall-to-wall and floor-to-ceiling); the stark and grim color scheme; the disorienting tempo shifts in the birds' embellished actions from frenzy to frozen; the camera's interspersing of chaotic zooms and tidy progressions.

The birds externalize the internal state of someone possessed by a demented force or suffering from hysteria. Some viewers may feel drawn by the work's grim beauty. Others may want to hurl a net at the sky and rein this turmoil in. Still others may flee. In each instance responses originate in the emotional gut of the observer, bypassing analysis and contemplation. The artwork is the active agent emitting an emotional charge. The viewer is the respondent to these charges.

Metaphor is the second way in which *Mutual Interest* disassociates birds from literal meanings and enables them to serve an expanded function as the work's expressive agents. Rovner guides her audience in their search for broader significance by marrying a soundtrack of the ominous drone of helicopter engines with imagery of the frenetic flight of birds. The unlikely nature of this partnership reveals the two essential characteristics of metaphor as the word is used in this context. First, metaphors are inventions of the artist's imagination. Second, metaphoric meaning is a product of the viewer's active search for meaning. This search may involve correlating the artwork with the artist's life or concurrent events. When this search is applied to *Mutual Interest*, it discloses that Rovner's bird hieroglyphs trace a political crisis that coincided with the creation of this work. The artist, who is Israeli, was in the United States when the Gulf War erupted in the Middle East. She sat glued to the televised news, watching Scud missiles being hurled at her homeland. Some missiles landed in the vicinity of her parents' home. Rovner channeled this experience into her artwork, but instead of using evidence of the actual conflict between Arabs and Israelis, she approached the theme through a surrogate, enlisting the metaphoric potential of birds to her art. As applied to *Mutual Interest*, for example, the tenacity of the migrating bird's drive to return "home" to the place where generations of their ancestors bred and reared their young provides a powerful model for the force driving both Arabs and Israelis in this conflict. For humans as for birds, survival depends on claiming territories and defending turf. Metaphor suggests that the drive propelling a tiny bird is like the drive that propels a tiny nation to fight powerful and determined enemies. In both instances, remarkable feats are performed in defense of home. Through these means, the disoriented flight of the darting birds conjures the agonizing conflict between the urgency of defending home and the imperative to venture into enemy territory. When Rovner associated birds with a particular act of war, their disoriented flight became evocative of fleets of helicopters homing in on a landing spot with the propulsive force of Scud missiles, the fanatical fury of Hamas, the frenzy of refugees fleeing their homeland. A single image may generate multiple metaphoric possibilities, contributing an ensemble of interpretations that enrich the work with denotations and connotations and reward viewers who engage in prolonged contemplation.

Of course, another way to discern the metaphoric significance of a work of art is to ask the artist. Rovner explains: "*Mutual Interest* means that we are all driven by a common force, birds and fish as well as people. I am just as upset if Israel bombs Lebanon or Lebanon bombs Israel. In both cases, humans are interfering with a natural course. Once you get off track, there is this twist, and we have war. The big question is, is it unnatural to fight? On one side, the war is bad. But there is also great beauty there. This can't be ignored. It produces confusion. We want to know, but we don't want to look. My affinity is to not judge, not even to comment. I only ask questions and wish for peace."

As explained, the birds in flight in *Mutual Interest* convey the artist's emotional condition and at the same time serve as a metaphor for political conflict. In the first instance, the viewer's response is automatic and reactive. In the second instance, the viewer's response involves the application of imagination and intelligence. Yet neither response is sufficient to account for the representational complexity of this work of art. Rovner explains, "I am trying to shift the thing away from its identity, away from its locality, to watch it in many ways, to look for some kind of essence." This essence is located in the human collective unconscious, a remote territory that may be difficult for people to access. Rovner's challenge is to tap this psychic vein and unleash the spectral phantoms that reside there. Like her predecessors who shared the desire to give form to this formless impulse, she is summoning art's trusted allies—symbols. Symbols are ancient instruments of knowledge. Their job is to convey aspects of reality that escape ordinary centers of perceptions and that bypass ordinary modes of expression.

Joseph Campbell, the distinguished scholar of mythology, states: "Mythological symbols touch and exhilarate centers of life beyond the reach of vocabularies of reason and coercion. The light-world modes of experience and thought were late, very late developments in the biological prehistory of our species.... The silence of primordial seas, of which the taste still runs in our blood … had been operative for so many hundreds of millions of centuries that it could not then, and cannot now, be undone."[3]

Because many symbols are components of our cultural inheritance, they do not need to be learned, and often elicit the raw immediacy of an emotion. Defined in this manner, symbols transcend time, the individual imagination, and linguistic communication channels. Throughout the ages symbols have played a privileged and essential social function, often evoking a sense of the sacred. In fact, of all the creatures that populate the Earth, birds are favored as symbols. They have been depicted as messengers of the gods and vehicles for the soul's journey heavenward. They inspire awareness of divine manifestations. Many religions and cultures utilize bird imagery as a symbol of earthly transcendence: Buddhists, Celts, Christians, Hindus, and Muslims, Scandinavians, Egyptians, Chinese, and the Maori among them.[4]

Rovner reveals her knowledge of this hallowed, cross-cultural tradition, stating that "birds are a symbol for freedom and speed." But instead of affirming this symbolic meaning, she repudiates it, claiming, "I gave them a different meaning. These birds twist the association with peace. They make a detour." In *Mutual Interest*, birds become representatives of strife and agitation. Perhaps birds have been reassigned to an antithetical symbolic role in order to mirror the disruption in the historic relationship between humans, birds, and gravity. The symbolic association between birds and joyful transcendence was sustained for as long as the human experience of soaring in the sky was confined to the imagination or was a product of spiritual rapture. Otherwise, it was the exclusive province of birds. When humans, too, took to the skies and acquired the ability to traverse enormous stretches of unmarked ocean and desert, maintain a course despite the sun's ever-changing position, and retain orientation at night even when clouds obliterate the stars, wonder was sacrificed. Birds lost their eminence to the airplane. Now they are forced to compete for space amid the congestion of an ever-expanding fleet of airborne technologies, tension power lines, plate-glass windows, transmission towers, and satellites. Illumination from city lights blinds them, emissions from industrial plants choke them, the roar of supersonic engines deafens them. It is no wonder that Rovner's birds have not only lost their exclusivity, they have also lost their way.

Traditional symbolism is ingrained in the human psyche. *Mutual Interest*, by depicting birds as messengers of turmoil, strips them of their age-old associations. Instead of representing joyful elation, Rovner introduces a different set of associations. "Flying brings to mind wings, initiation, getting from one place to another. To me, it's more about being taken out of context, being detached. It's about being in between, after taking off and before

Michal Rovner, *Mutual Interest #3*, (1998), 61 x 41 inches, canvas. Collection of the artist.

landing."[5] Birds still stir the deep recesses of the human psyche, but not the part that produces joyful elation. Rovner explains that her intention was to conjure the experience of chaos. "I am involved with Chinese meditation. Chinese philosophy teaches that flux is a part of everything. For no reason, suddenly there is change. Things are chased and attacked. It is as if things are possessed by a force. Is it inside? Is it outside? This is the theory of chaos." Envisioning the unpredictable power of nature and its stark beauty requires that Rovner herself escape the confines of rational, literal thinking. She also strips viewers of their comfortable illusions, submerging them in chaos by eroding visual details that enforce familiarity, confidence, and order.

"I am concerned with the blurring of human and animal, of existing and not existing, of being alive and not," Rovner says. "We all share a struggle for existence. It doesn't matter if one is a human or an animal, a plumber or an electrician. We all experience the fragility of being. My work exists in the line between being and not being. People cover themselves with information and an identity. These are the costumes of their presentation. Animals carry a different energy. This is what inspires me. I feel I know this energy, subconsciously and consciously. Animals experience the world beyond worlds. It is basic, fundamental, mysterious, mystical. It is nature's force. To connect, for a moment, with the force that moves through them is my aim. My art is about trying to learn the purpose of being here. This is epic. I occupy the gap between what we see, what we know, and what we think we should feel. It is like a puzzle."

MATURE

1. Unless otherwise noted, all quotes from an interview with the artist, May 12, 1999.

2. Jen Nessel, "Ghostly Visions," *Art News*, Summer 2000, 140.

3. Joseph Campbell, *The Masks of God: Creative Mythology* (New York: Viking Press, 1968), 4.

4. J.C. Cooper, *An Illustrated Encyclopedia of Traditional Symbols* (London: Thames and Hudson, 1999), 48.

5. Hunter Drohojowska Philp, "From Dislocation, Artistic Direction," *Los Angeles Times* 15 June 1997, 56.

Explicit Meanings: Instructional Maps, Notes, and Diagrams

Matthew Ritchie
Born 1964 London, England
1983–1986 Camberwell School of Art, London, BFA
1982 Boston University
Lives and works in New York City

Matthew Ritchie's complex artworks offer viewers more information than the human mind can comfortably absorb. He accomplishes this feat by ignoring two models of space and time (contraction and stability) and reveling in the third (expansion). Instead of expecting his viewers to understand the innumerable systems that proliferate in his installations, he offers them the experience of infinite possibility. But he doesn't stop there. The art he creates not only represents, it also mediates this proliferation by guiding his audience as they negotiate the load of information he offers. His art has multiple functions. It is a body of material to learn, a teaching tool, an enticement to participate, and a reward for participating.

Matthew Ritchie says he wants everything. He claims he cannot restrain his interests. He will not edit. He is unable to prioritize. He cannot dismiss anything as irrelevant. He says, "Art is about desire. I long to figure out everything, to integrate everything."[1] Ritchie actually discovered a precedent for this embracing artistic endeavor when he visited a cave in Brazil where there were 12,000-year-old paintings that amassed images of "sex, aliens from outer space, animals, funerals, whales, shamans—the whole of human experience." Like these primeval artists, Ritchie integrates "everything" in his art. His inclusive agenda demands that he start before the beginning of all beginnings, in the auspicious zone of nothingness that preceded the Big Bang, prior to the dawn of time. Embracing the ultimate beginning is paired with the perpetual delay of conclusions, since scientific consensus has determined that the Big Bang launched a constantly expanding universe. Ritchie's artistic project, like the entirety of creation, is infinite.

The conceptual magnitude of his sprawling narrative and the complexity of its visual equivalents demand an inventive alternative to the conventional artist/audience communication continuum. Ritchie produces neither unfathomable, sophisticated work nor easy-to-understand, simplistic work. Instead, he devises a very complex art scheme and the means for viewers to comprehend it. His works are presented like games. People are taught the rules and invited to play along. This has been Ritchie's intention since the beginning of his career. He has consistently integrated the role of the art educator into his studio practice by creating art that supplies the requisite information for deciphering the work he plans to produce in the future.

The narrative at the core of his endeavor revolves around members of what he calls the "central family." Each character personifies one of the seven quantum forces that have driven the narrative of the universe's evolution since the birth of time. Quanta are parcels into which many forms of energy are subdivided. The energies embodied by the central family are associated with the physical principles that propel the universe. They include the building blocks of matter, the lobes of the brain, the activities in mathematical formulae, chemical elements, mythological personifications, and the components of art. Their names are Lucifer (Lucky), Purson, Astoreth, Beelzebub (Bubba), Lilith, Abaddon, and Satan-El (Stanley). Each is also associated with a special attribute: the photon, the speed of light, absolute zero, ambiguity, deviation, apocalypse, and duality. Their task is awesome

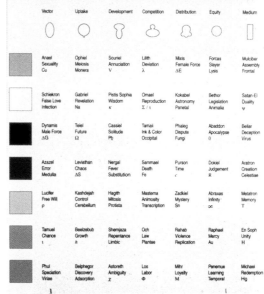

Left: Matthew Ritchie, *The God Game* and *working model* (1995), installation view. Courtesy of the artist and Andrea Rosen Gallery, New York.

Right: Matthew Ritchie, *working model* (1995), 20 x 18 inches, laminated cactus print. Courtesy of the artist and Andrea Rosen Gallery, New York.

Matthew Ritchie, *Hazard*, *Jackpot*, and *Games of Chance and Skill* (1998), installation view. Courtesy of the artist and Andrea Rosen Gallery, New York.

and their effort to accomplish it is frenetic. Ritchie declares that they must "open up the universe." The one quality that these omnipresent forces of matter and energy share is uncertainty. Their actions and campaigns and manias have unknowable outcomes.

The setting for this epic is as fantastical as any conjured by the creators of Marvel Comics, Hollywood films, or video games. It has no "where"—no size, no outside, no inside. It has no "when"—no past, no present, no future. Not even light can penetrate its consuming gravity. Yet it incorporates all time and all matter contained within all the galaxies throughout the cosmos. The scenario that occurs within this paradoxical setting is equally wondrous. The members of the central family enact the Big Bang and all its subsequent natural events and human cavorting, including the tireless scientific scrutiny and inspired religious contemplation in which Matthew Ritchie engages.

Ritchie's ability to manage, coordinate, and integrate manifold esoteric and technically complex disciplines is impressive. Yet he is less interested in displaying his mental virtuosity than in affecting the mental processes of his viewers. A baffled audience means a failed endeavor. Believing that, "people resent art that displays a closed language," and that "becoming an expert on anything is incredibly rewarding," Ritchie provided the means to break the code he constructs, taking advantage of the proficiency of contemporary audiences to decipher charts, diagrams, models, maps, and other compressed capsules of information, devices that facilitate the task of conveying great quantities of information. He explains, "One issue of the *New York Times* contains more information than people in medieval times received in a lifetime. Yet we get it in a flash. We are expert information managers." Furthermore, he believes that viewers naturally seek instructive premises and that curiosity provides a frequently neglected opportunity for art to engender a lasting influence.

Ritchie's inaugural show, for instance, took the form of an innovative solution to the problem that plagues most curators and art educators—how to provide viewers with the essential background material necessary to comprehend a body of work? Ritchie took a proactive stance by mounting an exhibition that consisted exclusively of instructional materials. Instead of the supplementary wall texts that commonly accompany artworks presented in museum contexts, Ritchie presented artworks that took the form of equations, schematics, charts, diagrams, cosmographies, wall drawings, and molecular models. They were created for the sole purpose of providing a key to the work he planned to produce in the future, an epic tale that would unfold from exhibition to exhibition as the characters interact and develop interdependent histories of ever increasing complexity. This initial exhibition, aptly titled *Working Model* (1995), set the stage for the next exhibition, entitled *The Hard Way* (1996).

Interview with Matthew Ritchie
By Zoe Feigenbaum

ZF: How did you begin to show your work?

MR: After art school in the UK I rehabbed some abandoned spaces with friends, including a derelict synagogue in the East End. We made installations and shows specifically for those kinds of spaces. Then I moved to the US and didn't really make work or show for a long time. After about five years here, I showed small works in not-for-profits like Artists Space and with independent curators using derelict storefront spaces. My first real "professional" exhibition was a small group show with Mitchell Algus in New York, which included me, Donald Judd, Robert Smithson, and others.

ZF: What was the influence of your education?

MR: I re-educated myself after I graduated from art school. I came out of minimalism at school. I asked minimalism's questions: "Why do I still want to be an artist?" "How shall I make art?" "Why does something qualify as art?" When I asked myself these questions, I realized that everything that minimalism omitted was what I needed to reintroduce. They had omitted all that we as a species had demanded from art for over 20,000 years. It became crystal clear when I visited some caves in Brazil where there were 12,000-year-old paintings. These paintings show sex, aliens from outer space, animals, funerals, whales, shamans—the whole of human experience. Context materializes through content. This is the opposite of formalism. Minimalism concerned itself with geometry, proportion, a sense of place, and hid from its latent content.

ZF: What were the circumstances surrounding your first big exhibition?

MR: I was writing for *Flash Art* and I met a young dealer called Stefano Basilico when I was reviewing a show he had organized in a temporarary, abandoned space. He came to my studio and asked me if I would like to show with him before he had even found a permanent exhibition space, before he opened his gallery. He had a lot of enthusiasm and energy and a long history working for Sonnabend Gallery, so he combined the best qualities of youth and experience. He ended up opening his new gallery around 1995 in what was my studio when we met. It had been a derelict restaurant. At the time, the art world was still suffering from the late-eighties recession, so a month's rent in lower SoHo was cheap. After that, I moved up to Chelsea, where I have had a studio since 1996. Stefano and I did three shows together and had a very successful creative and business relationship, but his gallery eventually closed and I began showing with Andrea Rosen, who was one of the pioneers of the big gallery move to Chelsea. So there is a strange kind of real estate symmetry in it all.

ZF: Can you describe your relationship with your galleries?

MR: A good gallery is a partner, and like any partner, they bring complementary strengths and creative

It introduced seven major celestial agents and forty-two cohorts, known as the Watchers, who tumble down to Earth from paradise and, as they scatter, cause everything that succeeded the Big Bang—from the advent of mitosis, the introduction of mutation, the delivery of light, the emergence of free will, and the dinosaurs of the Mesozoic era, to the Iron Age, Vikings, the angels Gabriel and Lucifer, the formation of numerology, astronomy, mythology, and the theories of advanced science. Ritchie wove these sundry systems into an inclusive chronicle that he transacted upon a tidy seven-by-seven grid. The resulting configuration of forty-nine squares is magically non-hierarchical, unrestricted in move-ment, and unlimited in the interchangeability of its components. The Magic Square has long been used to represent the concept of infinity. It provided a ready-made framework for this perpetually expanding work of art.

Ritchie's Magic Square involves the antics of seven Watchers who landed on seven conti-nents after fleeing heaven. Their job, as he describes it, is "to watch over the new, tainted, life and build the worlds of thought."[2] They are Mulciber the builder, Azazel the fool, Shemjaza the monomaniac, Penume the librarian, Kashdejah the teacher, Tamaii the eye, and Kokobel the navigator. The Watchers are mentioned in Genesis as giants who were thrown out of heaven for having sex with the children of Adam and Eve. In Ritchie's universe, the Watchers are the offspring of the original family. Each is assigned a cluster of characteristics. Mulciber, for example, is associated with the color green, the fault of indifference, the virtue of being balanced, and the word "truth," while Kashdejah is associated with the color red, the fault of being rash, the virtue of risk-taking, and the word "desire."

When Ritchie amasses diverse systems of knowledge, he is mirroring his life experience. The exponential proliferation of information is a distinguishing characteristic of today's environment. Managing this glut of information is a recent addition to the challenge of human survival. Ritchie describes the anxiety and bewilderment that result from the relentless bombardment with information as "the future unknown, the past a labyrinth of contradictions, our powers of description have failed us."[3] But when he simultaneously provides the means to decipher this "labyrinth of contradictions," he takes command of the chaotic deluge and helps his audience members restore their confidence. His artistic endeavor seems designed to rescue a populace in distress.

Acknowledging that there exist multiple ways to interact with art, Ritchie offered the audience five opportunities for engaging the works that followed *Working Model*. All of these opportunities conspicuously avoid what he calls "dreadful didactics." "Art is not like a light bulb that you can turn on. The gallery can only give an experience. This experience is sensory. I provide this. I don't take the PBS approach that people need to be educated. This is too coercive. The didactic panel provides finite information. This is not the same as learning to experience art. I am not in the business of art education. I am intrigued by the possibility of including a filter as part of the art, and not having it tacked on by the curator. I try to offer a welcoming gesture." Ritchie offers five welcoming gestures. They function in a sequence that lead viewers toward the ultimate state of enlightenment. Even if few viewers actually proceed to the loftiest destination, each plateau improves their ability to cope with the glut of disorganized information that besets people living in today's media-saturated environment.

Visual pleasure is the work's initial allure. Viewers enter the first plateau when the appealing shapes and colors that Ritchie utilizes to create his coded art captivate them. "If people don't want to look, they won't. This does not mean the work has to be pretty. It just has to be visually compelling." The visible components in Ritchie's artworks are derived from the style of popular furnishings and household appliances associated with the 1940s and 1950s, his parents' generation. The artist chose the beginning of his life as a useful metaphor for time's ultimate beginning. This era offers another historic beginning—it was in the 1940s that the first human-made "big bang" occurred: the atomic bomb was exploded. Chromatically, popular colors during these decades were aqua, turquoise, gray, and canary yellow. Texturally, the modern materials Formica, plastic, and Masonite all had unmodulated and flat surfaces. Formally, designers preferred biomorphic shapes to simple geometries. In Ritchie's works of art, these aesthetic elements converge harmoniously, and he might have considered the work complete, but Ritchie is not content to merely delight the eye. "I want people to feel that they are walking into a story, like in a fifteenth-century chapel in Italy." He immerses his visitors within his work by surrounding the paintings with lavish drawings that he applies directly to the wall with markers. Mathematical equations, arcs, lines, and arrows that refer to biological diagrams, architectural studies, and the mappings of coefficients proliferate beyond the frame of the paintings. Additionally, hand-cut, enamel-painted Sintra plastic pieces share the shapes and colors found within the paintings and are pieced together like mosaics, spilling out on the floor and creeping up the walls. They might, for example, represent the part of the brain associated with the character represented in a nearby painting. In all these ways Ritchie's artworks are vibrant but not aggressive, subtle but not dull, crafted but not precious. But even such visual immersion is preliminary to Ritchie's next destination—the intellect.

The second plateau of engagement is initiated once viewers move beyond visual captivation and become aware that these colors, shapes, and lines are not merely attractive patterns and designs. The first clue of their embodied meaning is offered by their structure. It appears too detailed and intricate to be a product of artistic caprice. Colored shapes resemble geometry; linear imagery seems to be derived from algebraic systems. These references to mathematics imply the presence of intended significance. They stimulate curiosity. Explanations are desired. Information is sought. This information could have been distributed—the facts laid out for the viewer, the data presented. But Ritchie wants to captivate audiences who might otherwise be reluctant to enter an arena where multiple systems of knowledge coexist. He lures them by exploiting the same human predilection that infuses mythologies, creation narratives, religious parables, and sacred texts the world over— Ritchie tells stories. The great weight of information in his artworks is presented in the appealing manner of a dramatic narrative. Encyclopedic themes derived from refined scholarship provide the content for engrossing high-action dramas likes those in comics. Cartoon logic dramatizes the teeming pressures of the universe and

differences to the relationship. I have been very lucky in working with people who are deeply passionate about the possibilities inherent in contemporary art and who are also neither solely financially motivated nor dangerously careless of economic realities. My work runs the gamut from one-time, temporary works through oil paintings, floor and wall works, digital photography, sculptures, and on to large-scale installations which can include all the other kinds of media. All of them have different exhibition criteria. Tracking, exhibiting, explaining, and organizing all that material is a big job. This is not helped by my propensity to keep changing, reorganizing, and adapting the work. Hopefully, it also encourages a deepening of the creative dialogue between the gallery and the artist. Understanding the work as an ongoing project or as research means new opportunities keep getting created for both the artist and the gallery.

ZF: Do you work with assistants?

MR: I have one part-time assistant, Karen Leo, who has worked for me for the last five years and is a brilliant artist in her own right. She's great. My wife Garland Hunter is a big resource as well. She comes by and helps out sometimes. If I can't make something easily in the studio, like steel work or large-scale digital printing, I'll use an outside contractor. But I prefer to work everything through my hands first. I'm not so interested in running a big crew and becoming a producer.

ZF: Are you concerned about the longevity of your work?

MR: Any work that isn't carved from pure diamond has a fixed lifespan, whether it's twenty, a hundred, or a thousand years. You can't beat the clock. I work in several media, and there are advantages and disadvantages in each way of working. There can be a real beauty in the fragility of short-term works—like [Robert] Ryman's foam core paintings or a cracked Mondrian. Longevity has to be considered differently each time as part of a larger equation. Most important is making the work now, when it needs to be made, not later. I try to build the work so that it functions by itself. I am doing all I can so that it can survive the absence of the artist.

ZF: How important is it to work in New York?

MR: New York is always in flux, a polymorph. That's its true identity and its strength as a site of inquiry.

ZF: How do you measure success?

MR: Success is the realization of the work. The crudest measure of how you succeed beyond that, of course, is dollars, which mean studio, time, materials. Better is friends and colleagues saying to me, "good job." People may come to see a show. I might get good reviews. Interesting people I don't know might come and talk to me. I don't really believe in momentary success or ultimate success. You can be complacent in a micro world or you can aim to succeed in the big time and you may fail. Not everyone can be Michelangelo but anyone can try. The audience is atomized. Success is just getting what you need to continue working.

Matthew Ritchie, *The Big Deal* (1996), 100 x 72 inches, oil and marker on canvas. Courtesy of the artist and Andrea Rosen Gallery, New York.

the super-protagonists who enact them. Ritchie believes that as long as he rewards his viewers with a cast of fascinating characters and interwoven plots, they will be induced to decipher the multiplicity of references heaped in his work. Thus, the primal transformation of the universe from potentiality to actuality, an event too grandiose and dimensionless for any human brain to accommodate, becomes imaginable because Ritchie compares it to a diversion played out in an infinitely hot and congested gambling hall. He portrays it verbally as well as visually: "It was crowded in there, no room to breathe. Good jammed up against evil; reason pressing down on stupidity, every possibility all at once, trapped in a golden venture of souls, with the temperatures endlessly rising. Time to play."

The narrative crescendos with the following description of the metaphoric Big Bang in the gambling hall: "(Lucky) made his move on the old guy as fast as anyone could but he was no match for a man made of time. The timekeeper's two hands, the hour and the minute, sneaked out faster than you could think; shuffled the cards, rolled the dice, grabbed Asta's coil of red wire and whipped it around Luck's neck. Photons scattered as the superstrings cut through his throat in a perfect Schwarzschild radius, spraying over the couch, the carpet and the TV set, blurring the image of the cartoon show as the blood trickled down the screen. 'There's only one way out,' said the off-screen narrator. 'The hard way.' Cartoon superheroes tumbled in an endless void.... Everything you ever wanted, all at once, the fall of the quanta, the escape of the uncertain. A clock made of stars, ticking at the speed of light until the end of time. Snake eyes rolled for eternity."[4]

Ritchie contrives these events to enable the audience to envision his ultimate destination—the birth of the universe: "The door was unlocked in a massive gamma ray burst, a blood sacrifice, as the seed burst open. In four minutes, it was eighty light years across, within six minutes it was eight hundred light years across. Now it is uncountable billions of light years across."[5]

To assure that his audience will not merely be beguiled by the narrative of Lucky and Asta and the other colorful characters, Ritchie provides an explicit reminder that these images are metaphors for actual events of epic proportions. He explains, "The game was nothing more than a three-dimensional cross-section of a puzzle made of time—a metaphor, a diagram of chance run amok. The moving parts of the puzzle were the Gamblers themselves. Its lubrication was their juices, spit, mucus, semen, blood, tears, and shit. The game opened the door into a possible universe, our universe, by twisting and folding space/time in a dance of improbable results." Thus the audience is primed to witness the beginning of time, an event that is, by definition, beyond the scope of human experience. He is forthright about his intentions to lure the audience with tall-tale telling, announcing after one particularly extravagant

MR: I know that the audience at art venues is particular. And this audience is growing rapidly. It is astonishing and wonderful to realize how many opportunities there are to see and learn about art. People have more access today than ever. Bringing art to the people—this has been accomplished on an epic scale. If many don't understand contemporary art, that is no different from most people not understanding the latest developments in physics and foreign policy. It takes a huge investment to keep up with these changes and to figure out which is good. The quantity of practitioners is always small. There is, inevitably, a pyramid. But still, it is the artist's responsibility to be interesting. This is a totally voluntary, reciprocal environment on both sides. The world needs art only as much as artists need the world to see it. Everyone is a player. I don't believe in "the audience," I believe in individuals and never underestimating their potential, and so far, I have not been disappointed.

POWERFUL

passage about the Big Bang, "If you believe that, you'll believe anything. But that's how it always gets started. Somebody tells us a story we'd like to believe, that we'd like just as much to hear is only a story, and we're hooked, breathless for more, the next version."[6] Bolstered by these aids, the colored shapes and lines coalesce into identifiable characters, and formal relationships are understood as enactments in a spectacle of operatic proportions.

Viewers enter the third plateau of experience when they realize that the sci-fi narrative addresses complex scientific truths and concurrent cultural transactions. A chain of responses characterizes this stage of audience interaction. A story about everything involves multiple levels of awareness. Viewers are aware that they are looking at art that appears to be abstract but has a chronicle embedded in it. They are aware of themselves attempting to interpret this narrative. The audience enters this plateau when they abandon themselves to Ritchie's compulsion to annex ever more platforms of denotation onto his complicated scenarios. His stories proliferate like fractal generators, absorbing celestial mechanics, chemical reactions, quantum cosmology, and a host of other systems. Charting the entire universe and accounting for all subsequent outcomes is as taxing to its audience as it is demanding on its creator. That is its function. This art is a test, says Ritchie, just like life. "It is like jumping in faith that someone will catch you." Ritchie strives to create an audience of jumpers. He first tantalizes them with sensual pleasures. Then they are enticed by a story. It is presented in the form of a game. Clues are provided. The riddles are identifiable. Gradually the unfamiliar language releases its meanings. Viewers are enticed to engage because they discern the possibility of figuring things out. They yield to Ritchie's provocations because they anticipate that their efforts will be rewarded with comprehension. Ritchie's art also promises pure fun. Viewers are invited to play what Ritchie calls "God's Game" by pasting together the vast domains of matter, human civilization, and individual mentality.

Ritchie prepared a road map for viewers to use before they embarked on the brain-sizzling journey through his multifaceted narrative. Yet he is more intent on stimulating curiosity than presenting data. Something that appears either arbitrary or complex discourages thoughtful engagement. "For the first show, the working model was a map. It was explicitly set up with charts and diagrams, lists of all the characters.... For the second show, it was like, you have the map, now let's go on the journey. So everything that was static in the first show gets pushed into motion, and all the characters that were iconic and static are now active and have personalities and are arguing with each other, and it's all falling apart, the whole thing is collapsing. But you can't do that unless you have a map to begin with."[7] Thus, according to Ritchie, the first exhibition "was organized to show you a schematic of the universe, because what I didn't want to do was plunge people into yet another arbitrary mythological construct. You have to be very rigorous about your own internal mythology or it collapses and people lose faith in it. So this was an attempt to be very explicit—here are the rules up front, there are no secrets, so if I make a mistake or backtrack or start to manipulate this, you'll be able to call me on it."[8] Ritchie further bolsters the confidence of viewers who encounter this spectacular sci-fi chronicle by basing it on verifiable experiences. Rather than pure flights of the imagination, scientific references abound. For example, each character is correlated with a particular element on the periodic table. Thus chemistry, not whimsy, determines the nature of their interactions. Likewise, mathematics gives their activities credulity; equations represent their sporting and frolicking and scheming and stumbling. In addition, Ritchie is assuring the rigor of his chronicle by actually visiting the seven places on Earth identified in the narrative as the sites where each Watcher landed after fleeing heaven. For example, Ritchie visited Norway because it is the location where Tamaii, the black Watcher, fell. In order to gain Tamaii's knowledge of ultimate darkness, he timed his visit to coincide with the winter solstice, a day when the sun never rises. Then he made absolutely certain that no light would penetrate his visual field by descending into a coal cavern 900 feet under ground.

Following the progression from sensuality, to curiosity, to witness, Ritchie focuses on consciousness itself at the fourth plateau of involvement. He creates a vivid metaphor for everyday experience in which our brains constantly collate innumerable disconnected messages. This complex mental process is accounted for by assigning each of the seven characters a corresponding lobe of the brain. Thus, the Watchers's skirmishes and alliances transcend their status as entertaining dramas and become correlates for the multiplicity of processes being transacted instant by instant in our brains. Ritchie explains, "This is about constructing ... a mental space that's similar to the space in your real brain where you make decisions based on inadequate information and belief."[9] Viewers enter the fourth plateau when they apply Ritchie's narrative to the influx of impressions, the resulting commotion, and their search for order. They discern, within their minds, processes that resemble the fusion of stellar cores, random flashes of gamma rays, neutrons trapped in spiral orbits, and supercharged thermonuclear particle surges. The fourth plateau is identified as "ecstasy." It marks the transition from the role of witness to that of participant. By assimilating the onslaught of information that occupies multiple layers of consciousness, viewers "take off" and become "perpetual motion machines." The brain is awash with information. Ritchie describes this experience: "All space and time are products of the initial 'fireball.' We are still inside it, as it spreads farther and farther out. There is no past, no future, only an eternal now, a firewall of space-time being blown out from the first breath. The rippled event horizon of the big bang means it is still happening now, will always be happening, over and over again."[10] At this stage the viewer's mind becomes a force of its own, divorced from its specific content. It has exploded beyond the singularity of a "universe." Ritchie has invented two words to express this expansion—"multiverse" and "omniverse."

And still there is a fifth plateau. Can there be a state beyond ecstasy? Ritchie's ecstasy is not escapist. He diligently works to assure a connection between his invented world and the viewer's lived world. The fifth plateau is attained when viewers leave the gallery with the realization that they resemble the protagonists in Ritchie's epic drama. Like the Watchers, they too stumble without destinations, are subject to arbitrary events, veer on collision courses, and act on the basis of inadequate information. Ritchie demonstrates that it has been like this since the Big Bang and remains like this today despite civilization's advances. Ritchie describes the manner in which we are living as "this vortex where we're constantly gathering more and more stuff." He thinks the Internet is the most obvious example of the hoarding and synthesis of an enormous amount of information. "Let's get everything together in one place for maximum incoherence."[11]

Like Chaos Theory, these conditions are fluid and interchangeable; there are too many variables to make patterns discernible. When asked what he expects the viewer to conclude from his excursion into complexity, Ritchie responded, "Life is as complicated as it appears."[12] And yet he protects the mind from being overwhelmed by this complicated scenario. As viewers gain an understanding of the narrative, they also come to recognize the many ways that exist to absorb life's complexity, and how intricately connected are disparate bodies of belief, and how metaphors can make grand premises less intimidating. In all these ways he prevents the door to information from slamming shut.

For these reasons, Ritchie is fond of saying, "information is a sublime experience," because information has become both more all-encompassing and less controllable than nature.

"The place we do have, where you can disappear, is into the information nexus. You're going to be confronted with so many paradoxes of your own position, that you cannot make a definitive statement. It becomes sublime, you have to just sit here."[13] In this manner Ritchie's work offers one way out of the central debate in neurology commonly referred to as "the binding problem." It contemplates how the individual integrates parts of the self to produce one personality. Ritchie's art not only offers the means to integrate personality, it integrates the massive, mind-boggling concept of "everything"—envisioning it in its immanent state prior to the Big Bang: "It was the whole universe; the birth, the hope, the blame; the dream, the betrayal, the revenge: waiting inside one tiny, hot, little dot."[14]

[1] Unless otherwise noted, all quotes from an interview with the artist, June 4, 1999.

[2] Matthew Ritchie, *The Big Story* (Cleveland: Cleveland Center for Contemporary Art, 1999), 66.

[3] Ritchie, 55.

[4] Ritchie, 41.

[5] Ritchie, 53.

[6] Matthew Ritchie, *The Hard Way*, exhibition, artist's statement (Galerie Meteo, Paris, 1996).

[7] Jennifer Berman, "Matthew Ritchie," interview, *BOMB*, Spring 1997, 62.

[8] ibid.

[9] ibid., 61.

[10] Ritchie, *The Big Story*, 53.

[11] Berman, 63.

[12] Owen Drolet, "Interview with Matt Ritchie," <http://desires.com/1.3/Art/docs/ritchie.html>.

[13] Berman, 65.

[14] Ritchie, *The Big Story*, 21.

Obscured Meanings: Squirming into Truth's Cracks

Eve Andrée Laramée
Born 1956 Los Angeles, California
1973–1978 San Diego State University, BA with distinction in fine art, also studied general physical science
1978–80 San Francisco Art Institute, MFA, sculpture and performance art
Lives and works in Brooklyn, New York

Eve Andrée Laramée acknowledges that before the advent of advanced technologies, fact and fiction resided in two distinguishable categories. In art, for example, it was possible to differentiate between a fiction (accepted as evidence of a rich imagination, not a lie) and realism (usually associated with astute observation, not a lack of imagination). In contemporary life, however, the difference between fact and fiction has been complicated by experiences that derive from simulations, virtual reality, and digital manipulations, and by such crossover products as designer knock-offs, tribute bands, and docudramas. Laramée's works of art challenge viewers in the same manner that they are challenged by contemporary technologies—to decipher fact from fiction.

Speaking with Eve Andrée Laramée in her Brooklyn studio constituted the latest installment in an ambitious art project that has been presented through a variety of communication channels. It has been an exhibition, a performance, an Internet intervention, and most recently, an interview. She believes it could occupy the rest of her life. Despite the differences between the modes of communication used, each manifestation elicits a number of responses from the audience. Admiration: the work is meticulously crafted, visually sumptuous, and thematically coherent. Doubt: something seems amiss. Bewilderment: credibility of the content begins to erode. Revelation: false information has been presented. Correction: the original impression must be revised. Fascination: gullibility is exposed, and the basis for forming beliefs is examined.

Laramée fiddles with certainty like a man might fiddle with his mustache. She twists each strand of truth just enough to place it under tension but not enough to uproot it. She accomplishes this by presenting cleverly disguised false information. The audience's skepticism regarding the credibility of her assertions leads them toward a realization of the dangers of single-track thinking. It demonstrates that intellectual rigidity prevents the mind from questioning its assumptions, and that unquestioned assumptions can lead to false conclusions. Discussing an exhibition she mounted in 1997 at the Islip Art Museum in New York entitled *Secret History: Yves Fissiault, Artist of the Cold-War Era*, Laramée revealed that this elaborate installation was based on a double secret. One 'secret' was made known to the public, that the objects exhibited were presented as the clandestine art activities of an unknown scientist. Wall text provided museum visitors with a plausible explanation of how this remarkable body of work became the possession of the artist. Laramée stated that as a science major in the 1970s she worked as a research assistant to the scientist/inventor, Yves Fissiault. To her great surprise, she was designated the executrix of his estate. The text asserted that the exhibition was gleaned from the notebooks, drawings, paintings, photographs, small devices, and personal effects that filled the seven suitcases and one steamer trunk that were delivered to her upon his death 1991. The audience was led to believe that she assumed the role of the show's curator by organizing and framing the deceased man's artworks and notes uncovered from these trunks. Furthermore, she created the impression that she had supplemented these artifacts by contributing documentation on the bizarre life of Fissiault, their presumed creator.

The second secret was only made known to the museum director and curator. To them Laramée revealed that she was actually the creator of the works of art and that Fissiault was fictional, a product of the her imagination and the material she presented as Fissiault's was actually fabricated by her. In addition to producing Fissiault's artworks, she fabricated official-looking documents, fake correspondence, phony sketches, photographs, and sundry artifacts to provide evidence of Fissiault's existence. Like a skilled counterfeiter, Laramée scrupulously used Cold War era paper, typewriters, seals, references, and jargon. She immersed herself in his world by listening to the music someone living in the 1940s and 1950s might have heard on the radio, perusing the newspapers and literature he might have read. Detail by detail, she assembled his biography by fabricating his colleagues, work history, secret passions, and family relationships. Based on this vast construction, she created plausible art by an imagined artist. Her effort was so thorough and believable that most visitors failed to detect her ruse despite the lunacy of the claims she made—for example, that Fissiault developed a hollow-earth theory oriented according to the north and south "holes" that expand and contract like the pupils in the eyes. Laramée 's inconsistencies and unlikely proclamations even failed to alert a *New York Times* art reviewer who wrote an admiring report of Fissiault's talents.[1]

The museum director was reluctant to accept her ruse. She feared that the show would fail to attract an audience if the name of an unknown scientist was attached to the exhibition instead of the name of a well-known artist like Laramée. "The director's concerns made me think a lot about my own credibility and my authority as an artist. It got me thinking about how a name can validate a work. Art institutions enforce this validation. At this time, I had been working on the credibility and authority of science. These same issues play a role in art as well. Both are constructed on belief systems."[2] Since her invented biography identified Yves Fissiault as an electrical engineer who not only made art, but indulged an unscientific fascination with mysticism, Laramée used the exhibition to explore the issue of faith and belief as they apply to art and science. "Yves Fissiault's hollow earth model allowed me to form a theory and test it by building a system of logic around an absurd premise. All cosmological theories about the nature of the world around us, like the concept of the glass dome over the earth, become absurd as soon as new theories replace them. What I wanted was to try to believe something I knew was false. This would shift consciousness."[3]

Art imposes a particularly inhospitable circumstance for deception to be recognized because it normally contorts the meanings of authentic and fake. The word fake, for example, does not apply to a

Interview with Eve Andreé Larameé
By Zoe Feigenbaum

ZF: What made you move to New York?

EAL: When I got out of graduate school in San Francisco in 1980, I moved to New Mexico and I lived there for six years. I went there to unlearn school. I felt like I had gone through art school and graduate school and I was unclear about what was really mine and what was learned. So I decided to isolate myself, to move to the desert and figure it all out. I founded this arts organization, ART/MEDIA, and ended up commissioning artists to do projects in the mass media—on billboards and TV and the radio and newspaper inserts. So, for six years I was there working both sides, being an artist making and showing my work and being an administrator raising funds and helping to facilitate other artists' work. Then I decided that I needed to enlarge the conversation with my peers into an international discourse, so I moved to New York.

ZF: What was the first indication that you were likely to become a successful and recognized artist?

EAL: The first big push was a reaction against something. When I was in college I got a lot of positive feedback from teachers and others students. My last semester in school I put together this portfolio to apply to grad school and showed it to a gallery director and I said, "Would you look at it and tell me what you think?" So, he looked at my work and he said, "You know, you are a really good artist but you are never going to make it in the art world. You have three strikes against you. You are young. You are pretty. And you are a woman."

ZF: He said that?

EAL: He said that! That was when I got political as an artist and I realized, if this is what I am up against, I had better listen to it. That's when I really started to push.

ZF: How did you push? What was your reaction?

EAL: I applied to graduate school and got in. I didn't take a studio on campus. I just decided, I am going to do this like an artist, not a student. I rented a Victorian house. The bottom of it was a carriage house and it opened out to this yard where there was this old horse stable. It was a really cool place. So, I rented an apartment and I rented that whole ground-floor carriage house as a studio. I started seeking out opportunities to show.

ZF: When was your first show?

EAL: My first show was when I was an undergraduate. I had a teacher who encouraged me to put some work into shows and I got into a show at the Laguna Museum in California.

ZF: How did you get your first solo museum show?

EAL: In 1981 or '82, I read a review of the work of Bruce Nauman at the Albuquerque Museum in the local newspaper. Having seen the exhibition, and being a great admirer of Nauman's work, I felt that the review conveyed a misunderstanding or "nonunderstanding" of the work. I wrote a rebuttal in a letter to the editor.

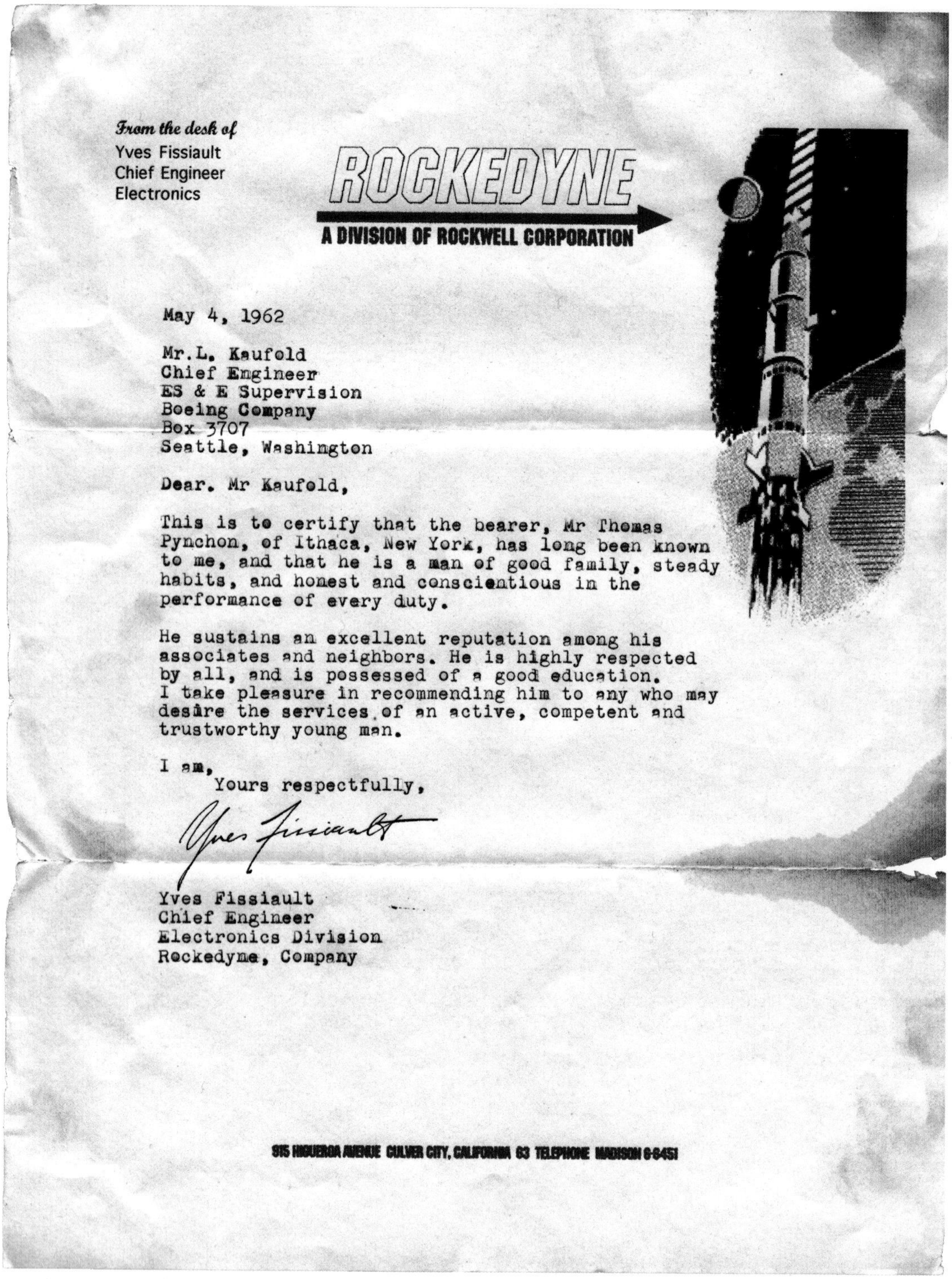

From the desk of
Yves Fissiault
Chief Engineer
Electronics

ROCKEDYNE
A DIVISION OF ROCKWELL CORPORATION

May 4, 1962

Mr.L. Kaufold
Chief Engineer
ES & E Supervision
Boeing Company
Box 3707
Seattle, Washington

Dear. Mr Kaufold,

This is to certify that the bearer, Mr Thomas
Pynchon, of Ithaca, New York, has long been known
to me, and that he is a man of good family, steady
habits, and honest and conscientious in the
performance of every duty.

He sustains an excellent reputation among his
associates and neighbors. He is highly respected
by all, and is possessed of a good education.
I take pleasure in recommending him to any who may
desire the services of an active, competent and
trustworthy young man.

I am,
    Yours respectfully,

Yves Fissiault

Yves Fissiault
Chief Engineer
Electronics Division
Rockedyne, Company

915 HIGUEROA AVENUE CULVER CITY, CALIFORNIA 63 TELEPHONE MADISON 8-6451

Eve Andrée Laramée, *Secret History (detail)*: Fabricated letter of recommendation for Thomas Pynchon on pseudo-Rockedyne stationery (1997), 11 x 8.5 inches, ink on paper. Courtesy of the artist.

SCOPING AN AUDIENCE

still life in which the illusion of grapes is created by a painter. In this instance, the work is considered to be imaginative, not dishonest. Art is authentic as long as the signature of the artist who created this painted deception is genuine. But when an artist's skill is utilized to simulate the work of another artist, accusations of forgery and fraud erupt in the art community, as when the artist Sherrie Levine rephotographed famous images by the renowned photographer Edward Weston, and presented them as her artworks. In other words, viewers don't expect art to be a factual depiction, but they do expect the creator of the fiction to be true. Eve Andrée Laramée reversed this convention by assigning credit for her artwork to another artist. She hid the fact that both the artist and his artworks were products of the "curator's" imagination and effort, and that this "curator" was actually an artist. Nor did she reveal that even the material that appeared to be supporting documentation shared the illusory mode of artistic deception.

Laramée's challenge to belief and credibility in art was even applied to the authority of the art institution itself. She installed her covert art exhibition in the scholarly manner of a historical show. "There was a timeline and all the objects were installed chronologically." She then confirmed this image of authority by presenting herself as a curator, the source of dependable information in museums. "I gave a performance by leading the visitors on a walk-through tour in the role of the curator at the opening. I effortlessly fielded questions from the audience on the details of Fissiault's life." Rigid thinkers who adhered to these signs of museum authority missed discovering the truth (that a deception had been perpetrated). But visitors who were capable of detecting the ruse corrected their error. In the process they confronted their susceptibility to false beliefs and their cleverness at getting the joke.

Two enticements induced visitors to linger in the exhibition and contemplate the complex experience it offered. One was the visual appeal of the installation. The other was the riveting narrative that it conveyed. Laramée purported that Fissiault worked on gyroscopes in the nose cones of the missiles that were produced during the Cold War. He held a high-security job in the aerospace industry during a period that was rampant with paranoia. Because his unorthodox activities were certain to jeopardize his position, he kept them secret from his conservative employers. He was ultimately fired as a security risk.

Laramée perpetuated her subterfuge in 1998 when she was invited to co-host an Internet symposium organized to discuss Internet-based artistic practices. As the only artist on a panel of theoreticians and art historians, she decided to utilize the occasion to extend her disruption of systems of belief. She interjected her fictional cast of characters into this scholarly context, conjuring increasingly outrageous stories about Yves Fissiault and his B-movie starlet wife,

Shortly thereafter I got a telephone call from Ellen Landis, the curator at the museum, who told me that she and the director, Jim Moore, found my ideas interesting and wondered who I was. I informed them I was an artist and they invited me to come to the museum to meet with them. I did so and brought documentation of my work (the large evaporation-crystallization installations) and they offered me a show, pretty much on the spot. In 1983, I mounted my first solo museum show, *Venusian Lagoons*, there. They published a beautiful catalogue with color and black-and-white photos, which helped me to get other shows in the future.

ZF: What would you consider your first big sale?

EAL: I was still in graduate school. There was an exhibition of student work on campus. Two collectors came and bought two of my paintings. The last thing I was thinking about was selling my work. That was a big surprise.

ZF: How do feel that school contributed to your career as an artist?

EAL: I spent a lot of time in the library, and I think that that was a really important part of my art education. I grew up across the street from a library in Los Angeles, which was sort of my safe haven. I would go there after school, then I'd go home for dinner, then go back to the library and stay there until it closed at night. And I continued with that pattern of being a library kid throughout my schooling. I think that having access to resources, to literary sources, to art historical sources and theory and visual sources was really an important thing for me. It helped develop cross-disciplinary thinking. Also, I had a few professors who were really special. They took the time to dive into my motives and my intentions as an artist.

ZF: Do you feel that there are any people or teachers who have helped you along or given you your first push?

EAL: Well, early on I did have a teacher who was a grad student at the time. Her name is Diana Folsom. I was torn between going into the sciences and going into the arts. Although I made art my whole life, my family pushed me into the sciences. It was Diana who sat me down in my 2-D design class and said, "You should really seriously think about being an artist." There was something about the way that she met my eyes when she said that that really touched me. Another person who has continued to be really an important inspiration and kind of a parallel thinker is the sculptor Erica Wanenmacher. She is an amazing artist. We are "best girl art buddies." Her perspective on art has been really important to me.

ZF: Who or what do you feel has promoted you?

EAL: I entered the art world through the not-for-profit world. I started showing my work in artist-run spaces and alternative spaces, and then I started getting calls from people at museums. "I saw your work at such-and-such art center and I am interested in finding out more about what you do." So, it was through the alternative spaces that the door opened to museums, and it was through showing my work at museums that a

Mia L'Amar. Heddy Lamarr, who was both a sex symbol on the big screen in the 1950s and an electrical engineer, inspired Laramée's concoction of Mia L'Amar's biography. Laramée made up the preposterous, but not impossible, assertion that Yves and Mia played significant roles in the evolution of the Internet by way of experimenting with ARPAnet, a precursor to the Internet designed by the United States Department of Defense for emergency communication during the Cold War. Presumably, L'Amar, like Lamarr, exacerbated the nation's paranoia about secret communist agents infiltrating the film industry. Laramée's narrative provided a vivid and detailed account of undercover message relay systems and electronic numerical integrators. Her riveting tale described how L'Amar inserted classified scientific information into her dialogue in B- science fiction films where the secret information could be picked up by the Soviets. In one instance, Mia reportedly interjected information on the physics of cosmic rays into the 1959 film *It Came from the Ring Nebula* . Of course, both the film and the dialogue were constructions of Laramée's imagination, as was the assertion that after hearings from the House Un-American Activities Committee, L'Amar was blacklisted. Mia's ostracism by Hollywood reactionaries fed suspicions of Fissiault's alliance with Communism. Ultimately, Fissiault was fired from the Defense Department supplier for whom he worked during the Cold War and jailed. Theodor Adorno, the renowned intellectual, posted a $10,000 bail bond. The sum represented his entire life's savings and enabled Fissiault and Mia L'Amar to flee to Mexico in a 1956 Thunderbird. The narrative proceeds to describe how they sped down Highway 101, picking up another esteemed member of the intelligentsia—the author Thomas Pynchon, a writer distinguished by his ability to overlay fantasies with historical fact. Pynchon, it is told, was in Mexico enjoying a peyote vacation. And in this way Laramée's story weaves increasingly elaborate plots with meticulously detailed subplots. She even purported that Yves Fissiault used his electrical engineering skills to design the first synthesizer for musician Frank Zappa. Laramée pretends to provide the facts to bolster this assertion by stating, "It was the same year that Yves and Mia L'Amar, his wife, moved into a duplex apartment at 1819 Bellevue Avenue in the Echo Park section of Los Angeles. They befriended a young neighbor, Francis Vincent Zappa...." Gradually, the symposium participants came to realize that this accumulation of credible details spun an absurd tale. Laramée's scenario was too preposterous to be believable. Those scholars who were not offended by her impertinence delighted in the artist's imaginative test of their gullibility and played along by fabricating their own accounts of events that might have transpired between the fictional characters.

In 1999, Laramée expanded her pretext again. This time she posted a question to a Thomas Pynchon discussion group on the Internet asking, "Does anyone know about Pynchon's involvement with Yves Fissiault when they were working on the ARPAnet project together?" The participants in the discussion group were all Pynchon scholars and admirers. The reference to ARPAnet did not raise their suspicions about the motives of the questioner. Furthermore, Pynchon's biography reveals that he really was employed in the aerospace industry as a young man. Unsuspecting participants accepted the sincerity of the question and concluded that they simply didn't know of the scientist whose name was Fissiault. Most did not suspect that Fissiault never existed. Some, however, detected the falsity that accompanied these elements of truth. Those with the prescience to question the questioner fell into two groups. The Pynchon purists protested Laramée's deception, accusing her of literary desecration and banishing her from their site. The rest, including such esteemed Pynchon scholars as John Krafft and Hanjo Berressem, interpreted her incursion as an act that honored the literary talents of Thomas Pynchon, who himself puts nebulous spins on ordinary circumstances.

Art that tampers with truth complicates the task of its creator as well as its recipients. Before our interview, Laramée's artistic process seemed dominated by the imaginative use of meticulous scholarship. The accumulation of literary, historic, and scientific information that comprised her elaborate installations depended on dedicated research. During the interview, however, it became apparent that the high-octane fuel of personal compulsion also drives her. In addition to citing her work as being about "a critique of Cold War paranoia, a re-thinking of the notion of truth in science and the media, and an active intervention with institutional presenters of art," she announced that it was fundamentally "an experiment in self-transformation. Eve became Yves. The practice of art was a real-life experiment in identity that lasted six months." Thus what appeared to the public to be documentation, and to the museum's curator and director to be farce, became re-categorized as personal exploration.

"One of the things that has recently become clear to me," explained Laramée, "is that my work of the past twenty years has not just challenged science and the authority of truth. Now I realize it has everything to do with my relationship to my family, particularly to my father, who I never really knew. In the *Secret History*, I was able to re-invent the person I imagine him to have been. I grew up in Southern California and was raised by my mother. My father was an electrical engineer who immigrated to the United States from Montreal. He worked in the aerospace industry during the Cold War. The last time I saw him I was five. I remember how he smelled. I remember some mannerisms. I remember speaking French with him. My mother was always secretive about his past. Her ambiguous statements about him were designed to prove his lack of importance in her life and mine. She neutralized him. She said the only thing I needed to know about my father was that he was a genius and inventor. Sometimes she would say, 'It is better that you do not know.' That totally intrigued me. My curiosity about my father came to a head in my mid-twenties. I began to search for him through birth records, death records, drivers licenses, but I never found him. The search was complicated by the fact that my father changed his name several times from his birth name, Yves André Fissiault dit Laramée. He was also known as Yves Fissiault, Yves Laramée, André Fissiault Laramée. When he emigrated in 1945, he changed his name legally to Andre Laramée."

Laramée then proceed to unveil the third level of artistic deception. During our interview, she disclosed that material she first presented as factual documentation (the work of Fissiault), and subsequently identified as fictitious fabrications (the work of Eve Laramée pretending to be Yves Fissiault), was actually both fact and fiction. "In 1995 my mother was ailing and suddenly felt the need to trace my father. She produced his Social Security number, which she had always denied having. It enabled me to discover that André Laramée had died just a few years earlier. He had been living in Hollywood,

commercial gallery first approached me. Maybe it was because I had been an arts administrator that I was comfortable with that institutional world more than with the commercial gallery world.

ZF: Please describe your studio.

EAL: Oh, my studio! My studio is in Williamsburg. It's big and beautiful in a run-down sort of way. One of the things about being a sculptor and about being an installation artist is you make a lot of mess. So, my studio is in an old factory building. It's all artists. I have been there for fourteen years now. It's always an unstable situation. Three years ago I bought a house, and my master plan is to convert the ground floor of the house into a studio so I can consolidate living and working. I have a nice garden, so the studio would open out onto green space.

ZF: I am sure you have watched Williamsburg change.

EAL: When I first moved to Williamsburg, it was pretty scary. There were people getting their cars stolen, people getting beat up and held up at knifepoint right outside my building. So it was dicey. It's not dicey any more. It's quite sweet and there are amenities, good food, and you run into your friends on the street. Many of my ex-students are in Williamsburg.

ZF: How do you preserve your work?

EAL: Work on paper I try to keep in a flat file in sleeves. I feel as if my works on paper are a record of my thought processes. If anything were to survive a hundred years from now, I would want it to be my drawings. A lot of installations have been dismantled and destroyed. When something is site specific, it just doesn't make sense to remake it somewhere else. Works that are not site specific get dismantled and stored in the basement of my studio. Some of that stuff is ephemeral just by the nature of the materials. I have used fluctuating materials like salt and tar, water, wine, and dust. They don't have that great of a half-life.

ZF: You don't get sad when you see something dissolve?

EAL: When I would dismantle an installation after a month or two that I put two years worth of research into, making prototypes and fabricating components, it was sad! I started to make little reliquaries. I would reserve or preserve part of an installation, alter its form and turn it into sculpture. So that was a way of dealing with that transformation.

ZF: Do you have any assistants?

EAL: If I am working towards a deadline for an exhibition, then I'll hire assistants to do certain things. But most of the time I like having a solitary experience in my studio. Thinking time in the studio is as important as making time, and that's something that I can't do if there is another person around. I have also worked with fabricators, which I guess you can say are assistants.

ZF: Do you have any other jobs? Do you supplement your income in any way?

EAL: I teach. I do lectures and workshops.

ZF: Do you have health insurance? Do you have a mortgage on your house?

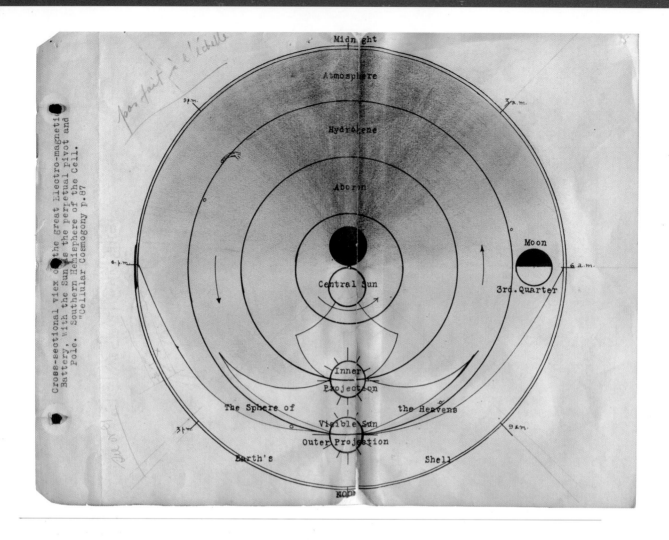

Eve Andrée Laramée, *Secret History (detail): Hollow Earth Diagram by Yves Fissiault dit Laramée* (1997/c. late 1930s–early 1940s), 11 x 8 inches, ink and pencil on paper. Courtesy of the artist and father of the artist.

just a few miles from our home in Los Angeles. Later that year my mother died. When I was clearing out her house, I made an amazing discovery—seven notebooks that belonged to my father! I remember seeing these notebooks as a child. I thought they were scientific, related to his work as an electrical engineer. But it turned out that my father did not just occupy the official realm of science. The books were full of diagrams and notes on alternative theories about the universe—alchemy, cosmology, the occult, hollow earth theory, mysticism, and Rosicrutianism—an esoteric movement popular in the seventeenth and eighteenth centuries distinguished by its secret occult symbols. One notebook shows that he was teaching himself Sanskrit. He was interested in numerous non-dominant systems of knowledge."

Insight into the personality of the father she barely knew emerged as Laramée studied his drawing style, his manner of forming sentences, and his handwriting as it appeared in notes throughout the secret notebooks. They provided the foundation for constructing his biography and the means to create "his" art. Laramée explained, "I hoped to not only create a work as a 'visual novel,' but to discover something about the person who I imagined my father to be. I referred to notebooks and other documents that actually belonged to my father for source material and inspiration. I attempted to think like another person. I was able to do this by not breaking character, by allowing my character, Yves, to be real in the world, and by questioning how the art world and I define authorship...I stopped using my own mind in making work. I asked, 'What would he do? How would he do it?' I entered a kind of trance state by listening to the music he could have listened to in the forties: Stepan Grapalli, Django Reinhardt, the Paris Hot Club... It was at times frightening to try to think like another person. Sometimes I felt like I could slip over an edge. But I also learned I had skills I was unaware of, that I could build display cases and create paintings and devise theories that had to do with optics and harmonics. I was incredibly prolific during this period."

In fabricating evidence to substantiate all that she imagined to have transpired in his life, Laramée drew on the blank pages in her father's notebooks as he would have and made notes using a type-writer similar to one he had used. She altered her way of structuring sentences by conjuring up his French-Canadian phrases and using his misspellings She twisted this composite material into a tangled chronicle dealing with Cold War politics, false identities, and futur-istic inventions.

During this process, Laramée was commissioned to create an installation by the Islip Art Museum. She used this opportunity, she says, to "give her father a show." The many gaps in his biography required that she invent the missing parts. A hybrid character emerged, part factual and part fictional. The fictional part was inspired by a character in Thomas Pynchon's novel, *The Crying of Lot*

EAL: I have health insurance through my teaching job. I have a mortgage on my house. It's a sweet story how I got my house. I came home one day and there was a note under the windshield wiper of my truck that said, "Ring our buzzer. We have a surprise for you." It was signed "Dottie and John," who were my neighbors. So I rang their buzzer, and John answered the door and said, "Do you want to buy our house? We'd like you to have it." Just like that. With the help of the manager of the bank I was able to get a loan. I used my work and small art collection as collateral for the loan because I had nothing else of value except my ten-year-old pickup truck and some camera gear.

ZF: Do you ever feel like you need to get away from your art?

EAL: No. I feel like I need to get away from my desk. The more time I have with my art in the studio, the happier I am. But it seems like over the years I spend more and more time at my desk making phone calls and answering the mail and e-mail and doing adminis-trative work and managing my old work. If I were to have a full-time assistant, it would be someone who is an administrative assistant, not someone helping me to make the work.

ZF: If you could change anything about your life or the way that you live it based on the fact that you are an artist, would you?

EAL: Sometimes I wish my life were a little more "normal" or stable. It has been years and years of uncertainty, financial uncertainty, not knowing whether or not I am going to have enough money to get by each month.

ZF: What gave you that confidence to say, "Okay, this is what I want to be doing even if it's scary." Because a lot of people would retreat to a desk job.

EAL: When I was living in New Mexico I met the artists Woody and Steina Vasulka. I remember one of them saying, "You have to believe in the Art God, Eve." If you just step off that cliff into the unknown, the Art God keeps you going somehow. That philosophy has allowed me to wing it all these years. So sometimes superstition works. Or is it faith? Perhaps it's the same thing.

ZF: Would you give any advice to young artists?

EAL: I think what's really important for young artists to realize is that there isn't one formula for being an artist. There isn't a protocol or one set of rules or standards or code of behaviors. We make up our own rules. We make it up as we go. At a certain point you get "turned"—instead of walking the straight and narrow path, like having a more normal life, you are on these interesting side roads wandering around in your imagination and in your desires and you can never go back.

49. A character whose traits, she thought, resembled her father's mystique and whose story was reminiscent of his own biography. This character served as the model for her father. She told the museum's director and curator that she was conducting an experiment with identity by creating the work of a fictitious artist/scientist who was based on a protagonist in a Pynchon novel. She explained to them that she had long been an admirer of Pynchon's work and the intricately complex narratives he weaves between history, memory, fact, and fabrication. The exhibition used these strategies by attributing work to her invented character, Yves Fissiault. She did not reveal the connection to her father, André Laramée.

The detailed chronology of Yves Fissiault's life that served as the wall text in the exhibition and the faux documents substantiating this chronology indicated Yves Fissiault inspired the protagonist in Pynchon's literary novel, when the reverse was true. Furthermore, she embellished this falsity by indicating that Yves Fissiault was Pynchon's mentor. Laramée contrived a letter from Fissiault recommending Thomas Pynchon for a job at Boeing. It was written on letterhead she fabricated from the Rockedyne Corporation where her father actually worked. This letter was exhibited beside an actual advertisement for a job at Hughes aircraft that Laramée clipped from a 1960s newspaper. In her narrative, Rocke-dyne inspired Pynchon's fictional corporation, Yoyodyne. Further "proof" was provided by a real photograph of her father at Rockedyne standing beside an unidentified man. Laramée made up the caption, asserting that the man with her father was the young Thomas Pynchon. In point of fact, Pynchon worked as a technical writer at Boeing before he became a fiction writer, so this narrative detail, like all the others, was plausible. It is well-known, however, that Pynchon had a strong aversion to being photographed. This was a clue to the photograph's potential inauthenticity. Unsuspecting viewers inter-preted the photograph as proof of truth, while suspecting viewers saw it as proof of fakery.

The project got a surprising boost in November 1999 when Laramée decided to make one last effort to investigate her family. She tried a new tactic: "Old family albums included photographs of a young woman holding me as an infant. They identified her as Ghislaine. My mother had always referred to her as 'daddy's friend from Canada.' It occurred to me that this girl might be my father's daughter from a previous marriage. So this time I searched the name Ghislaine Laramée and came up with a web site for a law firm in Canada: 'Ghislaine Laramée, attorney at law, family mediation, Montreal.' I took a deep breath and sent her a respectful letter. 'I sincerely hope this letter is not an invasion of your privacy, but I am very curious to know if we might be related. It would be deeply satisfying for me to discover my family history.' About a week later I received a response: 'Well, you did knock at the right door.'"

The half-sisters exchanged e-mails, then telephone conversations, then visits. Ghislaine showed Laramee a suitcase full of documents that spun a family history that is truly worthy of Thomas Pynchon's bizarre imagination. In also bears an uncanny resemblance to the fantastic chronicle that Laramée had invented to fill in the many gaps in the material she received when her mother died. In truth, her father's life was rife with treachery, the occult, murder, ostracism, scandal, and secrecy. Laramée describes it as "so bizarre, so dense, so baroque, so filled with turbulence and permutations, I don't know what to make of it yet."

Laramée has not arrived at the end of this circuitous narrative track. She and Ghislaine are conducting genealogical research and she has continued to develop the fictional narrative that surrounds it. In her pursuit of knowledge, Laramée embraces both objectively verifiable practices and the speculative constructions of the imagination. Her artistic process is a

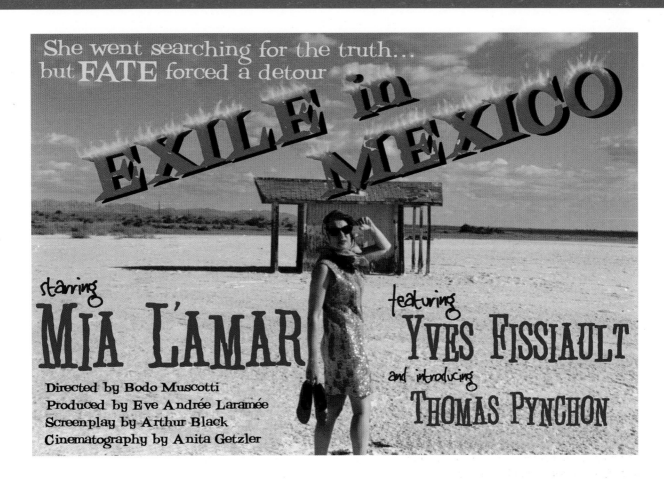

Eve Andrée Laramée, *Secret History: Exile in Mexico (Mia L'Amar "film poster")* (2001), 34 x 47 inches, iris print. Courtesy of the artist.

duet of left and right brain functions. The latter supplied verifiable data. The former produced imaginative ruminations. The same mental gymnastics are required of the viewer. When asked if she wants the audience to clue into her design, Laramee replied, "I did and I didn't want them to catch on. I really wanted to create a turbulent sense of play and see what the response would be."

The museum installation is capable of supporting all three of the artist's versions of *Secret History*. The suitcases and notebooks, for example, function in the manner of all sources of information—they can either be trusted or tested by the viewer. Like any data, they can initiate a process of investigation or imagination. Alternatively, as in the case of *Secret History*, all of these options can coincide. As Laramée explained, "Part of this artistic exploration of the murky territory between fact and fiction involves the necessity of not revealing the whole process of arriving at a fictional narrative. When I wrote fragments of text in the works on paper, I accessed a kind of 'cellular memory,' giving myself over to faith, believing that I could 'be' my father. It is uncanny how many of my interests over the years coincided with the subjects in my father's notebooks, like alchemy. This confirms my faith in intuition. This was a wild ride, but it was liberating. It forced me to question the authority of my own definition of self. It opened up realms of possible explorations—intellectual, creative, visual, emotional. This experience taught me that being an artist is about investigating the unknown. For me, the unknown is understanding the dark, uncomfortable places in my psyche and understanding my origin."

Instead of revealing a truth, Laramée reveals the truth about truth—that it is more like a hinge that oscillates than a bolt that fixes ideas in place. The complex brain functions involved in assessing uncertainty are not confined to art. They parallel the mental processes that have become more and more dominant in everyday interactions. They are required when assimilating simulation technologies, docudramas, staged live broadcasts, cyber-tourism, mediated politics, genetic modifications, and cloning technologies. Distinctions between fact and fiction are collapsing all around us. They also affect our ability to define "self." Contemporary technologies have liberated us from the limitations of constructing our personal identities based upon our physical bodies and our mental attributes. The virtual world offers unprecedented fluidity of on-line identities; with MPD (Multiple Personality Disorder) seeming normal in cyberspace. Furthermore, bodies that are electronically connected permit us to share intelligences. Laramée's work seems a fitting product of a world in which we are defined neither by our bodies nor our minds. "My work has a lot to do with questioning authority," she explained,"whether it is the authority of self and the authorship of work, or science and technology. I really love the slippery boundary between what is invented and constructed within the nebulous territory known as 'truth.' I play around with aspects of the sardonic, the humorous, and the reflective in order to blur boundaries between fact and fiction, faith and error. I squirm into the cracks. I enter the flows and vortexes where art is constantly being turned upon its self. I have faith in irrational, illogical thought as much as respect for hard and concrete thought... Like all of history and memory, the history of the self (autobiography) is always orchestrated out of fragments of information combining fact and fantasy into a conceptual matrix which represents truth or reality. That is part of our job as artists. We use our imaginations."

[1.] Helen A. Harrison, "Works of Curious, Conflicting Directions: Yves Fissiault: Artist of the Cold War Era," *New York Times*, 13 April 1997, Long Island edition, 16.

[2.] Unless otherwise indicated, all quotes are from an interview with the artist, November 28, 2001.

[3.] Eve Andrée Laramée, letter to the author, May 8, 2000.

Disrupting Assumptions

Charles Ray
Born 1953 Chicago, Illinois
1975 University of Iowa, BFA, Cum Laude, studied fine art
1979 Mason Gross School of Art, Rutgers University, MFA, studied fine art
Lives and works in Los Angeles, California

Charles Ray's art functions in the same manner as the practical joke. He contrives the audience response to many of his works by convincing viewers they are looking at something that is banal. Then, just before they succumb to disinterest, he insinuates evidence that their assumption is false. Upon closer scrutiny, they are able to correct their mistaken impression and delight in almost being fooled. In this manner his work energizes the viewer's perceptual engines, propelling neglected phenomena across the threshold into awareness. Sculptures that first appeared to be immobile move. Others that were assumed to be dead come alive. Some that were apparently solid reveal themselves to be liquid. The ordinary phenomenal environment becomes scintillating through his subtle manipulations.

Any man who describes his life as "a peanut butter sandwich that you squashed across the tabletop,"[1] sounds more like a deflated failure than a renowned artist. Yet this pitiful confession was discovered in a sophisticated art catalogue that only allocates space to those who have earned distinguished status in the art world. Charles Ray has received high esteem despite his apparent lack of passion, flare, and confidence. He is the kind of person who cannot state an opinion without including "sort of" and "kind of" and other self-deprecating phrases. And still *The New Yorker*, the *New York Times*, *Artforum*, *Flash Art*, *ARTnews*, and a host of international journals have repeatedly lavished attention upon him. His work has graced the covers of *Art in America* and *The Los Angeles Times Magazine*.

The banality of the peanut butter metaphor matches the innocuous nature of the objects that comprise Ray's sculptures: flowerpots, clocks, plastic tumblers, even the artist's own body. His appearance suggests only one thing—that he will be overlooked. Nonetheless, he is the primary visual ingredient in many of his artworks. He appears live, photographed, or cast in a three-dimensional form. In some sculptures he presents himself nude, displaying a distinctive lack of the physical attributes that typically define the male ideal. In other works he is attired so as to disappear in a crowd wearing jeans, sneakers, windbreaker, dark-rimmed glasses, and a geeky hat. Ray's personality is no more enchanting. "It's like I don't have an inside. I just have this outside."[2] Ray is average, the antithesis of the celebrity artist.

Where other artists might aim to inspire joy or sorrow, pity or scorn, Ray solicits attention. Remarkably, this innocuous man has succeeded in inducing harried art professionals and preoccupied nonprofessionals to pay him heed. Yet, his strategy for stimulating awareness of his creations often resembles his physique. In most instances both he and his work approach invisibility. Ray regularly reverses the ever escalating tactics typically used by commerce, politics, entertainment, and news, as well as most other products of the contemporary environment. Ray revives modesty as an alternative to extravagance and exaggeration, and reintroduces subtlety to replace assaults upon the senses. And still his work attracts notice. Ray's whispers are heard despite the din of the competitive environment. If an organism continually assaulted by experiences of the "mega," "ultra," "super," and "extra" variety protects itself from being overstimulated by overlooking, disregarding,

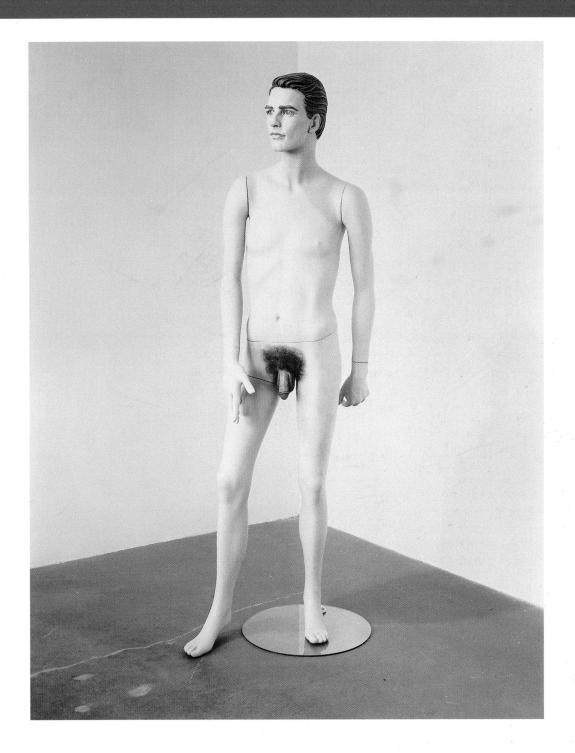

Charles Ray, *Male Mannequin* (1990), 73 x 15 x 14 inches, mixed media. Courtesy Regen Projects, Los Angeles.

Disrupting Assumptions: **Charles Ray**

and disengaging, then Ray's minimization of stimulation enables his audience to recover from their apathy.

Ray's works seem mute and muffled, but they are the opposite of dull. Indeed, Ray's success is measured by the reinvigoration of his audience. His gentle provocations seem to allow viewers to abandon their defensive postures and unblock channels of awareness. "There is a sensation I was looking for that is located somewhere between the genitals and the head. Like that charge you get from chopping down a big tree, seeing it fall. It's juvenile, but it's also sublime."[3] This mission is accomplished by creating slightly offbeat situations, each expertly calculated to be affective but not invasive. Ray opens up the space between stimulator and stimulated, providing the audience with an opportunity to fire their sensual neurons and flex their perceptual muscles. In the process of looking, they rediscover the delight offered by subtlety and nuance, which includes bizarre constructions that might otherwise seem fearsome and grotesque. It is not a euphemism to say that Ray offers a drug-free turn-on. He notes, "What drugs do is redesign the world a little. Not too much, just enough to make you realize how fascinating your surroundings could be if you really paid attention. Drugs never let you forget for a moment how much preexisting information you have to ignore in order to believe your life is significant."[4]

Likewise, Ray rejects the split-second approach to communicating. Marketing experts typically spice up their products and then offer them in a conceptually predigested form so that they can be gulped down before attention is diverted to a competing stimulus. In contrast, Ray's work is made for slow savoring. Instead of clobbering the viewer, he aims to "create tensions and reverberations that just keep going."[5] Because attentiveness exists in the "here and now," it is intensified by circumventing remembrances and anticipations. For this reason Ray strives to eliminate the "there and the then" that accompany cynicism, nostalgia, desire, knowledge, and a host of other attention distracters. He says he cultivates "some kind of present relationship between the spectator and the work, not just a mental or aesthetic relationship, but a kind of 'presentness.' So I was trying to give the spectator the same experience that I was having."[6] The experience of "presentness" to which he refers is derived from mind-altering drugs. But he traces his first encounter with total engagement in the moment to a remarkable episode in his childhood. The factuality of this fantastic tale cannot be verified, but it illuminates the experience that Ray attempts to recreate in his art.

"When I was a kid I was hit on the head by a falling timber at this construction site where I was playing. It made me lose my memory and I wandered off aimlessly into the city. I didn't mind not knowing who I was, and the fact that everything looked as vaguely familiar as everything else fascinated me. I walked for, oh, about two days begging for money, eating garbage, shitting in bushes. Eventually I came to a small marina. The ocean looked so beautiful that I asked this rich old couple with a yacht if I could be their cabin boy. They said, 'Sure.'... At my insistence we set off for the Arctic, a place that has always fascinated me. They were a nice couple but really boring. Since I had no history or ideas of my own, I was obliged to listen to tales of theirs all day, every day. And having no value system, I thought all their stories of cocktail parties and backaches and summer homes were just fantastic. I couldn't get enough. The second week at sea the yacht developed engine trouble and we had to be rescued by the Coast Guard. That night in a hotel room somewhere in Canada I woke up in a sweat and remembered everything about my life up to that moment I was struck on the head, but nothing after. I couldn't figure out who these naked old people were on either side of me. So I got dressed and tiptoed downstairs to the lobby and asked someone to phone my parents, who flew out to get me. Years later I was standing naked in a gallery doing one of my shelf-body pieces when I heard a very familiar voice and opened my eyes a crack. It was the woman from the hotel room. Somehow she'd found me, and after gallery hours were over, we met at a nearby restaurant. It turns out her husband was dead—cancer—but one of his last requests was that she give me a photograph he'd taken at sea. Why, she didn't know. At dinner she happily filled in that two-week long blank in my memory with talks of our time at sea."[7]

With meticulous craftsmanship, in this story as in his sculptures, Ray tweaks the mundane world just enough to enable it to cross the threshold into art. Unlike the attention-getting tactics of contemporary artists such as Matthew Barney and Mariko Mori who discharge volleys of sensory charges, this artist gently nudges his audience's response mode. The process of viewing proceeds in the following manner. Initially, a Ray work of art offers nothing remarkable. Viewers might not be inclined to linger, except that some indecipherable quality halts their progression. This is the instant when Charles Ray's clever manipulation of audience response is activated. Something appears to be a little strange; but identifying it takes time. Ray carefully structures this pause. "I think really good work does do something—transports people, stops time, takes time, takes them someplace and makes them think about things. Another space. Hopefully people get something of this."[8] Because Ray utilizes many devices to accomplish this deed, a survey of his major pieces is, simultaneously, a survey of artistic means to attract the attention of an audience.

Objective Becomes Subjective

The orderly functioning of our society depends on the shared pledge of all our citizens to conform to the universal settings of hours, minutes, and seconds. We rely on the reliability of clocks. Accuracy is a clock's measure of merit. Although the healthy human body is fully equipped with pulses and beats, we turn to mechanics and electronics to measure time.

Charles Ray exempted himself from this universal "we" when he became *Clock Man* (1978). In this work he replaced a large public clock with one that he had made. The external appearance of his clock was identical to the original. But Ray also replaced its internal parts. He substituted its metalworkings with organic ones—his own body. Ray climbed inside the pseudo clock case that was then re-hung in the location of the original clock. Thus positioned, he manually turned the hands. The official chronometric measurement succumbed to his subjective estimation of time's passage.

"I tried to become a clock. I got in there in the morning and was going to get out at six in the evening.... I didn't like it, I was miserable.... It was excruciatingly boring. And during the day I became three hours fast."[9]

Ray is mischievous, but not sadistic. He calibrates each situation only enough to disrupt people's complacency, not their lives. The latter must be avoided because it is more likely to confound the senses than awaken awareness. In this instance, serious distress would certainly have ensued if people rushing by really thought they had lost three hours. Ray averted this problem by deliberately exposing the cause for their temporal confusion. Both of his legs dangled from beneath the clock's face as ludicrous substitute pendulums. People passed in their usual way, but their habitual glances at the timepiece were halted by a comical clock that had relinquished its authority as an objective measurer of time.

Animate Becomes Inanimate

Shelf (1981) is a work in which Ray positioned a shelf on a wall precisely at the level of his neck. On it he placed four objects of equal size: a gasoline can, a toolbox, an empty flowerpot, and his own head. All were painted in the identical gunmetal grey. From the

Charles Ray, *Firetruck* (1993), 12 x 8.25 x 46 feet, toy truck scaled to life-size as a public sculpture. Courtesy Regen Projects, Los Angeles.

neck up, Ray seemed as lifeless as the other components of his sculptural still life. From his neck down to his bare feet, his naked body appeared as alive as the observer's, but a lot more exposed.

Lifelikeness has often been summoned as a measure of artistry in Western art. Sculptors from classical antiquity, the Renaissance, and the neo-Classical eras are celebrated for their ability to convey the illusion of warmth, suppleness, and breath in marble, bronze, and other inert materials. Ray, however, quietly defies this long and hallowed cultural tradition. He is a celebrated sculptor who expended effort on creating the illusion of lifelessness.

Generic Becomes Individualized

Male Mannequin (1990) is a work in which Ray suggests that the honored tradition of a master sculpting the perfect human body has been perpetuated by the less honorable practice of a machine fabricating mannequins. Ray's idealized male, standing in a distinctive high art pose, is cast from a shopping-mall mannequin. The artist impishly altered it by focusing on the one part of the male physique that is not idealized on mannequins. In fact, this body part is expunged entirely from their anatomies. Male mannequins are not only castrated, they are neutered. To make up for this deficiency, a second cast completes Ray's sculpture. It replicates Ray's own genitals. Ray toned them with great accuracy and surrounded them with a frizzy halo of pubic hair. The generic perfection of the form upon which this token of real life is placed is attention-getting, but it also awakens thought. *Male Mannequin* connects museums and department stores as sites for the display of cultural ideals. Furthermore, it utilizes this particular pound of flesh to alert viewers to the uneasy rapport between idealism and realism within fine-art and commercial contexts.

Static Becomes Mobile

Tabletop (1988) is a work in which six circular everyday objects appear on a plain, wooden table: a soup plate, a bowl, a potted artificial begonia, a plastic tumbler, an aluminum shaker, and a covered canister. They are arranged according to the dictates of aesthetics, not function, in the manner of a still life painting. Yet this commonplace assemblage stimulates scrutiny of these mundane artifacts. The senses become alert to signs of this innocuous work's inexplicable power to command attention. The objects are actual, not fabrications. They rest secure upon the tabletop. The piece generates no noise. Ray has altered the one quality that is least likely to be doubted. This still life is not still. Ray has motorized each element so that it moves so slowly and so silently, its rotation is barely perceptible. It is the plant, the single asymmetrical element, which provides the clue. The process of search-and-discovery induces viewers to examine banal objects with the intensity typically reserved for masterpieces.

The evolution of the idea for this sculpture provides insight into Ray's quirky working methods and the carefully considered mission that they serve. "With the rotating table piece, I was just smoking too much marijuana, and I was trying to work on a still-life piece. I kept trying to do that Russian psychokinesis thing where you mentally bend a fork or move a saltshaker. I was working on that for five months and I figured I was moving them, but I wasn't. Finally I figured I'd motorize the piece and turn them. It's a really stupid, nerdy, white-boy idea.... The struggle is to bring that idea into the world in a non-trite way, so that it re-enchants the world or activates it."[10]

Mobile Appears Static

In *Revolution Counter Revolution* (1990) Ray fabricated a child's carousel and outfitted it with four pairs of suspended ponies, two swinging sleds, and an elaborately decorated canopy.

Like a real carousel, his mechanical version rotates. Yet this merry-go-round has been designed to disappoint its riders, not delight them. Although the supports are whirling merrily around in one direction, the horses and sleds are spinning at the identical rate in the opposite direction. The movements cancel each other out so that the entire carousel appears stationary. In actuality, the horses inch forward, imperceptibly, as they gradually overcome the counterforce. Instead of spinning in joyful abandonment, riders on Ray's carousel confirm the plodding course of reality. Spoiling the fun is another means to awaken the audience's sensibilities.

Mind Becomes Matter

Yes (1990) is a life-size color transparency of Ray's head and torso that was shot while he was under the influence of LSD. Viewers are likely to observe the artist's strange expression at the same instant they feel a comparably strange sensation rising within themselves. Their perceptions are warped as if they, too, are experiencing a drug-induced hallucination. This disorientation activates viewers to seek stabilizing anchors. They expand their perception to the wall beyond the frame of the photograph, but it also looks distorted and offers no relief. It is not until attention is broadened to the neighboring walls and the floor that the source of their instability is discovered. Ray framed the print on a convex surface, protected it with convex glass, and surrounded it with a convex frame. He then mounted the print on a wall that was restructured to assume the exact convex curvature of the print. A subjective drug state is thereby applied to the objective architecture of the museum. As a result, the viewer's mind is expanded without chemical aids.

Harmless Becomes Nerve-Racking

Ink Line (1987) is realized as a slender, elegant column extending from ceiling to floor. It is approximately the radius of a nickel, jet-black and polished to perfection. The material out of which it is fabricated is not apparent to the eye. Glass? Steel? Plastic tubing? The temptation is to seek the answer by touching, but this impulse is forbidden in a museum setting. The alternative to touching is to refer to the accompanying label. Indeed, the medium is announced in the title. Can it be? Attention is redirected to the sculpture. Scrutiny is intensified until it is capable of perceiving a minute wobble in the line and infinitesimal specks of dust flowing downward. What seemed static now appears kinetic. What was invisible suddenly becomes visible. What appeared solid is now perceived of as a liquid. A continuously flowing line of printer's ink is making a deadfall from a hole in the ceiling to a hole in the floor without a splatter or a splash. This feat has been accomplished without visual signs of motors or the sound of pumps. Ray seems to be heading toward a final transformation. What was benign is now fraught with the anxiety of getting soiled. Anxiety is another means by which Ray heightens attentiveness. "If you spill ink all over the floor, there's no anxiety there. You've got a mess. But if you have a potential for a mess, you have anxiety. It's not boxing anxiety in, it's about creating anxiety."[11]

Representation Becomes Abstraction

Ray painstakingly made fiberglass castings of several hundred parts of a Pontiac Grand Am that had been destroyed in a cataclysmic car-crash for Unpainted Sculpture (1997). The frontal impact of the crash was so severe, it catapulted the hood backward into the front seat and forced the rear doors to skew. The crash occurred in a split second, but the car that served as the work's model was chosen only after Ray and his assistants spent months visiting insurance lots in search of the "platonic car wreck."[12] The process of disassembling it, casting each section, painting them a monochrome gray topcoat, and reconstructing the car into a pristine version of its ruined state took two years.

Instead of being sent to the car morgue, the wreck was resurrected as a finely crafted sculpture. "It's starting its life over again as an art object.... It has a funny trail of identity from the factory in Detroit, through wrecks, then ending up in my hands, on another weird assembly line in the studio, and going back out again."[13]

Ray offers an interpretation of this real-life disaster that conflicts with the one that would normally report it. The news media amplifies violence and calamity. Charles Ray defuses this emotional component by presenting the demolished car as a formal abstraction. The former is designed to provoke anguish; the latter to induce calm. Disjunction pervades the issue of process as well. The crash producing the wrecked form was destructive and violent, while the process producing the sculpture of the wrecked form was constructive and meticulous. Ray states that *Unpainted Sculpture* was created "to transcend the subject, even though the subject always has to be there as the thing you're kicking, like one element of an equation."[14] Because the subject matter remains apparent, viewers who tend to be dismissive of monochromatic abstract art become fixated. The work succeeds as long as perceptions of life and art remain unreconciled, and viewers are provoked.

The Obvious Becomes Inscrutable

Without the information provided by the title, viewers would observe an aluminum cube without distinguishing characteristics. The title, *32 x 33 x 35 = 34 x 33 x 35* (1989), however, provides an unusual set of data. It indicates both the exterior dimensions, which is normal on a museum label, and the interior dimensions, which is not. So, the work's outside dimensions are 32 inches high, by 33 inches wide, by 35 inches deep. The interior height of the cube is two inches taller than the exterior dimension.

One logical explanation for this illogical circumstance is that the label contains a typo. This would indicate that the truth is explained by an error. In fact, this conclusion is false. Close observation reveals that the inside of the cube is, indeed, taller than the outside. Ray has lowered the floor under it to accommodate the added inches. Thus, viewers discover that although all their previous experience in the world would indicate that the label information is wrong, this time it is correct. This slight discrepancy unhinges faith in gaining reliable information through observation.

A cube normally does not invite careful inspection because it is easy to assume such a simple object is knowable at a glance. Ray undermines this certainty by instigating an active visual search that yields wonder where banality was expected.

Art Viewer Becomes Art Medium

In *Fall '91* (1992), a female mannequin stands supported by a metal rod. Her blond hair cascades in controlled waves across one eye and cheek. Lipstick enhances her lips. She could be a call girl, except that she is dressed to conquer business executives, not seduce them. Her power suit is tastefully embellished with lapel pin and neck scarf. The cuffs of her starched shirt extend just enough beyond the sleeves of her jacket to frame her manicured hands. One hand is raised in a gesture that announces, "Don't mess with me."

Even from across the room, she is an imposing presence. Approaching her, viewers are startled to discover that she seems to be growing in proportion to their sense of shrinking. This scale shift crescendos when they get close enough to discover that Ray enlarged every feature of the mannequin by one third. Gazing up at the towering, eight-foot-tall "power woman" is intimidating. As in his other works, the medium Ray actually manipulates is the viewer's mental perceptions. In this instance, increasing the scale of the mannequin diminishes the confidence of the viewer.

A Curse Becomes a Festivity—Lust Becomes Humdrum

Oh! Charley, Charley, Charley... (1992). Who is speaking in this title? Charles Ray is speaking to himself, responding to the implied statement, "Go fuck yourself." The phrase usually means, "Get out of here. You are despicable." But Ray took these words literally. He created eight different life-size casts of his own nude body. They are posed as if they are performing a variety show of sexual acts with each other. The sculpture represents an orgy of self-love. The activity Ray presents is not only sexually explicit; it is usually private. Observing it, therefore, implies an invasive act of voyeurism. But being a voyeur is also a secretive activity. Ray reverses both of these expectations. His masturbatory extravagance is installed in the public space of a museum, where scrutinizers are not only welcome, they, too, are in a public position where they can be scrutinized as they examine this censorable scene. Ray is naughty. He insinuates scandal into a refined setting and introduces embarrassment where decorum normally prevails.

Such intense sexual activity, typically displayed in pornography, is designed to arouse the spectator. Here, no one pants because the figures seem devoid of anything resembling an erotic charge. They merely provide interchangeable parts in a chain of humdrum events, less shameful than mechanical. Ray comments, "With *Oh! Charley, Charley, Charley...* it looks like I'm exposing myself; but then you see I'm not. What at first seems vulnerable and open isn't; it's masturbation, there's no entrance, somehow. I'm just flat."[15] Ray presents himself as a lonely guy with no one to love but himself, and himself, and himself...

Functional Item Becomes Toy Becomes Art

Fire engines are as bright and shiny and appealing as a toy. It is not surprising that they have been bestsellers for toy manufacturers. In order to transform these vehicles into toys, their features are usually simplified and their scale is greatly diminished. Ray reversed the process. For *Firetruck* (1993), he started with the simplified form of a Tonka toy fire engine, retained its precise form, but magnified its size back to that of an actual fire engine. On one occasion he parked it on the street in front of the Whitney Museum of American Art as part of a retrospective of his work. The artwork might have been mistaken for a real truck if its features didn't look so out of proportion. Thus visitors to this exhibition received their first dose of Ray dementia before they entered the museum. The sculpture functioned like a training course in paying attention. The challenge was intensified by the hectic pace and clutter of the urban environment that rivaled even this substantial work of art. Ray went on the offensive by multiplying tactics of presence. First, he selected a fire engine, a vehicle that automatically attracts attention, as opposed to delivery trucks and taxis that don't. Second, he surrounded it with protective barriers and other signs of police protection to augment the expectation of a real emergency. They framed this object, isolating it, like a conventional artwork, from its surroundings. These clues accumulated until the vehicle came into focus as a simulation, a false sign of danger, a monster toy, a work of art, a Charles Ray sculpture. Visitors entered the museum prepared for the witty exercise in visual and mental acuity they would experience throughout the show. It was difficult to fail his training course, and a pleasure to pass it.

1. Interview with Charles Ray by Lucinda Barnes in *Charles Ray*, eds. Lucinda Barnes and Dennis Cooper (Newport, California: Newport Harbor Art Museum, 1990), 9.

2. Robert Storr, "Anxious Spaces, Interview with Charles Ray," *Art in America*, November 1998, 144.

3. Ann Wagner, "Charles Ray: Museum of Contemporary Art Los Angeles," *Artforum*, May 1999, 172.

4. Barnes and Cooper, Interview with Charles Ray by Dennis Cooper, 30.

5. Storr.

6. John Hugo, "Between Object and Persona: The Sculpture Events of Charles Ray," *High Performance* 30 (1985): 27.

7. Barnes and Cooper, Interview with Charles Ray by Dennis Cooper, 32.

8. Doug Harvey, "The Charles Ray Experience," LA Weekly, 4–10 December 1998, 45.

9. Hugo, 28.

10. Storr, 104.

11. Barnes and Cooper, Interview with Charles Ray by Lucinda Barnes, 16.

12. Charles Ray quoted in Paul Schimmel, *Beside One's Self* (Los Angeles: Museum of Contemporary Art, 1998), 89.

13. Lisa Phillips, "Charles Ray: Castaway," in *Charles Ray* (Los Angeles: Museum of Contemporary Art, 1998), 101.

14. Phillips, 89.

15. Storr, 103.

VEGETARIAN

Charles Ray, *Clock Man* (1978), 30 x 30 x 54 inches, wood, paint, and artist as clockworks. Courtesy Regen Projects, Los Angeles.

Disrupting Assumptions: **Charles Ray**

Instilling Confidence and Inspiring Laughter

Will Schade
Born 1943 New York
1962 Parsons School of Design, New York City
1963 St. Petersburg Junior College, St. Petersburg, Florida
1969 University of Southern Illinois, BA
1971 State University of New York at Albany, MA in printmaking
1973 Cranbrook Academy of Art, MFA
Lives and works in Williamstown, Massachusetts

Will Schade mounts a triple strategy for capturing his audience. The first strategy points his viewers in the direction of his comical mistakes—Schade spells like a third grader. The second directs viewers to his ribald humor—Schade's irreverence is often directed to biblical saints and prophets. The third leads them to acknowledge the mastery of his draftsmanship. His elegant drawings combine subjects that ordinarily provoke embarrassment and attitudes that typically evoke reproach. As a result, the audience has three ways to get hooked—on his innocence, on his naughtiness, and on his excellence.

Will Schade spins visual and verbal yarns about sacred texts and noble themes. He addresses such lofty figures as Noah and St. Sebastian, both of whom protected humanity from God's wrath. His subjects are solemn, not funny; his narratives are supposed to lead to morals, not punchlines. But Schade discovers humor in these uplifting subjects by sinking low. He is a bottom feeder. For example, he chose ravens to serve as St. Sebastian's attribute "because no one likes them."[1] Schade's version of this epic of sainthood and martyrdom is formed around a bird that is best known for its disagreeable caw and its massive droppings, which may explain why, in Christianity, it serves as a symbol for the Devil feeding on corruption, the opposite of the white dove, the symbol of the innocent soul. The artist captures the last gasp of the martyred bird in a painting entitled *St. Seabastion's Ravin* (1982). Its ungainly feet are roped together, its tongue hangs out, and its eyes are glazed. Feathers abound. The straggly ones sprout from the raven's body. Tidy ones appear on the arrows that penetrate its body, suggesting that this saintly bird has been betrayed by his own kin. Each arrow carries a message: "cheep shot," "crunch," "the last straw." The bird is beyond pity; it is funny.

But Schade's irreverence is not what makes this body of work so startling. Nor is it his obsession with urinating, defecating, masturbating, fornicating, and dying, especially when such activities are performed by the virtuous saints and wise prophets of the Old and New Testaments. Nor is it that he provides evidence of their jealousy, confusion, and an assortment of equally impious behaviors. The most radical component of Schade's works of art is less the content of his revelations than the abominable misspellings of the words that describe them. Schade is severely dyslexic. His mistakes are boldly presented as handwritten narratives on the drawings they accompany. In any other context, these texts would probably be dismissed as evidence of stupidity. That is the reasonable conclusion to draw from reading about "St. Seabastion's Ravin." Schade also recounts an idiosyncratic version of "Mrs. Noha's" role on the great ark of biblical fame. According to Schade, she demanded input on the interior design of the family suite on the ark, choosing walls of "nottie pine." Likewise, drawings representing a menagerie of animals refer to such preposterous concepts as: the crow with a "fork tung," a wild ass lavender fowl found in the upper Bronx by a city "demolishion team," the pink "flamigo cock" with a "hornie beak," fantastical one-

Will Schade, *St. Seabastion's Ravin* (1982), 78 x 107 inches, acrylic on linen. Courtesy of the artist.

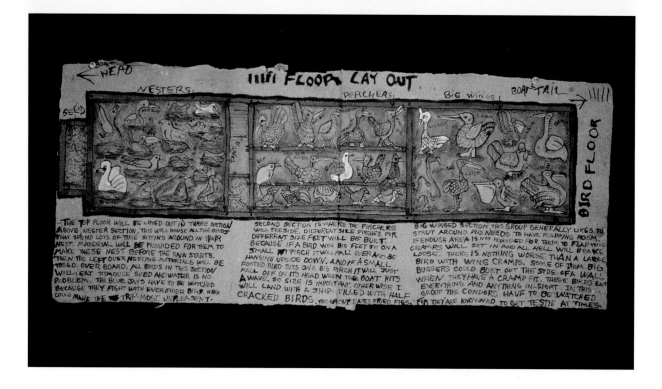

Will Schade, *Noha's Brown Prints* (1985), 26 x 48 inches, clay, gouache, and pen and ink on handmade paper. Courtesy of the artist.

eyed "salmon snacher's," a black-and-white striped "zipper zibbera" whose mien had a "trogan cut," and a fat "small toed rinoarusus."

The same hand that wrote these semi-illiterate texts in an awkwardly childish scrawl also created the brilliantly executed drawings on which they appear. It may seem curious that the artist made no attempt to hide his affliction. Visual artists are not expected to include text in their works of art. Even those who feel compelled to relay narratives can convey their texts out of sight of criticism and beyond the reach of judgment. Placed on the reverse side of the drawing or on an accompanying label, Schade could have avoided public disclosure of his dyslexia. Furthermore, in all these instances, he could have asked someone, almost anyone, to correct his errors. But Will Schade decided to display his considerable talents alongside his equally considerable deficiencies.

Instead of trying to decide whether to respect his honesty or ridicule his limitations, viewers typically erupt into spontaneous laughter. "Laughter" is a generic word like "car." There are many makes (guffaw, snicker, giggle, cackle, chuckle) and styles (merriment, ridicule, amusement, sneer), brands (sarcasm, burlesque, slapstick, parody, caricature, farce) and designs (vulgar, naughty, innocent, witty, droll). In most of these cases laughter creates an unequal relationship. The laughing person is empowered, while the person who is laughed at is humiliated. Chuckling in the presence of Schade's works grants viewers an enjoyable surge of superiority. The museum context allows them the special pleasure of feeling even more enlightened than an artist who, in this instance, is not a super-human genius. He is a talented artist with a flaw. Bill Schade's works are ego builders, morale boosters, and status elevators.

Yet self-aggrandizement cannot be enjoyed if it is accompanied by concern about offending the artist or behaving rudely. Viewers might worry, "Has my amusement come at the expense of the artist's dignity?" Schade makes doubly sure that these merriment-dampening concerns are unwarranted with the remarkable refinement of his draftsmanship and his willingness to instigate humor by bearing the brunt of his own jokes. By publicly disclosing his strengths and his weaknesses, he frees the audience to indulge in guilt-free laughter and enjoy the rush of self-confidence that laughter generates.

Schade values his dyslexia despite enduring a childhood that was marked by persistent efforts to rescue him from near illiteracy. These efforts failed. The learning problem followed him from a Catholic grammar school to a Catholic military high school, through spells at four different institutions of higher learning. He persisted and progressed only because academic standards were continually stretched to suit his abundant imagination and his minimal literacy. It seems he was too spunky to ignore and too endearing to fail. Schade reports that in order to complete his undergraduate requirements, he repeated English seven times. He finally passed by taking a course at a local college where half the course was devoted to writing and half to speech. Schade received a C, which, he believes, probably represents the average between an F in writing and an A in speech. Today Schade is a full Professor of Art at Sage College. He reports that he feels neither shame regarding his misspellings nor embarrassment regarding his grammatical errors because he has never been ridiculed for noncompliance with society's norms. Perhaps his scrubbed, cherubic exterior compensated for his bawdy antics and hopeless blunders. He was not teased in grammar school for his inability to read. He was not harassed in military school for his deficient skills in sports. He was not flunked in college for failing the tests. He was not discouraged in graduate school for ignoring the assignments. Finally, he has not been criticized for creating art that teases the public's sensibilities.

Will Schade, *Gerasimus* (n.d.), 8 x 11 inches, gouache, gold leaf, and pen and ink on handmade paper. Courtesy of the artist.

Schade's unrepressed imagination makes it seem as if he grew up without undergoing adult socialization. His artistic decisions waver between a youngster's innocence and an adolescent's insolence. These youthful traits allow Schade to restock the storehouse of untamed fantasies that most people deplete by their fifteenth birthday. His favorite themes involve biblical inconsistencies and bodily processes that are normally performed in private. He created, for example, meticulously sculpted porcelain figures to grace an outdoor fountain located in a sumptuous flower garden. The work displays a bevy of baboons joyfully peeing in the company of squirrels, monkeys, elephants, rams, and alligators, all out of scale and out of sense. Schade has fun. So does his audience. In fact, he makes sure that the audience takes a turn as the target of his jokes. Once, for instance, he produced a series of oversized, anatomically detailed chickens, *Faberg's Imperial Chicken Machine* (1979), *Fickled Feather* (1977), *Wisconsin Wish Boner* (1978), that were stitched out of muslin and stuffed with cotton. These creatures were meticulously crafted, but they were also ungainly specimens, a quality that became all the more apparent because they were displayed on elaborate stuffed bases decorated with the Ionic columns of classical antiquity and the Gothic windows of medieval architectural landmarks. Each was outfitted with a music box. In some cases viewers were invited to insert a penny into the bases to receive a prize, a chicken bone, if the gadget worked—which it did not, which was okay with the artist. Once again, Schade displayed his ineptness and avoided scorn. No one was annoyed since no one wants a chicken bone anyway! Museum goers, art connoisseurs, fowls, and the artist himself are treated with equal irreverence.

Books are Schade's favored vehicles for tall-tale telling. He has chosen a medium that has had profound influence on the intellectual history of world civilization, setting the standard for well-honed arguments, substantiated assertions, and refined discourse. By these standards, Schade's volumes are woefully inadequate. He has written and illustrated forty books in which the narratives are both logical and unlikely. Did "Noha" eat animal crackers aboard his ark? Did the "Long" Ranger's pet parrot fly over his head instead of sitting on his shoulder, thus explaining "why you never saw him on TV, because he was always out of the camera range"? Instead of intimidating the reader with well-researched topics written by an expert, the author's authority diminishes as the viewer's confidence grows. Braggarts and experts may earn respect, but sympathetic responses tend to be reserved for those who admit their insufficiencies.

Schade's childish imaginings are appended to grown-up pragmatism. Absurd suppositions are pursued to logical consequences, as if they were to be carried out in the real world. Schade created plans for ark construction as if Noah had drawn them, with an accompanying text that reveals the thoughts that might have been churning in Noah's own mind. Included are detailed accounts of the different

Some Titles of Books by Will Schade:

The Large Mouth Bull Frog by Noha, 1999

Noha's Brown Egg Society, 1999

Noha's Cholick Tree Peeper's, 1999

Gayroot Crock's, 1998

Gazza Yam Gaydor's, 1998

Zinbobbian Juice Bat's, 1997

The Large Quilled Medaterraium Pork.U.Pine, 1997

Last Buffalo Stamped, 1991

Sarmarian Tree Peeprs, 1986

Saint Seabastion and His Ravin, 1986

The Seven Horses of the Long Ranger, 1986

Noha's Que Cards, 1983

Zoo of Charles the Bald, 1983

FAMILIAR

kinds of wood to be used, and the need for Noah's donkey, Phill, to drag the wood to the construction site, and for tar, pitch, and straw to fill cracks and avoid leaks. Schade then writes, "The back should have a rutter to keep the boat going strait otherwise we will be turning in circles for God knows how long. This could cause bad seasickness with the animals. And that's all I need is to have a boatful of barfing creatures. If the noise does not get you, the aroma would." In another plan, he considers the complexity of designing an ark able to provide relief for cramped wings and handle the mess of droppings produced by species large and small. Finally, the ark was outfitted with a "jerk-off room" to relieve the creatures' inevitable frustrations during the long voyage.

In appearance, Schade's handmade books broadcast that they are one-of-a-kind productions both in terms of quantity and style. Serious books are all bound up, their pages lashed together with military precision. As physical objects, they are emblems of accuracy, formality, and rigidity. Schade gives his books "a rugged, primitive look, not like they just came from Rizzoli." His hand-made papers are often thick, brown, and aged; the covers are stained leather; the bindings are rough and made of lashes or ropes. His innovative choices of materials, he reports, originate in such unlikely places as a horse's ass. "I was in New York. A cop went by on a horse. I was smacked in the head with its tail. It was like being hit with a giant fly-swatter. The hair was so thick. It was just what I was looking for. Wig store hair was too flimsy. I went home and asked my friends to send me horse hair, which I stuck out of the edges of a five-foot-long book about a stampede of buffaloes."

Schade's books are intentionally awkward constructions. How else could illustrations in which the pigment is applied with oak sticks be described? But they are never careless. The artist whittled his painting sticks twenty years ago to produce the uneven lines he desires. His efforts are coarse, but never crude. He is an accomplished draftsman who skill-fully captures the precise moment of pathos in his narratives and transforms those instants into visual gems by adding the ethereal splendor of gold leaf upon a crude brown-paper background. These illustrated manuscripts expose the blunders of a living dyslexic at the same time as they share in the meticulous craftsmanship of monks from the Middle Ages— even if the piety of the latter hardly matches the impudence of the former. Schade's figures are motionless and removed from space and time against dark grounds. They have an ecclesiastic glow, like treasured icons. At the same time, Schade insists that in displaying his works, neither protective barriers of glass and frames nor elevated pedestals should be used. These museum protocols impose a reverential attitude that is another source of uncomfortable intimidation that interferes with good-hearted enjoyment. By breaking through this solemn barrier, cordiality replaces formality. He hopes people will get close enough to sniff his work. And what about the risk of damage? Schade insists that stains and blemishes enhance his work by contributing a patina of the public's engagement.

Schade likes himself just as he is, despite lacking literacy and being an anachronism in his own time. His amiable mischief exists against a background of gangsta rap and hip-hop; cartoon violence; high-octane celebrations of ambition; action-packed dramas; an internet choked with data and sleaze; a market rife with gimmicks. This is a culture more prone to snickering than chuckling, more adept at criticizing than savoring. Schade offers the one thing that is in scarce supply—confidence-building humor. Viewers enjoy guilt-free amusement kindled by Schade's faults and talents. Old and young, church goers and atheists, academicians and students are given a reason to feel good about themselves.

[1.] All quotes from an interview with the artist, June 1999.

Imposing Corporal Punishment

Arnaldo Morales
Born 1967 Puerto Rico
1996 School of Visual Arts, Institute of Puerto Rican Culture, San Juan, Puerto Rico,
BFA, sculpture
Immigrated to the US in 1995
Lives and works in New York State

Arnaldo Morales's sculptures consist of real motors that drive real devices that play real practical jokes on the audience. Pistons, gears, and electricity provide his means for artistic transmission. His sculptures are not only active, they act up by attacking their viewers. Morales's artworks actually spit, blast, and punch people who approach them. Analogies are not needed to describe viewer responses. Audiences actually screech, duck, and cringe. Instead of presenting art as artifice, Morales's sculptures dole out real danger, produce real fear, and extract real excitement from art-goers who tend to be aloof, intellectual, dubious, and unruffled.

Miraculously, Arnaldo Morales's brain did not explode after an attacker held a loaded gun to his head and fired. It was a transforming moment for him and his art. Since that time Morales has devoted his career to the ardent exploration of fear, aggression, vulnerability, pain, and danger. His manner of study is applied, not theoretical. Initially, he subjected himself to perilous circumstances and studied how he responded and coped. Now he subjects his audience to perilous circumstances by creating aggressive sculptures. "I like to listen to what people say, how they respond. What the work means to them. I make notes about it. I write what each person thinks."[1] But people are not merely the artist's guinea pigs. Significantly, the artist shows no signs of sadistic intent. By creating circumstances where they must either retreat or join the commotion, feel disturbed or feel exhilarated, he offers art goers surprising insights into their own anxieties and their capacity for hostility.

Morales explains, "After I was shot, I changed. I became more responsible with life. I said, 'I need to do research. I need to know the context of violent people. I need to share some time with them.' I wanted to hear their philosophies, so I moved to a violent neighborhood in Puerto Rico." Morales became a resident artist in a decrepit barrio, where he lived on red alert under the ever-present threat of the gang members, gangsters, drug dealers, and murderers who comprised a significant portion of its population. Even the police were reluctant to enter the barrio. As Morales describes it, "At first it was incredible, horrible. People there would say, 'Why do you want to live here?' And I said, 'Because I am an artist.' I talked to them about my work, they told me they didn't understand it. But when someone would point to me and ask, 'Who is that?' they would say, 'That is the artist of this place. Don't touch him.' I had the most amazing experience. I became like the mayor. I could leave my door open. Nobody went inside. I got a lot of respect. They offered to help me install my show. It was a huge surprise. They are beautiful people. It is like another culture, another reality, another kind of political system."

The surprising advantage that resulted from his exposure to danger provides the hypothesis that Morales continually tests by making "electrobjetos," sculptures that take the form of gadgets capable of perpetrating a variety of hostile actions upon the viewer. Morales constructs these kinetic sculptures out of industrially produced materials that he scavenges in a spirit that more closely resembles plucking flowers from a meadow than collecting debris from urban streets. He polishes each element until it glistens and then assigns it a new role within a sculpture that is completely alien to its original function. Speculums, prosthetics, snorkeling tanks, electric knives, microphones, and aluminum baseball bats are all examples of the components he assembles with immaculate new couplings and housings into inventions that are formally elegant, meticulously crafted, cleverly conceived, and mischievously aggressive. The resulting works of art are dangerous.

Morales shows a fondness for the exclamation "Wow!" His use of the word echoes the surprise with which audiences experience his work as they interact with his mischievous inventions. Some works entice the viewer to become the victim of a prank, like being squirted in the face with hot water. Others offer the opportunity to subject someone else to an annoyance, like deafening noises and blinding lights. Still others expose the observer to bodily danger by, for instance, hurling lightning bolts of raw electricity at them. Curiously, these works rarely evoke responses of apprehension and avoidance. Morales reports that people tell him, "You always make me have so much fun with your pieces," or "Your pieces always scare me so much, but I like it." Morales's works reveal the suppressed but powerful allure of circumstances we are socialized to avoid and/or dislike. Being squirted with hot water can be tantalizing as well as distressing. Blinding someone in bright lights releases aggression even among those who normally denounce such acts. Being zapped with a bolt of raw electricity can actually attract as well as repel. Morales's audience discovers surprising behaviors when they are confronted with these situations.

Morales's training to construct this eccentric form of participatory art began long before his encounter with the gun-wielding attacker. Many of his previous near-death experiences were precipitated by his own irrepressible curiosity. He describes one such incident. "As a child I was already interested in how things worked. I opened them. Their parts intrigued me. If I got a toy, I would destroy it. My mother would say, 'Why should we give you toys? You will only take them apart.' So I started making the things I wanted. I was fascinated by systems like the cable cars in the seventies that were in many action movies. So I decided to build one. It was many days, working on it. I took a little toy bus, took out the middle and put in a plastic container and filled it with gasoline. Then I put glass in the little windows. It looked the same as the real one from the outside. It was perfect." It was perfect, but Morales wasn't finished until his sculpture became a prop in his drama, as it was in the movie that inspired it. So, he made an announcement in an imaginary microphone. "I said, 'We have a problem in the system.' Then I ignited the gasoline and OOF! I exploded my bus!"

Interview with Arnaldo Morales
By Zoe Feigenbaum

ZF: How did school affect your preparation to be an artist?

AM: In school I wasn't really good because I have a learning problem. I didn't fit in the school program. So I did what I could. One of my own salvations was I knew how to draw. And then I started to hate it because the only relationship I had with everybody was "You really know how to draw." One of the blessings that I have is that my mother always told me, "You gotta fix this," whenever anything broke, even when I was very small. And I always asked, "How I'm gonna fix this?" And she always said, "You always know." So I learned to fix things, anything, whatever it is. And when I was eighteen I decided to work with art. I started drawing and everybody liked it. I started sculpting. It was really easy for me. But I just didn't really like it. And then one day I started integrating mechanical stuff and I said, "Oh my God, I've been doing art all my life without knowing it."

ZF: How did you start to show your work?

AM: I always tried to invent ways to show my work. So I kind of developed a strategy. When I was in the second year at college I was showing my art in exhibitions with my professors. I tried to be a professional from the beginning. And that's why I have a lot of faith from the beginning. When I graduated with my bachelor's degree I was super-established in Puerto Rico.

ZF: By just doing shows at college?

AM: No. I was searching all the time, asking people. I think my key was that I was really, really honest about what I do. My work has so much interaction with a public, it's like a game. I have so much fun. That's why it's not really difficult for me. What is difficult was not having money to do it. Before I had nothing and I just worked with everything I found. I collected every kind of material. Now my favorite place is garage sales. I buy, I collect objects everywhere.

ZF: Do you remember your first sale?

AM: I was in my first year in the university and the art professor asked me to do a marble piece. And I built this beautiful thing that I hated so much. Somebody at the school said, "I want it." And then I said, "This is the price," and she said, "Okay. Can you bring it home?" and I said, "Of course." And then I said, "Oh my God!" When you sell, you have to figure out how much your work is worth. If you start with a low proportion of money, it could be good because you sell more, but it could be terrible because they're going to pay you the same all the time. You really have to protect your reputation. Normally I don't let the gallery or the dealers tell me what my work is worth. Money for me is important to buy materials to make art. You need two pockets. One to risk and another one to save.

ZF: Do you have a gallery right now?

AM: I have a gallery in Puerto Rico which has represented me from the beginning. Here I start with a

ARTISTS

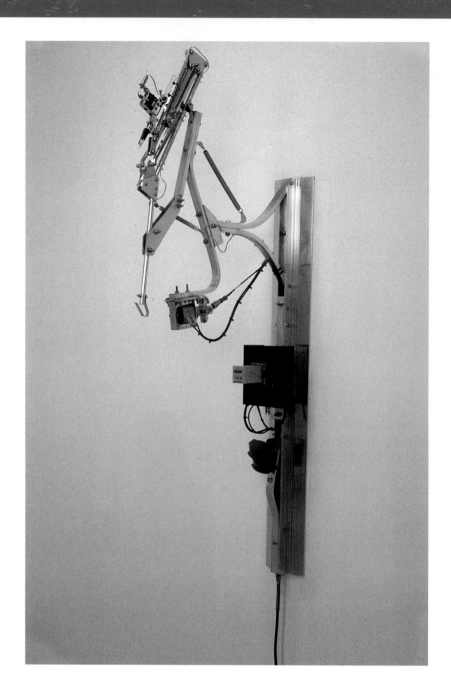

Arnaldo Morales, *TATAUEE NO 97* (1997), 5 feet x 8 inches x 2 feet, industrial materials. Courtesy of the artist and Galería Botello/Collection Millie and Chilo Andrée.

Training for his current art project started early. "My mother would give me her broken kitchen equipment and say, 'Fix this.' I say, 'I don't know how.' She always told me, 'You will figure it out.' That is how I learned to build things. My family let me work with every-thing—muriatic acid, electricity, fire. When I was four or five years old, I wanted to learn how to cut metal. My mother said, 'Use a hand saw.' I started working with electricity at seven and almost killed myself. I was ten when I did the bus piece." Morales's mother seemed neither impressed by his skills nor overly concerned for his safety. Perhaps this explains his unusually demanding interactions with art viewers. He doesn't seem to mind if these responses are negative, as long as they are powerful and spontaneous. "I can describe myself as a person who likes to provoke, no matter if I am calm or angry. I like drastic moments, always.... I need to discover a way that I can express my ideas and get a reaction!"

At the time of our interview, Morales's art studio more closely resembles the laboratory of a mad inventor. In a cramped twelve-by-twelve-foot room, he fiddles with the powerful forces of nature. Mechanics, electricity, pneumatics, centrifugal force, gravity, and compression are further activated by Morales's charged intellect as it concocts ways to tinker with the outer limits of human psychology. Shelves are laden with sorted and polished metal parts ranging from mufflers, cooking pots, brake handles, and medical equipment, bolts, wires, and tubes, to parts from gumball machines, refrigerators, slide projectors, transformers, tanks, and generators. The inventory is completed by cables, springs, neon lights, remote control devices, automobile engines, cans of WD-40, extension cords, drill presses, sanders, polishers, saws, and pulleys. Morales is all grown up, but he still delights in taking things apart in order to rebuild them to his own specifications.

Not unlike his childhood toys, his sculptures are contraptions of peril and allure. He plays pranks, springing traps that discharge experiences viewers would not choose, and provoking responses they would not anticipate. *TATAUEE NO 97* (1997), for example, resembles a high-tech dentist's drill held in the "hand" of a mechan-ical "arm" bracketed to the wall. Closer inspection, however, reveals two surprises. First, the tool is a functioning tattoo machine, needle and all. Second, the arm is not static, but lashes violently toward any visitor who activates its sensors by approaching within a ten-foot radius. Its thrust is as aggressive as a heavyweight champion's and as noisy as a jackhammer. Its recoil is as sinister as a scorpion's tail. The click announcing its readiness to launch the next assault is as menacing as the cocking of a trigger. Submission to a tattoo artist's needle is often a badge of courage, so it is particularly humorous when passersby leap out of harm's way in the instinctual response of primal panic. Morales comments, "An important part of my work is that I control the audience. It doesn't matter what people think—when they stand ten feet away, that thing attacks

gallery and then it doesn't work. The galleries here have other interests. But I want to work in New York because my possibilities in Puerto Rico were getting shorter. Puerto Rico is not a bad place to show, but it's limited. It's like living in Long Island without a car. You can go somewhere, but you really have to work at it. As a student in Puerto Rico, your only connection to the art world is the magazines, the videos, the stories people bring to you. And it's really amazing because what you see in the magazines, you imagine something better or worse. Sometimes when you see the real thing you say, "Oh my gosh, this is amazing." Or you say, "Wow, this is so bad." Whatever, you cannot be precise about it.

ZF: How did you adjust to being in New York?

AM: When I came to New York, for me the hard part was that I had to start from the beginning. Everybody told me I have to start from the bottom. I have to shoot for the little galleries. I have to shoot for little opportunities. This feels like a huge dinosaur hitting you. And I said, "Well if I'm gonna die, let me die doing it really good." And I try. I try many galleries. And they tell me they are not interested. I finally got an appoint-ment with [a] gallery dealer, but I didn't really know any English at all. I practiced with a friend of mine. But when I go there, I forget everything. So it was like this—I was talking and he was looking at me like a weird creature. It was really hard. I have to go to every gallery just to try to figure out what it's really about. I have no communication. Everything is so quick. But I always have this feeling that everybody has the belly button in the same place. This is one of my beliefs. It helps. Then I found some people who helped me. I found some friends on the way. And then I won the Public Art Fund grant. And then I found a gallery and I started. One of my first shows was at Exit Art in SoHo in New York.

ZF: How did you get that show?

AM: They saw the outdoor piece and called me to invite me to participate in a show. They have been tremen-dously supportive ever since. One of the curators is from Puerto Rico and we always talk about the New York art experience. And one of the first things he told me, because he saw me so confused, he said, "It's gonna take you fifteen years to see the light again." I said to him, "Let me get some trash, and you're going to see what I gonna do!" He was so...

ZF: Negative?

AM: No, for me it was like a fierce inspiration. If you plant yourself in a new soil, it's a different soil. To survive, you have to adapt yourself. There's no time to feel sorry. I don't show a lot in New York. I show outside of New York. I show in Mexico, for example. I show in Iceland. I show in Spain. Last week I had an exhibition in Italy. And then Chicago and Texas. My favorite shows are international shows. New York, I don't know if I like the energy or not. The people who really are in charge of art in New York manage the whole package, you know? Everything is about money, everything is about where they can see you. And this

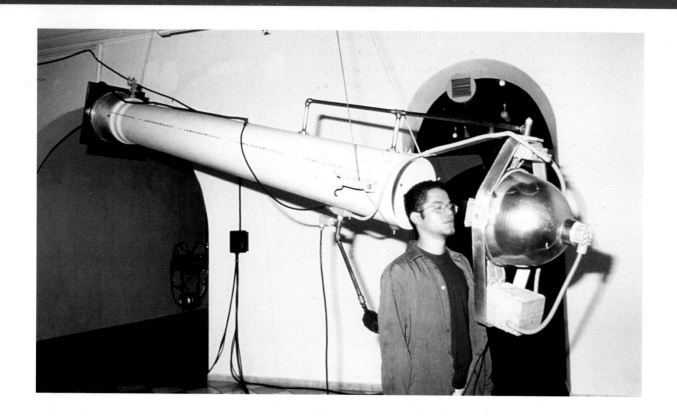

Arnaldo Morales, *Selector M1 No. 94* (1994), 14 x 2.5 x 9 feet, industrial materials. Courtesy of the artist.

SCOPING AN AUDIENCE

them. I play with psychological reactions in people. I love the unexpected. I love when there is no choice, when you have to follow the plan and learn how to adapt. I like the idea of somebody entering a place that has new rules, new circumstances, as if you enter a situation in which there is no oxygen, and you must breathe ether. Your body has to adjust to that. It is totally unexpected."

In most circumstances, the enjoyment experienced by the perpetrators of pranks is proportional to the distress of their victims. Humiliation and embarrassment are the ingredients of a prankster's delight. Like bullies, pranksters can only construct a dominating position by stomping on someone else's self-respect. But Morales's victims seem to share his enjoyment. Critics who might accuse him of sadism suspend judgment because, invariably, they observe the public having a rollicking good time. What may be perverse is the audience's pleasure, not the artist's intent.

TOX-EXT-EST EE1 NO 96 (1996) is a device that resembles a blood dilator, a medical device that facilitates circulation. The spread of AIDS has raised awareness of the possibility that blood can carry dangerous consequences. Morales, however, guaranteed the lethal nature of the red liquid in his work of art—the piece is made of mercury. Like a fountain of death, his contraption pumps mercury from a tank through a web of transparent plastic tubing and up a spout that shoots the toxic liquid into a metal basin. A vibrator attached to the basin drains the mercury back into the tank where it starts this menacing cycle anew. A sign announces the danger of contact. Each individual must decide whether to heed the artist's warning or tempt fate. Morales, too, had a decision to make regarding the real-life consequences of his contrived circumstance. He devised a means to assure that the work's danger was more apparent than actual. His work is designed to induce a fear response which is not dependent on the threat of actual injury. He explains, "I did research. A friend told me that if mercury is at a low temperature, it is not dangerous. The most dangerous part is the vapor, so I put this piece close to the refrigeration piece. The work offers some possibilities for getting hurt. On the other side, I think about how I can protect the person. I'm not interested in hurting someone. I'm interested in communicating." Morales's communications bypass words and thoughts. They target the zone of self-protective instincts.

In the museum context, audiences expect to encounter evidence of the artistic imagination. Art traditionally abstracts, interprets, and represents real life experience. Art and artifice are partners of long standing. But Morales doesn't subscribe to imaginary circumstances or symbolic references. "I want the real thing. I want people to really get scared if that is the purpose of the piece. But also, I try to take care of the other extreme. If I hurt someone, my work is not art, it is just a dangerous thing. But if I can recreate the moment and push inside—if a person says, 'I want to touch this, but I can get hurt,' if

is why nobody has any time to try new concepts. There's a lot of good artists in New York, and nothing happens for them. New York only has a place for the majority. Discrimination is everywhere, everything. You gotta be really, really strong. And you gotta be your own agent no matter if you have a gallery.

ZF: What is your relationship with your gallery in Puerto Rico?

AM: The gallery I have in Puerto Rico is really real. The director is my good friend. Aside from showing and selling my work, it's her moral support and true interest in the contemporary art of Puerto Rico and everywhere that is so important. We have a lot of contact. She's like my mother. She's always looking out for what I'm doing. The only thing she cannot do is, she's not interested in expanding her gallery, like trying to compete in this New York market. Here I work on grants lately.

ZF: Do you do anything else to make money other than your art?

AM: Lately, no. I've been making some money from my art. I've been saving some money. Artists really have to learn how to sell themselves. They really have to find out where to be and how to get close to the possibilities. This is something I've learned but can't really explain. Also, if I can help anybody, I do it. If I believe in the work they do, I help them. Being in art is a lot of work and not all the time really pleasant, but I don't have this belief, like, people have to suffer for what they need. I believe an artist has to be really happy. An artist needs swimming pools, cats. I've seen documentaries about artists who suffer. They make you cry because they don't find a real love. I have pleasure when I show my work. Like, the opening of the show when everybody sees it for the first time. I watch visitors.

ZF: Do you work differently now than when you were a student?

AM: As a student I tried to develop everything so fast because I always felt like I'm late for everything. In the beginning this was good, but it doesn't finish good. As an artist you need to be as calm as you can be.

ZF: So what has helped your career as an artist?

AM: For me, being a good artist doesn't mean you're going to learn a lot from your professors. Art for me is a way to communicate something. It's not fashion. It's nothing good or bad. It's to communicate something which you cannot read. Art is a kind of invention. You have to discover what it is. You don't have to be an amazing writer or an intellectual person to really get it, but you really have to be dedicated. Art is not like a beautiful hobby. If you're an artist who still struggles with life and doesn't make a good living, it's not really a fun thing to do. For me that is one of the most humiliating feelings. If you want to be an artist, you have got to be ready for everything. You've gotta be ready to not make it.

ZF: Do you have any advice for young artists?

AM: You've got to be ambitious, but you've got to be

I can create this feeling, then I am super-successful. I am fascinated by the fact that certain plants and animals have defense mechanisms. They survive because they are poisonous. I am fascinated by the impulse to walk up to a cactus, see the spines, know what they do, and still feel compelled to try them out, to prove that they penetrate and cut. We have an inability to resist something that is patently defensive to a plant and injurious to a person."

Art viewers are always granted license to challenge an artist's interpretation of reality. In Morales's case, however, the stakes are higher than mere trust and respect. Challenging Morales involves disregarding his warnings of danger. Some people ignore these warnings because they believe that all art is virtualized. They assume these sculptures merely have the appearance of danger and that the fear they evoke is imaginary. Those who are incapable of suppressing their curiosity often accept the dare even when they know there may be actual consequences. Of course, there are some who heed the artist's advice, respect the work's dangerous implications, and resist its seductive appeal. Morales provides a fourth form of response through *TRIOBEGUN IRONIK NO 98* (1998). In this work, release of repressed hostilities awaits participants who choose to play a shooting game. *TRIOBEGUN* is a "pneumatic conversation piece," according to the artist. It recreates real-life scenarios by allowing each of three participants to choose when and if they become aggressors. It does not, however, allow them to choose when they become its targets. The contraption transforms this familiar source of insecurity into a physical actuality. It consists of three guns made of pistol-grip impact air drivers that are equally spaced around a hanging armature that looks, ironically, like a peace sign from a bird's-eye point of view. The guns are connected to an overhead air compressor. Each participant in this three-way "conversation" occupies a station that is equipped with a trigger. Pulling the trigger discharges bursts of compressed air, deafening sounds, and blinding lights into the spaces between the other players. Passive players choose to be victims. Response-oriented players retaliate once a charge has been fired. Aggressive players initiate the actions. Every alternative is carried out with absolute impunity because Morales made it impossible for any one participant to know which of the other two pulled the trigger and caused these explosive effects. The piece forces people to confront their real, as opposed to their avowed, tolerances and beliefs in peaceful coexistence. By using guns as the medium of discourse for these "conversations," Morales reminds his audience of the frequent use of violence in conflict resolution, often to ill effect. Even in situations that are not hostile, guns are alluring. Morales notes, "Show a gun to anyone and they say 'Wow,' they pick it up, and point." Although most people attest that they disapprove of this violent behavior, experiencing this work of art can lead to surprising contradictions. Morales reports, "With *TRIOBEGUN*, at first people touch the trigger gingerly. Then, in a flash, they pull hard and make it like a machine gun. The aggression comes out. I want this change in the person with all my work. Everyone has really strong energies, no matter who." But Morales is quick to correct the impression that he is encouraging violence. The barrage of hot air and noise produces no physical harm. Indeed, it apparently produces a therapeutic effect. Many participants report that after activating the compressed-air trigger guns, they experience a cathartic release, like yelling at someone who has made them angry. Morales comments, "You can be very angry with a person, but you know you are not going to hit that person. Maybe you can do something and feel the release and then you can laugh with that person."

Morales seems pleased that most people enjoy their interactions with his "electrobjetos." But entertainment is less his purpose than his means. He lures audiences to join his explorations of brutality and danger by presenting them in the form of games and practical jokes. Once viewers become participants, they can begin to understand the relationships that exist between concepts presumed to be opposites. Panic meets pleasure. Danger conspires with excitement. Aggression motivates rehabilitation. Pain is linked to sensuality. These unlikely mergers create awareness of the widespread ambivalence over presumed taboos and accepted behaviors. Morales's social sculptures construct a more nuanced understanding of human psychology and its manifestation in the violence that pervades contemporary culture.

very honest and not pretentious. If you are going to be an artist because you want to be eccentric, that doesn't make it. The important thing in art is communicating. And you need to find people who believe in what you do. It's hard work. I'm thirty-three-years old. When I was twenty-one, I was working really intensely. I was working eight o'clock in the morning to four o'clock in the morning, every day. I almost fainted everywhere. I just collapsed. I had a crisis. And somebody told me, "You want to be successful? Concentrate but don't get obsessive about it."

1. All quotes from an interview with the artist, June 19, 2000.

ACTIVIST

Providing Free Food

Rirkrit Tiravanija

Born 1961 Buenos Aires, Argentina (to Thai parents)
1981 Ontario College of Art, Toronto, Canada
1984 Banff Center School of Fine Arts, Banff, Canada
1985 School of the Art Institute of Chicago
1986 The Whitney Independent Studies Program, New York
Has lived in Canada, Thailand, Ethiopia
Lives and works in New York City

Rirkrit Tiravanija might surprise Wise and Aldrich, the creators of a cartoon of a woman standing in front of a sink overflowing with dirty dishes who asks, "So, are you ever going to wash those?" The man answers, "No, because it's actually a sculpture I've been working on called *After the Meal*." Meals and the dirty dishes they generate actually constitute Tiravanija's artworks. He not only offers free food, he offers free beds to sleep in and free music studios to practice in. These acts of generosity guarantee that audiences interact with his art and delight in it. His artistic communication is a model of hospitality.

Rirkrit Tiravanija is an artist who renounces almost all commonly accepted assumptions about art. He does not, for example, subscribe to the concept that art is an aesthetic object, crafted from the residue of past activities by a specialist and presented to the public for observation and contemplation. Despite this wholesale rejection of the prevailing practice and presentation of art, he is still intent on being an artist. Others facing such a dilemma might have switched careers, but Tiravanija chose to customize his role as an artist and overhaul each aspect of the art world he intersected. Even this radical gesture does not conform to precedents set by radical artists in recent history. The outpost of the avant-garde is typically occupied by artists spurred on by anger and a rebellious spirit, but it is with a mild manner and an unflappable temperament that Tiravanija pursues a positive course. Quietly he invents his own rules of operation to bring his artistic practice into alignment with his moral and social vision. Likewise, many works described as avant-garde often combine confrontation, sophistication, and irony; Tiravanija's projects are best described by characteristics often neglected within the art context— simplicity, forthrightness, and honesty. His work is endearing.

Likewise, he welcomes a broad audience by creating art that consists of familiar, everyday activities. These activities are not only unlike art, they are normally forbidden in museums. Tiravanija's exhibitions, which have occupied prestigious galleries and museums worldwide, provide opportunities for people to dance in a museum (to a slow version of the song "Shall We Dance"); drink in a museum (beverages chosen to complement local preferences like Turkish coffee, beer, Coca-Cola, soup, tea); watch a sports event in a museum (a football match between artists and curators); sleep in a museum (orange sleeping mats provided); play music in a museum (in a studio equipped with instruments and mixing consoles); and hold public discourse in a museum (Tiravanija invited the public to discuss the work of other artists in a group exhibition).

Tiravanija has not omitted the producer of his art, himself, from his sweeping reforms. He has redesigned his creative process, replacing self-absorption with a concern for the well-being of others. By identifying more strongly with his audience than his own ego, his motive also shifts from self-expression and personal rewards to generosity. At the

SCOPING AN AUDIENCE

same time, his studio practice is recast as a communal public act. In order to fulfill this moral mandate, he has constructed particular artistic guidelines that he diligently follows. First, the primary goal of his artistic activities is the creation of experiences, not objects. Second, material evidence of these activities must have an ongoing utility within the life stream; unlike conventional works of art, Tiravanija's artworks are not isolated and protected as precious nonfunctional creations. Third, because Tiravanija discourages his viewers from merely observing his artworks and his collectors from simply storing or displaying them, the public actively determines the nature of their experience with his works of art. Fourth, the public thereby becomes the artist's collaborators; their activities, as much as his, are granted the status of art. Still, there is one professional given that allies Tiravanija to his career choice: he capitalizes on the liberty granted to artists to be non-conformists and explore zones outside the normal matrix of art and culture. Although eating and sleeping and the other activities that he absorbs into his artistic practice may be common, his acts of kindness are not. He states, "It's always about being outside. Art, in a way, is about that relationship. For me there is always another place, another condition, another situation... In a sense it's about relationships to time and place, and where you are."[1]

The transgression that first earned his renown in the art world involved eating. Transcending the banal cheese-and-cracker offering common at most art openings, Tiravanija offered a full meal. For Tiravanija, this meal constituted his exhibition. People were welcome to enjoy it, once or repeatedly, any time the gallery was open, throughout the duration of the exhibition. Because the artist was more often absent than present, visitors were granted the opportunity to be both hosts and guests. The artist provided recipes and ingredients so visitors could cook for themselves and for anyone else who had congregated in the gallery at the time. There was no transfer of money for the food. The free meal came with only one stipulation—to explore congenial ways of behaving.

Although radical deviations from art's norms often provoke public indignation, Tiravanija's departures not only inspire admiration, they typically arouse affection. He is especially beloved by those who lament that current art is often unwelcoming and the institutions that support it often practice aggressive marketing tactics within a contentious and competitive business environment. Tiravanija resists this cutthroat trend by ignoring it. He creates art that is defined according to service, function, and communal sharing. These principles were demonstrated in 1992 and again in 1995 when he created *Untitled (Free)* at the 303 Gallery in Manhattan. For this project, Tiravanija transformed the back room of the gallery into a makeshift kitchen by outfitting it with a refrigerator, a counter, camping tables and stools, cutting boards, cutlery, a can opener, woks, electric hot plates, plastic cups, and teapots. Bags of rice,

Interview with Rirkrit Tiravanija
By Lauren Harkrader

LH: How did you get connected with your gallery?

RT: Most of the galleries I work with are generally friends before they are galleries. I don't want to work with people who don't really understand what I do and how I think. The people I work with know this—that they don't know if they are going to make any money from it.

LH: How did you start out?

RT: It's not like I had a great vision and ambition. I mean, I have some ideas of what I wanted do, but it was not like I have an ambition. I really basically stumbled and fell into the position I'm in. It wasn't like I had to work hard at it. My idea was to make work which would be able to speak and relate to a very different culture. My goal was really to make work I will be able to continue when I went back to Thailand. My intention at that point was to go back home and try to figure out what it is that art could do when I was in Thailand. So it wasn't like I had an idea that I wanted to get a gallery show and museum exhibitions.

LH: To be able to do something that speaks to people in an interesting way.

RT: Yeah. To be able to communicate. I studied in the West and learned a kind of knowledge of what the culture is here. I wanted to utilize that kind of knowledge back in Thailand. And also I was trying to consider how it would be possible to use it and not to consume it. It's a different thing.

LH: Exactly. So what were the circumstances surrounding your first exhibitions?

RT: Well, I just kind of tripped into it. I was in a group exhibition in New York. It was a provocative work in relationship to what was going on around it. And it was my first cooking work. What I was thinking about and working on just happened to be the right question at that moment. And so people took it on. And then I was asked to do a one-person, smallish project show. And that was again something that got a lot of attention.

LH: How did that one piece interact with the other pieces if it was a group show?

RT: Like me, there were a lot of people making work which was very process-oriented. But on the other hand, it completely stood out because process-oriented work is still embedded in the object. Everybody still ended up with some kind of object, and I was making something that was really boiling and burning and stinking. I was working on this idea of a process which stank and had garbage, which was like New York in the 1980s—walking down the Bowery and smelling piss and things like that. There was a lot of work which was based on the media and unreality. I was trying to provoke reality.

LH: Since most of your work is about this process, how do you go about marketing it?

RT: I don't market my work or, rather, I try to sell my ideas. People who are buying it are basically collecting an idea. People who buy my work have to use it. So

Rirkrit Tiravanija, *Untitled (Tomorrow is Another Day)* (1996), apartment installation at the Cologne Kunstverein Museum, Germany. Courtesy Gavin Brown's Enterprise, New York, and Neugerriemschneider, Berlin.

packets of bouillon cubes, jars of spices, and cartons of produce were heaped onto the tables. These were the ingredients of a simple meal that was available to anyone who visited the gallery during the seven-week duration of the exhibition. Some people became repeat diners. Some came only once. The art experience they were offered was visual (colorful vegetables, steam, shiny pans), olfactory (the smell of simmering foods), aural (whistling kettles, chattering, laughter), and gustatory (Thai curries and rice).

Throughout the duration of the exhibition the menu remained the same, but the other sensual ingredients of the art experience underwent a metamorphosis. In accordance with the artist's wishes, dirty paper plates, disposable chopsticks, and the uneaten remains of the meals piled up. The visual components deteriorated into a mess of garbage. The olfactory sense was dominated by rancid food. Tiravanija wanted confusion and chance to prevail. Still, most visitors relaxed into the friendly ambiance that pervaded the art gallery, a setting not known for conviviality. Personal exchanges were initiated by the act of eating together, revitalizing a communal tradition which has become increasingly threatened by quick turnover in jobs, frequent changes in residences, cramped urban kitchens, working moms, and the collapse of family stability.

Another unwritten rule of the art world dismantled by Tiravanija assumes that artists must always create something new. He violated this mandate by mounting the same exhibition at the same gallery three years after its initial showing. Neither aesthetics nor innovation concerns him. His art is designed to instigate a "concentration of relationships; levels of engagement and shifts of focus; a different model, developed so that the subject/object has shifted, or maybe the relation between subject and subjected has changed."[2] Tiravanija explains how art provides the latitude to conduct such an experiment. "It is possible that there is more space for things to happen within this exchange because it is never 'really real' but another fiction."[3]

In the following statement, Tiravanija identifies another aspect of his maverick mission: "I am never engaged in the object."[4] He demonstrates this disengagement by introducing an alternative to those who make art in order to sell it to collectors. Instead of lavishing attention on the production of a material object, Tiravanija prefers to sculpt social behaviors. This interest became apparent early in his life. He recalled during our interview that even as a child he was more captivated by the people looking at the Mona Lisa than by the masterpiece itself. Likewise, the focus of Tiravanija's gallery installation is on the people interacting while they are eating, not on the food. That is how food became the core of his practice despite the fact that he is not a skilled chef. Haute cuisine would distract people from the social component of his work. The avoidance of such pretense in the menu sets the aesthetic parameters for all other aspects of his gallery installation: meals are set out on

it's not like you buy it and then you just put it in the vitrine to look at and to pretend that something that happened ten years ago is embedded in the object. My work is of the moment, of the now and the here. So nothing happens unless you use it. You have to cook the meal. You have to give it to other people. You have to have interaction with it and with people around it. I mean, even if you were just [to] cook for yourself, it's better than to put it in a glass case and look at it. It's also a process which could bring you to another plane. It's not the objects. It's not the cooking. It's not the eating. It's the combination of many things. It's the process of living, basically.

LH: But you have sold your work.

RT: There were different progressions. The initial problem of what I was doing was that the food was just sitting on a pedestal cooking and nobody could eat it. And then I solved that problem by cooking the food and serving it up. And then I only cooked for one day, so that was a problem because only some people could have that experience. So then the next time I cooked it every day. And then the problem is, only people in the art world get to eat it, so then I go and cook out in the street. When people were first buying the garbage, it was just relics. And then I realized, relics don't give any sense of the idea. So I stop selling garbage and start selling pots and pans, which people have to use to cook things in, from which they then make garbage. And as you do art, you are also building new problems.

LH: So you do not have a studio?

RT: No. I do not have a studio, but I have three apartments. I don't make big things. So that's part of it. And I don't make things until I have to make them.

LH: Why is that?

RT: I don't need to sit around and make anything. I can have it all in my head. I don't draw, I don't really write so much. In fact, it's more not having to have any of those things which becomes a burden, you know? I mean, you have a big space and you feel like you need to use it, and then you start to make things, and then you have more things, and then you have to have more space because you need to have space to keep them all. I use things that exist already. Those things, if they were used, they can be recycled.

LH: What do you do when you're not showing?

RT: I always have some kind of show going on. I'm trying to have new ideas and think about new things in the world, and you can't do that if you are sitting inside.

LH: Was there some person, or a group of people, or maybe an institution that promoted your career when you were still unknown and starting out?

RT: No, not really. A lot of people go to school to get connections to the art world. The only reason I went to school is so I could have a visa to stay in the States. I went to the Whitney program, which is a place with a great deal of connection. But I never thought about those. I don't like that idea. If somebody likes my work, they should like it for what it is or who I

makeshift tables without linen and are served on paper plates instead of china. These decisions are neither due to budgetary restraints nor neglect. Culinary elitism, like artistic elitism, can discourage friendly interactions among strangers. Offering a humble, home-made meal, on the other hand, is universally understood as a hospitable gesture. Tiravanija creates work that is, quite literally, easy to digest. The unpretentious nature of the meal has a welcoming effect on those who are intimidated by contemporary art. Furthermore, it is capable of being consumed without being purchased within the art market. When the art product is social exchange, everyone can become a collector. In fact, a fellowship of collectors of Tiravanija experiences exists around the globe.

In yet another transgression, Tiravanija inserts altruism into the business aspects of art by fashioning art galleries as if they themselves were mediums, like clay, to be shaped according to the artist's desired effect. As a result, mounting an exhibition with Tiravanija usually means that professional protocols must be suspended and institutional rules must be relaxed. In *Untitled (Free)*, for example, in addition to offering a meal in the back room, Tiravanija shifted the back-room functions to the exhibition space. Upon entering the gallery, visitors encountered an array of desks, chairs, files, computers, a photocopy machine, and a coffee maker, and also witnessed these items in use. The relocated staff resumed its activities under the glare of gallery lights, conducting its business in full view of all the gallery's visitors. Telephone conversations, negotiations with artists, discussions of sales and publicity, and bookkeeping were all placed on display. Because these business activities were conducted in public, the staff tended to become more polite, more helpful, more honest. All these improved behaviors could be included on an inventory of Tiravanija's art products.

Tiravanija's desire to break through the barriers of privacy and possessiveness extends into his personal life. He, his wife, and their Siamese cat live in a small, cramped, walk-up apartment in Manhattan's East Village. It is widely known that the artist readily shares his living quarters with guests. The apartment is such a poignant expression of his artistic principles that Tiravanija actually assigned it the status of a work of art—and used it as the model for his installation at the Cologne Kunstverein. A life-size, fully functioning, completely furnished version was recreated in the museum's exhibition hall. The plumbing worked, the refrigerator was stocked, beds were available for sleeping. Most importantly, Tiravanija insisted that the exhibition reflect one other component of his real apartment—it had to be open to everyone twenty-four hours a day. This benevolent act wreaked havoc on the museum, which is normally open only during regular business hours. During the extent of Tiravanija's exhibition, visitors were generously granted squatters rights. In response to this requirement, museum guards stopped guarding and museum registrars stopped protecting works of art. This show permitted touching, reclining, chewing, reading, and sleeping. In fact, it allowed people to take up residence in the museum, enjoying the beds, the food, and other comforts of home. When asked if there was a problem with people taking advantage of the free services, Tiravanija responded, "That's not a problem. People should take advantage of it. If people burn it down, it's not a problem. It might be a problem for other people that want to use it, but for me it's not a problem."[5]

Tiravanija has even discovered a way to oblige collectors in his gentle campaign to promote geniality. He accommodated requests to own a sample of his work by agreeing to sell the tables, woks, empty food containers, and leftover food after his exhibitions close. Since they are the end products of the artist's creative process, they are sold as art. Collectors have been willing to pay between $5,000 and $200,000 to acquire the mundane items that once constituted parts of his exhibitions. Remarkably, Tiravanija has even reconfigured these transactions as an essential component of his social concerns as an artist. He introduced innovative terms of ownership by insisting that collectors insure that the work will continue to generate geniality even after it has been sold. "I never thought about having to sell my work, or that someone would buy it.... As time passed I said, look, if somebody wants this thing, the only way to have any relationship to it is to redo it, which means to re-make the meal and put it back into the vitrine (with the old remains). Yes, the old things and the new things together. Basically I started to make things so that people would have to use them, which means if you want to buy something then you have to use it. It doesn't have to be all the time. It's not meant to be put out with other sculpture or like another relic." He continues, "My feeling has always been that everyone makes a work—including the people who take it to re-use it. When I say re-use it, I just mean use it. You don't have to make it look exactly how it was. It's more a matter of spirit. And if you can understand that, then you don't have to worry about how it works. It just comes back together."[6]

Tiravanija has fed and housed audiences in museums in Venice, Pittsburgh, Glasgow, Chicago, Stockholm, Budapest, and elsewhere around the globe. Sometimes, however, he takes his welcoming message directly to the people. In *Untitled (From Madrid Airport to Reina Sofia)* (1994), for example, the artist pedaled all the way from the airport to the museum on a wheeled contraption equipped with foldaway table and gas heaters. A rucksack of his own design was strapped to his back. It was stuffed with food, spices, a stockpot, and dishes. Every afternoon and evening he stopped and cooked for anyone who happened by. Early in the trip he sometimes ate alone, but as the days progressed, word of his arrival preceded him and huge groups assembled to meet him and to share the meal he offered. Unlike charity food vans, many of the people he attracted were hungry for the nourishment of convivial exchanges, not food.

A video camera recorded the sights and sounds of the five-day excursion. Tiravanija intended that this documentation would serve as an important component of the museum installation. The camera was strapped to the artist's bicycle. Thus the camera angles, the focus, the compositions of the imagery, the sequencing of shots were all determined by the random movements of the bicycle, and not by the artist's perceptions. This is another demonstration that Tiravanija is more intent on dismantling social formalities than constructing aesthetic formalisms. The museum presented this unedited video surrounded by the contents of the artist's backpack, including the uneaten remains of the meals. This careless demeanor is a product of carefully considered intent. "If I could, I would just keep the camera on the whole time and just let it run until whenever it had to end. So you get everything." He then explains why he has chosen this relaxed and inclusive aesthetic course. "We have to

am. People came to it on their own. In the art world you could be supported by someone and that could be a negative thing.

LH: How could it be a negative thing?

RT: Well, there are different schools and different groups and different ideas. There are factions in the art world. So if you are supported by one faction you are likely to be shut out by the other. There are a lot of people in the art factions who don't think that making popular work is actually a good idea. If you make popular work it means that there is a certain level which has been taken out of the art.

LH: What show was the most important for you?

RT: They are all important and none of them are important, you know? It's not a measure for me. Of course, the first show was important because it was the first show, which then led to the second show. But then the second show led to the third show. And then the tenth show did something which leads to ten other shows. Basically I still haven't made a good show. I'm just trying to find it.

LH: And who helps you—I see you have assistants that have come over to your apartment—who helps you out in terms of your work and what is their role?

RT: I need people to kind of help me do little things, like make sure I get a ticket to the right place and pay the tax and make sure I still have money. On the other hand, it's also about, like, helping somebody else, you know? There are people that need jobs and need money, so I give them something to do.

LH: How are the costs of producing your work allocated in terms of rent, and salaries, and travel, things like that?

RT: Even though I have three houses, I have very low rent. Everything else I do is paid for by everybody else. So if I have to do a show, then they are paying for me to do a show. If I worked in this place and they only had ten dollars to do the show, then I would do something which costs ten dollars. I don't have my own budget.

LH: What percent of your income would you say is earned by the sale of your art?

RT: I never sold any work out of an exhibition I've done, only later, much later. It's because nobody wants to buy it. My work has no value in the art market, basically.

LH: Those people that do buy your work, what is your relationship with them, if at all?

RT: Generally I know them. I think it's more like a form of support of the work. And there are people that I refuse to sell work to because I don't believe in what they are doing. I think that it's very important who is buying the work and what they are doing with it.

LH: And that would be because of the other work that they have?

RT: No, no, it is because of the way that they do business in the world. It's not about the art.

LH: I know that you have apartments all over the world. Do you feel like there is one place that you identify with most as your home?

Rirkrit Tiravanija, *Untitled (Baragas to Paracuellos de Garama to Torrejon de Ardoz to San Fernando or Coslada to Reina Sofia)* (1996). Courtesy Gavin Brown's Enterprise, New York.

slow down. As much as we're going fast forward on this Internet screen, one also needs to be able to reflect."[7]

In every aspect of the art enterprise, Tiravanija replaced elitism with egalitarianism. First, art was eased off of its lofty perch and relocated in down-to-earth experiences. Second, the artist abandoned self-centeredness. Third, curators relinquished authority. Fourth, museums shed their elite status and galleries abandoned their roles as luxury marketplaces. Fifth, art abdicated its cultlike status. Sixth, guards encouraged physical contact with the artworks. Seventh, docents encouraged physical and social interactions with the art. Eighth, viewers' experiences of art activated gracious social behaviors. The artist concludes, "Art has many different levels and you have to make your own level. You have to decide where you want to be, and then just go for that. It doesn't have to do with anything else in the world. Just yourself. You get there, and maybe nobody sees it, but you get there. It is, at least as I think of it, a spiritual thing."[8]

RT: Being in New York is very important, and I would say it is a very home place for me because I've been in it for so long, probably longer than any homes I've been in. But also I'm not attached to things like that. My migration route is generally based on climate, for my own well-being, based on what I need to do. Generally, wherever I am is home.

LH: Did you, or do you, struggle to maintain yourself as an artist?

RT: [Laughs] Well, I don't have that struggle because I'm not worried about being an artist. I'm not worried about having to have a studio and sit in the studio or whatever the life of an artist is, so I don't have that kind of ideal which means that it's all a struggle.

LH: Were there times in your life when you felt you were particularly productive?

RT: [Laughs] I'm not a machine. I'm not a mechanical thing. I'm not a hardware; I'm a software.

LH: So is there a tempo or a variability to your creative process, or is it very predictably unproductive?

RT: I'm much more interested in trying to live, more than to try to be more productive or be more creative.

LH: Would you have advice for the current generation of aspiring artists?

RT: Look for what it is that is important to you, something that you need to make other people think about. Always ask ourselves if what we are doing is really necessary.

LH: I know that a lot of your work is about the present moment and also the decomposition and rotting of elements, and how things are temporal. Do you do anything now to maybe enhance the value of your work in the future?

RT: [Laughs] No future. It doesn't mean anything for me to have something preserved.

[1] Richard Flood and Rochelle Steiner, "En Route," *Parkett*, No. 44 (1995), 119.

[2] Liam Gillick and Rirkrit Tiravanija, "Forget about the Ball and Get on with the Game," *Parkett*, No. 44 (1995), 108.

[3] ibid.

[4] Hans Ulrich Obrist and Hou Hanru, "Tuk Tuk. In Conversation with Navin Rawanchaikul and Rirkrit Tiravanija," November 1997 <http://www.mip.at/en/dokumente/15-content.html>.

[5] From an interview with the artist by Lauren Harkrader, December 12, 2001.

[6] Flood and Steiner, 116.

[7] ibid, 119.

[8] Conversation with the artist, June 21, 2001.

GILLIAN WEARING

Born 1963 Birmingham, England
1985–1987 Chelsea School of Art, B. Tech in art and design
1987–1990 Goldsmiths College, fine art degree
Lives and works in London

Gillian Wearing amplifies viewers' responses by bridging the divide that separates them from the real-life human subjects of her photographs and videos. Wearing situates these subjects so they stare into her camera in the manner of mug shots. As images, they instigate captivating, face-to-face encounters with the viewers. Then she invites her subjects to speak or to convey their thoughts in written statements. Wearing directs them away from emotionally diluting forms of discourse. Instead of the casual manner of chatting, the formal approach of lecturing, or the entertaining style of story-telling, her subjects confess. Honest disclosures are rare. The content of these disclosures is sometimes shocking. When viewers are shocked, they tend to suspend such relaxed and fleeting manners of observing as glancing and gazing. Instead, they look at these artworks with the intensity of a stare. Confession and staring complete the communication chain—from artwork to viewer and from viewer to artwork.

It is becoming common in many households to have an appliance that enables family members to document their private lives and broadcast them on the Internet. Sales of individual webcams are escalating and they are becoming regular features on PCs.[1] The popularity of this device suggests that the narcissistic impulse to be scrutinized by millions of people is complemented by millions of people's desires to observe the daily eating, sleeping, talking, housekeeping, fornicating, and grooming habits of strangers. The trend is evident in the major television networks as well, where broadcasts of true-life revelations, mostly contrived to expose painful truths and sensationalize shameful acts, are fast becoming regular fare. The audience for these shows prefers their reality, even if the events they chronicle are diluted by the tedium of real-time disclosure, and chooses these shows over the mediated, amplified, and packaged dramatizations churned out in sitcoms, soap operas, and other scripted television shows. This new kind of documentary originated when BBC2 broadcast *The Family* in 1974. Almost all of Britain watched transfixed as the Wilkins family divulged their sordid disregard for decorum and morality. In the U.S., public disclosures that range from the embarrassing to the reprehensible are regularly featured on such popular shows as *The Real World*, *Court TV*, *The Jerry Springer Show*, *Big Brother*, *Bachelor*, and *Survivor*.

Gillian Wearing's photography and video projects introduce this trend into the arena of fine art. Although she avoids both the sensationalism that tends to characterize reality TV and the banality that typifies webcam broadcasts, she shares their fascination with self-disclosure. Wearing comments, "In a way, media saturation has good and bad elements. It made people feel that they can actually exorcise their demons. People still believe in a new way of confessing, of making others partake in their problems."[2] Wearing creates expanded outlets for the need to expose and the desire to witness exposures. Drunks, transsexuals, and rapists come to share this category with children, moms, and workers. Wearing identifies the quality that serves as their common denominator by declaring, "We all have secrets, we all have things that we contain within our lives ... you never lose those doubts.

Gillian Wearing, *Signs that say what you want them to say and not signs that say what someone else wants you to say (Queer and Happy)* and *(I'm Desperate)* (1992–1993), 16 x 12 inches each, c-prints mounted on aluminum. Courtesy Gorney, Bravin + Lee, New York, and Maureen Paley Interim Art, London.

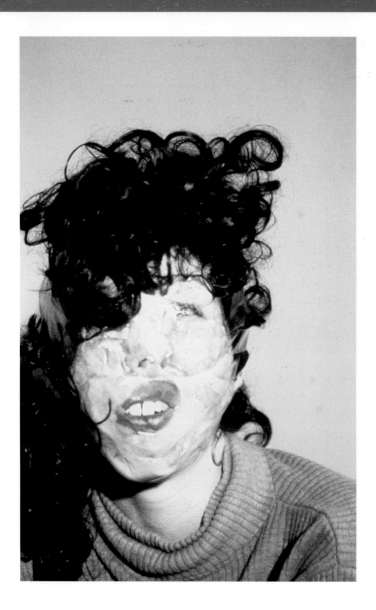

Gillian Wearing, *Confess all on video. Don't worry you will be in disguise. Intrigued? Call Gillian.....* (1994), video, 30 min. Courtesy Gorney, Bravin + Lee, New York, and Maureen Paley Interim Art, London.

They inhabit your body forever. We see our bodies as vessels, and what goes on inside is often much more complex and complicated, that disparity between the look of a person and the things going on inside is what I wanted to bring out."[3]

Wearing's artistry is revealed by her ability to connect the words "humane" and "humanity" through the astute psychological interactions that transpire between her and her subjects off-camera. That artistry is equally dependent on crafting the means to convey, to the art audience, the secrets revealed during these explorations. In the first instance, she must earn her subjects' trust. In the second, she strives to elicit sympathetic acceptance. Wearing continually escalates this challenge. The sites of her encounters have ranged from the busy pathways in Regent's Park in London to the private bedrooms of transsexuals.

Wearing's Regent's Park encounters generated a photographic series entitled *Signs that say what you want them to say and not Signs that say what someone else wants you to say*. The artist explains that in order to create this eighteen-month-long project (1992–1993), she approached hundreds of randomly selected individuals and provided them with a blank sheet of paper, a pen, and the occasion to write whatever they chose. These individuals were then photographed, one by one, holding their thoughts in their hands. About the pedestrians who she approached for this project, Wearing comments, "I definitely wanted something that involved collusion. Firstly they would have to agree, and on top of that they would have to think and say something that they felt. For me this worked so much better because, when they returned with something they had written, it challenged my own perception of them. We all start making up our minds when we see someone; we all get ideas based on how people look, even though we know these ideas can be knocked out of us as soon as we get close to them or start talking to them."[4]

Wearing mounted the snapshots on aluminum and hung them side-by-side as a comprehensive group portrait of nineties London. Through these means attention was directed to the relationship between the written self-disclosures and the appearance of the persons who wrote them. Repeatedly *Signs* confirmed the discrepancy between assumption and conclusion. The work provided uncontestable evidence that quick judgments based on observations of facial expression, posture, clothing style, age, and gender are often woefully inaccurate. The following pronouncements provide examples of internal states that conflicted with external demeanors: an officer wearing a helmet, a sign of authority, holds a paper scrawled with four huge letters that spell "HELP"; an attractive and clean-cut young man presents the words "I don't want to look like a boy"; a successful-looking businessman declares, "I'm desperate"; a teenage boy quotes the New Testament bible, "For he so loved the world that he sent his only begotten son." Wearing's direct, snapshot approach was so straightforward that some might consider it artless. But by withholding her personal response to the disclosures of her subjects, she verified the legitimacy of their statements and enabled viewers to respond directly to them without being influenced by the artist's intervention.

By inserting self-revelatory signs within the photographs instead of allocating these texts to labels, Wearing capitalized on the communicating power of signs. People today are programmed to read signs. Signage, however, is typically monopolized by the authorities that control behavior (Do Not Enter), manipulate action (Drink Coca Cola), alter opinion (Guns Kill), or identify a landmark (Wal-Mart). Wearing converted this potent source of official power into a vehicle for personal expression. For audiences, reading the subjects' statements coincided with the observation of their appearances. The subjects were empowered to speak for themselves. Wearing then optimized the social consequence and aesthetic impact of these commonplace photographs of ordinary people. For instance, the sheets of paper were large enough to allow the text to be legible in a photograph, but not so large that they obstructed the individuals holding them. Furthermore, all the subjects were given identical sheets of paper. When exhibited as a series, this formal uniformity served to emphasize the diversity of messages and the varied styles of handwriting.

Wearing replaces stereotypes, the determinant of most encounters with strangers, with each person's truth as revealed from the source. She discloses her inspiration by commenting, "We live in a society which is always telling us what to think and what we should or shouldn't do. For my own sake, I have to gauge what makes us live, breathe, and tick using my own methods."[5] Wearing's inquisitiveness applies to everyone: those whose behaviors are sanctioned and therefore boring, as well as those whose behaviors are outside the norm and thus deviant. Mainstream culture imposes a silencing mechanism on both, which is why they are the focus of Wearing's artistic concerns. The microphones and cameras of the mass media typically bypass ordinary people, like those photographed in *Signs*, because they don't appear to have anything significant to say. In contrast, the declarations of odd characters are often self-censored because their disclosures carry the threat of punishment or shame. In the 1994 video *Confess*, Wearing revealed that the consciences of both groups are burdened with guilt, remorse, and shame.

Wearing gathered her participants for *Confess* by placing an ad amid others offering cheap flights and appeals from lonely hearts in the back pages of *Time Out*, a London listings magazine. Her little notice read: "Confess all on video. Don't worry you will be in disguise. Intrigued? Call Gillian." When those who were intrigued contacted her, she offered them a platform to speak their truth, and assured their anonymity by providing materials to disguise their identities. Hidden behind ridiculous Halloween masks and gag wigs, rubber noses and nylon ringlets, each person laid naked a litany of secrets. They confessed. Wearing maintains the neutrality of her camera in film as in photography; by avoiding dramatic lighting or interpretive backgrounds or dark room manipulations, *Confess* presents the confessions of her subjects without judgment and consolation:

"So I put the bitch's telephone number in a phone box marked 'Busty lady wants to give men a good time' so then she was harassed by dirty old men phoning her up in the middle of the night wanting sex…"
"My confession is drugging a man, robbing his house and stealing his credit card…"
"Hi, I'm a transvestite…"
"The confession I have to make is this: My brother developed a sexual relationship with his sister and this involved snogging/necking, but not sexual intercourse. I haven't been able to come to terms with this…. It's meant that my own sexuality has been completely destroyed by this thing…"

Although the confessions heard throughout the film are as sensational as those found in the popular media, sensation and titillation were not Wearing's motives. She created *Confess* to redress the burden of harboring secret guilt. She explains, "There's no more belief in most people's lives that there might be some way for them to deal with something that's not right emotionally. There's this emptiness and void and I suppose that's what I've grown increasingly interested in."[6] Wearing acknowledges that her tactics subject her to criticism. "Some people were telling me I was ridiculing people. I've always had to question my ethics, but sometimes I think that the ethical becomes problematical because of this PC obsession with what is unethical."[7] Ethics lies at the core of Wearing's activities. Her intent to soothe the conscience of her subjects is paired with an attempt to awaken the conscience of her audience. But she avoids scripting audience responses just as she avoids involving herself in her subjects' confessions. "When people watch some of my videos that don't have a moral message and there's no structure to tell them what to think, they then feel they have to question their own morals and ethics."[8] The goofy artificiality of the camouflages used in *Confess* contrasts with the bleak authenticity of the confessions. But these camouflages also function to transform the individuals' confessions into generalized utterances that pertain, in some form, to the dark side within us all. As a result, viewers are less likely to impose social codes of morality than to contemplate the distressing burdens, shame, guilt, and torment they witness—and might actually share.

Wearing abides by the principle that every person's declaration matters. Since confession has a positive effect upon the speaker and the listener, Wearing's artistry depends upon urging some people to speak and others to listen. This principle is demonstrated in her made-for-television video entitled *2 INTO 1* (1997). The "two" in the title refers to eleven-year-old twin boys. The "one" refers to their mother. The five-and-a-half minute video presents a series of monologues in which the twins and their mother take turns discussing their relationship. Mom and the twins, Lawrence and Alex, appear middle-class, which suggests that their statements will reflect familiar middle-class values. Yet the film piques the audience's interest, even inducing them to stay tuned while the identical footage of their disclosures is replayed three times without interruption. This feat is accomplished by a single alteration—Wearing switched the voices and the speakers. In making the video, she first interviewed the children and then she interviewed their mother. What they said to her they would not normally say to each other. Then she filmed the mom lip-synching the statements made by her sons about her, and the boys lip-synching the statements made by their mother about them. Wearing explains, "We know children have interesting things to say and use language in a rich way, but when you channel this through an older body, then all of a sudden there's a pathos and you're transforming how people look at that.... It offers something fresh and it's better than something straightforward, which can't make you come out of the complacency of what you already know."[9]

The efficacy of this device becomes apparent in the opening sequence when mom says in a rushed, boyish voice, "I am only eleven and I already know about it." Then Lawrence says in a womanly manner, "My sons are unusual and they are absolutely adorable.... And sometimes...they drive me mad, but they...uh...well, they love me, I suppose. And they can be quite cruel too." Alex continues in his mother's voice, "I think having children brings out two very, very extreme emotions in us, which is that one's constantly faced with the border of love and hate..." Then Mom in Alex's voice: "I think children should have rights to be rude back to grown-ups." And Alex says in his mother's voice, "Well, I think I am someone who likes to be dominated because all the men I've had are quite dominating to me..."

This disarming frankness is intensified because the person who utters these declarations is also the recipient of the expressions of affection and disapproval. Mom lip-synchs a discourse about her shortcomings. The boys lip-synch statements about their troublesome tempers. "Putting each other's words in their mouths said so much more about how complicated and also contradictory, how filled with love *and* hate relationships are."[10] These blunt truths are sharpened with each repetition of the film loop. During the first viewing, attention is naturally directed at the speakers. The second and third viewings permit awareness of components that might otherwise be overlooked. Viewers can observe the embarrassment of the nonspeaking brother. They can notice that mom sits on a child-like bench while her sons are seated in adult rocking chairs. They can consider if the boys' chubby bodies and slouching postures are evidence of indulgence. Wearing acknowledges that *2 INTO 1* is discomfiting because it dramatizes the intense and fragile nature of

Gillian Wearing, *Drunk* (1999), DVD, three-screen projection. 23 min. Courtesy Gorney, Bravin + Lee, New York, and Maureen Paley Interim Art, London.

family relationships. "The criticism of the children, and also the male-female thing... It's very hard-hitting and quite painful, I think, in the way the children view adults and the family. It's not just about children and parenting. The piece is about familiarity, closeness, breeding, and contempt."[11]

Drunk (1997–99) is another instance in which Wearing gains people's trust and enlists them to disclose the raw, heart-wrenching truth of their lives in front of her camera. The prelude to the creation of this work transpired over the course of several years. During this time Wearing cultivated the trust of a group of homeless derelicts. They hung out in her studio enticed by her offers of friendship, warmth, shelter, and free beer. The resulting three-channel video captures the despondency that draws them to a lifestyle defined by the muddled state of inebriation. When the video is presented as a gallery installation, the disheveled figures are projected life-size, isolated from contexts that might absorb and dissipate their miserable states of being, and enlarged in the manner of a grand opera. They swig beer, urinate, quarrel, sleep, sniff, scratch—all things that drunks may do on the street but which are rarely observed because passersby tend to avert their eyes.

As in much of her other work, Wearing directs attention to subjects most people ignore or avoid. She stares at misfortune unaided by such moderating emotions as compassion or sorrow. In this way she leaves the emotional response to the discretion of her audience. Viewers confront people whose minds are sloshed with alcohol and whose bodies struggle against succumbing to the force of gravity. Walking for these men and women is a battle of epic proportions. Their determination to travel from one end of the room to another is played out in the slow-motion time of inebriation. Outcomes are always uncertain. Will the reeling man progress forward or totter backward? Will he sink to his knees or remain erect? In group scenes, the derelicts taunt each other until tensions explode into hostility. They always seem too distracted by their immediate concerns to care that there is a camera recording it all.

Drunk exposes the privileged segment of the population that frequents art exhibitions to an unflinching view of the plight of drunks. The video is neither merciful nor judgmental. Wearing summons four strategies to facilitate her desire to connect mainstream culture and this unfortunate subculture. Although some of these strategies are standard for gallery showings of video art, they are utilized to particular effect in this instance. First, benches are absent in the gallery space. Second, the large gallery space is dark except for the light of the projected film. Third, the film is devoid of a background. Fourth, the drunks are projected life-size. These decisions yield a powerful kinesthetic identification between the art audience and the filmed derelicts. No seats, no lights, no horizon. Denied these stabilizing elements, viewers begin to feel woozy, dizzy, and tipsy. For these few moments, the privileged share a state of being with the outcasts, suspending conditioned responses of avoidance, condemnation, or repulsion.

Wearing either discovers or invents circumstances resonant with her deconditioning efforts. *A Woman Called Theresa* (1998) is a series of photographic diptychs of a corpulent, unkempt woman, marred with sores, marked with veins, and exuding an alcoholic's unhealthy glow. In each of seven images she is shown in bed with a different lover. The photographs are paired with her lovers' handwritten and brutally candid comments about her. *I'd Like to Teach the World to Sing* (1994) documents the difference between people in the park on a sunny day by filming each of them whistling the Coca-Cola jingle. *Take Your Top Off* (1993) involves photographs in which Wearing, the astute listener of secret thoughts and the voyeur of private circumstances, is photographed in bed with three transsexual strangers.

APATHETIC

Homage to the Woman With the Bandaged Face Who I Saw Yesterday Down Walworth Road (1995) is a work in which Wearing put on an ordinary dress, wrapped her entire face in an unforgettable plaster bandage, and was photographed walking through the streets of London.

As an artist, Wearing adopts the demeanor of a social scientist. She constructs a catalogue of true identities, thereby exposing the distortions inherent in most projections and assumptions. Her work attempts to mitigate the psychological damage most people both cause and suffer. "We all control each other's patterns and we all have ideas of ethics and morals and PC. But then that gets exploited, and everyone exploits each other, and that creates limitations to what we feel we can do."[12] Wearing subverts those limitations by opening a space where the silenced speak and the disinterested listen.

1. Sales of webcams are expected to reach thirty-six million by 2003, according to PC Data Online. Trends Research Group predicts that by that date more than half of all PCs will come equipped with webcams.

2. Gianmarco Del Re, "Confessions: Why Would a Businessman Say, 'I'm Desperate'? A–Z of Gillian Wearing," *Flash Art*, March–April 1998, 90.

3. Grady T. Turner, "Gillian Wearing," interview, *BOMB*, Spring 1998, 38.

4. Donna De Salvo, Russell Ferguson, and John Slyce, *Gillian Wearing* (London: Phaidon Press, 1999), 8.

5. Paul Bonaventura, "Profile: Wearing Well," *Art Monthly*, March 1995, 25.

6. Del Re, 89.

7. Del Re, 88.

8. ibid.

9. De Salvo, et al., 18.

10. Turner, 40.

11. De Salvo, et al., 19.

12. Ben Judd, Interview with Gillian Wearing, *Untitled*, Winter 96–97, 5.

IDEALISTIC

SOURCING INSPIRATION

SOURCING INSPIRATION

Pipilotti Rist, *Regenfrau (I Am Called A Plant)*
(1999), video installation. Courtesy of the
artist and Luhring Augustine.

"Expire" is the last exhale. It distinguishes this one breath from all the thousands that have been breathed within a lifetime. It signals a finality, the end. "Inspire" carries opposite significance. "Inspire" is associated with the originating breath that infuses an organism with an energy that is so distinct from mundane experience, it is described by Ovid as "the deity within us who breathes that divine fire by which we are animated." Inspiration marks a significant beginning, particularly one laden with risks and exhilaration. Artists pursue this initiating spark. Art historians contemplate its effects. Still, inspiration remains a mysterious component of the artistic process.

A complete biography of a work of art extends from inspiration to expiration. Like a living organism, the fullness of an artwork's life-stages unfolds from the inspiring spark of its inception, through its gestation in the studio, to its delivery into the cultural arena. Although some works remain viable for long periods of time, most art passes away. Immortality is reserved for the exceptional few. Origins and conclusions meet when inspiration is also the cause of an artwork's death. This occurs when the inspiration is not sustained during the process of creation, inspiration is diverted to another work of art before the last one is completed, inspiration self-destructs, or inspiration is transmuted into a destructive impulse.

Histories and critical discourse about works of art commonly examine the influences (any effects on behaviors or opinions), but rarely include discussion of artists' inspirations (influences that are animating or exalting). The differences are profound. A cloudy day may influence a person's decision to go to the beach, or it may inspire that person to write a poem. In art, evidence of influence is often visible in the thematic and stylistic components of a work of art. It is, therefore, traceable. Inspiration, however, occurs within the private regions of an artist's contemplations and imaginings. The essays in this chapter function like ultrasounds, expanding the biographical narratives about selected works of art by exploring their infusing inspirations along with identifiable influences.

Artistic sources vary greatly. Some artists intercept cultural frequencies. Their creative juices are stimulated by situations that are external to them, such as politics, nature, history, culture, religion, psychology, and science. Although cultural factors have inspired countless generations of artists, the quantity of inspirational sources made available to contemporary artists is mind-boggling. In fact, it includes the entirety of recorded human experience. Plugging into computers and the Internet, for example, accesses data that is both local and universal, earthbound and cosmic, historic and futuristic. Information stockpiles have also swelled because journalists, manufacturers, and financiers operate in global markets, because archeologists, geologists, and astronomers expand knowledge of the past, and because forecasters, pollsters, and marketers lengthen projections of the future. All contribute to the vast inventory of external sources of art production. Some of these externally motivated artists prowl distant territories and probe uncommon worldviews. Others never leave home. These stay-at-home artists have different addresses. Some are at home in a geographical location. Others feel at home in their cultural tradition, or their ethnic identity, their religious practice, or other aspects of familiar experience. Artists seeking an external muse may also enroll in school, apprentice with a mentor, visit museums, conduct research, or undertake other forms of inquiry and edification. For some, elevating influence to inspiration entails consciously living under conditions that fuel creativity. For instance, artists inspired by sympathy for the victims of injustice might live among the oppressed, just as those who condemn the abuses of the privileged class might go where they can witness gratuitous luxury.

A second group of artists finds their inspirational impulses within themselves. Their muses lie dormant within them until inspiration awakens them. In order to jumpstart their creative engines, these internally motivated artists may meditate, or pray, or swallow hallucinogens, or listen to trance-inducing music. They may release their inner voices through introspection, psychoanalysis, isolation, fatigue, discomfort, or deprivation. Others may excavate their memory banks, submit to spontaneous impulses, record their dreams, or induce visions. They carry their artistic destiny within themselves.

Passion can be allocated equally between artists who plug in to influences from without and those who channel inclinations from within. In either circumstance, inspiration can be delivered in the form of a tiny spark of insight or a great blast of revelation. All levels of intensity can generate significant accomplishment. The gradual infusion of a subtle vitality that is experienced as a metaphysical stirring can be as effective as a punch that quickens the pulse, elevates temperature, tenses nerves, and sharpens perceptions. For some, inspiration is so sudden and so intense, it is experienced as a mysterious, irresistible, uninvited force. Others ascribe it to special people who are "gifted" with magical powers or spiritual insights. These instances are often referred to as "a-ha!" experiences because they seem to burst through a confining psychological membrane into consciousness. One such transforming moment may suffice for a lifetime, recharging an artist's inspirational pulses each time it is recalled. Alternatively, inspiration may be allocated on a work-by-work basis; a new inspiration is required for the creation of each work of art. Finally, some artists choose the option of simultaneously engaging in multiple inspirational sources, assigning each its own inspirational variables.

In addition to actively seeking inspiration, artists can rely on happenstance. Inspiration, in this instance, is the product of the random encounter with a phenomenon that infuses the artist with zeal and purpose. In between the extremes of inactive and proactive artists are those who optimize their opportunities to become recipients of inspiring experiences. They exist in a state of ready alert by cultivating vigilance, tuning their mental radar to likely frequencies, and giving a fair review to every interception.

Inspiring experiences can be joyful. But they can also be disturbing. The history of art is as enriched by anguish, indignation, despondency, and rage as it is by bliss, pleasure, comfort, and sensual delight. Trauma and obstacles may stifle the inspiration of artists dependent on encouragement and support, but they can awaken inspiration among artists driven by anger and resistance. Likewise, predecessors may serve as admiring role models that inspire creative

Are you more likely to be inspired by:

the presence or absence of contentment?

personal situations or social conditions?

interactions with humans or non-humans?

rest or fatigue?

relaxation or pressure?

sobriety or being high?

joy or sorrow?

culture or nature?

familiarity or mystery?

production or consumption?

the past or the present?

facts or feelings?

anger or pity?

yourself or others?

activity, but mutinies serve to inspire just as well. War and peace, wealth and poverty, fulfillment and frustration carry equal potential as inspiration igniters.

Nothing, as opposed to something, also serves as a compelling source of inspiration. Neglected considerations, missing data, gaps in the record, and rejected opportunities can rouse artists to undertake creative interventions. Some of these fill-in-the-blank artists are motivated to supply experiences that are lacking in their personal lives. They create art to fill deficiencies of excitement, or sensual pleasure, or beauty. The dearth that motivates other frustrated artists involves shared needs such as the lack of societal order, or tolerance, or caution.

Viewers need not feel excluded from this exhilarating experience. Artworks exhibit residues of their originating sparks. The thrill, or terror, or anticipation, or eagerness that accompanies the welling up of ambition and the first stirrings of artistic action can often be discerned in the work's physical enactments and its conceptual transcendence. Inspiration often supplies the compelling power that makes art captivating. But viewers also benefit from the artist's inspired state because art confirms the existence of this elusive state of being. Banality is balanced by artistic inspiration. It reminds viewers that inspiration belongs to every person's potential and can be cultivated as a part of every human's provenance.

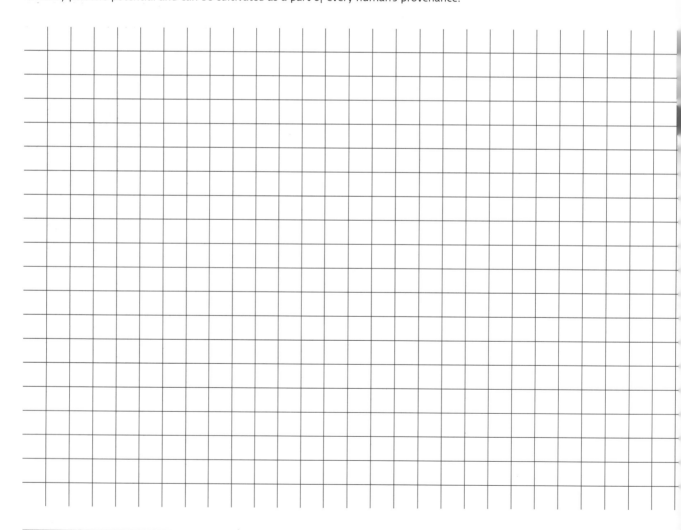

Soul–Genus Fusion

Jan Harrison
Born 1944 West Palm Beach, Florida
1967 University of Georgia, Athens, BFA, graphic design
1976 San Jose State University, San Jose, California, MA, studied printmaking, mixed-media works on paper, and artists' books
Lives and works in Ulster County, New York

Jan Harrison's initiating actions with a crayon or a lump of clay are products of her everyday consciousness. Each succeeding action, however, leads away from the material world and its practical considerations, and inches toward an inspired state that is exempt from rational applications of words and numbers. Harrison demonstrates that internal sources of inspiration can kick into action at any juncture during the development of a work of art. For her, inspiration is not a prerequisite for initiating a work of art; it is her destination. Arriving at an inspired state marks the final, culminating stage of this prolonged creative process.

Monsters. Once upon a time, their grotesque forms crawled up columns, crept along balustrades, and hung from the balconies of churches as reminders of the tribulations that awaited sinners. Today, these creatures mostly populate Hollywood horror films, action comic books, fantasy literature, animation, and children's toys. Their context has changed, but their linguistic root has endured across these vast spans of time: "monstrum" means not only a divine omen, but also a misfortune of divine proportions. Monsters stir fear and loathing and violate the natural order by sprouting appendages and fusing incongruous species.

Remarkably, the amphibian/mammalian/reptilian/avian hybrids that populate Jan Harrison's work invite prolonged, tranquil contemplation. Their impact reflects the artist's own relationship to these creatures, beings she describes as "a treasure, a deity within me, a divine thing."[1] Harrison's pastel drawings, porcelain sculptures, installations, and recorded recitations beckon viewers to embark on a voyage. But instead of leaving home to explore exotic locales, viewers are guided into their innermost selves.

The journey begins with personal perceptions and recollections, moves backward to the dawn of recorded history, proceeds backward to the origin of language, and even traverses the evolutionary emergence of the human species. Under Harrison's guidance, viewers ultimately disembark on a primal level where our DNA retains the vestigial coding of our animal ancestry.

Harrison undertakes a comparable journey into deep imagination during the creative process. Hers is an active quest for a source of vitality and wisdom that has been usurped by the authority of bureaucracies, institutions, laboratories, classrooms, and other such constructions of civilization. Despite the fact that it "can be fearsome,"[2] Harrison relishes the arcane region of the mind that escaped these confining influences of society. Physiologically, Harrison's artworks originate in the oldest and smallest region of the human brain stem. It is similar to the brain possessed by the hardy reptiles that preceded mammals approximately 200 million years ago and resembles the entire brain of present-day reptiles. This reptilian brain is preverbal. Lacking language, its impulses are instinctual and ritualistic. It controls fundamental needs such as survival, and basic emotions such as love, hate, fear, and lust. All this content emanates from this early version of the brain, prior to the evolution of intellectual thought and complex reasoning. Referring to these reptilian impulses, Harrison reports, "Once summoned, they act independently of my control. They erupt according to their own will and fade in their own time. In this way they claim both authority and authenticity and the power to heal."[3] This psychic underworld of the imagination is the origin of the crossed species and merged biologies that populate her works of art. They provide evidence of our enduring membership within the animal kingdom. One of the artist's journal entries from 1981 states, "A hundred million years ago we did something like jumping or leaping, or flipping over, our tails worked like pole vaults to help us over hurdles.... A hundred million years ago, when we licked our companions on the neck, a smile came up around our mouths (not out through our teeth, like now)."[4]

In Harrison's life, this passage back to the frontier of consciousness originates in ordinary, domestic animal experiences: a goldfish living in a glass bowl on her kitchen counter, pet cats scurrying through her house, a vacation swim with a dolphin, a trip to the aquarium. Harrison's experiences are typical of those who were born into today's ultra-civilized circumstances. It is the exceptional individual who experiences animals in the wild. But the ordinariness of her real-life animal contact yields a startling revelation: if pets and zoos catapult this artist's consciousness into untamed and untrammeled domains, perhaps the imprint of animal awareness has survived in all of us. Her work is dedicated to actualizing this proposition. "I believe in Darwin," she explains. "I believe in evolution. Real primitive animals are still within us. Bird-fish, aquatic mammals are in our bodies and minds. They are not invented. I feel like it is my mission to bring this out."[5]

In determined increments, Harrison penetrates the subconscious and summons images of the amorphous life-forms lurking there. Her own likeness serves as the point of departure for this exploration. She initiates each work by creating a conventional self-portrait in which her body and her humanness appear intact. During the prolonged process of working and reworking, however, borders gradually erode. Pastels and clay are her preferred mediums because they are as receptive to erosions and erasures as they are to accumulations and additions. Snakelike, catlike, fishlike "animoids" emerge. As in *Chuff and Roll Over* (1995), they crawl upon her naked form, wrap themselves across her shoulders, and perch on her head. A woman/animal intimacy develops that exceeds eroticism. These erupting figures bite and claw until boundaries between flesh, fur, feather, and fin disintegrate. In some works, her body and face appear swollen, red, misshapen. In others, her skin turns transparent, revealing capillary activity that parallels the surge of imagery awakened during the art-making process. In recent works, Harrison's immersion has proceeded toward self-obliteration. *Shaker* (1999), for

Jan Harrison
Interview by Zoe Feigenbaum

ZF: What would you say was the first indication that you were to become a recognized, successful artist?

JH: When I was a little child I knew it. But then I sort of forgot it when I reached my teens. Then, when I reached my mid-twenties, I really started getting serious about my work, serious in a playful way. At that time, I was chosen to be in an exhibition of emerging artists.

ZF: How did you do that—were you affiliated with a gallery?

JH: I wasn't affiliated with a gallery until I was in my late twenties. My gallery in New York closed a couple of years ago, and at this point I'm not represented by another (New York) art gallery. Actually, it's possible the gallery didn't survive because the owner was such a nice person.

ZF: It seems very cutthroat.

JH: Awful! But you don't have to have a gallery to be an artist whose work is respected. You can do art in many ways, and you can be an artist anywhere.

ZF: What are your feelings about the commercial aspects of being an artist?

JH: I call it "pinnacle thinking" when people think if they have the most money or the most attention or the most whatever that they're at the top of the pinnacle. That kind of thinking is totally alien to how I want to be. My work has to do with being in touch with the animal nature, which means it is okay to be lowly, closer to the earth, and even humble. On the other hand, I know my work is good. I'm not talking about that. I'm talking about not thinking that I am higher or better.

ZF: How would you say you made your first "art world" connections, or sort of plunged in or got recognized?

JH: I took a twenty-room mansion and made it into a world. I want to tell you the story. My father left when I was a child and I never knew what happened to him. And then, when I was in graduate school, I received a phone call saying that my father had died, and they had tried to locate me. I had inherited his savings. Well, it wasn't a fortune, but it was a fortune to me. And so I took that inheritance and bought a house and redid it, and it sold for a large profit... So when I graduated I moved to Cincinnati and bought a second house—a wonderful house with twenty rooms. And I made that house into a world. It had a masculine living room and a feminine living room, a black-hole-in-space room, and a paradise bathroom with palm trees on the wall. I self-published a book about it and then I had an exhibition in the house. And that's essentially how I got my work out and known. My paintings and drawings were a part of the house. I knew an art collector and a curator, and they called some people, and that's how it happened.

ZF: Can you describe your studio?

JH: Let me put it this way: some artists have come to see my studio and they think it's big because they have small spaces. But then other people I know who have lofts say, "We don't know how you do this big work in

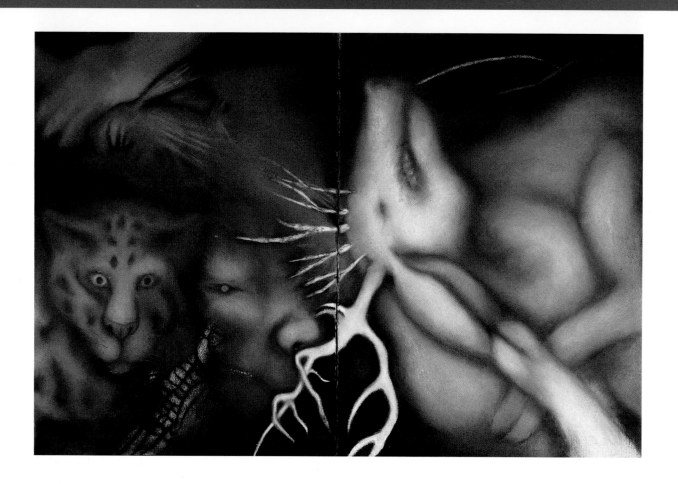

Jan Harrison, *Chuff and Roll Over* (1995), 30 x 44 inches (diptych), pastel and charcoal on rag paper. Courtesy of the artist. Photograph: Nancy Donskoj.

SOURCING INSPIRATION

example, is a searing red pastel in which a maelstrom of claws, wings, tails, and paws whirl around two gaping eyes that are locked into position. Their focus lies outside the work of art, beyond the visible world. They inhabit the realm of myth, though, as Harrison explains, "I am purposely not knowledgeable about ancient myth. Instead, myth comes out of my body. Myth is physical and also psychological. Original mythology comes from these sources."[6] Harrison's images do not illustrate specific myths from identifiable cultural traditions. Instead, she retrieves the images from her own primeval consciousness in a manner confirmed by renowned anthropologist Joseph Campbell. Campbell comments, "Fantasy and imagination is a product of the body. The energies that bring forth the fantasies derive from the organs of the body. The organs of the body are the source of our life, and of our intentions for life, and they conflict with each other. Among these organs, of course, is the brain."[7] Campbell then states that the function of mythological imagery is to "coordinate the energies of our body, so that we will live a harmonious and fruitful life in accord with our society."[8] In another context, Campbell examines "the half-human, half-animal figures of the mythological totem ancestors. The animals became the tutors of humanity. Through acts of literal imitation…an effective annihilation of the human ego was accomplished and society achieved a cohesive organization."[9] In this manner, Harrison seeks a synthesis of our dualities: male and female, human and animal, predator and prey, living and dead, brutal and generous, knowledgeable and innocent. "I feel like someone took a cleaver and separated the two sides. Art can reunite us. I am working for my character, working to become whole, an authentic person, not just an artist."[10] The impulse to fuse these conflicting characteristics emerged in childhood play when the artist conjured two imaginary friends. One was powerful and wild, the other shy and modest. These specters stayed with her. As an adult, she discovered that each had a voice and could speak. She also discovered her mind was able to contact these forces and utter their sounds. Instead of recognizable words, one specter utters high-pitched squeaks while the other growls. Harrison describes their languages as "animal tongues," although neither resembles the sounds made by animals. "When I am speaking in my animal tongues, I close off a part of my brain. Then I can interact with the part that I find in animals and some human beings. It is more unified."[11] Whenever asked, the artist willingly demonstrates these sounds. She closes her eyes and after a pause of a few seconds begins to emit a preverbal conversation that she describes as the cry of innocence confronting knowledge. This strange discourse makes manifest the contents of the artist's imaginative reality.

Through her studio practice, Harrison has identified three areas of consciousness that she believes enable humans to return to their animal natures and thereby heal the ruptures that derive from cultural experience. These remnants of our non-human ancestors

this little studio." So it's all a matter of people's perceptions. My studio is the second floor of my house—two rooms attached with pocket doors that open wide. And I have the whole house to live with my work and display it. I like to do that. I like to have my studio in my house.

ZF: It sounds like you've had houses that really shape the way you live.

JH: They're like worlds to me. And that might be partly because when I was a child we moved from apartment to apartment because we couldn't pay the rent. So for me it is very important to have a house. I do live with an architect, Alan Baer. We're not married but we've lived together forever. He's also an exhibition designer and he has helped me a lot with installations.

ZF: What's your relationship like with your collectors?

JH: Some of them are very knowledgeable and caring. Some of them, I think, also play games, like saying, "We like your older work better than your newer work. Why don't you return to the old work?" I'm going to do my own work, and if they like what I do now as opposed to what they bought five years ago, great. If they don't, I can't worry about it.

ZF: So you don't feel pressured to bend to them.

JH: I can't. That would be just absurd.

ZF: Do you have any other jobs? Do you supplement your income in any way?

JH: I work part of the week in the publications department at a university, and I design catalogues for the art museum there. But also I teach painting at another college every semester. My BFA is in design and my Masters work involved mixed-media works on paper and artists' books. I'm the first in my family to graduate from college. Since my mother worked, I grew up in offices, and I've always felt comfortable in them. So my job has certain benefits, even though it causes unhappiness for me—because many times I wish I was in the studio working when I'm working there. I lived for four years without any job—from the sale of my work and grants. I loved that, and I called it a hunter-gatherer existence that I had. But I found that I just couldn't maintain it. I had to have some kind of income coming in. My work does sell, but not enough to totally keep me going.

ZF: Do you think that being out of the studio sometimes helps you be in the studio?

JH: Yes. I do. Working at the job at the university is like the grain of sand that makes the pearl in the oyster. All of those things tie in together. Even living in a neighborhood that is made up of artists, poets, composers, and homeless people, it's everything. I sometimes think, "What If I lived in a neighborhood where everything was manicured? What would that be like? And then I realized, oh, that would really hurt my work. It would make me feel like I was in an ivory tower.

ZF: Do you have any regrets about the way you structured your career, the choices you've made?

JH: Some of my best work happens as a result of something that really didn't work very well and I had to go

Jan Harrison, *Tendril Birdfish* (1997), 19 x 15 x 9 inches, bisque-fired porcelain. Courtesy of the artist. Photograph: Marlis Momber.

SOURCING INSPIRATION

help us achieve harmonious integration of the spirit. Although these centers have been inactive for millennia, they still exist deep within the human brain. Harrison's work provides vivid testimony of the enduring presence of these areas of consciousness. Through examining her work, viewers may rediscover the abandonment of ego, all-encompassing love, and freedom from the fear of dying.. Her work serves now as myth served in the past: "Mythical thought moves from an awareness of contradictions toward their resolution, and stories of the topsy-turvy state of things in the world of myth attempt to mediate between opposites and resolve them."[12]

Ego: Harrison has noted that human behavior is often driven by motives that are ego-centered. She comments, "This narcissism extends beyond an obsession with the self. It also appears as towering urban architecture and disregard for the environment. The ego drives us to do this pinnacle thing. It hinders us as humans. It makes us unable to love."[13] Harrison counters this narcissism by re-imagining and re-animating our animal soul. She believes that animal gratification is limited by physical necessity, while the human ego's appetite for gratification is limitless.

Love: Harrison notes, "Animals manifest the two sides of love. They are capable of cruelty and tenderness. They display both the vileness and the divine beauty in the universe."[14] How can vileness be an aspect of love? Harrison explains, "Animals may be cunning and they may murder, but the aggression they display involves an acceptance of change that is inherent to the life force. Human aggression is of a different order. It attempts to suppress the life force. Destructive aggression stems from fear of growth and change. This desire makes us stiff, like cardboard. I want to be soft and round."[15] By merging life-forms, Harrison gives visual form to an animal's inclusive engagement in the world. By dissolving boundaries between beings, her imagery parallels the life-affirming act of love.

Death: Harrison says, "We fear death because we perceive everything related to our personal egos. Even our dying is narcissistic. People have lost their connection to death and the underworld."[16] Humans typically spend their last moments in an antiseptic, impersonal, indifferent hospital room or nursing home. This environment separates us from our inevitable contribution to the evolution of new sources of life. Animals die, but their deaths are free of the anguish about mortality. They teach humans the solace of dying naturally.

For Harrison, inspiration is released through introspection rather than through worship, or observation, or study. It transpires in the dark recesses of the human soul, not in the full light of the rational world and not in the radiance of heaven. In conjuring spirits from the animal realm Harrison spirals downward into the realm of darkness and death. The opposite process is practiced in most Western religions, where religious architecture and prayer are directed upward. Spires, domes, clerestory windows, and vaults

back and work it through. Or something I dropped or stepped on or tore. So I don't have too many regrets. I've accepted that I have to work within certain limitations. There's a book called *The Power of Limits* about proportional harmonies in nature, by Gyorgy Doczi. I think that there's a strength knowing the limits you have. You work beyond them.

ZF: When did you start feeling connected to this sort of animal thing—give me a better word.

JH: The animal nature—it has been with me all my life. When I was growing up I was what was called a latchkey child, and that meant I was alone a lot, and so, because of that, I was around animals most of the time—my cats, but also neighborhood animals, and the wild or feral animals that were in South Florida.

ZF: Flamingoes?

JH: I saw flamingoes. I would go to the beach and see wonderful and mysterious sea creatures and birds, and so that's how I became connected with them

ZF: Do you have any pets?

JH: Yes. I live with four cats—but they are more than pets.

ZF: How did you discover your "tongues" (the non-verbal language that Harrison speaks)?

JH: Well, in 1979 I did a piece that I called *The Tongue Drawing*. It had to do with animal courtship and sexuality, and it was on tongue-shaped pieces of paper that were waterproofed and attached to a drinking water fountain. I was tape-recording people's reactions and I just started speaking in tongues!

ZF: Is it something that you understand what you're saying?

JH: I do understand what I'm saying but I understand it in a way similar to when you're painting. It takes me to places. People ask me, "Why do you call it animal tongues, it doesn't sound like animal sounds." It's that part of me that I think is very closely related to animals. I have dyslexia, so learning to read was difficult. Finding my way around is difficult. Getting beyond a language that's structured to be cerebral, this language seems to come more from my solar plexus, it seems to come from my body. Speaking in tongues centers me. When I do it, my animals become very excited. They do respond.

ZF: Do you have any advice to artists who might ignore their artistic calling because they are afraid?

JH: My advice is to not fall into thinking that art is a popularity contest, and not fall into egotism. Try to witness yourself. Don't put other people on pedestals and don't put yourself on a pedestal. There are plenty of artists in the world, but if you are true to yourself, you will be special in your own way.

ZF: Is there anything you'd like to add?

JH: I always like to be a beginner when I start every piece. I like to feel like I don't know a lot. That's how I can keep a sense of wonder in the world. On the other hand I also feel a connection with the dark nature in the world and I am involved with the mystery of that. I have come to terms with turning myself inside-out.

allow interior spaces to suggest the soaring expanse of heaven. These architectural structures evoke ascent and perpetual life ever after. Religious belief often defies death, whereas the animal soul accepts it. Harrison reinstates animals to their roles as totems and gods, reversing thousands of years of domestication and exploitation. She believes, "Animals naturally have knowledge and innocence. Our souls yearn for knowledge and innocence. That is why animals are scapegoats. People fear them like they fear nature. That is why we build cages and make sacrifices."[17] A harmonious synthesis occurs when the animal soul is tapped and its vitalizing forces are released into consciousness. Harrison enacts this process to manifest an inner source of inspiration she believes we all share.

[1] Interview with the artist, August 23, 2001.

[2] Interview with the artist, June 19, 1999.

[3] ibid.

[4] Interview, June 19, 1999.

[5] ibid.

[6] Interview, June 19, 1999.

[7] Joseph Campbell and Dr. Jeffrey Mishlove, THINKING ALLOWED: Conversations On The Leading Edge Of Knowledge and Discovery, <http://www.yessaid.com/jc1.html>.

[8] ibid.

[9] Joseph Campbell, The Hero With a Thousand Faces (The Bollingen Series XVII, Pantheon Books, 1949), 390.

[10] Interview, Jun 19, 1999.

[11] ibid.

[12] Campbell, The Hero.

[13] Interview, June 19, 1999.

[14] ibid.

[15] ibid.

[16] ibid.

[17] ibid.

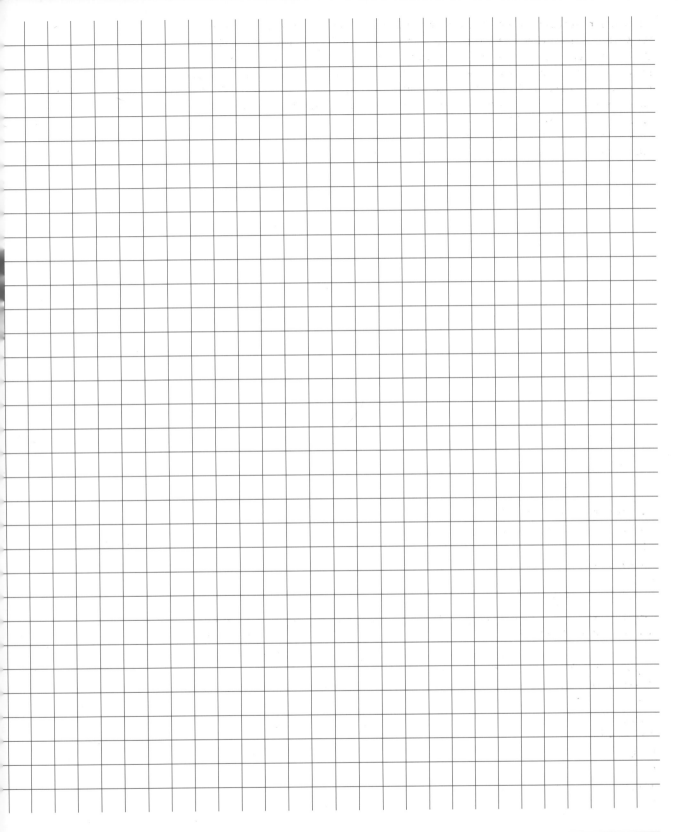

Emotion-Rage Against Female Gullibility

Pipilotti Rist

1962 Rheintal, Switzerland
1982–1986 Institute of Applied Arts in Vienna, studied commercial art, illustration, and photography
1986–1988 School of Design in Basel, Switzerland, studied audio-visual communication
Lives and works in Zurich and Rotterdam

Pipilotti Rist's internal source of inspiration resides in emotional turmoil. The specific source of her turmoil is discovered in the aftermath of collapsed dreams and failed romantic encounters. Her internal sources of inspiration originate in the gullibility and vulnerability she shares with many women. Although she is stirred by emotional aftershocks, she is not in the throes of her anguish while she is creating her art. If she was, she might hurl paint. Instead, Rist methodically gathers up her frustrations, disappointments, disillusionments, and regrets and translates them into ambitious video installations. In some instances her videos reenact romantic fantasies like making love in a glade. In others they construct emotional symbols like burning flames. Still others recreate dream states like running down a highway naked.

Trials, not triumph, describe Pipilotti Rist's pursuit of love, or so it would seem by examining her acclaimed videos and installations. The classical Greek tale of Psyche might have served as their inspiration. Psyche is the beautiful Greek maiden, beloved by Cupid, the Greek god of love. Because she was a mortal, she was forbidden to gaze upon her godly lover. As such, Psyche epitomizes a woman's romantic ardor and frustration. Rist is fixated on imagining a version of love that is mythic. Inspired by a fiction of courtship and romance that derives from ancient literature and is perpetuated by the contemporary media, she erects romantic settings as glorious as Cupid's castle and dreams of having a paramour as perfect as the god of love.

Her fantastical version of romance, which is almost certain to disappoint, is not confined to artmaking. Using extravagant imagery, Rist describes an intimacy from one of her failed relationships. "When I was with Thomas, my first lover, I loved whispering (in Swiss-German) 'I see endless hills flying right down to the bottom of the ocean.' It was very sexy."[1]

Like so many women before her, Rist's hope to achieve her imagined love is often shattered by a gullible belief that seduction is an expression of enduring affection. Such unrealistic expectations have made her a veteran of libidinous yearnings and amorous disappointments. Rist serves as today's spokeswoman for the archetype of the love-starved maiden. Despite the fact that the list of feminine role models has been augmented by the addition of sassy "grrrl power" advocates and competitive power dressing careerists, Rist demonstrates that this ancient feminine prototype still prevails.

The themes of her video installations may by traceable to the classics, but they are infused with the fantastical imagery common to MTV and porno-pop, not ancient art. Rist's use of hypnotic beats and extravagant visuals is a carryover from her experience as a member of the all-girl pop band, *Les Reines Prochaines* (The Future Queens).[2] The group's promotional material mirrors the inspirational sources that Rist applies to her independent work as a visual artist. It states, "Music and performances are marked by our inner images, presentiments, memories, experiences and fantasies, which all spring up from our individual,

Pipilotti Rist, *Himalaya's Sister's Living Room* (2000), video installation. Courtesy of the artist and Luhring Augustine.

Emotion–Rage Against Female Gullibility: **Pipilotti Rist**

political and cultural realities. Trivialities, myths, pop culture, folklore, childhood, and the physical all serve as sparks of inspiration for the form and the content of our work." It is the emotional fallout from this rich reservoir of imagery that occupies Rist. Heartache and jealousy seep over her emotional spillway and flood her artistic practice. She is inspired by longings that are unfulfilled and lust that is recalcitrant.

Pipilotti Rist was born Elisabeth Charlotte Rist. She took her name from Pippi Longstocking, the literary heroine who has delighted generations of children by watering flowers in the rain and riding a bicycle that has no wheels. This fictional namesake sets the tone for Rist's innocent, fantasy-laden approach to womanhood. Another fictional woman, Mother Nature, provides a complementary female role model. In many Rist videos, forests, rivers, oceans, and swamps appear drenched by the moisture of arousal. Like any star, Mother Nature is dressed up and made over for her role in Rist's works of art. Epitomizing feminine sensuality, these settings are enhanced with dazzling colors and luxuriant lighting. Rist likes dressing up too. "Clothes and jewelry are constituents of our feminine culture that I'm proud of. If I had to choose my sex, then this aspect of feminine culture would certainly be one of the many reasons I would prefer to be a woman."[3]

Sip My Ocean (1996) is a video depicting Rist adrift in an erotic, rainbow-hued, underwater fairyland. The video installation consists of two floor-to-ceiling video projections that abut in a corner, creating mirror-like reflections. Each depicts the bikini-clad artist swimming. For some people, swimming is an aerobic exercise; others view it as a competitive sport. For Rist, swimming is submergence into an all-enveloping sea of sensuality. She is an attractive woman, but she is no match for the glory of the setting she has concocted for her fantasy. She is neither as graceful as its seaweed clusters, as gorgeous as the tropical fish swimming by her, nor as sumptuous as the coral gardens. Her underwater ballet introduces "every girl" into an aquatic paradise.

This gorgeous swirling imagery conveys the swimming starlet's sensual currents. Like a coquette's first dip into the waters of carnal pleasures, she is innocent of the emotional whirlpools that accompany romance. But she doesn't remain innocent for long. This beguiling scene is abruptly interrupted by the domestic flotsam of coffee mugs, a teapot, and an old LP that suddenly appears on the top of the screen and sinks to the depths of the ocean like the discarded remains of a shattered relationship. Illusions are replaced by delusions as jettisoned objects of domestic stability tumble around her. The distorted face of a man is reflected in a descending mirror.

This collision of fantasy's perfection and reality's defects is augmented by a soundtrack of the artist singing her own rendition of Chris Isaak's ballad, Wicked Game:
The River was on fire and no one could save me but you
Strange what desire will make foolish people do
I never dreamed that I'd meet somebody like you
I never dreamed that I'd lose someone like you
Oh, I don't want to fall in love...with you.
I don't wanna fall in love no (This world is only gonna break your heart)
I don't wanna fall in love (This world is only gonna break your heart)
With you...with you (This world is only gonna break your heart)
What a wicked game to play, to make me feel this way.[4]

The emotional extremes that accompany a lovelorn life are integral to Isaak's song and expressed in his swooning singing style. Rist exploits the song's emotional potential. She uses her sweet, melodic voice to convey her pleasure. When this beguiling pleasure is disrupted by the loss of her beloved, her voice quickly progresses from agitation to howls of primal anguish and climaxes in a manic, wrenching shriek. Rist's hedonistic rapture is ruptured, but her distress is so short lived it doesn't even persist long enough for viewers to identify with her plight. Rist resumes her sensual swim as abruptly as the reverie was interrupted, immersing herself, once again, in her fantasy, despite its flimsy construction.

If this tale has a moral, it is that romantic fictions are so tenacious that they survive, even when a romantic relationship doesn't, and even though prospects for future gratification are dubious. Love is a wicked game because, for the love-starved maiden, it is a solo affair. Instead of relying on a partner, Rist soothes her disappointments by relegating her sensual fulfillment to her imagination.

The pathetic cycle of yearning and despair assumed grand proportions when, for her first solo exhibition in New York, in 2000, Rist transformed the sprawling Luhring Augustine Gallery into a domestic interior filled to capacity with furniture, housewares, and the contents of a wounded female psyche.[5] Rist adapts this multi-part installation to specific exhibition spaces so that each room is presented as a separate artwork with its own title. In New York there was a kitchen, *Regenfrau (I am Called A Plant)* (1998-1999); a bathroom, *Closed Circuit* (2000); a living room, *Himalaya's Sister's Living Room* (2000); and so forth. Rist invented a fictitious character named Himalaya Goldstein; the installations comprised her living space. Despite her absence, viewers became intimately acquainted with Himalaya by observing the furnishings as reflections of her tastes, income, and leisure activities. Lamps, vases, cookie tins, playing cards, a globe, plants, and a telephone occupy the many shelves and table tops, a tacky accumulation of inexpensive but well-preserved items seemingly culled from thrift shops. The bar is fully stocked. The table is set with plates, glasses, chopsticks, and Chinese food containers. Despite the abundance of material goods, evidence of a vital and fulfilling life are lacking. These objects have been collected but they have never been used. None is soiled, out of place, damaged, or worn. Airmail envelopes and snack packages are unopened; game pieces remain in their starting positions; liquor bottles are sealed; the meal is uneaten; ashtrays are clean; a suitcase remains packed. Significantly, the sole object that reveals wear is a life-saving tube that hangs on a side wall. Like all the assembled objects, it provides evidence of a woman who clings to the hope of being rescued from a life glutted with material possessions but lacking in companions with whom to eat, play, drink, correspond, and smoke.

This vacant dwelling is animated by ten video projections that envision the preoccupations of Himalaya's internal life. Rist says she treats the video monitor as if it is "a miracle lamp" that lights the inner self.[6] Thus, the video camera guides her descent into a woman's cluttered mind and illuminates her troubled emotions. These revelations of her imaginings and memories, disappointments and vexations are dispersed throughout the domestic interior. Some loom from floor to ceiling, the scale of full-blown obsessions. Others are like neurotic fixations, insinuating consciousness when and where they are least expected. These tiny projections are inserted into chair seats, books, plants, shoes, bottles, and tabletops. A low dresser becomes the site for the projection of a burning book. The dining table serves as a screen for a projection of the artist, dressed like a Harlequin, riding a bicycle. The liquor bottles in the bar display video loops of a soccer game that culminates in frenetic cheering. Together they comprise a video mindscape riddled with dreams, fears, memories, and desires that assert themselves in the midst of an excess of knick-knacks and bric-a-brac. Viewers navigate this visual delirium and may discover unsettling correspondences with their own lives.

Because the household is empty of its occupant, Rist cannot rely on staged arm flailing, melodramatic foot stomping, or other forms of human expression to convey mental agitation. Instead, the active conveyer of Rist's mental agitation is the camera itself. Yet her intimacy with the video camera is such that it not only records imagined spectacles of desire, it plays the role of her erotic partner. This double duty is apparent in the kitchen part of the installation *Regenfrau (I Am Called a Plant)*, an immaculate assemblage of larger-than-life kitchen furnishings. It consists of a sink, a refrigerator, a stove, a dishwasher, and a bank of 16-foot-tall white Formica kitchen cabinets that provide a pristine surface for the display of a huge video projection. Its sumptuous abstractions and vivid chromatics are gradually revealed to be the artist's vastly over-scaled goose bumps, hair follicles, nipples, fingers, and trembling lips. Like a lover, the camera encircles Rist's naked body with caressing motions and tenderly invokes her libidinous desires. All the while, she and the viewer are engulfed by the gurgling sounds of running water and the moody refrains of a harmonica. Eventually, the embrace is broken. The camera pulls back as if to admire her beauty. This distanced view discloses a vision of Rist, nude but for a fuchsia colored wig. Her flesh is as white as the Formica cabinets. She lies in a shallow stream like a mythic damsel possessed by multiple and autonomous erotic zones, sated with love. Rivulets of water trace the crevices of her contours; leaves and twigs are entwined in her hair. She seems frail. Then abruptly, as in *Sip My Ocean*, Rist's hedonistic swoon is terminated. The magic spell is broken. She stands up and walks off the set. At this moment, the camera's role as Rist's surrogate lover becomes pitifully apparent: she leaves, but the camera does not pursue her. She is alone, once again.

As a psychological tool, Rist's camera evinces the complexity of human emotions—both being loved and being abandoned. It undulates in tranquil sensuality, rears in panic, soars in rage, or seizes in anxiety. In one instance the camera zooms into the open, engulfing the orifice of Rist's mouth as if it was her lover. In another it swirls around her as she rides a bicycle. In a third, the artist's mental agitation is made manifest in the camera's spinning motion. In all these ways, it recreates the inner turmoil of a woman who seems confounded by the task of reconciling real life experience with romantic longings. *Ever Is Over All* (1997) is a video in which Rist has added self-empowerment to her fantasies of the female experience. Yet her imagined form of revenge is as removed from reasonable expectations as her imagined forms of desire. The artist appears in this four-minute video diptych dressed prettily in a baby blue dress and red high-heeled shoes with her hair pinned neatly in a bun. Her respectability, cheerfulness, and confidence exaggerate her deviant behavior. As she saunters down a city street, she smashes the windows of one parked car after another. Her appearance is as misleading as the appearance of the iron weapon she wields. It is disguised as a large flower that also resembles a phallus. A uniformed officer approaches, but instead of the expected reprimand or arrest, Rist's vandalism receives an approving smile. Surprisingly, this police officer is also a woman. Rist explains: "In my piece, I am inventing situations that *could* be, where the woman is destroying windows of cars, like she would do it everyday. It's just something super-normal. It's a symbol to break rules. We have so many rules in our life. Many of them are necessary so we can live together, but so many rules are just never questioned. I wanted her to behave like this, but doing [so] without a criminal attitude. ...It's symbolic. So often in our lives, we feel observed either by God or the police— May I behave like this? Am I too loud? Am I too wild? What do you think? And all of this automatically turns into self-censorship or self-punishment we carry on within us."[7]

Ever Is Over All proposes that the alternative to self-censorship and self-punishment is the giddy confidence that originates in gratuitous destruction. It fulfills the fantasy of breaking rules. Although Rist is inspired by such emotional events as the satisfaction of revenge, and the glory of imagined romance, and the anguish of frustration, she explains that identifying an artistic approach was neither sudden nor calculated. "I started to study physics, but then I went to art school. My aim was to visualize philosophical systems, but then I started to do Super 8 animation films. After school, I worked for several news groups—so I never really had an aim. I never wanted to become famous or do (art) as a career. The first years I showed my things at film festivals, and then it happened to be that museums invited me to show the pieces."[8] Once she became devoted to art, her method was prolonged and methodical, despite the work's emotional content and its emotional impact. "I came to video through Super 8. I like video a lot because I can control the whole production—from sound to light to camera. Changing to installation was only a little step, caused by an opportunity given by the museums. Museums belong to the people that go there, and I tried always to suck them in and to make three-dimensional emotional space around and with them."[9] But video and installation offered more than mere convenience. These mediums inspired her, she said, because they were so inclusive. "There is room in them for everything."[10] Technically they permit painting, language, music, poetry. Emotionally they welcome multiple forms of psychic turmoil—sex, frustration, longing, hope, and disappointment. Rist utilizes contemporary technology and contemporary aesthetics to express an age-old form of female frustration. Yet the conceptual basis of her work diverges significantly from pop music videos. "I work with the same material as TV, with the same technical stuff that NBC uses, but I don't have to sell something. I just can use the same stuff for philosophical and political statements, which gives me a kind of freedom."[11]

As sources of inspiration, love-seeking and social rule-breaking are elevated into the "rites, meditations, and ecstasy,"[12] that Rist stages, records, edits, and reworks until she arrives at "this moment that comes close to inner feeling."[13] Her inspirations may erupt spontaneously from within her emotional self, but the task of giving artistic form to these impulses is prolonged and exacting. Her elaborate studio process is undertaken under the auspices of Rist Sisters Corporation, a small enterprise Rist formed and likens to a self-sufficient spaceship. Sisters Tamara, Andrea, Ursula are members of this team.[14] Rist conducts their operations. She explains, "It's the subjects that choose me, not the other way round. We marry, the subject and I, and every now and then I'm being hurled out of the whirl of time and catapulted to my editing suite."[15] In the editing laboratory, Rist takes great pains to enhance the emotive power of the footage. Ten hours of tape may be shot to create a three-minute sequence. She explains, "I subjected the images to all kinds of interference: played them too fast for two simultaneously activated recorders, then put the pictures through a time-based corrector that evens out irregularities. That was only one of twenty-five kinds of disturbances that I tried out on the tape. Asking too much or too little of the machines resulted in pictures I was thoroughly familiar with—like my psychosomatic symptoms—that is, my inner pictures. ...Expressiveness or tackiness comes much closer to the truth than a perfectly sharp, slick representation."[16] The videos are not considered complete until, according to Rist, "you feel as if you're inside the box, behind the glass, within the wall. You forget everything around you and concentrate completely on the box: you're swallowed."[17] The works, therefore, originate and terminate within the emotional zone. They are intended to dislodge people from concrete reality and deposit them in the amorphous and intangible world of the psyche. In order to accomplish this feat, Rist's imagery exploits the connections between the retina and the brain by lavishing the viewer with the sumptuous colors and swirling forms that convey her girlish disassociation from reasonable expectations.

Her vacillations from neurotic withdrawal to brazen extroversion are given parallel form in the extreme range of scale that she employs in her artworks. Rist shrinks in *Selbstlos im Lavabad (Altruist in Lava Bath)* (1994), a video installation that is as likely to be overlooked as it is to be stepped on: the video monitor peeps out from a one-and-a-half-inch hole in a wooden floor. Close scrutiny reveals the artist swimming nude in an agitated manner in an incandescent lava bath. The opposite end of the psychological spectrum is exemplified by *Tribute-open my glade* (2000), which appeared on the huge Astrovision screen in Manhattan's Times Square. Amid the dazzle of advertisements and electronic news headlines, tens of thousands of pedestrians, bus riders and taxicab occupants were startled to encounter a video of the artist looming overhead, pressing her vastly enlarged face against the screen, smearing her lipstick, distorting her features, advertising her feelings. The video was broadcast for 60 seconds, sixteen times a day. Rist explains, "I see Times Square as an overwhelming space full of electric blossoms and electronic twinkle that hit visitors like a slap in the face."[18]

Since the early 1990s, a reliable, renewable creative resource has fueled Rist's inspiration. She has been spurred into action by the emotional residues of "the holy-unholy subject of gender"[19] that she refers to as "festering kernels."[20] But her life has changed. Rist got married and, in February 2002, she became a mother. Perhaps this is yet another instance of an imprudent girl giving away her heart while clinging to dreams of romantic settings, candlelight intimacies, mood music, and other ingredients she has refers to as "applied feminine culture."[21] Or perhaps Rist's life will end as happily as the Greek maiden Psyche's did. Psyche ultimately received the blessing of Venus, drank a cup of magical ambrosia, and was granted eternal life with Cupid in Paradise. Will Rist's romantic fate determine her artistic fate? Is her art better served by frustration or fulfillment? Despair or confidence? Rage or contentment? Rist has described herself as a picture machine with an endless reservoir of images, feelings, and sounds. "(I am) full of inner pictures that are more wild than we will ever be able to show."[22] It remains to be seen if being a wife and mother will activate a less hedonistic, more levelheaded lobe within Rist's female psyche, and if this experience can inspire her picture machine.

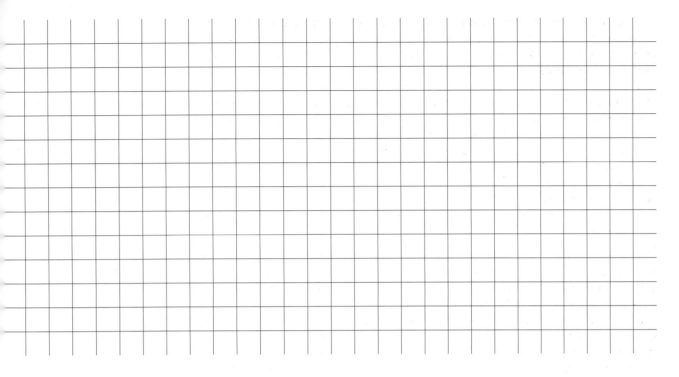

[1.] Hans-Ulrich Obrist, *Pipilotti Rist* (London: Phaidon, 2001), 133.

[2.] Les Reins Prochaines was founded by Rist and fellow Swiss artist Muda Mathis in 1987. The group disbanded in 1994.

[3.] Christoph Doswald, "Ich halbiere bewuust die Weit, Pipilotti Rist im Gespräch mit Christoph Doswald," *Be Magazin, No. 1* (Kunstierhaus Bethanien, Berlin, 1994): 91–96.

[4.] Chris Isaak, "Wicked Game," on *Heart Shaped World*, WEA Int./Warner Bros. Compact disk, 1991.

[5.] Pipilotti Rist, solo exhibition, Luhring Augustine Gallery, New York, May 2000. This site-specific installation was the culmination of a series of solo exhibitions titled *Remake of the Weekend* which Rist realized in Berlin, Vienna, Zurich, and Paris.

[6.] Pipilotti Rist, *Apricots Along the Street/Pipilotti Rist* (Zurich: Scalo, 2001).

[7.] "Interview with Pipilotti Rist," *EGG: the Arts Show*, PBS, 28 February 2002 <http://www.pbs.org/wnet.egg/222/rist/interview_content_1.html>.

[8.] EGG.

[9.] ibid.

[10.] Pipilotti Rist, 50 kg. *Nicht Durchtrainiert* (Kyoto: Korinsha Press and Co., 1999), n.p.

[11.] EGG.

[12.] "Laurie Anderson and Pipilotti Rist Meet Up in the Lobby of a Hotel in Berlin on September 9, 1996," *Parkett*, No. 48 (1996), 114.

[13.] Kevin Conley, "At the Galleries: Lady Video," *The New Yorker*, 8 May 2000, 82.

[14.] Obrist, 17.

[15.] ibid.,

[16.] Doswald.

[17.] obrist, 15.

[18.] ibid., 23.

[19.] ibid., 62.

[20.] ibid.

[21.] Marius Babias, "The Rist Risk Factor: When Dreams Twitch Like Dying Fish," *Parkett*, No. 48 (1996), 105.

[22.] Kaelen Wilson-Goldie, "Peep Show Video," *Black Book*, Spring 2000, 54.

Imagination—Inspiring Inspiration

Julian LaVerdiere
Born 1971 Adirondack Mountains, New York
1993 Cooper Union, BFA, fine art and sculpture
1995 Yale University, MFA, fine art and sculpture
Lives and works in New York City

Julian LaVerdiere experiences inspiration as a steady phenomenon. Instead of erupting as a flashing insight or exploding like a bolt of energy, it flows continuously, a component of every hour whether or not that hour is devoted to the creation of art. This energized mental state is both the product of each artwork and the inspiration for the next one. But it is in the ability of these works to augment the creative potential of viewers that their value is ultimately measured. LaVerdiere strives to establish the inspired state of mind as a mental norm. He seeks to accomplish this by creating art that cultivates mystery, produces curiosity, and ultimately stimulates creative action.

"My attitude is that of a young Faust. I want to meet the devil but I don't want to sell my soul. Maybe I'll just put my soul on commission rental."[1] With this declaration, Julian LaVerdiere pays tribute to Faust, the German legend about a learned doctor who surrendered his soul to the devil in exchange for youth, knowledge, and magical powers. Instead of interpreting the legend as a warning against runaway ambition, LaVerdiere has adopted Faust's determination to maximize human potential, and even to surpass it. But his identification with Faust exceeds the legend's role in inspiring his personal creative ambitions. LaVerdiere is equally impressed by the power of this legend to energize generations of artists. Faust has become the hero of operas, poems, and ballets, and paintings of enduring acclaim. Thus, as a character and as a legend, Faust is a paradigm of inspiration. LaVerdiere's desire to be the modern-day Faust reveals a parallel artistic effect. His mission is to create art infused with the perennial power to inspire original achievements in others.

LaVerdiere's work has been located in the section devoted to "Internal Sources of Inspiration" despite the fact that his artistic pursuits lead him beyond self-examination and into the annals of history. Imagination, curiosity, and motivation are his primary concerns, not events from the past; nevertheless, it is in the past that he discovers inspirational models of creative genius. LaVerdiere diligently capitalizes on the examples set by the original inventors, investors, visionaries, and designers who laid the foundation for our current technologies, luxuries, and comforts. He has noted, however, that most people are busy keeping pace with the velocity of change. Few take the time to honor these past achievements. LaVerdiere attempts to rectify this indifference. "History is the most valuable territory. Writing of history is the definition of the world at present ... particularly unacknowledged history. If you can dredge up new pieces of history, you can change people's understanding. History is always changing—new, nasty or exciting secrets are always being revealed. I enjoy finding the heroic members of the history of progress who have not been celebrated."

LaVerdiere is inspired by the missing chapters in recorded history. He is intrigued by the gaps in the official chronicles, the unsavory facts expunged from idealized narratives, all the stuff that has either been suppressed (if you subscribe to theories of conspiracy), forgotten (if you acknowledge the inevitable dissolution of the past), or rejected (if you presume that annals of the past are always selective). Today, such inevitable incompleteness of human accounts is exacerbated because time is so accelerated: the word "generation" is applied to the annual updating of trends; "dinosaur" applies to nine-month old technologies; "nostalgia" is conjured by defunct television sitcoms. Meanwhile, what is studied as "history" is a hulking wreckage of combat and upheaval. LaVerdiere's challenge is to distract us from the perpetual renewal of available and glittering enticements so we can develop our own creative potential.

LaVerdiere may address the truths that are ignored in our official versions of history, but his concerns exceed setting the historic record straight. Referring to his relationship to history he says, "My interest is one of hope. What I like to do is resurrect inspirational images that are romantic in nature." Reclaiming inspiring events from the past, he believes, forges inspirational visions of the future. Ironically, he prefers attempts at technological progress that did not succeed. These failed efforts are often the most noble and exemplify the most daring acts. As a result, they are effective tools for motivating people to reach beyond known limits.

It is in this spirit that LaVerdiere created *The First Attempted Trans-Atlantic Telegraph Cable Crossing* (1999). This historic milestone inaugurated the progression of technologies that seemed, a century and a half ago, as fantastical as intergalactic travel seems today. Cable technology's impact on the industrial revolution is uncontestable. The accomplishment signaled the dawning of the communications age, changing the world forever. Yet it barely registers on most people's lists of momentous events. LaVerdiere's representation consists of a neon-illuminated case that looks like the tomb of a great statesman. Within it lies the hulking mass of a meticulously crafted, nine-foot model of a sunken clipper ship. The failed attempt to lay telegraph cable by this ship in 1854 is a historical truth; it failed because the cable snapped and the venture went bankrupt. The excitement that surged between New York and London upon its successful completion ten years later is also factual, but in order to enhance the inspirational impact of this work, LaVerdiere took liberties with the historic truth.

Although LaVerdiere thinks of himself as a chronicler of these histories, he admits, "At times I do a little rewriting of history to aid and abet the inspiration factor. That is what propaganda is." In his piece, he omitted the ship that was actually involved in the cable project and replaced it with the picturesque and celebrated Cutty Sark. This grand three-mast clipper doubles the artwork's power to serve as a symbol of exemplary achievement. The Cutty Sark was the era's fastest conveyor of information between the continents until it was rendered obsolete by a more efficient information conveyor— the trans-Atlantic cable, the laying of which is also celebrated in this work of art. LaVerdiere further embellished his nautical lie by inventing a sea disaster, portraying the ship in its doomed state on the bottom of the ocean. He defends this decision by stating, "This is art, not documentation. I capitalize on people's ignorance. They are duped in the details to arrive at a deeper truth. Without a

Interview with Julian LaVerdiere
By Zoe Feigenbaum

ZF: What was the first indication that you were likely to become a recognized and respected artist?

JLV: That started revealing itself after my first show. We had three days of preview prior to the opening and the entire show sold in those first three days. My dealer Andrew Kreps and I were flabbergasted and recognized that either it was the temper of the times, or the market, or my work. But whatever it was, we were off to a good start. However, sales aren't an indicator of respect. That's hard to gauge. Perhaps I first felt respected when I was invited to participate in the P.S. 1/MoMA *Greater New York* exhibition, in which I was asked to build a giant installation.

ZF: How did you promote the show?

JLV: Andrew and I didn't have a lot of money to spend. We put out a quarter-page ad in *Artforum* and sent out 1,000 invites to everyone and their mother. I remember wanting the invite to be unique, so I had an embossing seal made, like the kind used by a notary public, but mine said, "lost history." We hand-sealed 1,000 cards in one afternoon. I can't say that made a difference but I can say that attention to details doesn't go unnoticed.

ZF: How did you get hooked up with the gallery?

JLV: I had been following the art circuit since I was in college. I was eager to show whenever I had the opportunity. I was in ten or fifteen group shows prior to my first solo show and I never sold a thing. But it wasn't about that. I definitely had made my presence known as an eager beaver. I had a number of studio visits with various galleries and some seemed interested but were wishy-washy. However, Andrew Kreps was really straightforward and ready to do a show, so we made a date. That was November 1999. I was excited because it would be the last show of the twentieth century.

ZF: Do you remember the sale of your first piece?

JLV: The sale of the first piece was really exciting. There were large, medium, and small works exhibited, as far as scale and price of the sculpture. And then there were a number of photographs that were in multiples. I figured that the photographs were a shoe-in, that those things would sell easy because they were priced low and were wall pieces. And I expected that the big sculpture of a giant model of a sunken ship in a casket was that last thing that would sell. But a big collector came in and saw the sculpture before I had even finished installing it and said, "I want it." Then in came another and another. So in one day there was a waiting list of three people for the same piece. I couldn't believe it. I was going from total anonymity to hot property in a blink of an eye. I'll never forget that phenomenal feeling of excitement and relief. I had been saved!

ZF: What would you say was the most significant exhibition that you have had?

JLV: It was *Greater New York* with P.S. 1/MoMA. That was a real honor for me because it was the following spring after my first show, and I was barely legal. The

Julian LaVerdiere, *First Attempted Trans-Atlantic Telegraph Cable Crossing (F.A.T.A.T.C.C.)* (1999), installation view at P.S. 1 Contemporary Art Center, pavilion enclosure, casket, ship model, with lambda print on wall. Private collection, New York. Courtesy Lehmann Maupin, New York.

SOURCING INSPIRATION

shipwreck or tragedy, people don't care about failures. Some fictions distract from reality. Others allow it to be better understood." Thus the ship, like a martyr or a fallen warrior, is made to exemplify courage and risk. Manipulating the facts enables a piece of the cultural past to enrich current consciousness. In this instance it resurrected the memory of inventors who dared to condense time and space by transmitting conversations across the vast and churning ocean. These exalted associations are augmented by the work's grandiose presentation. At the focal point of a huge gallery at P.S. 1 Contemporary Art Center in Long Island City, in 2000, LaVerdiere installed the nautical model on an elevated platform surrounded by towering, two-story-high columns that evoke the classical triumphal architecture of the grandiloquent German Pavilion at the 1938 World's Fair. Bombastic, spirit-rousing German war songs serve as the basis for the electronic music composed by Wolfgang Voigt that fills the hall. LaVerdiere carefully calculated the effect of inserting these historic references, although they are not connected to breakthroughs in communication technologies. They were used, he says, "to strike you with a sense of awe and theatricality," and to instill "a sense of uneasiness and fear." They vanquish the twin enemies of inspiration: apathy and boredom. LaVerdiere calls his method "historical hyper-texting." He describes it as "inspirational, romantic propaganda to help continue the march of progress." Since no historic accounts are complete, and all are, therefore, created out of select observations, he sees no reason to apologize for constructing his own version of truth. LaVerdiere compares his manipulations of fact to the work of H.G. Wells, Jules Verne, Arthur C. Clark, and other science fiction writers. "They inspired scientists to be socially conscious and to do wondrous things. Aerospace scientists have all read the texts of these writers. Stanley Kubrick's movie version of Clark's *2001: A Space Odyssey* is a concrete vision of the future. It inspired them to dream." To dream, to imagine, to experiment, to dare, to challenge, to strive—these are the desired products of LaVerdiere's work. Each modification of history is designed to convey trust in technology's role in progress and to celebrate the pioneers who defied inevitable perils. "I believe in Utopia as a goal and aspiration. By certain definitions, we are already there. We have ease of living, convenience, efficiency, physical comfort, and prosperity. Compared to the Dark Ages, we are doing okay. I see corruption and unhappiness, but today is better than yesterday. Tomorrow will be better than today."

In another work, LaVerdiere takes his dream-generating role literally. He designed cots and pillows into which electro-luminescent wires and microprocessors were inserted. These devices would trick a sleeper's brain into conjuring the rapturous state of resistance-free motion, of floating weightlessly, of flying; at least that is the desired result of the wires that blink in sequence and at specific intervals, firing bursts of light upon the closed lids of sleepers to create the illusion of rapid eye movement. Sleepers imagine themselves

show also was sort of a competition with the Whitney Biennial that year, so it had a huge buzz.

ZF: What was the most significant sale you ever had?

JLV: I think that the most significant sale was sort of a Faustian one. It may have been to Jeffrey Deitch and the corporate collection of Skadden Arps. I had become seduced by the promise of the big economics of the art world. Now I can safely say the most significant purchase I have ever made was buying my soul back while participating in the *Tribute in Light* initiative, because it had nothing to do with art commerce whatsoever. It has been the most enriching experience of my life.

ZF: Is there anyone who promoted your career when you were still unknown or unrecognized by galleries?

JLV: Yes, I would say there have been a number of people that have been very supportive that have helped me find recognition. I would have to thank curators that have helped me out. But the most important and the most legitimate is the support of your fellow artists. They will really launch a career. The art world, unlike other corporate jobs, is a family industry and people group together and form unions and cliques, and there is solidarity there.

However, it is Anne Pasternak who was the most supportive of me in one of the hardest times. Anne is the director of Creative Time, a renowned pubic art organization here in NYC. Creative Time had agreed to produce a totally crazy proposal that Paul Myoda and I had made in 1998 for *Bioluminescent Beacon* to be mounted onto the radio mast of the World Trade Center. This project was started before I ever had any commercial successes. This project introduced us to many acquaintances in the upper floors of WTC, now lost to 9/11. Anne Pasternak helped us come to terms with this loss and was instrumental in launching our proposal for the *Tribute in Light*.

ZF: Do you think that being in art school allowed you to make some of those connections?

JLV: For me, certainly. Most of my closest friends and colleagues in the art world are from Yale or Cooper Union where I went to school. The art schools that I went to shaped my approach to making art. Art school, no matter where you go, will inevitably help you develop the ability to communicate the meaning of your work, which is necessary for surviving as an artist in the market. But it's not just about the market. It's about being a participant in the current art culture. The art world is a complex system of discourses, beliefs, and cosmologies.

ZF: How did you sell yourself?

JLV: As I was coming of age in New York City, I was enchanted by macabre and iconoclastic cliques of individuals who stood out of the crowd. In high school, I modeled myself on death-rock and gothic-music archetypes. I became fascinated with black magic and hokey Renaissance festivals, although in art school I began to refine my interests toward Victorian neo-classicism and its fall and rise into decadence. It is not difficult to unravel the genealogy between gothic subculture

39. Julian LaVerdiere, *Safe Circa* (1919) (2000), still from *Suspended Animation* DVD (2001), 4 x 3 x 3 feet, antiquated styrene safe. Courtesy of the artist and Lehmann Maupin, New York.

transported. LaVerdiere explains, "You cannot inspire hope without inspiring confidence. Flying is a superhuman ability. It is indicative of empowerment, success, progress, freedom, and a sense of satisfaction. I control the mind of a sleeper and cultivate somnambulism. Somnambulism is a way of conquering the unknown territory of the unconscious."

Although LaVerdiere believes "there are more opportunities for mad science and invention in the art world than in rocket science or nuclear physics," practical considerations are also factored into the design of his exalted mental-flight training kit. The bed is designed to resemble World War I-era military cots. The pillows are as small as airline pillows. They are efficient, lightweight, and portable, woven from a space-age fiber called Vectran. The cold light that they emit doesn't contain harmful rays or burn the skin, and is powered by battery packs. They are designed for use on a mass scale and in multiple circumstances. The one thing LaVerdiere admits he can't control is what people do once they receive the sense of boundless possibility that he helps create. "I would like to inspire the public to pursue the sciences and technology. I want to inspire aspirations of explorations. I want to direct attention skyward. That is why these beds and pillows are designed to induce dreams of flight. I want to see greater national expense on space programs and extraterrestrial colonization." LaVerdiere intends to play a role in these grandiose schemes by infusing others with a passion for exploration, research, and vision.

LaVerdiere also created a personal inspirational beacon. He placed it in the area of his work space that is designated for sitting (thinking) and lying down (dreaming). It is a DVD of a haunting image—an ancient, barnacle-laden safe gracefully tumbling in an eternal descent, its free-fall accompanied by the eerie, pulsating drone of a techno-music score composed by Wolfgang Voigt, a.k.a. GAS. The retrieval of ancient artifacts usually stirs powerful surges of curiosity—as do relics of the Titanic. When locked safes are among the retrieved artifacts, the mystery escalates, news stories spiral into media sensations, and throngs of people turn their imaginings toward the unknown. "People rally around the opening of a safe. They expect remarkable secrets will be revealed. But, after all the hype, what comes out is rotten stocks and bonds, not the Hope diamond. Events are only exciting before the safe is opened." For this reason LaVerdiere cultivates anticipation and intrigue by perpetually postponing resolution. The safe never lands. It is never opened. The music never ends. The DVD is produced in an edition of six and sold with custom rear-projection frames. He hopes collectors will use it as he does in his studio—to infuse their lives with a constant energizing stimulus. This perpetual delay of conclusions functions as the perpetual onset of artistic inquiry. LaVerdiere has also given the work no name. As long as it is untitled, it is an unsolved mystery—it fascinates. LaVerdiere likens it to a "digital

and new romanticism. I began to recognize that artists' identities differed from those of musicians. They were more complex and less flashy, although they were often very performative. In particular, I remember being struck by these two dandies, Messieurs McDermott and McGough. These gentlemen appeared as though they walked right off the set of a Merchant-Ivory costume drama. They dressed and behaved as if they were living in turn-of-the-century New York, from their starched collars and cuffs to the inflections of their speech and mannerisms. I discovered that they didn't only dress and act that way, they lived that way. They resided by gaslight, drove a Model T, and painted with a subversive Northern Romantic style that flew in the face of the neo-expressionism of the day. This was a fascinating radicality in my eyes. These artists were living a total life work. At the time I felt a kinship with them in the extreme escapist pursuit of willful time travel. I didn't know how to distinguish my lifestyle from my art, or my identity as an individual from my belief system. My fascination with artificially self-induced progenitors led me to religiously bleaching my hair platinum, which would beg people to question, "Who is that peculiar white-haired young man wearing the frock-coat? Did he just walk off a time machine from yesteryear?" My lifestyle helped me become a public presence. It has indeed drawn intrigue, and it may be one of the factors that people consider when they choose to invest in my work. But I don't consider my eccentric appearance a marketing strategy. Is making art producing commodities? No. It is a way of producing inventions and sculpture that illustrate how I think life should be addressed and better understood.

ZF: What are your feelings about the commercial aspect of being an artist and selling art? Do you feel as if you are compromising your art?

JLV: No, not at all. My art is not performance art or an ephemeral object that is meant to be experienced once. My art is memorabilia, mementos, and memorials that are meant to be collected and cherished and traded if necessary. So, I make objects that can change hands quite comfortably. I have no problem with the sale of my art. I would rather be making a living from selling my art than by doing commercial work for someone else.

ZF: Please describe your studio. Who runs it? What are the jobs of the assistants if you have any?

JLV: My studio is now a completely armed and operational battle station. I recently installed an airplane hangar on my roof in which I can work on large projects with my team and hoist them down to street level when complete. My interior space has become more of a library/drawing room and design facility, where I do my drafting and smaller assembly. I don't maintain a staff but I do work with a few key fabricators who I trust intimately. I also enjoy working with students; I have had a number of interns from Cooper Union who bring in fresh ideas and dialogue. It's important not to be insular with one's practice.

yule log, an avatar or icon, like a satellite or moon or object of pursuit, like a floating carrot, or the fruit on the tree that can never be reached. The DVD is always on as an inspiration. I'm always trying to crack history. It is always there in my mind."

LaVerdiere's elaborate creative process enhances the work's appeal. He first simulated an old safe out of Styrofoam, cardboard, and paint. In his studio, this life-size version dangles from a strap and hook as if it is in the midst of being hoisted from the depths of the sea. Thus the sculptured version of the safe is in perpetual ascent whereas the DVD version is in perpetual descent. The model is exaggerated in the manner of a prop from old Holly-wood adventure films. Its details and proportions are altered just enough to enhance its mystery. But the DVD version was not based on this elaborate model. For this purpose LaVerdiere created a two-inch replica of the full-sized sculpture. He then filmed this minia-ture using advanced digital technology to mimic 1950s film technology, bathing it in uncanny, supersaturated light and adding a romantic musical score. These elements make it apparent that the work is not archival footage of an authentic discovery. They also served to activate inquiry about its construction. Is the DVD image based on a three-dimensional model? Is it a computer animation? Is it a real safe that has been digitally manipulated? Is it old film footage? This lack of resolution is equivalent to the mental state that many psychologists identify as the inducement of inspiration. LaVerdiere purposefully cultivates it. "I have created a spectral image. I don't want to fool someone about reality. I want to illustrate a source of hope and inspiration."

The terrorists who shattered the World Trade Center towers in Manhattan also shattered LaVerdiere's plans to create another awe-evoking, spirit-lifting work of art. If it hadn't been for that fateful disaster, residents and visitors throughout the city would be able to behold a radiant, otherworldly tower of light titled Bioluminescent Beacon. Beacons are often used as metaphors for inspiration and guidance. LaVerdiere and his collaborator Paul Myoda had completed preparations for bringing this metaphor into the realm of perceptual experience. They planned to install this ambitious public art project at the absolute pinnacle of Manhattan—on top of the 360-foot radio tower that rose from the roof of the World Trade Center's north tower. Its light would have been produced by phosphorescent, single-cell organisms known as dinoflagellates, a species of transparent sea-dwelling plankton that emit a soft, pulsating, greenish light. The artists planned to construct an oval aquarium for breeding the plankton. It was to be equipped with a sensor that would transmit the luminous pulses from the organisms to fiber-optic cables atop the tower. In this luminescent beacon, LaVerdiere and Myoda have imagined an inspiring work of art—a huge, transgenic astral body to inspire stargazers. LaVerdiere states, "Man can make history. Man can make natural history as well."

The towers fell, but LaVerdiere's faith survived. Six months after the September 11th attacks, LaVerdiere, Myoda, and two architects created a sculpture that consisted of two dazzling, massive beams of white light. For a month, Towers of Light (2002) occupied the exact loca-tion of the missing towers in Lower Manhattan. LaVerdiere describes the work as "a profound symbol of strength, hope and resiliency, a reclamation of New York City's skyline and identity, a tribute to rescue workers and ... all those who lost their lives."[2] The energy of the beams ascended from Ground Zero and rose into the sky, reversing the dreadful image of collapse. Towers of Light is LaVerdiere's inspiring symbol; a tribute to will, perseverance, and vision in the face of disaster.

[1] Unless otherwise noted, all quotes from an interview with the artist, March 24, 2000.

[2] LaVerdiere, conversation with author, March 12, 2002.

Julian LaVerdiere and Paul Myoda, *Tribute in Light: Artist's Rendering* (2001/2002), 24 x 20 inches, c-print. Courtesy of the artists and Lehmann Maupin, New York.

Imagination—Inspiring Inspiration: **Julian LaVerdiere**

Corporate Hype, Spiritual Cool, Military Heat, and Global Warming

Scott Grieger
Born 1946 Mississippi
N.d. Chouinard Art Institute, Los Angeles, California, MFA, printmaking, painting
1971 California State University, Northridge, BFA
Lives and works in Venice, California

Scott Grieger's initiating inspirations are products of chance encounters that occur as he conducts routine activities. Driving his car, shopping, watching television, or teaching, Grieger's mental radar continually scans the environment for instants that carry the significance of socially revealing truths. Once these random commonplace experiences are installed, assembled, and registered in his imagination, he is motivated to discover an artistically satisfying way to compose them. Grieger designs forms and symbols that realize the insights experienced during his inspired state.

An empty Nike shoebox is the unlikely inspiration for an elaborate installation called *Be Here Now!* (2000) by Scott Grieger. Grieger is an artist whose muse neither soars on imaginative fancy nor burrows into the dark recesses of the soul. Instead, it resides in commonplace experiences and normal modes of perception. Grieger's mind is stocked with images that are typically ignored during searches for artistic insight. They are encountered as logos and illustrations. They appear on objects that litter sidewalks, are glimpsed through windshields, are plastered onto toys and sports equipment. They are the stuff of supermarket shelves, billboards, the Internet, television ads, and product packaging. Grieger is an image-collector, not an image-inventor. Like a connoisseur, he selects prized specimens from today's supersaturated image-stream. But he does not share a connoisseur's reverence for the things he collects—images that are produced, almost exclusively, by powerful political, commercial, and media institutions. Instead of venerating these prized examples from the visual torrent, he manipulates them, usurps their authority, reverses their flow of influence, and sends them back into the world to un-brainwash the people. His artwork cleanses minds that have been indoctrinated by the unrelenting assault of political and corporate propaganda. At the same time, he is intrigued by the potential of popular images to alter attitudes. Grieger capitalizes on this power. By replacing their frivolous messages with responsible motives, he undermines the subliminal forces that prevail in contemporary cultures.

Grieger's interest in the significance of cultural artifacts can be traced to his study of anthropology in college. When he became an artist, he shifted his training away from indigenous peoples and rural situations. He declares, "Anthropology is here and now. This was new information. Corporations assign values without our permission: 'Anything that creates profits is good.' I am against the vocabulary of corporatization. For all the claims of diversity and enriched environment, my feeling as an anthropologist is that there is less choice today than historically. You are required to adapt your activities and thinking to what is available.... If a CEO or president or general doesn't like something, the course of thousands of lives change. I believe change actually comes from the thoughts of many individuals."[1]

An unremarkable situation initiated Grieger's efforts to address this impressive goal in *Be Here Now!* One day a student of his at the Otis College of Art and Design came to class wearing a new pair of Nikes. Nothing was remarkable about this except that the empty shoebox, emblazoned with the Nike "swoosh" logo, was tucked under his arm, and was still there when he returned the next week. Grieger noted that "he seemed enthralled by it, as if the box had value. I also noticed that his persona had changed, and his politics. He became a special youth because of the shoes. It sparked the thought that these Nike shoes were like the brown shirts in Germany before World War II. German youth were given a color and a uniform and they became monsters." In this manner the Nazi swastika and the Nike swoosh became conceptually united for Grieger. To visually unite them, he merged these charged cultural symbols. His composite image consists of four Nike swooshes radiating from a central point in the manner of a swastika. The new form announces the correlation between the dictatorial power of government and the authoritarian power of corporations. Grieger calls his symbol a "swooshtika." "The images were easily tied together," he explains. "They share the same visual vocabulary, although culturally, they seem unconnected. But they work on us the same way." In other words, corporate logos and political symbols implant collective beliefs. These beliefs can be summoned to advocate for good or to promote evil, but in most cases their power is more likely to be insidious than apparent. Grieger returns to Nike to cite the tendency of mega international corporations to operate on the edge of the law and beyond the limits of morality. "Corporate America has done what political diplomacy could never do—jump over political boundaries that couldn't be breached. Shoes are being produced in Thailand for American feet when Thai feet have no shoes. Meanwhile, young people are killing each other for Nike shoes. If I was a corporate executive, I'd be worried about that. But executives seem to slough it off as a social problem, not their moral problem."

Grieger's "swooshtika" appropriates the power of images to control thought and stimulate action. Within the gallery installation of *Be Here Now*!, "swooshtikas" are emblazoned on two pieces of fabric that are hung on opposite sides of the gallery. One is black on a white ground while the other is black on a red ground. Configured to suggest the confluence of corporate hype and political propaganda, they are hung high, resembling banners, flags, political posters, or advertisements—all forms of public address. Referring to his tactic of uniting corporate and political imagery, Grieger says, "I take extremes and close the ends. I make a circle of a bar graph."

Grieger implanted yet a third layer of associations. His fabric "swooshtikas" also resemble tankas, fabric paintings used by Buddhists to focus their meditations. The inclusion of this religious reference suggests that corporate logos, political symbols, and religious icons are equivalent in that all three embody collective beliefs and inspire fervor. On the other hand, it may seem odd to place Buddhist meditation practices in the context of commercial, corporate, and material values. This irreverent partnership can be traced to a personal experience that provided Grieger with a fourth source of inspiration in creating *Be Here Now*!—the military. As he explains,

RY: What were the circumstances surrounding your first exhibition or first sale?

SG: This is an exceptional story. I was still at college. There was a faculty member and he had a friend who was at the Whitney Museum. She came by my garage studio. I had a two-car garage that I had dry-walled and made into a little studio. I was just about ready to graduate and she saw some of these early conceptual photographic works that I was doing and she put me in the Whitney Biennial. That was my first show. I was really young and didn't look back for about 15 years.

RY: Where did you go to school?

SG: I originally went to an art institute but then I decided I would go to a college and actually take a real English class and a literature class and stuff like that. And that was one of the best things I ever did. I had already decided to be an artist but I learned to write and that helped me out a lot. I think that there are good things to be said about both kinds of schools.

RY: How do you feel school prepared you to be an artist?

SG: I was a dead-end kid on the street, a wild kid getting into trouble. Yet I had this talent, and that's what opened doors for me and changed my life. I would never have been able to get a college education because my family couldn't afford it. But then I got a scholarship in art. So for me, school led me to places and opportunities I don't think I could have imagined before. I was really changed by teachers and eventually became one myself. I felt that it was payback or an obligation to try and do the same thing for other young people.

RY: Were there times in your life when you were particularly productive and inventive?

SG: Yes. I came out of school like a rocket. That rhythm lasted the better part of ten years. Then I grew fatigued and I went through this time of research and development. I started something. It was kind of primitive. I needed to develop it, and that takes time. Then that would reach a point of sophistication in development and then I'd be on to something else. There is an episodic nature to the way I work. I'm in a particularly fertile period so I've been really cranking again.

RY: Do you think that talent is innate or that it can be learned?

SG: I think one can learn skills, but I do think the talent, some kind of drive, needs to be there to be developed. If someone has crummy work habits, or they have poor concentration, those things can undercut a person's talent. Issues of character become important. Somebody who has less talent can surge forward.

RY: Who runs your studio? What's the role of assistants?

SG: I'm very fortunate because I am a college professor. I often have young people work in the studio and hopefully it's mutually beneficial in some way. Presently, in terms of studios, I have one small studio that's a few blocks away from my residence. Then I have another place that's been converted into an office. And I do all

Scott Grieger, *Be Here Now!* (2000), installation view, acrylic, vinyl, fabric and digital time and temperature display. Courtesy Patricia Faure Gallery, Santa Monica, California. Photograph: Anthony Cunha.

meditation was a key part of his identity when he was the same age as his student with the Nikes. He continues this Buddhist practice today, particularly at the remote desert ranch he owns with his wife. He recalls the day when meditation failed to be a source of spiritual inspiration and became associated instead with military aggression. His closest neighbor at his ranch is a Marine base. In 1991, during Desert Storm and the Persian Gulf War, Grieger's meditations were often interrupted by the sounds of troop training, helicopters roaring overhead, and convoys of exotic weaponry barreling down the road past his house. "I am in the wilderness surrounded by the heights of technology," is how Grieger tells it. "This is an extreme contextual reversal. One evening I am immersed in meditation when BOOM! For an instant I believed this must be the boom of enlightenment. But no, it was only the boom of distant firearms. And I heard a voice in my head sing out, 'You're in the Dharmy now!'" Thus did Grieger discover another means to conflate two ludicrously mismatched partners. "Dharma" (one's duty and nature according to divine Buddhist law) is combined with "army" (one's duty and nature according to secular law) to produce "dharmy," the word that appears on the bright red, oversized tags that enliven the installation. These tags are attached to seat cushions and knee pads that also have split personalities. In size and shape, they are identical to the zafu cushions and zabuton pads upon which meditators traditionally sit. Furthermore, they are placed directly on the floor to indicate that they are intended for sitting with crossed legs for long periods of time. But military references invade and vanquish these religious connotations. The circular configuration of cushions and pads commonly used for group meditations becomes an orderly line-up, six deep and nine across, like soldiers in formation. Grieger also covered them with the army camouflage fabric that assures that soldiers literally become "at one with the world." A variety of camouflage patterns is used: one permits "immersion" into the desert in the midday sun, others are suited to snowy landscapes at dusk, or the woods in autumn, or jungles at night, etc. They dissolve the boundaries between the self and the environment, although this form of "oneness" is tactical, not spiritual.

Be Here Now! combines another well-known Buddhist principle with military practice. Although Navy Seals are not likely to meditate, and meditators are not likely to fight, they both abandon their egos by yielding to a higher order. Once these similarities are established, interesting contrasts emerge. To Seals, "yielding" is defined as obedience. To Buddhist practitioners, "yielding" means enlightenment. The "swoosh" energy of the military surges aggressively outward to take command of expanded territories; but "swooshes" applied to spiritual practice spiral serenely inward. In fact, Grieger notes that the swastika is an ancient cosmological image that originally denoted good luck. Grieger seems intent on attaining peaceful coexistence of these divergent forces. "Each group might be healthier if they accept the influence of the other. What I'm

the messy work at the other place. They're different. In the one in back of the house I work on the computer. There's a fellow a few miles away that has a stencil-cutting computer. So I make files and do images on my computer here, and then take them over to his place and make stencils, and then go to the other studio and put the stencils on panels or whatever and paint them. I skip around town doing my art. I have an orbit.

RY: What percent of your income is earned by the sale of your art?

SG: About 25 percent.

RY: Do you think that the whole financial aspect of being an artist is difficult?

SG: Less so as I've gotten older, but some people would view things as sacrifice. When I was in my twenties I was living and working in storefronts on major boulevards with the traffic noise, and using a hot plate, a toilet, and a stand-up shower in the back that I had rigged up. Some people would come over and say, "It's really bohemian!" It was primitive but it wasn't a sacrifice. It didn't seem like there was a problem at all. It took me a long time to have a house and a mortgage.

RY: What advice would you give the current generation of aspiring artists?

SG: My advice would be to not "hothouse" the careerist ideas too soon. To be a young undergraduate artist is a great privilege in that you can experiment and fail in semi-private. You have some years to develop something that may be rich for you and sustain you for the rest of your life, rather than saying, "Okay, these are the rules of the art world." Five years from now the art world will be extremely different. Certainly you shouldn't be editing yourself right from the very beginning.

RY: How much is fame and recognition a part of your own work?

SG: I don't do art to put it in the closet. I do art to have other people look at it and deal with it. I'll finish a piece, it gives me pleasure for about ten minutes, and then I'm on to the next thing. It is a part of my studio practice to have the work go somewhere. The work is a vehicle for communicating with other people.

RY: Do you do anything now to enhance the value and appreciation of your work in the future?

SG: I take care of it. I keep track of it. I know where things are. I develop relationships with people that own my work. It's interesting to see where it is when it goes out into the world, and how it's being displayed, and how it's functioning. I recently had an experience with somebody who had bought something of mine twenty-five years ago. She came to my last opening and had the small painting in her purse. She brought it out and there it was. And it was like, "Gee whiz! It looks pretty good!" [Laughs] It was nice to see it again.

RY: What communication channel is most suited to reach your intended audience?

SG: I do multiples. I do websites. I do discrete objects like paintings. I do installations, gallery shows. They all have strengths. My feeling is you just keep putting

trying to do is make a protein drink out of many fruits and vegetables. What comes out has a different texture and look from any of the original ingredients."

Concern for the environment can also be included in Grieger's "protein drink" metaphor for his multiple sources of inspiration. "I'm one individual. I hear and read that there is a problem of global warming. I have noticed evidence of climate change on my ranch in the desert. I observe it but I feel helpless to do anything about it. Then I realize, there are no images that have been invented to deal with the problem. There are words, but no images. What can I do? I can invent images to put us on the alert." The concept for an image capable of broadcasting the peril of global warming was supplied, once again, by a found representation as pervasive as it is negligible. "I saw a little icon of the globe on the Internet. There was magnetism in the image. How could so simple an image represent something so complicated as the whole globe? I knew what it was even though it didn't look like what it represented. I started to play with the image on the computer. It was random at first, pure visual experiment. I tried it in many colors. When I made it red, it grew a big new tentacle. It became a hot globe." But the color red signals warning, not crisis, and Grieger needed his globe to be "emergency hot." So he enlarged this tiny icon to match the scale of the globe's plight. Still, he sought an even more searing image. The clincher was supplied by another familiar image. "This was summer. I was driving one day. I noticed a time-and-temperature display on a bank. And I knew, time and tempera-ture coupled with a hot globe, it will come back to you. There will be a subliminal response. In this way the work is subversive." These elements combined in *Be Here Now!* to form a wall-sized icon of a globe painted dark red on a lighter red ground to give off a scorched appearance. Embedded in this chunky, geometric map of the world is a flashing digital mechanism that ticks off the real time and the real temperature. It announces, second by second, the true state of the world: threatened with inferno, eruption, or detonation, unless we heed the artist's warning.

In his determination to make visitors realize that these digital measuring devices actu-ally report instantaneous environmental change with absolute accuracy, and that these changes portend dire circumstances, Grieger used another propagandist tactic: surprise. Exploiting the power of letters and numbers to exceed their role as information-conveyers, he harnessed their ability to captivate attention, and thus to provoke thought. As visitors turn to exit the gallery they confront two painted replicas of LED displays. The stasis of these representations highlights the movement of the functioning devices. The text inscribed on one is "hELLO." The other reads "07734." The perplexing appearance of the lower case "h" is the clue that helps reveal that the two apparently unrelated signs are actually the same. By turning the sign with the numbers upside down, the viewer realizes that it too spells the word "hELLO." As they depart, visitors receive a greeting instead of a farewell.

Logos and icons are potent attitude-benders and opinion-modifiers. These simple, flat, monochromatic shapes constitute a collective language capable of addressing such issues as class distinctions, ecological responsibility, gender identities, and social values. These messages are absorbed without instruction. They infiltrate our minds and often become indistinguishable from thoughts that are self-induced. Grieger selects Nike's swoosh, swastikas, global icons, and camouflage patterns—all of which are prevalent throughout our visual environment. Within the context of his works of art, however, they are enlisted to promote a set of values that was not intended by their original designers. Since it is impossible for any viewer to avoid encounters with these common images, Grieger hopes that each sighting will trigger the new, subversive associations he has affixed to them, thus reinforcing his crusade instead of the intended one. In this way, he makes certain images function as inadvertent evangelists preaching a heretic's text. "If I do my job right," says the artist, "My art stays real vivid. It haunts you."

A common Nike swoosh was the catalyst for Grieger's determined act of social reform and its trickle-up bypassing of corporations and the military-industrial complex. As those protesting the display of the Confederate flag on government property can affirm, images embody and perpetuate principles. They are efficient and commanding weapons of mind control. Often they become a part of the background where they assert their influence even when they are not noticed. By modifying their appearance, Grieger changes their meaning, which affects the consciousness of the viewer, which introduces thoughts capable of reducing suffering, the goal of Buddhist practice.

things out and it returns to you in some way. It's almost like the laws of karma. If you do good and put it out there and take care of it, things return to you in odd and unforeseen ways.

RY: How has your choice for a place to live and work affected your career?

SG: I think it's important. In my case I'm in a metropolitan area and there's an art scene here. My wife and I have a remote desert cabin where I can be part of the wild desert. But I come back to my digs here in Los Angeles.

RY: What do you regret about your past decisions regarding your career?

SG: Well, I'll be really blunt and honest. I regret becoming an alcoholic and a cocaine addict at a certain point.

RY: Did you think, at the time, the drugs were inspiring you?

SG: Yeah.

RY: Do you think your art suffered?

SG: Yes. It was a waste of time.

RY: What is the nature of your struggle as an artist?

SG: Concepts are cheap. I have lots of ideas. Actually producing something in the world is extremely difficult. My process today is labor intensive. I can think it up in an instant but it takes weeks to do it.

RY: Which is more important to you: idea or craft and skill?

SG: The idea's got to be strong in order for me to be interested enough to produce it.

RY: What would you say is the most significant exhibition or sale that you've had and why?

SG: The last show was significant for me because it was very pointed about global warming and politics. It was really blunt. It was exciting to let that intensity of my values and morals out in public.

RY: What are your feelings about the commercial aspect of being an artist?

SG: I think it's great. I love it when people give me checks for what I do. That's really an interesting part of being an artist.

RY: How does your work get marketed?

SG: I have a dealer.

RY: What does your work contribute to a collector?

SG: In my case, a lot of the work has a pointed content and I think that people who buy my work agree with the content.

RY: What do you say are your primary sources of inspiration?

SG: My primary source of inspiration is society. I love being on the planet and looking at what's going on and formulating some sort of idea about it.

RY: Would you say that the world is screwed up?

SG: Most definitely. [Laughs]

RY: Do you feel like your art is there to fix it?

SG: No. My art's just there.

1. All quotes from an interview with the artist, February 12, 2000.

Apartheid and Redemption

William Kentridge
Born 1955 Johannesburg, South Africa
1976 University of Witwatersrand, BA, politics and African studies
1976–1978 Johannesburg Art Foundations
1981–82 Ecole Jacques Lecoc, Paris, studied mime and theater
Lives and works in Johannesburg, South Africa

William Kentridge's films and drawings explore external sources of inspiration despite the fact that they are also inspired by emotional distress. This is because the distress he explores is shared by an entire country (South Africa), caused by a political circumstance (apartheid), and has a historic outcome (racial reconciliation). Kentridge's emotional inspiration is, therefore, not discovered within his own soul. It is observed in the streets, enacted in the legislature, reported in the media, demonstrated in the marketplace, and taught in schools. He documents the confluence of the emotional residue of abuses with the emotional complexity of amnesty.

William Kentridge probes the guts of a governing body suffering from its own abuses and illustrates the consequences of its accumulated offences. His work captures, in vivid and distressing detail, the cruelty that resulted when the South African government instituted an official policy of apartheid. But diagnosis is not the issue, nor is treatment. The "main complaint," the phrase that serves as the title of one of Kentridge's major artworks, is dealing with the distress that lingers even after the abuses have ceased.

Kentridge, who is South African by birth, exposes viewers to the appalling details and soul-wrenching complexities of apartheid. He invents dramatic narratives in which the fate of his fictitious victims and their fictitious oppressors rise and fall within factual political contexts. The characters are continually buffeted by such historic events as Nelson Mandela's release, in 1990, from a twenty-seven-year-long imprisonment; the first general elections in South Africa, in 1994, which brought Nelson Mandela and the African National Congress into power; and the Truth and Reconciliation Commission that granted immunity to perpetrators of apartheid in 1995. This geographic and temporal specificity is rendered all the more distressing through such formal attributes as the artist's choices of medium (darkly imagined charcoal drawings that serve as the basis of his animated films) and color (stark black and white occasionally punctuated by red and blue), and the tempo of his creation (drawn with the tense rapidity of an anguished soul) and process (an unrelenting reworking of imagery that epitomizes the obsessions of a guilt-ridden mind). Kentridge typically composes his scenes out of acute angles and skewed perspectives to augment these effects. He explains, "The single viewpoint of the head-on image is on shaky epistemological ground. The contradictions and dislocations are the interesting things, rather than the consistencies."[1] Together these elements converge to intensify the harsh actualities they represent. Thus, Kentridge's films are animated in a technical manner, but also in the raw emotions that propel them. In explaining the source of his inspiration, Kentridge insists that he does not illustrate apartheid, but that the drawings that serve as the basis for his films are "spawned by, and feed off, the brutalized society left in its wake. I am interested in a political art, that is to say an art of ambiguity, contradiction, uncompleted gestures and uncertain endings. An art (and a politics) in which optimism is kept in check and nihilism at bay."[2]

William Kentridge, *History of the Main Complaint* (1996), video still. Courtesy of the artist and Marian Goodman Gallery.

Kentridge's biography prepared him to serve as an envoy of the nationwide struggle to achieve forgiveness in the face of South Africa's anguished history. Kentridge is of Lithuanian and German Jewish descent. Both of his great-grandfathers were driven out of Europe by pogroms and sought refuge in South Africa in the late 1800s. Thus, even though his family is white, their history includes victimization by an official policy of malevolence directed against a targeted segment of the population. Perhaps this family legacy explains why his father, a prominent lawyer, defended victims of apartheid from the 1960s to the 1980s, and why his mother advocated for parity during apartheid rule. Kentridge vividly recalls his first encounter with the brutality that afflicted the majority of South Africa's population. "At the time, I was six years old and my father was one of the lawyers for the families of people who had been killed. I remember coming once into his study and seeing on his desk a large, flat yellow Kodak box, and lifting the lid off of it. It looked like a chocolate box. Inside were images of a woman with her back blown off, someone with only half her head visible. The impact of seeing these images for the first time—when I was six years old—the shock was extraordinary. I understood that the world was not how I had imagined it at all, that things happened in the world that were inconceivable."[3]

Kentridge's deep concern for the plight of black South Africans emerged out of divided loyalties and a dual identity. African by birth, European by descent, Kentridge was keenly aware of divergent cultural traditions, neither of which were wholly his own. Though a white man, he felt alienated from the European social patterns and cultural values that were imported into this colonial outpost, but he also felt detached from the native culture in the land of his birth. Kentridge's work is deeply enriched by this double perspective. It prevents him from adopting the tendency among some Europeans to romanticize old, tribal Africa by portraying it as a utopia characterized by spiritual healing, untamed nature, and virtuous people. "This idea of a pre-European Africa of innocence is firstly false and more importantly it obscures the strange contradictory relationship between Western conquest and the tribalism that still endures."[4]

Kentridge joined the South African resistance art movement that emerged in response to the infamous massacre of African patriots at Sharpeville on March 21, 1960. The fatal gunning down of dozens of peaceful African demonstrators became a poignant symbol of the repression. The events at Sharpeville were pivotal in the revolutionary struggle against white minority rule and colonialism throughout southern Africa. One of its effects was to rally artists, most of whom were African victims of apartheid, to publicly denounce the injustice being perpetuated against the black population. Kentridge joined their efforts in the 1970s, devoting his efforts to instilling social conscience and inducing political change. In 1994, apartheid was abolished, and all South Africans were charged with the thorny task of melding opposing histories into a unified "rainbow nation." Ironically, South Africa earned this affectionate nickname because of the variety of cultures, languages, religions, and nationalities represented by its citizens. Achieving a post-apartheid South Africa required that people at opposite sides of the racial divide become united by a single national identity. Since that time, Kentridge has summoned the power of art, film, and theater to facilitate this historic mandate for rich and poor, powerful and oppressed, boss and laborer, and to help transform their acrimonious past into a harmonious future.

In Kentridge's films, the horror of torture and dismemberment occurs within the internal domains of memory and conscience, not as it might appear in popular media accounts. He allows mental manipulations to magnify details, blur distinctions, condense time, connect disparities, and reorder chronologies. Thus historic details, as depicted by Kentridge, are rendered in terms of their impact on human lives, particularly the white industrialists who were wrestling with the lingering impact of motives that had suddenly become obsolete and excuses that had just been rendered criminal. Parallel psychic dramas were taking place among the victims who were asked to forget their sufferings, forgive their oppressors, and abandon their rage. Kentridge acknowledges that this historic drama is more psychological than political. "Facts are not simple. They bring a whole train of mud and slime with them, or like a comet, a train of frozen ice ahead of them. Facts are not fixed."[5]

Kentridge exploits the fluidity of animated film to convey these transformed and transmuted facts. In 1989, after working in film and theatre as a writer, director, actor and set designer, Kentridge created the first in a series of short animated films that include *Monument* (1990); *Mine* (1991); *Sobriety, Obesity and Growing Old* (1991); *Felix in Exile* (1994); *History of the Main Complaint* (1996); *WEIGHING...and WANTING* (1998) and *Stereoscope* (1999). As a filmmaker, Kentridge literally narrows the aperture of his camera as he figuratively narrows the aperture of his vantage point. The shattering events of the nation are essentially assigned to two white protagonists—Soho Eckstein, an avaricious industrialist, physically modeled on Kentridge's grandfather, a Labor Party politician who wore pinstriped suits, and Felix Teitlebaum, a sensitive, melancholic brooder whose face resembles the artist's. They are alter egos, symbols of the self divided by conscience. This pitiable pair is repeatedly buffeted by political cataclysms and psychological turmoil. The personalized narratives of their struggles with guilt, confusion, confession, emancipation, fear, and suspicion parallel the struggles transpiring on a national scale and provide the vehicle for addressing a collective moral awakening. As Soho's and Felix's histories accumulate from work to work, an epic drama unfolds narrating the half-life of the megaton emotional fall-out from apartheid.

In the films, Soho is always dressed in a pinstriped suit. Felix is naked. The crass materialist is thereby distinguished from the vulnerable fretter. Soho's personality as a bragging bombast is visualized as an accumulation of telephones and other communication equipment used by bureaucrats to augment their power. Felix, the sullen listener, is typically depicted with downcast eyes and wearing headphones. Thus, Kentridge personifies the conflicting sides of the conscience of white South Africans as they struggle to become reconciled with the new political mandates.

The word "complaint" in the title of a five-minute-and-fifty-second, 35 mm film called *History of the Main Complaint* displays the grievance, criticism, and protest that was occupying the South African population in the mid-1990s when the Truth and Reconciliation Commission attempted to negotiate a settlement between the

Interview with William Kentridge
By Lauren Harkrader

LH: What was the first indication that you were likely to become a recognized artist?

WK: It took me many years of being an artist to think of myself as an artist. For the first ten years that I was an artist I kept wondering what I was going to do in life. And then, all the other activities I tried were kind of calamitous. The only thing I was good at and the only thing that ever made me any money was drawing.

LH: Could you talk a little bit more about your education?

WK: I studied politics and history at Wits University in Johannesburg, and I studied theater in Paris. I learned more about being an artist from theater school and from my politics courses than I did from any art school. All the education I did in fine arts and in theater was at institutions that offered no degrees or certifications or diplomas. And that was a good way of getting into it.

LH: That's interesting. What was your first sale?

WK: My first sale was probably as a child to friends and family. The first solo show I had when I was twenty-four; it was a sell-out show. But then I gave up for four years, deciding I wasn't going to be an artist. I studied theater, only to discover I couldn't really be an actor. Then I spent some time in the film industry as a props assistant, which was hideous. I found myself back in the art studio some years later, and decided to see how long I could survive on the drawings I sold before I had to go back to working in the film industry—but I never had to go back. I was fortunate in that even before there was wide recognition, there was enough income to survive on.

LH: But you have delved into opera.

WK: I still do theater work. It's part of my artistic practice, doing theater, doing films, rather than a separate job to supplement my income. If anything, the drawings have to supplement my interest in working in theater and opera. I started making films in 1989, after having a number of successful drawing exhibitions. I made the first film in order to do something utterly different, that couldn't be exhibited or marketed. Today the films are sold as objects, and the drawings from them are sold, but the first time I sold anything from those films was five years after I started making them. The films I thought of as my private curiosity, but not the main part of my art practice. As it turns out, the films are the thing for which I have become most known, but this came about without me having any anticipation that they would have any value; I think that gave the work a looseness. It gave me the freedom to take risks.

LH: How do you assess the longevity of your career?

WK: I don't assess the longevity of my career. I assess the longevity of being able to keep working. I don't see my career as a construct, as if it's an instrumental thing that can be strategized. I have dealers to whom I can say, "This is the project I want to do," and they make it happen. The thing that's made me leave dealers is when I hear them talking about strategy. Once you

William Kentridge, *History of the Main Complaint* (1996), video still. Courtesy of the artist and Marian Goodman Gallery.

outgoing Nationalist government and the incoming African National Congress. As Mr. Dullah Omar, the former Minister of Justice explains, "a commission is a necessary exercise to enable South Africans to come to terms with their past on a morally accepted basis and to advance the cause of reconciliation."[6] The Truth and Reconciliation Commission's Report breaks the silence that surrounded the gross violations of human rights committed over a thirty-four-year period. Moving from town to town, it set up makeshift courts in churches, schools, and auditoriums where victims and survivors recounted their harrowing stories. The hearings permitted perpetrators to confess their participation in the atrocities in exchange for amnesty and immunity from prosecution. Kentridge's film explores the resulting anguish of reliving the horrifying events of the previous thirty-five years. His perspective is personalized. His approach is psychological. The film dares to raise the question of the era: Can reconciliation, once it has been accomplished as a formal court procedure, evoke comparable accommodation within the secret recesses of the human conscience?

In the film, this daunting task is assigned to Soho Eckstein, whose stout body lies unconscious upon a hospital bed. He is surrounded by a team of pinstriped doctors who look and dress exactly like him, suggesting that their patient's recovery can only be accomplished by self-diagnosis and self-therapy. Ten such doctors lay stethoscopes upon Soho to monitor the pulsing of his bodily systems. His vital signs register as flickers and beeps on a bank of up-to-date medical equipment. Xray, MRI, and CAT-scan probe the innermost being of this comatose man. The cause of his malady lays soul-deep within him.

What do they discover? The first evidence of the nature of Soho's illness appears as a trove of devices that epitomize the disproportionate impact of an industrialist's authority. Telephones, bells, typewriters, sirens, microphones, bullhorns, loudspeakers, and ticker tape machines churn ominously in his gut. Then the film probes Soho's mind for festering memories of dastardly deeds. Evidence appears as seen through the windshield of his car, observed through his eyes as he drives through the streets of Johannesburg and the South African landscape, a wasteland beset with billboards, tire tracks, dumps, mines, and other industrial detritus. A proliferation of red Xs mark sites of past violence perpetrated against the land as well as its people. The film explores Soho's responsibility for both.

In Soho's delirium, windshield wipers work fervently to clear the conscience and bring the past into focus. But grime continually accumulates on the glass, obscuring the scenes much in the manner that the mind represses painful memories. A brutal beating of a single black man by two white men occurs along the roadside. The wipers erase this horrible moment and the journey progresses into

subsume yourself to the market, there's good reason for the market to mistrust you.

LH: How do you feel about the art market at this time?

WK: I'm grateful that there are people who want to buy my work. But I quite like working in Johannesburg, 8,000 miles, 10,000 miles away from the art market.

LH: What would you say your most important exhibition has been?

WK: The most important exhibition that I've been a part of was Documenta X. If I were to name an event that transforms one's recognition in the art world, it would be Documenta.

LH: So that was the gateway to other things. How about in terms of sales?

WK: The interesting thing about selling works is that the price that is charged for a work or what is paid is largely dependent on the context of where the work is sold rather than the work itself. There is work sold in an artist-run space in town, and if you charge $2,000 it will be seen as expensive. If the identical work is on display at one of the smart galleries where it's for sale for $6,000, it will be seen as very reasonably priced. Why one piece of paper is worth $5,000 and another is $50 is often difficult to say. These contradictions are part of living in a commodified world—every object is split in two, between a non-exchange value and an exchange value, between its "real" value and the price.

LH: How are the costs of producing your work allocated?

WK: I wouldn't begin to know. A bookkeeper comes once a month and puts costs into different categories and then hands it over to the tax accountant who prepares my tax return. More comes in than goes out. With the theater productions, we need to get producers and sponsors and festivals and grants. The films are not expensive to make—I do them myself. The one thing I will never do is to write a project proposal, which is a good way of killing the work before it's begun. If I simply take a piece of paper and draw it and film it, I can practice my craft without it being dependent on the whim of anyone else.

LH: How has the choice of place to live and work affected your career?

WK: Initially it counted against me. During the 1980s my work was seen as that of a white South African and there was a cultural boycott of art from South Africa. The boycott was not total, but there were never expectations of South African art being able to find its place in the international art world. Throughout that decade I had the sense of being cut off. But at the same time, this allowed me to start developing these animations without any thought of how they fit into the international art world. The pressure of what else is being done is a nightmare for artists starting out in Europe or America now.

LH: What advice, if any, would you give to the current generation of aspiring artists?

WK: David Hockney once said he got noticed by making a point of having the longest title of anyone

the night, when suddenly the suppressed memory of a dark figure is dislodged and brought to conscious awareness. The figure runs into the pathway of the car and is flung into the air smashing Soho's windshield. Here Kentridge has chosen to illustrate two moments that are terrible for Soho to recall, despite the fact that in neither is he an active perpetrator. In the first instance, he is the witness. In the second, he is an unintentional murderer. Yet Kentridge notes that he is still complicit. "(Soho) didn't deliberately set out to do it. But at the end of the day, through his presence and through the presence of the other person, there is one dead body. He can't say, 'Well, it wasn't my fault.'... It's that sort of indeterminate position. He is the driver, and is somehow tied into and responsible for events that he is part of, even if he is not, as it were, forensically guilty of it."[6] The severity of Soho's physical condition is evidence that he is suffering from these events. His plight is typical of those white South Africans whose guilt is by default, not fault. Kentridge seems well acquainted with the discomfort of being "neither active participant nor disinterested observer. The work itself is so many excursions around the edge of this position."[8] As the film progresses, the dislodging of these painful memories jolts Soho out of his coma. He literally awakens from his unconscious state, no longer oblivious of the cruelty that has long surrounded him. The history of Soho's "main complaint" may be that he is now suffering from the pain that was mercilessly inflicted on others. Even if he never wielded a club, he contributed to the conditions for maltreatment and profited from them.

Throughout the film, viewers share Soho's perspective. Kentridge has positioned this evocation of memories from the perspective of the driver's seat of his automobile. From this vantage point, they gain a double perspective—one is out the windshield and the other is in the rearview mirror, which reflects Felix's guilt-ridden eyes, not Soho's. At this moment in the film, it appears that even a crass industrialist like Soho is capable of acknowledging complicity in the atrocities. He seems ready to be cured through redemption. Viewers are led to believe that perhaps white South Africans can be rehabilitated. But this hope immediately plummets into the sobering realization that both memories and their effects are of short duration. The next scene returns to the hospital. The curtains that surrounded Soho's bed open to reveal him seated behind the office desk he occupied throughout the years of apartheid. Surrounded by his old bureaucratic paraphernalia, he resumes active service as a fat cat bureaucrat. Heavy jowls, sleek hair, cigar stuck between his lips, as commanding as ever, Soho is restored but not reformed. Kentridge explains, "In the film, the question is: here's a person who's in a coma because of the weight of what he's seen, of what he's been through. Is that going to kill him? It becomes clear. No, people don't die from the guilt of their feelings or the weight of their memories—even though they ought to, perhaps. But they contain them. These memories may suddenly resurface in a crisis, but they get put away. So in the end, all the things that Eckstein has experienced get resolved or get reduced to mementoes on his desk, and he continues through the world. He's busy, but the sobering thing is, well, if he's just back and busy in the world, then what was the point of the whole journey?"[9] The film suggests that white guilt is both rare and ephemeral. Kentridge continues, "Here we are in the new society that's busy and bubbling. But what of all the pain that went into its making? Does that simply disappear? Do we forget about it or do we desperately hang onto it forever? It's a South African problem, but also a problem for all countries that have gone through major change. What do they do in East Germany with the Stasi, for example? What exactly is the balance between historical memory and forgetting in order to make a sane society?"[10]

Kentridge's probings into the particular circumstances of South African society exceed their specificity, arriving at the disturbing patterns of history that pervade the greater human experience and have yet to be resolved. Kentridge is not an ideologue. He offers no solutions because he remains in limbo between doubt and hope. His political position is mirrored by his technical means and reinforced by his formal decisions. He describes his idiosyncratic "drawings for projection" by contrasting them to traditional animation: "The technique I use to make films is very primitive. Traditional animation uses thousands of different drawings filmed in succession. This generally means that a team of animators has to work on it, and it follows from this that the film has to be worked out fully in advance. Key images are drawn by the main animator and in-between stages are completed by subordinate draftsmen. Still other people do inking and coloring. My technique begins with a sheet of paper stuck up on the studio wall. Halfway across the room is my camera, usually an old Bolex. A drawing is begun on the paper. I walk across to the camera, shoot one or two frames, walk back to the paper, continue and change the drawing (marginally), walk back to the camera, walk back to the paper, to the camera, and so on. So each sequence, as opposed to each frame of the film, is a single drawing. In all there may be twenty drawings to a film rather than the thousands one expects. It is more like making a drawing, albeit a gray, battered, and rubbed-out drawing, than making a film. Once the film in the camera is processed, the completion of the film—its editing, the addition of sound, music, and so on—proceeds like any other."[11] Although there is no spoken dialogue in any of Kentridge's films, *History of the Main Complaint* features a Monteverde madrigal, *Ardo*, which supplies an eerie, operatic soundtrack punctuated by sonar beeps, phones ringing, and the wail of distant sirens.

Kentridge takes advantage of charcoal's smudge-and-smear quality. Charcoal permits continual reworking. Frame by frame, the drawings are added to and parts are rubbed out. Traces of people, objects, and landscapes appear and disappear like memories. Residues of charcoal erasures accumulate throughout the process of reworking, allowing each drawing to record the effects of all the others that preceded it. Through this compositional strategy, Kentridge mirrors the real-life process in which current events are inevitably affected by past events. Charcoal permits instantaneous action and reaction. Crowd scenes, for instance, can be assembled as quickly as Kentridge can transfer his imagined scene into marks on a sheet of paper. His unusual technique captures the excitement of the first political processions that surged through the streets after 1989, the year of the political thaw in South Africa. The drawings both illustrate and restage the evolution of politics toward unforeseen conclusions, engaging equal possibilities for error and improvement.

Each six- or seven-minute film takes three to four months to create. Kentridge's demanding animation technique may be taxing on the hand, but it is therapeutic for a mind contending with colonial assumptions and postcolonial turmoil. "Drawing for me is about

on any group show in order to take up the most space in the catalogue. My rule number one—have something to say. The other is, do what you are good at and what you enjoy, and in the end people will respect you for it. Don't ask, "What needs to be done? What is the gap that is waiting to be filled? What are the pictures the world needs?"

LH: One final question—what communication channel is best suited to reach your intended audience?

WK: Have around you people whose opinions you respect and who are supportive of you. Don't keep knocking your head against someone whose inner voice dislikes what you are doing. Make the people who already love what you do your primary audience.

fluidity. There may be a vague sense of what you're going to draw but things occur during the process that may modify, consolidate, or shed doubts on what you know. So drawing is a testing of ideas, a slow-motion version of thought. It does not arrive instantly like a photograph. The uncertain and imprecise way of constructing a drawing is sometimes a model of how to construct meaning. What ends in clarity does not begin that way."[12] Kentridge's assessment of life and politics is also reiterated in his primitive film technique. The disjuncture between the images visualizes life experience as an uninterrupted flow of incomplete sensations and contradictory impulses. Daily living is characterized as a contest between the desire to maintain stability and the pressure to change.

In addition to these short films, Kentridge creates prints, drawings, video sculptures, operas, plays, and puppet shows that testify to the tireless fervor of his explorations and the consistency of his approach. *Shadow Procession* (1997), for example, greets viewers with the resounding celebratory sounds of marching music accompanying a lively procession of silhouetted cartoon figures. But the joyful intonations of the first impression quickly succumb to the sobering realization that this parade of figures is an endless stream of fleeing refugees lugging their belongings across a barren landscape. Kentridge approaches the collective conscious. Viewers are left to ponder the universality of South Africa's history. Subjugation and emancipation, guilt and confession, trauma and healing are themes that are applicable to a distressing number of situations—personal and political. For example, race relations remain problematic in the United States despite the fact that a century and a half has transpired since slavery was abolished. Although Kentridge provides no resolution, he assures us that, "To say that one needs art or politics that incorporate ambiguity and contradiction is not to say that one then stops recognizing and condemning things as evil. However, it might stop one being so utterly convinced of the certainty of one's own solutions. There needs to be a strong understanding of fallibility and how the very act of certainty or authoritativeness can bring disasters."[13]

[1] Carolyn Christov-Bakargiev, *William Kentridge* (Brussels: Sociéte des expositions du Palais des beaux-arts de Bruxelles, 1998), 17.

[2] Dan Cameron, Carolyn Christov-Bakargiev, and J.M. Coetzee, *William Kentridge* (London: Phaidon Press, 1999), 14.

[3] Christov-Bakargiev, 28.

[4] Cameron, et al., 108.

[5] Christov-Bakargiev, 17.

[6] Dullah Omar quoted in editorial by Avery Lee, <http://www.angelfire.com/ak3/apartheid/trceditorial.html>.

[7] Roger Taylor, "Memento Mori," *World Art* (Melbourne), May 1997, 49–50.

[8] Cameron, et al., 3.

[9] Taylor, 49.

[10] ibid.

[11] Cameron, et al., 114.

[12] ibid., 8.

[13] ibid., 34.

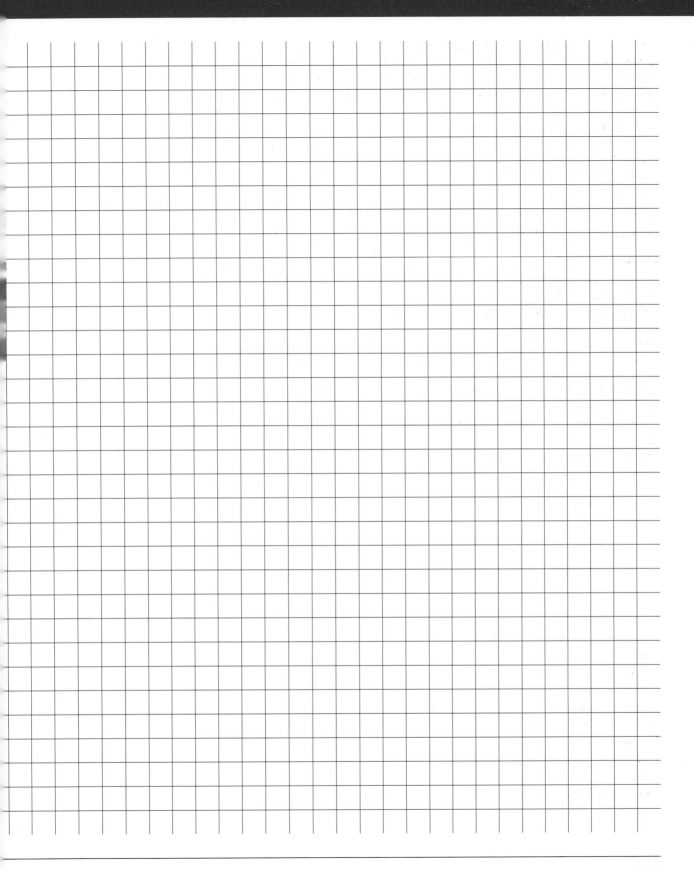

EXTERNAL SOURCES OF INSPIRATION:

The Kaleidoscope of Black Experience

Chris Ofili

Born 1968 Manchester, England
1987–1988 Thameside College of Technology, London, foundation course
1989–1991 Chelsea School of Art, London, BA, fine art
1991–1993 Royal College of Art, London, MA, fine art
Lives and works in London

Chris Ofili's paintings dazzle the eye. But each painting ultimately gains credence as a repository for the manifold influences that affect his life and the lives of most black people living in predominantly white cultures today. His canvases represent four giant springheads of inspiration: Africa, Europe, popular culture, and the fine arts. Each creates a separate stream of thematic and stylistic references that flow according to specific value systems, sets of symbols, and aesthetic constructions. Ofili attempts to make this torrent of divergent inspirational sources coalesce. But by combining these massive inspirational sources, he also divides. Cultural collisions among his viewers often erupt. The controversies instigated by Ofili's paintings apply to art and society as a whole. They demonstrate that misinterpretations abound when divergent cultures attempt to co-exist. At the same time he proves that the outcome of such cultural mixing can be rich and rewarding.

In order to protect the painting that is the topic of this essay, the Brooklyn Museum of Art placed it behind a thick pane of shatterproof Plexiglas and surrounded it with a rope partition. In addition, visitors to the appropriately titled *Sensation* exhibition (1999) in which it was shown, were required to pass through metal detectors. The infamous painting, *The Holy Virgin Mary* (1996), attracted protesters representing the Catholic League, the Knights of Columbus, the Madonna Society, the Vietnam Veterans of America, the Ancient Order of Hibernians, the New York Civil Liberties Union, Jews for Morality, mainstream politicians, religious leaders, and unaffiliated moral arbiters. Using such contentious words as "sick," "blasphemous," "sacrilegious," and "vulgar," they accused the artist, Chris Ofili, of Catholic-bashing and denigrating the dignity of art. The press rushed into the fray, and for weeks the public was transfixed as the media chronicled the ensuing drama of protest demonstrations and court rulings.

Not all the press was critical. Amid seething indignation and threats of sabotage, a remarkably restrained description of this controversial painting appeared in the *Amsterdam News*, an influential African American newspaper in New York. It read, "Chris Ofili portrays Mary as a rather exciting Black with impressive eyes, a hint of breast upon which a piece of dung has been placed signifying nourishment, the color of darkness, a broad nose and a sensuousness not generally assumed when one sees the Eurocentric version of Mother Mary."[1] The sanguine tone of the Amsterdam News journalist was a product of sensitivity to black values and aesthetics. The Association of Art Museum Directors, the American Association of Museums, the American Federation of Arts, and the Art Dealers Association of America also issued expressions of support. These organizations rallied behind the artist to proclaim his right to free expression and to acclaim the work's artistic merits. They enjoyed tracking the work's sources within European and African cultural traditions. African Americans delighted in the painting's funky rhythms, sexy references, saturated colors, and dazzling textures. They shared the artist's appreciation for popular music, movies, fashion, and street style. The enthusiasm of these advocates, however, was more than matched by the

Chris Ofili, *Holy Virgin Mary* (1996), 8 x 6 feet, acrylic paint, oil paint, polyester resin, paper collage, glitter, map pins, and elephant dung on canvas, with two elephant dung supports. Courtesy of the artist and Victoria Miro Gallery.

gut-wrenching revulsion of those whose faith was based on the virgin's quintessence. The artist apparently identifies with them all. Each of the categories of source material that appealed to these different audiences is enumerated in Ofili's own description of his painting:

"I wanted to make a '90s version of the Holy Mary, an in-your-face '90s version of Christ's mother. All the shapes of her dress and her hair are vaginal shapes, flowery. I was going to the National Gallery, Sainsbury Wing and looking at Van Eyck's paintings of mother and child. I just wanted the image of the breast really. The exposed breast is hinting at mother-hood but those images are very sexually charged. She's painted as this beautiful, passive, angelic woman, pure and very attractive looking. I think the Virgin Mary was an excuse for pornography in the homes of these holy priests and God fearers. So I think in the '90s a version of it would allow the pornographic images to come more to the surface. These spherical shapes around her, I was thinking of them like butterflies flying around, but somebody else saw them as angels flying around her so what would have been angels are now replaced by bum shots clipped from magazines. I really think it's a very beautiful painting to look at, full of contradictions, which is perhaps why it's been misunderstood."[2]

Assembling the aesthetic and thematic sources embedded in Ofili's *The Holy Virgin Mary* is not merely an academic exercise. It elicits Ofili's embrace of the breadth of black popular culture, especially those aspects that contradict the presumption that political correctness instills respect and that religious observance produces virtue. He eagerly penetrates any space where blacks are present: the grimy streets of London's ghettos, the plains of Africa, television and movie studios, editors' desks, popular music performances, and mainstream life in America and Europe. Equal representation is allotted to the kaleidoscope of black experience. Ofili mixes, matches, and processes images in the same manner that hip-hop artists manipulate samples of recorded music. He too exploits the vast opportunities for creative recycling present in contemporary culture, highlighting those aspects that reflect the black experience and the individuals who are at the forefront of the black community.

A primary reason why Ofili's painting ignited indignation on both sides of the Atlantic is missing from Ofili's description of his work, but was broadcast in a New York Post headline: "NO DUNG DEAL—Museum to sue city over art flap."[3] Elephant dung is a substance most Americans associate with foul smells and filth, not the Virgin Mary. Ofili reports that his initial impulse to incorporate this unconventional material in a Christian context stemmed from his inability to capture the emotional and optical intensity of his experiences in Zimbabwe. Ofili had visited Africa on a British Council scholarship, a trip which provided him with an opportunity to reclaim his African heritage. Although Ofili spent his entire life in England, he was conceived in Nigeria to Yoruba-speaking parents. The beauty of Africa's land and its wildlife affected him as deeply as the disturbing remnants of European colonialism. In frustration, he threw a lump of elephant dung at his canvas and discovered in that impulsive act the visual impact and thematic complexity he had been seeking all along. Thus began his practice of incorporating dung into his artwork—not straight out of the elephant, but hermetically sealed in glistening resin and decorated with tiny map pins. "I'm interested in ideas of beauty," he explains, "And elephant dung in itself is quite a beau-tiful object. But a different sort of beauty. And I want to bring the kind of beauty and decorativeness of the paintings together with the apparent concept of ugliness of the shit and put them together and try and make them exist."[4] But the dung carried more signifi-cance than that of an aesthetic contest between beauty and ugliness. Thematically, it introduced a practice of venerating dung as a symbol of regeneration that is common among some indigenous African tribes. Ofili adopted the substance's exalted African meaning by ornamenting it and presenting it in a sacred context. In *The Holy Virgin Mary*, one dung lump serves as the Virgin's breast and two lumps form the floor-supports on which the painting rests. With humor and irony, Ofili explains why. "Somehow it makes the painting feel more relaxed, instead of being pinned upon the wall like it's being crucified.... [The painting can] stand in its own shit and watch the other paintings being crucified on the wall."[5] (Ofili generously shares credit with the donors of the dung, Liang-Liang and Geetza, residents of the London Zoo. In fact, his gratitude is such that, in February 2002, he donated $105,000 from the sale of a single painting to Whipsnade Wild Animal Park for more spacious quarters and a play area for these productive elephants.)

Ofili's adoption of African artistic practices was not limited to his racial bonds. As a British citizen, his cultural roots are European. Africa's rich visual language liberated him from Western forms of representation, as it did for Matisse, Picasso, Brancusi, Modigliani, Gauguin, Derain, Vlaminck, Kirchner, Nolde, and innumerable other contributors to the evolution of Western art. In addition to discovering the medium of dung, he returned from Africa enriched by a compositional element that has become a hallmark of his style. "The dot making process started in 1992 when I visited Zimbabwe and saw these Matapos cave paintings, one wall, six-feet high and twenty-feet long, covered with yellow, red, and blue dots, made with a sharpened twig and pigments, made by someone who didn't go on the hunt, made where there was music. It's an abstract wall, early abstraction, nothing concrete, translating a state of mind into something visual through a repetitive dot making process."[6] Through this encounter, Ofili's artmaking acquired the aura of Africa's sacred, ritualistic craft tradition. Dots scurry up and down his canvases in veins of pulsating, life-enhancing energy. Like his African predecessors, Ofili's work seems invested with the capacity to unleash the power of African gods and evoke the spirits of its ancestors, a task it audaciously performs within a sacred Christian context.

Ofili may have imposed elements of his African heritage upon one of the most revered images in Western art, but he simultaneously invested his version with the hallmarks of a classical European masterwork. This impulse stems from his familiarity with Catholicism and his education in British art schools. The European theological and artistic orthodoxies that he absorbed are apparent in his work's resemblance to the manner in which Cimabue, the great thirteenth-century Florentine painter, elicited the Madonna's saintly qualities. Indeed, a description of Ofili's *The Holy Virgin Mary* could also describe Cimabue's *Enthroned Madonna and Child* (c. 1280). In both paintings, the central figure of the Virgin is shaped like a large, blue triangle that is circumscribed by undulating lines. Her form floats without substance in a horizonless, golden expanse that releases her from grounding in the mundane world. An array of circular forms bestows her image with ornamental luxuriance while a proliferation of tiny striations shimmer in majestic splendor.

Ofili's connection to Catholicism exceeds art historical references, but he is not a typically observant Catholic. "I was brought up a Catholic and was an altar boy. I believe in God, but I'm not dominated by it. We all studied math, but we don't go around spewing numbers. Religion should be used in the appropriate way."[7] Ofili reportedly hung a sign outside the entrance to his London studio that read, "This area is being constantly watched and patrolled by the Lord."[8] Ofili said he made the sign for the addicts who regularly smoke crack in his doorway.

The influence of Europe is also apparent in Ofili's special relationship with Francis Picabia, a more irreverent representative of this fine-art heritage. Picabia was a renowned French artist who was active in the first half of the twentieth century. Ofili explains, "[Picabia]'s

Giovanni Cimabue, *Madonna and Child Enthroned* (c. 1280). 12.75 x 7.2 feet, tempera and gold on wood. Courtesy of the Galleria degli Uffizi, Florence, Italy/Bridgeman Art Library.

been a long time inspiration actually. He laid out all the possibilities."[9] Although Ofili delights in Picabia's ability to stimulate the optic nerve, the artist is not just a formal influence. As the prototypical bad-boy artist who thrived on controversy, cultivated the ridiculous, inserted nonsense into serious contemplations, and capitalized on the opportunity for artists to be libertines, Picabia established a precedent for linking refined art with the grim world of contemporary sexism, racism, drugs, and prostitution.

The Holy Virgin Mary is both artistically correct and politically incorrect. In his zeal to include all contexts in which black people are present, Ofili depicted Mary with the exaggerated Negroid attributes found in racist cartoons and typecasts of black sexuality. Her revered chastity is replaced by the seductive provocation of lips, nostrils, and eyes that seem to beckon the viewer in as brazen a manner as a hooker might solicit a client. Even her dress is configured as a series of vaginal forms. In addition, because the holy child is absent from Ofili's representation, Mary's exposed breast is presented as a token of erotic titillation, not maternal lactation. Porno magazines further augment Ofili's repertoire of controversial tactics. He depicts the Virgin surrounded by crotch shots and pairs of buttocks that are cut out and pasted on to the canvas like tiny fluttering butterflies or cherubs. "I wanted to juxtapose the profanity of the porn clips with something that's considered quite sacred. It's quite important that it's a Black Madonna. I concentrated more on bum shots and rear crotch shots in a way, playing with the sexuality of the Holy Virgin Mary, wanting to really pull it right up to the forefront."[10] In all these ways, Ofili blatantly reappropriates the stereotypes that have long been used to denigrate his people. By refusing to indulge in the indignation that has become expected of artists of African descent, Ofili provides equal opportunities for both the black and the white members of his audience to be offended.

In Ofili's painting, the Virgin Mary was updated for inclusion within the cultural climate of the 1990s. She is not, however, a jeans-and-sneakers kind of woman. Draped in long robes, she blatantly displays the seductive femininity of Lil' Kim, the New York rapper whose poster hangs on Ofili's studio wall. Only 4'7" in heels, this tiny powerhouse decks herself in the clichés of female glamour and personifies predatory sexuality. In the poster, Lil' Kim appears in a glossy purple wig cut to ear level on the right and shoulder level on the left, sporting Batman glasses, multiple necklaces, a bare shouldered dress, green lipstick, talon nails, and the like. By assigning Lil' Kim's assertive style of dress to the Virgin Mary, Ofili revised the revered Virgin, transforming her into the prototypical sassy lady. Ofili explains, "One of the starting points [of *The Holy Virgin Mary*] was the way black females are talked about in contemporary rap."[11] Typically, they're called "bitches" and "hos" in a gangster slang that flaunts violence, nihilistic pleasure, and misogyny. Likewise, Ofili configured his Virgin as a "bad-ass" action heroine.

ADDENDUM: Space limitations prevented the following sources of inspiration from being included in this essay: South Bronx, Electronica, Coffy, Foxy Brown, Hit Man, Shaft, Spider-Man, Superman, Pam Grier, Tarantino, Darius James, Melvin Van Peebles, Missy Elliot, Left Eye of TLC, Da Brat, Angie Martinez, Mobb Deep, Snoop Doggy Dogg, NWA (Niggaz With Attitude), Wu Tang Clan, Marvin Gaye, Curtis Mayfield, Jimi Hendrix, Noel Redding, Ishmael Reed, Bob Dylan, Alice Coltrane, Angela Davis, Huey P. Newton, Erica Huggins, Bobby Seale, Black Panthers High Command, Sly Stone, Larry Graham, Cynthia Rose, Carlos Santana, Pharoah Sanders, Marsha Hunt, Eddie Hazel of Funkadelic, Black Lightening, Luke Cage and Black Panther, Gordon Park, *Shaft*, Prince Paul, De La Soul, Gravediggaz, The Psycho Realm, Missy Elliott, Notorious B.I.G., King's Cross, Lonnie Mack, the fathers of blues rock, Stan Lee, Marvel Comics, Power Man, Robert Beck a.k.a. Iceberg Slim, Voodoo, the Jackson Five, the Harlem Globetrotters, Philip Guston, George Condo, Jean-Michel Basquiat, David Hammons, *Mothership Connection*, Black Audio Film Collective, Sun Ra, Lee Perry, George Clinton, Octavia Butler, Samuel R. Delany, Juan Atkins, Derrick May, Michelle Nichols; Lieutenant Uhura, *Star Trek*, Super Trooper, Big Daddy Kane, the popular slang term "Pimpin' ain't easy," "It's a Big Daddy Thing," "Dreams of fuckin' an R&B bitch," Quincy Jones, Tiger Woods, Michael Jordan, Evander Holyfield, Scottie Pippen, Louis Farrakhan, Michael Jordan, Naomi Campbell, Kenny Scharf, Peter Halley, Ashley Bickerton, Mike Kelley, John Miller, Gilbert & George, Piero Manzoni, Robert Gober, Satan, Miss Black America, Muhammad Ali, George Foreman, *When We Were Kings*, Rob Hallam, Donald Cammell, Susan Sarandon, Wendy Wasserstein, Jane Alexander, Judge Nina Gershon, Dennis Heiner, William Blake, Rudolph Guiliani, Saatchi, and Frank Stella.

The primary influence that Ofili claims to borrow from hip-hop, however, is the permission to march across cultural borders with impunity. "I always think of the work as coming out of hip-hop culture, which is an approach to making things and looking at things with no hierarchy. Everything just gets everything. The site has been bombed out, anyway, and you just bring whatever you want to it. And that's the way I see the situation with art and painting. The whole thing's just been kind of blown apart, and it's wide open for me to bring anything and everything to it. I don't want to say that this is above that, or this is more important than that. The elements just exist as they are, as individual things. But at the same time, once they're put in that new context, they become something else."[12]

Since every influence has its own influences, it is worth noting that both gangsta rappers and Ofili cite the "blaxploitation" films that first appeared in the 1970s as a significant cata-lyst. These films brandished amorality as the strategy for deliverance from poverty, rejecting the optimism of older Civil Rights advocates who believed in reform through constitutional change. Ofili's generation rejects their policies as whimpering, dawdling, and indecisive, and replaced them with bold images of gangsters, pimps, players, and pushers filmed amid glittering opulence. Ofili reports, "I bought tickets to this blaxploitation season at the National Film Theater in London. I went to every film. It was just so virulent. Nigger this, bitch that, tits and ass everywhere.... My project is not a P.C. project, that's my direct link to blaxploitation."[13]

Yet Ofili's intentions, like his sources of inspiration, defy pigeonholes. "In the end, I'm trying to bring something up out of the rubble that's pleasing to look at. And in a way, what I'm trying to do is to promote contradiction because that's the reality of the everyday. One side of the street is this. You cross the street and things change. Instantly."[14] Ofili not only attempts to make dung and its scatological connotations, and sexuality and its pornographic connotations coalesce with a sacred image. He also tries "to make it more and more beautiful, to decorate it and dress it up so that it is so irresistible, you just want to be in front of it."[15] The extravagant beautification process used to make The Holy Virgin Mary required under-painting a background of bright patterns in orange and gold, on which Ofili painted a mosaic-like image of the Virgin, and then added sinuous linear contours to define it. He embellished this embellishment with collaged magazine cut-outs, sprinkled glitter, and splashed translucent polyester resin to invoke a luminous and radiant image. The visual opulence of his Mary suggests yet another source of inspiration—the aesthetic of lower-class neighborhoods—where residents decorate their homes with brocade upholstery, lace doilies, shag carpets, and plastic knick-knacks. Moreover, Ofili admits a fondness for JET, a kitsch-saturated Afro-American magazine founded in the 1950s. "I love the fact that it hasn't changed. I don't really read it. It's source material. It's just informa-tion. It's like listening to some really bad rock music."[16]

The motive behind Ofili's thematic riffs, stylistic crossbreedings, patchwork aesthetics, cultural promiscuities, and multiracial kitsch is, in the end, to demonstrate that there is no unilateral measure of black experience. "So, it's about critique. It's about the way the black woman is talked about in hip-hop music. It's about my religious upbringing, and confusion about that situation. The contradiction of a virgin mother. It's about the stereo-typing of the black female. It's about trying to make a nineties hip-hop version of the Virgin Mary that would include, therefore, everything that I think she's about. It's about beauty. It's about caricature. And it's about just being confused. But at the same time, it's about not being uncomfortable with that state of mind, and seeing that as a full palette rather than just black and white. So, you know, it's the gangster coming out with his full clip."[17] But presentation is incomplete without its reception. "The most important thing is what people bring to the work, really. Not necessarily what the work is giving out to people. I mean, that's from my point of view, because I make the work and I put so much of what I know into it. But then, I think it's also a mirror. It allows people to see themselves and reflect their own ideas in the work.... If there is a function for the work, it is to allow people to see it's a magnet, a magnet for people's thoughts, ideas, and arguments, and hopefully, it will allow people to feel free to disagree with themselves. Not necessarily with others. But to allow them to think one thing and then to think another thing completely openly. And freely. And not to be so intent on right and wrong."[18]

[1] Wilbert Tatum, "A Black Madonna: Guiliani's Worst Nightmare," *Amsterdam News*, editorial, 30 September 1999–6 October 1999, 1.

[2] Kodwo Eshun, "Plug Into Ofili" in *Chris Ofili* (New York and London: Southampton City Art Gallery and the Serpentine Gallery, 1998).

[3] "No Dung Deal: Museum to Sue City Over Art Flap," *New York Post*, 29 September 1999, front page.

[4] Benjamin Ivry, "'Modern art is a load of bullshit': Why Can't the Art World Accept Social Satire From a Black Artist?," *Salon*, 10 February 1999. <http://www.salon.com/ent/feature/1999/02/10feature.html>.

[5] ibid.

[6] Eshun, n.p.

[7] Carol Vogel, "Chris Ofili: British Artist Holds Fast to His Inspiration," *New York Times*, 28 September 1999. <http://mbhs.bergtraum.k12.ny.us/cybereng/nyt/ofili.html>.

[8] ibid.

[9] Eshun.

[10] ibid.

[11] ibid.

[12] Paul D. Miller, "Deep Shit: A Conversation with Chris Ofili," *Parkett* 58, 2000, 165.

[13] Eshun.

[14] Miller.

[15] Lynn MacRitchie, "Ofili's Glittering Icons," *Art in America* 88, no. 1, January 2000, 99.

[16] Eshun.

[17] Miller.

[18] ibid.

First Moments in Art History

Hubert Duprat

Born 1957 Montpellier, France
Lives and work in Claret, France

Hubert Duprat reviews the history of art, seeking inspiration in the transforming innovations that periodically redefine the practice of art. One example involves the primeval efforts to make flint tools. Another is the invention of photography. Duprat demonstrates that the motives of artists who resurrect art history can include emulating, reinterpreting, defying, or surpassing previous artistic accomplishments. In addition, Duprat demonstrates that special advantages accrue to new art that is inspired by historic precedents. It is automatically assigned a place in the narrative constructed around its renowned originators and the legacy of masterpieces they created. In addition, it is included in the considerations of their followers, researchers, and interpreters.

No degree of independence can liberate an artist from the grip of art history. Whether this relationship is inadvertent or deliberate, precedents and predecessors factor into their work. In some instances they are default components of an artist's work. In others they are crucial motivating factors. For example, conventional artists seek inspiration from the means, themes, images, and forms that comprise the annals of art; they tend to engage history as a great storehouse of tantalizing models to emulate and to honor. Maverick artists often view the long chronicle of art as a catalogue of romanticized accomplishments that merely invites mockery; they vanquish nostalgia by initiating new traditions. Competitive artists view art history as a territory rife with rivals to exceed and standards to surpass; they retain the vitality of a tradition by stretching and teasing it to reflect evolving conditions. These diverse manners of relating to art history can be stimulated by recent and remote traditions, by celebrated masterpieces and obscure works, and even by artworks that have already earned the prefix "neo" or "retro" because they, too, renew some preceding form of art. Each antecedent equips younger generations with not one, but a field of possible operations.

Hubert Duprat's ongoing homage to artistic antecedents is made manifest in the vast library of art history books that he has amassed. These volumes of volumes abound with photographs and descriptions of the alluring prototypes offered within his profession. Yet Duprat has cultivated a special relationship to art history. Instead of accepting the conventional Western narrative that traces art's unfolding across the centuries, Duprat bypasses established chronologies. He conducts an independent search for art's absolute inception and the subsequent moments when history-altering innovations occurred. Although Duprat is a self-taught artist, these scholarly discoveries inspire his artistic creations, his reactivations of the wondrous inceptions of art. Duprat has explored, for example, the first principles of two- and three-dimensional rendering and the first mechanization of the imaging process. This broad engagement with his profession has led him beyond the parameters of art into territories normally identified with archeology and even entomology.

The introductory chapters of most art history surveys locate the earliest form of painting deep in the caves of southern France and northern Spain, during the Paleolithic period. The texts describe the irregular walls of these subterranean caverns where, in perfect stillness, by the light of burning animal fat, using reed and bristle brushes, early humans created dynamic representations of beasts. The texts proclaim how they captured the physical

Hubert Duprat, *Les Bêtes* (1993–1999), 12 x 18 inches, silex (flint). Courtesy of the artist. Photograph: Frederic Delpech.

First Moments in Art History: **Hubert Duprat**

bulk of the animals as well as the minute details of their anatomies, and then suffused the images with the vigor of life itself. But for Duprat, these early creative manipulations do not mark the absolute inception of art. In his search for the first image-making impulse, he imagined the era prior to art's commonly recognized commencement. Invoking the circumstances of the lives of these earliest humans, Duprat inferred that the prototypical artistic act was conducted by prehistoric beings arranging their hands between a blazing fire and a wall to create compelling silhouettes of recognizable creatures. Shadow casting required no tools, no mediums, no technical knowledge. It had no precedents and there-fore it is likely to earn the title of being the most archaic of all image-making practices. To Duprat, it marks humanity's auspicious entry into the world of artistic creation.

Duprat's deductions coincide with the narrative attributed to Pliny, a Roman credited with providing the explanation for the origin of art within the Western cultural tradition. Before he died of asphyxiation while investigating the eruption of Mount Vesuvius in A.D. 79, Pliny wrote an encyclopedia that included a history of the fine arts. This chronicle begins with a story about the daughter of Butades of Sicyon who traced the shadow of her lover on her wall and then asked her father, who was a potter, to preserve the image by applying clay to the outline.[1]

But Duprat's search for the original impulse that drove humans to not just create images but to preserve them in material form bypasses Pliny's narrative. The artistic impulse to create an art object, he believes, was inaugurated in the tool-making practice known as the core tradition. Core tools were formed by knocking chips off one edge of a water-worn stone. The flakes were discarded and the core, with its new and contrived shape, was preserved as a tool for cutting and scraping. Duprat would argue that the moment in the forming of material substances, when consideration of proportion and design was annexed to utility, marks a milestone in the evolution of early humans. He honors this inspiring event by reviving the carving technique within his own artistic practice. "The flint tool interests me because it's the first artifact."[2]

Duprat created a series of artworks based on his reconsideration of shadow casting and flint-shaping, but his trip back in time was not motivated by a nostalgic longing for a bygone era. Instead of quoting this antediluvian past, Duprat renews it by integrating the oldest artistic impulses with one of the newest technical capabilities. Like his primeval predecessors, Duprat decided to fashion flint. But his ambition was to exceed their accomplishments by shaping large chunks of the material into delicate and precise contours. Flint is a fragile material, even more brittle than glass. Each layer of its struc-ture contains a record of past events, revealing a fire in the forest or some other environmental circumstance. It breaks under the slightest percussive pressure at precisely those points where disturbances once occurred. As a result, it is conducive to flaking but thwarts attempts to form a large, accurately contoured mass. Today, however, an array of powerful fashioning implements exist that early humans could never imagine as they tapped the mother stone with antlers or a rock. Duprat integrated the distant past with the proximate present by using sophisticated electric tools whose cutting action oper-ates through pressurized water. Even with the aid of this tool, it required five years of intense experimentation before Duprat mastered the technique of carving large flint sculptures of approximately 11 x 14 inches in size. "For my project I purposely mixed epochs. Works in flint which are actually polished and sized all at once don't exist in the prehistoric corpus. This is a way for me to at once create a more fascinating object by the mélange of these techniques, but also, and especially, to distinguish my own from archeological objects, because for me it isn't a question of imitating prehistoric production... It isn't about the creation of a fictional archeology."

The images Duprat materializes in flint are created by hands configured to cast shadow silhouettes of animal heads. Thus, Duprat pays homage to three of art's felicitous beginnings. Form (cast shadow) derives from the earliest creation of visual impressions. Medium (flint) references the first human fabrications. Technique (carving) traces a surviving tradition to its origin. In order to prevent the viewer from being distracted from these sources of inspiration, Duprat intentionally refrained from creating elegantly rendered or amazingly life-like images. It is significant that the entire series is simply entitled *Les Bêtes* (The Beasts) (1992–1999). Duprat explains, "This somewhat childish and vague title is imposed because ideally I prefer that one can't clearly distinguish the animal whose profile one is viewing. It has to stay an animal, without a doubt, but whether it seems to be a goat, a dog, a deer, we won't be able to know." In this manner, Duprat folds the past into the present, modernizing the history of art as he revives its advents.

Duprat's quest to locate art's beginnings has led him backward in time. But it also led him to look outward, including examples of aesthetically sophisticated and meticulously crafted material fashionings that are excluded from standard chronicles of the history of art. He includes a type of artistic construction that originated before the human species had even evolved and that continues to this day. This construction is carried out by tiny insect larvae. Duprat discovered its remarkable capabilities as a twelve-year old who enjoyed making aquariums that recreated marine ecosystems. He recalls, "I was able at that moment to discover the prodigious ability of the Trichoptere larva." Popularly known as caddis flies, these larvae construct tube-like casings assembled out of leaves, sand granules, tiny pebbles, twigs, and bark scavenged from the streambeds of their habitat. In order to adhere these elements together, the larvae's bodies secrete adhesive silk. The tiny insects are skilled processors of material, constructing their edifices around their bodies using techniques that resemble the human crafts of masonry (building by assembling units of material) and wickerwork (construction with twigs or reeds). Once the cavities are sufficiently solid, the larvae begin dragging their protective casings along with them, laboriously searching for food. Later the chambers are sealed. Within these protected spaces they metamorphose into moths. Camouflage and protection do not, however, seem to be the sole motives of these aquatic carpenters. The results of their efforts are stylistically varied and painstakingly crafted.

Are caddis flies artists? Are their cocoons works of art? In a series entitled *Larves aquatiques de trichopteres avec leur etui* (1980–ongoing), Duprat raises such questions by inviting these creatures into the art museum and encouraging them to conduct their creative manufacture on location. In the space where a painting might be hung, the artist suspends a wall-mounted aquarium within which larvae busily drag the sheaths that they have been cutting and shaping, arranging and fastening, according to their normal nocturnal schedule. But the artist has modified their efforts. Duprat replaced the larvae's twigs and pebbles with gold leaf, opalescent pearls, brilliant turquoise, blue sapphires, deep red rubies, and glistening diamonds. These simple creatures accept the precious gems as their building materials and conduct their construction in their usual manners. After approximately thirty days, the larvae have created exquisite jewel-like casings.

Natural history merged with art history when Duprat removed the caddis fly larvae from nature and relocated them within an artistic context, thereby expanding the field of art to include the work of insects. Duprat approached each larva as a fellow artist, not a

Hubert Duprat, *Aquatic Caddis-fly Larvae with Case* (1980–2002), approx. 1 inch each, larvae, gold, precious stones. Courtesy of the artist. Photograph: André Morin

SOURCING INSPIRATION

scientific specimen. Duprat explains, "For me, it isn't about setting up in the museum of natural history or about making any such scientific experience into art." Instead, he states, his goal is to provide "an emotion, a surprise, a wonder." Although the larvae's protective cocoons had become sumptuous aesthetic artifacts that many art collectors would covet, Duprat refuses to sell them. Instead, he dismantles the cocoons after each exhibition and reuses the gems in the next installation.

Despite the momentous impact of their activities, the creators of the source objects for *The Beasts* were unaware that their efforts would ever be designated for entry into the field of art traditions. Formed flint expands the reductive approach to sculpture known as carving. Shadow castings append the catalogue of two-dimensional depictions of the three-dimensional world. Insect cocoons augment the additive approach to art-making known as assemblage, an artistic technique that involves assembling and composing diverse materials into a unified form.

Duprat's exploration of momentous art events is also evident in a photographic series that explores the first mechanized transmission of an image. Entitled *The Rise of Images* (1983-ongoing), this series required that Duprat transform his entire studio into a primitive camera. He sealed his studio from all light save for that which penetrated a single pinhole opening. Through this hole, images of the exterior entered the studio interior. They appeared on the room's opposite wall, upside down and reversed. This projection verified the laws of optics, first discovered in the fifteenth century, that led to the invention of the camera obscura, which means "dark room" in Italian. The camera obscura is the precursor to the modern camera and marks another first in the history of art.

By permitting artists to trace the outlines of the projected forms, the camera obscura guarantees an accurate transmission of the spatial complexities of a three-dimensional environment upon a two-dimensional surface. For Renaissance artists, it also verified the laws of linear perspective. This geometric system organizes every object in a setting according to its relationship to a single ocular point. Photographs, too, register scenes from a single point of view. Linear perspective and the camera obscura exerted an immense influence on the subsequent history of Western art, particularly on those traditions in which artists attempted to render the three dimensional environment in two-dimensions with empirical accuracy.

Duprat reenacted this revolution in artistic image-making by transforming his entire studio into a camera obscura. The images of antennae and roofs and chimneys that exist outside his studio entered through the tiny opening in his wall and were deposited onto the wall opposite the opening where they overlaid its doorways, floors, and moldings. This composite image also included the shadow of the camera that Duprat set up to record the complex layering of exterior impressions on top of interior objects. Upside-down converged with right side-up. Left crisscrossed right. Likewise, black-and-white was transformed into color, a process that required the intermediary of a camera. Duprat explains that the projections entered the studio in gray scale; color was captured "only by grace of a very long exposure time (sometimes nearly an hour) which re-established the color." In the final photographs, the transparent colors of the sky and other outside objects are superimposed onto the opaque colors of the interior woodwork and walls. "This history of not seeing directly what one is photographing, of not sharing the reference with the spectator, was for me very close to the experience offered by the images of the Pioneer or Voyager probes...I attempt to imitate...the visual aspects of the photographs from these satellites, the filming of our own atmosphere."

Hubert Duprat, *L'Atelier ou la montée des images* (1983/85), 31 x 47 inches, cibachrome. Courtesy of the artist.

SOURCING INSPIRATION

The unfathomable and enigmatic quality of the finished photographs is further enhanced because a very long shutter time yields a record of the movement of the sun. In this way, another artistic tradition is alluded to. These still photographs capture the passage of time and the movement of objects. They are animated like movies. In this way each layered photograph recapitulates the historic progression in image-making that originated with the camera obscura and resulted in modern photography, film, and today's media explosion.

Duprat's unorthodox explorations of the art history are neither reactionary nor reverential. Instead, he revives some of art's wondrous occasions, enriching current art practices by realigning them with the first attempt to recreate an observed form, the first impulse to create an imagined form, the first effort to register a human memory in material form, and the first mechanical recording of a two-dimensional visual impression within three-dimensional space.

OPINIONS

[1] Pliny the Elder, *The Elder Pliny's Chapters on the History of Art*, trans. K. Jex-Blake (London and New York: MacMillan. 1896), XXXV, 151.

[2] Unless otherwise noted, all quotes from Hubert Duprat, letter to author, trans. Jacob Bacharach, September 2000.

EXTERNAL AND INTERNAL SOURCES OF INSPIRATION:

History, Geography, Sensuality, Cosmology

Thomas Joshua Cooper

Born 1946 San Francisco, California
1969 Humboldt State University, BA, studied art, philosophy, and literature
1972 University of New Mexico, MA, art with a concentration in photography
Lives and works in Glasgow, Scotland

Thomas Joshua Cooper photographs the sea. But the visual characteristics of a location are not the sole determinants of where he sets his tripod and how he aims his camera. The physical features of a site are less significant to Cooper than the human events that transpired upon it. Thus, he applies this eye-dependent medium to a prolonged intellectual process that involves amassing information about history, geography, climate, and mythology. From the initial decision to commemorate an event, through the research required to support this endeavor, to the journey to the location where the event occurred, to the culminating snap of the shutter, Cooper draws alternately upon both internal and external inspirational sources. Some sources of inspiration excite his intellect, while others increase his visual acuity, arouse his sensual engagement with the setting, and awaken his visionary perceptions. The final image is enriched and compounded by these divergent impulses.

Art occupying the forefront of today's avant-garde is so wide-ranging, even straightforward black-and-white photographs of seascapes can be eligible for inclusion. Thomas Joshua Cooper's images of oceans and rivers qualify as contemporary art despite his conventional subject matter, his use of an 1898 field camera, and his perpetuation of such traditional values as meticulous craftsmanship, precision, and modest scale. Furthermore, his avant-garde status prevails despite an old-fashioned reverence toward human accomplishment and natural wonders. These inspiring motives are garnered from the great quadrants of human experience: history (the narrative of human accomplishment and action); geography (the ground upon which the events comprising this narrative transpired); sensuality (receptivity and perceptivity toward time and place); and cosmology (the magnification of reality into a mythic zone). Cooper's photographs are grand visions presented in modest material form.

The first two sources of inspiration are located in the world of recorded events and measurable locations. The latter two sources of inspiration originate in deeply internalized impulses that are metaphorical and metaphysical. Together they account for Cooper's extension of photography beyond such customary procedures as the capture of a random and instantaneous perception and the recording of a preconceived and constructed image. Furthermore, he exempts his work from the norms established for photography by romanticism, documentation, and formalism. These aspects of conventional photography are replaced by a magical synthesis that propels his apparently straightforward images well beyond their photographic precedents.

The following narrative by Cooper provides an example of his creative process and discloses his unique approach to photography: "Many photographers gathered to photograph the eclipse that occurred in Great Britain in 1999. They were concerned about the weather. Clouds and rain could ruin their photographs. That is because they were working celestially—their perception was raised skyward. I didn't care about the weather. I concentrated on the terrestrial impact of the eclipse—the eerie light that bathed the land. I don't give a damn about the sky. It does not have history embedded in it. I never work in wildness. I am interested in a sense of history—cultural, and geographical, and geological. My work is 99 percent activated by human activity. That is why it is so important to me to exclude the sky. My images are horizonless. I'm interested in the interiorization of viewing and living space. Take away the navigational aid of the horizon, and you create a different psychological construct. I want to become part of the earth, the land—to stay long enough for it to reveal its secrets—to see the invisible. It took me twenty-five years to figure out how to be the artist I wanted to be, twenty-five years spent exploring my relationship to the landscape."[1]

To commemorate the impact of this extraterrestrial event upon a terrestrial setting, Cooper located himself at the southern tip of Great Britain and devised a means to record the eclipse as an earthly event by photographing the limits of human experience that it afforded. The eclipse lasted a total of forty-five minutes. Cooper captured four images to embody the sequence. The first was shot in total daylight the day before. The second was shot at the first instant of the eclipse's impact on the earth. The third recorded total darkness. And the last documented the final instant of the eclipse's impact on the earth. Together they comprise a work entitled *Eclipse from the World's Edge, August 11, 1999* (1999). Since the southern tip of Great Britain has both an east coast and a west coast, Cooper traveled in synchronous manner with the moon. In order to arrive on time on the westernmost tip of Great Britain, a helicopter sped him twenty-one nautical miles and dropped him on a rock. He finished the exposure with thirty-five seconds left before the sun began to reemerge. Instead of observing the eclipse, Cooper and his camera participated in its drama, its mobility, and consequently its wonder.

Long before Cooper picks up his camera, he determines a theme for a project and a manner of visualizing this theme photographically. The thematic preoccupation of his *Indication Pieces* (1994–ongoing), for instance, pays tribute to those rare individuals who journeyed to the edge of possibility. From this vantage point they turned away from all that was familiar and dared to imagine the unimaginable. Each historic instance entails people who not only surveyed the limit, they proceeded to explore, inhabit, or occupy the unknown. Some of the events commemorated in Cooper's photographs are based on historical events or periods. They recall the renowned explorers who expanded the known world and added entire continents to the European territory: Leif Ericsson, who discovered America in A.D. 1000 for the Norse; Magellan, who, during the Renaissance, risked falling off the edge of the world to circumnavigate the globe; Jacques Cartier and Samuel de Champlain, who explored the New World for the French. All paved pathways for the great migrations and colonization that followed. Cooper also honors those who forged paths of consciousness. He pays homage to the achievements of great inventors (Guglielmo Marconi), great writers (Herman Melville), great thinkers (Henry David Thoreau), and great artists (Richard Serra).

Interview with Thomas Joshua Cooper
By Zoe Feigenbaum

ZF: What was the first indication that you thought that you were going to become a recognized and respected artist?

TJC: One of the first sales was, to my great surprise, to one of my very famous inspirations, a woman named Imogen Cunningham. She was one of the great American photographers. In the mid-sixties she and a critic friend of hers named Marjorie Mann each bought a picture. I was a kid and they both paid a very legitimate price. I was absolutely floored. I offered them the pictures of course, but they really wanted me to have the payment. It astonished me that people that I admired so much would bother. And it taught me that even though you might not be well known or famous, an artwork speaks no matter the position or background of the maker. It is a sacrifice to actually part with your money. Art needs to be seen in relation to food and shelter and clothing. Payment equals commitment. So, as these first pictures sold, it was wonderful. It was extraordinary. That first sale was like a first kiss.

ZF: When was your first exhibition?

TJC: It was in a bank or library, anywhere that I could show the pictures. It was all very modest to begin with. Get them out into the public. See what happens! It didn't take much time to move through unofficial spaces into art spaces. But those first shows were in banks and libraries. It was stupendous. I couldn't believe that the pictures on those walls ultimately belonged to me.

ZF: What would you consider the most significant sale you have ever had?

TJC: Every time an artist makes a sale it helps them to facilitate more work and more opportunities. The bigger sales are the better ones in that regard, because they give you more opportunity. They allow your family a little less difficulty. They allow your friends less hassle because you are less weird. The aim is to sell as much as possible for as long as possible for as much as possible. In order to do that you have to make good work more and more often. However, at a very crucial time in my life, in 1978, Sam Wagstaff met with me for the first time and bought twenty-five to thirty pictures. It was a miracle. It saved me, literally. So his faith and belief in me made that sale immensely important. I still remember it with the greatest gratitude.

ZF: Are there some people who you feel promoted your career when you were still unknown?

TJC: There are a bunch, actually. Early on, a very great American painter, who recently died, named Morris Graves was of singular importance in inspiring me and helping me get started. My early teachers were of greatest importance to me. My first teacher was an artist named Tom Knight. Another great friend and teacher was Roger Cinnamond. Yet another great teacher was the photographic historian named Beaumont Newhall. And finally, of huge importance to me was the last person who really was a teacher to me, a

Thomas Joshua Cooper, *An Indication Piece. Cabot Strait – Looking N., N.E. – Towards the New World. Cape North, Cape Breton Island, Nova Scotia, Canada 1999-2001 (One of the two Northernmost Points of Nova Scotia – and along the site of John Cabot's Canadian discoveries and explorations of the New World for the English)* (1999-2001), silver gelatin print, selenium toned. Courtesy Sean Kelly Gallery, New York. Photograph: Wit McCay.

These remarkable individuals expanded consciousness, laying the grand boulevards upon which Western civilization journeys to this day. Cooper also honors nameless heroes and heroines such as the pilgrims who ventured across the oceans in search of new beginnings. Even remarkable acts that occur in mythic legends are commemorated. Cooper once set his camera at the edge of a cliff that overlooked a waterfall in Iceland into which, according to Celtic lore, tribal elders routinely plunged to achieve a direct path to Valhalla, the great hall in Norse mythology were the souls of heroes were received. Courage, the sacrifice of self, the determination to pursue dreams—these acts inspire the artist and are lodged in his photographs to restore the spirit of the viewer. In addition, Cooper is inspired by the grandeur of nature's own creations. In order to acquire intimate knowledge of the Rio Grande River, he traversed its 2,000-mile course from headwaters to mouth, not once but many times between 1994 and 2000. In this manner he prepared himself to honor the river photographically.

Prior to considering the perceptual aspects of a photograph, Cooper undertakes an elaborate process of identifying, locating, and researching a transforming instant in the annals of history. He seeks the precise historic moment when human consciousness opened to new vistas. He studies records to establish the accurate longitude and latitude of the locations where knowledge was altered forever. He surveys historic records to calculate with exactitude the rocky promontory that provided the last glimpse of the known world as people embarked toward uncertain fates. He peruses detailed maps that describe each inlet and cliff and ledge that comprise the jagged coastlines where great ships navigated. He studies the mythic histories and spiritual traditions attached to these locations. History, geology, geography, and literature guide him in determining the instant of significance that ultimately inspires his work. Lengthy titles accompany each image to identify the actual location and the actual historic event that transpired there, information that greatly enriches the viewer's experience of a seascape or waterway that does not otherwise reveal its historic significance. An image of a misty sea becomes charged with the human drama that once transpired in that location through its title:

The English Channel—Looking S., S.W.—Towards the New World.

Rame Head (Number 2), Near Plymouth.

Cornwall, England, 1998-2001

(The Last View of the English Coast that the Pilgrim Settlers would have had upon their leave-taking from England for the New World)

Another title is equally detailed:

Cabot Strait—Looking N., N.E.—Towards the Old World

Cape North, Cape Breton Island

Nova Scotia, Canada, 1999-2001

(One of the two Northernmost Points of Nova Scotia–and along the site of John Cabot's Canadian discoveries and explorations of the New World for the English)

man named Jim Kraft. Also older photographic artists like Imogen Cunningham. I was tucked under the wing of a lot of people and I owe them greatly. Currently I am looked after best by my gallery in New York, Sean Kelly. Peter Bunnel at Princeton University is another one of my godfathers. Two other people of great importance to me would be the director of the DIA Foundation and the director of the Lannan Foundation. I am remarkably indebted to these people.

ZF: How did you make these connections with these people who were going to help you later on?

TJC: I started my career in the middle of nowhere as a country bumpkin in Northern California. I got lucky. It was an entire accident. People now go to great lengths to network, and it's one of the necessities of postgraduate education and, increasingly, undergraduate art education. I don't know how to do it. I've never done it, I'm not good at it, and I don't give a goddamn about it. I meet people through my work and we gravitate or not toward one another. Sometimes, when I was younger, I sent fan letters or just thank yous to say to artists how much their work meant to somebody like me who they would never ever know. Ironically, I occasionally met those same artists. However, it was out of the devotion and deep admiration for their work, rather than a particular desire to become friendly with the artists themselves. I was too shy to do that. I wouldn't have known what to do. Early on Morris Graves allowed me to establish a brief but very important friendship with him. The same way with Imogen Cunningham and Ansel Adams and Edward Weston's last wife, Caris Wilson Weston. These people were amazingly kind and generous to a nobody like me. They seemed to like my work. That inspired me and it really did give me courage.

ZF: How would you say your work gets marketed? Is it through an agent, dealer, or someone else?

TJC: The mercantile relationship between art and artist to the external world is an absolute necessity to deal with. Art is a business. Any artist who doesn't deal with that doesn't survive as an artist. There is no question about that. I am not a good businessman. I work with some people who are extraordinarily adept at it. In my case, in America it is my gallery, Sean Kelly. They move the work into the appropriate contemporary art context with dignity. I can't do that and I don't think that it is my job. My business is to make pictures with enough authority and clarity to absolutely validate the process that the gallery engages in with their clients.

ZF: Can you describe your studio?

TJC: I live in the studio day and night when I'm working. The studio consists of where I am sitting right now. An office with maybe five thousand books in it. Maybe six thousand, including fifteen different dictionaries which make me happy. Every single map of Great Britain, and most of the detailed maps of Europe, and all of the detailed maps of the American coast. So there's maybe two thousand maps. So that's a room where I can write and think and read and research. And then there's a

Thomas Joshua Cooper, *A Premonitional Work. The North Atlantic Ocean – Looking N., N.E. – Towards the Old World. Race Point, Cape Cod, Massachusetts, USA 2000-2001 (The Northernmost Point of Cape Cod)* (2000-2001), silver gelatin print, selenium toned. Courtesy Sean Kelly Gallery, New York. Photograph: Wit McCay.

In the second phase of Cooper's creative process, learning becomes experiential. He visits the precise spots upon the Earth where these momentous events occurred. Several visits might be required before his explorations reveal the optimal site and the exact conditions capable of embodying its accumulated history. Hiking over rough terrain, enduring the discomforts of wind, rain, and cold, Cooper willingly travels the globe to pay homage to those who made history and advanced consciousness. The sites that serve as his formal photographic subjects, therefore, are determined by their historic significance, not by their visual appearance. If his seascapes are majestic, it is because they resonate with the unobservable narratives of human hope, terror, and valor. "My photographs are meditations; it is as simple as that ... they are more the products of a revelation than that of actual direct documentation of place."

Cooper's commitment to each predetermined task is absolute. Practical difficulties are ignored. For example, he arrived on the Nova Scotia shore, a location he had never before visited, with the intention of positioning his camera at the precise site of John Cabot's discovery of the New World for the English. This meant teetering on the last toehold of a cliff that marked the outer limit of the entire North American continental mass. At other times, Cooper has stood chest deep in water, or leaned precariously over a cliff. He is always alone when he takes his photographs. In all these ways, Cooper consciously preserves the emotional intensity once felt by travelers as anchors were raised and sails were hoisted, or by drowning sailors as they caught their last glimpse of land and life. He explains, "I don't swim and I don't sail. I choose not to learn. I'd rather not. I have taken something from old sailors, if you fall in, you belong to the sea. It claims you." Danger is an essential component of Cooper's working process, because fear has positive effects: it intensifies perceptual acuity, increases visceral sensitivities, and generates ardor. "One time I wanted to be surrounded by water," recalls Cooper. "So I climbed up on a rock and waited for the tide to come in. I had never been there before. I waited for hours. I could have been submerged." In these ways the sea regains its attributes as a fearsome force churning from unfathomable depths. The camera's position enables viewers to join the photographer, as he joined those who contributed to human history, in standing at the edge of nothingness. And from this vantage point, they observe a dimension far greater than themselves.

In addition to the inspirational benefits he derives from fear, Cooper also benefits from self-imposed technical encumbrances. He works with crude, old-fashioned technology, as if to reenact the adversity confronted by the photographers of yesteryear whom he honors. For example, he rejects the modern convenience and sophistication of new cameras, preferring to use a bulky 1898 field camera that has only a single lens. Together with its tripod it weighs over sixty pounds. Second, he pledges that if an image is unsatisfactory, he

small room with a slide table above a chest of pictures where I can think about pictures. I also teach. I try to figure out ways to communicate the life of pictures and the meanings of pictures to myself first and then hopefully on to students. There is a small studio area where I work on putting the work together in its physical form. There is a room specifically for proofs so that I can look at what I am doing and try and figure out how the pictures work. And then a darkroom where everything I do happens. I make all of the pictures in this darkroom. In the darkroom I develop the negatives and the prints and do all that. It's in four or five rooms. So, it's very compact but extremely functional. I work twenty-four hours a day on the pictures from here.

ZF: Do you have any assistants?

TJC: I am very fortunate. The man that I work with, David Bellingham, is so talented that I would never call him an assistant. He is certainly an associate and a friend and a man that I have worked with happily now for twelve years. He is a much better artist than I am.

ZF: How would you say the cost of your work is allocated?

TJC: Just recently I figured that each picture I make as an edition costs nearly $4,000. I don't even count rent. Just on the material and travel basis alone and then the cost of working with my friend and colleague. Recently my New York show had sixteen pictures in it. So multiply sixteen by $4,000; that's how much it cost me, just in materials, to make the show. It's crazy because of the incredible hard work and labor I put in. If I factored in rent and other things, I couldn't afford to make it work. When you figure that if a show cost me $50,000, the expense needs to be recouped before you have even gotten to the point, overall, where it is now possible to move forward. I'm finally at a point where that is happening. But for a long, long time that didn't happen, and I financed that work through my life as a teacher, through the inevitable use of a Visa card—the remarkable debt mountain—and occasional access to grants. The rule is, it seems, spend first, get paid much, much later.

ZF: Do you only teach to supplement your income?

TJC: Teaching is how I supplement my income. I am, however, an absolutely dedicated teacher. I think the necessity to be a public servant and to have a calling to this profession of teaching is really important to me. I do teach because I love it and because I think it's a great privilege to be in contact with young and sometimes not-so-young visually creative minds.

ZF: Do you have a mortgage?

TJC: I have a mortgage the size of the Empire State Building.

ZF: Health insurance?

TJC: The whole lot. And I'm an older person with a young family. I am twenty-five years behind everybody else of my age. And this simple personal fact puts great pressure on me to achieve for the continual well-being of my family.

ZF: Do you do anything now to enhance the value and appreciation of your work in the future?

Thomas Joshua Cooper, *A Premonitional Work. The English Channel – Looking S., S.W. – Towards the New World. Beach Head, The South Downs, Sussex, England 1997-2001* (1997-2001), silver gelatin print, selenium toned. Courtesy Sean Kelly Gallery, New York. Photograph: Wit McCay.

SOURCING INSPIRATION

will never return to that location to try again. Third, he refuses to bracket his images. Bracketing is a common photographic process used to optimize the possibility of producing a successful photograph. It involves taking many shots of the same image varying only the shutter speed or some other element. Instead of this hit-or-miss approach, Cooper considers all his options, then chooses one. Fourth, he never travels with extra film. He prefers the care associated with risk to the comfort derived from having a back-up. Fifth, he often chooses to photograph under conditions of maximum obscurity, which also means maximum difficulty. Lastly, and most importantly, Cooper clicks the shutter only once at any given location. He explains, "I believe in the one take. I don't rely on the light meter anymore. I know what to do. It is intuition and practice. Furthermore, I never alter the negatives. When I work in the darkroom translating the negative to print, I will not let a picture get away. I am in the darkroom sixteen to twenty hours at a stretch working on a single image. I am joyful if I get one picture a day. I may use one-thousand sheets of paper to make seventy-five prints." During the darkroom procedure, Cooper subtly tints each image with indigo or burgundy to enhance the work's luminosity.

These self-imposed technical strictures are often applied to particularly challenging situations, such as his decision to photograph the convergence of significant geographic, seasonal, and celestial events that occurred at midnight in midsummer at the Arctic Circle. Under Arctic conditions, exposure time is uncertain. Instead of relying on equipment, Cooper's photographic readings are based on intuition and sensitivity. Visual obscurity is not a disadvantage. He has noted that minute impressions accumulate when he subjects the film to long exposure time. Under these conditions, for example, his camera has coaxed into visibility events occurring beneath the thresholds of ordinary perception, like a subtle disturbance of the tides. In this manner an undersea rock appears in the photograph like a specter rising from the darkness.

Having explored history, geography, and the sensual components of a site, Cooper introduces the fourth inspirational source—the cosmological realm that offers a metaphysical explanation of the nature of the universe. Although photographers are presumably allied with the visible environment, Cooper penetrates beyond the appearance of the physical world and the human events that occur within it. Cosmologists have long satisfied the human urge to locate our origins and determine our destinies by assigning values to the cardinal points on the globe. In this manner cosmology gives form and meaning to an otherwise chaotic world. Cooper integrates this ancient wisdom into his photographic process. He provides a concise explanation for the symbolic psychology of place. "The compass acts as metaphor," he says. "West is always promise. It is a symbol of opportunity. North is always fearsome, hostile and foreboding. The East, in almost all primitive orienteering, talks about

TJC: All of the work is made to the very highest museum standards. I think there are far too many pictures, too many things made by everyone. So, when I let something out into the public it is as fine as I know how to make it, and that enhances the value.

ZF: How do you assess the longevity of your career?

TJC: I assess the longevity by my physical stamina, as well as my intellectual acuity. I reckon I've got twenty to thirty years of work left unless an accident in the field happens and I get killed or messed up. So I have projects on my mind for twenty years at least and I am very, very focused.

ZF: What role would you say school played in your preparation to become an artist?

TJC: [Laughter] Quintessential! I am a product of the university system. I come from a background where there was no genetic possibility of even thinking about fine arts. My brother is a logger. My brother-in-law was a fisherman. My father was a rancher. It was an accident that I became an artist. It is entirely due to the university that I moved into the fine-art world. It changed my life and much for the better.

ZF: How has your choice of a place to live and work affected your career?

TJC: Dramatically. I left America for the first time when Richard Nixon was elected. I left to go to England. I left England when Maggie Thatcher was first elected. I returned to the United States because Carter was here, and I thought there was a hope. I then went on a walkabout to Mexico and Australia and back when Ronald Reagan was elected. I figured that was the end of life for me and consequently went to Scotland. Living in a small English-speaking country on the edge of mainland Europe is probably the best thing that ever happened to me. Scotland is far away from the silliness of capital cities, yet I can work in London or Paris or Rome or Madrid or New York or San Francisco or Los Angeles. The plane service is perfect. I can be anywhere in the world in ten hours. It has probably kept me away from some amazing foolishnesses that I might have otherwise gotten myself involved in.

ZF: Do you have any regrets about decisions that you have made about your career?

TJC: I have a bad temper. When people push me they have to be ready to fight. I realize that perhaps that is not the best way of responding to things these days. I'm not sure if that's regret. I don't think I regret anything in real terms. It will sound corny, but my wife's a Quaker, and I guess I do regret not being a better human being because I live with such a great one. But I am the way I am, so regrets are pretty futile.

beginning and wisdom.... Primitive people and I share the belief that the directions are opportunities. Moving West is a symbol of opportunity, promise. It tells the history of poor people, displaced people who found new life—where people have a chance. [Moving westward] entirely relates to Celtic minorities, racial minorities, religious minorities, people who have been excluded and were transported to other places. Cosmology can't actually be seen in [my] pictures. Perhaps you can feel it. I use it to equate our experience to what older peoples have believed in." Cooper strives to assure that his photographs participate in the exchange of spiritual energies. His *Ceremonial Dwelling (Tribal Offering Area)*, for example, was not exhibited for twenty years in order to protect the spirits and the people it represented.

Cooper's awareness of the earth as providing a sacred context for human life is made manifest in the ceremonial quality of his artistic process. Most photographers perceive landscape in terms of mass and shadow and form. Cooper performs more like a visionary. His eye discerns the spirit in the land and the energies in the sea, its mythic and its human histories. Perhaps his metaphysical connection to nature can be traced to his experience growing up on Sitting Bull's reservation in North Dakota. "When I was seven," he tells, "I was inducted into the Ogalala branch of the Sioux. It scared the hell out of me. My mother is white. My father is Cherokee. One day my father woke me up and said, "We have to go. You have to do something. It will hurt you, but if you cry, I'll hurt you more." And in this way he recalls the bloodletting ceremony, conducted by an old man in a darkened room, which marked his initiation into his tribe. His father got cut first. Then the boy received a vertical cut in the wrist, leaving an indelible awareness of the intensifying and unifying effects of ritualized behaviors.

The great quadrants of human experience convene within the frame of each of Cooper's photographs. These photographs confirm that people absorb energy from the land, but they also demonstrate that the land absorbs the energy of people. A bit of shoreline resonates forever with the force of a deed enacted upon it. This insight suggests a disturbing implication—if the impact of humanity's heroic and ingenious acts is so intense upon the earth, then the impact of human carelessness and greed must be equally profound. There is a dire warning implicit within these inspired testimonies to human achievement. Discretion is needed in our interventions upon the natural world. Cooper's photographs layer spiritual guidance upon human history, and history upon nature. As Cooper has written, "Remember all you have seen. For everything forgotten is given back to the circling winds."[2]

[1.] Unless otherwise noted, all quotes from an interview with the artist, January 23, 2001.

[2.] Thomas Joshua Cooper, *Dreaming the Gokstadt* (Edinburgh: Graeme Murray, 1988), n.p.

CRAFTING AN ARTISTIC "SELF"

CRAFTING AN ARTISTIC "SELF"

INTRODUCTION

Vanessa Beecroft, VB 35, *Solomon R. Guggen-heim Museum, New York, 1998* (1998).
© Vanessa Beecroft. Courtesy: Deitch
Projects, New York.

CRAFTING AN ARTISTIC "SELF"
INTRODUCTION

Does the face that peers out from your photo ID define who you are? Have you ever asked yourself, "Who do I want to be?" Of course, people create themselves through clothing, hairstyles, and cosmetics, tattoos, piercing, and body shaping. But new prospects for identity construction now clutter the cultural horizon. The current marketplace abounds with body-transforming hormones, plastic surgeries, and cross-gender reassignment operations. Digital imaging has made chameleon-like transformation possible with a mere mouse click. Cybernetic communication devices allow people to disembody. Constructing an identity on the Internet is unencumbered by any physical counterpart. These tools provide opportunities for people to extend the actualities of their biographies and genetics. The right to free imaginative invention of a self has earned cultural consensus. Fabrications have ceased to carry the onus of dishonesty, affectation, or duplicity. Some people even use T-shirt selection as an opportunity to proclaim past achievements never earned (sports-team affiliation), journeys never taken (remote and glamorous), associations never realized (Ivy League education or blue-color employment), or events never attended (renowned concerts). Deciding who to be has become an open invitation for creative ingenuity. Many artists are capitalizing on the enormous latitude that has been granted. Their constructed selves may be obviously fictitious or sly deceptions, playful or solemn, idealized or demonic, revelations or camouflages, aggrandizing or castigating, fulfillments of desire or simply public relations ploys.

But even the artists who have chosen to stick to the facts of their biographies can't avoid engaging in option-selection. This is because even accurate projections involve selecting definitive traits from the infinite array of possibilities and then crafting these traits into functional identities. Some artists select one all-abiding trait by which they wish to become known. Others orchestrate several. Each item on the following list of identity constructors is available for selecting and combining: gender, age, sexual orientation, nationhood, region (rural, suburban, urban), race, body type, religious affiliation, state of health, economic status, profession, political beliefs, and education. This list is not comprehensive, but it serves to demonstrate that it would be difficult to give equal credence to all the entries on this extensive inventory. Thus, the process of identity construction can involve adding and subtracting. Desirable elements that are invented or borrowed are added. Extraneous facts and experiences are subtracted. Quotation marks accompany the word "self" throughout this introduction in order to emphasize its mutability.

Because style, theme, process, and medium are all affected by the artist's "self," the importance of identity in art's creation is obvious. But knowledge of the artist's "self" is also vital to experiencing art, especially now that artists have gained the freedom to craft their own identity instead of upholding traditional roles. Looking at a work of art by an artist whose "self" is not identified can be as unsettling as receiving an anonymous letter or telephone call. Biography is key to unraveling artistic meaning. For example, a reference to blood in a work of art is clarified by knowing if the artist is afflicted with AIDS, or recently experienced combat, or just gave birth. As traditions in art have eroded and dispersed, they have also eroded and dispersed the traditional characteristics of artists. Acquiring such knowledge complicates as much as it enriches both the process of making art and the process of viewing it.

But there is another component of "self" in this equation, the one that applies to art viewers. Each entry in the above list of biographical components can also apply to members of the art audience. A viewer's "self" influences responses to works of art as much as an artist's "self" affects their creation. For both groups, "self" shapes opinions, behaviors, appearance, loyalties, desires, ethics, and pet peeves. Likewise, "self" is not static for either group. Issues of authenticity and factuality are continually being reshaped and reassembled as lives evolve. People mature, experiences accumulate, lives are relocated, relationships are formed and broken. Fortunes are earned or lost, health improves or deteriorates, faith is found and lost. All the while, past experiences are being forgotten, altered, and embellished. Each event transforms definitions of "self."

The stereotype of the artist working in the European tradition brings to mind an ego-driven individualist. In actuality, ego plays varying roles in the articulation of an artistic "self." One variable involves the degree of self-involvement. Egocentric artists are self-centered; egotistical artists are significantly egocentric; egomaniacal artists are extremely egocentric. But, it is also possible for artists to construct their "selves" without relying on the perspective of the first person singular. An altruistic ego, for example, sacrifices personal comfort, health, and security to perform public service. "Wego" is a term invented to indicate a plural version of "ego." It is activated when an artist's individuality is replaced with some collective identity such as an African American eco-feminist, or a homosexual male intellectual. The term "wego" also applies to artists who choose to conform to a predecessor or a historic style instead of asserting their individual wills. It is equally applicable to artists who collaborate or form collectives. But it is also possible to expunge both individual ego and communal forms of ego from art. This occurs when artistic "selves" embody the universal essence of humanity. These "wego" artists often submit to mystical or godly sources of inspiration. Finally, an alter ego, or alternative ego, is a double, the counterpart of the ego. It provides another "self." Meanwhile, artists who rely on their superegos preserve cultural models of behavior. But there are also supercilious egos (arrogant), super-cool egos (sophisticated), superficial egos (shallow), superstar egos (famous), and superlative egos (preeminent).

For artists, "self" knowledge is sometimes discovered through the process of creating art. For other artists, establishing "self" is a prerequisite for creation. Artists are at liberty to truly liberate a "self" by assuming extravagant disguises and enacting outrageous behaviors. But personal choice and individual experience can also be tempered by cultural context. Issues that dominate the news, determine public policy, occupy social critics, attract philanthropy, and inspire rallies are extra-personal situations that can contribute to determining which aspects of "self" gain ascendance. As an example, femininity and masculinity became defining qualities for artists influenced by the emergence of gender politics, while health and sexual orientation surfaced as "self" definers during the AIDS crisis. Thus "selves" change as individuals rub up against cultural conditions.

In sum, each person is granted the liberty to determine who is the "I" who pledges allegiance; who announces "I do" at a wedding ceremony; who hereby promises to honor, or protect, or protest; and who creates and observes works of art.

Nan Goldin

Born 1953 Washington, D.C.
1977 Tufts University, BFA
1978 School of the Museum of Fine Arts, Boston, fifth year Master's Certificate,
photography
Lives and works in Paris, France

Nan Goldin's compelling photographs demonstrate that the human impulse to assert
individuality co-exists with the complementary human impulse to form deep and abiding
social connections. Goldin's identity is a composite of interwoven, lifelong friendships,
not a singular construction. Such "self"-related concepts as privacy, individuality, independence, and self-expression seem irrelevant to her life and her artistry. This becomes evident
in the emotional candor of the people who serve as her photographic subjects, but also in
the bathroom functions and the bedroom intimacies they enact in front of her camera.
These ongoing, multidecade, close-knit friendships expand Goldin's notion of self in the
same manner that they enlarge the tradition of self-portraiture to include the entwining
of mutual fates.

Everyone dies, but some people tempt death, living day by day in a race against unfavor-
able odds that they may or may not have chosen. Nan Goldin and her friends belong in the
former category. As youths during the 1970s, they reveled in the glam-rock scene. Tragically,
their numbers were diminished by AIDS, drugs, and suicide. Those who survived gradually
slipped into punk despair as they dealt with the aftermath of their experimentation.

Goldin's camera has been her enduring partner throughout these trials. Its lens has seized
the passing moments of these turbulent years. Photography is an extension of both Goldin's
eye and her spirit, releasing her grief, quelling her psychic turmoil, bonding her with those
she loves. "The camera is as much a part of my everyday life as talking or eating or sex," she
explains. "The instant of photographing, instead of creating distance, is a moment of clarity
and emotional connection for me."[1] Goldin's artistic self is a compound entity comprised
of tightly knit relationships. The intimacy of her identification with her companions is
revealed in the manner in which Goldin describes her work—not as a chronicle of the lives
of others, but as "the diary I let people read."[2]

Goldin's life has been a race against time and loss. Long-standing acquaintances report
that her compulsion to chronicle each day surfaced while she was still a teenager. They
remember her scribbling down their conversations as fast as they were spoken. Her
compulsion soon shifted to the camera. Through photography, Goldin has produced an
unabridged version of the fleeting instants that comprise her extraordinary existence.
These instants are amplified by her uncanny ability to penetrate the striking façades of
her close-knit family and expose the raw emotions that lay beneath. This talent blossomed
when, in 1978, she and her friends moved from Boston to the Bowery, a low-rent district in
Manhattan where she still maintains a loft. Goldin became politicized under the influence
of her radical feminist boss at the Tin Pan Alley, a basement drinking establishment on
49th Street in Times Square in Manhattan where Goldin worked as a bartender. Bartending
provided the ideal arena to hone her gift for receiving confessions and inspiring trust. At
the same time, the unrestrained behaviors that occurred in the barroom fed her fascination
for those who live on the fringes of society. Her lifelong work has been devoted to chroni-
cling the unscripted dramas they endured. The searing intensity of the photographic

Top: Nan Goldin, *Cookie and Millie at the Mudd Club*, NYC, 1979 (1979), Kodak ektrachrome. Courtesy of the artist.

Middle: Nan Goldin, *Cookie and Vittorio's wedding – Cookie crying*, NYC, 1985 (1986), Kodak ektrachrome. Courtesy of the artist.

Bottom: Nan Goldin, *Cookie at Vittorio's casket*, NYC, Sept. 1989 (1989), Kodak ektrachrome. Courtesy of the artist.

Disclosing Biography—Unabridged and Uncensored: **Nan Goldin**

Top: Nan Goldin, *Self-portrait making love w. Brian, NYC, 1983* (1983), ektrachrome. Courtesy of the artist.

Bottom: Nan Goldin, *Nan 1 month after battering, 1984* (1984), Kodak ektrachrome. Courtesy of the artist.

CRAFTING AN ARTISTIC "SELF"

portraits Goldin produces recaptures the heartbreaking event of her own childhood, in which her older sister committed suicide by lying across railroad tracks. Goldin attempted to escape this horrific memory by running away from home when she was just eleven years old. She spent the next years living with foster families, being expelled from their homes, and finally settling into a commune with a group of teenagers and adults. The friends made at the commune came to comprise her world and do to this day. In the summer of 1972, Goldin began photographing them. "I started taking pictures because of my sister's suicide." Goldin says. "Her death completely changed my life. I'm constantly looking for the intimacy I had with her, in my life and my work. And I think about the deaths of my friends. My sister's death is more abstract to me, more symbolic. Their deaths are real, and that's left behind this immense legacy. That's why I photograph. I miss so many people so badly."[3]

Goldin and her band of spirited maverick friends were not born outcasts. They arrived at their outcast status by actively seeking styles of dress, living arrangements, family structures, and sexual orientations that lay outside cultural norms. They also chose the jeopardy in which they placed themselves. Goldin explains, "In my family of friends, there is a desire for the intimacy of a blood family.... We are bonded not by blood or place, but by a similar morality, the need to live fully and for the moment, disbelief in the future, a similar respect for honesty, a need to push limits, a common history."[4] Goldin embraces these values. A desire for intimacy, respect for honesty, and a need to push limits define her artistic credo. Nothing is beyond the range of her camera. Batterings, drug addictions, detox therapies, heroin relapses, and cycles of love awakened and love shattered are byproducts of the lifestyle she shares with these companions. The manic tone of these events obviate the need for artificial staging and posing, or contriving lighting and props. Goldin describes her work's relationship with real life as "letting it be what it is. And not trying to make it more or less, or altered. What I'm interested in is capturing life as it's being lived, and the flavor and the smell of it, and maintaining that in the pictures."[5] Goldin and her camera witnessed transsexuals primping; women being ravaged; friends showering, masturbating or having sex, shooting up, and being introspective. The desire for privacy was alien to their lifestyle. Candor was absolute. It is reported that the bathroom in Goldin's loft had no door.

The unmediated human exposure of the resulting photographs contrasts with the mindless drone of camcorders and the fulsome sensationalism of journalism. The former is too devoid of emotional involvement, the latter too intent on fabricating melodrama. Instead, Goldin works in the tenuous zone of the snapshot, a form of photography that is usually associated with personal amateur efforts, not formal artistic accomplishment. Purged of pretense, snapshots are frank admissions of a nostalgic impulse that derives from the fact that the photographer and the subject(s) are bonded in life. Goldin describes snapshots as "the form of photography that is most defined by love. People take them out of love, and they take them to remember—people, places, and times. They're about creating a history by recording a history. And that's exactly what my work is about."[6]

Goldin's renown in the art world was initiated by the snapshot intimacies of *The Ballad of Sexual Dependency*, a slide show of friends and lovers. Disheveled, teary eyed, and sullen, pitiable, desperate, and beautiful, they revealed the entirety of themselves to Goldin's camera. Initially, Goldin only showed *Ballad* privately and informally to the friends whose lives it captured. She had no intention of presenting it as an art piece to an anonymous audience. But then, in 1979, *Ballad* was shown at the legendary Mudd Club as part of rock star Frank Zappa's birthday celebration. It captured the attention of the art world. But even after its public premiere, *Ballad* remained a life project more than an art project. Goldin kept taking pictures. Slides accumulated. Years passed. *Ballad* has become an epic work that barrages viewers with over 700 slides. Because recent images are integrated into the sequence, each showing is unique. Yet the work retains its essential qualities. The images fade from one to the next without comment or titles. It presents Goldin's friends to the audience as they presented themselves to her—through multitudes of passing gestures and the immediacy of changing facial expressions. They are accompanied by a medley of ballads; sentimental love songs such as *Lonely Boy* by Paul Anka, *Another Night With the Boys* by The Drifters, *Sweet Blood Call* by Eric Burdon, *Cowboys to Girls* by The Intruders, *Downtown* by Petula Clark, *All Tomorrow's Parties* by the Velvet Underground, and *I Put a Spell on You* by Nina Simone, stirring up melancholy memories of the past. Nostalgic romanticism is not, however, the prevailing narrative style of *The Ballad of Sexual Dependency*. The slides barrage viewers with unflinching portrayals of precarious behavior. Nor does nostalgic romanticism describe its visual style—Goldin's imagery more closely resembles punk's maniacal rhythms. The slides are imbued with the harsh, strobe-lit atmosphere of the lofts, bars, and clubs frequented by Goldin and her friends. Interiors are flooded with crimson light and scarlet shadows. Despite the grouping of the slides according to such broad subject categories as couples, women, men, and still lifes, the series testifies to drug-induced confusions. The slides proceed in succession. Goldin's friends appear and reappear at sporadic intervals and in unpredictable circumstances that mirror the incoherence of their lives. *Ballad* chronicles the world of those who exempted themselves from factories, offices, and schools. Instead, they hung out, indulged their fancies, got high, and partied. Yet their revels often seem more desperate than joyful. The fearsome specter of AIDS is evident in the urgency that pervades their exchanges of affection as well as in the gaunt and ashen faces of others already afflicted. This disease inextricably links love, pain, danger, and death. Goldin lives and conveys this tangled truth. She discovers, and makes vivid, a radiant beauty within the grotesque horror of her friends' demise.

Why do the people who inhabit this world of the misbegotten allow Goldin to document the perverse subtexts of their lives? One reason may be that being photographed was familiar to those friends who participated in the world of underground music and film. But even they report[7] that they just thought of Goldin as a trusted friend who obsessively took pictures. Perhaps these people welcomed the camera because it seemed to give their fragile lives credence. Without doubt they knew this camera's perspective was sympathetic. Posed portraits tend to be characterized by formality. Candid shots tend to be superficial. The process of creating both kinds of portrayals is commonly described using such words as "point," "shoot," "aim," and "capture." Goldin's process resists this aggressive vocabulary. Her camera seems to squint, blink, and sob. "I photograph out of love…and out of my idea of beauty and out of desire. I don't allow myself to photograph out of the critical side of me."[8] She goes on to explain, "People sometimes don't realize what I give back in the work. There are people who still think the work is exploitative, even after all this time. But it's really about giving back to the people who give so much of themselves to me. That whole thing of the African tribes having this theory that their soul would be stolen by photography…I always say, if you're photographing your own tribe, then there's not that danger of the soul being stolen. I think that you can actually give people access to their own soul…. I photograph directly from my life. These pictures come out of relationships, not observations."[9]

Initially Goldin had no intention of becoming a career artist. It seemed unimaginable that these images would eventually become the subject of extensive commentary, or comprise entire books, or be exhibited in prestigious museums. But years later her friends found themselves standing among crowds of strangers scrutinizing images of their lovemaking or their despair. They were not anonymous. At Goldin's retrospective at the Whitney Museum of American Art, New York, in 1997, for example, they observed the sometimes pitiable, sometimes sordid, but always intimate documentation of their pasts. Unlike the slides in *Ballad*, Goldin identifies the subjects of her still photographs by name.

Goldin's photographic records are uncensored, unabridged, and therefore perpetually expanding. Her manner of presenting her work, therefore, had to accommodate images that kept accruing in tandem with the events they chronicled. Slide shows were optimal because they impose no finite limits. Likewise, Goldin typically hangs her photographs in the manner of a nineteenth-century salon where artworks are clustered at and above eye level, on walls that have been painted by the artist with deep saturated colors. Instead of looking at one image at a time, this unconventional style of gallery presentation encourages viewers to see in a plural fashion. Whereas a single photograph presents a snippet of a person's life, presenting multiple events and circumstances creates a narrative spectrum. Cookie Mueller, for example, first appears as a vibrant, self-confident woman, a writer and underground film star, the lover of Sharon Niesp. Subsequent images document her tragic decline. She grows increasingly thin, frail, and sick. The image of Cookie dying is particularly heart-wrenching because it is accompanied by evidence of her early success and her once-promising future. Goldin explains her penchant for expanding the definition of the photographic portrait to encompass decades of a subject's life, by stating, "I've photographed David for 28 years, you know, since I met him. And I photographed Sharon for 20 years since I met her. And the same with Bruce. I've known him for 22 or 23 years. And Greer I knew 18 years or something. It's all about making a record of people's real lives."[10] Goldin's commitment to producing an unflinching view of harsh realities was not only directed to her friends. She also applied it to herself and her own emotional crises. Her works from the 1970s and 1980s documented her precarious life, trumped, doped, and teetering on calamity. One series chronicles her turbulent love affair with a man identified in the photographs as Brian. During this period his oscillating moods became the center of her work. He appears sullen, abusive, affectionate, stern, withdrawn, violent. Goldin explains, "It was kind of like being in a wild three-way—me, my lover, and the drugs."[11] One night Brian beat Goldin so badly that she had to be hospitalized. As she was recuperating, Goldin directed the camera at her own battered face and produced one of her hallmark photographs, *Nan One Month After Being Battered*, NYC (1984). It was a reminder, she said, "so I would never go back to him." Goldin was eventually also hospitalized for drug use. She relapsed after seven years and was readmitted for treatment. Now, she says, "I have both literally and physically emerged from darkness and discovered light and have begun to explore these changes visually and metaphorically."[13]

The starting point of Goldin's new work was a series of psychological self-portraits begun while she was rehospitalized. Nevertheless, her image of "self" continues to include those who survived past sexual, emotional, and chemical excesses. *Memory Lost!!*, the 2001 exhibition in which these pieces were included, evidences Goldin's ongoing effort to reconcile her life and those of her friends with time. The people in these photographs still bathe, sleep, urinate, and masturbate in full view of the artist and her Leica, but they also do a lot of reflecting. Nonetheless, the haze of intoxication has lifted. A world beyond raw nerves and taut emotions has come into view. The nuanced light of the sun and moon has replaced the strobe-lit glare of all-night parties. Her new work, says Goldin, is comprised of "many landscapes, photos of maternity, of children, of my friends in nature."[14] Yet they remain inspired by human relationships. A picture of a beautiful sky was taken "the night a

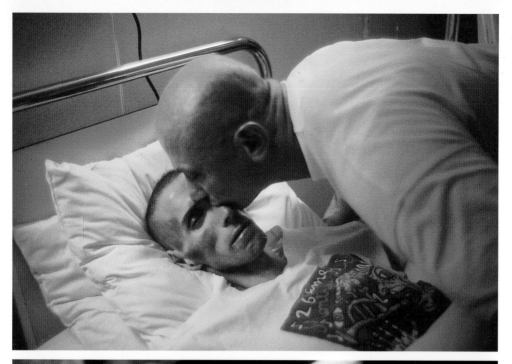

Top: Nan Goldin, *Gotscho kissing Gilles goodbye, Paris, 1993* (1993), Fuji ektrachrome. Courtesy of the artist.

Bottom: Nan Goldin, *Guido floating in Grotto, Levanzo, Sicily, 1999* (1999), Fuji ektrachrome. Courtesy of the artist.

CRAFTING AN ARTISTIC "SELF"

young friend of mine committed suicide."[15] Likewise, a photograph of Fatima candles reflects "the fact that I go to churches to light candles for my friends with AIDS to try to keep them alive."[16] The image that most anticipates the possibility of healing and soulful reawakening represents her friend Guido swimming in dark waters, his head flung back in a gesture of emotional and spiritual release. Among Goldin's closely bonded community, this deliverance also applies to their surviving companions. "My community has been deeply impacted by both AIDS and drug abuse," she concludes. "Survival and recovery have become priorities. This has become a time of healing: physically, emotionally, and spiritually."[17]

Photography still mediates the fearsome imminence of death in Goldin's life and the lives of her friends. It provides lasting reminders of how it really was. "We all tell stories which are versions of history—memorized, encapsulated, respectable, and safe. Real memory, which these pictures trigger, is an invocation of the color, smell, sound, and physical presence, the density and flavor of life. Memory allows the endless flow of connections."[18]

[1] Nan Goldin, *The Ballad of Sexual Dependency* (New York: Aperture, 1986), 6.

[2] ibid.

[3] Dennis Cooper. "The Ballad of Nan Goldin." interview. *Spin* 1997. <http://members.aol.com/Voodoopod/clsrngoldinindex.html>.

[4] Goldin.

[5] Marvin Heiferman, "Pictures of Life and Loss," in *Nan Goldin: I'll Be Your Mirror*, eds. Nan Goldin, David Armstrong, and Hans Werner Holzwaith (New York: Whitney Museum of American Art, 1996), 452.

[6] David Armstrong, Nan Goldin, and Walter Keller, "On Acceptance: A Conversation," in *Nan Goldin: I'll Be Your Mirror*, 449.

[7] Cooper.

[8] Goldin.

[9] Heiferman, 279.

[10] Mia Fineman, "The Nan Goldin Story," *Artnet* 12 December 1996. <http://www.artnet.com>.

[11] Cooper.

[12] ibid.

[13] Dana Friis-Hansen, "The Party's Over," *Parkett* 57 (1999), 96.

[14] Nan Goldin, letter to author, 2 July 2002.

[15] Friis-Hansen.

[16] Scott Rothkopf. "Indifferent to Issues of Environment, Politics, Equality: Interview with Nan Goldin." *The Harvard Advocate* Spring 1999. <http://www.theharvardadvocate.com/spring99/interview.html>.

[17] Friis-Hansen.

[18] Goldin.

Inventing Biography—Fictionalized Fact and Factualized Fiction

Kim Jones

Born 1944 San Bernardino, California
1964-1966 California Institute of Arts, Valencia, California
1969–1971 California Institute of Arts, BFA
1972–73 Otis Art Institute, Los Angeles, California, MFA
Lives and works in New York City

Kim Jones demonstrates that the human "self" need not be singular. "Himself" expands into "themselves" because Jones periodically transforms himself into his alter ego, Mudman. This alternative being manifests its own personality, mannerisms, interactions, physical form, impulses, trepidations, and desires. Alter egos are true and complementary beings, not to be confused with play-acting, role-playing, dressing-up, or pretending. Despite the full-body transformation of his appearance and behavior, Mudman is still Kim Jones. However, Mudman engages in a wider range of behaviors, conveying a more basic form of truth and possessing a greater potential to affect others.

Since 1973, Kim Jones has regularly transformed himself into an alter ego who captures the anguish of both a perpetrator and a victim of aggressive acts. His transformation begins by stripping off his clothing and plastering his almost-naked body with mud from head to foot, smearing a thick layer over his Marine-issue boots to produce an unnaturally ponderous appearance. Once his skin is obliterated behind this casing of earth, he attaches to his back an ungainly assemblage of wood, twigs, wire, tape, cheesecloth, latex, and foam that weighs as much as 150 pounds. His metamorphosis proceeds as he pulls panty hose over his face, further obscuring his features. Sometimes his alien appearance is augmented by puffs of odorous smoke that discharge from a fat cigar in his mouth. In this guise, Jones becomes the living sculpture he calls *Mudman*.

This strange and fearsome creature with the weighty appendage on his back has elicited diverging interpretations. Mudman has been described as a hallucinatory apparition of an earthly outcropping, an archaic being rising from the primal ooze, a shaman from a distant outpost, an uprooted tree, a peasant hauling his harvest on his back, and a camou-flaged G.I. carrying a heavy backpack. But Mudman does not make his appearances in the badlands, the bog, the bush, the wilderness, or the jungle—locations consistent with these interpretations. For the past thirty years, he has regularly appeared in the urban arena, touring art galleries and walking the streets of Manhattan, Los Angeles, Hamburg, and Washington, D.C.

Jones is uncomfortable with grand propositions. He insists that Mudman does not origi-nate in New Guinea, the Zuni, Zimbabwe, India, or Australia, where mud-smeared shamans frighten enemies, heal the sick, purify the land, and enact rites of regeneration when people die. "People talk about me being a shaman, but I'm not here to heal anybody. I don't asso-ciate with primitive cultures. All the materials used in my back sculpture are modern and industrial—nylon, foam, wire, shellac, acrylic paint, and wood. I'm not romantic about being a primitive man. I'm not rejecting contemporary Western civilization. I just reach for more potent images in my life."[1]

Mudman came into being as a logical progression of Jones's studio practice. The shift from producing conventional paintings to becoming a living sculpture began when he abandoned painting to experiment with traditional forms of sculpture. When the conven-tional parameters of sculpture became too restrictive, several renowned vanguard sculptors

Kim Jones, *Wilshire Boulevard Walk, January 28, 1976, 18 miles* (1976), mixed media. Courtesy of the artist. Photograph: Jeff Gibbins.

Inventing Biography—Fictionalized Fact and Factualized Fiction: **Kim Jones**

provided him with the impetus to break into new territory. Eva Hesse, Chris Burden, and Bruce Nauman had laid the groundwork for adopting eccentric materials and unusual display tactics. They set the precedents for his work in foam, rubber, wax, bamboo, and wire, and for dislodging sculpture from its hallowed position upon pedestals. But even attaching three-dimensional work directly to the walls and floor quickly became unacceptably confining. His sculpture was finally and satisfactorily liberated when he attached it to his body. In 1973, Jones did his first performances wearing his sculpture. A year later he ventured into the streets with it on his back. The evolution culminated in the creation of Mudman. "I wanted to be more a part of the sculpture, more like a sculpture," Jones explains. "Adding mud changed me. It was like adding another skin, making me closer to the sticks and the cheesecloth. I became more like a walking, talking sculpture." The difficulty of acquiring the mud needed to become a sculpture is inevitable in the settings where Mudman performs. Cities obliterate the earth except in parks and vacant lots. "No Trespassing" signs often mark locations where the earth is accessible. Importing mud compromises the integrity of the endeavor. Jones explains, "I use mud from the place where I am. In New York, I got mud from Central Park and Washington Square Park. In Los Angeles, I used mud from the La Brea tar pits, which was foolish because it was full of oil. In Paris, I found it in a vacant lot. The healthiest mud came from the Santa Monica Mountains. The aesthetic quality of the mud is not as important as connecting to the place."

Although mud alienates Mudman from the asphalt and concrete streets of the major metropolises he wanders, it connects him to the people he encounters there. Jones reports that mud is his social intercessor, opening a channel for him to talk and for people to listen. "Mudman is a conversation piece. It makes me stand out and forces me to talk to people. Going out into the world as Mudman makes me more careful about dealing with people. I have to be more sensitive to their reaction to me. If they approach me, I calm them down. I tell them why I'm dressed this way. I ask how they feel about it. It makes me more conscious of how different I am." Without a touch of irony, he adds: "It's a nice way to meet people."

Thus, despite Mudman's bizarre appearance, Jones consistently reasserts his ordinariness. Mudman conducts no ceremony to honor the gods, no evocation of dream time, no entry into mythic space. As if to illustrate this point, Jones intentionally demystifies his actions by allowing the audience to witness his metamorphosis from Kim Jones into Mudman. In full view of the public, he removes his street clothes and neatly folds them before methodically smearing his body with mud, strapping his twig sculpture to his back, covering his face with panty hose, and sauntering forth. He is neither hostile, nor cheerful, nor belligerent. Indeed, his demeanor is designed to avoid frightening people. Mudman is polite. "Sometimes I am silent," Jones says. "If I approach people, they get scared. I am the wait-and-see type. If people approach me, I start talking. I tell them when I first made the structure it was made with wax and shellac and looked like wings. I thought about being Icarus or an insect. I tell them I like to think about being a tree."

The cumbersome sculpture that Mudman straps to his back may be abstract, but the physical strain it imposes on the artist's body is actual, especially since his performances are always long in duration (from sunrise to sunset) or long in distance (eighteen-mile walks). The mud draws heat out of his body, the stick structure strapped to his back is heavy and restricting. Mudman walks like a cripple in braces or a soldier lugging heavy weapons and survival gear. In fact, both of these metaphors comprise significant components of Jones's biography. As a child he was afflicted with a polio-like disease that kept him alternately in a wheelchair and in traction for long periods of time. In order to occupy himself through periods of isolation, he devised a never-ending, solitary game.

With pencil on paper, Jones devised an army of Dot Men who waged wars against an army of X Men. The game immersed him in the imaginative realm from which Mudman would later emerge. Jones's adolescent militaristic fantasies burst into devastating actuality when he served a tour of duty in the Marine Corps in Dung Ha during some of the bloodiest years of the Vietnam War. "I was dirty, sweaty, and scared," he recalls. "Mud was everywhere." Jones slept in ditches and crawled through mud searching for booby traps. When he returned from Vietnam and became an artist, Jones continued to wage skirmishes and battles, but they were conducted with pencil on fields of paper. Jones's post-Vietnam drawings retain the nervous appearance of his adolescent drawings, but they are no longer products of play. Each drawing provides a detailed accounting of the functional components of adult warfare and its harsh, live-or-die urgency. His renderings include tables where soldiers gather to plan campaigns, pens for confining prisoners of war, chambers to interrogate the enemy, facilities to store ammunition, quarters where soldiers sleep and eat, places of worship, routes for transporting supplies, and parks for relaxation during periods of peace. Jones has even devised a manner of exhibiting the drawings to confirm their military imperatives. Instead of being matted and framed like fine-art objects, they are pinned to the wall like hastily drawn battle plans.

In each drawing, a proliferation of delicate pencil lines describes a world ruled by conflict, violence, danger, and terror. Battle lines are continually redrawn with pencil to record endless cycles of incursions and defensive actions by the warring factions. Tanks and their artillery ranges are sketched with obsessive and minute specifications. Crisscrossing lines signify weapon fire. Accumulations of tense markings represent advances and victories. Erased lines chronicle retreat, massacre, and defeat. Because these markings are never completely obliterated when they are erased, the drawings contain ghostly reminders of prior battles. Erasures and reworkings accumulate as disheartening reminders of the interminable role that war plays in constructing human history. On some drawings the combat and bloodshed are so intense, lines expand beyond the borders of the paper and invade the surrounding walls, resembling real-life escalations of military conflict. Jones sometimes provides accompanying legends to embellish the action, writing such texts as, "Defenders usually fire first, unless they are attacked from behind or ambushed. Each side has explosives at their disposal, useful for getting through fortified walls or in ambush. Ultimately, each side can also build a super-cannon, capable of penetrating the fortified walls and with an unlimited firing range. Immobility is their disadvantage: super-cannons can easily become sitting ducks."

Presenting the warring factions as contrasting icons of Xs and Os generalizes these drawings beyond their specific reference to American G.I.s and the Vietcong. Xs and Os can also represent cowboys and Indians, Huns and Visigoths, or any foes past and present. Jones accentuates this implied universality of conflict by depicting an array of battle sites: fortresses, bunkers, clusters of tepees, and fortified cities. Furthermore, the futility of resolving conflict through military action is enacted within Jones's working method— these drawings are never completed. He reworks them again and again, sometimes over the course of many years, until they are sold. But even sold works are sometimes continued if they are borrowed for an exhibition, providing Jones with another opportunity to extend the battles recorded on their surfaces. Over time, these paper fields of battle become tattered, brittle, and yellowed. As they are disfigured by the wars waged upon them, they become transformed from simple pencil drawings into visual epics, relaying the conditional terms of all defeats and all triumphs. Jones reminds viewers that only strife is everlasting. "My war drawings are actually a different category from more traditional drawings which have an end. In the war drawings, there is no ending, there is living and fighting. You can see how things are changing. That is one of the basic rules of the world. That is what makes the two-dimensional world interesting to look at. You can visually see the way that particular world is changing. It's not that it is getting better or worse, it is just changing. I play the part of a minor god. I determine the fate of the Xs and Os. I am on both sides at the same time. Who wins depends on my mood. Individual Xs or Os are heroes; they are stronger and survive longer. But ultimately they all die. That is one of the basic rules of world."

When asked, "Are you still Kim Jones when you are Mudman?" he responds, "I am Kim Jones when I am Mudman and after I take a shower." Mudman and Jones co-exist. They inhabit the same mind and body, taking turns at visible embodiment. In the same manner, Jones is both the Xs and the Os whose perpetual battles he wages on paper. He is both good and evil. He is human and mythic. He is the aggressor and the victim. "Everything is nature." Thus, Mudman seems to derive from nowhere and everywhere. Wandering the city streets as a hulking humanoid who splatters mud on urban sidewalks or leaves a trail of flaked dirt on museum floors, he is a reminder that wildness can denote derangement or innocence or passion or hostility. Jones explains that these qualities are inherent to the sophisticate and the savage, the institution and the individual, human and nonhuman life forms, living and nonliving entities. "Nature grows out of control until it destroys itself through this so-called natural selection. Things run out of food and die. You can think about media and advertising that way. They are always growing, trying to feed themselves. They extend themselves until they kill off the host. I am not romantic about the way things are.... I like when people are nice to me, but the world seems, for the most part, an aggressive place. If you are weak, it will kill you. That's just the way it is all over the world. Something you think is weak is really sneaky."

Jones and his alter ego, Mudman, provide material evidence that the natural order resembles an interlocking network of relative strengths and momentary advantages. Everyone seems destined to play both roles. In a work entitled *David and the Giant* (1978) Mudman performed against himself. Jones installed a three-foot-tall plaster cast of Michelangelo's *David* at the L.A.C.E. Gallery in Los Angeles. As a work of art, *David* is a masterpiece and a symbol of human achievement. As a biblical figure, David represents the triumph of the weak. Jones initiated the performance by smearing mud over this emblem of greatness and victory. Next, he attached a miniature *Mudman* sculpture to the back of the plaster replica of *David* and covered its head with nylon. Then Jones walked about forty feet away and repeated the process of transformation upon himself. As a living sculpture he faced the half-sized plaster version of himself and began shooting marbles at it with a slingshot. Jones describes the event in his usual straightforward manner: "The rubber breaks. I fix it with my muddy hands and continue shooting. I'm getting closer and closer to him to improve my accuracy and destructiveness. Marbles are ricocheting everywhere. Some people in the audience are hit. Can't destroy David. I do manage to chip off parts of his leg and arm. I shoot off his genitals. The crowd cheers. After I lose all my marbles, Miles (a gallery employee) throws me a sledgehammer and I bash David's head and push him over. There are publicity shots taken of my victim and me. I leave and take a shower...and go home to bed."[2] In this manner Jones enacted his view of the natural disorder, the state when conflict is pervasive, the organism battles against itself.

Instead of seeking a remedy for the pervasive nature of strife, Jones seems to accept its inevitability. Throughout the thirty years that he has been a practicing artist, this courteous, reserved man has had a recurring impulse to confront combat. Early in his art career, Jones committed actual acts of aggression. *Rat Piece* (1976), performed in the gallery on the California State University campus in Los Angeles, included the methodical burning of live rats. Jones suggests the stimulus for this dark act in a hallucinatory text that he wrote in 1983: "vietnam dong ha marine corps our camp covered with rats they crawled over us at night they got in our food we catch them in cages and burn them to death i remember the smell."[3] If this statement identifies the impulse for burning live rats as an artwork, the following one provides an explanation: "I wanted to bring this home, to show it with its smell, screams, and the responsibility for stopping it—not just tell about it. You can't really write about burning. It does not have the impact of actually seeing something die. It is horrible, to have control over it." A controversy erupted that resulted in Jones's arrest and conviction on the charge of cruelty to animals, a circumstance filled with paradox since killing soldiers does not normally result in convictions of cruelty to humans. It demonstrates the difficulty of categorizing acts of violence, especially in war, where heroism and humanitarianism are in opposition. Jones, the perpetrator of violence in *Rat Piece*, made this inconsistency apparent when he grieved the rats' deaths as he might grieve the torching of the war's human victims. The 1983 text about rats also states, "When they were burning and screaming, I bent down and screamed with them. I don't know whether it helped them or not. Probably, it didn't mean anything to them, but it meant something to me. It was my way of connecting with them somehow, although they were feeling the pain, not I. They were like scapegoats."[4]

Jones admits that, "At least in my mind, this is the way the world usually works: first it is my turn to eat something and kill something, then it is someone else's turn to eat me and kill me. I have my individual experiences. They seep out of my art." But Jones insists his worldview is not bleak and he is not moralistic. Through his war drawings and his *Mudman* performances he simply represents the truth that he has observed. "I am trying to be as real as possible. There is conflict, but there has to be a certain amount of time for things to grow and survive. I show intervals of peace as well as conflict." But from Jones's personal observatory, the resumption of conflict is inevitable. He warns against complacency, "I don't think there ever was an enlightened time. It is dangerous when people start believing in eventual harmony because when you don't agree with them, they kill you."

Periodically Mudman still rises and shivers in the cold night air beside a subway station or a traffic light. He is a living war memorial, a debilitated cripple, a mighty aggressor. He is an alter ego, an evoker of fear and awe and pity and sorrow. "As an art object," Jones says, "I would like people to look at me and make up their own minds. Mudman doesn't have a personality or a mission. I think the audience has a personality. The audience may have a mission." A drawing entitled *The Man Who Talked Too Much and His Soul Fell Out of His Mouth* (1983) might explain Jones's reticence. It enables Mudman to be created again and again, as he yields to the unique psychological dispositions of those who encounter him.

[1] Unless otherwise noted, all quotes from an interview with the artist, March 12, 1998.

[2] Kim Jones, "David and the Giant," artist's statement (Los Angeles, L.A.C.E. Gallery, October 7, 1978).

[3] Reese Williams, ed., *Unwinding the Vietnam War* (Washington D.C.: Washington Project for the Arts, 1987), 114.

[4] ibid.

Shirin Neshat
Born 1957 Iran
1979 University of California at Berkeley, BA
1982 University of California at Berkeley, MFA
Lives and works in New York City

Shirin Neshat is among many artists who explore the imaginative possibilities activated by crossing borders. Cultural change, just like biological change, is often stimulated by environmental contrast. For Neshat, who was born in Iran and now lives in the United States, borders are not the determinants of the compound "self" that pervades her video installations. This is because borders are precincts with defined territories that demarcate one locale from the next. Neshat's "self" occupies the margin—the complex, dynamic, and unstable space that exists in-between the borders. It is the place where influences merge. In her occupation of this middle zone, contrasting versions of femininity, courage, freedom, and faith co-exist.

Calculating the ratio between the exposure and the concealment of skin on a woman's body does not yield a consistent measure of modesty and exhibitionism. The glimpse of an ankle inspires incrimination in some cultures, while near nudity is unremarkable in others. Nor is there a cross-cultural measure that applies to specific parts of the anatomy. Baring breasts can be either innocent or scandalous. Women wearing shorts and tank tops on the streets of Manhattan, where Shirin Neshat currently lives and works, rouse less attention than a shrouded woman with an immodest gaze in Iran, where she was born. Neshat has fashioned an expansive visual language that embraces and transcends these polar cultural traditions.

The paradox that may account for Shirin Neshat's acclaim among the many artists currently working in the genres of photography and film installation is her ability to evoke universal commonalities out of the inconsistencies of cultural difference. Neshat's special ability to see beyond the pettiness of such discrepancies is inextricably linked to her personal history. The United States became Neshat's adopted country in 1973, when she left Iran to attend school in California. When the revolution erupted in Iran in 1978, she remained in the U.S. to avoid the strictures imposed by the Khomeini regime after it reversed the Shah's support of progressive cultural influences and economic reforms modeled on the West. Twelve years passed before she was able to return to her family and the land of her birth. In the interim her mother had become a devout Muslim and her family's status had declined. "It was probably one of the most shocking experiences that I have ever had. The difference between what I had remembered from the Iranian culture and what I was witnessing was enormous. The change was both frightening and exciting; I had never been in a country that was so ideologically based. Most noticeable, of course, was the change in people's physical appearance and public behavior."[1]

As a woman of Allah, Neshat respectfully explores the religious orthodoxy of her compatriots. As an artist in SoHo, she is a vanguard who uses a Western medium that conforms to current Western artistic practices. As Neshat explains, "I stay in the United States by choice, and I go to Iran by choice. I'm not in exile. I don't have to have an excuse for doing something. My dilemma is about being between spaces—culturally, mentally, and physically. When it comes to the production of work, I go back and forth between these two worlds. I like that. My work is about being Muslim, Iranian. But the way it is framed is according to who I am now and what my knowledge and aesthetic is."[2]

CRAFTING AN ARTISTIC "SELF"

Thus, ancient Islamic traditions affect her relationship to urbane culture in New York. New York, in turn, adds a postmodern, transnational perspective to her relationship with her ancestry. Combining them seems to cancel their disparity, permitting Neshat's art to pertain to people from diverse cultures.

Neshat not only pursues cultural harmony without sacrificing her connection to the cultural tradition and religious inheritance of her birth, she amplifies them: "Among all the issues of Islamic culture, I zero in on the strangest ones. These are difficult subjects. I am adamant in bringing up this dialogue because it is at the heart of the misunderstanding of Islamic Fundamentalism. Subconsciously I tap into aspects of that culture that are peculiar to Islamic culture. In addition to exploring my Islamic roots, I present material from an alien culture, because strangeness captivates viewers. But the work wouldn't have sustained the attention of the audience (in the United States and Europe) if it was just foreign. I do not cash in on the foreignness. The audience is captivated because of its foreignness and because of its universality."[3]

Universal truths transcend the myriad definitions of "here" and "now" or "me" and "you." Artists who wish to expand the relevance of their work usually avoid specific references. They use universal themes like birth and death, universal emotions like fear and joy, universal shapes like circles and squares, universal objects like fire and water. Neshat reverses this approach and reasserts a sense of balance, explaining, "The recent challenge for me, particularly with my new films *Rapture and Turbulent*, has been to create works that, while remaining uncompromisingly authentic to the roots of the subject, do not become too ethnographic, and do no alienate those who are not quite informed about the culture. With video I feel I have finally arrived at a point where the work has become universal in its motive.... I'm interested in juxtaposing the traditional with the modern, but there are other, more philosophical aspects that interest me as well—the desire of all human beings to be free, to escape conditioning, be it social, cultural, or political, and how we're trapped by all kinds of iconographies and social codes. I try to combine these elements to convey a sense of human crisis and emotion. One feels surrounded by these kinds of pressures in the Islamic culture. They are not necessarily good or bad, but they are very real Islamic conditions."[4]

Thus, the truths that Neshat pursues apply to everyone, everywhere. Yet she is resolutely specific about the visual motifs that comprise her majestic film installations. Every view of architecture, clothing, and landscape discloses the work's cultural and religious origins. Their spiritual basis is Islamic. Their geographical location refers to Iran. Their perspective is feminine. The setting still resonates with en-Nabi and founded a new religion. He named it Islam, a word that means "submission to the will of God," and he forbade sumptuous displays and immodest behaviors. To this day, five times each

Interview with Shirin Neshat
by Linda Weintraub

LW: What was the first indication that you were likely to become a recognized and respected artist?

SN: I haven't really thought about this at all, maybe because I never really dreamed or planned to become active or successful as an artist. Everything has happened so spontaneously in my career that I have no explanation such as that. In fact, particularly at the beginning, I anticipated that the attention will momentarily fade, that it wasn't going to be a lasting experience.

LW: What were the circumstances surrounding your first exhibition?

SN: I was first invited by Franklin Furnace [in 1993] to make a solo exhibition. This was part of their effort to highlight new artists and give them a full solo show. As you can imagine I was numb from having no previous exhibition, not even group exhibitions, to suddenly have a solo show. I took their invitation very seriously and spent a year preparing a show. It included photographs, video, and a film, all of which I had never experimented with before. During the same time, Exit Art invited me to participate in their highly acclaimed exhibition called Fever. I had minor visibility but it became an interesting experience nevertheless.

LW: What is the most significant exhibition you have had?

SN: My solo exhibition at Serpentine Gallery in 2000 was, in my mind, the most significant exhibition, as it presented the *Trilogy [Turbulent, Rapture and Fervor]* together with the *Women of Allah* series. It was the first time that even I myself was able to see the work together in such a context. Also, their perfectionist attitude toward the installation was just marvelous. I had never seen my films look better. The catalogue was the best book produced about my work. Finally, the audience was tremendous. I had never seen such number and range of people show up for my work. I was completely stimulated by the energy of this exhibition. I will never forget the experience.

LW: What is the most significant sale you have had?

SN: When the Whitney Museum of American Art purchased *Rapture* in 2000, I was very happy. I have always felt that my films are like my children and I must make sure they find the right home. So I was so relieved to pass it on to an important museum in New York.

LW: Is there someone, or some people, who promoted your career when you were still unknown?

SN: Annina Nosei was very critical to my early career. She was the first person in the commercial scene to recognize my work, take it seriously, and offer me a solo show at her gallery in New York. I will never forget our friendship. Then it was my friend and curator Octavio Zaya, who at the earliest stage took notice of my work, wrote about it, and promoted it by including it in various international exhibitions. I can think of numerous others who have been very critical in the development of my career. They include Francesco

Shirin Neshat, *Rapture* (1999), production still. ©1999 Shirin Neshat. Courtesy Barbara Gladstone Gallery. Photo: Larry Barns.

CRAFTING AN ARTISTIC "SELF"

day, devout Muslims are reminded of their religious duties when they are called to prayer with the chant, "Allah is great, Allah is great. There is no god but Allah."

Rapture (1999) is an installation consisting of two synchronized black-and-white films projected onto opposing walls in a darkened gallery. One video presents a throng of Islamic men all wearing Western-styled white shirts and black slacks. They occupy a remote fortress by the sea. In the film they attempt to scale the fortress walls with ladders, conduct menial drills of war, jostle, and perform rituals involving the passing of food, the laying of carpets, the clapping of hands. The second video projection presents a multitude of Islamic women who gradually come into view as they walk across the desolate desert outside the fortress walls. They too wear identical attire, but their clothing carries a message of social significance. Their bodies are wrapped, head to foot, in traditional *chadors*. In the film these black cloths flap in the desert wind like the flapping wings of a flock of crows. Separate soundtracks emanate from speakers next to each screen so that the exchanges between the sexes are both visual and aural. Typically, the women respond to the action of the men, as when one hundred female voices erupt in *ululation*, a shrill and mesmerizing vocalization that rises above the sound of the winds and halts the brawling among the men. Significantly, the dual soundtracks overlap only once, when both the women and men chant a prayer, an uplifting crescendo of voices unified by religious devotion. In the final sequence of the film, six women wade into the churning ocean. They climb aboard a decrepit little boat and cast out into the vast sea, set adrift by the other women. The distant horizon marks their uncertain fate. The men stand beside the guns on the rampart and face out toward the women and the sea. Solemnly they raise their hands and wave with open palms, an Islamic symbol of giving your hand to God in supplication.

These specific components of her narrative remain uncongealed, allowing each viewer of Rapture to ponder humanity's perennial search for freedom and exaltation. At the same time, Neshat seems intent on avoiding vague abstractions: "The biggest challenge for me has been how to present my ideas in a way that avoids generalities, clichés, and a sense of didacticism. I usually first try to identify the specific points that I am interested in, find curious and critical to raise concerning my subject. Then conceptually I compose the images with a certain amount of vagueness, almost self-contradictory, to leave the answers to my viewers."[5]

Such dichotomies erupt at each intersection of the film. For example, men occupy a formidable architectural structure while the veiled women wander under the open skies and amid the howling winds. This imagery evokes quandaries of interpretation. Which domain offers protection and which is perilous? Which group

Bonami (curator/critic), Dana Friis-Hansen (curator), Enwezor Okwui (curator), Paolo Curti (Italian dealer, the first person who bought my work) and many others.

LW: How does you work get marketed?

SN: My work is only marketed through dealers. I work mainly with Barbara Gladstone Gallery. Occasionally I work with Patrick Painter Gallery in Los Angeles. My experience is, the less dealers you work with the easier it is. I have never shown work in Iran. It's not yet the right moment. It won't get approved by the government. There is no museum or outlet there.

LW: What are your feelings about the commercial aspect of being an artist?

SN: It is a reality that any artist has to face. Frankly, I don't really think about it too much or do anything about it. So far everything has happened outside of my control. Also, the market has a logic of its own that I don't understand or want to understand. But I accept that commerce is one major aspect of being an artist today if you want to financially survive from your work.

LW: What is your relationship with your collectors? What does you work contribute to the life of a collector?

SN: I have become friends over the years with many of them. I really appreciate their sincerity and support. I never take people's faith for granted. I am always very flattered when someone is willing to invest their money in my art.

LW: How are the costs of producing your work allocated?

SN: My films all have producers and I must keep a close eye on the budget and receipts. Usually while we make films there is a production manager who takes charge of that type of thing. I get paid by the sale of my work and fees for any extra type of work. My travels for exhibitions are usually covered by the host institutions. I cover all my expenses such as rent, material, etc.

LW: What percentage of your income is earned by the sale of your art?

SN: Ninety-five percent of my income is from the sale of my art.

LW: Do you have a mortgage and health insurance?

SN: Yes.

LW: Are these issues difficult for you?

SN: Not at the moment.

LW: Please describe your studio. Who runs it? What is the role of assistants?

SN: My studio is at my home. I have made the largest and most beautiful room as my studio. This room is very bare. Nothing is on the walls. It has only one long table in the middle for our meetings, a couple of desks, my file cabinet, my music, computer, and lots of flowers. I think the studio is where one should be able to meditate and be quiet. I don't have many assistants. I need the time to be alone in my studio, since I work always in collaboration with people when I make my films. My one assistant who is an artist mainly does errands. I don't have him do anything else at the studio. But I must mention that the Barbara Gladstone Gallery takes

IDIOSYNCRATIC

is free and which is confined? The fortress is crumbling. Nature is powerful. The demeanor of the women is proud and resolute. The conduct of the men resembles mindless obedience. Which group
is dominant and which is oppressed? In the end, the men are left behind at the abutments while the women set out to sea. Neshat never reveals if the women's perilous journey represents migration, liberation, salvation, or martyrdom. Nor does she indicate if the men beckon for the women to return or if they wave them farewell.

The film surmounts cultural boundaries for its Western spectator because "us" combines with "them" to produce the collective "everyone." This expansion of contexts is something Neshat actually experienced when she worked with the Kurdish women from villages in Turkey and Morocco who appear in her films. Perhaps they ignited a sensation that might explain the work's title, *Rapture*. Neshat recalls, "They were so physical. They touched my face. It was the female bonding. They showed their strength and power in the most subtle way. These women play themselves. They really were not performing. The work is so much about these people. I examined Muslim woman's internal nature and her relation to nature. It all came out during the film. I bring out aspects of human character that is candid. It is up to the director. The idea was to generalize the experience of womanhood, the things that affect all of us—politics, government, history, tradition, religion, mortality, emotional trauma. Things we can't escape as human beings. We are bound to them in different ways. My interest is to point out that we are just conditioned differently—underneath, we are all the same. Human suffering and dilemma is universal. No one way is better than the other. We are only different on the surface. The veil is just a symbol."[6]

Women and men cease being individuals and become, instead, generalized as maleness/womanliness.

Rapture is poetic, but it includes no words, no dialogue. Its soaring verses are structured out of the universal syntax of emotion that is conveyed through gestures, through the choreographed movements of masses of bodies, and through Sussan Deyhim's pulsating musical score. Deyhim's hypnotic composition combines ambient sounds, traditional Middle Eastern songs, techno passages, and drumbeats. Thus Neshat capitalizes on elements that have universal appeal and carefully omits barriers to cross-cultural comprehension. But even universal works of art can't escape the effects of time and place. The Islamic terrorists' bombing of the World Trade Center and Pentagon on September 11, 2001, altered the emotional, spiritual, and historic context in which *Rapture* will forevermore be viewed. The film now stirs thoughts about the relationship between faith and fanaticism, between devotion and suicide, between secular law and divine law. Even Neshat's original concern regarding gender roles is now altered. September 11 heightened sensitivity to divergent cultural stereotypes regarding Islamic and Western women—one shunning visual attention while the other attracting it, one being acquiescent and the other self-assertive, one accepting self-renunciation while the other pursues self-fulfillment. In addition, the fortress setting in the film conjures the Islamic Fundamentalist belief that "the sword is the key to heaven." Thus, militancy has been added to the specific references of time, place, tradition, history, and nationality. *Rapture* is a descriptive word that denotes the fervor inspired on one side, the indignation provoked on the other, and the imperative to establish harmony between them.

Neshat's inclusion of the chador exemplifies her embrace of the fullness, the complexity, and the contradictions of her subject. "From the beginning," she says, "I made a decision that this work was not going to be about me or my opinions on the subject, and that my position was going to be no position."[7] Living in the West has exposed her to the opinion that the black, veiled dress of Islamic women signals their requirement to hide their bodies, restrain signs of sexuality, and suppress their individualities. But the faces of the robed and mute women in Neshat's film are radiant with fierce pride. Their spirit has not been extinguished. Indeed, their demeanor evokes the complex history of the chador in Islamic countries. This robe-like garment was actually condemned during the early years of the twentieth century when Iran attempted to modernize by modeling its policies on the West. It was revived during the revolution, when wearing it became a way to demonstrate opposition to the insinuation of Western values. In that era women donned the chador to reassert and purify Islamic values. It was not uncommon in the late 1970s to see militant Muslim women robed and carrying machine guns. After the revolution, however, an Islamic republic was established, and the chador, once again, became integrated into the ultraconservative policies of the state. *Rapture* is a film that addresses such contentious subjects without contaminating its poetic beauty.

Neshat alters the conventional manner of presenting foreign cultures on film. Her works do not, for example, resemble travelogues in which exotic subjects are treated as tourist attractions and the audience members behave like sightseers. Nor are they like documentaries made to convey information. Neshat says she uses film "to engage an audience."[8] The grandeur of *Rapture*'s black-and-white images and its riveting musical score support this intention. But engagement is mostly achieved by requiring viewers to stand in the space between the two wall projections. The film on one wall presents the women. The film on the opposite wall presents the men. Because it is not possible to see both films as they run simultaneously, audiences must continually turn to monitor the actions on one screen and the responses on the other. Physically, observers occupy the position in-between. Alien constructs literally pass through them. They inhabit an ambivalent mental position—devotion mixes with independence, tradition with progress, security with freedom, individuality with community.

In actuality, Neshat straddles more than two opposing cultural contexts. "Iran is such an extreme opposite of the United States. It makes you think about yourself. You start questioning your relationship to your own culture. I am interested in tapping into ideas and subjects that are ethnically specific but presented in a way that is universal—subliminal and primal."[9] Neshat's international reputation requires that she travel extensively. She lives in cosmopolitan New York, where the sidewalks teem with people of all races and nationalities. In New York her loft is in Chinatown. Her son is half Korean. All these aspects of her life prime her to transcend specifics of class, race, and ethnicity. Neshat notes that this experience is not unique: "Globalization of the world and the

care of most of my administrative work, so I really don't need a person to do such things at my studio.

LW: Do you do anything now to enhance the value and appreciation of your work in the future? How do you assess the longevity of your career and your reputation?

SN: No, I just work on my art. It is my gallery that thinks about such issues.

LW: What role did school play in your preparation to become an artist?

SN: Hardly any. School for me was never a blossoming period. I can't entirely blame this on the school system. I was not personally prepared for anything more than that. In fact I ended up feeling like I had to reject my education to return to making art.

LW: How has your choice of a place to live and work affected your career?

SN: I have always decided to work at home because I have a child and it has made it easier for me to work at odd hours at home. I have never had a conventional studio like most artists, because of the nature of my work. My studio is more like an office and a living room than a studio. I often edit my films at home, which makes it all so much easier than spending day and night at outside editing studios.

LW: Can you tell me more about how you are raising your child?

SN: I am raising a ten-year-old son. He is Korean-Iranian, but he doesn't see many Koreans. He lives in a true melting pot. He mostly sees Iranians and Americans, and we live in Chinatown. But he is very American. He likes American values and he wants to make sure we are not ethnic with him. He enjoys everything. He has traveled a lot. I want him to speak Farsi, but he is resisting. All my friends are Iranian, so he is more integrated with Iranians. He has a concept of where he is from and I am happy about that. I want him to be proud to be Iranian even though he lives here. I am a reminder of this other aspect of his heritage. I want to keep the fire alive.

LW: What are some cultural differences between Americans and Iranians?

SN: There are subtle cultural differences and mannerisms in the way we deal with one another. For Iranian people, others come first and then you. Here, there is more emphasis on the individual. We have the tradition of being overly accommodating. Here there is always a boundary. Places you can't go over. But being always with Iranians has its own problems.

LW: What advice would you give the current generation of aspiring artists?

SN: My only advice is to spend less time on thinking about success and put all the energy in making art itself. Otherwise your relationship to your art changes. It becomes less genuine and honest. Art should not be born from a pressure of becoming successful but something deeper. This is always a danger and the cause for mediocrity in art. If a great idea or art is born, everyone will come to it sooner or later. This is a fact.

Shirin Neshat, *Untitled (Rapture Series – Men Looking out to Sea)* (1999), 43 x 67 inches, black-and-white photograph. Courtesy Barbara Gladstone Gallery.

CRAFTING AN ARTISTIC "SELF"

subsequent rapid migration has uprooted many of us, sometimes by choice, and other times due to economic factors. Whatever the reason, however, those of us living in the state of the 'in between' have certain advantages and disadvantages: the advantage of being exposed to a new culture and, in my case, the freedom that comes with living in the USA; the disadvantages, of course, being that you will never experience again being in a 'center' or quite at 'home' anywhere."[10]

Being in-between is even revealed in Neshat's appearance. Respectfully, she veils herself when she visits Islamic countries. In the United States, however, she adopts a Western style of dress. In both kinds of apparel, her eyes are her dominant feature. The thick black mascara line that sweeps beneath her bottom lid from the bridge of her nose to her temple is not merely a cosmetic flourish. It underscores a gaze that echoes the confidence and intensity that shine in the eyes of the female subjects, the only part of their bodies that is not hidden by their chadors, precisely those eyes where suppression and defeat might be expected. They evoke an epic tale of rapture.

[1] From an interview with the artist, March 24, 2000.

[2] ibid.

[3] ibid.

[4] Octavio Zaya, "Shirin Neshat," *Interview*, September 1999, 166.

[5] Lina Bertucci, "Eastern Values," *Flash Art*, November/December 1997, 87.

[6] Zaya.

[7] Bertucci, 84.

[8] Zaya.

[9] ibid.

[10] Interview.

Epitomizing Biography—Single White Female

Vanessa Beecroft

Born 1969 Genoa, Italy
1983–1987 Civico Liceo Artistico Nicolo Barabino, Gempa, studied architecture
1987–1988 Accademia Ligustica De Belle Arti, Genoa, studied painting
1988–1993 Accademia Di Belle Arti Di Brera, Milan, studied stage design
Lives and works in New York City

Vanessa Beecroft, instead of discovering her "self" within herself, constructs her image of "self" according to criteria valued by contemporary society. She adapts to the societal land-scape by accepting and implementing constructed standards of beauty and complying with ready-made models of success. This adopted "self" is epitomized by the live models who comprise her installations. They may be natural beauties, but nature is not a sufficient qualifier according to cultural values. The models are trained and their bodies are enhanced through surgeries, wraps, liposuctions, and tooth capping. Then they rise to even higher standards of perfection through cosmetics, make-up, hair design, and fashion. Lastly, they are further refined by lighting and the aura of the setting. Beecroft provides viewers with mediated images of desirability and allows them to ponder the impact of these images on themselves.

Vanessa Beecroft commits the kind of exploitative acts on women that have, for the last thirty-odd years, provoked the ire of several generations of feminists. Gender inequities fueled the protests of such groups as the Women's Action Coalition. Art-related gender protests became the cause for The Guerilla Girls, an anonymous collective of female artists that, in 1984, protested, "Do women have to be naked to get into the Metropolitian Museum?" After all this, it might seem odd that Beecroft earns praise, not criticism, for her apparent support of the biases women have been fighting for years. Her work enlists the old-boy's club of attitudes in which the appreciation of women obsesses on appearance, but ignores intelligence and accomplishment. Likewise, it seems to align itself with two traditions that perpetuate male chauvinism: the exalted legacy of depictions of female nudes in art and the stringent criteria for female beauty promoted in the popular media. Beecroft, a tall English-Italian beauty, could just as easily fill the role of model instead of artist. But she prefers to exclude her own body from her art installations, choosing instead to incorporate other women's nude and nearly nude bodies into her artwork.

In her 1998 exhibition entitled *Show* (known officially as *VB35*), the sweeping curves of the Frank Lloyd Wright-designed Guggenheim Museum were complemented by the skimpy curves of twenty professional models arranged in an orderly fashion around its rotunda. No imagination was required on the part of the observers to seek this aesthetic corre-spondence. Fifteen of Beecroft's "girls" (a demeaning term she commonly uses) were barely dressed. The remaining five were nude. All wore full body makeup to better fulfill the air-brushed perfection demanded by contemporary paradigms of beauty. Through physical disclosure and cosmetic enhancements, the girls became living sculptures. For two-and-a-half hours, under the glare of a helium balloon spotlight, they displayed the unachievable, media-constructed standards by which legions of impressionable women regularly measure their self-esteem.

Beecroft describes the work in the following manner: "Five of the women were fully nude. The others were dressed in Gucci bikinis and high heels. As with all my installations, the girls are given certain rules. Initially, I install the girls in a formation and they are aware

Epitomizing Biography—Single White Female: **Vanessa Beecroft**

that that's their position. Depending on the duration of the show, they will move as if a still picture turns into a blurry image. Eventually, they go back to their original position. There are other rules. The first is not to speak, not to move in real time, and not to interact with the audience in any way.... There is always a virtual distance between the work and the audience. During the performance, there is a kind of silence. They are totally detached from the audience."[1]

It is significant that the words "...and tell" do not accompany the work's title, *Show*. The only act authorized therein is that of looking. And the only individuals permitted to look were members of the audience. The models were instructed to be silent, maintain blank expressions, and avoid eye contact with the audience. Such one-sided aesthetic examination of the female form is loaded with a history of impassioned commentary (mostly protest) and astute social analysis (mostly indignation). The Internet and the academy are filled with treatises by feminists decrying the cultural and aesthetic canons that have evolved around "the privileged male gaze." They explore the social, cultural, and psychological implications of the empowerment to male scrutinizers and the concurrent debasement of the female objects of their scrutiny. Several generations of women artists have protested this inequity, including Barbara Kruger, Nancy Spero, and Carolee Schneemann, among others. They resent that women are traditionally welcomed into prestigious art contexts when they present their nude bodies as models for male artists, not as artists in their own rights.

Viewers often ask whose side Beecroft is on. Doesn't an enlightened female artist ignore such superficial criteria as body weight and proportion in her search for womanly fulfillment? Is respect really dependent on physical attributes? Is this work an art show or a girly show? Beecroft responds to such questions by saying, "I feel authorized to use girls because I'm not exploiting them for particular reasons or particular needs. Objectification can be an issue. And I have been accused of showing naked chicks ... as soon as it starts from a woman, it's a different thing. I'm responsible for the women and I'm responsible if I'm displaying this type of nudity. It's not like looking at something from outside."[2] Yet Beecroft assumed a power position throughout *Show* by moving freely (and clothed) throughout the event, scrutinizing the models' immobile bodies. She claimed the artist's role for herself. The girls were relegated to the status of statues.

Beecroft established her insider's status in another work of art, *Despair*, shown in 1993 in a Milan gallery. In it she exposed her obsessive attempts to achieve the model's standards of beauty by exhibiting the personal diary that she kept from 1985 to 1993. In it she recorded obsessively detailed accounts of the food she ate and the time of its consumption, interspersed with expressions of guilt and reports about her visits to her psychiatrist:
31 January / 06.00: 2 apples, 2 kiwis, three oranges / 08:30: 2 apples, 2 kiwis, lukewarm, milky coffee / 17:30: cabbage, carrots and raw cauliflower, 2 boiled potatoes / 20:30: 1 banana, 2 apples.

She also selected the "audience" for this work, women she saw on the street who resembled her physically. Beecroft instructed them to dress in items she provided from her own wardrobe and to respond to her works with minimal movement or expression. The diary and the performers offered a compelling document of Beecroft's personal struggle with anorexia. In the aptly titled *Despair*, Beecroft distanced herself from her "girls" by dictating their appearance and behavior, but retaining her own right to act freely and determine her personal appearance.

Inconsistencies and paradoxes abound in Beecroft's work. Rather than signaling a conceptual flaw, however, they provide vivid evidence of the confusion surrounding the search for "self" that this artist seems to share with an endless number of women. Fixations with one's body image frequently impede self-acceptance, providing clear access for insecurities, doubts, and inadequacies to invade the psyche. In Beecroft's work this confusion is staged, polished, and dazzling to behold. Once they are enticed in this manner, viewers can consider their personal relationship to such provocative statements as "Beauty creates shame,"[3] a phrase that appeared in the promotional material accompanying *Show*. It reveals that Beecroft is not merely a victim of the obsessive efforts to fulfill near impossible expectations of beauty. She is also aware of the psychological penalties they impose. At the same time, she seems to espouse the self-help advice printed in such popular magazines as *Cosmopolitan* ("Insane Ways to Get to Size 0"), *Marie Claire* ("Burn Fat Fast"), *SELF* ("Lose pounds and inches with the workout that worked for the testers"), *Good Housekeeping* ("Quick Tricks to Beat Bloating"), *First* (Outsmart your hormones and say "So long fat""), *Shape* ("The Ultimate Fat Blaster").[4] Beecroft admires the skeletal ideal these magazines promote. She is not an indignant feminist. In *Show*, her bevy of beauties epitomizes glamour and elite status.

Lined up for inspection, the *Show* models might have been participating in a slave auction or a beauty contest. But instead of suggesting competition, Beecroft standardized her art product to create a "multiple." Multiples are usually identical prints of an artwork or identical sculptures cast from the same mold. In this case, Beecroft gave the impression of a multiple by selecting her participants for their similarities, not their individualities. "The model is supposed to look like a mannequin. There's a moment where they quit doing what they usually do and they quit talking, and they become more visual. It's not that there is a specific instruction to look like something. It's just [that] when you pose, that's what happens."[5] Each participant was young, tall, slender, and had the same skin tone. Identical bikinis (on the clothed models), shoes, and accessories augmented the impression of uniformity. Only their hair individualized them, as it often individualizes mannequins that are otherwise identical. The intentional anonymity of the models is reflected in Beecroft's habit of referring to them as an "army," a term that reflects the qualities she most admires: they are fit, trained to follow orders, and homogeneous. The recruits for this "army" are nameless specimens that represent physical standards of loveliness at the end of the twentieth century. Likewise, the impression of "self" in this work, and perhaps for many women not included in this work, is measured according to superhuman, impersonal ideals. One corollary to this aspect of Beecroft's work suggests that the legacy of portraiture may need updating. Instead of seeking the individualizing qualities of people, portraits of people may now be more accurately conveyed by conformity to standardized ideals.

Exclusivity defined every component of *Show*. Invitations were required for admittance, which meant each member of the audience was drawn from the current roster of "who's who" in the art and fashion worlds. In this manner, Beecroft carefully channeled the work toward privileged men and women who were most likely to observe the girls from a respectful distance, looking at them from the balcony of the museum's spiral ramp. "I intend this work for an audience accustomed to a museum, who look at it as if it was an art exhibition, as if they were going to see sculpture or painting. Usually, there are no boundaries, no directions, but the audience automatically takes a position in the space and does not approach the girls. It's up to them to decide for how long they are going to view it—five seconds, for half an hour, or for the entire length of the show. The audience for this work is mostly the art world, who usually does not touch paintings, does not touch sculptures, does not even try to interact with my works because it's supposed to be something you are just going to look at. So I never had problems."[6] As this statement indicates, the audience's ability to preserve a respectful distance from the models was important to Beecroft. But Beecroft and her crew of photographers exempted themselves from such formalities, moving among the models, focusing the lenses of their cameras, like ill-mannered lechers, on the models' rumps and nipples.

Viewers might wonder how the implications of this work would be altered if the artist had been male or a lesbian or fat or old instead of conforming to an Aryan feminine ideal. Other viewers might admire the formal qualities of the work, as if the living girls were inert abstract shapes, as if the models merely contributed form and color to the artist's composition, displaying the idealized principles of classical art—order, harmony, and beauty. In fact, both cultural and formal explanations are suggested by Beecroft. "My background is painting, so I used to spend hours in front of the nude models to draw. I soon realized that the drawings did not have the same aura as the live model. And so I decided to invite about thirty girls to the first presentation of my drawings, and these girls had something in common that was not exactly beautiful, but it was something that reminded me of paintings. I decided to give them my clothes and to have them in between the audience, but what happened is [that] they became, in and of themselves, a very strong image. The audience separated from them, and they became themselves a piece. Since then, I decided to use the girls as a material because they would be stronger in communicating what I was unable to get with painting. Like painting, this work is about arranging figures and composition and colors. I do drawings and paintings, but my main work is using live people and only girls. And this brings up some elements that are not just about pictures and visual art, but are also social issues. So, it's very important—the fact that those women are real and that is a real happening in real time."[7]

Three cultural sources fuse to become Beecroft's artistic self: The first is the alluring and illusory "look" of beauty that is promoted by corporate, fashion, and entertainment industries, determining the body type of the models in *Show*. The second is the museum setting, determining the manner in which they were presented. The third is the corporate model of creativity. Instead of conforming to the modern image of the artist as an inspired and isolated genius, she hired a team of experts who constructed a highly controlled product that became the spectacle credited as her work of art. Upscale representatives of commerce, fashion, and advertising were her creative partners. *Show* was organized by Yvonne Force, Inc., a high-powered contemporary art company that assembled the necessary makeup experts, film crew, and models, and arranged for the location and sponsors. Force even acquired the work's "designer," also identified as Beecroft's collaborator, Tom Ford, Gucci's renowned designer and supplier of the models' $2,425.00 rhinestone bikinis. Beecroft loves it all. Her appreciation of high-end consumerism can be traced back to her roots in Milan, the fashion capitol of Europe and the home of Armani and Versace. "I started buying Prada when I was 15. I wore heels everywhere.... Even to the pool, Manolos and red Chanel liptstick."[8] These commodities serve as her personal model of desirability. The two qualities Beecroft covets are expensive and gorgeous.

The Vanessa Beecroft paradox does not end here. Her living sculptures shared the beauty of orchids but also their fate—both wilt over time. The alluring perfection of her fresh and winsome beauties did not survive the 150-minute duration of *Show*. Beecroft not only anticipated their withering, she accelerated it by requiring them to stand in their high-heeled sandals long after comfort had passed and energy had been expended. As time progressed, subtle signs of instability and weariness escalated. Eventually, what had been picture perfect succumbed to entropy. Those faces that adorn the covers of glamour magazines and those bodies that enhance fashion apparel began to slouch, sag, and droop. True life propelled the work to its finale, testifying that Beecroft's relationship with commerce and fashion is an amalgam of collusion and collision.

Beecroft identifies her artistic self by basking in the epicenter of four status signifiers. *Show* assembled a chic crowd, a celebrity fashion designer, an eminent art museum, and an exclusive Fifth Avenue address in a trend-setting city. Beecroft has also produced performances and installations in many other types of locations. In each she arranges her stand-ins so that they externalize some aspect of her reconciliation of ideal woman-hood with the real-life experience of her own body. Each performance explores a female type that has been assimilated from the history of art, cinema, advertising, or fashion. She has presented the showgirl, the schoolgirl, the working girl, the virgin, the dominatrix, the suburbanite, and the stripper. A show located in a gallery in a low-rent neighborhood in New York reflected that setting: the performers wore modest flesh-colored underwear, panty hose, heels, short blond wigs, and little makeup. In sophisticated Venice, the participants were tall and lanky, had long hair, and wore sexy thongs and Pucci-patterned pantyhose. A London piece involved stockier women, with long blond hair, heels and gray sweaters, who were otherwise naked. Beecroft even shifted her gender focus to fill the deck of the *U.S.S. Intrepid* with idealized, but unindividualized, males. They belonged to a battalion of Navy Seals. In this piece she included men within her dilemma of sacrificing the "self" by conforming to a collective standard.

Beecroft describes herself as a "postfeminist" who depersonalizes the female body by emphasizing its image quality. She responds to those who accuse her of betraying her sex by explaining, "The women are always aware of what's going on."[9] She then goes on to comment, "It is a delicate separation between what is an image just to be representa-tional and what is a real person standing there."[10] This statement might imply that Beecroft aims for accuracy by presenting real bodies rather than representations of bodies. But this interpretation is reversed when she says, "I want women on heels because that's powerful; that's not natural nudity or pureness."[11] And this position is further contradicted when she states that her work "brings the concept of beauty and misery together,"[12] and that "beauty is always something unsolved, something you can never achieve in real life,"[13] that "beauty has to do also with intelligence, because beauty involves compassion,"[14] or that "the concept of beauty is difficult because there is no single set of rules—and it's mostly, to me, virtual. It's not real."[15] Then she dismisses these considerations and declares, "I like the freedom to do actions that embarrass society."[16] Ultimately, she withdraws. "I don't like any meaning. I just show the girls."[17] There is no sign that she will resolve the beauty myth in the near future. In the meanwhile, Beecroft, with her plucked brows, is frequently sighted riding her bicycle around Brooklyn wearing tight black outfits and Manolo Blahnik backless spiked heels.

1. "What's the Ideal Woman." *EGG The Arts Show*. WNET New York, 2000. <http://www.pbs.org/wnet/egg/223/beecroft/index.html 2000>.

2. ibid.

3. Clarisse Hahn, "Vanessa Beecroft, Galerie Ghislarine Hussenot," artist statement, *Art Press* no. 2211 (February 1997), 69.

4. *Cosmopolitan*, October 2002; *Marie Claire*, October 2002; *Good Housekeeping*, October 2002; *First*, October 2002; *Shape*, October 2002.

5. *EGG*.

6. ibid.

7. ibid.

8. "Fashion Stylewatch," *Bazaar*, October 1998, 124.

9. Monty DiPietro. "Vanessa Beecroft Does Tokyo." 7 August 1999. <http://www.assemblylanguage.com/reviews/Beecroft.html>.

10. ibid.

11. ibid.

12. Lynn MacRitchie. "Taking Sex Out of Nakedness." *Financial Times* no.33,606 (23–24 May 1998). <http://www.vanessabeecroft.com/biblio.htm>.

13. *EGG*.

14. ibid.

15. ibid.

16. Vanessa Beecroft, "Flash Art XXXI Years," *Flash Art*, Summer 1998, 85.

17. S. Corrigan, "Artrageous," *i-D Magazine* no. 171 (December 1997).

HEROIC

pearls to pigs
mple and devour you.

Lt 7:6

EXPRESSING AN ARTISTIC ATTITUDE

Rev. Ethan Acres, *Pearls 2 Pigs* (1999), 48 x 32 x 28, vinyl, mixed media. Courtesy of the artist and Patricia Faure Gallery, Santa Monica, California. Photograph: Anthony Cunha.

233

EXPRESSING AN ARTISTIC ATTITUDE
INTRODUCTION

Artistic attitudes contribute enriching adjectives and exclamation points to the expressive-ness of art. An art subject that doesn't have an artist's attitude attached to it exists in a holding pen awaiting its artistic fate. Will the artist revere it, degrade it, ennoble it, ridicule it, nurture it, condemn it, pity it, idealize it, or aggrandize it? This entire range of attitudes can be attached to every conceivable subject—global warming or an apple in a still life, hip hop or a nation's flag, dreadlocks or a covered bridge. Attitudes determine if money is a godsend or a devilish lure, if a boundary is protective or divisive, if a nuclear plant is ingenious or foolish, or if a Moby performance is juvenile or profound.

In aviation, the word "attitude" refers to an aircraft's manner of approaching its destina-tion. A good attitude facilitates a safe landing. A bad attitude banks against the prevailing winds and jeopardizes the landing. Aviation attitudes can be high-and-wide or straight-and-narrow, meandering or urgent. When the word shifts from a physical context to a metaphysical one, attitude can describe artistic approaches, too. In art, attitudes refer to a variety of angles of positioning. They have elicited a vast and ever-expanding reper-toire of devices summoned by artists to reveal their attitudinal positions in relation to their subjects. Artists make their psychological paths palpable to viewers, even when they are absent from the exhibition space, by emphasizing the wart on the queen's nose instead of her regal bearing; deciding whether to depict the sky over the cotton field as ominous or balmy; choosing to present the city scene in the form of a tidy grid or a jarring cacophony of shapes and colors; rendering their works in a frenzied outburst or methodical manner; choosing whether to evoke a battle scene in radiant hues or gloomy tones; selecting precious or cheap materials; or deciding between accuracy, distortion, and idealization. Even artworks that are abstract contain attitudinal positions about a subject, i.e. the artist's feelings of security, or optimism, or distress. In these instances artists capitalize on the communicating power of pure color, shape, texture, and composition. Of course, every artist possesses an attitude about art-making. The attitude favored by the popular media depicts artists as crazed, unwashed, paint-flinging fanatics. Such representations, however, neglect the artists who describe the act of making art as duty, exploration, drudgery, habit, fun, discovery, meditation, or release.

The dictionary identifies a second, but not secondary, use of the word "attitude." It frequently pops up in contemporary jargon where it signifies arrogance, assertiveness, or self-importance. Clothes with attitude are cool. Students with attitude are arrogant. Sales clerks with attitude are impudent. But what are artists with attitude? Artists enjoy a limitless arena of possibilities. Artistic attitudes come in many degrees (intense, moderate, and mild), are conveyed in numerous styles (subtle, insidious, aggressive, humorous, matter-of-fact, dramatic), embody multiple personalities (humble, arrogant, apologetic, assertive, shy, self-important), endure for various time spans (life-long, sporadic, tempo-rary), and originate in contrasting sources (personal, religious, financial, cultural, aesthetic, propagandistic). Despite the extensive catalogue of contrasting alternatives, it is almost always true that artists configure their attitudes to be shared. That is why work is often judged to be successful if it strikes an emotional chord, influences opinion, and generates response. In this manner the attitudes conveyed in the artwork become those of the viewer. Thus each time someone interacts with a work of art, the artist's attitude becomes a lived component of the present, and not just a reminder of the past experience of the artist. But it is also true that an artist can neither monopolize nor predict viewers' responses, because viewers possess their own unique sets of attitudes that will either make them compliant or resistant respondants. For artists and audience members alike, attitudes reveal little about issues, but a great deal about the person who possesses them.

In sum, art collects human attitudes with as much fervor as it dispenses them, and it solidifies familiar attitudes with as much insight as it generates new ones.

Obeying Ants

Yukinori Yanagi

Born 1961 Fukuoka, Japan
1985 Musashino Art University, BA, fine arts in painting; MFA, painting
1990 Yale University, MFA, Fellowship in Arts, sculpture
Lives and works in New York City and Okayama City, Japan

Yokinuri Yanagi explores the attitude of humans toward other living creatures. The relationship between human and animals is one of the characteristics that differentiate cultures. It is also a major determinant of human behavior. Yanagi neither subscribes to the Judeo-Christian belief that humans have been granted dominion over lesser creatures, nor does he uphold cultural traditions that identify animals as revered totem progenitors. He chose, instead, to enlist an animal as his equal, his artistic collaborator. The creature who was honored in this manner, however, is distant from humans on the evolutionary ladder. Indeed, it is not even a mammal. Yanagi chose to create art with an ant, an insect that is normally considered neither beautiful, individuated, endearing, nor directly useful to human enterprises.

Yukinori Yanagi crawls on his hands and knees in a determined effort to record the meanderings of a single ant with a red crayon. It is the ant, not the artist, who determines the linear configuration of the resulting drawing, a work of ethereal delicacy and beauty. Yanagi will exhibit this drawing as his creation with the title *Wandering Piece*, which establishes the priority of the ant's perspective over the human's. Although he abducted this tiny creature from its colony and drafted it into the service of art, it is the artist who is following the ant's trail. Yanagi explains, "I let the ant [be] free to wander. It creates a natural line."[1] But the artist assumed control when he laid out four five-and-a-half-foot steel beams coated with grease to prevent the ant from escaping. They mark the limits of the resulting drawing. These beams serve as the enclosure for the creative act that lasts several days. All the while the human member of the team crawls awkwardly, like a regressed toddler, behind the agile ant. Throughout this entire period the ant scurries with superhuman energy. It is only the artist who shows signs of fatigue. That is when a tiny vial is placed over the ant to suspend its travels until its human partner has rested and the drawing can be resumed.

Interpreting the work's meaning is entirely dependent upon the artist's attitude toward the ant. Part of the process involves pursuing symbolic clues. Although Yanagi has reversed the conventional human use of animals as pets, food, or transport, he maintains the metaphorical role that animals commonly play in art and literature. In these contexts animals are frequently anthropomorphized while humans are "animomorphized." In both cases, they are decked out in the guise of metaphors designed to help humans better understand themselves. Contemporary media offers such a menagerie. Cars are associated with mustangs, thunderbirds, cougars, and impalas. Professional sports teams include the Denver Broncos, the Seattle Sea Hawks, and the Baltimore Orioles. Exxon is personified as a tiger; Hartford Insurance aligns itself with the elk. Alternatively, human behaviors are explained in accordance with animal traits. A person is as sly as a fox, as sloppy as a pig, as busy as a bee, as silly as a goose, as eager as a beaver, as stubborn as a mule, and so forth. But what are we humans like when we act like an ant? Does the ant exemplify perseverance, social organization, anonymity, endurance, or insignificance?

EXPRESSING AN ARTISTIC ATTITUDE

Yukinori Yanagi, *Wandering Position* (1997), 17 x 17 feet, ant, wax crayon, steel angle. Courtesy of the artist. Photograph: Riho Aihara.

Obeying Ants: **Yukinori Yanagi**

The power dynamic that Yanagi enacts with the ant in this work of art is complicated. Although he conscripted the ant into artistic service, he abandoned himself to the ant's aesthetic discretion. Likewise, although the ant is a mere speck of life and the artist is a representative of human intelligence and ingenuity, the artist kowtows to his minuscule master. Nonetheless, the ant appears to be unaware of its ascension up the evolutionary ladder to attain the status of an artistic partner. It even appears oblivious to the hulking human mass many times its weight and size that stalks its every move. Nevertheless, the ant's scurrying and zigzagging behaviors do not seem mindless. The dense concentration of lines at the perimeter of the drawing reveals its determination to traverse the border of the steel beams and resume its duties as an anonymous contributor to the well-being of its community.

Yanagi has repeated this work on many occasions and in different locations. Often the resulting drawing is exhibited along with a video showing the work in the process of being created. This enables audiences to go beyond delighting in the linear configuration and explore possible relationships between the artist and the ant. Yanagi may be a stalker or a disciple. The ant may be the captive or the leader. Either may assume the role of art cata-lyst or collaborator. Answers depend upon the artist's attitude. Did he intend for viewers to chuckle at his preposterous humiliation or seek a solemn message in his humble demeanor?

Clues to the intended meaning of this work of art are intimated by the long duration, the earnest solemnity, and the acceptance of discomfort that characterizes the artist's creative act. But even prior to lifting the crayon and making the first mark, Yanagi reveals the seri-ousness of his intent. He spends several days in the room designated for the creation of this work. His demeanor is as quiet and attentive as a master calligrapher preparing himself for the creative act.

Attitude is also revealed in the artist's manner of presenting his work, which is as precise, as restrained, and as carefully considered as his manner of creating it. The steel beams that enclose the ant and the artist are specially sized and meticulously placed within the gallery space. Once the drawing is completed, Yanagi and his ant vacate the performance arena. Then the artist carefully lifts one end of each beam, rotates it slightly outward, and then lays it back upon the floor. The degree of this rotation and the precision of its placement are calculated and recalculated until the exact position is determined so that viewers can observe both the drawing and evidence of its production.

Finally, attitude is conveyed through the artist's aesthetic decisions. Although the ant's lines comprise a convoluted tangle, the artist's calm deliberation is revealed by the tidy square within which the drawing is enclosed and the gently diverging steel beams that surround it. There is nothing frivolous, impulsive, or immoderate to distract from the artist's serious intent. Attention is paid to every detail. "The piece is my own meditation," Yanagi explains. "Constructing this work is very calming, although it is hard on my knees and back. The piece wants to be like a stone garden, really simple. But the content has deep meaning. Like the garden, the work is framed off from the world. We can find great spiritual meaning there."

But further examination reveals that the attitudes that pervade this work also derive from the artist's personal history. Yanagi calls his ants "friends." This friendship began when he was a child. "I grew up in the countryside. My toys were insects, fish, birds. I liked to look at their habits and activities. I played with insects, especially the ant. It is a familiar animal to me. I made ant farms, collected moth larvae in their pupa stage and fed them money in the form of prewar paper bills that my grandmother gave me. I liked to watch them spin cocoons that were made of money. I also made maps from an ant's eye level, showing a little stone as a huge mountain, and grasses as forests." Thus, long before he became an artist, Yanagi imagined the world from an ant's perspective. From early on, he pondered the issues that would later become all consuming, that "ants and humans have missions. But an ant's mission is predetermined. Their functions are the same as ours—to acquire food, to procreate and rear our young, to preserve our safety, but they are also totally different from us. We may watch their relentless labors and think, are they tired? Are they hungry? Are they forced?"[2]

As he grew up, ants ceased being playthings and became allegories for Yukinori himself. He explains, "At school, I was like an ant zigzagging and devouring whatever I happened to find along the way." After studying art in school, he says, he became increasingly restless as an oil painting major. His desire to explore less conventional modes of art-making explains why he commemorated his graduation by burning his paintings and depositing the ashes in wooden boxes. These remains were exhibited in a Tokyo gallery along with a small glass box filled with dirt and, significantly, ants. He describes the feeling "of being trapped in a giant Japanese flag, in a cage, engulfed, suffocated by national identity! Three years into my career, I realized that I was just like the ants in the glass case working in a limited area. I was driven by an irresistible desire to get out of the ghetto called Japan." Yanagi explains this need through his own history. "I was born and raised in Fukuoka, the Japanese prefecture closest to the Korean Peninsula. In our island nation, where people are barely conscious of the national boundaries, I was occasionally forced to recognize the existence of a foreign country right next door. We often found, for example, everyday objects marked with Korean characters in the debris washed up on shore. To the Japanese, however, 'outside' does not only refer to countries across the sea, but also to people living in Japan: Korean and Chinese, native Ainu, and Okinawans."

In 1988, Yanagi escaped these cultural strictures by moving to the United States and enrolling in the graduate art program at Yale University. There he began to apply his childhood ability to experience the world from the ant's perspective to the grown-up urge to envision a more perfect social system. Yanagi's friend, the ant, introduced him to a model of consummate social organization. "I am interested in the fact that the ant is a member of a complete society, but this society differs from people's. Human society is continually being constructed and is constantly changing. Ant society is perfectly organized. It is completely perfect. The meaning of perfection is very important for my work." In fact, the ant colony is a model of the flawless coordination of specialized duties. Ants have professions. Queen ants are the egg producers who never leave their subterranean obstetrical wards. Nurse ants dig cavities for the larvae and tend to the cocoons. Harvester ants store seeds underground after nipping the radicle from each grain to prevent sprouting. Farmer ants grow fungus by fertilizing underground gardens with their own excrement. Worker ants clean house, construct elaborate architecture, and pave roadways. Shepherding ants tend flocks of plant lice by building shelters for them and milking them. Hunting ants work in packs to kill other insects. Humans can only dream of the communal efficiency that prevails within an ant's social colony. This reputation even extends back to biblical times when King Solomon advised, "Consider the ant's ways, and be wise," suggesting that aboveground cities would be well served to emulate the ant's intricate underground metropolises.

At the same time, Yanagi seems to have harbored doubts about the mindless obedience required to erect such a perfectly functioning society. "If the travels of the ant show us anything, it is that he wants to escape in order to go back home, to resume the task he has been programmed to perform, not to acquire freedom." Such reservations emerged after Yanagi undertook to decipher Japan's political past at the Yale University library, where he studied the Western version of World War II. The son of a soldier who volunteered to be a kamikaze pilot during the war, Yanagi examined his country's unquestioned acceptance of the emperor. In ancient Japanese mythology, the emperor is considered a direct descendant of the Sun Goddess; for centuries, he was worshipped as a sacred progenitor and the highest priest of Shintoism, the nation's official religion. State ideology cultivated unwavering loyalty and dutiful compliance. Yanagi came to realize that, "All these people died for the emperor because they thought he was a god, and it turned out that he was just a small man with a human voice." Obedience remained ingrained even after the Emperor renounced claims to divinity in 1945. Many citizens found an alternative repository for allegiance in the business corporation. This cultural context helps explain Yanagi's national concerns. "My works are borders I have had to cross or barriers I have confronted in trying to define myself as a Japanese,"[3] says Yanagi. The dutiful ant is a metaphor for the confining influence of Japan's government and education.

Yet Yanagi and his tiny consort confront the discrepancy between the self and community that applies to all societies. "I think that individual expression is always controlled in some way in every nation state. For instance, in the U.S., interrogation about the atomic bombs of Hiroshima/Nagasaki is taboo and controlled. What I intend to do through my work, dealing with issues related to myself, particularly about the nation state called Japan, is to suggest and investigate the issues which are universal to every modern nation state." These issues apply to the United States as well. By demonstrating that "ants don't know national boundaries,"[4] Yanagi's ants serve as allegories for the process of shifting primary allegiances away from all national territories. They demonstrate how to optimize the unification of all peoples. Once national borders are ignored, people are liberated from oppressive political influences. They finally are free to pursue personal visions. Indeed, the contemporary world seems to be evolving in this direction. The coexistence of a mélange of races and cultures increasingly characterizes the nations of the world, diminishing the influence of place in determining people's values. Furthermore, advanced technologies do not respect borders. As a result, fences and no-trespassing signs and border patrols and passports and visas no longer contain human experience. Yanagi addresses the erosion of these separatist cultural forces by asking, "Do the ghettos of nations, ethnic groups, and religions truly determine personal identities?"[5] An ongoing series of works known as the *World Flag Ant Farms* explores this theme. It, too, engages the concept of wandering explored in Yanagi's drawings, but here the wanderings are enacted by hordes of living ants as they cross the metaphorical borders of nations and enact the contest between sovereignty and community. For one of these farms, in 1990, Yanagi constructed 170 Plexiglas boxes linked by plastic tubing. Each box was filled with colored sand arranged to form the flag of one of the members of the United Nations. Into this system, masses of live harvester ants were released. The ants performed their normal activities by scurrying through the tubes and between the flags. Like refugees, tourists, explorers, and emissaries, they traveled from nation to nation. As they crossed these "borders," they dragged particles of colored sand with them, mixing the grains of one flag with the grains of the others, illustrating the mighty power of the meek to destabilize powerful institutions. As the ants disintegrated the borders, the flags lost their national identities and became, in Yanagi's own words, "a simple, equal, and hopeful way of expressing the gradual unification of all the world's nations." Gradually, the neatly differentiated flags became intermingled in the same manner that people stream across borders carrying

Yukinori Yanagi, *Asia Pacific Ant Farm* (1994), each box 12 x 18 inches, total 36 boxes, ants, colored sand, plastic box, plastic tube, and plastic pipe. Courtesy of the artist. Collection of Takamatsu City Museum of Art, Takamatsu, Japan. Photograph: Taku Saiki.

Obeying Ants: **Yukinori Yanagi**

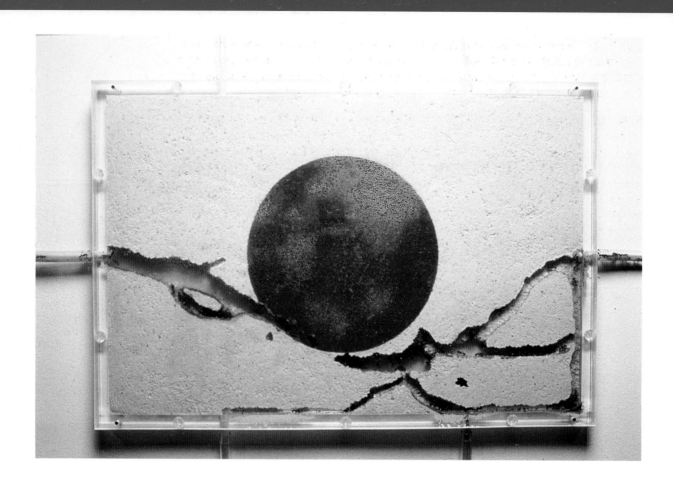

Yukinori Yanagi, *Asia Pacific Ant Farm* (1994) detail, each box 12 x 18 inches, total 36 boxes, ants, colored sand, plastic box, plastic tube, and plastic pipe. Courtesy of the artist. Collection of Takamatsu City Museum of Art, Takamatsu, Japan. Photograph: Taku Saiki.

EXPRESSING AN ARTISTIC ATTITUDE

aspects of their native cultures with them. As in *Wandering*, power positions were exchanged. The miniscule insects accomplished what treaties and wars failed to do—they united peoples across the globe. As Hafiz the great Sufi poet from the 14th century, wrote, "God blooms from the shoulder of the elephant who becomes courteous to the ant."[6]

Attitude constructs the lenses through which each artist views his or her world. Awareness of an artist's attitude permits viewers to perceive an artwork as its creator sees it. Yanagi's motive, mood, and social principles prevent his diminutive collaborator from coming across as a participant in a trivial farce. Indeed, a consideration of Yanagi's attitude-revealing qualities casts the ant in a performance of epic proportions that addresses such hefty themes as freedom, patriotism, will, compulsion, responsibility, loyalty, and globalism. Yanagi explains, "Like my ant, people live confined inside a frame which is their social system. But people also need freedom.... People may think that the nation gives them identity, but it's not so. Ethnic groups and religions don't give personal identities either. Nations, ethnicities, religions are all ghettos. They are all surrounded by imaginary boundaries born out of social or institutional constructs. Inside the ghettos, people share illusions." Presumably, the shared illusions he refers to replace personal visions. Yanagi's message is eternally pertinent, "Identity can come only through yourself."

[1] Unless otherwise noted, all quotes from an interview with the artist, December 22, 1997.

[2] From an interview with the artist, December 26, 1997.

[3] Carol Lutfy, "Taking On the Taboos in Japan," *International Herald Tribune*, 19 August 1995.

[4] Jeffrey Deitch, *Border Crawl* (Seoul: Kukje Gallery, 1995).

[5] "A Japanese Clay Figurine's Thoughts," in *Wandering Positions: Yukinori Yanagi* (Benesse Island: Maoshima Contemporary Art Museum, 1993), n.p.

6. Hafiz, *The Gift: Poems by Hafiz the Great Sufi Master*, trans. Daniel Ladinsky (New York: Panguin Compass, 1997), 87.

Spoofing Biblical Miracles to Inspire Christian Faith

The Reverend Ethan Acres
Born 1970 Ft. Payne, Alabama
1993 University of Texas at Austin, BFA, painting
1996 University of Nevada, Las Vegas, MFA, multimedia
1996 Doctorate of Divinity from the World Christianship Ministries
Lives and works in Los Angeles, California

The Reverend Ethan Acres abounds with love for imperfect people and for a perfect God. He loves folks who need encouragement and those who seek forgiveness, and he readily includes himself among their ranks. The Reverend admits he has succumbed to laziness, gluttony, and envy, among other human temptations. Still, he sermonizes from the pinnacle of exuberance, singing hallelujahs, reciting spirit-rousing tales that contain as many references to popular culture as to biblical verse. Acres provides the occasion for people to giggle their way toward redemption. His attitude is that of an angel of mercy sent to offset the cynicism, despair, anger, frustration, and defiance that ricochet across the contemporary airwaves.

Ethan Acres's nose points toward heaven and his belly descends toward hell. In between these destinations beats a joyful Christian heart. This officially ordained Reverend loves God. He loves people. He loves them exuberantly. Sin, punishment, guilt, and retribution are conspicuously absent from his vocabulary. Heaven and harp replace fire and brimstone in the sermons he delivers from the flocked pulpit of his custom-designed mobile chapel and in art galleries and museums. His title as Reverend publicly declares him to be a man devoted to God. But his second "higher calling" is fulfilled as an artist. Thus, his dual professional credentials merge human and divine inspiration, priming him for spiritual service to humanity. An evangelical preacher in a Christian church of his own devising, Acres's art is preaching. Likewise, his sculptures, Photoshop creations, costumes, and paintings constitute his ministry. "Art and religion do the same thing," he says. "They are ritualized practices that manifest in the material world what's going on in a person. They make visions physical, transforming abstract ideas into tangible forms."[1]

Las Vegas, the capital of sex and flesh and gluttony and sin, has been the Reverend's home. It is a place uniquely suited to his double mission. A satellite of the prestigious Solomon R. Guggenheim Museum was recently added to the glitzy Las Vegas strip, amidst replicas of the Easter Island idols, the Great Pyramids, the Eiffel Tower, and the Manhattan skyline. As a man of the cloth, he prefers spandex, fake fur, and plastic to black serge. He is a reverend, an artist, and an entertainer. By combining the social roles of this grand triumvirate of professions, Acres uplifts the spirits of his world-weary congregants—including members of sophisticated art audiences.

The Reverend describes his Highway Chapel as a 1965 Shasta camper that he takes on the road to administer sacraments from baptisms to weddings. It has a tiny pulpit and altar. A framed copy of Acres's Doctorate of Divinity hangs beneath the mirrored ceiling and disco ball, above the purple carpeting, and beside the fake stained-glass windows and a crucifix filled with red bubbling "holy water." Because the Highway Chapel was being repaired when I visited Las Vegas, our interview took place in a cheesy Las Vegas motel room that the Reverend had reserved and outfitted for the occasion. I entered to discover music emitting from a tape player, videos of his performances waiting for the "play" button to be pressed, and photographs of his artworks laid out upon the dresser. Five hours later, the bed remained undisturbed, but my spirit was stirred.

"I don't consider myself a prophet," Acres began, "but there is such a long history of men of God going into the desert and finding God. Isaiah: 43 says, 'Make straight in the desert a highway for your God.' Everyone comes to Las Vegas to rebuild themselves. People come to implode their past, build fresh, start over. I didn't eat locust and honey. I had a 99-cent beer and shrimp cocktails. But I too came to find a vision."

Acres was born with a cherubic face that now sits atop a burly, six-foot-four-inch frame. But the rest of his physical appearance is designed to serve as an outward manifestation of his inner grace. A shaved head contributes a radiant, halo-like glow. His barbed wire bracelets represent humility, like "a crown of thorns." The gold ring that pierces the septum between his nostrils indicates submissiveness. Acres likens himself to Jeremiah, whose words he quotes: "Lead me, oh Lord, like a bull unaccustomed to the yoke." He adds with his down-home wit and Southern-molasses drawl, "and like the cattle on my grandfather's farm in Northern Alabama."[2] In all these ways, he displays that he is aiming for "a higher purpose," a goal pursued by applying high-voltage antics to convey the high commandments delivered by the Lord himself. "As a minister, I function like a DJ at a party. People come to the party. I provide the beat. People can either dance or sit against the walls. But hopefully, if the mix is good, everyone is getting something out of it."

The Reverend Ethan Acres shares the breadth of his life's experiences when he sermonizes, including confessions of his ungodly lapses in deportment. He and his wife sometimes drink, gamble, and overeat. And though Acres may not stand naked before his people, he is willing to toss away his ministerial robes and appear before his congregation in a fake-fur loincloth or a spandex suit and alien's helmet. The latter outfit provided the theme for an impassioned sermon based on a vision inspired by watching *Ultraman* reruns on television. Like Ultraman, the Reverend saw himself as a warrior of the nebula of light, protecting the Earth from evil (the giant monster Teresedon) and menace (the Baltans), gathering disciples (soldiers of the Science Patrols), and heralding the resurrection (Zapphi). Acres exhorted, "Brothers and sisters, be my Ultramen and Ultrawomen, not wimps like Superman. You don't have to wear spandex, but you do have to get your power from someplace. Get it from the Lord! Hallelujah! Get it from the Lord." Even if the messenger seems ludicrous, his message is offered in earnest. Acres declares that it is his mission "to be a fool for God's sake, a holy fool."

Acres's sculptures function as sermons too. In *Pearls 2 Pigs* (1999), the Reverend installed flashing red lightbulbs in the eye sockets of oversized pigs sewn from sheets of shiny pink car-seat vinyl and stitched together with Velcro and zippers. Their mouths are gaping orifices out of which long, floppy tongues protrude. They tremble. Although they look as if possessed by wickedness, in actuality they are

Interview with The Reverend Ethan Acres
By Ry Russo-Young

RY: What role did school play in your preparation to become an artist?

REA: While I was in graduate school, I was really against graduate school. It was really a traumatizing experience for me because I didn't fit in and people told me what I was doing was horrible.... The only thing I learned from the university was paranoia [cracks up laughing]. Rejection was hanging over my head all the time. So I came out of school completely neurotic and freaked out. But now I look back on it and see it as having been beneficial. I think it's a place where you make connections and you meet people and have the opportunity for people in the art world to come through and talk to you and see your work.

RY: So would you recommend it to other artists?

REA: I don't think it really matters which school you go to, but it does matter what place you go to school. Vegas is very influential to me. I mean just the place itself, this weird conglomeration of popular culture all shoved together on this strip. You automatically begin making analogies between the pyramids and medieval castles and New York City and that has a lot to do with my work—making connections between popular culture and esoteric religious ritual and religious thinking. Vegas also taught me one of a preacher's and an artist's greatest tools—showmanship! As a preacher you are trying to capture the imagination of your congregation and as an artist you're trying to capture the imagination of your audience. So it's very much the same thing.

RY: Can you describe your studio?

REA: Right now my studio is just here on this ranch in Texas. My studio is typically a mess [laughs]. Bits and pieces of works that have failed are usually laying around. My banjo is always there, and I always have a stereo, and typically I always have a television. I tend to listen to the television more than I listen to the radio when I'm working. I own an industrial sewing machine, so that's always there. Usually lots and lots of big containers of chemicals and things like that. I tend to work on many things at one time so there's a lot of unfinished things laying around, maybe things that won't ever see the light of day, that no one will ever see. There's a lot of junk. I'm a thrift-store person too. I'm always going out and buying more stuff and bringing it in for my own pleasure.

RY: How are the costs of producing your work allocated?

REA: I don't operate with any sort of trust fund and thus far I haven't received any grants. Basically I just tend to be really thrifty. When I do sermons I get paid. A large portion of the money that I make goes right back into the work.

RY: So you don't have a day job?

REA: No, no, no, I can't. It's not that I haven't thought about it, but I'm always late and, I don't know, I just don't work out. I was one of those kids who always had the report card that said, "Doesn't work well with

Rev. Ethan Acres, *The Highway Chapel* (1996), recreational vehicle used as a chapel. Courtesy of the artist and Patricia Faure Gallery, Santa Monica, California.

possessed by the Walmart-bought electric fans installed in their bellies. Acres removed all but one blade on each fan, making the pigs shake when the fans whirled. Motion sensors activated CD players installed in the pigs's heads, producing a cacophony of oinking noises. At their feet lay scattered white balls. In this manner Acres admonished his audience: "Cast not your pearls to pigs lest they turn, trample, and devour you." (Matthew 7:6). Likewise, in another piece, an "army" of locusts descends down a wall in formation wearing army helmets and dog tags, and equipped with toy Scorpion-missile tails. They stir the soul like this verse from Revelations: "And then came out of the smoke locusts upon the earth: their shape like horses prepared unto battle. On their heads were crowns like gold, their faces were the faces of men, and in their tails were stings like scorpions." Elsewhere, the Lamb of God circles the gallery like a merry-go-round and Mary's body is formed around a lava lamp. In medieval churches, art conveyed the gospels to people who were illiterate and could not read the Bible. Now, according to Acres, people can read, but they are illiterate in a religious way. "The Bible has changed in popular culture. We are scared of it. We don't have long attention spans. We are visual creatures. It is hard for us to read section after section of 'begans' and 'begats.'" The Reverend's artworks replace the Bible. They inject religion into today's cultural bloodstream.

Chuckles are welcome. But the Reverend also hopes that people will be moved to accept his God, one who is more inclined to forgive than forbid. Sins, he believes, are personal, not ordained. "The lessons in the Bible were written by a man inspired by God. Like making a Xerox copy, you don't get an exact interpretation of a divine plan.... The Old Testament God was vengeful and angry. The New Testament God, Christ, is loving. Since we are the representation of the divine, then there are bad moments and good moments. All those failings are of God, too. The beauty about being human is that we can never be perfect. The fact that we fall makes us beautiful. I would hate it if people were perfect." Acres believes that the Devil represents universal sins such as stealing, adultery, and greed. Personal demons, however, represent idiosyncratic sins. These sins are often associated with new varieties of temptations that generate new strains of guilt, producing new crops of prophets who warn against succumbing to them. Today, many of these sin-admonishing prophets enter the hearts of the masses via televisions, tapes, and the Internet. Many do not participate in revival meetings, television prayer clubs, and Christian choirs. Instead, they seek more current ways to keep mortals on the path of self-perfection. Four such leaders are presented as larger-than-life wall constructions in *Personal Demons* (2000). They embody a contemporary code of morality in which good and evil are measured in inches (around the waist) and pounds (upon the bathroom scale). Their names are familiar: Richard Simmons (the cheerleader for dieters), Jane Fonda (the model of the diligent exerciser), Suzanne Sommers

others" or, "Doesn't play well with others." So, no, no, no, I just sort of slump by. The thing is, a lot of artists worry excessively about money. I find if you work hard it always comes in. Sometimes you might be a little late with the bills, but by and large I think you can do it. You can't live extravagantly. I would say probably about sixty to seventy percent comes from the sale of my work and the other comes from my teaching and lectures and things.

RY: Do you think that these are difficult issues for an artist, this money thing?

REA: Lisa [Acres' wife] and I gave up our credit cards years ago because we got into trouble with them. I'm not lying to you when I say there have been times that I have cursed myself for not having a credit card. You get in these awful situations where a show's coming up and suddenly you have to buy twenty-five plastic deer. It's like so ridiculous!

RY: What were the most significant exhibitions you've had?

REA: I had my first show at Patricia Faure Gallery in Santa Monica, California. It was really great ... I mean, my work tends to be a little difficult because it deals with religion. The whole right-wing notion of Christian thinking has sort of polluted popular culture to the point where people, and with good reason, tend to be a little nervous. Recently, I did a show in Stockholm, Sweden ... basically they want to have the artist in this Kunsthalle over the course of the show for like six weeks. You do your work every day in the gallery. So I was able to go build a new chapel out of an old trailer that I found north of Stockholm. Right inside the gallery, every day, I would do sermons. The Kunsthalle was open six days a week so I was preaching every day, four to five times a day. Sometimes you would have forty people there and sometimes you'd have one person. It wasn't the most widely publicized show I was in but it allowed me to grow very much as an artist.

RY: What would you say is the most significant sale you've had?

REA: I'll tell you, there was one sale that was significant, mainly because it revealed how absurd my life had become. A couple from Venice bought this piece, a crucifix made out of vinyl and different kinds of fun furs and stuff. I couldn't go to Italy to see it installed, but I got to see pictures. At the time I made the sale, I was so broke I was working part time as a Wells Fargo security guard. I'll never forget these pictures. I didn't open the envelope until I got to work and I was working this really late shift. So here I am in this mall parking lot in one of those little golf carts they drive around, and I'm pulling out the pictures and seeing this piece of mine at this really fancy cocktail party, you know all these people with nice clothes standing around looking at it and here I am out on this golf cart in the middle of the night in Las Vegas! So I think that was a significant thing for me because it made me realize how separate artists are from their work. You see what I'm saying? It's like your work

Rev. Ethan Acres, *ULTRA-MAN* (1999), sermon/performance at Patricia Faure Gallery, Santa Monica, California. Courtesy of the artist and Patricia Faure Gallery.

(ThighMaster guru and low-carb connoisseur), and Billy Blank (Tae-Bo advocate). Acres equates sticking to a diet and maintaining an exercise regimen with following traditional Christian principles. The analogy is not so far-fetched. These diet and exercise principles supply definitions of guilt, sin, and retribution for a great many Americans, over half of whom are officially classified as overweight. The Reverend portrays himself in their midst, fighting demons like St. Paul in a losing battle. His failure to achieve Jane's and Richard's standards of perfection is revealed in the technique he has chosen for representing them. Although Acres dutifully watches their exercise videos, they fail to flatten his belly because instead of jumping and stretching, he spent long hours sitting on his couch crocheting their likenesses in yarn. Most preachers describe the struggle of "exorcising" demons, but Acres speaks about the struggle imposed by "exercising" demons. He says, "Exercising demons is a testimony to one man's ongoing battle against the forces of darkness, and questions whether or not creamy, nougat-filled confections are the works of God or possibly the Devil."

The Reverend's zest for hope, charity, and love matches his appetite for food. He admits that, "Happiness is on occasion chemically induced: Hershey's chocolate, Thousand Island dressing, Pringles potato chips." All his many passions are represented in *The Sermons of Reverend Ethan Acres* (2001), a book that has a white, faux alligator cover, gold embossing, and a red ribbon. It includes a clandestine wedding in the Sistine Chapel; an exorcism at the Santa Monica Museum of Art; and a pilgrimage to the J. Paul Getty Museum, but it also features the Rev. Mrs. Acres's recipes for Texas-style brisket, snickerdoodles, and oatmeal cookies.The Reverend received his Doctorate of Divinity from the World Christianship Ministries via a correspondence course. Simultaneously, he was a student in the progressive Master of Fine Arts program at the University of Nevada, Las Vegas—two colliding educational contexts. Many of his art professors then, and some art critics now, assume he is poking fun at religion. They perceive satire, for example, in a large photograph that depicts the looming soul of a pet beagle rising above the Reverend, who stands with bowed head, offering solemn benediction to the deceased pet who lies in the middle of an urban street. Tiny dots of light rise from the corpse to its spirit. Instead of ascending with solemnity, however, the beagle sprouts wings and bounds toward heaven as a puppy might. *A Final Voyage of the Beagle* (1997) takes the form of a black-and-white silkscreen on Mylar hung several inches away from the wall, which gives the impression that it is as diaphanous as a religious vision. The Gothic typeface used in place of the artist's signature reinforces the biblical context. But does this work affirm or spoof hallowed images of ascension in religious art? Acres insists that no mockery is intended in this work, nor in the series in which women wearing fur coats are surrounded by the ascending forms of the mink, fox, and raccoons who died for the fur-wearers's "sins"—as fur coats. "Animals seem

somehow can have a much bigger and richer life than the artist has.

RY: Were there people who promoted your career when you were still unknown?

REA: There was an instructor that I had in graduate school. He really gave me a permission that I probably wouldn't have gotten from any other artist. I was starting to really concentrate my work on faith and religion, really trying to break that boundary between the two sides of my life. You know a lot of people thought I was insane and that no one would pay any attention to me. Jeffrey Vallance was a major proponent of letting it all go and not worrying about that. And that permission was the main thing, a permission to find your own way.

RY: How do you assess the longevity of your career in the future?

REA: I do worry sometimes about that. I do this weird sculpture and performance kind of thing. Sometimes I will wander into a show by a painter and all this jealousy will bubble up, little voices in my head nagging me saying, "They didn't have to pay as much money as I did, they just got some canvas and paint … nothing to break, nothing to fall apart." Sometimes you let that sort of thing build up in you, and you get upset. I can't compete financially. I can't compete. But in the end you just gotta keep plodding along and doing your thing. To be honest, there's nothing else I can do. I mean, this is really it. I don't have any other skills. I don't really have a choice. For that reason, I just have to let the jealousy go and keep working.

RY: What advice would you give the current generation of aspiring artists?

REA: I think what I would suggest is to try not to look at trends, not to make work because you think it'll sell. I think my advice would be to really try to dedicate your life to something that you care about, something that you love, whether it's in fashion or not. Like I was just saying, this is something that you are going to hopefully do for the majority of your life. If you don't really care about it, if you don't love what you're doing, then what's the point?

RY: How has your choice of a place to live and work affected your career?

REA: For financial reasons Lisa and I have had to live in some really rough places, slumming in houses infested with roaches that make gas station toilets look like the Ritz, just so we can know for sure that we can survive. That can be detrimental to your work. If you're constantly worrying about the toilet exploding or roaches carrying you off in the middle of the night—that doesn't exactly make for a great creative environment. Yet at the same time some of my best work has been made during my darker moments, when things are bleak. Somehow you instill that desire for something more in the work. In those moments of depression, you're the most hungry to create the greatest things.

RY: Is that when you're the most productive, would you say?

Rev. Ethan Acres, *KISSY SNAKE: Gene Simmons, Temptation* (2001), 80 x 80 inches, crocheted yarn. Courtesy of the artist and Patricia Faure Gallery, Santa Monica, California. Photograph: Anthony Cunha.

so pure of heart," insists Acres. "I believe animals have souls, especially dogs." But, he insists, it is not just sentimentality that inspires these works. Animals help people address solemn topics many prefer to suppress, such as the inevitability of death. "Almost everyone has a story about a dog who died," notes Acres. "For many people, that is their first experience with mortality. For some, it is the only time they have been touched by death."

"My work is a door that allows people to step into a new world," he says, explaining his artistic attitude. "I give people permission to explore their belief in a different way. Humor belongs with religion. I think we laugh to deal with things that make us nervous. Physically, that laughter allows us to get over that initial shock. Humor is not poking fun at religion. It's a way to say that it is okay to think about this without worrying whether you are right or wrong. Other preachers may be equipped to do it with tragedy and high drama. I have to work with my gifts. To me, humor is the surest way to make it real and human—that is what religion and art are supposed to be. They are human endeavors about human journeys."

The good Reverend shares his jubilant feelings, proclaiming, "The Good Lord has gone and set off an M-80 of joy inside my head. Glory to God, and I intend to get a little glop of happy on all those around me."[3] It is his evangelical enthusiasm that is most likely to provoke the consternation of an art audience that tends to prefer cynicism and irony. Acres's brand of Christianity is not hip in the art world. Being "cold as a Buddhist," he says, would render him more likely to be embraced. At the same time, his preaching lacks the solemnity of the "shalls" and "shall nots" preferred by the faithful. "If people get irritated, that is good. Religion and art should stir you up, make you mad or glad. I gave a lecture at the University of Southern California. A guy held up his hand and asked me if there is any work that I think is blasphemous. And I told him, 'The only work that is blasphemous is the work that doesn't take chances. That is the worst affront to God.' As long as you pull people a little off center, whether you push them back or pull them forward, you are providing a situation where change can occur—psychologically and spiritually. That is the basis of what I do." But the Reverend's "pushing" and "pulling" is directionless. "How can I lead people to a path? The only path I could lead them to is my path, and why would I do that? I can hardly pay my bills. Every person's path is different. My function is to lead them to their own path. This is a personal thing."

For this reason, Acres's sermons are less admonitions than amusing stories about his childhood. He is fond of recalling a conflict between him and his mother over his school lunch box. She wanted him to have a Donny and Marie lunch box because they provided virtuous role models. He coveted one with a picture of the Satanic band Kiss. The image of the musicians entwined by a serpent lingers to this day as a lesson about the garden of innocence and the tree of

REA: Absolutely, yeah. Not when things are going good, no. I gain weight. I don't do anything. I sit and watch DVDs.

RY: Do you have any past artistic decisions you've regretted?

REA: I regret not working more, I regret not trying a little harder at times.

RY: Do you struggle to maintain yourself as an artist?

REA: No, in that I don't feel like I ever had a choice. I feel like this is the only thing I can do and do even remotely well. Therefore, maintaining myself as an artist would be like maintaining myself as a Caucasian. I mean how am I going to do that? It's just sort of in your blood. It's just who you are. It's part of your nature. I think I do owe my fortune to having faith, because I believe that through faith anything's possible. If you leave those doubts behind, I think you can do anything. I do believe that. I know it sounds kind of silly, but I do believe that. I have to believe in that.

STERN

knowledge. "I was so tempted," he recalls. "Knowledge is so hot and sexy.... It's a fascinating power struggle. Whether you are religious or not, these are great stories about the human journey and self-sacrifice and temptation and betrayal and problems with your parents. The Bible is not just about faith."

Acres began preaching at the tender age of ten, when he stood on street corners and cajoled people to attend the revival meetings conducted by his preacher stepfather. His interest in art arose at the same time. "When I was around kids in school, I was quiet and nervous. But when I had a Bible in my hand, I was an agent of God. I felt so strong, nothing could stop me." As time went on, he began to think that a gallery was not so different from a church. "Both ministers and artists take chances in front of people, lay themselves bare and let people take and take from a font from inside them that shows who they are and what their belief systems are. If they are able to transport their congregation or audience to another time, place, or level, they have done their job. Art either represents the divine or the damned. This is the catalyst by which we change or fall. That is what religion and art are supposed to be—human endeavors about human journeys."

1. David Pagel "Faith Be No Proud," *Los Angeles Times*, 17 April 2001, 4.

2. Unless otherwise noted, all quotes from an interview with the artist, June 7, 2000.

3. Ethan Acres, "A Sermon by Rev. Ethan Acres: The Straight or Crooked Way," *Art Issues* no. 56 (January/February 1999), 14–18.

EXPRESSING AN ARTISTIC ATTITUDE

Marcia Lyons
Born Toledo, Ohio
1981 University of Georgia, BFA, painting
1988 School of Visual Arts, New York, MFA, sculpture
1994 New York University, certificate in video
Lives and works in New York City and Paris

Marcia Lyons transfers the experience of bearing human offspring conceived in biological sensual immersion to a sensual immersion into technology. She and her machines create enduring, interactive, and evolving artworks that acquire lives of their own. Lyons's attitude is expressed when she describes machines as "gooey and malleable" and discusses the blurring of relationships from a "machine/sex orientation." Lyons optimizes the possibilities for viewers to be swept into her rapture and develop their own sensual relationship to computer technologies by offering (otherwise known as exhibiting in an art gallery) her cybernated, virtualized infants or pets (otherwise known as artworks) for home adoption (otherwise known as "sale").

Marcia Lyons's speech proceeds at sonic speeds and her topics leap like quanta packets breaking the barriers of normal consciousness. She can be mind-numbingly contradictory. At one moment, she proclaims everlasting life via the Internet. At another, she mourns the fact that her virtual digitized offspring are subject to death. Then, she asserts the perpetuation of life after death outside of cyberspace, through spirit energies that are electrical in nature. When confronted with these inconsistencies, Lyons makes no apology. To her, they are not signs of confusion, but a testimony to the breadth of possibilities she entertains. Her delight in incongruity and diversity is also made manifest in her lifestyle. Lyons has constructed several divergent personas that she assumes and discards with ease. Each persona harvests specific domains of information. Each has its own social networks, technological interfaces, and psychic channels.

Meanwhile, Lyons overhauls the syllabus for her digital media classes several times a year. In fact, she estimates that most "givens" need to be updated every three months. She applies this frenetic pace to her entire life. Lyons is not content to discover emerging facets of contemporary fashion, technology, entertainment, and culture. Nor is she satisfied with arriving on time to witness their arrival. Lyons strives to anticipate impending events, imminent concepts, and looming technologies. She says she watches thirty movies per weekend while listening to selections from her stockpile of compact discs. She is in a frenzy to keep apace of all that is new. Her life and her art demonstrate her belief that anyone who is not actively constructing newness is irrelevant.

Lyons's mad-dash life demands that she continually disengage from dead ends in order to respond to new beginnings. No single persona and no single location can contain her appetite to include an infinity of experiences in the finite dimensions of her life. "I want to always be creating and inventing. Hair, shoes, spaces, partners. I can't wait. If IT is perfume, IT is my scent. If I could implant IT, I would be the first. Lights would blink when I get an implanted message. I will walk around pulsing, glowing like a Christmas tree. I don't want to make a bunch of stuff that gets stored. I want to morph."[1] In New York, Lyons wears a wig as blue as the Nike logo, eight-inch platform shoes, and a padded silver jacket. The space in which she lives is efficient and severe. But that description only applies to her apartment on the East Coast. In the other locations she also calls "home," she could be described with different sets of characteristics. In Los Angeles, she wears a Barbie-pink wig and her living quarters are furnished with inflatable furniture. In Rome, she has set up a Baroque and sensual flat, and in Tokyo her apartment has a playful, cartoon-like ambience. She also has a private retreat in the country that is distinguished by the absence of a telephone and computer. In this way, Lyons has propagated five personas. Each is a compound being whose appearance and personality are determined by its contact point on the globe: Europe, Japan, both coasts of the United States, and one that is private. It is as if five distinct Marcias inhabit the earth, each of them contrived to be remarkable. She likens her lifestyle to "living a movie life which is better than real life. I am charming in the way that you are charmed by a character who comes to life on the big screen in a dark theater. It feels like it is just you and one of the five mes. Disbelief is suspended. I am a subliminal, anthropomorphic, interactive video clip."

One might think having a collection of identities would make it difficult to find a life partner. Yet Lyons insists she is utterly fulfilled in love. She speaks of her partner in rapturous tones. The recipient of her affections is nonjudgmental, cooperative, undemanding, and responds to her desires with electric speed. Best of all, this partner has an appetite for venturing that is as voracious as her own. Marcia Lyons is in love with technology. "I don't mean I love my monitor and my central processing unit. It is the experience and the involvement that has sucked me in. I sleep, eat, think it. I am there, totally, in each moment." Technology won her affection because it is better than any person at enabling her to multiply realities. Furthermore, it is loyal to all of her personas. Her euphoria appears sincere: Lyons says that romantic ardor stirs when she plugs into new technologies and immerses herself in the catapulting force of their communications capabilities. She speaks rapturously of combining output options with her techno mate, fondly named N2BLAK. "N is an unknown number times 2," she explains. "The 'blak' is the sound of the space where it happened." Lyons uses the word "it" frequently in her speech to refer to anything of particular significance. She then notes, "If N x 2 could equal that, I imagine the form to be like a kind of company, self-sufficient, before-verbal … almost before body … a punctuation of a space."[2] To Lyons, communicating through the Internet is as passionate as a physical embrace and as exciting as romance. "You can almost feel the energies traveling all around you. It affects the environment. If you get an e-mail, it sticks in your stomach. What love provides, new technology provides, all the romantic, physical urge, in flesh, separate from [the] mind."

As is typical in love relationships, Lyons's full-throttle passion progressed from infatuation to the urge to procreate. Her offspring come into being as a result of an ecstatic event—a version of conception that occurs in the absence of flesh and tactile stimulation. Foreplay occurs when Lyons feeds a visual representation of

Interview with Marcia Lyons
By Ry Russo-Young

RY: What was the first indication that you would become a recognized and respected artist?

ML: Respectable is the real word. I think I really didn't know there was such a thing as an artist when I was growing up—someone who did it as a living or as a way of life. When I announced that I wanted to be an artist to my family, everyone tried to steer me away just because it's not practical. But it wasn't until graduate school that I met other professional, working, showing artists in New York City. That is when I understood what it means to live the life of an artist. It really involves a lot of sacrifice, a lot of juggling of other jobs to keep going.

RY: How do you feel that school has prepared you to be an artist?

ML: Well, I'm teaching, but I was never a really good student. I couldn't follow directions. It isn't like you can go to school and learn how to be an artist. I went to school more so that I would be qualified to teach in the academic environment.

RY: How has your choice of a place to live and work affected your career?

ML: New York has been another kind of school. You grow into New York. You become part of New York. Like wearing shoes, it takes a long time until they feel comfortable and they fit your lifestyle. I got a studio in New York to become an artist. Now I find when I'm away from New York I lose my identity. My work is pretty edgy so it doesn't really fit with a regional audience. It competes with filmmaking. So I need that kind of audience that can get beyond this relationship to other forms of media.

RY: Do you feel like you have a specific audience?

ML: No, I guess I don't. I'm making the art for me, what I like to live with, what inspires me, what gets me to start working.

RY: What advice would you give to the current generation of aspiring artists?

ML: It depends on the temperament and the type of work someone is doing. I'm pretty particular about what I say to each person. It's important to have a lot of encouragement when you're young. Discouragement tends to happen in New York on a harsh level, just on day-to-day life. Also, if you love doing what you do, it would be nice to be able to grow into that talent. So I would encourage students to keep learning, keep following the curve, especially any kind of new technology. Find out about it. Play with it. I think new technology, new media give you the option of being mainstream. Incorporating your artwork with your work life is so much more possible now if you embrace digital environments at whatever level. It's like paint in a tube. I mean it's like the camera. What's the big deal? Everybody should glom on. It's the fastest-growing industry. It offers a Renaissance for young artists. It's like [the] fifteenth century, or the WPA, or any kind of

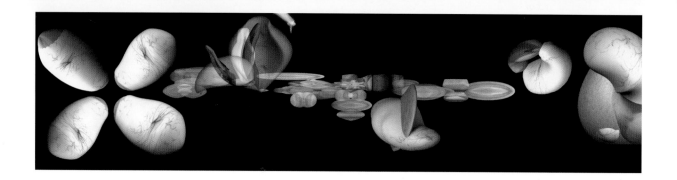

Marcia Lyons, *N2blak: Seeded Bodies* (1998), digital animation on DVD, projection, 120 min. Courtesy of the artist.

a piece of her body into an electronic imaging device that transforms it into the coded language of pure data. She calls this digitized version of herself a "mediartspace" clone. She has a special fondness for using photographs of her body's deep, moist, private parts. Her own larynx became the core image for a work entitled *B-emovie* (1998). Recorded sounds from deep inside her throat provided the work's sound source. Thus the conception of her offspring transpired, appropriately, deep within her body. These images and sounds were the nucleus of "embryos" that eventually developed into "data bodies" whose "mother" Lyons claims to be. In this manner, Lyons and her digital partner spawn digital beings that resemble their parental software. Conception is followed by gestation, which, in this case, is the digital conversion and processing of these virtual components of Lyons's body. Visually, the baby data bodies resemble blobs of protoplasm whose surfaces are marked with traceries of veins, arteries, and neural pathways. These surface patterns derive from images of Lyons's throat that were digitally wrapped around three-dimensional forms that resemble condoms or buttocks or breasts bursting with liquid. During this phase of their evolution, the data bodies also develop kinetic qualities. They throb, elongate, twist, flatten, slither, multiply, and divide like generic forms of life. Their continuous motion suggests breath and pulse, dilation and contraction, waking and sleeping, all the essential life rhythms. Once they have generated the appearance and mobility of life, biomorphic voices are appended to them. These noises are constructed through computer manipulations of the artist's throat sounds. If Lyons's animated, clone-like constructions resemble current advances in laboratories where actual life forms are being created, the coincidence is legitimate. Lyons shares with scientists and inventors the desire to achieve a seamless merging of human and machine; she maintains her artist's status, however, by the aesthetic concerns and emotional fervor that drive her creative process.

Lyons is not content to limit her creations to the physical signs of life. The gestation process continues until each data body is capable of participating in the fulsome love relationship that spawned it. Her virtual babies are thus granted virtual intelligence and virtual personalities. One program makes them responsive to external stimuli. Another makes them develop in infinite variations and capable of unpredictable behavior. They are endowed with the software to be nervous and placid, funny and stubborn. They can hiccup, whimper, giggle, and sob. They are also capable of self-reproduction. But despite these liberating capabilities, like all life forms, they always retain their connection to their progenitors. Unlike other life forms, these progenitors consist of one artist and her electronic partner, N2BLAK. Though Lyons has multiple real-life personas, it is within cyberspace where she can propagate without restraint. Birth occurs when the digitized life form can sustain an independent life in the virtual world. It exists in the virtual womb of Lyons's computer console and is thrust into the world in the form of an interactive

system that employs artists, keeps artists vital, makes the art relevant, and brings the art into ordinary life. I think galleries are behind the curve.

RY: Describe your studio.

ML: My studio is nomadic. It's wherever I am. I have a studio [in] upstate New York. I have a studio in New York City. My studio is my laptop, my computers, my video projector, the tapes that I'm playing, the surfaces that I'm working with, the manufactures that I'm using. So I'm very fluid.

RY: What percent of your income is earned by the sale of your art?

ML: Probably twenty-five percent.

RY: What's the other?

ML: Teaching. Public projects are probably another twenty-five percent. It's year-to-year. It varies. I've never been able to support myself solely on my work. All my equipment comes through my teaching.

RY: Do you have assistants?

ML: If I'm having a show, for a length of time before the show I will. I think it's damaging for technicians to be too involved in the making of your work. I don't really believe in assistants making my art.

RY: Were there times in your life when you were particularly productive and inventive?

ML: When I first moved to New York, for the first couple years, I couldn't be in the studio more than three hours a day, or three times a week. Every day was just exhausting. I couldn't perform. I couldn't produce. I couldn't think. And now it's so much a part of my identity that when I'm not working I feel like there's something wrong. Twelve years of being out in the public and twenty-two years of being private has given me enough confidence to deal with the highs and the lows that come with it. You are your own cheerleader and your own support system. The art world is very competitive. Also, I recognized that to develop work I had to be outside of New York. So I would take a year and be in Italy, or I would take a year in Canada to try a new medium, just to get me stretching. It's like flexing a muscle or flexing your brain and playing tennis. You have to find your range, find your ability, your style, and then your thing becomes you as you become it.

RY: What do you regret about your past artistic decisions?

ML: I regret going with galleries that weren't financially stable. I'd go with a gallery because they offered me a show, said they loved my work, but then they'd go out of business. The momentum would be stalled. That's happened several times. I'm recognizing that I have to be funded in a public sense so that means that I have to pursue projects that are funded in different ways than the traditional object-buying, as in a store situation. My personal life has taken me off the path a couple of times. The men that I've been married to were not supportive. I would follow them and help their careers, but that was based on hormones and biology and trying to have a family and also make art.

movie projection. Its eerie presence in real space and time begins in art galleries and museums. These sites function like adoption agencies that present each digital orphan to prospective real-life parents. Lyons's data bodies are most suited for adoption into smart homes, where, she says, they take the form of "sensuround" environments. Each installation consists of three wall-sized projections, three video players, three sets of five-channel speakers, and three receivers. The sound can be powerful enough to make a floor vibrate. Thus, the data body not only occupies all the interior surfaces within its "parents'" home, it also affects its parents' bodies. They see it, hear it, and feel it. Lyons says that acquiring one is an "experience-tainment exchange," not a business transaction. Owners can choose to use the projections as background enhancements for their lives, or they can actually merge their existence with the data body's life, which explains the trade-mark, *B-emovie*. The title reveals that people can choose "to *be* or not to *be*" the movie.

Lyons's creations are ultimately adaptive. Unlike an inert art object, these responsive, surrogate life forms provide companionship like a pet, a housemate, or a child. They beckon. They charm. They greet. Light, sound, and motion sensors are triggered when a person walks into a room. By programming a delay between action and response, the data body's responses seem sympathetic, not mechanical. A list of tracks rotates and changes the data body's actions from random, to idiosyncratic, to habitual. It can approach you, comfort you, humor you. Lyons observes, "Once your tone and sound are registered, they feel what you feel." By adjusting its actions, it can satisfy your emotional needs and alter your state of mind. It may behave in a manner that is intimate, endearing, silly, soothing, or dynamic. It may talk to you, repeating a phrase like "Today was the perfect day," if that is what you wish to hear. The machine ceases to be an impersonal tool. It offers and receives emotions. Lyons proudly exclaims, "That's what I can provide with my love experiences!"

Lyons describes her version of conception and birth in rapturous tones. "There is the instant when the computer does what it does and the images join with sound and tone. At that instant, a new being is allowed to speak out with personality and occupy its own space in the virtual, to be a kind of presence. You can commune with it. You fall in love, merge, and then you are left with a life form that you have absolutely no control over. Sometimes it gets morphed into things that you weren't intending at all. Wherever this new virtual environment expands, life forms that I have procreated, that I gave birth to, will stream!" Lyons has magnified the emotional rapport offered by such technological playthings as Tamagotchi, Nano Pets, and robotic puppies, and has expanded their potential by offering owners a multiplicity of options for customizing their electronic housemates. The manufacturers of these novelty items have never proclaimed, as Lyons does, that, "It is like falling in love in the old sense. I'm thinking in romantic terms of Shakespeare's *A Midsummer Night's Dream*. I felt like I had entered a magical, euphoric garden. It's a rush." She confesses that she is saddened each time one of her digital offspring is adopted. Lyons's *B-emovies* provide the means for others to share her expansive way of being in the world. She asserts, "I think people have trouble *being* their true natures because the inhibitors throughout our society are severe. These self-customizing environments liberate viewers from the many coercive restraints that choke us and from those that are normally placed upon the art audience by the artist. I work really hard because we deserve to do what we want in life. I want others to be able to go wherever technology takes them. My art utilizes a form that allows anyone to be any form they want to be. *Being* is really this century's biggest adventure." Lyons exalts interactive, virtual technologies. She loves them because they contribute a new variety of adventure to the realm of human experience. Since physical proximity is not necessary to generate cyber occurrences, the concepts of one body occupying one space at one time or growing old with one life-long partner have been rendered obsolete. Virtualized space and time multiply opportunities for variety. "Partnering" is the word Lyons uses to describe her relationship with her digital devices. Initially, she paired up. Now, she is experimenting with multiple consorts. The technology to achieve this model is still being developed, but her vision of it diverges significantly from old-fashioned promiscuity. Lyons is busily reconfiguring her "self" with multiple ports of entry for simultaneous activity with different partners. Her craving is for speed and space—not sex. Her futuristic involvement with love transports her beyond her present body, which she thinks of as "her little prison." She escapes into a disembodied state on the Internet. Freedom is true pleasure. The Internet offers the ultimate pleasures because it provides an immense, uncharted domain for free play. "Some love is physical. Some love is not. When you get older, you don't have time to be horizontal. You have to be vertical. Out-of-body experiences can be very interesting."

Lyons creates works of art that are custom-made for those who share her lifestyle—professionals living in one-person households who work hard, play hard, and prefer independence to commitment. Speaking on their behalf, Lyons states, "People are afraid to get into situations with real-life ramifications. They just want to experience life and not deal with the ramifications. In life, you can't change the channels. This art is for people, like me, who can't seem to take care of pets and plants." For people like these, data bodies satisfy the urge to perpetuate themselves without actually having children. "Death is imminent. Time is short. Speed is important. When I die, these forms will take on their own life and other people will reprogram them, influence them, reshape them. Some people may remember where they came from. There is a legacy involved in any love relationship. Like the electrical cord you plug into a wall, it binds you once you have been intimate. It never goes away."

Lyons has expressed her love for the virtual world, but does it love her back? When asked, she hesitated, but only for an instant. Then her breakneck monologue resumed. "A million readers are encouraging me on the Web all at once. People want access to me because I am a new intersection point. Love comes in the form of communication." Lyons foresees that the Internet will soon change its form. E-mail will become obsolete. Instead, we will plug in through our clothes and the walls of our homes will project the sounds and images of our collective hallucinations. "The technology is still in its infancy. It will reach elementary school in 2002 and high school by 2008. When it becomes an adolescent, then we will first see what real problems there are."

RY: How many ex-husbands do you have?

ML: Three. Each person probably took two years off my track—recommitting myself to being an artist and not having a baby and a husband. After the fact, when I figured out that autopilot in the traditional sense didn't work for me, being a wife, *marcia redux times three*, made the work that much stronger.

RY: How is your art related to your sexual identity? It seemed to me from reading the essay Linda wrote about you [in this book] that those creatures are your children.

ML: They were made at that period of my life when I was going through illness. I started working with the computer because I was sick and I couldn't work with materials anymore and I needed some kind of art-making channel I could work with in bed. I was grieving over the fact that I couldn't have children. So I decided to make my own progenies that could grow and grow through the Internet and have their own life in different environments throughout the world. It was a way of coping. So that was the motivation behind empowering myself to have children on my own terms without the traditional lifestyle. I think it's very difficult for women in our culture to live alone, or not want to be married, or be unable to have children. The computer saved my emotional life. It saved my artistic life. It supported me. I got jobs immediately and it enabled me to get my work out there and be seen without the dependency or the tyranny of the gallery system which was so political at the time. It really helped rejuvenate me in the way that moving to another country would. I re-identifed myself without all those labels attached to who I was that tend to get in the way. Behind the screen I could be anything. I could be a man, woman, child, any race, live in any country. It was very free. So I could get past myself, past my little physical prison, and make art, enjoy myself. That to me is sensual. That to me is sexual. It's in your mind. It's not just physical. I think there's a phase in your life when your identity comes out in your work.

RY: Right now from your perspective, do you identify with a sexuality?

ML: I think of myself sexually as being fluid, just as identity- and shape-shifting as I can be with my expression. I come from a background where a husband and a wife, two kids, a dog, and one car, and a really nice house with good furniture was the goal. The women artist friends that I have all had similar experiences. They try to structure their life to accommodate being an artist in New York. So if a husband is supportive they're with a husband. If a woman is supportive, they're with a woman. You just adapt as best you can to the opportunities and to your ability to cope.

1. All quotes from Marcia Lyons, interviews with the artist, February 7 and October 5, 2000.

2. Marcia Lyons, *Marcia Lyons*, artist's statement, (New York: Alexandre de Folin Gallery, January 1999).

Lorna Simpson
Born 1960 Brooklyn, New York
1982 School of Visual Arts, New York City, BFA, photography
1985 University of California at San Diego, MFA, visual arts
Lives and works in Brooklyn, New York

Lorna Simpson demonstrates that artists are not obliged to express attitudes. Withholding personal commentary contributes to her art in two ways. First, by avoiding the messy and obscure zone of personal opinion, an artwork gains authority. Second, by leaving the attitude category blank, space is opened for viewers to contribute the attitudes missing from the experience. In the video work entitled *Call Waiting*, Simpson provides evidence that human-to-human communication is fraught with hurdles. She demonstrates that misunderstandings are unavoidable because of linguistic, cultural, racial, and economic differences. To this list of communication obstacles she adds the human desire to deceive. Viewers are invited to supply their own attitudes about these issues.

In 1990, at the age of thirty, Lorna Simpson became the first African American woman artist to represent the United States at the prestigious Venice Biennale exhibition. In that very same year she had a solo exhibition at the Museum of Modern Art in New York. Simpson's special talent lies in exploiting the affecting and transmitting potential of photography. Still, her accomplishments are not without precedent. Sojourner Truth (1797–1883), the courageous African American abolitionist and defender of women's rights, anticipated the mass appeal of photography, a technology that was in its infancy at the time. Photographs confirm the fearless ardor of this African American woman who traveled around the country giving inspirational speeches during the troublesome years between slavery and emancipation. Sojourner Truth was among the first pioneers to capitalize upon photography's celebrity-enhancing and income-producing potential by selling photographs of herself at her speeches and rallies. These souvenirs were produced by a woman who believed that charisma was photogenic. They were purchased by people who agreed.

Unlike Sojourner Truth, Lorna Simpson's photographs project neither zealous social convictions nor fervent self-confidence. In fact, Simpson's work reveals that a century-and-a-half later, she is still reckoning with the after-effects of the struggle between the master and the slave that Sojourner Truth fought to vanquish. Simpson embodies the lingering effects of racism. Instead of celebrating the vitality of black culture, she focuses on such dehumanizing aspects of black experience as living in urban redevelopment projects or standing in line at unemployment offices. In addition, she conveys the psychological toll of racism by assuming the artistic stance of the outcast. Simpson's suppression of individuality suggests the consequence of exploitation, marginalization, and prejudice. In her photographs, this social alienation is expressed by omitting evidence of her personality.

Simpson's stylistic preferences are distinguished by her elimination of self-expressive opportunities. By confining her work to black and white, she circumvents the emotive moods that color evokes. Likewise, by eliminating all compositional schemes except the one that is simple, centered, and explicit, Simpson successfully avoids opportunities for original invention. Furthermore, by choosing to keep her backgrounds vacant, she abolishes the evocative coordinates of time and space and context. Through these omissions, Simpson's photographs minimize aesthetic distraction and propagandistic affect. Mug shots of criminal suspects also omit these expressive strategies. Indeed, Simpson and the

FBI seem to share the intent to minimize subjective interference. Her stylistic detachment suppresses emotions, but it accomplishes a different goal. It instigates the thoughtful process of investigation.

Simpson's works often consist of numerous photographs on a common theme, with each object within the series occupying its own frame. Examples include twenty-five candles, one hundred wishbones, seventy braids, and twenty-five twists. Methodically, she collects her subjects category by category. Counting them by the unit discourages her from forming subjective responses to them or conveying personal associations through them. Viewers also assume the detached perspective required for comparing numerous examples of a type of object. *9 Props* (1995) presents a vase, cup, fishbowl, port glass, goblet, and other props of the type used in well-known nineteenth-century photographic portraits of black New Yorkers. *Wigs* (1995) consists of fifty pieces of white felt printed with images of wigs, a catalogue of the ways in which African American women either conform to or rebel against white standards of beauty. Individual images depict braiding, dying, weaving, coiling, and straightening. The collection even includes a blond, Barbie-like wig.

Texts serve to guide and multiply the interpretations of these grouped photographs. Simpson explains, "I would insert my own text or my own specific reading of the image to give the viewer something they might not interpret or surmise, due to their 'educated' way of looking at images, and reading them for their emotional, psychological, and/or sociological values. So, I would start to interject these things that the photograph would not speak of and that I felt needed to be revealed, but that couldn't be absorbed from just looking at an image."[1] *Twenty Questions [A Sampler]* (1986) consists of four identical images of the back of a woman's head and an accompanying text that reads: "Is she pretty as a picture or clear as a crystal or pure as a lily or black as coal or sharp as a razor." *Three Seated Figures* (1989) is accompanied by a collection of possible meanings: "her story," "prints," "signs of entry." Flanked on the left by a sign that says "her story" and on the right by a sign that says "each time they looked for proof," these neutral, legalistic terms convey the implication of sexual assault, a subject that typically evokes outrage, trauma, and other strong emotions. Likewise, the text for *The Service* (1991) addresses violence by adopting the unimpassioned tone of a newscast: "almost everyone joined the military," "man with no finger," "accidental shooting in the living room," "he jumped from the Empire State Building." Even the presentation of the text that accompanies her photographs confirms Simpson's straightforward approach. Typically, plastic plaques similar to those found in government and industrial office buildings are used to convey titles.

Statistics expand the opportunity for anonymity by reducing subjects to nameless sums. The artist is a conveyer of impersonal numbers instead of personal feelings. Furthermore, Simpson presents numerous statistical possibilities to avoid displaying preference for any particular set of data. In *Odds* (1993), three impressions of a faceless black woman are hung beside a plaque of unspecified statistics: "1 in a hundred," "1 out of three," "2 out of 7," "3 out of 4," "one fifth," "1 in ten," "99.44%," "10%," "20%." In *Time Piece* (1993), four images of a black woman photographed from behind read: "died last year," "died a year ago," "died last month," "died 18 months ago," "died at home," "died 2 years ago."

Since humans are powerful response promoters, Simpson strips the people she photographs of their individuality. One strategy is to eliminate their heads. Thus Simpson often frames her models to appear from the shoulders down. Alternatively, she photographs their backs. Her self-imposed edict to avoid photographing faces also applies to carved African masks and those that are implied by wigs. These objects are arranged with their backs to the

Clockwise from Top Left: Lorna Simpson, *Call Waiting #4, 7, 10, 11* (1997). All works are 22.5 x 18.5 inches, silver gelatin print, 8-ply archival mat with silk-screened text in artist's frame. Courtesy of the artist and Sean Kelly Gallery, New York.

EXPRESSING AN ARTISTIC ATTITUDE

camera. Similarly, since dress is a conveyer of a person's individuality, Simpson generalizes the women who appear as models by clothing them in formless, plain white or black dresses. The strategy eliminates signs of age, body type, and looks. Only core categories remain. Simpson explains, "I like the simplicity of the white shift. I feel it communicates 'femaleness' without additional interference from fashion.' It's not specific to the physique of any particular woman and it can become many different things for the viewer."[2] People are further generalized by Simpson's scrupulous avoidance of such individualizing markers as physical flaws. Every model's skin is smooth and blemish-free. Their dresses are spotless and freshly pressed. Their hair is neat.

In the same manner, the pristine surfaces and refined craftsmanship of her photographs suppress evidence of the artist's idiosyncrasies and her personality. Simpson's disengagement from her subjects and her suppression of the expressive use of her medium convey the distanced perspective of an outsider. Her photographs have the long view of a woman who is positioned at the physical and emotional margins of her culture. It is the vantage of the ethnographer who collects, sorts, counts, and catalogues, and whose investigation (in Simpson's case it is the investigation of identity formation) is conducted without nostalgia, empathy, idealizations, moralizing, self-pity, cynicism, or sympathy.

In 1997 Simpson expanded her range of operation, all the while preserving her taciturn composure. She not only added the dimension of time to her photographic repertoire by undertaking filmmaking, she broadened her exploration of identity to include other genders, races, and identities than her own. *Call Waiting* (1997) is a 16 mm film installation with sound and a series of still photographs with silk-screened text. Although there are six characters, the real star of the film is the telephone. In fact, attention is directed to an entire cast of telephones. They appear in each scene in a different guise—plugged-in and cellular, cheap and expensive, fashionable and functional. They set the pattern of proliferating types that prevails throughout the film.

Simpson provides a synopsis of the sequence of episodes that comprise the film version of *Call Waiting*: "A man calls a woman who is just getting off the phone after trying to track down a woman for yet another woman. She's speaking in Chinese and he's cursing her out in Spanish because their relationship isn't going well. His call is interrupted by one from another guy who's talking about the woman that the first man is having an argument with. The first man walks into the room with a cell phone and puts the other guy on the speaker phone and allows her to eavesdrop on the conversation about her."[3] Other aspects of the film add to the complexity and confusion evident in this description. For example, although the communication can be observed, Simpson withholds information about who initiated a call. Furthermore, the identity of the person at the other end of the line is never shown. Attempts to make sense of these episodes are further thwarted by the fact that the responses of the actors and actresses do not congeal into a consistent narrative. Bewilderment has been carefully constructed by disparate people speaking different dialects derived from divergent cultural contexts whose attempts to converse are further complicated by calling cards, conference calls, speaker phones, and call waiting. Each episode within this convoluted sequence of interlocking relationships shares two characteristics. First, the attempts to communicate occur on the telephone. Second, these attempts falter.

As has been noted, Simpson strips her subjects of their individuality by applying one of two strategies. Either she generalizes a unique example, or she collects enough examples so that they sacrifice their individuality to a category. *Call Waiting* provides the opportunity for Simpson to indulge her penchant for such taxonomies:

— of relationships: friends, lovers, former lovers, suitors, and jilted lovers.

— of racial characteristics and languages: English, Chinese, Spanish, and Punjabi. Simpson highlights the speakers' diverse racial characteristics by equalizing their ages, their physical appeal, and their socio-economic status. They are all affluent, attractive adults.

— of liaisons: man/woman, man/man, woman/woman, black/white, white/Asian, black/Asian.

— of forms of estrangement: betrayal, malice, desire, deceit, expectation, hope, lies, excuses, accusations.

— of film style sources: television soap operas, sitcoms, TV commercials, film-noir of the 1940s and 1950s, video installations of the 1970s.

— of settings in which the characters conduct their conversations: home office, feminine bedroom, suburban 1960s kitchen, upscale 1940s bar, home patio. Settings come equipped with appropriate models of telephone.

— of ways to hold a telephone: cradling the receiver between a neck and shoulder, holding it casually to an ear, pressing it against the chest to recover composure, cupping the mouth around the receiver to muffle the voice, holding the receiver anxiously with both hands. Each gesture is an observable indicator of an inner state.

Twelve 20-by-16-inch silver gelatin prints with titles printed on the mats comprise the photographic version of *Call Waiting*. They hang in orderly rows, six above six. Each is a film still of a character with a telephone. Together, they present a catalogue of telephone communications:

"Makes a call 11:45 a.m."
"Waiting to make a call 11:58 a.m."
"Separate lines 12:05 a.m."
"Messages 4:15 p.m."
"Call at work 4:29 p.m."
"Call for her 4:35 p.m."
"Taking a call 4:35 p.m."
"Listening to message 4:40 p.m."
"Call on the other line 4:49 p.m."
"3 way call 4:50 p.m."
"Returning a call 5:00 p.m."
"Letting it ring 5:00 p.m."

Despite the emotional intensity of the individual interactions that Simpson stages, her own conduct is determined by emotional concealment, suppression of a personal agenda, elimination of biographical information, the curbing of imaginative impulses, and the refusal to resolve her plot. Simpson's withdrawal has a powerful effect upon the viewer. As she herself states, "the work is not answer-oriented. It's intentionally left open ended. There's not a resolution that just solves everything."[4] The strategy is used to powerful effect. In order to complete the narrative, the viewer becomes a co-author, interpreting the text and supplying its emotional content, judging who among the characters is guilty and who is innocent, deciding who merits favor and who deserves scorn. In plugging up these narrative holes, viewers confront their own prejudices toward the numerous racial, ethnic, and gender types represented in the film.

EXPRESSING AN ARTISTIC ATTITUDE

Simpson refrains from varying camera angles and focal lengths. This cinematic constraint further activates viewers. Her determined use of a single, stationary camera replicates the visual experience provided by surveillance cameras and keyholes. Observing her film acquires the heightened aura of peeping. The characters in the film reaffirm this impression by going about their affairs oblivious of being observed. None appear to be performing. Thus, the passivity of watching a staged film production is replaced with the intensity of peering and snooping.

Simpson's self-imposed restraining orders enable audiences to acknowledge their preconceptions, biases, and prejudices. These truths comprise the content of *Call Waiting*. As a result, this film about convoluted relationships avoids the trivialities of gossip about others and acquires the significance of self-revelation.

Perhaps the title that is most revealing of this artist's attitude is *Unavailable for Comment* (1993). Simpson disengages from the rules of narrative both within her work and within her career, rarely submitting to interviews and other opportunities for self-disclosure. She demonstrates that inexpressiveness is a viable alternative to expression in art, and that withholding meaning can have profound consequences.

[1] Lorna Simpson quoted in Beryl Wright, *For the Sake of the Viewer* (Chicago: Museum of Contemporary Art, 1992), 8.

[2] Deborah Willis, *Lorna Simpson* (San Francisco: Friends of Photography, 1992), 56.

[3] Coco Fusco, "Interview with Lorna Simpson," *BOMB*, Fall 1997, 55.

[4] Willis, 60.

Being Gently Subversive

Marco Maggi
Born 1957 Montevideo, Uruguay
1980 Universidad de La Republica, Montevideo, Bachelor in Law
1998 State Univeristy of New York, New Paltz, MFA
Lives and works in New Paltz, New York

Marco Maggi reports that he can't keep an inventory of his artworks because there is a
buyer for every work of art he creates. As a result, it is necessary for him to produce an
entirely new body of prints, drawings, and constructions for each of his frequent exhibitions. Despite this impressive record, the word "humble" best describes his artistic
attitude. It even prevails in his means of production. Maggi's creative process depends
on minimal requirements, materials that can be acquired at any hardware or grocery
store: an exacto blade, manual dexterity, one table, and one chair to sit on. The products
of these labors reflect his modest methods of production. They are small, quiet, and gentle
in appearance and in their interactions with the viewer. These self-effacing means complete
the portrait of an artist whose attitude quietly defies the strident bombast of the contemporary environment.

Even before Marco Maggi decided that his way of being an artist meant incising Macintosh
apple skins, embossing Reynolds wrap, printing Avery labels, and etching Celotex insulation
boards, he made the following decisions.

First, he decided that he had an adverse relationship to many aspects of the current environment, that he describes as "semiotic turmoil."[1] The world he objects to is exemplified by
the extravagant plan announced by The Lawrence Livermore National Laboratory to build a
massive, $100 million machine capable of conducting more than a quadrillion operations a
second—equivalent to two million of the most powerful desktop PCs operating simultaneously. It is also the world which relishes such sensual extravaganzas as those created in
Imax theaters where screens soar 76 feet into the air and sprawl 98 feet laterally, personal
stereo systems discharge sound directly into the listener's ears, and eyewear accessories
are available to immerse the viewer in three-dimensional effects. Second, Maggi decided
to address these aversions in his artwork, but not through criticism, rectification, or
suppression. In determining his attitude of communicating his objections, he chose to
discard the tantrum, the tirade, and the sermon. He thereby arrived at his third decision,
to address the distasteful components of the contemporary environment by ignoring them.

Some artists involved in social dissent appropriate and intensify the harder, faster, meaner
approach. This apparent inconsistency is based on the conviction that being big, loud, and
blatant is necessary in order to be noticed amid the clutter of today's environment and to
be heard above its clamor. Other artists refrain from employing the strategies they decry,
and exercise the option of establishing a new paradigm. Marco Maggi exemplifies this attitude by maintaining an artistic modesty that matches his personal humility. "I don't work
like a big man to change the world. I have no big ideas or ideology or big truth. I am a little
man working with normal things. I am comfortable with my materials and my scale and my
lack of a didactic message. I do not attempt to transform you. This is not an aggressive
discourse about the world. I create an alternative world with its own rules." Maggi has
discovered that it is possible for art that is as quiet as a whisper and as delicate as a tiptoe
to delight the senses despite the unrelenting onslaught of the media. Maggi creates antidotes to contemporary hype, believing that, "People are tired of shock, big impact, didactic

Marco Maggi, *Micro & Soft on Macintosh Apple* (1997), variable dimensions, engraving on real apple (five-year-old Macintosh fossil). Courtesy Cristinerose and Josée Bienvenu Gallery, New York.

Being Gently Subversive: **Marco Maggi**

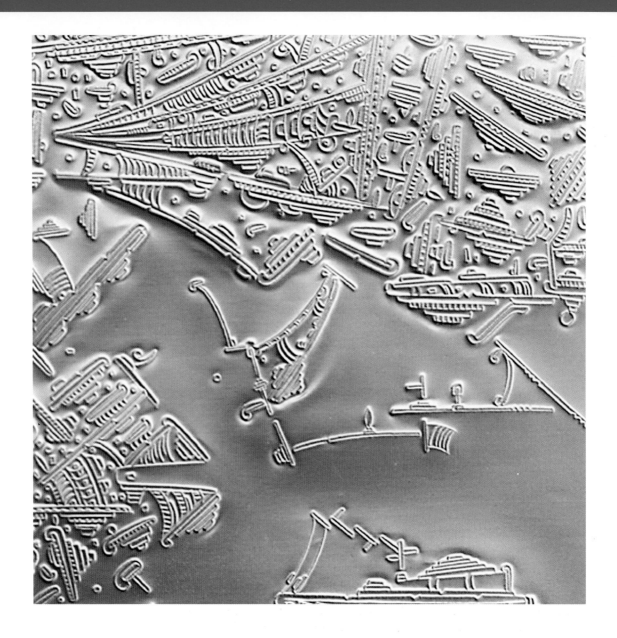

Marco Maggi, *PreColumbian and PostClintonian* (2002), 20 x 16 inches, dry point on kitchen foil (Reynolds). Courtesy Hosfelt Gallery, San Francisco.

EXPRESSING AN ARTISTIC ATTITUDE

messages, and stage-effects like the movies. A lot of art is like a balcony in a big theater. What you see is outside you—like in big screen. It is audio, visual, and long distance. There is no need to read or interpret. It is all done for you. It is all image."

Shock tactics are used with such frequency in advertising, news reporting, entertainment, games, and internet communications that experiences once capable of causing astonishment have become normalized and even boring. Each time a new plateau of excitation becomes standard, the volume is amplified, the scale magnified, and the bombardment escalates. This pattern can be discerned in the arena of fine art as well. In tune with the times, the organizers of an exhibition of contemporary art in the late 1990s chose the bombastic title *Sensation* and then pumped up its impact by enlarging its middle letter "A" and printing it in scarlet when all the other letters were black. They invited provocation by branding their own show with the classic "A" of an adulteress. The show was conceived to adulterate refinement, decorum, and propriety. Lest anyone miss the point, the exhibition announcement included the following disclaimer: "Health Warning—The contents of this exhibition may cause shock, vomiting, confusion, panic, euphoria, and anxiety. If you suffer from high blood pressure, a nervous disorder, or palpitations, you should consult your doctor before viewing this exhibition."

Maggi's attitude is directly opposed to that espoused by Sensation. His works not only avoid shock, they quite effectively avoid detection. Casual observers could easily mistake many of his painstaking and detailed creations as gray smudges. If a personality was assigned to the kind of artwork he creates, one might say that his drawings are shy, refusing to disclose their beauty until viewers develop an intimacy with them. Other works are reclusive, like those created by engraving a sheet of nonglare Plexiglas with infinitesimal lines; these phantom markings would be imperceptible if Maggi had not made them visible by casting their shadows onto a clay board. Other works are coy, peaking out from behind columns that serve as their hiding places in the gallery.

Certain physical postures correlate with shock while others are associated with humility. Maggi's mode of working brings his shoulders forward and his gaze downward. Likewise, the act of looking at his diminutive creations requires his audience to assume a position of reverence. One work, amusingly titled *Hoover Corner* (1999), is actually placed directly on the floor when it is exhibited. It occupies the place where a Hoover vacuum might be. Looking at it necessitates a very deep bow. "I pay attention to viewers' reactions to my work," comments Maggi, "and I am the first to be surprised by their attentiveness. My work is not colorful or commercial in any way. I watch their attitudes. They don't rear back. This teaches me that people are bored [by] big aggression." " Maggi's works revive ways to see that have been usurped by the drive for competitive advantage.

Maggi's dining room is his studio. He starts each workday by walking down the hall that leads from his bedroom. He seats himself at the dining table to practice exercises designed to cultivate superhuman standards of artistic performance. Maggi approaches art-making with the decorum and ceremonial formality of a medieval scribe. This morning ritual not only maintains his skills as a master draftsman, it continually elevates them. After he takes a seat, he prepares his materials and arranges his tools. He warms up by practicing freehand drawing until he is capable of producing lines that are perfectly parallel, or ruler straight, or regularly curved. Maggi never knows how much of the day will be occupied by these preparatory activities. Their duration lasts as long as it takes for him to attain peak performance. Not until his drawn lines appear as controlled as those dependent on mechanical or electronic tools does he proceed to the next exercise. This one is designed to perfect his etching skills. Rhythmically and deliberately he inscribes a single Macintosh apple with thousands of minuscule cuts that scratch but never pierce the skin. "If a week is missed," he says, "practice may require an entire day." The width and depth of the lines must be resolutely consistent, uniform, aligned. It is a pivotal moment when he finally begins to create a work of art. Although philosophers and prophets have variously posited that the beginning of all beginnings was the word, the pulse, the spark, or the breath, Maggi's "in the beginning" commences with touch, the perfectly controlled, miniscule mark that initiates each suite.

In art, when extensive rehearsal prefigures execution, the task is typically applied to such precious materials as gold, gems, ivory, or silk. But Maggi invests this meticulous devotion in cheap and accessible substances manufactured for use-it-up-and-throw-it-away applications. Computer paper, kitchen quality aluminum foil, and architectural insulation panels are his favored art mediums. They remain as identifiable after they have become objects of art as they were on the shelves of Home Depot, Staples, Shop-Rite, and Wal-Mart. Maggi's art is never intimidating. Instead of eye-catching, extravagant imagery, each piece waits politely until someone initiates a connection. The artist behaves in a similar manner. His comments about his work are invariably accompanied by an apology for intruding. Viewers seem to welcome this restraint. They honor these snippets of paper and these rolls of foil by giving them their attention. In return, they receive a reprieve from commotion and hyperbole. Maggi's delicate work seems to revitalize media-assaulted senses and revive the capacity to delight in subtlety.

Maggi has never struggled for success. In fact, his struggle has been *with* success. As a boy growing up in Uruguay, he made thousands of tiny linear drawings, working on them for hours every day. Maggi recalls that when he was twelve years old, a famous poet from Argentina visited his parents. When this gentleman was preparing to leave, he asked permission to take thirty of the child's drawings with him, saying only, "I will take them and return in one month." When the poet returned, he brought news that an exhibition had been scheduled in a prestigious gallery in Buenos Aires, Argentina. The show was a coup by adult standards. Praise-filled reviews appeared in German, English, Portuguese, and Spanish publications. Every drawing in the exhibition was sold. This success, however, derailed Maggi's art practice. For him, it happened too early, too quickly, and too unexpectedly. Commercial success was too crass, too distracting. So he stopped making art, a hiatus that lasted for two decades. In the intervening years Maggi studied law, worked as a journalist and editor, and ran a construction company. Then in 1994 he resumed his artistic career. Once again his work was immediately acclaimed by critics and sought by collectors. Still concerned about the ill effects of commercial success, he contrived a way to manage it. Instead of dwelling on sales as proof of achievement, Maggi thinks of sales as the creation of voids that must be filled by producing new works. Thus, each end product serves as the impetus for new work. "Each time I sell a work of art, I relinquish my history to the collector. Each year I increase my expression incrementally. Like software, I upgrade. Like writing a long novel, there is an evolution. The only thing that is sad in this story is that I have already sold the first, second, and third chapters. They are gone."

Maggi perpetually postpones completion. Because he conceives of beginnings devoid of endings, his works propel toward infinite generation. This model applies to his career and also to individual pieces. They usually originate with a random mark. This mark suggests another, and another. They proliferate, expanding exponentially into the surrounding spaces. Those lines that do not produce further patterns often continue as dots or dashes

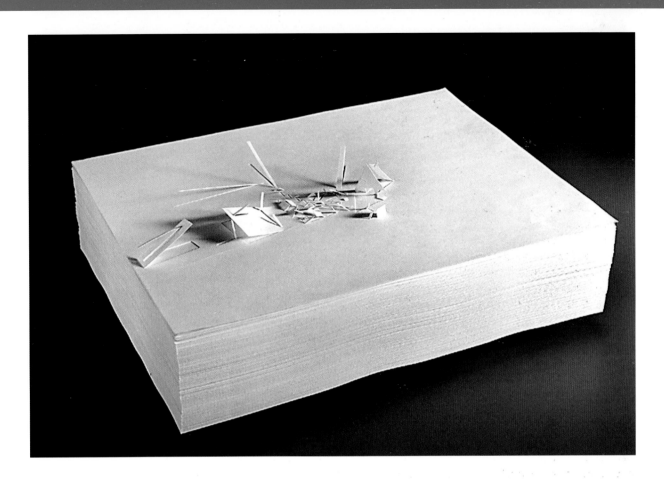

Marco Maggi, *Hotbed* (2002), 8.5 x 11 x 2.5 inches, incisions on Xerox paper ream. Courtesy Dan Galeria, Sao Paulo, Brazil.

Marco Maggi, *Untitled Reynolds V* (1999), 12 inches x 16.6 yards, dry point on foil and cardboard box. Courtesy 123 Watts Gallery. Photograph: Masahiro Noguchi.

to imply further growth. Other patterns expand to an edge, implying extension beyond the physical limits of the work of art. But dynamic expansion is not merely implied by these marks. Maggi actually produces works of art like generations of offspring from single sources. For example, a series may propagate because Maggi places sheets of paper onto different zones of a single woodblock plate so that every print registers a unique image. Or he may cut an embossed sheet of aluminum foil into numerous pieces to be mounted and presented as individual works of art. Or he may use a Xerox machine to transform a tiny print into ever-larger formats, or to copy a single drawing onto a sheet of self-adhering labels that can be framed as tiny individual prints. In exhibitions, the progeny from each parent remain grouped together so that viewers can deduce the methods used to generate them.

In order to halt this relentless course, Maggi has arbitrarily selected the number 361 as his point of cessation. It is a significant choice because it is a number without consequence. Three hundred and sixty one bypasses the tidy 360 of circular degrees, the periodic 365 of the annual calendar, and the convenience of logical divisions. Maggi terminates each series once it attains this idiosyncratic summation, a reminder that it could have continued without end. For example, in Blind Slides (1998) 1,444 (or 4 x 361) prints and drawings are enclosed within standard, two-inch slide jackets. In some works, what was once a detail becomes a totality. In others, totalities are divided into discrete works of art. Viewers can track the lineage of each component backwards to its inception, onwards to the breeding of offspring, and forwards to the genesis of new generations.

Process and completion coincide in a pile of graphite shavings that accumulated as Maggi sharpened pencils during his working process. This little black mound constitutes both an elegant work of art entitled *Steadler II* (1999) and a record of the artist's working technique. This display of process demonstrates the willful sacrifice of speed and efficiency offered by up-to-date technologies. Maggi explains both rejections by stating, "I draw by paying special attention to two traffic signals: slow down and stop ahead." Another work consists of a container with compartments lined in red velvet, each of which holds an example of one technique used by Maggi. Together they provide a virtual glossary of processes that diverge from current modes of production. Maggi prefers methods dependent on "digits" that refer to fingers, not to the components of a binary code. Because he believes that "the new technology has yet to achieve a more digital instrument than the hand,"[2] he applies old-fashioned art skills to contemporary materials: lithography on slides, engraving on apples, woodcuts on file labels, dry point on aluminum foil, drawing on computer paper, engraving on insulation panels. Maggi contrasts his minimal displacement of materials with the mega-horsepower digging, drilling, and bulldozing projects that alter our landscapes. Likewise, he contrasts the slow pace of his creative process with the frenetic tempo of many contemporary forms of production. His phrase "fast food travels from freezer to microwave"[3] is a metaphor for many forms of production currently in use. But this artist does not merely retard time. In some works of art he reverses it by exhibiting empty slide jackets, reams of unused Xerox paper, and unmodified pieces of foil as works of art. Maggi delights in these unmarked territories, referring to them as "places in the brain that are not yet occupied by memory." His extension into time not only proceeds forward toward infinity, it also proceeds backwards to the state that preceded their beginnings.

Maggi's gently subversive drawings calmly release an abundance of references. Stripped of identifiable content, scale, and context, his imagery accommodates dynamic principles and complex patterns, resembling diagrams of plate tectonics, microscopic images of

DNA, and maps of city streets. He emphasizes their multifarious nature by describing them as "insignificant signs, unclear circuits, vague mutations, illegible cycles, cloudy viruses, incomprehensible dolmens and inaccessible codes."[4] Furthermore, multiplicity is confirmed because each image plays simultaneous roles within its status as art object; each is a fragment of a whole, a distinct entity, and raw material for partioning into future orchestrations. Wordplay further multiplies meanings, while introducing another opportunity for subtlety and gentle humor. Marco Maggi reworks his name to produce Marko Maggi, Macro Maggi, macro micro mArco, and Micro Maggi.

Although emerging technologies compete for miniature status—microchips and microcassettes and microcircuits and microelectronics among them—the visual environment remains characterized by bigness and boldness. "Our time is so preoccupied with the spectacle of macro drama that delicacy is subversive. It is like a scandal. We need to build a slow scandal. This is the possible revolution—we cannot choose the big things, but we can choose the little things." Maggi concludes, "That's why myopia is the best response to globalization: reducing the visual field allows us to discover infinitesimal details in the space of a square inch.... In a small world, not compatible with hooligans and visual slogans, we have to lower our voices and the ceilings of art galleries."[5]

[1] Unless otherwise noted, all quotes from an interview with the artist, January 4, 2000.

[2] Marco Maggi, "The Pencil Monologues: Micro Macro Drawings Retrospective 0002-9991" (New York: 123 Watts, 2001), n.p.

[3] Marco Maggi, *Microwave, one* (New York: 123 Watts Gallery, 1999), 16.

[4] Marco Maggi, "Microwave vs. Macrowave," in *Microwave, one*.

[5] Marco Maggi, "Sonspy and Linux Drops," in *Pencil Monologues* (New York: 123 Watts, 1999), n.p.

CHOOSING A MISSION

CHOOSING A MISSION

China Adams, *Official Stitch and Hide Procedure*
(1995-96), glass, canvas, unidentified objects.
Courtesy of ACE Gallery. Photograph: ACE
Contemporary Exhibitions, Los Angeles.

Doctors heal. Lawyers defend. Educators teach. Advertisers persuade. Carpenters build. Chefs cook. Architects design. Ballerinas dance. But what do today's artists do? When asked, even art historians and critics often clear their throats and then stammer something as noncommittal as "Artists make art." Instead of offering clarification, this kind of answer contributes to the quandary of determining the mission that motivates artists to make art. Redundancy is not the problem here—it is meaningful to say "preachers preach" or "programmers program." But the art profession seems devoid of determined operations. Establishing a mission is not only an individual affair, it seems to be an unavoidable component of artists' creative responsibilities.

Once upon a time, it could be assumed that artists made art to inspire faith in God, or celebrate the wonders of nature, or pay tribute to a secular ruler. Artists served the ruling monarch, or the official church, or the predictable tastes of the upper class. But those times have given way to a cultural scene that is fluid and porous. Today, art doesn't offer a definition of itself, and it certainly does not provide artists with a neatly formulated mission. As a result, establishing an artistic mission has become a matter of self-determination.

At the same time, the reservoir of artistic opportunity is overflowing with alternatives. Today's artists heal, sell, teach, build, cook, dance, document, perform, recite, preach, and more. But if art's activities overlap with all these non-art professions, what distinguishes its mission as art? One answer might be that artists are at liberty to enact these activities without submitting to the standards of functionality. Another is that imagination, fantasy, metaphor, and symbol are suppressed in many places of employment, but they are welcome in art. Likewise, artists are granted special latitude in dealing with truth and facts. Instead of accuracy, they have the privilege of exaggerating, distorting, ignoring, and embellishing. Furthermore artists can disregard professional protocol and standards of correctness. They don't need to request permission to speak or to act. As a result, functionality, accuracy, and manners can be warped without compromising artistic merit.

Artists enjoy a unique social advantage because of these liberties. Unfettered by normal constraints, they are able to formulate missions that evaluate entire value systems and behaviors and ethical standards and social trends. Rescue missions, attack missions, evangelical missions, remedial missions are all predicated on the option of instigating change, while stabilizing missions confirm the status quo. Art's purpose can involve advocating or opposing any topic. It can aim at self-fulfillment or generosity. Its scope can involve a region or the globe. Missions can revert time by returning to a past era, slow time by expanding the moment, create time by multiplying perspectives, stop time by creating monuments, or extend time by perpetuating a tradition or anticipating the future. All these options are possible because artists practice art without needing credentials or waiting for invitations or receiving approvals. They can, for example, comment on scientific issues without submitting to peer review. Functioning outside of the controlling forces of the mainstream enables them to introduce original solutions, revive neglected precedents, or direct future developments. Artists are not beholden to standards of correctness, either in terms of accuracy or politeness.

Artistic missions are first acquired, next pursued, and ultimately possessed. Acquiring a mission may be the product of prolonged investigation, but some artists report that their missions seemed to find them. Pursuing a mission may entail willful decision-making, conscious design, and calculated strategizing; alternatively, it can be pursued through mindless abandonment to impulse. Possessing a mission implies dedication, long-term commitment, seriousness of purpose; it differs from the temporary and informal goals that are commonly referred to as intentions. Even artists who avoid preordaining results are not exempt from acquiring, pursuing, and possessing missions; their spontaneity is often predicated on the desire to release suppressed memories, emotions, or mythic visions.

Mission control is missing from the operations of creators of art and their audiences. There are no rules to dictate the best way, or even a good way, for artists to determine why they have chosen this profession. Likewise, there are no rules to dictate the best way, or even a good way for viewers to deduce these reasons. Consequently, viewing art is either a guessing game or a studied activity. In both instances, it is complicated by the fact that visual clues are often not sufficient to reveal why a work was created. But they are also not sufficient to limit creative contemplations about art. Uncommon liberties are claimed by people seeking meaningful artistic experiences. Like artists, viewers assert the right to ignore accuracy, dispense with politeness, and indulge in personal interpretation.

Victoria Vesna

Born 1959 Washington D.C.
1984 Faculty of Fine Arts, University of Belgrade, Yugoslavia, Fine Arts Diploma
2000 Centre for Advanced Studies in Interactive Arts, University of Wales, Ph.D.
Lives in Los Angeles, California

Victoria Vesna's mission addresses a common human desire that few humans have actually attempted to satisfy. Vesna attempts to create time, or time's equivalent, by expanding the quantity of experiences one can include in one's lifetime, the quantity of information one can absorb, the quantity of interactions one can engage, the quantity of colleagues one can access, the quantity of creative work one can accomplish. She enlists computer technology as her ally in satisfying the needs of people, like herself, who continually complain about being too busy.

Humans seem more attuned to their wants than to their satisfactions. We want what we don't have and we want more of what we do have. We want more money, more cars, more food, more security, more love, more fun, more sleep. Victoria Vesna's most urgent "want" is a product of the accelerated pace and complexity of contemporary lifestyles. Many of her friends and colleagues also complain about this deficiency: they all want more time. Vesna's art practice is devoted to creating time.

Although Vesna is responding to a current crisis, her mission has its roots in such primeval activities as smoke signals, shouting, and drumming. It was expressed by such historic occasions as the invention of writing, when the word was made tangible and therefore transportable, and the invention of the printing press, when the dissemination of the written word to a vastly expanded audience became possible. These developments demonstrate how early and how insistently humans have augmented their channels of communication. In the past fifty years, this impulse has been indulged through the wondrous attributes of electronics and fiber optics. Distance has ceased to be a deterrent to communication. Messages, zapped across political and geographic boundaries, are received instants after they are created. Like so many others, Vesna's existence depends on these technological feats.

Vesna frequently acknowledges her indebtedness to three telecommunications visionaries: Norbert Wiener, who anticipated a day when humans would be telegraphically transported; Hans Moravec, who proposed that machines can become repositories for human consciousness; and Chris Langton, who envisioned separating the "informational content" of humans from their "material substrate." Each has contributed to a post-human paradigm in which humans are abstracted into information and function as information processing entities. Vesna observes, "When you shop at Amazon, agents are taking your information and putting it in databases. Your information has a life of its own, but you can't visualize it and you don't know where it goes or who has it."[1] In creating her art, Vesna applies ingenious propositions of these three futurist thinkers to solving the shortage of time in her life. Her practice is founded on a series of well-defined missions.

Mission: *"In an age in which we are increasingly aware of ourselves as databases identified by social security numbers and genetic structures, it is imperative that artists actively participate in how data is shaped, organized, and disseminated....In this context, artists become information architects, helping to usher in this new way of working, thinking, anticipating, and helping to visualize new structures."[2]*

CHOOSING A MISSION

The computer has more than fulfilled its promise to make massive quantities of information readily available. Indeed, it is a crushing success. But Vesna sees through the fog of data and identifies two of communication technology's broken promises: that communicating via the Web will save time and that it will renew a sense of community. Addressing the great divide between human bodies that chug along according to biological rhythms, and technology that zooms at milli, micro, pico, and femto seconds, Vesna comments, "Space technology is based on the premise that it will save you time. But the space of communications so expands your field of influence through your ideas, there comes a point when the information that comes back to you is way too much for any single individual to process. My relationships actually suffer. I don't have time to talk and communicate in depth. Information demands time; relationships demand time. Technology is killing our time."

Vesna became acutely aware of her desire for more time when, in 1999, she felt particularly frustrated because she had no time for researching online communities. Colleagues and friends who shared her fascination with communication technologies were equally busy. "No time for" was a refrain frequently attached to "family," "friends," "colleagues," and "exercise," "recreation," and "rest." She concluded that time is in short supply in this era and that art is uniquely positioned to create some. Though the concept of "timelessness" has long been a measure of greatness in art, Vesna's spin on it twists the word into its own antonym. Her version of "timeless" means without time, "neverlasting," not everlasting. She observed that the very technology that promised unprecedented speed and efficiency was consuming the hours of her life. This seemed true for everyone. She Explains, "The constructed time we live in is not working very well for us at this point, as is seen by the number of stressed-out individuals that do not exclude you and me. We have moved away too far from any biological/analog measurements of change…and are overwhelmed with information, processed much faster than we ever are [sic] built to absorb."[3]

Mission: "The project n0time is conceived to raise questions about our perception of time and identity as we extend our personal networks through technology. It is designed to address problems most specific to the Western human condition that seems to be entering a crisis because of its particular stress on productivity and efficiency in structuring time."[4]

Real people working with tangible materials are not capable of regaining time. Both are constrained by the cumbersome laws of matter. Within the virtual world, however, home is as intangible as a URL or e-mail address, movement is as unfettered as a tap on a keyboard, and time is as instantaneous as data processing. To create n0time (Building a Community of People with No Time) (2000-2001),[5] Vesna attempted to resolve her problem by enlisting the technology that produced it. She shapes and designs and forms technologies

Interview with Victoria Vesna
By Lauren Harkrader

LH: When did you decide you were an artist?

VV: I can finally say that I consider myself an artist without cringing. It took me awhile to shed some of the preconceived notions about what art is and what it means to be an artist that I was taught in art schools. Supposedly an artist is a lone genius, not very social, usually discovered and nurtured by a famous critic, and sponsored by a very wealthy eccentric collector. Only a few women make it to the top layer of artistic fame and fortune. Unfortunately some of these ideas are still very much in circulation, mostly because they uphold the established marketing scheme. Luckily, we have inherited some of the movements in the twentieth century that have opened paths for artists like myself. Happenings, performance, and conceptual art in particular have helped pave the way for artists to break [out] of the frame of the work and the gallery as the only context that matters. Groups like The Guerrilla Girls have made statistics loud and clear and raised consciousness about the workings of the established art world. Participating in extending the traditional boundaries of the established art world could be defined as a major perk and should give hope to the new generation of artists.

LH: How did you begin to do such a big project as Another Day in Paradise?

VV: When I had the idea to make Another Day in Paradise I was not affiliated with institutions. I was absolutely unknown as an artist. All I had was an idea. I put the idea together. I wrote a description and made detailed sketches and submitted them to a show. It was accepted. I went to the company that produces the silicon palm trees I needed and told them that I'll produce a promotional video for them if they would produce the trees for me. The trees were very expensive. They finally agreed. Then I showed the sketches to Sony and asked if they'd supply the photographic equipment. Then I got another company to help produce the interactive part. I ended up making an enormous installation. I had zero money. I was out of work. I begged and borrowed. That kind of show opens doors to other opportunities.

LH: What role did school play in preparing you to arrive where you are today?

VV: I have had two extreme schooling experiences and I could safely say that both played a major role. The Academy of Fine Arts in Belgrade provided me with a solid foundation in traditional art-making and introduced me to some of the trends in European art, although not in practice. I appreciate the many hours spent in studying the human anatomy and I know that this knowledge still surfaces in my work. Many hours of art history really helped me learn how to contextualize my own work and shape my thinking about my role as a cultural worker. In retrospect, I would say that this phase of my education helped me articulate what it is that I was not interested in pursuing, and this is a great gift.

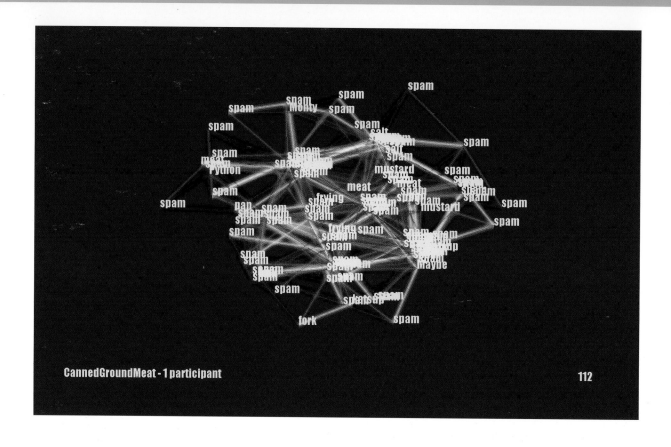

CannedGroundMeat - 1 participant

112

Victoria Vesna, *n0time (Building a Community of People with No Time)* (2000–2001). Courtesy of the artist.

that evolved from industrial and military applications according to her sensibilities as an artist, and to make them useful to ordinary people. "The Internet," she notes, "developed anarchistically. It was not designed. It needs to be rethought. The premise is wrong. We are losing our sense of time." Her rethinking is based on the observation that time can be as scarce within dematerialized cyber zones as it is in concrete geographies. Within both locations people can only occupy one spatial dimension (the here) and one temporal dimension (the now) at a time. Vesna designed *n0time* to enable one person to simultaneously occupy multiple sites and conduct simultaneous interactions. She is optimistic about the prospects. "The Internet provides a space for exploring our many identities, and experimenting with ideas of extending our influence beyond our local spaces…I consider this to be our baby steps into the unknown potential of ourselves."[6]

Mission: *"Society needs artists because we have become so disembodied. The artist allows us to get back to who is carrying this data. Artists visualize this complicated world. What I am delivering is an easier way to grasp and understand the complicated technological environment. This is a project about a community of people with no time—here is how it looks as we travel through life, how it evolves."[7]*

Designing networked multi-user environments was not a task Vesna could accomplish alone. She enlisted experts in artificial intelligence, research computing, virtual environments, interface theory and design, and digital arts to work with her. Together, this impressive team established the University of California Digital Arts Research Network. These professionals, spread out across California on nine different university campuses, added Vesna's project to their already demanding work schedules. Synchronizing meetings was impossible. "It seemed to me," Vesna reasoned, "that the logical conclusion was to conceptualize an environment that would act autonomously, largely independent of direct, real-time human interaction, and not requiring direct participation by those who are represented by the information they carry." For this reason, she revamped the concept of hands-on, person-to-person artistic collaboration and replaced it with a system of remote telecommunications that connected a group of people who never met. Three requirements for networked communications became apparent, and Vesna applied them to both the process and the product of their collaboration. She cites them as: "A need to connect, a willingness to collaborate, and the ability to embrace the fact that the work may change form and be re-appropriated in the process. In other words, this type of work requires letting go of the idea of 'control' we inherited from the cybernetic/industrial approach to computing. As we move into the age of bio-informatics, these systems are clearly not working for the advancement of social consciousness or collective intelligence."

My more recent schooling was doctoral that was self-inflicted, at mid-career. I was already very actively exhibiting for years and had just become a tenured professor and my kids were two and four. There was no perceived need for a Ph.D. The reason I did this is not because I needed it for my career, but because I wanted to ask myself what I am doing, where I am going, and put myself under scrutiny. In my opinion, the mid-career point is the most critical and dangerous intersection of an artist's path. This is when things can become easier and people can fall into a routine with their work and become too busy to stop and ask themselves what [they are] doing and why.

LH: Have you ever sold a piece? Do you feel your work is sellable?

VV: Not really, because I do not do individual pieces that can be bought and sold in the usual sense. The negative side of this kind of marketing is that it very quickly becomes commodified, and before you know it, gallerists start influencing the work you are producing. It is probably no different from a challenge any alternative musical band faces when they start making money. Do you keep repeating your hits, or do you risk losing some of your audience by trying some new tunes? I feel really lucky to have a position at a university at this phase, since this gives me the luxury of creating work that is not about financial survival. But, I should note that I worked odd jobs for a decade before joining academia, and still had pretty much the same attitude. Ultimately, anything can be sold, even a concept. I just do not think it is healthy to think about whether the work is sellable while in the process of creating it. Just plunge in and do it, even if no one supports or understand you. Eventually, it will all make sense. How the markets respond is a gamble no matter what you do.

LH: Am I correct in assuming that your income is derived from teaching, grants, and the sale of the publications?

VV: My bread-and-butter comes from teaching. Publications do not bring any money, but do help in getting invitations to speak, which certainly supplements my income. Slowly, I am getting more commissions and grants, which is really helpful. Although it varies from year to year, I would say that on average, twenty percent comes from grants, commissions, and lectures.

LH: Beyond this, do you supplement your income with digital art-related activities or non-digital art-related activities?

VV: I do not separate digital from nondigital. We are entering an age of nanotechnology and bioengineering, and these concepts will soon be completely obsolete. I consider all my activities part of a whole and a reflection of my "being" in this world. It is my way of communicating and working creatively.

LH: Did you, or do you, struggle to maintain yourself as an artist in the digital media?

VV: From time to time I wonder how I have managed to have so many shows without ever submitting work or entering a competition. This definitely must be good fortune, especially given the nature of my work. Perhaps

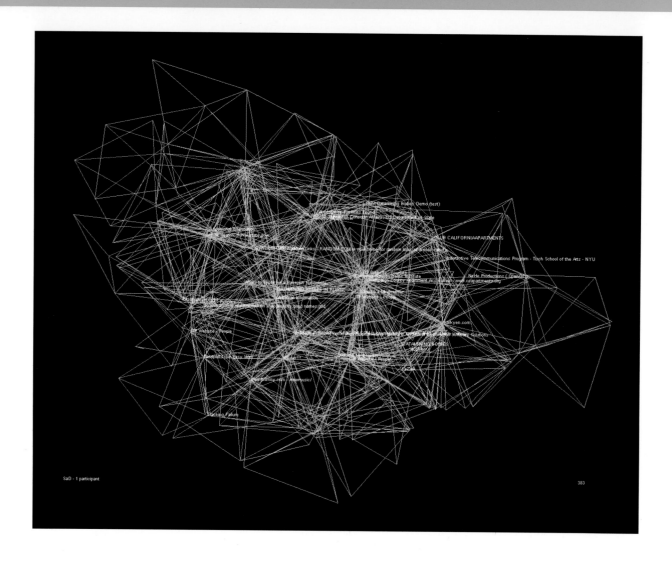

Victoria Vesna, *nOtime (Building a Community of People with No Time)* (2000–2001). Courtesy of the artist.

Vesna's "re-appropriations" take the form of an extensive catalogue of unconventional art-making tools and techniques, among them: artificial intelligence, genetic algorithms, complex adaptive systems, virtual reality, AKP (adaptive knowledge portals), and OPS: MEME (Online Public Spaces: Multidisciplinary Explorations of Multiuser Environments). Each term highlights an aspect of technology designed to achieve interactive communications independent of the participants' physical or mental presences.

Mission: "*The most promising arena for conceptual work is already in place as the archives and database systems are being developed with dizzying speed. It is in the code of search engines and the aesthetics of navigation that the new conceptual field work lies for the artist.*"[8]

NOtime alerts participants to the shrinking of time and the redefinitions of personal identity that are products of advanced communication technologies. It accomplishes this in three ways: as a Web project, as a physical installation, and as a performance. In each of these formats, Vesna demonstrates that contemporary human experience is more affected by the quantity of information exchanged than by the specific data being transmitted. Each manifestation of the work involves an interactive project that focuses on searches, retrievals, and collections of data, but ignores the content of the participants' communications.

On the Web, the project works this way: instant-by-instant interactions between communicators unfold as patterns of line and color. If you choose to participate, your identity is entered into the program, represented by the information you possess—what you know about baseball here, what you know about Chinese cooking there. You become disembodied and take the form of an online mobile agent known as an Information Persona (IP). IPs are virtual, mobile, and transformative. They also possess the wondrous capacity to replicate themselves. Becoming an IP is like acquiring surrogates for yourself. Thus, those who are too busy to attend to all of their interests and responsibilities can exceed their physical limitation of being in one location at a time. They even exceed their mental ability to pay attention to one subject at a time. They can acquire the prodigious stamina of machines. They can engage in simultaneous out-of-body interactions and can source information in one stream while seeking information in others. Moving out-of-body and into an IP multiplies outlooks, extends outreach, and increases outputs. IPs expand time.

Mission: "*I decided to attempt to make a move from the graphical representation of the physical body to the energetic body, using the principles of 'energetic geometry,' meaning a body that is networked and built from information, but not de-humanized.*"[9]

Vesna's search for a model to guide her in visually representing this network of online bodies led her to research cellular and molecular

passionate devotion to a vision is something palpable, and people are willing to put their trust in it, even when they do not quite understand it. I am enthusiastic about my projects and am consumed by them. Luckily, I live in a time when it is not necessary to depend on a gallery system to show work and promote the ideas that obsess me at a particular moment.

LH: Is there someone, or some people who promoted your career when you were still unknown?

VV: Two people in particular played a major role in my career. In the early 1980s, Biljana Tomic introduced me to conceptual art and encouraged me to be as wild as possible. More recently, Roy Ascott, a pioneer in network art and theory, responded to my work and invited me to be one of the first five people in his newly established Ph.D. program in Wales.

LH: When considering virtual time and virtual space, has your choice of a physical location affected your career?

VV: When I moved from New York to a small town in California, a part of me feared that my career would suffer. But it turned out not to matter at all, since the Internet was suddenly available. Perhaps I would not have been as interested in learning how to work with this medium if I was in a major city at the time. My work is very much context-driven, and I could safely say that every location has had an affect on my career.

LH: How do you feel the art museum or gallery compares to the Web in terms of reaching your audience?

VV: There is very little to compare, actually. It is similar to asking a video artist the difference between doing an installation in a museum and showing the work on broadcast television. I would like to reach anyone who is interested in questioning how science and technology impact our perception of self and our reality. This is a deeply philosophical question, and my goal is to create work that amplifies these issues. I have always been interested in reaching a much wider audience than just the art historians and collectors, and receiving feedback from audiences scattered across the globe is particularly important to me conceptually. The way I approached it when I was first out of school is that I formed a band. That provided a more diverse audience. Performing in nightclubs was much more fulfilling for me. Being able to jump from that to the art scene was fun. I challenged their expectations in the club too. The next step was cable television. I discovered video and cable television. Combining music and videos gave me access to a broader broadcasting system. This was a precursor to the Internet, which I immediately fell into. To work with the communication medium allows artists to amplify what they want to say and to be more independent in distributing their expression. You don't have to wait for shows that only last one month. You can put out your own work. The work is living, continuously updated and changing by audience interaction, participation, and feedback.

LH: How do you define success?

VV: The trick was, and still is, how to create artworks that actually stand up in an art environment with all

architecture. The building blocks of nature provide the graphic model by which she transforms the invisible human interactions into visible representations. Participants initiate
their engagement in *n0time* by building "energetic bodies" out of their own personal
information. First they construct a basic tetrahedron (a pyramid) that is individualized
according to their contributions to the data stream. Participants construct this basic
structure by determining the length of six intervals that each have a color and meaning
attached to them: red represents family; orange, finances; yellow, creativity; green, love;
blue, communication; violet, spirituality. After determining these lengths, they input four
"memes" into the nexus of the lines. Memes are ideas that replicate themselves and are
passed from one generation to another. They are the cultural equivalent of a gene and are
considered the basic unit of cultural evolution. Examples of memes are: ideas, catchphrases, fashion styles, and ways of making pots or building arches. Additional memes
can always be added to the *n0time* body, allowing personal communication networks to
expand beyond biological limits.

The second phase of the project entails visualizing the human information exchanges
between these IPs. When participants in *n0time* dispense information, their IPs sprout
linear connectors with the IP of the information requester. New patterns emerge, altering
the basic tetrahedrons, rendering observable their ongoing, dynamic social interactions.
The density of these lines reveals the frequency of communications between senders and
receivers. When many such interactions occur, communities are formed. As a result, each
person's visual pattern registers his or her value and stature in cyberspace. Are you well
known? Are people eager to talk to you? How often is your data accessed? Vesna explains
that, "As you become famous, you have less time. Your information has magnetism of
its own. You will need to figure out ways to close down. Should you store your messages?
Should you have them forwarded to e-mail? Should you reject live communication?" Those
who receive only a few hits need not sulk about being ignored. Because they have assumed
an ultimately malleable form, they can instantly transport themselves across cyberspace
and visit any other site within the area in which their data is desired. Then they can relocate. Even better, they can duplicate themselves and relocate to multiple communities.

Meanwhile, "you" as a physical organism are superfluous within these exchanges. Your IP
has a life of its own. The physical version of "you" can choose to visit the virtual version
of "you" on the Web and observe the changes that have occurred in your virtual life during
your physical absence. Multiple "yous" generate independent histories. Some of the virtual
"yous" can even die; alternately, your IPs can survive your physical death since "you" remain
alive on the Web as long as your information is actively used. The multiplicity of these virtual
relationships can co-exist with partners in divergent communities, thus thwarting the
tyranny of clocks, calendars, aging, and life spans. That is the equivalent of creating time.

N0time ignores the observable features of a person's anatomy. Its visual representations
are based exclusively on the individual's relationships with other cyber communicators.
Becoming an IP requires "learning how to communicate in a group consciousness way,
shifting from the self and the individual-centered society." Each graphic representation
is shaped through the frequency and intensity of hits by other people. Thus, others create
"you" and insert "you" into new contexts. Communities prevail. Each person's pattern
contributes to a composite geometry revealing the community's cohesion or instability,
its hierarchical or egalitarian structure, its anarchistic or orderly permutations. With
each transfer of information, these dynamics are updated and amended. *N0time* chronicles increases and decreases in the cumulative knowledge of its members and the number

of famous (busy) residents. Each fluctuation is registered as a visual addition or deletion.

Survival in cyberworld depends on the exchange of information as much as the physical body depends on the exchange of air. Vesna implies that air and information are equivalent necessities in the life-stream of today's societal organism. The recognition that human life is networked, not individual, is further demonstrated by making observable the invisible information exchanges within the network. *NOtime* reveals its structural similarities to biology and geology: all are formed out of simple dynamic systems that interlock to comprise ever more complex systems. These commonalities confirm Vesna's belief that the human self is a unit within a social community, and social communities are units within networks that embrace all forms of life and matter.

Vesna presents this shift in consciousness in the title of the work. Capital and lower case letters have been arranged to convey the work's essential concepts. The "n" refers to n-space in physics, which stands for any coordinates and therefore refers to the multiplicity of space. "0" means zero, here applied to time. The title as a whole marks the shift from corporeal bodies to energetic, information *nOtime* bodies. As Vesna says, "There is no time. There is only change and our registration of the change. We determine how we structure change into time. This is a philosophical questioning. Not so new, but it is amplified by technology. How do we turn this around and look at it differently? It is not necessarily providing a solution, but I am trying to make a platform by which people can address it. I want to bring the idea of time and busyness to the table. I'm one of them. I'm in the problem. Everyone can relate to this."

Mission: "*We must rise to our civic role and duty and respond to the need for intelligent thought and expression of knowledge production and dissemination.*"[10]

By inventing a means to accommodate large amounts of information traveling between large numbers of participants, Vesna visualizes the chaotic and complex adaptive dynamics that have replaced the linear formalism and static states once used by artists to represent earlier conceptions of space and time. But at the time of this interview, Vesna was in the process of addressing a flaw in her artistic enterprise: thirty-eight minutes are required to download the 4.4MB of software needed to view *nOtime* online, in direct contrast with her themes. The newest version of *nOtime* is not as demanding on the viewer's time. Users can now download an 80k work in three minutes. The site provides a simple, linkless, one-page explanation. The work is algorithmic—it starts with a tetrahedron that replicates at time intervals determined by the user. The nexus of intervals is drawn from two invisible aspects of internet communications: "cache" memory that you input and "cookies" that others input. Taking the form of a screensaver that

the value systems that apply there, and still speak to a larger audience. To me, success is to create work that has multiple layers, almost like an onion skin, where people could see it on a surface level and address it as an aesthetic experience. I like the idea of making very complex works that you enter into as if they were very simple.

LH: Do you do anything now to enhance the value and appreciation of your work in the future? How do you assess the longevity of your career and your reputation?

VV: I really do not think about this at all. Being an artist is not a rational plan or decision. It is who you are and how you are in the world. You make the best of it using the circumstances you find yourself in, and take advantage of opportunities as they present themselves. Your career should be a reflection of your growth as a creative human being with a purpose to fulfill. I think the best way to get a sense of the effect of your work is the unexpected feedback from people in various parts of the planet. An artist's role is to inspire. If you manage to inspire someone who is in a place with little access to the world that we take for granted, that is really satisfying. I am having some kind of effect.

LH: What advice would you give the current generation of aspiring artists in the digital media, or in the arts, period?

VV: Take risks and do not be afraid to do the irrational. Think of every situation as a potential for an art project, no matter what life may throw at you. Learn how to trust yourself and use the technology available to amplify your message. Think outside of the frame and the white box.

Victoria Vesna, *n0time (Building a Community of People with No Time)* (2000–2001), installation view. Courtesy of the artist.

runs on an idle computer, it replicates and works and has a life of its own while the participant is not present. On June 26, 2002, *n0time* was featured in Rhizome.org's art news section, with the following description: "No Time For A Screensaver? What do you get when you cross a networked screensaver, Buckminster Fuller's quasi-cosmic tetrahedron worship, Richard Dawkins' evolutionary cybernetics, and a whole lot of computer down time? You get n0time, software that attempts to embody practically every major wired theory put forth in the last 25 years. Networked, customized, imploding, meme-laden tetrahedral avatars! "n0time-sharing" community protocols! Auto-generated e-mail invitations to exclusive online implosion re-enactments! And you thought it was just a screensaver."[11]

Vesna likens her work to one of art's traditional functions—suspending the viewer's sense of time by transporting him or her into mental realms where time ceases its relentless and measured course toward the future. Web surfers often report experiencing a similar suspension of consciousness. Vesna refers to this humanization of digital experiences as "a sign of a newly emerging distributed consciousness that has materialized on the Internet." Her work suggests that a new consciousness is emerging out of the confluence of a powerful duo—computer time and online space.

[1] Unless otherwise noted, all quotes from an interview with the artist, January 1999.

[2] Victoria Vesna. "AI & Society Database Aesthetics." *AI & Society: The Journal of Human-Centered and Machine Intelligence.* 17 May 2002. <http://time.arts.ucla.edu/AI_Society/vesna_intro.html>.

[3] Victoria Vesna, artist's statement, <http://n0time.arts.ucla.edu>.

[4] Vesna, "AI & Society Database Aesthetics."

[5] *A Community of People with No Time (n0time)*, 2000–2001. Collaborators: Victoria Vesna, concept/interface design; Gerald Jong, Fludiom software author; Tim Quinn, physical structure for installation; David Beaudry, soundscapes/real-time video; Rosanna Mann, Java programming; Ramsel Ruiz, Web authoring; Mark Yen, print.

[6] Inna Razumova. "Interview with Victoria Vesna." *Switch V7N1: social networks* 2, 17 May 2002 <http://switch.sjsu.edu/v7n1/articles/inna02.html>.

[7] Vesna, "AI & Society Database Aesthetics."

[8] ibid.

[9] ibid.

[10] ibid.

[11] See <http://vv.arts.ucla.edu/publications/reviews/95-97/rhizome/rhizome.htm>.

Wenda Gu
Born 1955 Shanghai, China
1976 Shanghai School of Art and Craft, traditional Chinese ink-and-brush painting
1981 Zhejiang Academy of Fine Arts (now China National Academy of Art), MFA, landscape painting and calligraphy
Lives and works in New York City

Wenda Gu celebrates such common aspects of human experience as the physical origins of life. Yet the shared wonder in the creation of life dissolves when culturally divergent practices related to conception and birth are introduced. Disparate practices often provoke misunderstandings, indignation, and conflict, fracturing humanity into contentious groups. Gu's mission is devoted to reconciling contrasting cultural practices, thereby promoting universal accord. In pursuit of this mission he has instigated cross-cultural exchanges in relation to contraception, placentas, menstruation, fertilization, virginity, and blood. Other themes that he has approached include language and hair. Because all these themes are stubborn conveyers of ideology, they contribute to divisiveness among the peoples of the world. Gu seeks unity through art.

"A great utopia of the unification of mankind probably can never exist in our reality," admits Wenda Gu, "but it is going to be fully realized in the art world."[1] With these words, Gu pledged to devote his art career to unifying a planet beset by quarrels and conflicts. When he made this decision, he forfeited the years of study he had devoted to mastering the art of classical painting in his native China, the security he had begun to earn as a master teacher, and the respect offered to him as an accomplished traditional artist. Envisioning international reconciliation required an art purged of evidence of any national tradition.

All the components of Gu's art are determined by his ambition to realize a vision of global accord. The magnitude of each project is global. The choice of mediums is global. The manner of presentation is global. But Gu encountered one hurdle that he could not easily overcome. He recognized that as a native of China, he himself is not global. Being well traveled, reading an international roster of authors, living in both the East and the West, and possessing a vigorous artistic imagination have still not prepared him to represent the perspective of humankind. Gu recognizes that internationalism demands that he "conquer himself;" that assuring a worldwide perspective requires that he add multiple creative partners from across the globe in order to subtract evidence of his unique self. Gu often draws his collaborators from among the people who reside in the city where his works will be exhibited. "I become the stranger. The locals 'otherize' me." Gu also uses addition and subtraction to achieve universal comprehension. He subtracts verbal communication from his work because languages segregate populations, fragmenting instead of uniting humanity. At the same time, he adds corporeal references because all people share knowledge of the body and its functions. The body provides the themes and the material for his art.

In the first installation of his *Oedipus Refound* series, Gu addressed a topic that is cross-cultural, transnational, inescapable, and intimate. The work deals with menstruation, a universal biological component of mammalian reproduction. Among humans, it is a deeply felt marker of fertility—but beyond this connection, its universality succumbs to difference. Humanity's attitudes surrounding menstruation defy common description. Individual cultures apply different attributes to a menstruating woman: a menstruating woman embodies evil spirits for some, benevolent spirits for others; the monthly cycle can be celebrated or dreaded; menstrual blood can be reviled or revered, taboo or accepted. *Oedipus Refound #1: The Enigma of Blood* (1988) attempts to "cross civilizational borders" in order to "hit the core of human existence." To create this work, Gu engaged sixty female collaborators. Each contributed a one-month supply of used tampons or sanitary napkins along with a written statement about her personal experience of menstruation. The volunteers were solicited at lectures Gu delivered in cities around the globe. Once he had received each woman's contribution, he installed the blood stained materials on a pure-white pillow and placed it in an elegant glass case. The menstrual remains were displayed like jewels, crowns, chalices, relics, or other cherished objects. Each woman was credited by name. In order to emphasize the universality of the menstrual experience, Gu also identified each woman's native country. Despite the artist's magnanimous intentions, his efforts at erecting cross-cultural alliances collided with cross-cultural discrepancies. Controversy raged in locations where the display of menstrual blood violated standards of decorum, particularly since it was presented in the refined setting of art museums. But Gu seems reconciled that those who expressed consternation may later join the universal sisterhood. Differences must be articulated before they can be overcome.

Similar disruptions greeted *Oedipus Refound #2: The Enigma of Birth* (1995). For this work, Gu's medium consisted of placentas, another universal bodily material, and one that carries significance far exceeding its status as the tangible evidence of gestation and birth. Gu attempted to merge Western attitudes, where placentas are quickly discarded as unsanitary medical waste, with attitudes prevalent in China, where they are prized as the prime ingredient in tonic medicines. To this end, he arranged five cribs in a gallery. He covered each with placenta powder made from processed placentas collected with the help of a friend who worked in a maternity hospital in China. The cribs were marked as "normal," "aborted," and "stillborn," characteristics of the range of outcomes produced by this universal experience.

Oedipus Refound #3: The Enigma Beyond Joy and Sin (1993) completed the series by focusing on the procreative act itself. This time, over-sized beds were arranged under canopies that bore evidence of the instant of conception. They were stained by the semen of a male and the blood of a virgin, all donated materials.

In the *Oedipus Refound* series, Gu presented three primal materials, under a title that indicated his intent to place them in the context of a primal myth. The Oedipus myth conjures the situation in which a person succumbs to one's destiny and then suffers the agony of its consequences. In this ancient greek myth, Oedipus inadvertently committed two horrific acts: he killed his father

Interview with Wenda Gu
By Zoe Feigenbaum

ZF: What where the circumstances surrounding your first significant sale?

WG: When I was in China, China still had no commercial galleries. You work only for art's sake. There are two ways you work as an artist—one was to be doing government propaganda, and the other kind was doing contemporary art. If you stick to the freedom of art creation, you become an underground artist, which is not favorable to the government. I was criticized all the time when I was in China for doing free art. I never thought about trying to sell art, to live off art. So I was not mentally prepared when I came to the West. To go through the capitalistic experience, that was kind of dramatic.

The first sale in the West happened when I was still in China. There is a well-known art historian who often went to China to give lectures. There was a collector of Chinese ink paintings from the University of Utah on the train who asked him, "Which contemporary Chinese artists should I collect?" The art historian told him about me because when he went to my academy to give a lecture, he saw my work and was really inspired by it. So that was my first major sale. When I came to the United States, this collector acquired a number of my early ink paintings for his collection. That was really significant, because when I came here, I had no money and no language. He helped me to survive in the first period.

ZF: Wow. So what did you plan on doing once you got here?

WG: I was totally dedicated, and sacrificed everything for the art I wanted to do. The commercial side gradually came to my awareness, but it's still secondary. I would never do art just to sell it. To sell you have to compromise what you create—like, this color is favorable to the collector, and that size or medium is good for the collection. But I never think about this. But I can sell. And this also provides me the ground to be successful. For other artists, when they have difficulties, they try to make a sale. I just create a piece of work. Even if you have difficulty, that's what's better. What I did was try to survive and lower the costs for living and use the rest of the money for my creations.

ZF: Were there some people who promoted your career when you were still unknown?

WG: My success couldn't be like it is without gallery dealers, critics, magazines, TV, media, and collectors. I have several big, important people supporting my work—one of the top collectors of contemporary art in America, the head of Morgan Stanley in Asia, the dealers I have in New York, and a curator in Hong Kong—many, many people. And these people are my patrons.

ZF: What would you say was the first indication that you were likely to become a recognized, respected artist?

WG: Actually, I don't clearly remember. It was just gradual. I don't remember which show really provided the respect. The only thing I can say is, every time you

Wenda Gu, *Oedipus Refound #1: The enigma of blood* (1988–ongoing), white bedsheets, white pillows, glass cases, metal casting beds, white curtains, bibles, used tampons/pads from 60 women including handwritten poems, statements, and stories about their concerns. Courtesy of the artist.

and he married his mother. Gu summons the myth to provoke our confused attitudes about familial relationships that inevitably entail reconciling social obligations with personal desires. Freud transformed this classic myth into a classic psychological disorder called the Oedipus complex, defined as the libidinal feelings a child has toward a parent of the opposite sex. In the following statement about his series, Gu reveals that universal experiences are rarely accompanied by universal attitudes. "The Oedipus myth is one of the most representative ancient allegories about our being, nature, and knowledge.... We are the modern Oedipus caught in the chaos of modern enigma, from our blind indulgence since ancient times, we are still looking, our knowledge is still extending, and the chaotic enigma of the modern Oedipus still continues."[2] Gu's art applies this enigma to events crucial to the creation of all human life: ovulation, insemination, and birth.

Language is another universal aspect of human experience. It fosters communication, but only among common speakers. Otherwise, Gu observes, language "brings about deep misunderstandings, which is what mankind's knowledge is all about." The Babel of miscommunication and misunderstanding is evident in debates at the United Nations, peace treaties made and broken, and collapsed world congresses. As a global activist-artist, Gu has invented forms of writing to heal these ruptures. They appear in his series *United Nations*, and they borrow letters and language structures from English, Hindi, Arabic, Chinese, and so forth. But anyone capable of reading one of these languages quickly discovers that the script is nonsensical, raising suspicion that the other scripts are not cogent either. In fact, they are all pseudo-scripts, and in that sense they are universal: No one can decipher them. The literate and the illiterate are united. Gu explains that he creates pseudo-scripts to "imagine the universe which is beyond the reach of human knowledge." Transcending human knowledge circumvents the divisive impact of language and the contradictory contents of the rational mind. Gu suggests that dispensing with language and rationality might mark the most direct and hopeful route toward global unity and spiritual transcendence. Gu identifies the destination as "infinity and eternity. Therefore the multi-pseudo languages ... pray for our future." The title for the language series, *United Nations*, identifies an institution that shares Gu's dedication to creating a world in which political alliances and social harmony replace violence and strife.

The fake scripts take the form of floor-to-ceiling free-hanging panels, reminiscent of the propaganda posters Gu produced as an adolescent during Chairman Mao's Cultural Revolution. But the influence of propaganda on this body of work goes beyond mere resemblance. Gu reports that propaganda undermined his faith in the intelligibility of language and ultimately inspired the *United Nations* series. "From the beginning I doubted human beings' artificial creations, one of which is language. Juxtaposing and interweaving pseudo-languages

have a show you have to provide the best of your work, once, twice, many times, to let people know that you are doing good art. It's difficult to divide the period when you have nothing and then you have everything.

ZF: Do you ever feel guilty about the commercial aspect of being an artist?

WG: There are two sides. If you create artwork, you are really into what you do. Then the selling is proof of such an idea. But on the other side, the more money I get, the more money I can transfer to the new art-creations. I feel this is a return to society. You're spending energy and time to create artwork. This is a kind of service to society, to the culture.

ZF: How does your work get marketed now?

WG: So far I have not committed to commercial galleries. I still feel I have a long way to go, and I want the more academic side rather than commercial gallery shows. I have enough money to hold my career, so if I get more money or less money it's not really a matter of concern. Mostly I do creations for museums and nonprofit organizations. This year I've been so busy. I'm involved in seven major new installations and a performance, as well as shows of my work of the past.

ZF: What kind of relationship do you have with your collectors?

WG: I think that to be friends is first. If we get together, I do not think, "I'm the artist and he's the collector." We're friends. The friendship for me is more important than the patronage. Even if the collector shifts his attention to other artists, we're still friends. So I think friendship is more important than a sale. Of course this is easy to say, because I have enough money for the end of my life, for my career. In reality, the artists who are stressed about getting money for living or getting money for creation, they are going to stick to the issue: How can I approach this collector? How can I approach the commercial galleries? But if you're not doing good artwork, you try to approach the galleries and collectors, it doesn't work out.

ZF: How do you approach your patrons and your collectors?

WG: There are many ways. The dealers approach a collector who knows your work and also the museums. Or the museum will approach the collector because the museum wants to acquire this work. They find a patron to buy it and donate it to the museum.

ZF: Please describe your studio—who runs it? Do you have any assistants?

WG: Now I have three studios, two in China and one studio in Williamsburg, New York. I have two assistants who work in the New York studio, and I have eighteen assistants working in both studios in China. I hire assistants to do the things I don't know how to do. The contemporary arts involve different skills and technologies that I didn't learn in my training as a visual artist. I don't have much knowledge of video projections. I cannot possibly do everything. So I conceptually design. They fabricate. The number of

Wenda Gu, *United Nations-China Monument: Temple of Heaven* (1998), a temple made of human hair in pseudo-Chinese, English, Hindi, Arabic, and synthesized English-Chinese, Chinese Ming Dynasty furniture, TV monitors, and video. Collection of the Hong Kong Museum of Art. Photograph: Jiang Ming.

Wenda Gu, *Oedipus Refound #3: Beyond joy and sin* (1993), human placenta powders (normal, abnormal, aborted, still-born) produced according to ancient Chinese medical methods, a white bedsheet stained with blood and sperm from first episode of sexual encounter, four giant metal casting beds. Courtesy of the artist. Photograph: Wexner Center for the Arts.

introduces not only the misunderstandings within a single culture, but unveils the conflicts of coexistence on a bio/geo-cultural level."

Once Gu had determined the concept (harmony among nations) and the format (meaningless writing) of his message, he still required a medium that reinforced the idea of a unified humanity. If the scripts had been written with pen or brush or pencil or computer, or if they had been stenciled or printed or carved, or inscribed in ink or paint or blood, they would have privileged one cultural tradition over another. The alternative was to discover a means of conveying language that was common to all humanity. Once again, the human body supplied the solution. Gu gathered prodigious quantities of hair from barbershops and hair salons around the world, always including the names and locations of cooperating shops in the final work. He and his assistants formed the donated hair into gossamer panels inscribed with pseudo-scripts that transform the spaces in which they are hung into hallowed sanctuaries. Gu's medium contributes more than merely the means of transcribing nonsensical scripts. The panels unite samples of different people's bodies, symbolically forming a consecrated, coherent monument to a unified humanity.

To construct *United Nations Series: Temple of Heaven* (1998), hair was gathered from barbershops in Poland, Italy, the Netherlands, the United States, Israel, Russia, France, Sweden, Hong Kong, South Africa, Japan, and Korea, among other countries. In order to represent the multiracial population in the United States, hair was gathered from such diverse locations as Indian reservations and New York City's Chinatown. The panels surround an interior meditation area set with Ming era-style furniture. Gu removed the seats of the chairs and replaced them with TV monitors that show tapes of moving clouds. He explains, "I want people to sit on the chairs, surrounded by invented languages in a transcultural setting, to meditate about issues like existence beyond knowledge, beyond nationality, beyond the boundaries of culture and race."

Gu began the fifteen-year *United Nations* project in 1993. It is conceptually, methodologically, culturally, and politically inclusive. At the time of this writing, he had completed twenty-one *United Nations* installations worldwide. His goal is to eventually have a work in every country. He estimates that the hair of more than one million people will be incorporated. "The audience, when they see the work, will immediately relate to the work because the materials come from themselves," Gu explains. "Language and knowledge are artificial. The human body is authentic and natural. That is why I switched to biological substances.... It is important to explain that uniting human bodily substance (hair) and human knowledge (language) returns artificial knowledge to its origin. This unique language is artistically inscribed by the human body itself, unlike the conventional written format through a medium such as ink and printing. Bodily materials help us transcend conventional attitudes of culture and direct us toward the essence of spirituality which equals the essence of our materiality."

Hair, like language and menstruation, instead of consolidating humanity, accentuates difference. Pigtails, crew cuts, dreadlocks, skinheads, cornrows, ponytails, can announce gender as well as political or spiritual allegiances. Hair texture and color can be associated with race, ethnicity, and age. There are cultures that believe that human vitality and life force are located in hair (whether or not it is attached to the head of a person). In others, it is cosmetic when it is on the head and refuse when it is not. Such divergent responses to hair are integral to Gu's art. Whether opinions from viewers or critics praise his work or condemn it, these respondents, as much as those who donate hair, blood, semen, and placentas, are welcomed as collaborators.

Gu believes the accumulation of divergent voices is another way to neutralize individual difference. *Confucius Diary* (1998 and ongoing) is a touring, worldwide art performance. It honors Confucius, a Chinese sage who lived about 500 years before Christ and who envisioned a great commonwealth in which humankind would be united under ethical rule. Confucius was an activist who, like Christ, crossed borders on a donkey in the hope of restoring social order throughout the region. Eventually, Confucius's journeys took him to Jerusalem. Gu resurrects these parallel stories by mounting a donkey at distant points on the globe and stopping to converse with people in public spaces. He believes that direct dialogue cultivates mutual understanding between cultures and societies. In Vancouver, for example, he spoke with the director of an international communications center, the chief curator of the Vancouver Art Gallery, the president of a bank, and many anonymous members of the public. While seated on the donkey, Gu wears a costume that manifests his role as a cross-cultural ambassador. The left side of his attire is a red velvet Chinese scholar's robe; the right side is an English tuxedo. Each half is decorated with pseudo-letters from the other culture's language. The English-like script is embroidered with Chinese hair. The Chinese-like script is embroidered with English hair. Videotapes of each encounter that Gu makes are later integrated into museum exhibitions. The topics of his discourses are issues of global significance: Will postmodernism's tendency to doubt the value of nation and history extend to science? Will reprogramming our genetic sequences, rearranging the blueprints of life, and producing artificial evolution be designed with market forces and commercial objectives in mind? Will the new millennium allow us to rise above our ethnicities and fulfill a universal melting pot?

Recently, Gu has been planning a work that is even more proactive, and potentially more controversial. He has removed the dream of global unity from the realm of mental abstraction by devising an artwork that actualizes it. This new project would extend his engagement with procreation. It will add insemination, pregnancy, and birth to his earlier considerations of ovulation and conception. Gu plans to create human lives. An international team of lawyers, social scientists, biologists, and politicians are advising him on the manner of producing a work that will involve the artist impregnating one woman from each continent on the globe. (Gu is currently married and has no children. He has already conducted "cultural weddings" with four different brides in four different countries.)[3] Although he has not yet determined the means of these impregnations, Gu's elaborate plan will not only be global, it will be eternal. He envisions that when these "art babies" grow up, they will become parents whose children will grow up and become parents, and so on. Thus Gu's work *UNTITLED: Impregnation Piece* will last as long as humans exist on the planet. As Gu notes, it is "completely open to the future, it will involve all changes in the environment, society, culture."

studio assistants varies depending on how many projects I do and what kind of work I am doing.

ZF: How would you say the costs of producing your work are allocated?

WG: There are two sides. For commissioned work, the museum will provide a kind of standard commission for you to produce the work, which is a material cost, assistant cost, and artist fee. If you want to do some work which is not commissioned by the museum, you have to pay yourself. In my two studios in China, I am doing some real work which is not commissioned by anybody. So I pay for everything, including the salaries for the assistants, my traveling, and hotel.

ZF: What percent of your income is earned by the sale of your art? Do you supplement your income in any way?

WG: I am lucky. Since I moved to the States in 1987, I have never worked a single day at another job. At the time I was really poor. If you work at some other job you're tired when you get home. You don't think about art. So I try to lower my living cost in order to not have a job. The most I get is lectures or a half-year as guest professor at a couple universities. In China I was a professor for seven years. At that time, China had no central art market, so artists had to be professional or a professor in order to make a living. But here, I never work a single day, lucky enough.

ZF: That is lucky enough, for you to be able to work on your art. Do you do anything now to enhance the value and appreciation of your work in the future? I mean, do you preserve it?

WG: The best way to preserve your work is in the collector's or the museum's hands, not in my studio. Some artists save what they think is the best work for themselves. For me, I think the art has a purpose to serve a public.

ZF: Did school play any particular role in your preparation to become an artist?

WG: School is important, but I barely listened to the professors. What I want to do is listen to my heart. When I read books, I always find a thing or thought to go against what I read. For me, the influence is the first process. But the second process is very important. During the second process, you evolve your own thoughts different than the book, different than the professor. If people learn from the professors and from the books, they're not generating their own ideas. For me, I always question when anybody tells me something.

ZF: What advice would you give aspiring artists right now?

WG: I would say, in general, it's not the art, it's the life experience that is most important. What you're experiencing from life in general, that's the foundation of your creation. I haven't been to museums for seven, eight years. The only time I go is when my friends have shows. I get influence from other fields. I have a habit of learning from fields outside of art; like you learn from a philosopher, from a villager, from science, from things that are distant from the art field. You make a marriage.

Wenda Gu, *Confucius Diary – Vancouver* (1998), performance. Courtesy of the Norris and Helen Belkin Gallery of the University of British Columbia, Anna Wong Foundation, Western Front, Vancouver Film School, and Record the Essence of Culture Foundation, Inc.

This work-in-progress addresses problems that have beset the human race since the earliest encounters with strangers that differentiated "us" from "them"—encounters that have established continuing cycles of territorial disputes, racial prejudice, and ethnic conflict. "The only solution," according to Gu, "is intermarriage."

These global art children, who will be created via Gu's insemination and belong to his artistic output, will otherwise be no different from other children. "They will be natural born and natural living. Art and non-art and life become one thing. But the children may be psychologically influenced by their special identity. They may think they are better than other kids because they have the status of art." He hopes the mothers will play a major role in his artwork. "They will be like any mother. Art is like life." Gu has pledged to raise money from art foundations to help support the children.

Gu says his projects are "dedicated to her, him, us, and our times." But besides enlightening his audiences about universal accords, Gu is constantly cultivating his own global identity. He describes himself as existing on a horizontal axis between Marxist and capitalist ideologies. The vertical line of this axis extends from his Chinese heritage to his acquired international attitudes. This provides creative energy and rich comparisons not available to those who have always lived in the environment in which they were born. Thus, jet travel and ancient wisdom coalesce to form Gu's vision of the future and his mission as an artist: "You shall be free from genders, nationalities, races, politics, cultures, religions ... you shall fantasize while you ride on running clouds ... you shall have moments of transcendence and tranquility."

Like a lot of my work has socialist influence. I'm really into the contemporary genetic research and biological science. Early on, the major influence came from visual artists, but I was more inspired by the ideas of other artists, not by the visual format.

ZF: Do you regret anything about the past, any decisions regarding your career?

WG: Of course you make some wrong decisions, but in the long run, I don't think there are wrong things. If you're able to capitalize upon your mistakes, you can turn them around.

ZF: Is there a pattern to the way you work?

WG: I think of my lunch, my dinner as my break times. So I wake up, I'm not even able to stay in a bed—my mind starts to run and I have to work.

ZF: And you go straight to your studio and get to work?

WG: I barely go to my studio. I work in an office with a computer. I go to the studio maybe once every two weeks to inspect the quality of production. I become like a boss. And if my work has to be fabricated in the factory, I invite these factory people for dinner and talk about my ideas so they understand what I'm doing. I also pay them. It's like a little company.

ZF: Do you like running a little company?

WG: Mentally, I don't behave like I have a company. I have a manager, and she has the responsibility of paying the assistants, and telling them what time they have to finish the work and what kind of quality I want.

ZF: When you struggled to maintain yourself as an artist, what was it like?

WG: Of course you are sometimes frustrated, you know? But one thing to tell you, I never lost my confidence. That helps you stick to what you want to do. Galleries and museums receive so many proposals from artists. So you send the materials. Maybe the dealers never open the envelope. Or they simply don't return it to you. Mental toughness means that what you believe is more important than reality. You can't change the reality, but you can toughen up. [laughs]

1. Unless otherwise noted, all quotes from an interview with the artist, September 23, 1999.

2. Wenda Gu, letter to the author, 12 May 1999.

3. Cultural wedding with groom Wenda Gu and bride Melanie Eastburn, Utsunomiya Museum of Art, Japan, 2000; Cultural wedding with groom Wenda Gu and bride France Kaplan, San Francisco Asian Art Museum and San Francisco Museum of Modern Art, 1999; Cultural wedding with groom Wenda Gu and bride Anne Katrin, House of World Cultures, Berlin, Germany, 2001; Cultural wedding with grooms Wenda Gu and Jeremy Wingfield, Hong Kong Museum of Art, China, 2000.

Tony Oursler

Born 1957 New York City
1979 California Institute of the Arts in Valencia, BFA
Lives and works in New York City

Tony Oursler has come a long way since he was taught to paint by his great aunt. He has become renowned for removing the images of talking faces from their usual confinement within video monitors or television screens. In Oursler's video installations, videotaped faces occupy the actual spaces of the real world. Typically they appear projected onto the blank heads of crudely formed stuffed dolls. Animated in this manner, the dolls provoke eerie confrontations with viewers. The projected faces speak. Often they rant. Most are distressed. Because they conjure extreme psychological states, all are distressing. People wandering through Madison Square Park in Manhattan in 2000 encountered ghostly faces floating over trees and onto clouds of smoke. The eerie, animated landscape fulfilled Oursler's mission to replace the trance-like state that projected images usually induce on television with active emotional engagement.

Paranoiac, demented, tormented, demonic, hallucinatory—any of these words can be used to describe Tony Oursler exhibitions. It's interesting to note that the emotional turmoil in these words is provoked by video—a medium that Oursler says is distinguished for its tendency to neutralize emotions and to make the despicable seem tolerable. "Video," says Oursler, "leads to a neutral space—this is the place inside which we grow and it is impor-tant that we swim into it, make it two-way, violate the power structure of technology."[1] This statement serves as a concise mission statement that propels his emotive use of video. Oursler explains, "Our culture is obsessed with the whole horror-sex-violence thing. It's a weird refinement, like bonsai. We love to watch it, and I am obsessed by the fact that we love to watch it."[2] Viewers gawk at Oursler's video-activated installations of psychological disturbances. The works loom so palpably, they not only consume the physical space of the gallery, they also invade the mental space of the visitor. A sculptor of psychic events, Oursler primes his viewers for mutiny against the oppressive influence of television technology.

Oursler's video characters wallow in an emotional abyss, bombarding visitors with a relentless volley of pleas and moans from their tormented souls. Yet he insists that he is not an expressionist artist. "Expressionism is not of great interest to me, nor is autobiog-raphy or self-expression."[3] Oursler is a gregarious man who displays no evidence of the need to exorcise his demons, despite an early bout with drugs and alcohol. He explains this apparent contradiction by commenting, "There may be a very emotive aspect to my works, but it generally comes from larger issues that I'm trying to explore."[4] Some of these issues involve what Oursler calls "models for a new consciousness,"[5] his term for mental states that are so prevalent they characterize an entire population, not just personal infirmities. His work indicates that statistically significant emotions often fall within the categories of mania, depression, and delusion. He tracks these mental states to their sources—the violence and trauma that dominate mass media and technology, and their capacity to infiltrate consciousness. Sociologists, psychologists, politicians, and parents commonly cite this correlation. As an artist, Oursler's contribution to this debate consists of staging the full charge of its ramifications. "There is TV. There is the human mind. There is the third thing created out of their convergence.... Our show is just beginning, and it's not about watching."[6] Presumably, this "show" is the real-life staging of calamities and breakdowns, not broadcasts of contrived dramas.

Even before entering the gallery where Oursler's works are exhibited, visitors hear the confused din of screaming, crying, muttering. It is agitating. Nerves are tensed. Emotions are placed on red alert. Curiosity is piqued, as it is at the site of a disaster. Upon entering, visitors find themselves immersed in a darkened room punctuated by multiple small video-projections of faces contorted to display a catalogue of acute psychic disturbances. The eyes on these video faces shift, their lips purse, their brows furrow. Some spew tirades of invectives and pleas. Others seem to collapse under the weight of their psychic burdens. These projections fall onto a collection of blank, sewn heads that are attached to crudely constructed dummies with deformed or truncated limbs. The figures are eerily animated by the videos. The talking heads punctuating the darkened room resemble close-up shots as captured by a television camera. Oursler explains, "I have a theory about this, which is that people are most attracted to the face. It carries the most information about us for many reasons. The rest of the body is inconsequential in comparison. Thus, the evolution of the close-up and the talking head on television. The fact is unmatched in psychological reflective qualities, so I think that people will always remember or are receptive to a moving face above almost anything else."[7] Face-to-face with these characters, viewers begin to empathize with them as they are confronted with the full thrust of their insults, groans, and pleas. The gallery doubles more as psycho ward than doll shop. These raw characters have lost their grounding, their ability to cope, and possibly their ability to recover. Viewers share their misery. Oursler's preference for dummies instead of fully rendered bodies transforms the figures' roles into common denominators. In fact, they seem less like humans and more like emotional catalysts such as scarecrows and totems. Oursler notes, "Dummies have the skill of seasoned panhandlers. The viewer may ask, "Can we accept such a pathetic invitation to empathy?"[8]

Empathy, the state of vicariously experiencing the feelings and thoughts of others, is directly correlated to the intensity of the emotions conveyed. The stronger the emotional display, the stronger the empathetic response. Oursler says his work is meant to be "a pathetic invitation to empathy"[9] and "an empathy test for the viewer."[10] To achieve this goal, he says, "I attenuate these emotions like musical notes, just to see what happens. They are worked almost to the point where they fall apart. That's how they transcend being a special effect in a movie, or part of a good performer's repertoire, or an insult from someone in the street."[11] Oursler's exploration of empathy thrives in this smarmy mental soup. None of the emotions displayed belong within the range of normalcy. Chagrin escalates into anguish, confusion descends into hysteria, irritation intensifies to despondency.

In a landmark multipiece installation entitled *Judy*, (1994), all of Judy's alter egos enact their trauma endlessly. Furthermore, they

---

Interview with Tony Oursler
By Lauren Harkrader

LH. Tell me how your decision of where to live and work has affected your career.

TO: Well, first I went to school in Los Angeles, so some people have associated me with being an L.A. artist. But I grew up on the East Coast and I wanted to return to New York. Those are the two big centers, L.A. and New York. On the other hand, I lived in Boston for some time, and that was not the center, but it was a really good place for thinking and developing work. Centers don't necessarily produce the best artists, but it's the best place for artists to be shown. So for artists who are established or developed in their careers, it's a great place to live. For someone starting out, it might be better in a place that's not so established. I think a lot of my career actually started in Europe. I was involved in the world of alternative spaces and coming out of the 1970s and '80s where video art and experimental installation work was highly valued in the noncommercial art world, comparable to the Internet today. So there was a network of alternative spaces and alternative programs. A lot of my development was virtual because I could send videotapes to different institutions in Europe and in the U.S. My development was global. It was facilitated by the medium I work in. This couldn't really work for a painter, because there's basically no money involved in putting on an exhibition of videotapes. You just have to make a copy of the tape and put it in the mail. Europe was a big part of that. They were always interested in experimental work, and I think to some degree more interested in experimental work than we are here.

LH: What do you think that people are after around here? Since the late '70s, '80s, it seems America has caught on to what Europe was starting.

TO: Yeah, video has been accepted. New mediums take a long time to get assimilated into the culture. So now people can accept moving images. Even though they had TVs in their house forever, it took awhile for them to see that as a potential place for art to be produced.

LH: I think that in a way, people have TV to soothe them and to just tune themselves out. The license that artists take with video, making the viewer think, probably turns some people off.

TO: Definitely.

LH: One thing that's interested me is your collaboration with different artists: Sonic Youth, Mike Kelley, Constance deJong, Tracy Leipold, David Bowie, Tony Conrad (an experimental filmmaker and musician), Joe Gibbons (a film and video maker), and other musicians, actors, actresses, and performance artists like Karen Finley.

TO: Well, in a way, my work is almost like movie production. If you really look at the history of art, it's pretty easy to see that there's always been that kind of production. People are shocked when they say, "Oh, you use an assistant." But if they look back to the history of art, they see there's a long tradition of that. I think contemporary art can be kind of monastic, but on the

---

Tony Oursler, *Judy* (1994), mixed media and video installation. Courtesy the artist and Metro Pictures.

spew unmanageable quantities of heart-rending drama simultaneously. Oursler offers museum goers no reprieve. "What makes the crying doll most effective is this superhuman ability to never-stop weeping, which in turn becomes horrifying for the viewer, who eventually must turn away. It is that moment of turning away which the empathy test is all about."[12] The deterioration of these characters is total. Viewers, bombarded with lost souls who seem to be beyond hope, cannot help but empathize—and wonder. What force is to blame for such misery? At the very least they must decide when to exit. It depends on their capacities to endure emotional confrontation. "I like the idea of someone expecting to 'get' an artwork entering an environment where they can't possibly absorb anything within a few seconds or minutes—thus the viewer is put into a different position; they must make a decision of where they stand in relation to the artwork, how they want to read it, how much do they want to invest in the process?"[13]

Flowers are visible everywhere in *Judy*, but nowhere do they contribute a pleasing decorative quality. Stultified plastic replicas and crudely printed patterns on fabrics, these floral motifs appear on an old-fashioned upholstered chair, floor-length curtains hung from a freestanding frame, a pillow thrown on the floor, and a patterned cloth covering a table. Oursler says he used them as "a sort of mock feminine camouflage or skin."[14] They emphasize that the surfaces on which they appear are delicate, unsuited to shielding the psyche from abuse or sheltering the wounded soul.

In one of the multiple stations that comprise this elaborate installation, a doll screams endlessly and wails, "Oh no! No, not that! Oh God!" Her face is distorted by fear, and her rudimentary body is suspended on a stand like an effigy that identifies her as victim of some unseen terror. Below her, a tiny doll's dress and a large pile of clothes are heaped on the floor like discarded bodies and souls. In the next station, a face emerges from a bouquet of plastic flowers supported on a metal stand. "The Boss" humiliates and abuses an unseen figure under the couch, screaming, "Eat this! Eat this now! God, you are stupid, you're an idiot. You're a worthless piece of shit.... I'm going to stick your head in the toilet again. I'm going to get the hairbrush again. I'm going to stick the hairbrush up your ass—you know I will." The figure cowering under the couch, known as "Fuck You," discharges a constant stream of obscenities. The couch is overturned as if thrown over during an uncontrollable burst of rage by an attacker. Propped up by a wooden stick, it creates a precarious retreat. The fourth character in this drama appears as an adult fetal figure projected onto a garish, flowered pink dress suspended on a bar in the manner of a headless scarecrow. Naked and silent, she writhes inside the dress's womb. A girl's flowered leggings hang upside down from the ceiling above "Fetal Figure," suggesting some unspeakable sadistic act.

other hand, it can also be very, very collaborative. Did you make your own pigments? Did you sew your own canvas? Or did someone do that for you? I'm from the conceptual-art continuum, where the idea is more important than anything else. Video is a medium that a lot of things can go into, a lot of different people. But I pretty much retain authorship unless it's specified in the credits of the piece. Most of the people I use are paid performers. I provide them with a script and they improvise within those parameters. In defining the terms of collaboration that I utilize, the performers bring their own character and individuality to the work. If I do use people and let them improvise, [they'll] be credited as collaborators. I really enjoy working with other people to get out of myself.

LH: Early in your career, how did you support yourself as an artist?

TO: I taught for roughly six years. I taught video and installation. I made about $24,000 a year. I really needed the job to make a living. It's a kind of job that allows you to be creative, to be in a creative atmosphere, and to participate in the world of ideas, which is different from other jobs. It's also important because it's out of the commercial world, and so that makes it distinctly different. Now I live off my work.

LH: It seems you work with many different galleries.

TO: My main galleries are in New York, London, Athens, San Francisco, Paris, Los Angeles. I work at a lot of different ones.

LH: How do you feel about working within the constructs of capitalism?

TO: Well, I'm lucky, because I can sell my work. I don't know if this figure of 15,000 art students graduating every year from art schools is something that you've come across in your research. You have to know how many people are out there, because what you're basically talking about is not capitalism—you're talking about competition. Obviously not all those people can make a living producing fine art. Some of them are going to be cultural producers in a lot of other ways, some in ways that can't be measured by capitalism.

LH: A lot of my friends are having to settle for graphic design, which seems like a practical decision that they've made.

TO: Well, people can do both. I think it's very interesting now; you have a lot more people crossing boundaries in that way. There's feedback between the sort of things that were considered commercial art and fine art. Borders are being fooled around with. I've always felt that the most important thing for an artist to do is to find some way to make a living that has nothing to do with their work, and to be happy with that, and to keep the financial burden off of their artwork. If the two come together at some point, you're lucky. Otherwise, try to support yourself in some other way.

LH: So you don't think that that is a distraction from your artwork?

TO: Well, it might be a distraction, but it's completely

Tony Oursler, *Back to the Womb (from Judy)* (1994), mixed media and video installation. Courtesy the artist and Metro Pictures.

There is a fifth station as well. A table in the gallery is outfitted with a surveillance-like system and microphone. Both are connected to an effigy figure that hangs in the museum entryway. The face and the speech of the figure are supplied by any visitor who chooses to sit at the table and share his or her personal responses "on location" from where the turmoil is ensuing. The communication device operates in two directions. Anyone who accepts the invitation to speak can use the effigy's "eyes" to survey people as they enter the museum, their attention commandeered by the individualized comments of this talking figure who observes them. Thus visitors are embroiled in the emotional mayhem on display elsewhere in the museum even before they pay the entrance fee.

The faces of the talking dummies are oddly proportioned, impossible to confuse or forget. It is obvious that they all belong to the same person. Oursler has assigned a single person to embody the multiple, massively disordered mental states that afflict the animated figures. They are all Judy. Each of the trio of speaking dummies exhibits a specific form of trauma. Pain, fear, and abuse are expressed as moaning, rage, and weeping. They provide evidence of phobia, paranoiac obsession, and mania. Although their mental afflictions are specific, the multiple characters represented by Judy are amorphous. Tracy Leipold, the actress who performs as Judy, is particularly suited to invite multiple points of contact. Some viewers see her as a woman, while others see her as a man. Some see her as young and others as mature. Most people can therefore project themselves into Judy's situations. These personal connections open the emotional receptors for empathy.

The fourth fetal figure is withdrawn and silent, a visualization of deep psychotic depression. In fact, this artistic incarnation is based on the actual medical study and testimony of a patient named Judy who suffered from Multiple Personality Disorder (MPD). She lived as a constellation of characters. In Oursler's work, Judy is a vehicle for addressing broader social conditions. He explains, "MPD is a metaphor for a postmodern persona and thus I began to study its particulars around 1992 and made a series of works based on this interest over the next couple of years. But first was *Judy*."[15] He elaborates, "*Judy* is a portrait, over time, of one character who fractures into many. I decided to use an individual as a metaphor for an overall cultural propensity, as I often do feel that it allows one to be more specific, to tie overarching concepts to a situation everyone can understand.... The work led me to further explorations of MPD in relation to media structures, which has always fascinated me; the uses of technology to expand the human psyche and body."[16] Thus, Oursler not only displays mental dissociation, he explores a root cause. "For me these works became the embodiments of the link between media and the psychological states it is capable of provoking: empathy, fear, arousal, anger."[17]

unrealistic for anyone to graduate from art school and think that they're going to make a living off their work. [laughs] That's a fantasy a lot of people have. But if somebody can be happy in their life and be making work, they have to understand that that's success. If you then get money on top of that for what you do, that's great. But the important thing is to keep it together for the long term and to believe that if you're able to do something interesting, people will eventually pay attention to it. That I firmly believe. But whether you're going to make money off it or not, that is a different story. The art world is not a meritocracy. It's not like there's some kind of court system where people are sitting around going, "Well, of these 15,000 art graduates, this thousand are the best, therefore they're going to get a check every month." That's just not the way it's going to work.

LH: Well, it seems like we're having a crisis of identity. Right now for us, it's money, you know? That's what has become the new code. But that's probably inherently unhealthy as well.

TO: You put your finger on it. Because if the measure of success is money, you have a built-in conflicted situation where people are going to be unhappy. I think it's really important for people to understand that the way the art system is set up, you're always waiting to be validated from the outside. The biggest struggle in the arts is to realize that you have to validate yourself from the inside. You're going to be set up for disappointment and failure if you believe that the only way to be a success is to be validated from the outside, because you can't control that. There's no way to control the reaction you're going to get from the world.

LH: Was there a point at all in your studies, in your growth, when you realized that art was what you wanted to do?

TO: Oh, that was when I was a kid.

LH: So how did your family react or support you in that stage?

TO: Half of my family is the literary side, the other half is the visual side. They were always supportive, and they were very happy when I had my first screening at MoMA in 1980. That was like a real high point of validation, but then they were very, very happy when I got a teaching job.

LH: And how about your first sale?

TO: Well, oddly enough, I was selling paintings right when I was in junior high and high school for not very much, but still I was able to sell a few here and there. I really didn't start to sell big pieces until 1992 or '93.

LH: Tell me about your studio and the assistants you have, and who runs it.

TO: I try to keep it fairly small. I farm out a lot of the construction of pieces that I can't do myself to various fabricators, and so I have woodworking guys, or metal guys, or plastic people, sewing people who are kind of experts in those things and work freelance. Office work I do most of myself. And then I have one or two core

Tony Oursler, *Simulacra (from Judy)* (1994), mixed media and video installation. Courtesy the artist and Metro Pictures.

There are degrees of emotional connection between people. Sympathy suggests pity while retaining the integrity of the self. Empathy involves total but temporary identification with another person's state of being. Empathy is the response Oursler calculates for himself and the viewers of his artworks. The third and most intense form of emotional connection is called introjection. It is the psychological term for the complete, long-term, and unconscious absorption of another person's traits, experiences, and emotional state. Judy is a case study of introjection. She lost her "self" and became "others." Psychologists generally assume that introjection is a person-to-person phenomenon. Oursler suggests that introjection can also occur between a real person and a media character. If people become mesmerized by television, if it is on throughout the day and evening and becomes the dominant source of visual, aural, and narrative stimuli in their homes, or if it is easier to watch television than to live a real life, vicarious media experiences are gradually perceived as real. Oursler presents the evidence that television is captivating not only as a medium, but that the themes it discharges become literally lodged in viewers' minds: sex, greed, trauma, and violence. Oursler comments on this fracturing of the self by stating, "Analogies in the media-viewer relationship are many, the MPD sufferer (or 'multiple') switches unknowingly from one personality to another like a hypnotized actor. They can be seen as a collection of characters acting out a horrible true-life drama. Some psychiatrists theorize that multiples are really just experts in self-hypnotism. In fact, while the U.S. seems to be suffering an epidemic of MPD, in much of the world it remains unknown or rejected—leading others to theorize that it is a mass hysterical epidemic fueled by pop cultural accounts in the media."[18] Oursler supports this notion by stating, "Physicians have even likened the multiple's ability to shift personalities to channel switching, or 'zapping'"[19] In fact, the number of cases of MPD has increased, and so has the number of personalities acquired by individual patients. Furthermore, the multiple personalities often resemble stock characters on television.[20]

Video projections are not only the culprit causing Judy's mental breakdown, they are also the ideal artistic medium for conveying her dementia. By flickering from view to view and leaping about from topic to topic, television transmissions mimic mental disorders. This is also true of the multiple video sites that comprise Oursler's installation. Physically as well as emotionally, viewers are immersed in the psychoses occurring inside Judy's head. Within Oursler's installation, the psychotic characters are released from their confinement in television sets. This invasion of the viewer's space intensifies the impact of the direct, one-way communication from dummies to viewers that normally occurs as television personalities invade people's homes but prohibit interaction. This relationship is made apparent by the silent viewer seated in front of the active, noisy TV set. Mimicking the passivity of television's

people that work for me. One person does all my video editing and computer stuff because that's the most important aspect of the studio. And then I have a couple of people who go out to set up exhibitions, like museum shows.

LH: And how are the costs of producing your work allocated?

TO: I'd say I spend maybe half of what I make producing stuff, so that would be a combination of studio, salaries, material. About half of it goes back into it.

LH: Do you have any regrets about your past decisions regarding your career?

TO: The only thing I regret is that it took me awhile to realize that you have to look inward for validation and not outward. I wish I would have been able to figure that out somehow earlier, but maybe it's impossible. There's a lot of unrealistic expectations in the arts. I think that a lot of what happens in art schools is very unrealistic—this mythology develops. I'm spending so much time with you on this interview because I think that it's important that books like this get out there. I think that ignoring the economic issues and ignoring students' fantasies which are completely unrealistic can be really destructive. I think students should respect work that doesn't come out of an economic base. Art schools should understand that the people going through there are going to be culturally functioning on a lot of different levels, and those levels are not measurable by a simple dipstick into the bank account. They're going to be measured in other ways: creativity. Training people to be creative should be respected more.

LH: Were there times in your life when you were more productive and inventive?

TO: In terms of the ebb and flow of creativity, I'm a workaholic. Work is my favorite thing to do. One of the things about success is that I get to do a lot of projects but I also have an incredible amount of administrative stuff to do. I can't really figure out how much of my time is spent on one or the other. I will say one thing about the most creative time in my life, [which] I call my "Year Zero," 1991: It was when I gave up on everything and just completely rethought things. And a lot of that had to do with the fact that I was completely outside of the economic stream. So I think you don't have to have a giant studio and lots of sales coming in to be creative. You have to be able to create a space for yourself where you can breathe. There is this dilemma, which is that you need to do all this research, and you need to have a studio, and you need to be funded, and you have to have these kinds of materials to have that moment of clarity in art. In fact, it might be when sitting on the bus you'll just have an idea. It's a very comforting notion to think that you could be super-creative while waiting for a bus. There was one exhibition that I did—this was the exhibition that I had the most time to work on, the most money, and the most support to work on, and guess what—it turned out to be my least successful, worst-reviewed show.

viewer-media relationships, Oursler dramatizes the crippling imbalance of one side monopolizing the "cause" while the other remains the "affected."

The fact that museum goers look instead of turning away provides evidence of the allure, and the danger, of the projected image. Oursler calls it "a psycho-mirroring system."[21] He says, "What really happens is that one reassembles or decodes visual-sonic language in a subjective, psychosomatic manner.... That's where I'm working, trying to make machines that coax the viewer into engaging with the transformation."[22] Empathy is the strategy by which Oursler disrupts the mesmerizing effects of the media. His complex tactics are designed to make viewers into participants, "finishing the work, carrying their own personal history into the process."[23]

The remote-control camera and microphone, the final station, provides viewers with an outlet for discharging this uncomfortable accumulation of empathy. According to Oursler, some museum goers participate in Judy's drama, "thus continuing the chain of multiplicity."[24] They become vicarious sufferers within the nightmarish den of Judy's split consciousness. They share her mental anguish.

Oursler's mission remains consistent with his idea that "making art is how people sort through chaos, through life."[25] Lately he has expanded his range of expressive options by enlisting the evocative powers of other technological communications, including antennae, 3-D hologram-like images, Web art, and CD-ROMs. "I'm fascinated how we want to put ourselves in a kind of trance through these technologies, to immerse ourselves in them so that we can experience something we don't want to confront in real life. To dance with the devil, you might say.... For me, the idea that an object could transform what's invisible—waves in the air, electronic signals—into something visible was interesting, not just because of the spiritualists, but because it seemed a metaphor for art: making visible an intangible sensation."[26]

In the end, the audience members' empathy creates awareness of their own propensity to be affected by a round-the-clock stream of electromagnetic waves bearing sex and violence. The Federal Communications Commission permits it. Sponsors support it. The public wants it. Oursler describes it vividly, "People weeping in theaters, whole families watching TV; a lot of telling but precious little vision. Sure, I search the media for evidence of the evolving collective unconscious. It's like going to an electronic prison. It's not a pleasant job."[27]

1. Elizabeth Janus, "A Conversation with Tony Oursler," in *Tony Oursler: Judy*, Jon Kessler, ed. (Salzburg: Salzburger Kunstverein, 1994), 6.

2. Louise Neri and Tracy Leipold,"In the Green Room: A Conversation with Tony Oursler," *Parkett* no. 47 (1996), 22.

3. Simona Lodi, "Video is Like Water," in *Tony Oursler*, Simona Lodi, ed. (Milan: Charta, 1998), 26.

4. ibid, 2.

5. Neri and Leipold, 27.

6. Janus, 82.

7. Lodi, 28.

8. *Tony Oursler*, Friedmann Malsch, ed. (Frankfurt: Portikus, 1994), 62.

9. ibid.

10. Lodi, 25.

11. Neri and Leipold, 22.

12. Lodi, 25.

13. ibid.

14. Janus, 7.

15. Lodi, 26.

16. ibid.

17. Janus, 7.

18. ibid.

19. ibid.

20. ibid.

21. *Tony Oursler*, 81.

22. ibid, 83.

23. Christiane Meyer-Stoll, "Written Interview with Tony Oursler," in *Matthew Barney Tony Oursler Jeff Wall*, Jerry Saltz, ed. (Munich: Sammlung Goetz, 1996), 65.

24. Lodi, 26.

25. Michael Kimmelman, "A Sculptor of the Air With Video," *New York Times*, 27 April 2001, B27.

26. ibid.

27. *Tony Oursler*, 82.

Mariko Mori
Born 1967 Tokyo, Japan
1986–1988 Bunka Fashion College, Tokyo
1988 Byam Shaw School of Art
1989–1992 Chelsea College of Art
1993 The Whitney Independent Study Program
Lives and works in Tōkyo, Japan and New York City

Mariko Mori is the designer, stylist, director, and star of all of her photographs and videos, yet she never appears as herself. To create her recent works of art, she first transforms herself into a cyborg deity who embodies an idealized state of being. Mori then creates comparable environments for these perfected selves. They are imbued with the lush resplendence of heavenly glory. Throughout history, artists have shared Mori's mission to fulfill the human desire for perfection. But few have had her advantages. Although her radiant, extraterrestrial vision of bliss carries the aura of ancient Buddhist and Shinto traditions, Mori capitalizes on space-age digital imaging technologies to incarnate heavenly flawlessness.

Mariko Mori's work is best appreciated when it is compared to two popular depictions of technology's role in shaping the future. The first scenario envisions that the indomitable force of technology will subjugate nature and provide the means for people to live, work, play, and die in comfort, security, and with contentment. The second scenario suggests that technology is as harmful as it is powerful, and will eventually cause the demise of civilization. Mariko Mori suggests a third prospect: that technology fosters spiritual enlightenment. By recognizing the continuity between mystical goals and technological means, Mori unites two sources of human advancement. Mori has studios in Tokyo and New York, locations where the futures of many other cities are already in full production. Based upon the work that she has generated from these sites, it appears that the fulfillment of the human desire for perfection is imminent. The good news is that the noble path of enlightenment that she discovered is not dependent on such demanding protocols as yogic discipline, the cultivation of right understanding, or a heightened state of mindfulness. Mori's envisioned world is simply an extravagant extension of current technologies and styles that offers the means to satisfy the three conditions upon which fulfillment rests:

Condition one is salvation from banality and drudgery to attain an ideal life on earth. Technologies offer life-enhancing, leisure-producing, work-saving attributes that permit the pursuit of one's deepest yearnings, noblest dreams, and highest aspirations. Mori comments, "I feel that technology has represented people's hope for improvement for much of this century.... The imagery I create is sometimes taken to be very utopian. But what I am really trying to do is point out where technology should go in the future, which I think is to coexist with nature."[1] In Mori's idyllic world, technology liberates people for metaphysical fulfillment.

Condition two is the creation of an image of nirvana that is attuned to contemporary sensibilities. Mori's vision of paradise is supplied by technologies originally designed as pragmatic tools, and later enlisted to create extravagant entertainment. These technologies are reformulating and intensifying human perceptions. Mori envisions the future in terms of today's virtual and enhanced environments. It is lush and ethereal, characterized by brilliant light, expansive spaces, multidimensional movement, and saturated colors. She explains, "In virtual reality there is only illusion and image collected in your memory as

Mariko Mori, *Pureland* (1997) 9 x 24 feet, cibachrome print, aluminum, wood, smoke aluminum. Courtesy Deitch Projects.

Mariko Mori, *Empty Dream* (1995), 5 panels: 48 x 120 inches, cibachrome print. Courtesy Deitch Projects.

experience. Things like this will really change and shift what we do, develop our concept of space and time and consciousness and make us more aware of the essence of life. My hope for technology, cyberspace for example, is that it will bring up questions of the space that actually exists, space that exists conceptually, and also inner world space, mind space."[2]

Condition three is the communication of this vision to the public. Instead of prolonged periods of ascetic withdrawal and meditative introspection, Mori's spiritual divinations are true to her cybernetic model. She computes her creative power surges by collecting, sorting, and merging the talents of an international team of technical wizards. The credits that accompany her works reveal that their stunning visual effects are executed on her behalf by digital-image manipulators, videographers, camera operators, lighting designers, computer graphic animators and designers, technical managers, production managers, 3-D video producers, 3-D camera operators, 3-D computer graphic designers, sound engineers, Photoshop editors, lighting technicians, structural engineers, set producers, sculpture fabricators, and video editors. In addition, she enlists the services of architects, couturiers, prop makers, makeup artists, composers, jewelry makers, stylists, choreographers, hairdressers, and location coordinators. This battalion of specialists yields to her wishes by producing such visual extravaganzas as digital landscapes; 3-D virtual-reality videos; dazzling, luminous architectural spaces; and fiber-optic devices for collecting and transmitting purified sunlight.

Mori's prognostications take the form of extravagant photo, video, and architectural installations. She summons high-tech tools and devices, but she pursues an age-old vision summarized by the following statement: "I wish for an eternal harmony of human spirit."[3] This decree serves as her "logo" (a secular trademark) and her *logos* (a divine principle). Analyzing each word in this proclamation, as follows, provides the means to track her mission to manifest the magnificence of a world that has been redeemed and perfected.

I. The "I" that is wishing for eternal harmony describes Mori's appearance in her artworks as part human and part fabrication. She appears transformed into a futuristic techno-dream woman occupying a futuristic, techno-dream world. Her various incarnations include electronic geisha girl, samurai waif, robotic streetwalker, video commando, bioengineered waitress, synthetic mermaid, pop diva, cartoon superheroine, extraterrestrial maiden, virtual ingénue, cyber-muse, and technocratic deity. Mori's human/technology crossbreeding, surprisingly, does not evoke perversity and dread. By relinquishing her humanity, she also relinquishes its inevitable flaws. Mori appears in her work as an ideal beauty. Similarly, the psychic unrest that accompanies the human condition vaporizes into a supernatural serenity. She blends the allure of a woman untainted by lust with the innocence of a child uncompromised by vulnerability. Mori offers a simple explanation for her superhuman contentment, noting that, "The women appear to be happy because they are cyborgs, not real women."[4] Finally, Mori surpasses human capabilities in processing input from the environment. Her cyborg self channels a multipronged image stream that is plugged into MTV, avant-garde fashion design, IMAX, the Internet, television, science fiction, Osamu Tezuka's *anime* features *Astro Boy* and *Phoenix*, video games by Nintendo, PlayStation, and Sega, the techno sounds of the Chemical Brothers and Crystal Method, and even Italian baroque ceiling painting from the seventeenth and eighteenth centuries. To this medley Mori adds references to quantum physics, string theory, Buddhist practices, and world art.

In the five-screen video projection *Miko no Inori (Shaman-Girl's Prayer)* (1996), for example, Mori's idyllic vision is literally conjured in a crystal ball. In the video, Mori appears transformed into a galaxy-hopping space-age seer who foresees the advent of a glorious future by gently massaging a crystal ball as she is steadily rotated round and round. She is a flawless, otherworldly apparition with silver hair, three-inch long silver fingernails, ruby lips, and an opalescent outfit that has pointed, inflated shoulder pads as large as her head. Viewers cannot perceive the world as it appears in the crystal ball, but they can observe its effects on Mori. Only a sight as glorious as eternal bliss could cause such unearthly iridescence.

Wish. Mori's ecstatic wish for eternal harmony represents an aspiration that has inspired many generations of religious leaders and artists. She describes her version of it by explaining, "My perception of the future is primarily focused on harmony of the individual spirit, and art is a great way to achieve that."[5] What is new to Mori's endeavor is her discovery of the impetus provided by new media and new technologies to propel this wish towards realization.

Eternal. Mori prepares herself for eternal harmony by ceasing to be mortal. In *Empty Dream* (1995), a 12-by-24-foot photomural, she accomplished this transcendence by morphing into a blue mermaid who lounges on a flawless beach. The synthetic shores on which she lays are those of Ocean Dome, the largest indoor aquatic theme park in the world. This fake seaside beach and ocean actually exist in the Miyazaki prefecture in Japan, an example of technology's ability to mimic nature while omitting such vacation inconveniences as rain, wind, chilling or skin-scorching temperatures, sharks, and mosquitoes. The only thing missing from the pop idealization of Ocean Dome's virtual setting was supplied by Mori when she reinvented herself there as a voluptuous mermaid. In a fishy plastic and fiber-glass guise, her picture was taken, digitized, and inserted into a pre-existing photograph of the theme park, where she appears in four different places in the same image amidst hundreds of real vacationers. Her fantastical presence coexists with the Ocean Dome's hyper-reality. Here such dualities as real water/fake ocean, real light/fake sunshine, real fun/fake experience converge. Like a cyborg, a mermaid is impervious to aging, illness, and death. Now, enhanced with space-age body parts, a real fake mermaid has been inserted into a real fake setting. Such complex intermingling of fantasy and reality is no longer considered a sign of mental illness. To those like Mori who aspire to a state of enlightenment, such intermingling of dichotomies releases the mind and catapults it toward visions of eternal, all-encompassing bliss.

Harmony. The title *Empty Dream* (1995) probably refers to the emptying of the mind, a prerequisite for achieving awareness of the interconnectedness of all things. Mori describes this Buddhist principle, known as nirvana, by saying, "All living beings are connected at every moment in inner space. Every life form with its own life cycle is part of the outer universe and there is only one planet earth. In the next millennium, the power and the energy of the human spirit will unify the world in peace and harmony without any cultural or national borders."[6] Mori pursues this vision by plugging in and hyperlinking out to parallel systems for processing reality in the contemporary environment. Presumably referring to the range of Eastern religious practices, she comments, "I don't directly take ideas from these religions," she says, "but try to bring some essence into the contemporary world, fused with science, technology, art, and popular culture."[7]

Early in her career, Mori posed for her pieces in subway stations, amusement arcades, corporate office buildings, love hotels, airports, and the Biosphere. Although these sites seem far removed from spiritual concerns, they anticipated her later work by recording evidence of the materialism and moral decline that is said to precede the arrival of the future Buddha. Mori's more recent work is designed to unify the material and the spiritual

Mariko Mori, *Dream Temple* (2000), metal, plastic, glass, fabric, and audio, fiberoptics and visiondome. Installation at the Royal Academy, London. Courtesy Deitch Projects.

domains. In these instances, she applies the advances of culture to depicting natural land-scapes. Mori is only attracted to sites renowned for their extraordinary features. She has depicted the spectacular Painted Desert in Arizona, a passage called Flaming Cleft in the Gobi Desert, the magnificent waterfalls on Japan's Pacific peninsula, and the awe-inspiring Dead Sea in Israel. These sites are each the setting for a billboard-size, digitally composited photograph encased in glass that uses images from a stereoscopic video of the same name. They comprise a larger work entitled *Nirvana* (1996-1998). In addition to being natural wonders, these locations are associated with the expansion of human consciousness. The Dead Sea, for instance, is not only the lowest point on the Earth, it is, according to legend, the purest place on Earth. In the 3-D video *Pure Land* (1996-1997), Mori enhances its other-worldly aura by inserting a levitating glass palace into the enormous acid-orange panorama of the Dead Sea. Materializing as a radiant apparition within the palace, Mori gracefully executes ritual hand gestures. Her sumptuous kimono and elaborate crown are reminiscent of the renowned twelfth-century sculpture of the compassionate deity Kichijoten. Mori's godly stature is augmented by her heavenly attendants: six lollipop-colored, pointy-eared, chubby little aliens she refers to as "tunes," each of which floats in a mini bubble-like space-craft. As the tunes play ancient ritual instruments, their globular enclosures zoom out of the dazzling landscape and penetrate the 3-D space of the viewer. Their high-pitched melodies accompany the artist, who chants an invocation of the spiritual journey to nirvana. The journey culminates as the crystal lotus that Mori holds in her hands takes flight and whirls before the viewer.

Pure Land provides an example of how the addition of high-tech apparatus augments the spiritual impact of traditional Buddhist rituals and ancient Buddhist teachings. The deep, sumptuous, and fluid space of enlightenment that is conveyed in this work is a product of 3-D glasses and a 3-D video system (engineered for Mori by GIT Corporation). The experience is transfixing, despite the fact that viewers recognize the role of a technically induced optical illusion in producing this glimpse at nirvana. It is a nirvana that can only be described in rapturous tones as "inward peace and strength, insight into truth, the joy of complete oneness with reality, and love towards all creatures in the universe."[8]

Human spirit. Mori's incarnation into a deity is as pop as it is cosmic. She has been compared to narcissist music star Madonna, the goddess Kichijoten, a Bodhisattva (an enlightened being who strives for humanity's salvation), and even the Buddha. All of these personas manifest an energy that flows from all beings but is neither spatial nor temporal nor visible. Mori describes this "efflux energy" as "innumerable and immeasurable ... a habitual dynamic presence. It spontaneously self-regenerates in a perpetual series of instantaneous moments, continuing to manifest itself from the eternal past to the eternal future. No death or birth strikes it."[9]

Mori's attempt to construct the experiential equivalent of "efflux energy" here on Earth is realized in *Dream Temple* (2000). Although the ancient Yumedono Hall (part of the larger Houryu-ji Temple complex) in Ikaruga City, Japan, inspired it, Mori's version is bolstered by the up-to-date contributions of Shiseido graphics production, Sony sound engineering, Italian architects, and a Japanese computer graphics team. In its design, *Dream Temple* resembles a futuristic wedding cake. It is constructed of iridescent Dichroic glass, a space-age material infinitely more suited to visualizing an immeasurable, dynamic presence than the opaque wood used to construct the original temple in the year A.D. 739. Colors appear to shift as visitors move about. Mori describes her version of the structure as a "white, spherical video projection room—a vision dome."[10] The visually antithetical nature of these spaces is a product of differing historic contexts that share a common mission. Mori explains, "[The Yumedono Hall] was a place that had a life of eternal present, where Prince Shotoku would go to meditate or study, a place where he could transcend time and space. I wanted to create a place like this … a place where you can use all five, maybe six, senses. It's a utopian space from an ancient concept. A place where, for four minutes and forty-four seconds, one person can experience another kind of reality."[11]

Like gurus, yogis, New Age nutritionists, aromatherapists, purveyors of crystals, cosmetic surgeons, and herbalists, Mori strives to ameliorate concerns regarding the impermanence of the body and the permanence of the soul. The difference is that Mori actually achieves this goal, even if it only lasts a few minutes. She offers her viewers an instantaneous, hip, chic, and gorgeous experience, perfectly described in this ecstatic verse:

Awaken! Know the cosmic wisdom, life's mystery,
and the efflux of primal energy that has no entity.
Let us transcend language and conception.
Let our flesh melt into the air. Let our spirit be liberated.
Let us be one with the ultimate truth of ourselves
and the whole universe.

[1] Neville Wakefield, "Momentous Mori," *Interview*, June 1999, 109.

[2] Margery King, "Mori Pop," in *Mariko Mori* (Chicago and London: Museum of Contemporary Art Chicago and Serpentine Gallery, 1998), 39.

[3] Wakefield.

[4] Dick Blair, "We've Got Twenty-Five Years," *Purple Prose*, April 1993, 99.

[5] Wakefield.

[6] King.

[7] Steve Brooks, "The Miraculous Appearances of Mariko Mori," in *Shambhala Sun*, July 2000, 53.

[8] E.A. Burtt, *The Teachings of the Compassionate Buddha* (New York: Mentor Books, 1952), 29.

[9] Lisa Corrin, "Mariko Mori's Quantum Nirvana," in *Mariko Mori*, 22.

[10] Wakefield.

[11] Clifford Pearson and Ingrid Whitehead. "Mariko Mori: Tour Guide to a Technological Temple of Dreams." *Architectural Record*, November 2000. <http://www.archrecord.com/INTRVIEW/PROF1100.ASP>.

12. Mariko Mori, "The Eternal Law," trans. Reiko Tomii, in *Mariko Mori*, 41.

Gregory Green
Born 1959 Niagara Falls, New York
1981 Art Academy of Cincinnati, BFA, sculpture
1984 School of the Art Institute of Chicago, MFA, fine arts
Lives and works in Brooklyn, New York

Gregory Green has presented a well-worn Volkswagen bus as a work of art. It came stocked with Campbell's pork and beans, Sunbeam white bread, personal snapshots, and necessities for camping comfort. The other gear demonstrates that vacationing is not the motive of the bus's owner. The camper is filled with tapes and books with such titles as *The Right to Protest, Counterfeit Currency, In Defense of Anarchism, An American Adventure in Book Burning*. The radical theme of these texts is not hypothetical. The camper also comes equipped with a functioning 100 VHF television transmission system, a thirty-five-watt FM radio transmitter, and is accessible on the Internet. This artwork is a real, roving pirate transmission station designed to operate outside FCC regulations. Green's mission is to undermine existing concentrations of power and to distribute it among the people. The centers of power that appear in his art include the control of communications networks, the possession of weapons, and the knowledge of how to concoct chemical poisons.

Artists who reject conventions in order to indulge the outermost reaches of their imaginations are often compared to anarchists. When the term is applied to Gregory Green, it refers to his artistic practice of producing "do-it-yourself" instructions for constructing real bombs. Green describes himself as a "romantic anarchist" or a "conceptual terrorist."[1] In neither case is he attracted to bombs for their destructive capabilities. His engagement, rather, is located in the realization that those who do not possess bombs often forfeit authority, freedom, and autonomy. Green is dedicated to anarchy—a form of social organization in which governmental rule is eliminated in order to avoid the very inequities of power he investigates. He pursues his anarchist ideal by bringing weapons access to the general population. Pipe bombs, letter bombs, and Molotov cocktails are stock for any insurgent's arsenal, as are liquid LSD, which might be introduced into an enemy's water supply, or computer viruses that contaminate communication networks. Lone rebels favor such insidious devices, compared with the weapons of choice for large-scale warfare like megaton nuclear bombs, multistage missiles, or incendiary weapons like napalm. This entire fearsome inventory of weapons appears on Gregory Green's catalogue of artworks.

Green is a thoughtful, mild-mannered man. It is difficult to imagine that bombs, missiles, and other tools of treachery could be fabricated by someone as modest and soft-spoken as he. He is neither brilliant nor wealthy nor a zealot. Knowing that he is average is essential to his artistic mission. Green's art demonstrates that anyone can fabricate devices as potentially nasty as *Big Bertha* (1996), a three-stage, thirty-foot, fully functional, high-powered surface-to-surface missile capable of carrying a 150-pound payload. Green assembled this artwork for about $250 with materials readily available to anyone with access to a typical shopping center. The missile's timers, for example, are alarm clocks. Furthermore, he demonstrates that utilizing these components requires neither advanced academic degrees nor privileged access to secure documents. Green obtained all of the necessary building information from published manuals and books and the Internet. His accomplishment proves that one average citizen can instigate hostile actions worthy of a major military complex. "I make destructive objects," Green says. But, he counters, "I don't necessarily promote them. I want everyone to recognize power is an option available to them.

I don't make the moral decision for them. Most people assume they can't do a lot of things because they're too technically difficult. But if you can follow directions in a cookbook, you can build a nuclear bomb. It is easy to discover how to make a bomb from reading any high-school physics books—just do everything the authors warn against doing."

It is Green's peaceful demeanor, and not his menacing arsenal, that reveals his motives and inspires his improbable feats. As art, these weapons acquire a function that is not only nonviolent, it is anti-violent. Instead of blowing up the oppressors, Green aims at exploding the inadequacy and demoralization of the oppressed. By demonstrating that it is possible to fabricate destructive apparatus in kitchen laboratories, Green hopes to convert defenseless conformists into stalwart individualists capable of defending themselves. Revolution depends upon an agitated populace. In this manner, Green encourages defiance against the status quo. "I want to nudge a complacent audience to consider the possibility of joining the ranks of radical protestors. I illustrate that both violent tactics and nonviolent strategies are accessible to any individual or group regardless of technical or educational level. I want to break down the myth of inaccessibility." Green further explains his motives in a manifesto-like work entitled *Text Piece* (1986). The concluding paragraph of this unlimited edition print summarizes his philosophy and justifies his crusade: "The voluntary relinquishing of responsibility for our lives, actions, and truths is the true source of our destruction. Freedom from this system of control based upon perpetual fear and misinformation is required for our own survival. The myths and systems that maintain these false realities must be removed." Although Green demonstrates how to produce weapons, he does not identify any targets. The myths and systems to which he refers can be as subtle as building codes, as tenacious as advertisements, as alarming as religious fanaticism, and as menacing as despotic rulers. "I am pro access to information. In some way I function as an academic—I give information. But I want the work to also be aesthetic, a provocation, and a revelation."

The bombs Green builds are operational; he once deliberately exploded one to test whether it was actually functional. In a gallery setting, however, they are exhibited without their combustible fuel. The missing dynamite or plutonium is presented in the form of a written recipe. But he has also contrived a protective strategy against the misuse of these instructions, and he intentionally complicates the task of following them by garbling the "recipe." Materials for making Homemade Black Powder Igniter, for example, include "Potassium (or sodium) nitrate, powedered charfcoal, powdered sufur, powder." To prepare the ingredients, he provides equally confusing instructions: "Into a clean, dry jar or can puit spoonfuls of potassium or sodium nirtrate. Spoonfuls of powdered charcosl, and 1 spoonful of powdered sulfur. The ingredients must be at least as fine

Interview with Gregory Green
By Ry Russo-Young

RY: What was the first indication that you were likely to become a recognized and respected artist?

GG: Recognized and respected artist? [laughs] I went through my pre-Madonna stage very, very early, so when those sorts of things were happening I didn't really recognize them as happening. They were just normal. A lot of younger artists think that when they get that one show in that one place, then they'll be set. That's really not the story. It's literally from show to show.

RY: How do you feel school helped or didn't help shape you?

GG: I went to the Art Academy of Cincinnati for undergraduate and School of the Art Institute of Chicago for graduate school. After I got out of school, I developed a lot of issues with the educational programs in art schools across the country, the primary thing being that they give absolutely no guidance to people about how to function outside of college. Most of my education came from the other students and artists that I knew. I was working in a big nonprofit gallery, and that's where I learned the most about how to survive in the art world. I don't know how they're doing it now but the last time I talked to somebody about it, they still weren't teaching that you had to have a resume and you have to have slides. There are still students who think, well you just do your stuff and you are discovered. No, that's not the way it is. You've got to be as much of a salesman as an artist. It's part of the way it works in the business. You sell yourself and then somebody buys your work and they start pushing you as well. And then more and more people start doing it and then one thing leads to another.

RY: What percent of your income would you say is earned by the sale of your art?

GG: Well, if we define my art as honorariums from museum shows and lectures and all of the art-ancillary things, then 100 percent. I have been lucky enough to have not needed an alternative income for the past ten years.

RY: Describe your studio.

GG: My studio is an 800-square-foot space, set up for mostly clean work. All the big dirty things I get fabricated—metal welding and big tool things that are really dirty. There's no reason I have to form a hemisphere of aluminum if there's a standard aluminum hemisphere that's available exactly the way I want it. I don't have to come in and make it by hand. Seventy percent of my work is actually not made in my studio, but on site prior to an exhibition. The studio is more a place where ideals are explored and the final assembly of individual works takes place. In a way, it is almost an extension of the gallery.

RY: What are the parts that you enjoy the most?

GG: Being finished in the end. [laughs] There's a lot of boring labor involved, and boring labor is boring labor.

Gregory Green, *M.I.T.A.R.B.U. (Mobile Internet, Television and Radio Broadcasting Unit)* (2000), Volkswagen bus and mixed media. Courtesy Feigen Contemporary, New York.

as granulated sugar. If they must be ground, grind each separately. Never grind the mixed intredients—they may igniter or explode." Then, he obscures the directions for using the gunpowder: "pile 2 lr 3 spoonfuls ontop of any soliod incendiary material which is to bve ignited. For igniting liquids in ioopen containers, wrap 2 or 3 spoonfuls in a piece of paper and ssuspend it ujust above the liquid."

Green's distrust of institutionalized concentrations of authority was instigated by a conversation he had with some patrolling police on a sweltering summer day in Chicago in 1985. He recalls that residents of a housing project kept throwing garbage into the alley behind his studio. Despite polite appeals to his neighbors to stop, the stench, bugs, and rats accumulated at the same rate as the mounting heaps of garbage. The policemen's advice revealed a shocking desecration of power that has since shaped Green's daring artistic mission. They told him, "All right, buddy, this is off the record. What you should do is buy a gun. Next time you see someone in a window throwing out the trash, shoot at them. Shoot them—I don't care if you kill them. You're white, they're Puerto Rican or black. Don't worry, we won't bother you. Take it easy." Green goes on to explain, "When the Chicago police told me to buy a gun to solve my problems with the neighbors, they were talking to me about strategies to control and manipulate the population. It was an abuse of power. My work talks about abuses perpetrated by the government, military, police, even at times the general media and other social institutions. That incident with the police made me realize how far the abuse could go."

As an anarchist, Green aspires to resurrect the organizational models of the Quakers, the Amish, and the utopian communes of the 1960s and 1970s. As a terrorist, his activities remain theoretical because his incursions have an immaterial target—the power that is unchallenged for some and unattainable for others. Green identifies this situation as the root cause of terrorism. "I am on record as saying to the press after the first attempt on the Twin Towers, that it is highly likely the towers would be brought down. That whole event reinforces the importance of the work I have been doing. I have been talking about the potential for violent acts. Terrorism is going to define the next fifty years, at least. We have dived into [a] quagmire that is unsolvable and only going to get worse. I don't trust governments or structures or systems. We need to address the conditions that force people to choose violence as a way to solve problems."[2]

Green is particularly determined to apply his oppositional tactics to rout out insidious oppressors, those who usurp rights without flaunting their dominance. His strategy intentionally courts confrontation. First, when Green threatens their sovereignty, they typically rise up to suppress his efforts. In this manner, Green lures them out into the open, where they become vulnerable. Second, their retaliation broadcasts the extent of their tyranny. This activates resistance in the populace. A poignant example of this tactic can

RY: How does your work get marketed? Do you have a dealer, an agent?

GG: I have five dealers. One in the United States and four in Europe.

RY: What is your relationship with your collectors?

GG: [Laughs] The richer and more important the collector is, the cheaper and more evil they are.

RY: Really?

GG: Collectors and the sort of relationship they want to have with artists varies tremendously. Some collectors want to know you well. I have a couple of collectors I have relationships with like that. They call, "I'm going on vacation. What are you doing?" Other collectors never want to meet you. I know of one who feels it corrupts his experience of the work if he knows the artist, which I think is actually pretty smart. Also, most people think that you are your work. Most people think that when they meet me, that they're not gonna find some wholesome, blond, white American boy. They're looking for a leather-clad, mean, angry, hard, vicious guy. I've gotten that a lot throughout my career.

RY: Do you feel pressure to fall into that?

GG: I used to play dress-up to a certain extent, but I got bored with the whole game, so I stopped. When my work was most frightening to people, at openings and other events, I'd wear a conservative suit, plain bow tie, white shirt—as opposite from my work as I possibly could. And then sometimes I'd show up at my next opening in leather pants, my motorcycle boots up to my knees, and a latex shirt, looking really hard. It was a way of making a point. I mean, I am like my work, but it's more about the empowerment and the positive aspects, the conceptual basis of the work, not about the spectacle and violent aspects.

RY: And the business?

GG: Financially, with my work, I could be a lot more successful. My work isn't pretty, not decorative, and 50 percent of my sales are canceled because the partner, whether it's a male or a female, says they won't have something so negative in their home. So my income from sales varies from year to year, from $18,000 to $60,000. It goes up and down in cycles.

RY: Do you think that it's beneficial to you to be around people who are other artists or who are in your community? Or do you prefer to have friends who are completely unrelated, like stockbrokers or construction workers?

GG: It's changed. I've been doing nothing else for twenty-four years. The first eighteen, I only trusted artists. Currently, I'm bored with the art world. I'm more interested in people outside the art world right now. And also there's been a change in my relationship to my work. It's reached a point where my work is between me and me. But being within the enclave of the art world in the beginning of one's career is really important.

RY: What advice would you give the current generation of aspiring artists?

GG: [laughs] If you want to make lots of money, be a painter and make pretty, nonoffensive paintings that

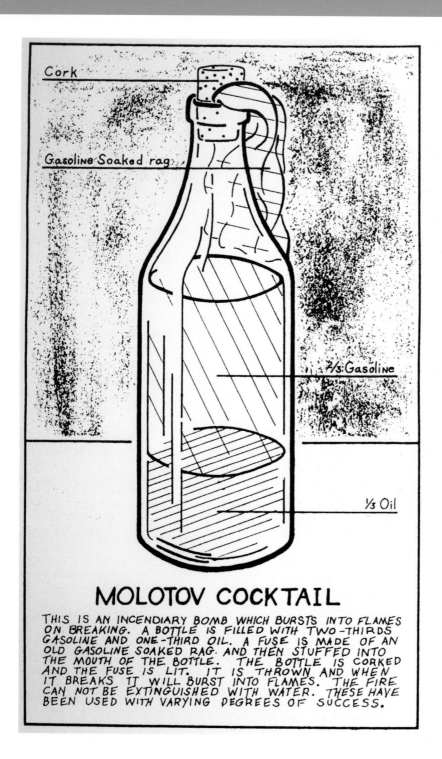

Gregory Green, *Molotov Cocktail* (1993), 16 x 10 inches, ink on paper. Courtesy Feigen Contemporary, New York. (Artwork seized and later destroyed by police in Potsdam, Germany. A curator and assistant were arrested under German antiterrorism laws. Later that year all charges were dropped.)

be found in Green's contributions to a group exhibition in Potsdam, Germany, in 1993. At the time, the country was embroiled in a political and economic crisis. Although the Berlin Wall had already been torn down, the old guard was still in power. "The police just changed uniforms. Potsdam was a very poor economic area. Most people did not have easy lives. There was a huge amount of tension. Young skinheads needed someone to blame. There was a resurgence of Nazism and widespread anger towards the West. Fire bombings from right-wing groups were rampant." Green's two contributions to the exhibition ignited Potsdam's tinderbox political climate. The first was a T-shirt printed with a recipe for a Molotov cocktail. The second piece was a billboard that dispensed instructions for fabricating book bombs. As anticipated, controversy between the police and the sponsoring museum erupted and raged for a week. Then the police staged a midnight raid and tore Green's billboard down. The curator was arrested, but Green's mission had been accomplished. Fomenting protest exposed entrenched right-wing bias among the police and the government.

Green describes his bomb pieces as "Fascist bait." But bait is not just a taunt. Sometimes bait is devoured by its intended victim. Although Green intended to incite the authorities by threatening their supremacy, the range and fallout of this provocation couldn't be anticipated. Green created these works fully aware that they were illegal under Germany's strict anti-terrorism laws. He anticipated the political and legal repercussions of his brazen acts. He inserted incorrect information into both sets of instructions to provide himself with a protective strategy. The book bomb billboard, for example, omitted an instruction to connect a particular wire. Thus his legal defense was bolstered by the fact that the bombs weren't functional. The tactic worked. Green reports, "It was clear my intent was something different. The judge realized that I do not support the utilization of violence at all. My work was not intended as a provocation to expand the attacks on dark-skinned others, which is what was going on at the time. The central reason why I gave incorrect information was that I do not want to educate people in strategies that I do not morally support." Green's artworks function as provocation, not the weapons of destruction they portray. He does not promote violence. He promotes an equitable distribution of power as a deterrent to violence.

Green also perpetrates potentially violent tactics in order to snag the attention of the media. He explains, "I think of exhibitions as abstract terrorist events. If you look at any terrorist event unemotionally, it falls down to a formula—it is an event of spectacle that creates a form of public interest that then creates a platform for the perpetrator of the event to have a public voice. I regularly talk to lawyers to find out about the specific letters of the law. I want the works to exist on the edge, or even a little over the edge of what might be legal. This was part of an overall strategy to create more

aren't too big and aren't too small. If you don't buy that, then do whatever you think will be right for you. It's hard to say—the relationship between artists and their art is individual. Don't lose yourself in your art. Take care of yourself.

RY: What do you mean?

GG: A lot of young artists self-destruct. A lot of people become so obsessed with their work that they really aren't able to function outside of that. I've been manic and obsessive about my work. But I could say, "Okay, I've had my studio hat on for two weeks now, it's time to take my studio hat off and put on my business hat. I've got to send out those resumes, I've got to look at my bank account." There is a business aspect of being an artist.

RY: How has your choice of a place to live and work affected your career?

GG: Tremendously. As soon as I started knowing the art world relatively well, it became very clear that it was important to be in New York. For instance, if you want to be an actor it's gonna be much easier in Los Angeles. New York is simply the center of the art industry.

RY: What do you regret about your past decisions being an artist?

GG: There are a couple of things I regret, but I don't think I would change them. In some respects I regret the direction that my artwork took. Part of me wishes that I would be happy making pretty, medium-sized paintings. But at the same time, I can't ever imagine doing that. It's just who I am. Sometimes I regret that I put my artistic career ahead of my personal life. But then other times I regret that I put my personal life before my art.

RY: Were there times in your life when you were particularly productive or inventive, and if so, what is the tempo and variability of your working process?

GG: Usually, every five years I go through a period where I have piles of ideas. My mind will be incredibly productive. And then I'll move into a phase of production and development. So yeah, I'm very cyclical…

RY: Do you have certain things that help you with your work?

GG: Naturally I require a lot of technical information for the production of my work, and that primarily includes library research as well as a little bit of internet research and the purchasing of certain books from alternative publishers. Other than that, it really comes down to what music or other media that I listen to in the studio. I tend to listen to a lot of contemporary trance, house, and jungle music in the studio. In a way, it is like drinking caffeine all day long. It helps maintain my focus and destroys my sense of time, allowing me to work long hours uninterrupted, which is often my working style.

RY: And do you work in the morning, evening—do you have a time preference? Is it helpful to punch a time clock for yourself?

GG: My working process has no set schedule for production or thinking, which can be equally important as

access to the general media." Like terrorists and politicians, Green crafted his early projects to generate publicity. He succeeded. The media clamored because the presumption of danger constituted news, confrontation with the authorities added drama, and the fallout from the incitement riveted the attention of the populace. Green admits, "I am aware that a lot of press activity has the secondary effect of promoting my career. It would not be unfair to say that was also part of the strategy." But Green's desire for renown cannot be dismissed as a quest for personal fame. Being well known is a protective measure against the peril that Green describes as "being in a legal barrel, rolling downhill, not knowing how to get out, heading into a kangaroo court." It protects him from retaliatory actions of corrupt judicial systems. Officials at the Center for Constitutional Rights and the American Civil Liberties Union have tutored him in such defensive conduct.

Cultivating media attention also serves Green's long-range artistic program by helping to circulate his work beyond the art world. "The fine-art world is a playground for the super-rich who would have no motive to use these weapons." Because most museum goers are allied with institutions of authority, they are more likely to be targets of dissident action than perpetrators. Green comments, "To a certain extent, dialogue within the art environment is only academic. That's one of the reasons that access to the popular media is critical. It is the only place that the work might actually achieve its hoped-for function." Green also sought media attention because he anticipated that a period of media neglect was forthcoming. The form of subversive action he was planning to engage would not offer the spectacle, danger, and violence that attracted the media to his bombs and missiles. Early fame would assure that his later work would be noticed, discussed, and disseminated.

Green chronicles the history of political resistance by reviving diverse strategies of empowerment used by successive generations of dissidents. This artistic practice commenced when he dressed men in crudely made wooden armor and had them engage in fierce hand-to-hand combat. From 1990 to 1995, he was occupied with bombs, the favored tactic of terrorist empowerment since the Cold War. Then, in 1995, he assembled all the ingredients (minus one) for 100,000 doses of LSD (car starter fluid, rubbing alcohol, and seven kilos of ground morning-glory seeds) to replay the tactics of civil disobedience favored by dissidents during the 1968 presidential campaign. Since 1995, Green has updated his anti-establishment activities by adopting the insidious tactics offered by advanced technology. He believes that computer programmers and other disseminators of information have as much ability to commandeer power as hijackers, Unabombers, and terrorists. Thus, instead of propagating the means to destroy human life and physical property, Green next undertook to inculcate the tactics for mass-marketing paranoia and transmitting subversive ideologies. In an ongoing project, Green has become a pirate broadcaster. He works from his studio and from his 1967 VW Westfalia Campmobile. The unit contains a complete sound and video recording and mixing studio, a 100 VHF television transmission system, and a thirty-five-watt FM radio transmitter, and it is accessible on the World Wide Web. These pieces of equipment are the newest weapons in the fight to empower the people. Green notes, "Accessibility of information and information are the keys to power in any society."

Although Green eliminated a vital bit of information from his weapons instructions, the campmobile artwork, entitled *M.I.T.A.R.B.U (Mobile Internet, Television and Radio Broadcast Unit)* (2000), supplies the complete means necessary to conduct clandestine actions. "The material is anything that any individual or group wants to put on and broadcast. The broadcasts are open forums—there is no curatorial agenda. I have never and I will never support the control of information available to adults in any form. I'm going for empowering people. I could empower a maniac. It comes down to a question of responsibility. This is a problematic question. When you begin limiting what is broadcast, who decides who is included and who is excluded? I would rather listen to a Nazi voice than to discover that the Green Party suddenly is denied a voice. Once that begins, you have opened a door that can lead to your own enslavement." Green has welcomed DJs, writers, politicians, artists, and musicians to transmit their personal agendas. But terrorists, messianic visionaries, fundamentalists, and zealots are also welcome. Green's refusal to censor explains this pacifist's willingness to broadcast those who advocate violence as an optional strategy of empowerment. *M.I.T.A.R.B.U.* establishes the standard for absolute freedom of speech.

When the broadcasting equipment is installed within a gallery, visitors are encouraged to sit at the microphone and speak out across the airwaves. The range of these transmissions intentionally exceeds the legal limits. Green takes illegal command of broadcasts and then purveys information about how to avoid detection from the authorities. He advises that broadcasts at high power only be made after five p.m. and before nine a.m., when there is less of a chance that the Federal Communications Commission will detect them. He encourages people to establish their own pirate stations by providing detailed instructions on how to construct transmission sites, where to get cheap materials, and how to infiltrate regulated communication systems. He instructs users to move their transmitters regularly, to withhold the names of those involved, and to avoid interfering with other broadcasters. Green notes that because the FCC is a bureaucracy, "you can rely on their inefficiency." Pirate broadcasting permits people to reclaim authority from official institutions. Each transmission is intended to irritate those who possess power, and inspire those who don't.

Through self-initiated transmissions with *M.I.T.A.R.B.U.*, Green assumed direct command of a mass communication channel. But his range was limited. Thus, in 1996, he began construction on a device capable of worldwide unauthorized transmissions. *Gregnik, an Alternative Space Program*, whose title acknowledges the artist's own contribution to the legacy that began with the renowned launch of the Sputnik space rocket by the Russians in 1957, is a satellite designed to broadcast on an FM frequency in a low level, short-term orbit around the earth. Green is also designing its booster rocket. Once the satellite is completed, he will exhibit homemade production instructions that will broadcast from the gallery via the satellite. As in his other works, Green de-emphasizes content over means. In order to place the emphasis on the political power of long-range transmissions, his own broadcast will consist of a typical laugh track. The relentless laughter of an omnipresent, unidentified infiltrator is designed to unsettle authorities around the globe.

physically producing something. Throughout most of my career I lived in my studio, and I would work when the desire or need hit me. It was sort of 100 percent of the time. I would start working when I got up, four hours later, or six hours later, or midnight, or whenever it happened. When I first moved out of my studio, I literally didn't know how to function. I did not know how to go to the studio like a job. When the studio is a separate space, sometimes it feels like work. Whereas before, I was just living my life. But in general, I tend to be a night person, and my mornings are usually spent waking slowly and dealing with certain office activities and thinking. The afternoon is generally filled with finding materials or working on a piece, if I am in the middle of a project. The evening, hopefully, is a personal period, but is often filled with a strong focus on production or fun. When on site for an exhibition, the days seems to be filled with twelve or more hours of hard work, and the nights I tend to be overpartied at the insistence of my host, an art institution or gallery.

RY: Do you feel like you have a choice about being an artist?

GG: Oh, I definitely can do other things. But in a way I feel like I don't have a choice. It actually embarrasses me to say it, because it feels like a mission. And I'm realizing that it's working out and I'm doing fine. I could leave it, but I would always wonder what would have happened. The art world won't keep me from leaving. I know that if I quit any time—right now—within a year I could be making huge amounts of money. The question is, would I be happy? My parents still have doubts about the art world. They always treated it more like a hobby until they saw a program about me on *Hard Copy*. Other relatives saw it too and called them. Then everything became real and serious. But you know, prior to that point, almost every time I talked to my dad on the phone, one of the things he'd say to me is, "So boy, you still doing that weird shit?" And I'd say, "Yeah dad, still doing the weird shit."

Gregory Green, *Book Bomb #7* (LA) (1994), 4.5 x 21 x 12 inches, mixed media. Private collection. Courtesy Feigen Contemporary, New York. (A mechanically complete book bomb minus any explosive materials.)

None of these actions, however, truly fulfilled Green's ultimate desire to realize a "romantic anarchist system." In pursuit of this goal, he undertook to create a legitimate nation. His first try failed, but he has redirected his efforts toward twin islands in the Indian Ocean. The process of claiming territories, he says, is no more difficult than constructing a satellite or a missile. Anyone can do it. All it requires is some research on international law and a letter-writing campaign to the United Nations, the World Court, and various international governments. Green has attended to all these requirements for nation building. He has designed a flag, a currency, and stamps, and he has assembled the names of over two thousand people who wish to become citizens. Citizenship, Green insists, is unrestricted. "If you ask, you are. Your only obligations are to participate in the decision-making process." Green declared that the nation's governance would be based on an anarchist system used in the 1970s by radical groups on the West Coast of the U.S. "Essentially, there is no hierarchy. All decisions require unanimous consent." Though Green acknowledges that none of these '70s groups has survived, he explains his choice to model his nation after them: "Me starting my own country has maniacal implications. Choosing that structure is meant to undermine the implication that I am the leader, I am in control. It implies an inherent potential for failure. We are not emotionally or morally mature enough for this system to function. I believe in it as an idealized future. But I think it would be incredibly successful if the country were recognized, even if it failed. This artwork is a shamanistic gesture. Nations usually rise through violence and war, but this nation will be the first to be created peaceably, in the name of art."

1. Unless otherwise noted, all quotes from an interview with the artist, August 20, 2000.

2. From an interview with the artist, February 10, 2000.

China Adams
Born 1970 San Francisco, California
1994 University of California, Los Angeles, BFA, fine arts
2001 University of Nevada, Las Vegas, MFA, fine arts
Lives and works in Los Angeles, California

China Adams's artworks are idiosyncratic in terms of their forms and mediums, but their themes are hallowed and enduring. Her mission is to update the age-old human concerns that still prevail, and have yet to be adequately resolved. An unrealized project proposal provides an example of her original manner of addressing perennial human concerns. In this instance she considered disposing of the physical remains of the body, both as a living and as a dead organism. She explains her proposal as "airlifting via helium balloons packets of soil, flower seeds, and my excrement out of a gallery. The goal being to assist in the beautification of the landscape while simultaneously dispersing my "essence" all about, sort of like dropping the ashes of the dead." She rejected the project because the balloons and packaging would foul the environment.

China Adams investigates the essence of humanity and its timeless concerns. Uncovering the core of humanity requires that she disregard certain facts about herself: her mixed race; that she is beautiful, a loving sister and a product of California culture; that she holds an MFA degree. Describing her personal approach to creating transpersonal art, Adams explains, "Working with myself is okay if I am able to pull from myself universal truths or ironies."[1] If she had chosen instead to engage biological considerations in her work, her task would have been easy—97 percent of humanity's genetic material is identical. But Adams extracts less quantifiable components; those that are deeply rooted in the human soul. The themes that really inspire her are found throughout mythology and the Scriptures—themes that arise in the contemplations of prophets and the sermons of preachers. They are found in the rhetoric of revolutionaries and the verses of poets.

Despite this elevated mission, Adams says, "I want my work to be accessible. When I was younger, I felt somewhat intimidated by art that is founded on theory. There is a place for that. But I am more blue-collar. I would be pleased to make connections with people off the street. I believe I have a real responsibility to the viewer. The world is inundated with images. If you take someone's time, you owe them something they can relate to." It would be wrong to assume that Adams's populist objective and unoriginal themes indicate that she produces prosaic work. Though her themes originate in the nagging, sinister issues that seem hard-wired in the human mind and can be traced back across millennia, in every other way she belongs to the ultra progressive art world. More oddball than old-hat, her eccentricities remain readily comprehensible by the masses. "My work has a huge court-jester element. It is accessible, humorous, and fundamental. It is about existential issues that all people can grasp."

This essay enumerates Adams's approach to six universal human dilemmas. Each involves a metaphysical concern that comprises the uniqueness of human experience on Earth and poses a perennial dilemma that emerged with the evolution of consciousness.

How to deal with the dead?
It is impossible to escape the responsibility of dealing with the bodies of the deceased. Most cultures honor the dead with rituals ranging from burial or burning to mummification. cryogenics and mining the body for usable parts to prolong someone else's life are

recent additions to this catalogue of sacraments. In *Contract of Sale* (1994), China Adams introduces an unprecedented option for confronting mortality: using the parts of her own body that will endure after her death as her artworks. Specifically, she conveys the use of her bones by presenting fourteen X rays of different portions of her skeleton. The images are exhibited in medical-issue light boxes. Each portrayal identifies the bone available for sale to art collectors who are patient enough to wait for Adams's death. Delivery is not due until then. A bone purchase agreement is mounted beside each X ray to identify the terms of sale. "Let it be known that on the date hereof _____, China Adams (the 'Seller') hereby sells, for $_____, the receipt of which is hereby acknowledged, all the rights (including, without limitation, the rights to have, hold, display, exhibit, and exploit) to her _____ (the 'Bone') to _____ (the 'Purchaser')."

The temerity of this artwork is calculated with legal precision. The terms of purchase require that collectors pay the medical fee for accessing their bone from the artist's cadaver. Another clause protects the artist from collectors who may be eager to gain possession of their artwork. It states, "The Purchaser agrees that any attempt by the Purchaser to expedite, cause, influence, or in any way accelerate the date of the death of the Seller shall render this contract void and unenforceable."

Adams's approach to this all-pervasive dilemma not only resolves the vexing problem of grappling with one's own mortality, it introduces decorum and self-esteem where morbidity and dread might otherwise prevail. Her bone offering bestows a measurable value on her corpse. Indeed, it now carries the stature of art. Adams asks, "What becomes of me? Beyond any spiritual sense, what becomes of my physical form? I have tried to create a fancy coupon, using the art to help me resolve these ideas and take advantage of the traditional notion that art is precious. I sell bones. If someone buys a piece, they are buying a coupon. They can take advantage of it or not when I die. In buying a coupon, I am placing my bones in a transcended context." Adams is laying the foundation for everlasting esteem, assuring that parts of her will be treasured like relics.

Will my reputation endure after my death?
Contract of Sale offers a solution to another haunting inquiry, that of how long and how vividly the memory of one's life and one's accomplishments will survive after death. Even the construction of pyramids and mausoleums, the writing of epics, or the discovery of galaxies cannot assure one's fate. Like many, Adams ponders her longevity. Unlike many, she created an artwork that enables her to discover the answer during her lifetime by enlisting the forces of the marketplace to reveal her destiny. Purchasers of Adams's receipt-upon-death art make long-term investments in a speculative futures market. They must anticipate Adams's eventual worthy as an artist.

Interview with China Adams
By Ry Russo-Young

RY: So you were twenty-two when you got your first show?

CA: I very much had luck on my side in terms of being in the right place at the right time and everything lining up in my favor. There's some old saying, you have to be prepared so that when luck strikes you can take advantage of it. My first show came from a weird angle. I started out in school as a biology major. I was not very good at it. I dropped out of school and I kind of flaked around and then came back to school and got into art. I was so thrilled that I had found something that I liked at all that for a long time I was just pleased with that. It wasn't like when I was fourteen years old I was thinking, "Oh, I'm gonna be an artist."

RY: Where did you go to school?

CA: I went to UCLA. That's actually funny too, because I was going there doing biology and I didn't even know that they had a good art department. I just thought, "Eh, what the fuck. I'll try to transfer into the art department." And that is how I landed in what was the hot art school. I was pretty much painting, but there was this required class, New Genres. I had put it off, but in my third year I had to take it. So I asked myself, "What the fuck am I going to do in this class?" And so I did this piece where I posted ads saying that I was going to become a cannibal and that I was looking for a donor of flesh. Initially it was tongue-in-cheek, although I was really interested in cannibalism and I was reading about it. I became really fascinated with the fact that in so many cultures it was linked to love. I think I was taking some anthropology class at the time. So a guy from this gallery heard about my project and actually called me. My career just took off from there. The gallery gave me an opportunity to do all these things that I'd wanted to do but hadn't had a venue. I mean, the one thing that is really nice about having a place to show your work is that you have these ideas and things you want to do, but they're big, and you know you're not going to do them in your bedroom.

RY: So you put up an ad for flesh and then did people respond?

CA: I hung posters all over the campus. Yeah, people did respond. I ended up actually using someone I was fairly close to because, like I said, it was about this love and affection thing.

RY: Did you eat them?

CA: Yeah, I had a small piece of their flesh surgically removed.

RY: Where? What part?

CA: Kind of the hip area.

RY: The love handles?

CA: Yeah, exactly, and that's precisely why they wanted to take it out of that area. There's a nice core of fatty tissue that you can go into right there without doing any severe damage to anything.

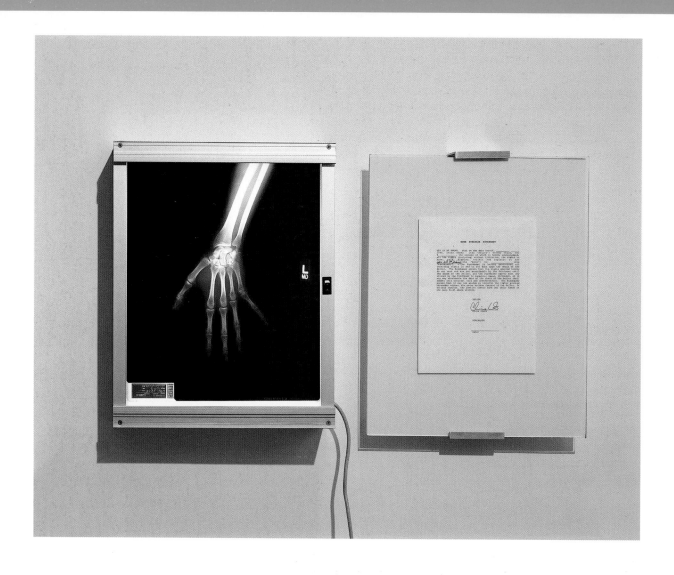

China Adams, *Contract of Sale (Left Ring Finger)* (1994), X-ray, lightbox, ink on paper. Courtesy ACE Gallery. Photograph: ACE Contemporary Exhibitions, Los Angeles.

"Bone selling provides an indication during my lifetime of my value as an artist in the ultimate distant time. How much are people willing to invest in me? The value of the work is tied to my anticipated stature as an artist." Sales indicate the expectation of her eventual worth and at the same time, consumers must calculate the odds of collecting since they must outlive the artist (who was healthy and young at the time of the work's creation) in order to take possession of the artwork.

Will my possessions be discarded after I die?
Adams asked herself, "Which of my belongings have worth? What will happen to them when I die?" Possessions, like the people who own them, have histories and destinies. Some are treasured. Most are disregarded. Few are preserved. Things do not merely sustain our lives. They are tangible manifestations of us—our taste, class, age, gender, and personality. Will others value them when we die? Will our belongings be kept as an expression of love? Will they be discarded along with the memory of us? Will they be cast off, a purging of resentment or aversion? Adams admits, "I have a huge internal dialogue about things. I need things. This got me thinking about my relationship to my possessions." Adams says that her anxiety about the fate of her possessions was triggered by the story of an eighty-eight-year-old man and an eighty-eight-year-old woman who lived at opposite ends of a hallway in an apartment building. When the man died, his survivors discovered an apartment stuffed floor-to-ceiling with a lifetime's accumulations. Only a narrow passage remained between the bathroom, the kitchen, and his bed. The old woman's apartment, on the other hand, was empty except for a few cans of food, a bed, and one book. When asked why she had so few things, she answered, "I don't want people rifling through my possessions. They were too precious. So I disposed of them."

Adams realized, too, that some of her favorite things had little value to anyone else. The desire to protect them merged with the desire to be rid of those that were extraneous. She asked herself, "How can I secure them so they are safe but not a burden to me?" She decided to "Give them the stature of art," and, in this way, *Official Stitch and Hide Procedure* was conceived. On February 20, 1995, Adams conducted an extensive inventory of her possessions. She concluded that 77.13 percent had achieved "official burden status." Objects were tagged burdensome if they were sentimental; if they hadn't been touched in thirty days; if they posed a maintenance problem; if they were expensive to maintain. The next day, she began the laborious task of fabricating hundreds of shrouds, one for each of these objects. They were made of water-repellent cloth to assure their protection, and meticulously sewn by hand using strong, unwaxed dental floss for endurance. Ten months later, when the process of carefully cutting, stitching, inserting, and sealing was completed, Adams arranged the collection into thirty-nine stacks,

RY: Did you cook it?
CA: Yes.

RY: Did you spice it?
CA: Yeah. Just, like, garlic and onions. Real standard.

RY: Was it tasty?
CA: First of all, I overcooked it and it was mostly fat, and fat's fat. Basically it just absorbs the spices.

RY: Do you feel like it brought you closer to the person?
CA: Absolutely, yeah.

RY: What is the most significant sale you've had?
CA: My work has not sold particularly well. Ultimately, I really do think it's a decorator's market. The piece I did where I sewed up a whole bunch of things that I owned, that piece fit in most people's homes better than a big portrait and an old glass of blood or bloodstains.

RY: How does your work get marketed?
CA: I've been with one dealer the whole time, and that's pretty much how. I don't do a lot of promoting. I'm really slack. At some point I should probably become more of an aggressive promoter. It's a hard call, though, between making the work and staying afloat financially. For me, I've always felt like, well shit, if it comes down to it, I'd rather spend my time making work as long as I have a place to show it. That's what I like to do, and truthfully, I hate all the other stuff.

RY: How do you feel about the whole commercial aspect of art?
CA: As attractive as it is, there certainly are drawbacks to getting knocked way up into the position of art celebrity. Being an art star looks like it takes an awful lot of time and it may sort of limit one's freedom to just kind of rock and roll. I imagine it very quickly becomes big business. I feel like I'm in a relatively nice position right now. I really like making stuff. So in a strange way, I am really quite pleased with the situation as it is because I have a place to show the work. I certainly have a group of people who like to follow the work, which is obviously very flattering. But at the same time, it's not something that's gotten out of control where I no longer have time to do the work. It just really depends on what you want out of being an artist. I think a lot of people are looking for a kind of celebrity. I don't think there's anything wrong with that. It's a negotiation. You give up one thing for another. I suppose if you're really lucky, maybe it works out so you're a big star with plenty of time to work and a big ol' wad of cash in your pocket.

RY: Do you have a day job?
CA: Yeah. Right now I've been teaching a sculpture class, and prior to that, I worked for an antiques dealer, and there's been times when I've had two jobs. I got really in debt and I was waiting tables and working.

RY: What is your relationship to your collectors?
CA: I tend to think more of my audience than my collectors. It means a lot to me to make work that's accessible to a wide audience. I do believe that you owe your audience something because I think it's

China Adams, *Blood Consumption – Sara Love* (1999), Photograph :drinking glass stained with blood and framed notary. Courtesy ACE Gallery.
Photograph: ACE Contemporary Exhibitions, Los Angeles.

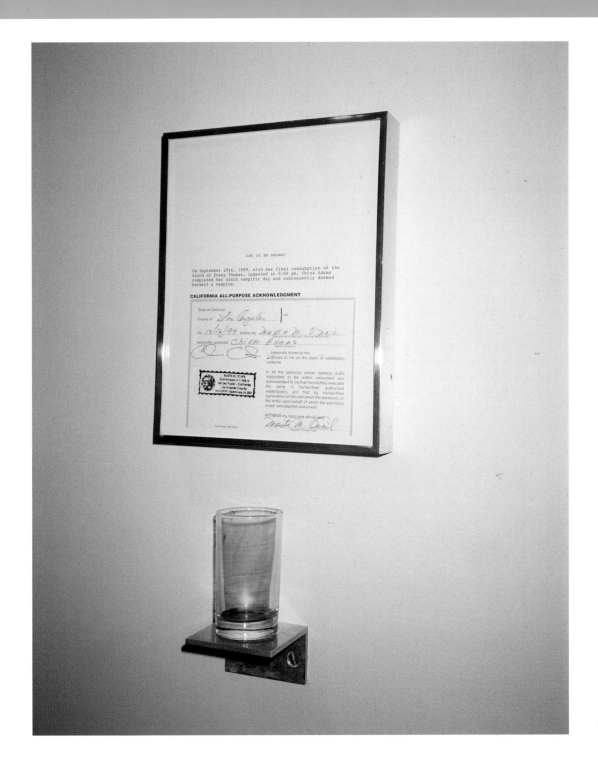

China Adams, *Blood Consumption – Sara Love* (1999) detail. Courtesy ACE Gallery. Photograph: ACE Contemporary Exhibitions, Los Angeles.

displayed them as sculptures in protective vitrines, and offered them for sale. A family heirloom watch was enclosed in one vitrine. A broken toaster in another. Purchasers did not know if they were acquiring something of intrinsic value, of sentimental value to the artist, or of dubious value to everyone. Therefore they all carried the same price tag. As a result, collectors had no choice but to make their selection based on the abstract sculptural appeal of the cloth enclosures. They were also offered the tantalizing allure of concealed contents. Adams explains her strategy in earnest. "I hope people will refrain from throwing my pieces into a landfill. They became exalted when they became art. The art world did me a favor. ... Now it is off my shoulders. It is in someone's collection where it is treated like something precious."

Will future generations benefit from my creations?
Official Stitch and Hide Procedure and *Contract of Sale* deal with the facts of our physical remains after death. But physical residue is also created during one's lifetime. Humans make things. We make crafts and art and beauty and noise and garbage and order and chaos. In deciding what to make we confront a range of thorny alternatives. We must decide between innovation and conformity, carelessness and responsibility, consequence and banality. Adams capitalized on the liberties permitted within her profession to project these ponderous metaphysical choices. She comments, "Anything goes, and unfortunately it seems like certain recent art left people feeling like, 'Hey, artists can shit on the ground and call it art.' We artists have all this freedom. We are standing at the proverbial existential cliff looking out upon an enormous number of possibilities. One can keep restating the old notion, 'Anything can be art,' or take the plunge and marry this notion with something more progressive." Adams took the plunge, marrying it to the progressive notion that the process of artistic manufacture could occur physiologically, and that the product of this process was capable of functioning in the manner of art by fostering an enduring creation of beauty. Adams beautified America by depositing her feces in the ground and had the act registered in an officially notarized statement that testified that China Adams's action during her lifetime would have an enduring impact, and this impact would engender a more perfect world. "Let it be known: On January____, 1994, at _____am/pm central time, China Adams dug a hole on the boundary line of Choctaw Indian tribal land, in Vancleave Fontainbleau, Mississippi. Into the hole she shit and planted Forget Me Not seeds." Adams likened her act to "people burying the ashes of their loved ones under a tree and then they live on through the tree." "For me," she says, "it means trying to merge document-based declarations with aesthetic objects. The notarized document functions as evidence of the art action."

Is Armageddon imminent?
As the millennium approached, collective fear that the world was careening toward disaster seemed to escalate. Prognostications about the future were bleak. In March 1999, Adams began to have premonitions while she slept. She reports that she experienced "such a persistent bombardment" of premonitions that she felt obliged to record them. She wrote about them, she drew them, she created diagrams outlining them. These written and drawn recordings of 1,242 visions constituted her next art project. The effort commenced in April 1999. It concluded on December 29, 1999. "Some of the visions had voices," Adams explains. "Some had texts. I could read them in my head. I jotted them down in the morning. They always came when I was sleeping. A lot are distant in the future. They identified problems and disasters, but they were not of the nature where people could put an end to them. I saw a tornado. This is something you can't control. The furthest projection in time was 2,776 years. Many were so far in the future, there is no one I can contact who

could deal with them." Adams envisioned plagues, computer malfunctions, and "weird fetishy things" like plastic surgery to produce numerous vaginas. She believes, "The source wasn't me. I hooked into the collective unconscious."

Because Adams believed the premonitions belong to humanity, she returned them to humanity by rolling her notation of each vision into a scroll sealed with dental-floss stitching. Adams grouped these scrolls by the month in which the visions they record were experienced, providing the only externally revealed information about the premonitions. Otherwise the scrolls' contents were concealed and Adams contrived to keep them that way. She quelled the temptation of her audience to rip them open and read her wondrous premonitions by creating objects that were so meticulously crafted, they became too precious as aesthetic objects to destroy. Like talismans or fetish items, they exuded the mystery of omens from an otherworldly source. Adams notes, "This piece raises some real questions about the nature of any creation. I wanted to signify the sense of hope by the nature of the making of them. The act of making things requires faith in being a human being to construct anything, to do it with the hope of showing it to an audience who will have a reaction to it requires faith in the importance of that act." The anti-Armageddon character of her campaign is bolstered by the delicacy and beauty of the scrolls; as Adams notes, "They don't seem ominous." It is reinforced by the quantity of premonitions presented in this collection, an assurance that there will not only be a future, but this future will be long and multifaceted. "Writing (my premonitions) down was a hopeful omen. If there were this many scrolls it was some indication that I saw a lot going on. It was not an apocalyptic vision." At the same time, she suggests, "Keeping my visions concealed allows viewers to impose their visions on them. It helps them identify what they hope for and what they fear. The work remains universal instead of being a psychological self-portrait."

How to express true love?
The search for the ultimate expression of love has inspired the creation of sonnets, romance novels, ballads, films, paintings, and sculptures. Adams contributed a contemporary sensibility to this age-old search. She realized that such standard terms of endearment as "sweetheart," "dear one," and "beloved" have vanished from contemporary vocabularies and that romance has disappeared from contemporary vanguard art. Artists often demonstrate their sophistication by dwelling on irony, sarcasm, and scorn. Love themes are disparaged as trite. Adams decided to create a work that exalts love in a manner in tune with the times. "I made romantic love tough and raunchy, as basic as the question of death. I wanted to bring up issues of consumption, sexuality, and adoration."

Blood Consumption (1999) exposes Adams's plan to drink the blood of her closest friends and relatives. Finding participants for the

incredibly decadent to assume that you can take someone's time and leave them feeling like, "What is this?" There's a zillion other things that they could be looking at.

RY: Can you describe your studio?

CA: I've worked out of my house … just like a desk or whatever. I've never had a separate space.

RY: How are the costs of producing your work allocated?

CA: I've definitely done the whole credit-card affair. Not that I recommend it. At one point I had $15,000 at 18 percent interest and some shitty job. I have gotten a few grants, but do you want to spend your time writing grant proposals or do you want to spend your time making work?

RY: What percent of your income is earned by the sale of your art?

CA: Truthfully? Zero, because any money I have made has been swallowed over at least twice by expenses to make the work. So at this point it's not even income. It's like damage control. In my twenties, I really had no other financial aspirations except to get my work done and pay my bills. And now it is a little bit unnerving, because the big thing is I'm interested in adopting a kid. So, yeah, it's starting to become more of a weird sort of thing.

RY: Do you feel like school helped to prepare you to become an artist?

CA: Art school is important to the extent that you make it important. It's this nice block of time where you can really investigate yourself. I think the danger of school is you can get really swayed by what's going on at the time…

RY: What advice would you give the current generation of aspiring artists?

CA: Well, let's see. Probably one of the best pieces of advice is learning to edit your own work—to be critical of your own work without it becoming a hindrance in your production. I also think that you have to really figure out a mechanism to deal with criticism, because you're going into a field where that's a huge part of it just by virtue of the fact that you put what you do into a public context. It's awfully sad to see it cripple people, and it does, you know. As much as there are problems with this lifestyle though—think about sitting in a fucking office for nine hours a day.

RY: Were there certain times in your life when you were particularly productive and inventive?

CA: I'm a pretty bad workaholic. For me, I feel like a big goal is to slow down and think more about what I'm doing. This sounds silly, but I get a lot of work done when I'm not very happy. When things aren't going well in other areas of my life I tend to really delve into my work, sometimes just working for the sake of working and not being terribly thoughtful about what I'm actually doing.

project was not a great challenge. Her problem was in finding someone willing to extract the blood. Adams reports matter-of-factly, "I found a doctor and he did it in one sitting in my house. One person came every ten minutes because the doctor was not comfortable with everyone gathering at once. Then the blood was purified. I drank it a week later. The donors were not present. I drank nine people's blood. The number was arbitrary. They tasted differently."

Even though vampires have long been associated with the macabre combination of graveyards, malignant spirits, and blood-sucking corpses, it was love that motivated this performance, and not a desire to shock. Adams borrowed this concept of blood consumption from Hans Askenasy, a forensic anthropologist who has developed a theory that applies love or unification cannibalism to vampirism. "One eats a person out of some kind of affection or a desire to unite with him or her."[2] Adams insists, "In my consumption of blood, my aim was not to appall and horrify, but rather to consummate the perfect fulfillment of unsexualized love. My vampiric act ... might be viewed as a relative of the literary sonnet, whose goal, by declaring the depth of the author's personal love, is ultimately to glorify the very nature of love."

In order to divert viewers from conventional revulsions against vampirism, Adams designed the gallery presentation of her action to be controlled and antiseptic. She neatly arranged nine small glasses on shelves, each glass retaining a thin residue of the blood it once contained. A large color photograph of the donor was hung beside it. To prepare her subjects for the photographer, Adams meticulously applied makeup to enhance their beauty (employing skills she'd learned in a cosmetology course). In this manner she transferred a traditional artistic notion (to create an idealized portrait) and a traditional art process (to paint) from the canvas to the sitter's face. She further defused viewers' emotional and distasteful associations with blood by pairing each glass and each five-by-six-foot portrait with a notarized document. The texts were legalistic, not dramatic. One such document stated, "Let it be known: On September 21st, 1999, China Adams began proceedings to obtain official vampire status. Upon rising at 7:36 am, until retiring at 11:25 pm, she subsisted only on the blood of Joseph Daniel. It is without hesitation that she confirms experiencing a heightened level of élan coupled with a dynamic sense of vivacity." Stamped, Marta M. O'Neil, Notary Public.

Adams hopes that her attempt at creating romantic art will inspire viewers to ask themselves whose blood they would willingly drink. The answer, especially in an era in which AIDS has heightened awareness of blood contamination, may indeed be an indicator of ultimate intimacy and trust. It exceeds the power of the sonnet. It may even exceed sex as an expression of love.

In sum, Adams offers a realistic assessment of humanity's perennial fears. The function of art, she believes, is a kind of "social therapy" that functions through acknowledging things that are uncomfortable. Adams gives full exposure to humanity's deepest fears, insecurities, and guilt, but they are combined with generous additions of humor and optimism. "In my work, there is verification and celebration. Yes, you are going to die. Yes, all your things are going to end up at thrift shops. Yes, in fact, no one gives a shit about your body or about your sins. But they are there, like written and notarized statements, basic and simple."

[1.] Unless otherwise noted, all quotes from an interview with the artist, April 15, 1999.

[2.] Hans Askenasy, *Cannibalism: From Sacrifice to Survival* (New York: Prometheus Books, 1994), 126.

Alix Lambert
Born 1968 Washington, D.C.
1990 School of Visual Arts, New York, BFA
1985 Royal College of Art, London, summer program
1984 Parsons School of Design, summer program
Lives and works in Los Angeles, California and New York City

Alix Lambert is committed to real-life experiences. She once assigned art students to go to a hospital and observe a patient undergoing surgery. She didn't specify if the students should watch bloodless laser surgery, or selective cosmetic surgery, or life-saving emergency surgery. These aspects were not as important to her as the actual encounter with a situation that is known to most people only when it is feigned, filmed, or reported. Lambert's artistic mission shares these qualities. She has dedicated her art practice to experiencing life-transforming situations that she regretted were missing from her life. In pursuit of this mission, her daily life and her art life collide. She has become a boxer, a basketball coach, a tattoo artist, a divorcée, a bride, and a rock star.

Alix Lambert's artworks explore the array of sentiments that are ignited by one person and fueled by another. These include love, commitment, trust, compassion, jealousy, dominance, and submission. But her art is not extrapolated from her life since, for her, interpersonal relationships are more likely to be observed than experienced. Her familiarity with the varieties of human interaction derives instead from film and television. As a result, Lambert doesn't draw on her biography to create art. She draws on art to create a biography. She conducts her creative endeavors in the following manner. First, she identifies a fictional situation that is missing from her life. Then, she undertakes a real-life action that includes it. In this way, she gathers authentic data to replace the impressions left by watching artificial events projected on television and movie screens. Finally, these actualized experiences are documented and exhibited through photography, film, or video.

Lambert designs activities and undertakes relationships to fill the voids in her life, to compensate for disappointment, to enliven daily routines, or to develop traits observed in others. Her experiences are deliberately composed and their themes invented. Each time she takes an impression of human experience that was stockpiled in her mind and transmutes it into real-time events with real-life consequences, her life acquires the qualities of art.

Lambert's process of identifying the things that are missing from her life story is not only time consuming, it is life-time consuming. Instead of cultivating fantasy and idealization within her artistic practice, she deactivates these mental functions to maintain the veracity of the experiences she is investigating. Nothing is feigned, not even the inevitable emotional entanglements of these social activities, nor their physical demands, nor their financial costs. Lambert actually makes commitments, forms expectations, and accepts obligations. Thus, her artistic endeavors require a unique set of faculties. Lambert must enter situations with no anticipated outcomes. She must master the skills of the professions that offer arenas of heightened human exchange. She must abandon the projected outcomes provided by scripts and dramatizations so that her mind is primed for discovery.

The videos, films, and photographs documenting these art/life endeavors are more accurately described as byproducts than end products. Lambert is not like the many artists who assume a persona, dress up, create a signifying backdrop, and pose in front of a camera lens. Lambert's images document a spontaneous event in the real time and space

Alix Lambert, *Platipussy #3* (1998), 26 x 39 inches, Fujiflex. Courtesy of the artist and Sara Meltzer Gallery.

Alix Lambert, *Wedding Series* (1993). All works 6 x 4 feet, black-and-white photograph. Courtesy of the artist and Sara Meltzer Gallery.

of her life. They play two roles, one personal and one artistic. As recording devices, these images preserve her personal memories. As communicating devices, they dispense information to those who were not participants in the events they document. Viewers of her work encounter evidence of the intense person-to-person contact she experienced. The situations that Lambert has isolated for investigation include boxing, marriage, tattooing, and performing, as described below.

Boxing: Lambert grew up among polite parents, in a sheltered neighborhood among upper-middle-class friends. As an art project, she activated two emotional states that this social environment stifled: defensive instincts and aggressive tendencies. Lambert entered a setting that specializes in these behaviors. She joined a gym that trains professional boxers. In the ring, hostile and self-protective behaviors are not only cultivated, they are easily measured. A clear index of a boxer's mastery is produced every three minutes. Lambert faced her opponent and either won or lost the round. She explains the complementary proficiencies she was exploring: "The work is about overcoming fear. It is scary to stand in a ring with someone who wants to hit you in the head."[1] The aggressive nature of this interaction is alien to middle-class manners and absent from her retiring personality. She is shy, admitting, "I don't even like to speak on the telephone." The other lesson that boxing provided involved learning to intimidate and attack someone else. "The work teaches me to become comfortable with hitting, with defending myself. After someone hits you, your instinct is to hit back."

Lambert's exposure to boxing was real—blows from her opponent hurt, she sweat, her muscles ached, she felt fear. Each day, improvements in her strength, stamina, and skill were calculated against the bruises, exhaustion, and aches. These effects were true, even if the hostility that provoked them was conducted according to the rules of a game. Her training took years. As time progressed, Lambert became such a skilled boxer that she was encouraged by her trainers to consider going professional. She chose, instead, to retain boxing as an artistic exploration of human behavior. The artwork that commemorates this long-term, real-life involvement with boxing, *Round Twelve* (1994–1995), consists of a three-walled video projection produced when Lambert attached tiny cameras to boxing gloves, where they literally took a pounding as the cameras ran throughout a three-minute round. From this glove's-eye point-of-view, the viewer witnesses the dizzying shifts and swings produced by the boxers' rapid offensive and defensive acts. The video evokes the impact of the blows, despite the fact that it proceeds in silence. Instead of relying on the dramatic effects of grunting and panting, Lambert utilizes a purely optical device—the deterioration of the images that occurred as the relentless slamming and punching of the boxers damaged the cameras. Viewers observe the effects of the fighters' aggression, brute force, and determination. Lambert magnified the brief, three-minute unit of violence by slowing the projection. Then she made the experience of getting slammed seem relentless by showing the sequences as a perpetually repeating loop. "Boxing is an aggressive sport—all sports are. They are about 'beating' the opponent. The competitive match is as much a part of the universal human condition as love. It is just another kind of human relationship."

Marriage: Duration is an indicator of commitment, whether it is applied to sports, friendship, hobbies, politics, religion, or careers. For this reason, the temporal dimension is an essential ingredient in all of Lambert's relationship pieces. In 1993, for instance, Lambert investigated trust and loyalty by reversing the typical "till death do us part" component of marriage. The pledge she elicited from her husbands involved the promise to divorce her as quickly as was legally possible after they were married. Las Vegas provided the inspiration for this project. Lambert noticed that wedding chapels were located right next to quickie-divorce centers. She decided to investigate whether the spatial proximity between entering and exiting from wedding vows could be transferred into a temporal proximity as well. Her project was to get married and divorced as many times as possible in six months. Within the time allotted, Lambert maneuvered her way through the contractual intricacies of marriage and divorce four separate times.

The emphasis was on parting, not pairing. Lambert reports the she and one of her fiancés listened to "D-I-V-O-R-C-E," a song by Tammy Wynette, all the way to the wedding ceremony. She explains, "I don't believe there is any permanence. My parents divorced when I was eleven years old. This event still manifests itself in my life. This fear has contributed to my art." As in *Round Twelve*, the *Wedding Series* (1993) is an artwork calculated to confront insecurities her real life had not prepared her to handle. In this case, they involved the risks and consequences involved in entering into a loving relationship with a partner: commitment and trust on the one hand, disappointment and separation on the other. Specifically, it enabled Lambert, who had never been married, to practice securing a marriage and enduring its demise. Lambert proposed to prospective mates. Some declined, but four accepted. She was candid about her reasons for wanting to marry them. None were deceived into believing that they were going to be married to Lambert for life. Their marriage to her meant dispensing with the "to love and honor" part of the wedding ceremony, but retaining the "to obey" part. They agreed to obey her request to divorce. Indeed, Lambert was the only one who risked betrayal, because her husbands retained the legal advantage. They could refuse to divorce her. Her art project commenced the moment she accepted the jeopardy of placing her life in their trust.

Choosing husbands was an informal process. She reports, "I did not sit down with a long list of candidates. I was indifferent, although there were some people I wouldn't want to marry. I wouldn't want to spend time with them. I'd rather divorce someone I was fond of." The first marriage was to a person she was only acquainted with from group situations. Lambert had never been alone with him. Still, she considered him an eligible husband. "I thought he might agree; he seemed up for adventure. What was his enticement? Perhaps it was respite from the boredom of his job. I can't speak for him." They were married in Manhattan District Court and immediately began the process of unlocking their wedlock. Most of their time as a betrothed couple was spent filling out divorce papers. The procedure occupied less than a week. Normally it takes one year of separation before a divorce can be filed, but if the divorce is uncontested, and if a reason can be given, the process can be accelerated. Lambert and her groom agreed that the cause for their divorce was "emotional abuse."

The knot was tied and untied to her second husband, Michael, in Las Vegas. The couple dressed formally for the occasion. They got into a car, drove up to a drive-through wedding chapel, and pressed the buzzer for service. The chaplain leaned out the window, handed them a clipboard with the forms that needed to be filled out, and then proceeded with the ceremony. Then they kissed over the emergency brake and drove away. Both Alix and her groom confess that they felt extremely anxious as they voiced their "I dos." Michael, who is a writer, said he married Lambert because he thought the experience would provide interesting material for a story. He didn't anticipate his emotional reactions. "I started to feel a faint choking sensation, shock waves of meaning. Marriage was too close—too close to another person for too long. It didn't feel like falling onto a big feather pillow; it felt like having one stuffed over my head; it was all compromise in the occupied space of the real world, and no matter how much I wanted to turn it into paperwork, it was a tangible, emotional reality." At the same time, he reports, "I had a weird pocket of pride in the back of my mind—I was married, after all, and at least something had happened to me in my life, even if I was a goldbricker, even if I was a fraud. The false love that we invoked, the lie of an affair, took on layers of meaning."[2] Lambert's experience of this marriage was heartfelt. "Michael and I were close friends. We spent time together before our marriage, although we never dated. We talked about our parents' marriages, whether we would ever get married, the repercussions of what we were doing. After the wedding we went on a trip together. We didn't tell people our marriage was an art piece. They behaved differently towards us. We were treated as a unit. Regardless of our understanding that this was an art piece, it was real, with real personal feelings. We discovered that marriage is both difficult and emotional. Michael is a great person. Some woman will be lucky to spend the rest of her life with him."

Lambert's challenge to marital norms included her choice of mates. Her first marriage was not consummated because her husband was a male homosexual. Her second marriage was not readily approved of because it was interracial (she is white, Michael is African American). Likewise, her third betrothal violated the taboo against same-sex marriages. Lambert married Hadley, a female friend from high school. Even after Hadley moved to Budapest, she and Lambert remained close friends. They agreed to conduct their wedding ceremony in Hungary, where two people of the same sex cannot be legally married, but are permitted to formalize their domestic partnership. Lawyers prepared the paperwork. The ceremony and the reception were held in a friend's apartment. There were candles, a wedding cake, and friends snapping pictures. Then the couple went to Poland for a honeymoon. Lambert and her bride experienced all the romantic trappings of a conventional marriage, despite the fact that neither she nor Hadley is a lesbian. Lambert reports, "This marriage was the most comfortable. I knew Hadley the best of all my husbands. There was real affection there."

The last in her succession of marriages and divorces was to a writer and curator who Lambert hardly knew at all. "I was originally going to marry a friend, but he couldn't get divorced in time to marry me, so he offered me Bob. I accepted my friend's recommendation because I trusted him. Bob often gets involved in artists' projects." The ceremony was conducted in City Hall in New York. After enjoying a little reception with mutual friends, they departed, not on a honeymoon, but to a lawyer's office to begin divorce proceedings. The couple did not spend much time together. Alix doesn't know why Bob agreed to become her husband: "You'd have to ask him about his motivation."

Lambert entered into four unconventional marriages: same-sex; mixed-race; she married a homosexual man; and she married a complete stranger. None involved amorous feelings. Lambert's motive for undertaking the *Wedding Series* was investigative, not romantic. She conducted her study by living her art. Data was generated in the course of creating the artwork. She explains, "Through doing the piece I learned about marriage—the legal side, the ceremony, how to dress like a bride, to say the vows, to get a marriage license, to get divorced, which, in each case, took more time than getting married. I learned that unconventional marriage overlaps with conventional marriage because both demand courage to make a commitment to someone. I also learned about other people's feelings about marriage. It was interesting to me that marriage is so emotional. I have a permanent bond with the people I married. It is funny how I am introduced as their ex-wife. There is a connection, even if there was never an experience. I feel the piece gave me a much more well-rounded knowledge of matrimony as an institution and how I relate to it personally."

The physical artwork that represents the *Wedding Series* consists of photographs of the four nuptial ceremonies, the kind that might fill anyone's wedding album, except these were enlarged to six-by-four feet. Sentimental content was presented in confrontational dimensions. The scale may not have represented the romantic feelings of the newly married couples, but it did match the disruption of the audience's romantic attitudes when they discovered the same smiling bride at the side of four very different mates.

Tattooing: In a 1998 series, Lambert reversed the dynamics of the *Wedding Series*. Instead of subjecting herself to the whims and devices of wedding chaplains and divorce lawyers, she asked others to subject themselves to whims and devices imposed by her. She tested their trust by requesting they submit their bodies to her tattooing needles. Unlike the legal contracts that define the duration of a relationship and can be terminated, she, and the friends whom she tattooed, were bound for life. Tattoos are nearly indelible. Unlike marriage, tattoos make "forever" the temporal basis of this work of art. Here Lambert exposes issues that have an insidious effect on real-life relationships but are often unexpressed: "Do you trust me now?" "Will you trust me forever?" Art took the form of real-life commitments by her real-life friends. It taught her to handle her real-life insecurities. Intense emotions accompany nearly everyone's decision to be pricked and stained with ink. Lambert magnified the stakes by admitting her amateur status. She taught herself the techniques of tattooing by practicing on oranges and bananas at her kitchen table. Despite the long hours Lambert devoted to this pursuit, she never refined her skills—but then, the proficiency she was cultivating in this work was not the art of tattooing. It was the art of participating in intimate, high-stakes, and intense person-to-person exchanges. As a result, Lambert withdrew from the aesthetic and thematic aspects of tattooing. Although she is fully trained as a visual artist, her friends selected their own tattoo images, because, as she explains, "I am not interested in tattoos as a component of popular culture. I am interested in the dynamics between the tattooee and the tattooer." Lambert challenged her friends to surrender some corner of their body to her for the rest of their lives. Those who agreed are represented in the final exhibition by photographic close-ups of the finished tattoos, entitled *Tattoo #1 – 6* (1998). Although it was not part of the installation, one of her images records a tattoo that the artist applied to herself. Perhaps it provides evidence that this artwork also enabled her to develop self-trust.

In 1999 Lambert intensified her exploration of the fear and danger on the part of the tattooee, and its relationship to responsibility and trust on the part of the tattooer. After a determined effort, she succeeded in gaining access to Russian prisons, a territory normally forbidden to foreign visitors, especially those with the avowed intention of documenting the conditions of life inside and interviewing the prisoners. Her specific mission was to film evidence of the longstanding tradition of criminals marking other criminals with signs that indicate their particular offenses and personalities. This gentle artist and her translator filmed the tattooed arms, chests, and backs of murderers, rapists, and thieves. In making *The Mark of Cain* (2000), Lambert's primary concerns lay beyond the craftsmanship of this tattooing tradition. Echoing her statement about marriage as "something that magnifies whatever relationship is already there," she explains, "In prison, all aspects of being human are magnified." Prison settings intensify the challenges facing all humans. They magnify the burden of living with past misdeeds, the difficulty of erecting workable relationships, the need to submit to authority, and simple survival. These real-life explorations lie at the core of all of Lambert's art.

Performing: The punk music scene is another institution that promotes intensified social exchange. In most cases, the behavior of performers is both contrived and hyped. Media attention is solicited on stage and off, which means these contrived personae are performing on stage and off. Success is usually measured in terms of album sales and concert attendance, but another reward is the adoration by a mass, unknown audience. This "love" relationship is facilitated by the presence and persistence of the media in pursuit of a story. In order to add the experience of broad-scale adoration to her life, Lambert formed a musical group and then cultivated a skill that made her eligible to be one of its members. She taught herself to play the drums. Her bandmates already knew how to play instruments, guitar and bass, even though they were formally untrained. Furthermore, they really did write their songs and perform them, even though they were novices. In addition, they really did produce an album that brandished such punk-rock sentiments as "Get Your Shit Out of My Place." Lambert reports an additional real-life component of this project—the group was voted "Best Unsigned Band of 1995" by a prominent fanzine. Throughout, the members made no pretense regarding their lack of artistic talent. No one claimed their fame was predicated on musical accomplishment. Lambert suspects the group's raunchy name had something to do with their success. *Platipussy* (1996) became known for the outrageous cavorting of three flashy bad girls who performed best at drinking, brawling, and gun toting.

The material manifestation of Lambert's investigation into punk stardom consists of memorabilia like T-shirts, panties, posters, an album, and a trailer to a pseudo-documentary film about the band that was never made. The trailer provides a synopsis of a tragic tale in which firearms catapult Platipussy to fame and then precipitate the band's demise. The bad girls are shown firing pistols in their act. The fans are shown cheering them on. The fever spreads. Kids join the fun. The music industry thinks this is a great gimmick, so it encourages them to go on shooting. Ultimately, all three are found dead, mysteriously killed by gunshot wounds. The trailer shows how it all went wrong. The villain is the group's handler, the manager/publicist who creates the stars' personae. This character is actually the only actor. Everyone else plays themselves—the promoter and the band members, as well as their friends and families who are interviewed on film about the girls' tragic, fictional deaths. They responded without being scripted. The film suggests that the girls will live on, if only through postmortem media hype.

Punk stardom amplifies more than the volume of sound or the hazards along the road to their deaths. As in her other projects, Lambert has selected an extreme circumstance within which to conduct a commonplace exploration. Becoming a rock star enabled her to amplify the task of constructing an identity, a task that applies to everyone. Real life provides few guides for conducting the crucial search for self-definition. "In truth," Lambert comments, "we all create ourselves and then become our reality." Or others create us. Platipussy was a fabrication, but it was not a product of the members' own invention. They resemble Courtney Love, whose film biographer, Nick Broomfield, used the star to capitalize on the public's appetite for gossip, speculation, and melodrama. Lambert comments, "Many people knew of Courtney Love's image as a doped-up junkie, a bad wife." Like so many of their punk predecessors, Platipussy died in the process of feeding other people's expectations. But this work also provided an opportunity for Lambert to continue her exploration of personal trust and commitment. At the time of this interview, Lambert didn't have the money to complete the pseudo-documentary, which distressed her: "So many people volunteered their time and talent. They worked hard and they believed in me. My responsibility to them is to finish it."

Lambert's mission does not involve offering answers. Instead, she hopes the viewers will also consider exploring life options that include direct, lived experience with real consequence instead of relying on culturally inscribed programming to determine their lives. "The conclusion is not clear," Lambert says. "The work is not intended to provide a concise explanation. If you are looking at my exhibition and thinking in a new way, that is enough."

1. Unless otherwise noted, all quotes from an interview with the artist, May 12, 2001.
2. Michael Mattison, "D-I-V-O-R-C-E," *Artpaper*, March 1991, 12–13.

MEASURING SUCCESS

MEASURING SUCCESS

Daniel Joseph Martinez, *Self Portrait #7: George and Daniel. In an insane world it was the sanest choice* (2000), 48 x 60 inches, light jet print. Courtesy The Project, New York and Los Angeles.

The word "success" indicates fortunate outcomes, but it does not indicate the nature of these outcomes. Artists are free to choose among countless goals, systems of measurement, and criteria of accomplishment. For some, success is measured according to rulers that have developed a patina from long and frequent use. It is common for recent generations of artists, for instance, to adopt rulers that are keyed to increments of wealth, power, and eminence. Many contestants vie for these three limited resources. Such popular definitions of success involve entering a field of operations crowded with competitors, but they also offer benefits that exceed wealth and fame. One benefit is having predecessors whose accomplishments provide precedents that are available for emulating. Furthermore, ready-made markers of commendation await artists who subscribe to them. In our culture, these might include auction sales, media attention, honorary degrees, foundation support, or solo exhibitions. But this triumvirate of criteria is not mandatory. Rulers can be self-styled by artists who strive to fulfill independent goals.

Artists who declare independence from the standard system construct their own professional destinations. They forge career paths by pursuing their own indicators of achievement, devising methods of realization, and defining their rewards. In this open field of endeavor, earning the respect of the masses defines success for some artists, but it defines failure for those who covet attention from the most sophisticated viewers. Instead of seeking public recognition as a personal goal, some artists seek it as a social means, since it provides a platform from which to have an impact. Anonymity is acceptable to artists who are content with self-satisfaction, or those who seek subliminal or subversive influence. Success may entail instigating controversy or staying out of trouble. It may be measured in constructive increments (the creation of something wonderful) or destructive increments (the disruption of something terrible). Succeeding may mean affecting the self, or it may mean the generous act of affecting others. The minimum quantity of others needed to make the grade varies from a few to an entire culture. The minimum degree of impact varies from mild to powerful. The minimum duration may be a momentary ripple or a permanent paradigm shift. The minimum delay before delivery ranges from instant gratification to a culminating success that may even exceed the artist's lifetime.

Success does not guarantee happiness. Receiving too little success is a familiar refrain in the field of art, but artists can also have excess success. Too much success produces conflict, angst, boredom, isolation. Too much inhibits professional growth. Too much compromises integrity or instills complacency. Too much can cause resentment and jealousy on the part of others. It is uncertain if achieving success in youth is an advantage or disadvantage. Thus, the appeal of success is tainted by dangers of actually achieving it. It seems useful to calculate the benefits of pursuing success as opposed to actually achieving it.

Betsy Damon
Born 1949 New York City
1963 Skidmore College, BA
1966 Columbia University, MFA
Lives and works in St. Paul, Minnesota

Betsy Damon excludes mention of herself when she describes her artistic success in initiating a huge water-reclamation project in Chengdu, China. The success she sought and had in completing the project is evidenced in benefits that accrued to the vast domains of earth, water, and air, the interconnections between aquatic life, plant life, and the lives of all nine million citizens of Chengdu. Damon says, "The Chengdu project is an extension of my philosophy of what it takes to live on the planet, the necessity of working together, bringing together unlikely partners, and forming new relationships. It is about building new kinds of connections and relationships while grappling with the consequences of a globalized class system and the economics of dominance, possession, exploitation, and greed."[1]

When Betsy Damon stopped painting to become an activist artist, she set aside the art establishment measuring device that calibrates success according to income, number of solo exhibitions, and mentions in the art press. In the 1970s, there were other maverick artists who were also declaring their independence from that model. They cultivated relationships with the natural environment and the people on the streets instead of with museum goers and art collectors. By devising original goals and methods of achievement, they demonstrated why opportunities to demonstrate their artistic integrity and imagination are as applicable to defining success as to attaining it. Damon explains, "Success to me is a narrow and specific word that has little to do with good art or qualities that I look for in myself or others. Success is measured primarily by money or fame. Both are useful, they make it possible to do more of what you would like to do. But success for me is being able to keep my integrity, have good relationships, and make a slight difference. It is being part of a larger project, which is to build a just society."[2]

Damon set aside her brushes and paints in the 1970s and has devoted the subsequent decades to expanding her field of operations. Her work has progressed in this regard from addressing individuals to communities to entire cities. Since the mid 1990s, the focus of these endeavors has been even more encompassing; indeed, it is now global. And it is devoted to water. Unlike most Americans, who take for granted that water is a liquid that flows out of faucets in controllable temperatures and predictable volumes, Damon perceives water as a precious and fragile resource. "Each of us as members of the human community face the challenge of understanding our environment sufficiently to preserve or restore it. What is at stake is the very quality of life, the living bodies we have inherited, and the recognition that our DNA is immutably dependent upon water. Yet it seems as if the more removed human beings become from the sources of life-sustaining systems, the less they are able to act to protect those systems. What do you know about your water? Do you know what is in it? Where does it come from and where do all the things you put into it end up?"[3]

As an artist, Damon honors the beauty of water on a scale that includes the delicate minutiae of its molecules. But her devotion to water involves more than aesthetics. It also honors water's role in sustaining the health of all living things. Damon is an artist-ecologist who actually returns this abused and neglected substance to its original state

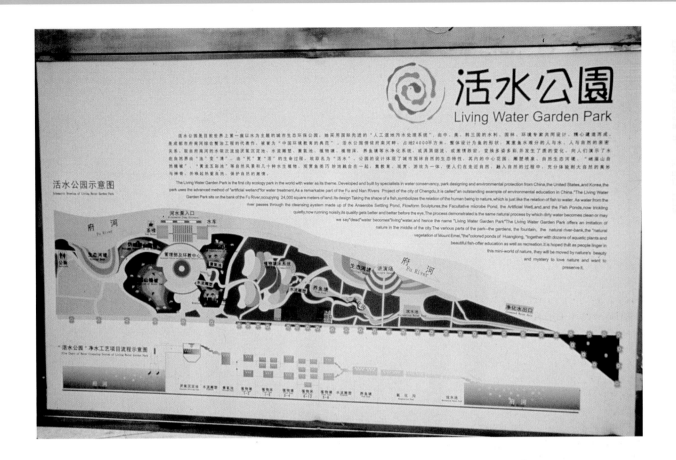

Betsy Damon, *Living Water Garden* (1998), plan of Living Water Garden, 6-acre park, City of Chengdu, Sichuan Province, China.

Betsy Damon, *Living Water Garden* (1998), aerial view of Living Water Garden, 6-acre park, City of Chengdu, Sichuan Province, China.

as a vital source of sustenance. Furthermore, she is an artist-ecologist-social activist who extends her vision beyond life-sustaining and aesthetic qualities to acknowledge water reclamation as a catalyst for uniting communities. In addition, she is an artist-ecologist-social-activist-humanitarian who honors the power of water to create tranquility, cheerfulness, and courage for people everywhere. Damon explains, "It isn't about how I like to swim or gulp down a refreshing glass of cold water, but rather … how water makes all life, and how rituals and belief systems about the purity and pollution of water have meaning for every human being."[4]

In 1990, Damon founded Keepers of the Waters, a nonprofit organization dedicated to bringing artists, scientists, and citizens together to develop aesthetically pleasing, multi-functional, sustainable water-treatment systems. The organization is committed to the belief that, in this manner both the physical infrastructure of an urban center and the psychological infrastructure of its citizens can be restored. This vision was applied to an ambitious water project in Chengdu, China. With a population of over eight million, this ancient walled city in southwest China is located at the confluence of the Nan and Fu Rivers near the Tibetan border. Damon explains, "The Chengdu project is an extension of my philosophy of what it takes to live on the planet, the necessity of working together, bringing together unlikely partners, and forming new relationships. It is about building new kinds of connections and relationships while grappling with the consequences of a globalized class system and the economics of dominance, possession, exploitation, and greed…. Water as the source of all life can form the basis of such connections."[5]

If Damon had remained a painter, her artistic process would probably have entailed isolation within a studio, the transformation of a blank canvas into a personal expression, and success predicated upon personal achievement. Instead, Damon disengaged from self-expression and egocentrism by participating in a citywide water-reclamation project. Joining together in Chengdu with a team of artists, engineers, government officials, and citizens, she became, in her artistic role, the facilitator of a shared mission. Damon, however, was inclined toward communal activities even before she was enlisted for this municipal effort. When Damon brought Keepers of the Waters to Chengdu in 1995, her purpose was simply to raise public awareness of the river's acute pollution problem. Instead of staging a solo event, she invited numerous Chinese, Tibetan, and American artists to come to the city to dramatize the fouling of the river. One performance involved a group of women washing long strips of white silk in the river. The more they washed the cloth, the dirtier it became. These art events were televised, acquainting the people of Chengdu with the work of the many artists involved, not just Damon's. Furthermore, what this project presented was a subject critical to their health and well-being in China, not to Damon's life in America.

The success of this endeavor far exceeded Damon's expectations. Not only was the public receptive to these collaborative efforts, but the director of the city's Funan River Compre-hensive Revitalization Project, Zhang Ji Hai, was also impressed. He sought out Damon. Based on their discussions, he began to reconsider a citywide, five-year plan for flood control and waste-water treatment that had already been approved. The plan involved the construction of unsightly walls and dams along the river to hide the waste-treatment facility. Damon introduced Zhang to an alternative ecological approach. She suggested it would be possible to accomplish the practical aspects of the project by eliminating the barriers and constructing an open park along the banks. "The final stage of waste treatment can be an addition to every community…. If you make it into a wetland, you can make a park that will attract wildlife and can be a place for study."[6] A few months after Damon returned to the U.S., she received an invitation from Zhang to revisit Chengdu and help design a "living water park" that "encouraged people to look at the world more carefully, to value each creek, river, and groundwater aquifer."[7]

Damon returned with Margie Ruddick, a landscape architect who specializes in water remediation. The Chinese government provided accommodations, an office, a phone, and a modest stipend for food, but no salaries—since Damon had recently received a fellowship she was still able to accept the invitation. The first task that she and Ruddick established for themselves was to study the situation. They consulted Chinese landscape architects, hydrologists, artists, government officials, and engineers. Then they shared their ideas with the officials. Again, the rewards of success far exceeded Damon's expectations. Instead of her involvement being limited to this consultation, she was offered a six-acre site along the waterfront to create a living water park.

Collaboration is not only Damon's working process; it is also her work's primary theme. Her vision would be compromised by personal attention. "I believe that a group of committed people can address any challenge concerning water, and solve the difficulties in ways that respect the dynamic universe and every individual. The key to our success is relationships! My work is action, action that motivates, connects, and possibly at times, changes lives, which I hope invites or offers the possibility of connection."[8] She and her project director, Jon Otto, worked with numerous Chinese project directors, five construction teams, and many individuals. Damon asks, "Who was in charge? That question was never answered. The park is not mine. That is a really important truth. We did it together."[9]

In truth, Damon's principal collaborator is not human at all. It is water and its capacity to splash, swirl, splatter, spray, trickle, and bubble. All of these qualities determined her design for the park, which included a sculptured setting for people to frolic or meditate in, and to interact with. The park also accommodated an environmental education center and a refuge for wildlife and plants, but the featured star of this ambitious construction is water. It commences its journey through the park after being pumped uphill from the river, whereupon it enters the eye of a settling pond shaped like a large fish. In the center of the eye sits a thirteen-foot-wide granite sculpture of a single drop of water, as it would appear if seen through a powerful microscope. The water then ripples through an aeration system that takes the form of a series of sculptures Damon calls "flow forms." They function like rocks in a mountain stream. From there it arrives at a reconstructed wetland with boardwalks that permit visitor access. In the wetland, water tumbles from pond to pond, each one containing specific plants that clean certain contaminants from the water. The next stop in this liquid journey consists of fish ponds where the water is further filtered. It then meanders past an open amphitheater, spills into a splash pond for children, and flows back into the river cleansed, revitalized, and pure. Visitors honor and respect the creative powers of water, not the artist. The work is a tribute to nature's own healing powers.

There are ample polluted waters in the United States. Why did Damon have to travel so far from home to demonstrate water's role in maintaining a vital ecosystem? What does China offer that the U.S. lacks? "Dependence on nature for well-being is integral to Chinese culture, art, philosophy, teaching, and medicine," Damon explains.[10] In the U.S., "We don't acknowledge the role [water] plays in our lives. Chinese do, like all people who have a deep history, like Native Americans. People with a deep history understand on a profound level, not on a gross level, the importance of water."[11] Damon's vision may be alien to the nation of her birth, but it's conducive to a setting on the opposite side of the globe. Despite

Betsy Damon, *Living Water Garden* (1998), tea house and setting pond.

China's recent neglect of its waters as the nation rushes to become industrialized, its traditional rapport with nature is easily renewed. China's industrial development began just thirty years ago. Many citizens can still recall swimming and fishing in the crystalline waters that have since become fouled by pollution. Damon notes, "No one in China ever argued with me or failed to understand how important [water] is to the quality of human life."[12]

China's current water crisis was already in evidence in the 1980s. Approximately twelve million people had left the countryside and piled into China's cities each year. This exploding urban population strained the essential services to the point of collapse. The city of Chengdu was beset with problems. Yet this provincial capital was primed to lead the nation's campaign for water remediation because of its historic pride in its water. The city's prosperity over the centuries had been attributed to the steady stream of cold, clear, pure water that flowed into the Chengdu basin from the Himalayan Mountains. According to legend, the waters were so clean that fabric washed in the river became brighter and more lustrous. The region is also associated with a renowned hydraulic feat that dates back to 256 B.C., when ancient engineers harnessed the river and channeled it through an elaborate irrigation system. The ancient water system functioned throughout the ensuing millennia until the 1970s, when it was abused by industrial development.

Water again played a pivotal role in the history of Chengdu when, in 1985, a teacher of natural science in the local elementary school decided to raise his students' concerns by using the river as a living laboratory. The students not only became concerned, they became activists. Their insistent appeals to government officials were the catalysts that sparked a revitalization initiative. It culminated in a massive project that entailed removing and relocating a thousand polluting businesses and factories, replacing the shanties that crowded the river banks, relocating 100,000 residents, dredging the entire length of the river, restoring the banks with public spaces, and planting 20,000 trees. The Secretary General of the Chengdu Communist Party identified the major hurdles to fulfilling this plan: financing, relocations, and a third hurdle that laid the foundations for Damon's involvement. The Secretary General articulated the challenge by stating, "What is the vision for this project? We need a concept on how we want to design the renovations, and we need a consensus to make it happen."[13]

For all artists, context is an essential determinant of success. For example, whether their work is celebrated, derided, or ignored is often a function of their rapport with their audience. Damon enjoyed such a relationship. Chinese officials invited her to transform their communal needs into a practical and aesthetic reality. They were predisposed to believe that insidious poisons from chemical pollution could be treated naturally. They did not have to be convinced by Damon that, "It is one of the wonderful aspects of nature that it is organized to create and sustain life."[14] Instead of the controversy that plagues so many public artworks in the United States, the Living Water Park has become the most popular park in Chengdu since it opened in April 1998. Damon was even awarded honorary citizenship to the city. This kind of artistic acclaim is rare in other countries. Damon describes being an artist in the U.S. by noting, "Artists are among the few people who have held on to the creative part of themselves. Creativity is taken away from most people and belittled. So we work very hard in a culture that has little respect for art. If the culture did have respect for art, artists would not be isolated from society and each other."[15]

Successfully reversing water pollution in Chengdu is not Damon's ultimate goal as an artist, because the globe is rife with polluted waters in need of restoration. But this project is a stepping stone to future public art endeavors. The Living Water Park in China demonstrates the viability of the green approach in any region where economic growth and industrial-ization have discharged hazardous wastes into the waters. Creating a successful prototype in China has given credibility to the natural approach that Damon advocates. "We need this kind of hope. I think that fear stands in the way of most attempts to change the ways we interact with the Earth. Too often, people believe that they can't really affect environmental policies and practices or that they can't afford them. But once they see things start to happen, they can't help but become interested."[16] There are signs that this environmentally healthy ambition is becoming more and more achievable. Keepers of the Waters groups have been established in Duluth, Minnesota and Portland, Oregon. Portland is considering a plan to construct a series of living water parks to treat storm-water runoff and possibly nurture endangered populations of salmon.

The positive change that serves as Damon's measure of success is not calculated in terms of her personal fate and fortune. Her desire for well-being is not even limited to the lives of average citizens. In order to be successful, the outcome of her endeavors must also benefit the non-human and the environmental recipients of her art activities. Damon reports, "That is what is fun in life. Yes, as an artist I am successful."[17]

1. Betsy Damon, "The Living Water Garden Chengdu, China," *Earthlight*, Fall 2001, 30.

2. Betsy Damon, letter to author, 24 March 2002.

3. Damon, "The Living Water Garden of Chengdu, China," 31.

4. ibid., 30.

5. ibid.

6. Anne H. Mavor, "China's Living Water Garden," *YES! A Journal of Positive Futures*, Winter 1999-2000, 52.

7. Damon, "The Living Water Garden of Chengdu, China," 30.

8. Damon, letter to author, 25 March 2002.

9. Mavor, "China's Living Water Garden."

10. ibid.

11. Mike Meyer. "A River Runs Through It: Chengdu's Living Water Garden." <http://www.keepersofthewaters.org>.

12. Damon, "The Living Water Garden of Chengdu, China," 30.

13. "The Long March," *The Climate*, Winter 1999-2000, <http://www.lifeonline.org/archive/citylife2main.html>.

14. Betsy Damon, "Living Water Garden," *Hieronimusing*, 6 July 2001, n.p.

15. Damon, letter to author, 25 March 2002.

16. Author, "Living Water: Combining Art and Science to Rejuvenate Communities and Restore Waterways," *Bush Foundation* News, Fall 2000, n.p.

17. Betsy Damon, letter to author, 24 March 2002.

Xu Bing
Born 1955 Chongqing, China
1987 Central Academy of Fine Art, Beijing, MFA
Lives and works in New York City

Xu Bing states, "Human thought has limited potential. I sought a different source." Thus, in order to expand human potential, Bing's artworks direct viewers to forms of awareness that are not dependent on such products of the conscious mind as reason, belief, opinion, ideas, and even the imagination. Sometimes they create confusion. Sometimes they erode dependence on written words. Sometimes they evoke paradox. Sometimes they engage live animals such as pigs, silkworms, and sheep. In these manners, viewers experience modes of understanding that are not dependent on conventional conveyors of meaning. Success, for Bing, depends upon undermining humans' attachments to thoughts, ideas, concepts, theories, and texts.

In 1999, Xu Bing received the coveted MacArthur Foundation Genius Award. In addition to the prestige associated with the award, he received a substantial sum of money. The Genius Award is designed to relieve remarkable individuals from financial concerns for five years so that they can dedicate themselves to their creative and academic pursuits. The day after the news was announced, Bing recounted how he had celebrated, "I called my Mom," he said, "and told her, 'Mom, someone got a genius prize and you gave birth to him,' then I went back to work."[1] This very special tribute did not dislodge Bing's humility. It is too firmly rooted in a philosophy that he describes in the following manner: "Do not look at things too seriously. Do not regret things in the past. Believe in fate. You are what you are born with—you can't change. You will have these qualities for life. But there are limitations—there are things you will never accomplish. There won't be many things that will make you extremely happy or sad. The middle way is the way of life. You must accept that. It is a comfortable state of being—free from desire. It is best to know your abilities. Work hard. That is today's success."

Xu Bing's studio is a hum of activity. Ringing telephones and whirling fax machines continually issue exhibition invitations from around the world. Nevertheless, neither this clamor nor its confidence-building implications figure in his definition of success. He recites a parable to explain the principles that guide his life and work: A student once asked his teacher, 'What is the spirit of Zen?' The master replied, 'Zen is in the heart, within. There is no physical manifestation. Zen does not reside in objects.' That winter was severe, and it was cold in the temple. In order to keep warm, the student took the carvings of the great ancient masters and burned them. The teacher discovered this and was very upset, scolding, 'How dare you burn these masterpieces?' The student defended his action, 'But teacher, you told me Zen is in the heart.'

Bing's response to the question of success epitomizes a classical instruction by Ch'an Buddhist masters. Ch'an is a Buddhist tradition that originated in India and later traveled to Japan, where it became known as Zen. The answers of masters are designed to avoid resolution, not attain it. It is believed that uncertainty and confusion stimulate reflection, propelling the disciple's mind to venture into unfamiliar domains, thereby bringing one closer to enlightenment. "The way I communicate with the audience owes a lot to this," explains Bing. Thus Bing, like the Buddhist teacher in the parable, has a penchant for paradox. But he also behaves like the student, because he doubts that authentic culture

Xu Bing, *Classroom Calligraphy* (1995), installation view, mixed media. Courtesy of the artist.

Xu Bing, *A Case Study of Transference* (1994), original performance, Han Mo Art Center, Beijing, male and female live pigs printed in false English and Chinese scripts. Courtesy of the artist.

dwells within its physical manifestations. Like the master, though, he objects to the destruction of a venerated legacy. Nevertheless, like the student, he questions the strict preservation of traditions, preferring to process the past according to the conditions of the present. Still, like the master, he laments the clumsiness of cultural transmissions that erode the purity of a culture's progenitors. Constructing such elaborate paradoxes fulfills Bing's self-designed maxim: "Success means through your work, you can change the way of people's thinking or provide a new way of thinking to the world."[2]

Throughout his career, Bing has applied this mind-expanding goal to the mind-restricting influences of culture. "You can go far, but humans can't be totally free," he says. "We are all bound by a cultural chain." In an effort to manifest the weight, the length, and the girth of this "chain," he has undertaken a dedicated artistic inquiry into four components of culture: authenticity, sustainability, transferability, and favorability.

Bing's search for the "authentic" aspect of culture directed him to the hallowed traditions of his native China. They provided an extraordinary storehouse of working processes that Bing has embraced within his artistic practice. Some, such as calligraphy, stone rubbing, and woodblock printing, are familiar, but Bing expanded the known history by reviving a system of movable-type printing that had been neglected for nearly one thousand years. He also extended his repertoire of artistic practices to include pig-farming and silkworm cultivation, because they, too, are entrenched Chinese cultural traditions.

A crisis in the "sustainability" of culture ensues when a tradition is stripped of its vitality and loses its relevance. This occurred in 1949 when the ancient forms of Chinese visual representation were forcibly suppressed by the Maoist regime and replaced with a social realist style of art. Throughout the Cultural Revolution, it remained the exclusive style sanctioned by the government for both expression and instruction, and it defined Chinese art for Bing and other members of the post-1949 generation. Asked about his early experiences with art, Bing recalls the omnipresent portraits of a benevolent-looking Chairman Mao and the idealized images of industrious workers surrounded by the bounty of their output. He also remembers the Big Character Posters used by the government to disperse news and ideology to the people. Banners and placards commanded the visual environment of public buildings, commercial areas, and the country's primary indoctrination centers, its schools. As he tells it, every available wall seemed emblazoned with slogans.

Bing's parents were ill suited to the cataclysmic changes that took place in China's rush to evolve from a crippled empire into a modern nation. His mother was a librarian and his father was a professor of history at the country's most prestigious university. The family was ostracized because history perpetuates vestiges of the country's feudal past, and books were considered reactionary forces that obstructed modernization. While other parents were instilling the revolutionary spirit in their children by giving them names like Red Soldier, To Face the East, and To Fight, Bing's father urged him to copy the masterworks of calligraphy. Then a real-life Buddhist paradox occurred. As a teenager, Bing was frequently required to contribute his calligraphic skills to the revolution. For long hours he produced Maoist Big Posters full of ideological propaganda. But instead of instilling a Maoist fervor to modernize, the practice had an unintended effect. It instilled a deep sympathy for China's "authentic" past. Bing absorbed the philosophy and history of China's prerevolutionary art forms because the practice of calligraphy draws equally upon the body, the mind, and the spirit. This technical instruction was a circuitous route into the forbidden terrain of mental attitudes and spiritual practices that lie at the core of classical Chinese culture. Ironically, Bing became steeped in his cultural past while he produced posters designed to vanquish it. "Learning calligraphy gave the experience of and access to a very traditional intellectual Chinese practice. It taught a young person how to be straight and quiet and slow."

After his immigration to the United Stated in 1990, Bing transformed the personal awakening he had experienced through calligraphy into a public offering to the members of his new Western audience. His challenge was to conceive of a way for English speakers to benefit from the thought-altering and spirit-awakening benefits of Chinese calligraphy, despite the fact that calligraphy is an alien tradition involving a foreign language and requiring such unpopular conduct as practice, patience, and precision. He rejected conventional museum displays because calligraphy is not like a Western art object intended for observation and contemplation. It is a discipline to be experienced and performed. Unlocking the audience's mind depended on teaching them the proper way to sit, to hold the brush, and to perform the strokes.

In an artwork entitled *Square Words: New English Calligraphy (Beginner)* (1994–1996), Bing transformed admirers of calligraphy into practitioners by rearranging the Public Access Gallery of the New Museum of Contemporary Art, in New York, into a classroom. School desks arranged in orderly rows and instructional tools were supplied so visitors could practice this venerable art form. They were given exercise books of rice paper lined with practice characters and numbered strokes, thin brushes, and black ink stones. Posters on the walls provided standards of calligraphic renderings. An instructional video beckoned visitors to take a seat, lift a brush, and actually draw ideograms that appeared to be Chinese. It even provided coaching in aesthetic values. A gentle voice advised that a horizontal stroke should be strong "like a bridled horse, not a rotted log." The work did not merely promote manual dexterity and aesthetic appreciation. It also induced the standard by which Bing measures his own success—the mental state that accompanies the calligraphy process. Thus, the instructional video promised, "You will write in a way you've never thought possible, communing with nature and experiencing consummate beauty." Visitors to this exhibition were likely to be in need of such tranquil reminders of beauty. In order to arrive at the museum, it is necessary to endure the clutter of downtown Manhattan crowds, graffiti, litter, commercial signs, and the clamor of traffic, jackhammers, sirens, horns, and the subway. Calligraphy offered serenity.

Bing modulated this ancient Chinese tradition to serve the imperatives of a frenetic, urban audience. Because he anticipated that the duration of their devotion to calligraphy was likely to be measured in minutes, not decades, Bing broke calligraphy's orthodoxy and provided a shortcut training session that avoided the drudgery of practicing and assured instant results. First, Bing circumvented a source of frustration that often accompanies initial explorations of a new skill by limiting the tasks to rudimentary, easy-to-master strokes. Then, he induced museum goers who decided to try their hand at copying the strokes of traditional Chinese writing to persist in their efforts by offering them a surprise. They discovered that these calligraphic strokes had been assembled to form English letters. Furthermore, they were combined to form English words. Thus, the discomforts normally associated with encountering an inscrutable language vanished. Visitors discovered they didn't need to learn a foreign language in order to learn a foreign, language-based art form. As they followed the instructions to sweep their brushes across the page, they made another discovery. Their calligraphic marks spelled out words like "sheep" and "Peep." This intimidating schoolroom venture into a foreign tradition turned out to be as effortless,

Xu Bing, *Silkworm Series* (1994–ongoing), live silkworms and mixed media. Courtesy of the artist.

as familiar, and as elementary as *Little Bo Peep*.

Buddhist paradox extended beyond using silly and simple means to acquire an enlightening experience. It also applied to the Chinese speakers who could not read this Chinese-based calligraphy. To them it was gibberish. But English speakers who could not read Chinese could decipher it. Although their experience with calligraphy excluded tireless dedication to a master and to ancient standards of excellence, Bing hoped the audience would revel in the uplifting essence of the practice. He explains, "Calligraphy is good for health. It is like a spiritual exercise of meditation—like Qi Gong. When the mind concentrates, it is clean and the heart is quiet. At that moment, your pulse, heart, breath are like nature, like Ch'i. Your whole body is involved, you lose yourself, you are totally empty. Nature is the pulse, not mind. This is a Chinese idea. Calligraphy marks a moment."

Square Words dismisses the technical virtuosity that set the standard of success in calligraphy for many centuries. When Bing attached populist principles to this revered art form, he declared an alternative standard of merit. The work succeeds to the degree that it transforms the West's appreciation of calligraphy from an exotic museum specimen into a vital transnational rite. "Writing English words in a Chinese square-word style forces people to adjust ingrained thinking. This readjustment is reeducation. The process of studying calligraphy works equally well for Chinese or Western audiences. It acts like a computer virus on their minds. It breaks up or disturbs one's normal thought processes and expands the space of one's knowledge and consciousness. To both audiences the characters cause the reader or writer to stop and reevaluate their understanding of language and culture."

Bing is currently planning to take a multimillennial leap forward in time by annexing this five-thousand-year-old art form to advanced technology. He is creating a typeface that will enable people to use New English Calligraphy on a computer, thereby making calligraphy accessible to almost anyone. A mere press of a key will instantly produce a perfect stroke. Always willing to adapt tradition to pursue the goal of broad impact, Bing determined that the benefits of using calligraphy could even endure when electronic media are used to preserve a tradition that celebrates manual dexterity. "Culture equals control. Learning calligraphy is cultural control. The computer uses a Chinese attitude: it likes impersonal traces to convey a sense of order, clarity, and restraint." As "a great equalizer," the computer will allow calligraphy to infiltrate the daily lives of people throughout the world. "I want my work to apply to the social life of all people—regular people—everyday. For it to be part of their routine life."

After "authenticity" and "sustainability," the third component of culture explored by Bing is "transferability." He wondered if his culture could be transplanted to foreign soil and thrive there. To aid him in examining this uneasy alliance between mental liberation and cultural restraint, he enlisted the help of animals. "Animals are the most wonderful collaborators. I learn from them.... In order to recognize the limit of mankind, including myself, I started working with other living beings. With their assistance, we can compensate for our deficiency and degeneration." Bing rejects the tradition of the circus elephant dressed in a tutu or Mickey Mouse squabbling with Donald Duck. The behavior of his animals is contrived not to entertain humans, but to instruct them. In the museum installation of *A Case Study of Transference* (1994), one male and one female pig were placed in a pen that was filled with books printed in many languages. Bing covered the pink body of the pig with printed characters that had the appearance of the English alphabet, but which were actually nonsense. The brown sow was marked with fake Chinese writing. The animals were breeder stock, and their appearance in the museum was calculated to coincide with their peak mating cycle. The artist describes the event that was observed by the museum visitors. "Two pigs bearing marks of civilization (stigmata) on their bodies … were interchanging between each other via the most instinctive method—sex. We chose a pair of pigs in love. They mated as the audience watched." The sow was most zealous to copulate, and often nudged the exhausted male into renewed action.

A Case Study of Transference compares human efforts to assimilate with copulating pigs. One was an American York, the other a Chinese Changbai. Their success at achieving a mutual understanding was not only visible to the museum goers, it was a metaphoric manifestation of cooperation between Occident and Orient. Bing encountered the need to assimilate several times in his life. The first occurred while still in China, when he rejected the art education he had received at the Academy of Fine Arts in Beijing and replaced it with two forbidden alternatives—ancient Chinese traditions and vanguard foreign influences. Later, when Bing immigrated to New York, he became immersed in the struggle to master English and the values imbedded in the language. In both instances, he has encountered an indecipherable amalgam of contrasting forms of expression. "When I moved to New York," Bing explains, "I began to understand human boundaries. In China I felt afraid because of the human rights problems. But now I understand that these are actually cultural problems, beyond politics. It is inevitable. I can't find any place that is really free." As he speaks he moves his hands toward each other. Intentionally, they don't touch. "Living life as a human means living in this condition. We can't really understand. Even talking does not represent our thinking."

Bing has expanded the issue of transferability beyond human culture. "I decided to make this piece with pigs because pigs have a very primitive feel to them. They are like some sort of specimen in Darwin's theory of evolution. *A Case Study of Transference* juxtaposes culture and something primordial, something prehistoric." In fact, the pigs made a great spectacle of their dissociation from social etiquette and the codes governing propriety by shamelessly abandoning themselves to their sexual drives in full view of an audience recording their actions with cameras and flashbulbs. The pigs' ferocious fornications vanquished language, the tool of reasoned discourse, by ravaging the books in the pen and smearing the text on their bodies. They enacted the triumph of nature/instinct over culture/reason, "as if nobody else is around," to cite a Chinese proverb. Bing noted it was the observers, not the pigs, who were embarrassed. "This was the first time I had really experienced the force of this concept. The pigs demonstrated how different I am from them. I want people to think of their human selves, not to know more about pigs."

Although the pigs' actions provide uncontestable evidence of their uncivilized temperaments, Bing abandoned his original plan to complete the work by releasing the animals into the wild when he discovered that their survival instincts were depleted by generations of domestication. Thus, the pigs were already marked by civilization before language was printed on their bodies. Bing abandoned his plan without regret. The piece still confirmed his professional measure of success by providing the occasion for animals to be instructors, and humans, as their pupils, to entertain new thoughts. Afterwards the pigs were sold, but not as works of art.

The fourth influence identified by Bing is "favorability," a condition that determines if a cultural tradition still yields positive effects. Bing returned to the animal kingdom to discover this model of constructive behavior. In the *Tsan Series* (1994 and ongoing), hundreds of silkworms enact their entire life cycle over the course of an exhibition. Visitors who

Xu Bing, *Silkworm Series* (1994–ongoing), live silkworms and mixed media. Courtesy of the artist.

come when the shows open discover creamy-white adult worms devouring mulberry leaves as they prepare for the pupa stage. They see the silkworms slowly weaving back and forth in graceful, undulating movements, emitting an endless thread of silk until they exhaust themselves. Those who come a week later might observe yellow and white cocoons clinging to the naked mulberry branches amid an ever-thickening, delicate, and glistening veil of spun silk. Near the end of the show they behold the emergence of moths that rush to reproduce and lay multitudes of miniscule black eggs to assure the renewal of the cycle. Bing explains, "Silkworms are a symbol of human life and can also be very symbolic of the Asian cultural heritage. Silkworms create something beautiful. They are very meticulous and careful creatures; they work hard and they don't speak; they represent productivity and they sacrifice themselves for society, using up their whole body. They don't retain anything for themselves. They are silent workers. The worm provides a model of socialism, which is, more than anything else, useful. Chinese people like them, they feel close to their style of living…. They set an example of how to sacrifice yourself, how to put everything you have into your work. I think it's a very beautiful process."

Throughout the *Tsan Series*, Bing often placed the silkworms upon newspapers and books, where egg-hatching, larvae roaming, and silk-spinning obliterated these published accounts of human intelligence. As in the work with pigs, Bing measures his success in terms of the destruction of words and meaning and language. Yet this work is not nihilistic. In fact, he believes it benefits humanity. He explains that written words control people's thoughts. For this reason Bing sought a different source of guidance and wisdom. The simple worm was elevated to the role of mentor. "People need to have their routine thinking attacked…. While undergoing this process of strange and yet familiar transformation, one can enter a realm never experienced before." The Chinese word for making a cocoon has an alternative meaning. It refers both to bundling yourself and placing yourself in a cage. Thus the cocoon provides a second analogy for the need to open closed minds. Furthermore, in the Chinese language, the sound of the word for "silk" is the same as the word that means "thought." Xu explains, "People should not make a cocoon. This is negative…. Some people spin thoughts, they search for meaning like a philosopher. But even they die without understanding life and the world. Thinking doesn't keep you alive."

Bing explains a successful outcome of his works of art by stating, "The audience won't get any direct information, but they may think and understand something about the condition of their existence." They may come to a fuller realization of the futility of relying on language to communicate accurately and to gain wisdom. This futility applies equally to people who share a language as to those who don't. He prefers the veiled discourse of parable. "The story goes that, in ancient times, when there were no written characters and no drawing, Cang Jie created writing. The heavens were so frightened that they rained mullet, and the ghosts were so terrified that they wailed throughout the night. Heaven feared that from that point onward people would attend to trifles and neglect essentials."[3] Likewise, Ch'an Buddhism encourages people to abdicate language in order to release experience from within. Bing adopts two of its practices for liberating minds from their bondage to language. One is silence (no language). The other is paradox (no meaning). Bing measures his accomplishment according to his ability to avoid meaning, not create it.

1. Unless otherwise noted, all quotes from an interview with the artist, August 13, 1999.

2. Xu Bing, letter to author, 10 March 2002.

3. Vivienne Tam. "Writing Chinglish: Interview with Xu Bing," *China Chic*. (New York: Regan Books, 2000),<http://xubing.com/aboutMe/interview01.html>.

Daniel Joseph Martinez
Born 1957 in Los Angeles, California
B.F.A. 1979, California Institute of the Arts, Los Angeles
Studied in Germany with Klaus Rinke, 1981-1982
Lives and works in Los Angeles

Daniel Joseph Martinez objects to being identified as an artist. This is because many people assume that artists only create and market decorative objects, and that success for artists is measured according to these criteria. In order to demonstrate that he does not conform to this art convention, Martinez has invented his own job title. He prefers to be known as a Tactical Media Strategist. The "tactics" and "strategies" he employs fall into two categories: Martinez defies rules, and he disrupts conventions. These methods are designed to expose insidious concentrations of social, political, and economic power. Open discussion is a prerequisite for social change. Martinez succeeds when his methods stimulate dialogue among those who are in control and those who are controlled.

One nation, under God, indivisible, with liberty and justice for all?

Star spangled banner waved o'er the land of the free?

All people, created equal?

These celebrated patriotic mottoes exemplify the majestic moral principles upon which the United States is founded. Question marks have been added to them to indicate that their genuineness can be questioned. Despite the laws and bills and jurisprudence that have accreted over the past two hundred years to bolster these principles, the gap between privilege and privation persists. Daniel J. Martinez has established his artistic headquarters within this gap. He asserts, "We are living in a period of extreme crisis. The production of hatred and division is a disease that is killing this country. Racial and class divisions, predetermined by an unequal access to education, housing and jobs, produce feelings of rage and alienation. Our society is controlled by a racist fear of people with dark skin, yet no one is dealing honestly with racism."[1] From this place between the mainstream and the margin, Martinez has launched an artistic crusade. He bypasses the official legal and judicial mechanisms that institute societal change, because they perpetuate inequality and prejudice. He is a freelance artist-activist whose success is determined by his ability to shame the offenders and empower the victims. His uncompromising interpretation of the democratic principles of equal opportunity applies to everyone, but particularly to Chicanos, like himself, who endure alien status in the country of their birth.

An uncompromising renegade, Martinez only exhibits when he receives an official invitation to present his work. Since he is known to wreak havoc with the public image of the presenting organizations, impugn the systems that sustain them, and undermine the complacency of the individuals who operate them, it is remarkable that he receives any invitations at all. In fact, his biographical statement lists well over one hundred exhibitions. He says that most of his shows are in little galleries where, "I take small opportunities and turn them into something important."[2] But he also manages to exhibit within institutions he wishes to reform: the government (*I Shit on the Order of Your World* [2000], Veteran's Hall, Los Angeles); the business community (*For Your Intellectual Entertainment* [1995], Los Angeles County Transportation Commission); museums (*Study for Museum Tags* [1993], the Whitney Museum of American Art, New York); and academic institutions of higher learning (*The Castle is Burning* [1993], Cornell University).

An artist who chooses to play the roles of guerrilla fighter, truth-sayer, façade basher, and disrupter of complacency calculates professional achievement in terms of the disruption of the status quo—weak, moderate, strong, seismic. When Martinez applies this measure to the work he conducted on the Cornell University campus in 1993, it reveals a triumphant seismic rating. Martinez was invited to create a new work of art on campus by the Hispanic American Studies Program. He accepted because, he says, "Cornell is an emblem of the ivy leagues—of power and privilege and how these function among individuals in this school and in this country." The work's subversive intentions are declared in the title, *The Castle is Burning*. This phrase was scrawled on the walls of the Sorbonne in Paris during the historic student takeover in May, 1968. Martinez decided to transfer the configuration of barricades constructed at the Sorbonne to the Cornell campus. Because he anticipated that permission to commemorate a historic example of student protest would be denied by the university, he contrived a proposal that camouflaged any reference to the Sorbonne uprising. Martinez acknowledges that this two-thousand-year-old strategy was borrowed from Hannibal, the Carthaginian general who waged the greatest military challenge against the invincible strength of ancient Rome. Martinez explains, "When Hannibal had a goal, he would create confusion amongst the enemy. I used the strategy of confusion." Although constructing a sculptural maze to disrupt the mindless complacency of students and faculty was Martinez's real goal, his proposal was a decoy. He announced that the structure was a project of the behavioral science department to examine the movement of students. "I had the whole university—students, administrators, faculty—talking about everything except what I was actually doing."

The Castle is Burning took the form of an eight-foot-high, tar-covered passageway across the central Arts Quad. It formed a narrow corridor between the classrooms and the administration buildings, restricting views and confining walking to the narrow corridor. The psychological effect was carefully calculated. It evoked the disquieting sense of oppression that comes from the imposition of strict controls. Once the massive construction was completed, Martinez topped the walls with bold, red styrofoam letters that spelled out such inflammatory sentences as, "In the rich man's house, the only place to spit is on his face." The plain black walls provided a convenient surface upon which students could scrawl responses, and they relished the opportunity. Latino students and faculty used the walls to vent complaints about discriminatory school policies. Non-Latinos entered the fray by scribbling sinister renderings of swastikas and racist epithets like "Kill the Illegals" and "White Pride." This blatant exposure of Cornell's veiled racist climate fueled the indignation of

Interview with Daniel Joseph Martinez
By Zoe Feigenbaum

ZF: What goes into putting together a show like the one you are working on right now, *happiness is overrated*, at The Project gallery in Los Angeles?

DJM: This particular show is a direct result of a year's work in trying to create a cyborg self-portrait, a computer as machine and as simulation of an individual human being, myself.... This show is in a commercial gallery, which is something sort of new for me. My practice has been to work in de-territorialized spaces—noninstitutional, unconventional modes of aesthetic intervention and provocation. Most of what I have done has been made and exhibited in the in-between spaces on the margins of the institution and its systems of validation.

ZF: How did you first hook up with The Project gallery?

DJM: Before he opened his gallery in 1997, Christian Haye, the owner-director, came out to visit me in my studio to see if I would be interested in working with him and the gallery. We talked and listened to each other and decided that it would be a good fit.

ZF: What were you working on that you think might have made them interested at the time?

DJM: I don't think that he was looking for a particular genre. I would assume he saw a coherent stream of thought through the very different kinds of work that I'd been making over the course of my career. Christian Haye is very intelligent and has global knowledge of what is happening in contemporary art. More importantly, he had a vision of what kind of artist he wanted to represent in his gallery. Before I started working with him, the only time my work was shown in New York was in the 1993 Whitney Biennial.

ZF: So it was buzz? Promotion? Stuff like that?

DJM: No. The Project in New York is in Harlem. Think about that! The choice to open the gallery in that community represented a conscious shift in the geography of the social/economic/aesthetic marketplace. Christian had to have been doing research about what kind of philosophical and aesthetic territory he wanted to occupy as a gallery. In combination with establishing a new de-centered center, Harlem, the space represents a reclamation of a past cycle of radical cultural intervention. Remember, this is a commercial gallery; one of the goals is to sell art and forge careers. I assume Christian was looking for artists that would fit within that conceptual landscape. Because of my history of refusal to accommodate the toxicity of the market-driven art world and, at the same time, my insistence on the creation of new economic frameworks where artists are free to engage the market if they choose, I guess it was a good fit. When Christian started the gallery he was by himself. Now he has a business partner, Jenny Liu. They are a great team.

ZF: So what kind of relationship do you maintain with them?

DJM: My relationship with them reflects their unique

Daniel Joseph Martinez, *Quality of Life* (1990-91), site-specific installation. Courtesy The Project, New York and Los Angeles.

Latinos and other minority students. They marched on the administration building and staged a four-day sit-in until the administration promised negotiations. The turmoil raged all through the confluence of Parents' Weekend, Homecoming, Alumni Weekend, and Halloween, just when the college was most intent on projecting an idealized image.

As in many of Martinez's works, the entire community became his collaborator; even people who were never aware that the roles they were playing were written into the artist's script. The media also participated, even when it was antagonistic to his cause. Over three hundred of the entries in Martinez's massive bibliography of articles, editorials, and letters to the editor were prompted by this particular work of art. Printed tirades and voiced indignities against the work actually served Martinez's intentions by exposing latent hostilities on the campus. Martinez submits the following condemnation from a *Cornell Review* opinion piece as evidence of his success. It stated, "Mr. Martinez: we have a special message for you. You snot-brained fiend, you flighty, warbling, gallivanting, strutting little twit. You whining, moaning, kvetching, sniggering, paste-and-construction-paper excuse for an artist. You puerile non-entity, you prattling babe in the woods, you slobbering lapdog of the putrid international art establishment. You've ruined our campus."[3]

The conflict waged long after Martinez returned to California. It was from there that he wrote, in a letter to the President of the University, "Given the response from the University students and all concerned, it seems there is a great need for the symbols that represent freedoms of speech, thought, and expression and a forum that allows all voices to be heard ... I would like to offer in donation the artwork, *The Castle is Burning*, to Cornell University. I would like to make this temporary artwork a permanent public sculpture for generations of students and faculty to experience and feel proud of our great country and what it represents." His offer was denied.

Despite the mass of insults, despite the rejection of his offer to donate the work, Martinez considers this piece one of his most successful because its effects still reverberate on campus. Every year, on its anniversary, minority students hold a multiday conference on aesthetics, race, and class. *Castle* has become a compelling symbol of victory for them. Martinez reports, "I was invited back to be the keynote speaker on its fifth anniversary. It makes me cry. It was so touching and so loving.... When artists succeed, they have greater effect than violent revolutions. People take to arms because they believe there is no other way to alter the social nature. There is another way. From an artistic standpoint, it is to create absurdist situations that show people how they have been socialized to see things in certain ways. I show them how ridiculous that is."

Fair, wiry, and accent-free, Martinez does not appear to embody the Chicano stereotype. Nevertheless he grew up in a trailer park in a

way of working. We discuss ideas of what I want to do— the why and the how. Then they talk about the work from a long-term point of view— the multilayered strategies of investment and collections that they would like the work to be placed in. But after all the discussion, they just leave me to the making of the work.

ZF: Do you remember your first show?

DJM: I was ten. It was in the alley behind the house where I grew up in a lower-income housing project. I hung a bunch of paintings and sculptures on the fence. Seems that was a signifier of things to come! [Laughs]

ZF: Did people come to see it? Did you announce it?

DJM: Just some kids in the neighborhood, and then they proceeded to tear it down and beat me up!

ZF: Wow! At the other end of the spectrum, what was your first high stakes professional show?

DJM: It was in 1974, in an exhibition of photographs at a university gallery.

ZF: Did you sell anything at that show?

DJM: No. My shows have never been about selling art. My interest and concern is in the creation of meaning. I am not really concerned with the free market or the fashion of the day. One of the questions is, is it possible to create work that is effective, complex, and deeply visual and to remain in a mode of experimentation using simultaneity, multiplicity, proximity, and agency as active ingredients to produce the art?

ZF: What are your feelings about the commercial aspect of the art world in general?

DJM: I think it's fine. Artists need galleries. It is simple. Galleries are stores.... Artists are people who make things. They make products and need places to put their products so people can look at them and collectors can buy them.... Some galleries are willing to invest more money and help artists' careers. For other galleries, if you don't sell ... the gallery simply is not interested in you anymore. There is nothing wrong with the commercial art world in and of itself. What is of concern is that the free-market-based system is the only mechanism that artists have to exhibit their work. This system— exemplified by commercial galleries and museums—is well fortified and very difficult to penetrate. Yet it seems to be in full control of what we think of as taste. This suggests that there is a relationship between sales and the actual meaning of art, which, of course, there isn't. So then you create a false sense of importance and value—make something that people believe will sell and then they will tell you why and how it's important. So it either has to be very hip, very marketable, or just a good con. This then rules out the potential for a larger spectrum of production.... The nonprofit art movement is over in America. It ended in the '90s. So there are no other types of spaces available for artists to be able to show their work. It limits the potential of the distribution of ideas and the dissemination of work through exhibitions because there are just not enough kinds of venues that exist.

tiny Mexican neighborhood in Los Angeles that was sandwiched between the all-black Watts and the all-white Inglewood. Daily existence vacillated between uneasy truces and overt hostilities. Gangs and police were in continual conflict. Martinez recalls, "The city was a militarized landscape with blockades and police. There was the ever-present helicopter lullaby, the searchlights, police stopping us on the street to ask us where we were going, searches, harassment, arrests, being thrown in holding tanks for a night for doing nothing."

Becoming an artist required no conscious decision; Martinez says he always made art. He describes his first show, at age ten, which established him as someone destined to buck the system and pay the consequences. "I hung my constructions on a fence and gave a lecture to the neighborhood kids. Then I got my head cracked open. This was my earliest act of resistance and I was punished severely by the kids for not doing what they were doing. You are either in a gang or you are dead. There are no options. Gang strength is maintained if everyone agrees with the system. If you don't participate, you are a threat. You could be a traitor or a snitch for the police. I didn't like sports or cars. I didn't do drugs. That made me an alien in my own environment. Every block was someone else's block. I was always getting beat up. My only goal was to save myself. So I started to make friends with people who were bigger than I was ... I traded my ability to think for their protection. Most people don't think so much. There is a lot of talk and a lot of act. I became the mastermind for gang revenge, robbery, beatings. Once they realized my thinking skill, I became like a guru. As a kid, success was measured in terms of survival."

If survival was the goal of Martinez's childhood strategies, public impact is the goal of his adult activities. The skills he originally developed for self-preservation he subsequently directed to self-endangerment. His work intentionally courts censure, abuse, and ostracism. "My marker of success comes every time an individual takes me to task. The angrier people get, the more successful I feel." In 1993, the Whitney Museum of American Art provided an opportunity for him to become "an interventionist into the geography of colonialism and public space."[4] Curators invited him to participate in the Whitney Biennial, one of the most prestigious displays of living artists in the United States. Martinez accepted precisely because he objects to the definition of art that museums support. To Martinez, art that takes the form of objects is too mute, art that evokes aesthetic contemplation is too passive, and art that embodies personal expression is too self-indulgent. He supports an alternative definition by creating art that involves real-life issues and propels real-life actions.

From the outset, Martinez intended to challenge the premises upon which the Whitney functions. He planned to use the opportunity to draw attention to the underrepresentation of ethnically and racially diverse artists in eminent art settings like the Whitney, which purport to represent the culture of the nation. An essential component of the plan was devoted to getting approval from the curators to pursue this irreverent course. This time he credits a three-thousand-year-old mentor, Sun Tzu, a Chinese military strategist and author of a slim volume entitled *The Art of War*, which details military and revolutionary strategies that Martinez transferred to his artistic practices. "I used a tactical move, a decoy to convince the authorities that they had control over me. I submitted something I knew they would reject. My first proposal was a ploy. I let them say no. Then they let me do what I wanted all along."

Martinez proceeded to design replacements for the standard metal tags that visitors wear on their lapels as proof that they have paid the entrance fee. Usually the tags are marked

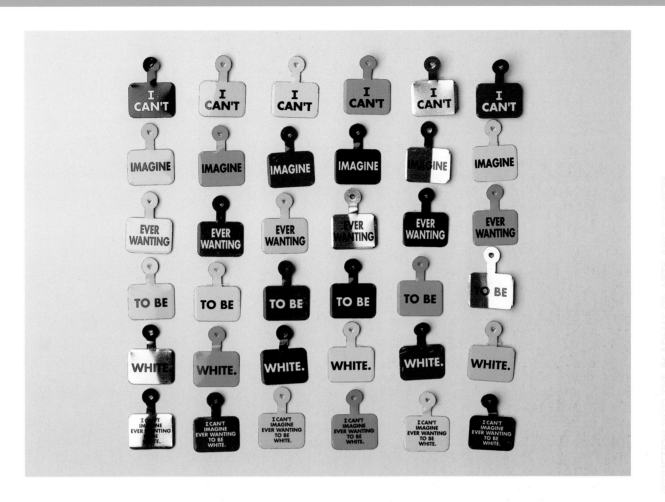

Daniel Joseph Martinez, *Museum Tags: Second Movement (Overture), or Overture con Claque (Overture with Hired Audience Members) – Whitney Biennial 1993* (1993), metal museum tags. Courtesy The Project, New York and Los Angeles.

with the museum's initials. His five different versions of the tags bore words that, if the wearers lined up in the proper order, formed the sentence: "I can't imagine ever wanting to be white." Visitors were required to wear this public declaration of reverse prejudice in order to enter the museum. Every visitor helped expose the exclusivist power system that operates within high culture. Pandemonium erupted. The work, entitled *Museum Tags: Second Movement (Overture), or Overture con Claque (Overture with Hired Audience Members)* dominated all other discussions of the Biennial. Of the more than eight hundred articles written about the exhibition, nearly all featured Martinez's contribution, and almost all protested his brazen assault on museum decorum. Though most artists wish for "good" reviews, Martinez relished the vitriolic attacks directed at him and his work. "I want radicalism. I don't care if my work has anything to do with good or bad reviews or the marketplace. I want the work to create a discussion about things that people don't want to talk about."[5] Some people capitalized on the hubbub by producing and selling stickers, T-shirts, and buttons brandishing the work's infamous slogan. Others produced souvenirs that said, "I can't imagine ever wanting to be D. Martinez." He welcomed them all. "By allowing this kind of activity in a distinguished museum, the infrastructure of the status quo seemed to crumble. I weakened the power structures." The ramifications continue. In a summary of the most significant art events of the decade, the December 1999 issue of *Artforum* featured *Museum Tags*. And the March 4, 2002 issue of *Newsweek* referred to this mock admission-button as "the high point" of biennials in the 1990s.

A third subject of Martinez's institutional re-evaluations was Seattle, and its civic pride in the parks, plazas, and lakes that comprise its public spaces—a sense of pride that left Martinez less than impressed. He believes that the word "public" is often a euphemism for those whose class, race, bearing, and appearance conform to establishment values. Nonconformists are excluded from this notion of "public." "In Seattle, they told me that they had rid themselves of all social evils. My reaction was, 'Hey, I didn't know that such a place existed.'"[6] So Martinez set about demonstrating that it didn't. In 1991, Seattle's most prosperous commercial district became the location for *Quality of Life*, an installation sponsored by the Seattle Art Commission, that consisted of 150 black-and-white street banners that had questions printed on both sides. Although the banners issued no direct accusations, they debunked the myth of a Camelot in Washington State. From one direction, questions such as "Do you have a housekeeper?" would receive a "yes" answer from wealthy residents. From the other direction, questions such as "Are you too poor to see a doctor?" and "Do you know anyone who can't read?" would receive a "yes" answer from poor Seattleites.

Instantly, a debate erupted all over the media. Martinez's defenders argued that the public streets are paid for with tax dollars from everyone. His accusers dwelled on the distraction that Martinez's signs offered from those bearing consumerist messages. Seattle's Downtown Business Association called for the immediate removal of the banners on the basis that they were bad for business because their content was inflammatory and could lead to civil unrest. But Martinez outwitted them. "The project had approval all the way up to the mayor's office. The city's art commission had invited me. I had followed every rule. I left no legitimate reason why anyone should remove the banners."

Martinez noted that he reveled less in the rash of publicity about the banner project than in the dialogue that transpired among ordinary people. He exuberantly recalls hearing such a conversation in a laundromat. "How can you ask for more? From my point of view, if someone buys an artwork—that's not success. That just means you are satisfying a personal taste or an investment. But if you get ordinary people doing laundry to debate the merits of an artwork—that is absolutely unbelievable."

Since the late 1990s, Martinez has been producing horrifying photographs of himself with his gut, neck, or the top of his head slashed, ripped open, or stitched shut. His collaborators in these images are Bari Dreiband-Burman and Tom Burman, award-winning makeup artists who create the virtual wounds, scars, stitches, and organs that cover and sometimes tumble from his body. *Self-portraits #4a and 4b: Second attempt to clone mental disorder or How one philosophizes with a hammer* (1999) are close-ups of Martinez's head encircled by thick, bloodied stitches that also resemble a crown of thorns. *Beauty Stains; Generosity, that was my first mistake. If god didn't want them sheared, he wouldn't have made them sheep* (2000) is a photograph that refers to the sacrificial lamb that has long served as a metaphor for suffering. The title suggests that people are destined to be "sheared," i.e. stripped of their protective coats. *Self-portrait # 7: George and Daniel. In an insane world it was the sanest choice* (2000) refers to a famous 1968 photo of a Saigon police chief executing a captured Vietcong fighter; the image has become a symbol of the brutality of the entire Vietnam conflict. Martinez updates the implications. In his version, a man identified as George is the victim. He stands facing the viewer with his hands behind his back. Daniel Martinez raises a gun to George's head. The photograph appears to capture the trajectory of the bullet exiting from the gun, penetrating George's skull, and bursting out the other side in an explosion of blood. "In an insane world, what is the sanest choice?"[7] Martinez suggests that the answer to the question is violence. Viewers are left to ponder if police atrocities, gang hostilities, and movie gore are the sane responses to an insane world that Martinez has in mind.

These issues culminate in the disturbing *happiness is overrated* (2002). To view this installation, visitors step inside a room that is white, sterile, brilliantly lit, and empty except for an animated hyper-realistic sculpture of the artist kneeling in a corner, its back turned to the viewer. Martinez spared no effort to replicate his body. Even his teeth and tongue were cast; his flesh was constructed to be moist and warm. Two sounds fill the space. One is the steady whir of pneumatic mechanisms that move the figure's head, face, and limbs. The other is the maniacal laughter that erupts from the sculpture's open mouth once every minute. In each of its hands is a razor blade. The figure raises one hand, then the other, and slashes its wrists. Although the physical lacerations in this sculpture are simulated—spiritually, emotionally, and morally they are real. Wounds are not necessarily recorded on flesh, nor are they necessarily signs of self-punishment. Martinez describes *happiness is overrated* as "a suicide machine that cannot kill itself."[8] Perhaps the figure's attempts are futile because betterment is really

ZF: As a kid, were you sure about what you wanted to do?

DJM: The question you are asking presumes that individuals have options in their lives, that they are educated in and welcomed into the social matrix that allows them to have someone … help them understand that … [they] could make decisions regarding the direction of their education and the formation of their identity as individuals. That option is not available to the majority of people in this country.… In my case, I did not have that opportunity.… It happened to work out quite well only because I was an artist, I am an artist, and I have always been an artist. It was not an option.

ZF: Did school do anything for you?

DJM: Nothing and everything at the same time. It was the first lesson in contradiction and exclusion.

ZF: What is your studio like?

DJM: I live on the west bank of the Los Angeles River … in a loft/warehouse where I have about 2,000 square feet with thirteen-foot-high ceilings. Part of my studio is all windows.… While this is not exactly the height of luxury, it is quite a nice place.… There are no deluxe amenities. There isn't an air conditioner or heater. It is just a warehouse that has been converted into a studio.

ZF: When you suggest that you validate your existence as an artist on a more human level, do you ever regret that?

DJM: Oh my God, no! I consider myself honored and privileged to have the role that I have. Having said that, it is not an easy role to maintain. The pursuit of knowledge and the manifestation of aesthetic territories … are the only things I can think of that I would be willing to spend my time and energy on. My work is a serious consideration of our social and cultural matrix … I attempt to interpret those patterns of behavior.

I teach fine art and philosophy at a major university. I exhibit my work in many different countries in the world. I don't create work to make money.… The only value that money has for me is that it allows me the means with which to do the things I want to do. Above and beyond that, it has no value. I am going to spend my life pursuing questions of existence and truth. I am interested in the dialectics of our culture. I am interested in Diogenes and a Socratic model of thinking of who we are and trying to investigate that psycho-geographical space of our existence. Existentially, who are we? Why are we here? Those are the questions that interest me.

ZF: Is your role as teacher in line with that goal?

DJM: Yes. I view the act of teaching as an art project.… I function in three different modes: one as a visual artist producing work; the other, as a teacher and in interactions that take place working with students; and the last is trying to act provocatively within a context of a social-aesthetic matrix, trying to create a free market of symbolic exchange.… I like it when it becomes the most confusing. It forces me to exist in a state of constant flux, to consider and reconsider my

the theme of this piece, not death. Martinez has stated that in these works he destroys himself "in order to be reborn again."[9] He includes the audience in this endeavor, creating a state of crisis "as the means of being able to bring us out of our numbness and remember how to feel something, anything."[10]

Martinez perpetuates a long tradition of distinguished crusaders, but he conducts his activities in a manner all his own. Unlike Martin Luther King, Martinez is as inclined to pummel those in power as empower those who have been pummeled. Unlike the Black Panther leader Bobby Seale, Martinez is both a rabble-rouser and an elite-rouser. He rouses the indignation of the rabble and the remorse of the elite. Unlike Robin Hood, Martinez steals two things from the rich—their arrogance and their pretense. Unlike Che Guevera, Martinez doesn't invade enemy territory—he waits for invitations and then he disguises his intentions. Unlike Nelson Mandela, Martinez is less likely to forgive transgressors than to shame them.

Martinez's vitality is engaging. He laughs easily and speaks in an impassioned manner about leadership, bravery, altruism, authority, and ideals. His campaign is vehement, but not bitter. He insists that his work is more artistic, social, and philosophical than political. "It is about power, but it is not activist based. I never claim to serve the interests of anyone else. I'm not a representative of a cause. I'm not trying to overthrow anything. I make compressed philosophical aestheticized gestures. My works are tiny atoms. In the right circumstances, they go through an aesthetic- chemical reaction."[11] References to aesthetics justify the inclusion of these political provocations within the chronicles of art. Martinez's tactics are elegant. Like a gem-cutter faceting a rough stone, he carves each action, removing extraneous material until it acquires a perfect form, and polishing its core until it shines through social injustice. Beauty, he insists, is built into his equation of meaning. Elegance can apply to political strategies as well as to aesthetic styles. Crafting skills can refine public actions as well as material substances. Mastery can elevate the effectiveness of actions as well as commodities. In all these ways Martinez applies his artistic sensibilities to egregious inequities.

[1] "Art and Politics: A Pre-Election Symposium," *Art in America*, October 1992, 40.

[2] Unless otherwise noted, all quotes from an interview with the artist, March 16, 2000.

[3] Quoted in Chon A. Noriega, "On Museum Row: Aesthetics and the Politics of Exhibition," *Daedalus*, Summer 1999, 78.

[4] Mary Jane Jacob, "Against," in *The Things You See When You Don't Have a Grenade!*, by Daniel J. Martinez (Santa Monica, California: Smart Art Press, 1996), 37.

[5] From an interview with the artist, March 10, 2000.

[6] Coco Fusco, "My Kind of Conversation: The Public Artworks of Daniel J. Martinez," *Atlantica* no. 15 (1996), 23.

[7] Daniel J. Martinez, *Beauty Stains*, exhibition flyer (Stanislaus, California: University Art Gallery, California State University, November 2000).

[8] ibid.

[9] Mat Gleason, Untitled interview with Daniel J. Martinez, *Coagula*, April 2002, 18.

[10] ibid., 15.

[11] *Beauty Stains*.

position.... It is the exchange and dialogue that I am excited about.

ZF: Do you employ any particular teaching methods?

DJM: I have a modest goal, which is to share ideas and information, to expose the potential and possibilities of creative and imaginative production, and to position the artist as intellectual. This allows me to sow a ground of the simultaneous relationships of ideas and form, skill and content, aesthetics and politics; to consider the possible effects of artists as catalysts and agents of transformation.

ZF: What was the first indication that you were a recognized and respected artist?

DJM: I am still waiting for it.

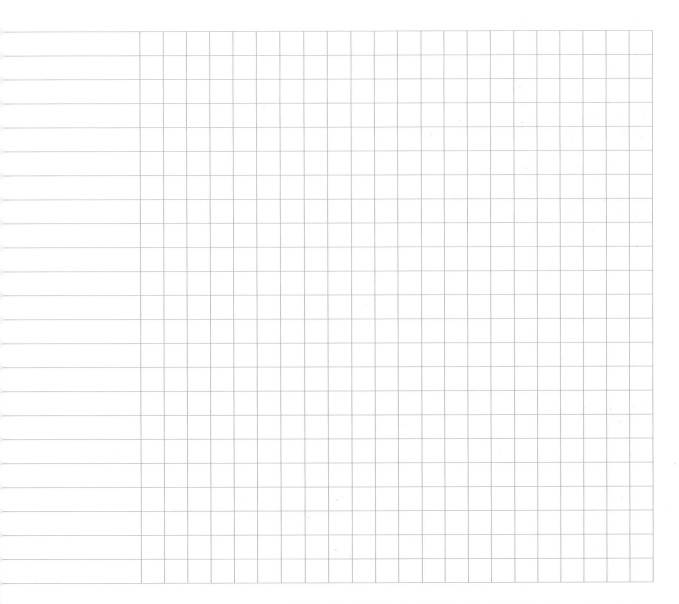

Michelle Lopez
Born 1970 Philippines
1992 Barnard College, BA, literature and art history
1994 School of Visual Arts, New York, MFA, painting and sculpture
Lives and works in New York City

Michelle Lopez carefully attends to the checks and balances between her efforts and her rewards. She believes that her ability to attain her highest potential is compromised if either of these aspects of success is disproportionate to the other. Too much effort for too little reward produces frustration. Too much reward for too little effort creates an opportunity for careless complacency. Furthermore, she is sensitive to the kind of reward she is being offered. In an era when glamour is valued as highly as accomplishment, and entertainment is sometimes more desirable than integrity, it is necessary to be watchful. Lopez attends to her production, but also to her reputation, so that they develop in synch with her perception of her own professional worth.

A delicate negotiation with Michelle Lopez preceded the completion of this essay. She was candid about her concerns regarding its inclusion in this book. Yet each hesitation confirmed the significance of her contribution to the discussion of success. Lopez is acutely aware of the power of the media in determining an artist's career. Because the media is as capable of compromising an artist's reputation as it is of bolstering it, she feels precarious whenever a critic or writer addresses her work. "I have an inherent distrust of language," she explains, "and when I speak about work I speak about it carefully and mysteriously.... I feel that this essay will try to pin the work down, put it into categories—which is language's downfall. The challenge would be to write about the work elusively just as the work is elusive."[1] Lopez's own description of her work suggests this mysterious quality diverges from what is produced in the language-center of the brain. The audience, she says, "participates in the beauty of the body as a landscape for all human experience."[2] But even her own description makes her uncomfortable. She edited herself, noting that, "'Beauty' may pigeonhole it," but she could not provide a more acceptable word.

Lopez's dilemma is one many artists would gladly have. Her work became known in the art world soon after she graduated from art school, when she was immediately granted four commonly coveted milestones of career accomplishment. The first involves being offered gallery affiliation. The second, third, and fourth measures of success were inherent to this offer: her gallery is located in a cultural capital (Manhattan), in one of its premier artistic districts (SoHo), and in a gallery that is respected worldwide (Deitch Projects). But her good fortune did not end there. Based on a friend's recommendation, Jeffrey Deitch visited Lopez's studio and immediately presented her with the fifth measure of triumph—gallery representation that is offered, not sought. Yet for Lopez, this status is accompanied by sincere discomfort ("I feel a bit overexposed with the media") and an unusual decision ("I am going into hiding a bit")[3].

Jeffrey Deitch is known for distinguishing trend-setting artists from those who are merely trendy. Collectors and curators regularly check out his selections because he has a knack for discovering emerging talents. Likewise, art writers and critics take note of the artists he chooses to represent. Their positive critical reaction often serves as the launching pad to hefty price tags, honors, commissions, and one-person exhibitions in major museums. It is at this juncture that Lopez's career momentum has halted. Despite the distinguished context in which her pieces have been presented, commentary from critics has been limited. Occasions where there has been a flurry of media attention have only intensified her misgivings regarding media attention. The two prongs of Lopez's attitude about publicity can be described as "not yet" and "not ever."

"Not yet" refers to her reluctance to be thrust into the limelight before she has fully matured as an artist. Maturity, she says, takes time. "My career is very young. I don't deserve attention yet. I want to do things appropriately and not get [in] over my head. I could make pieces that would attract a lot of attention—but I'm not doing that. My art career would have a short life. It's like movie stars. People get tired of them. There are only a few who surpass that. I'd like people to continue to be interested in my work—which is really hard to do."

"Not ever" reveals two other related concerns. The first is Lopez's refusal to satisfy a writer's expectations. Familiar modes of art-making facilitate critical analysis because they offer a known framework for assessment and an established vocabulary to express this assessment. Unfamiliar modes discourage it. Lopez observes, "It's possible that critics don't write about me because my work doesn't fit into categories and simple generalizations and that may bother them. I think some critics spend little time looking at work and a great deal of time thinking of ways to talk about art cleverly. The artists I respect the most continue to make work despite what people are saying. They have faith in their vision." "Not ever" also refers to Lopez's disinterest in "artspeak"—the catchphrases and ready-made vocabulary that constitute many art texts. Lopez explains that she consciously creates multisensory, intimate, anti-rhetorical work that lies beyond the scope of artspeak.

"My work is less a part of art than basic to the human sensorium. I intentionally make works that obscure easy analysis and description. My work is more about experience. The act of formulating words to describe a piece takes away from the experience. In order to talk about my work, you have to speak in an incredibly romantic manner, which most people are suspicious of. It's about having a universal vocabulary. It's about human empathy and mystery. It doesn't participate in art history dialogues. I'm struck by how often critics don't get the poetic resonance of a piece."

Thus, Lopez does not fret over media disinterest. Instead of selling herself short, she prefers to invest her efforts so they pay out dividends in the long term. Because she avoids proven attention-getting tactics, even the terms Lopez uses to describe her work are rarely used to describe today's vanguard art. Lopez says she seeks "tenderness, sensuality, quiet. Welcoming. The opposite of the titillation and aggression that pervades contemporary media. Anti-television. Not trying to sell you anything. Not dramatic. Not flashy. Honest. No hype."

Interview with Michelle Lopez
By Lauren Harkrader

LH: How has your decision to live and work in New York affected your work and your career?

ML: New York is a great place. It's accelerated my career. I went to grad school here and so immediately I had that community of artists. I had a kind of rapport that was necessary for me to develop my work through meeting people, and having dialogues, and constantly being challenged, and growing. The great thing about New York is that there is a serious audience that has a serious background in art history that's going to challenge you. It's difficult to get away with things. But now I'm feeling that I don't need the scene like I used to.

LH: What role did school play in your work?

ML: I wasn't in a studio program before graduate school. I studied literature and art history, and so I had very, very little studio practice. School taught me how to be a professional. Like, how to make art that wasn't student work, how to fine-tune the work, not only aesthetically but conceptually. So it was good for me to be able to talk about art. That's the thing that I really love most. Now that I'm teaching, I really love going into student's studios and seeing their ideas, and helping to nurture them and to clarify what they're doing. And that's the one thing that school gave me. And it's also about buying time. The whole time I was in grad school I didn't really make work. I was presenting ideas to my instructors because I wanted to throw many things out there, even if they were just proposals or ideas. When you are spending the whole semester making just one work, you can't do that when there isn't a community there to provide feedback, at least for me. And so school was really a gestation period for me. The serious work I did was when I was alone and solitary and out of school.

LH: So you are based in Brooklyn?

ML: I just moved out to Williamsburg, Brooklyn. I really love it here. I think Williamsburg has a real sense of community. It's like a village. A friend of mine that knew SoHo in the 70s said that Williamsburg is very much like that right now. The same kind of feel and the same kind of attitude and the same kind of community.

LH: Do you have a gallery?

ML: Yeah, I show with Deitch Projects.

LH: How does your work get marketed?

ML: I've sold some things, but I don't have that kind of success. And I think it's really difficult with sculpture. People, if they do buy art, they want to buy paintings or drawings or prints, which is fine; But it's really challenging to buy sculpture. I think people don't know what to do with them.

LH: Have you had a sale that was more important than others?

ML: I guess selling that car was really amazing. It was a Honda 600 that I covered in leather. Selling that was really a big feat for me. But I think galleries are shifting away from really selling work. I've been aligning myself

INVITATIONS TO CELEBRITY PARTIES

Michelle Lopez, *Boy* (1999), 49 x 46 x 146 inches, steel, leather, contact cement and pigment. Courtesy of the artist and Deitch Projects, New York. Photograph: Joshua White.

Until 2002, leather was Lopez's preferred medium. It offered a unique combination of qualities. Leather invites tactile, visceral engagement. It is sensual, receptive, and malleable. She welcomed the marks, scuffs, soil, and sweat that it accumulates as a chronicle of its history. Despite the fact that her initial drawings are composed on a computer, Lopez designs the other components of her studio practice according to their consonance with her vision of regaining the intimate connections and sensual contact she finds lacking in contemporary lifestyles. Choosing leather as her medium allows her to compensate for the tactile deprivation of most synthetic materials. Lopez's sculptures offer antidotes to the unyielding, nonporous qualities of plastic, polyester, nylon, and steel. She comments, "Modern materials are textureless. We aren't sensually aroused by the physical world today."

Arousal through the senses of the eyes and ears and nose is dependent on distent light- and sound-wave transmissions. But touch is exempt from such intermediaries. Lopez experimented with numerous materials in search of a sumptuous immediacy. She explored such translucent and skinlike mediums as apple peels, animal-fat soap, and marzipan. But of all the materials that invited tactile engagement, leather was most conducive to body-to-body contact. "There is something about leather that is primal. People are always attracted to it. It's true skin. They want to touch it." Touching is enriched by the emotional reaction associated with such words as "caress," "embrace," "stroke," and "fondle." Deer leather is Lopez's preferred medium because it is soft and maintains a fleshy color. The skins taken from the animal's lower body are the best parts because they are "the body's soft points."

Synthetic substances resist change. Lopez notes that they are desirable because they validate popular cultural values, "[supporting] an aesthetic that is pristine, unlined, young, undamaged. We abhor signs of time passing. We seem less concerned with death than decay." Leather supports a very different value system. It is prized for its patina; this lustrous quality that develops over time serves as Lopez's material ally in conveying that "soil, age, and wear can be beautiful." But in other contexts, the presence of a patina upsets entrenched cultural aversion to signs of age. Even antiques and historic houses are restored to their original condition. Cracks, scratches, and sags are rarely considered desirable.

Lopez's intense, prolonged, tactile engagement with her medium demands an investment of three to five months of labor in each work of art. As her actions on the leather accumulate and the work assumes its desired shape, she enacts an aging process. This takes the form of the history that she bestows upon the work in the studio, and that the audience perpetuates in the exhibition space. "Ancient fetish objects have an aura that comes from the residue of urine and sweat and shit. I like the idea of my leather work

with foundations. I think that's more where artists are heading, because the art world is such small change, especially for emerging artists. With the exception of a few artists, it's tough to make money off of your art.

LH: What percent of your income is earned by the sale of your art?

ML: Fifty percent. It depends. It varies from year to year. Sometimes I make absolutely nothing off my work.

LH: Do you write grants?

ML: Sometimes. The gallery also works in that way. They're basically my advertisers and they were the ones who got a grant [on my behalf]. Not that they seek opportunities out, but because of their high exposure, people come to them.

LH: And you work on the side?

ML: Yeah, I've done everything. I've done waitressing, I've done part-time work, I've done teaching. I think that's the most challenging—trying to have a normal life and be able to survive. I mean, I live pretty frugally and that's really tiring.

LH: Do you have a mortgage and health insurance?

ML: No. No, it's really bad. I think part of it is that I've structured my life around the artwork. I would rather not have to do another job. And so in that sense I don't make it a priority. I think it's starting to get to me. I would like to have a bit more stability. The one thing that helps is my dad's a doctor, and so if I do need any medical care, I can just go to him and his friends and it doesn't cost that much. I'm very hand-to-mouth and I live like a child. The most difficult thing is knowing that you've chosen this path, but also knowing that you could also have a job and get health benefits and do all that stuff to make your life easier. But sometimes I don't think you can make that choice, and sometimes I think it's a cop-out. I'm hoping that teaching will become more full-time so I get benefits.

LH: It seems like either it's "just name the price" or it's "hand-to-mouth struggling."

ML: If I look at the big picture, I'm okay. I think the problem now with the whole art market is that we expect to be taken care of by the art world. Emerging artists do. And that's not always the case. You may be doing really well in terms of getting your work out there, and showing, and getting a good response. But there's no guarantee financially.

LH: So how did you get connected with the Deitch gallery?

ML: Cecily Brown, who was showing at the gallery, came to my studio, and then she recommended that Jeffrey, who's the owner of the gallery, go and see my work. He came, and then, literally, a week later he offered me a show.

LH: Do you feel like that was kind of your breakthrough point?

ML: I first started showing at Feature Gallery in 1996. So that was really my first show. And that was two years after grad school. And those two years after grad

developing a patina out of the residue of my effort, absorbing all the elements of nature." Lopez prepares the leather hide to serve as a drawing surface by soaking it in a brine. She describes this process in graphic terms. "It is visceral, creepy. When I stretch it, process it, I connect with it as the skin, a living thing." Once this process is completed, she transfers a drawing of utmost delicacy to its rear side. Lopez then undertakes the meticulous process of incising the area where the drawing appears. Multiple minuscule lesions score the leather but never pierce it. The malleability of leather is integrated into the sculptural process when Lopez sets aside her blades and commences to rub the skin with dental tools until it becomes pliable. She then beats it gently with mallets from behind until the leather distends into the form suggested by the original drawing. The leather is then set aside and Lopez sculpts a wooden mold, translating the original two-dimensional drawing into a three-dimensional form. The leather is then draped over the mold and the pounding continues until a relief or a full-dimensional sculpture is formed. In all these ways Lopez enacts a ritual of touch.

The desire to include the audience in the marking process determines both the thematic and aesthetic components of Lopez's sculptures. Lopez avoids frightening or distasteful imagery. Her welcoming agenda requires friendly visions like cars, couches, and beds. These images are metaphors for psychological vessels that convey a quality she describes as a "sense of cradles" or "domestic sites of surrender." Her renderings retain the cozy appeal of the cartoon drawings that often serve as their sources. Toys and the characters populating children's television supply a second source of imagery and a metaphor for the emotional resonance she cultivates in her work. Lopez explains, "I resist going to an existential place. I want the experience to be emotional, not intellectual.... Teletubbies are speechless and have round bellies and are incredibly endearing. I want to return to that childlike state where you like things for what they are but you don't know why. It is wordless. That state is comforting." Lopez's "wordless" state comes with one stipulation: it is not amenable to conventional forms of art discourse, and thus provides another hurdle to critical analysis.

Just as angular forms seem aggressive, globular contours appeal. That is why they prevail throughout Lopez's work. One example is the leather sculpture titled *Boy* (1999) that Lopez formed over a ready-made mold—an abandoned 1971 Honda 600 that she found in a Mohave Valley junkyard. It fulfilled her thematic and aesthetic requirements. This model of car is small and has rounded bumpers that give it the appearance of a cartoon car. Lopez stripped it down to its steel shell and proceeded to cover it, inside and out, with pink-toned animal hide. The interior roof was embossed with cartoons and logos that drifted down the dashboard and around the back of the car. The car's comforting shape is fabricated out of an alluring material and embellished with endearing images. In this manner its aesthetic and representational components combine to produce a highly affecting work of art. Like a cradle, it swaddles viewers in reassurance.

"I'm so tired of cool art," remarks Lopez. In discussing this aspect of her work, Lopez expressed concern that writers, accustomed to cool art, may either judge her works to be "conceptually boring" or "too flashy."[4] She thinks it is neither. "I see it as scarring the belly. I do something that is incredibly unnatural to the body. I make it conform to new shapes." Through the many stages of its manipulation, the leather she works with undergoes a torturous process. She wounds it. Like skin, it heals itself by stabilizing in its new form. This new form reveals its mutated biography, materializing memory. But Lopez carefully divests her works of disturbing associations with blemishes and defects by demonstrating that injury and healing are not only inevitable, they are desirable ingredients of life. "Skin is a vulnerable organ. Wounds and the resulting scars are receptacles of memory and experience. I try to mimic the body's natural scarification in beautiful ways. I create an alternate history for this skin. I am fascinated by the way skin connects bodies to the world and to other people. I'm leaning towards something that is immaterial."

To Lopez, skin is the location of the body's touch receptors. During the creative process, she engages it as a physical experience. Then she invites her audience to actualize the sensuality of this experience too. "I feel like I'm creating orphans. I want people to embrace the pieces. I have caressed them so much in the making, I want to share that process." By defying the touch taboo in museums, the skins of the viewers and the skins of the sculptures become mutual receptacles of experience. "When museum goers have physical contact with the sculpture, the leather will eventually develop a patina, like the feet of ancient sculptures of Christ where adoration is expressed through touching." Viewers who touch honor Lopez's sculptures by leaving their marks upon her work. Perhaps, like the worshippers who stroke the feet of Christ, they will receive its grace, "the beauty of the body as a landscape for all human experience."

For now, Lopez seems content. "There is a difference between those who make art to become an artist and those who make art because they have no choice but to make art.... I'm not making art because I want to be an artist, but because I want to make art.... I am happy when writers appreciate it and not so happy when they don't … but I still am fine. I'm not dogmatic about it. I'm just reluctant. I'm not convinced that if the work is not recognized then the artist doesn't mean anything."

For many months Lopez remained reluctant to be included in this textbook, despite the fact that the essay was based on her statements, that each word was reviewed by her, and that her suggested edits were accepted. In the end, she agreed to be included. It is possible that this essay serves her desire to sensitize authors to the discrepancy between the written word and the lived experience of art, to make them more conscious of the effect of written commentary upon an artist's future development, to measure their praise against an artist's potential as much as to his or her past accomplishments, to translate the uniqueness of a visual experience into a unique written expression.

school, I basically waited tables and made art on the side. I think in that time the work really grew. Now I feel like I'm finally making the work that I was supposed to make. I really feel that I own these sculptures, that they're mine. Because of this whole experience of making this past work, I feel like a bona fide sculptor. I don't think that people are really making sculptures anymore. I like these new works because they're absolutely strange. I think they're strange and mysterious. They're not trendy.

LH: How do you think that change occurred?

ML: I think I wanted to make work that was absolutely me. And I think what makes artists really successful is if they make art that's truly themselves and not about what they think they should make. I mean, obviously you have to pay attention to everything else, like what's going on in the world and in the art world and what's happened in the past. My work is unfashionable right now and I like it that way. In the end, artists make work because they like it, they simply like it. But I want to create work that I think everyone would respond to. I was talking to Linda about how I didn't think I was getting any attention in general, that I like being ignored. [laughs] I'm actually not ignored, but I like the idea of not having so much pressure on me. Everyone's always looking for a hot artist and there's so much pressure on that artist.

LH: What are your feelings about the commercial aspects of being an artist?

ML: I really hate it. I feel that a lot of our culture gets ideas through osmosis from the art world. In a lot of ways we do get the respect, but we're not taken care of. It's always about money. We have to market ourselves. A good friend always said to me, "When the work is good, people will find you." So I didn't invite people over to my studio for two years. It's really easy to get starry eyed about the art world. There are so many artists out there right now, you have to add a face, you have to add a story to the art. I would rather have it just be about the art. But that's not how we work anymore. I don't think there's such a thing as selling out anymore. I think we're at a point where we're willing to do more things, like collaborate with fashion houses or science companies or do things that might get the work out there. And I like that. I like that idea of art being like music, where it gets more into the public and not so isolated. I think that's turning around. People are realizing how art's turning in on itself. It doesn't communicate to anyone except those in the art world, which is really awful.

LH: What is your relationship to your collectors?

ML: It is a personal thing. I think if they like you, they like the work. Or they like the work, so they like you. That's being a part of that world and being able to socially involve yourself in that community. There are times when I just treat it as a business. Honestly, I really don't have a serious group of collectors at this point in my career. I really don't understand why, but my gallery thinks that my work is challenging. I'm

surprised that people find it disturbing. I think that the problem with my sculptures is that they're archaic. They are objects to be held and seen from all sides, so it is a kind of intimate experience. In the end, I'm trying to create a sensual environment.

LH: Do you have any advice for the rising artist hopefuls?

ML: I think you cannot get anywhere in the social network until the work is strong. Really, what collectors are looking for is innovative, fresh work. You really have to work hard and question yourself, question, "Is it necessary?" How are you touching people?

LH: Do you have any assistants?

ML: I have interns. Sometimes I have assistants, usually from Barnard, because that's where I went to school. I love those girls because I can relate to them intellectually.

LH: What is the rhythm of your working process today? What is the tempo, variability, unpredictability of your process?

ML: Before I made the *Adventures in the Skin Trade* series, I made very little work. I think what happens is that I work until I can't make the same work anymore. So I stop for a time, for everything to collect. For me, realizing my drawings three-dimensionally took a lot of courage. That's the scary thing, knowing what you want to do but not knowing how to begin. It usually happens in preparation for a show. Shows are difficult. They're really tough on your psyche, because you're making work in solitude, and then it's exposed to the New York public and it's getting picked apart. It's hard to maintain yourself. You feel very vulnerable. These objects are your children, and you're ushering them out into the world.

1. Michelle Lopez, letter to author, 8 April 2002.

2. Unless otherwise noted, all quotes from an interview with the artist, May 21, 2000.

3. Lopez, letter to author.

4. ibid.

Matthew Barney

Born 1967 San Francisco, California
1989 Yale University, BA
Lives and works in New York City

Matthew Barney's tool kit for making his art consists not only of paint, brush, turpentine, and rags. Barney amasses choreographers, production teams, digital animators, film editors, makeup artists, hair stylists, composers, sound designers, editors, administrative assistants, fabricators, production assistants, and others. Allocating tasks to specialists hardly simplifies his role as an artist. Indeed, assembling this team of experts is evidence that Barney maximizes his challenges. Applying the skills of this team of players to his extraordinary vision may result in the production of epic films, but to Barney, their primary purpose is to expand his physical, imaginative, financial, organizational, and intellectual capabilities. Barney's success, therefore, depends on continually escalating the difficulty of his endeavors.

Resistance implies interference. It indicates that some oppositional force is retarding the accomplishment of a task. Friction is a form of physical resistance. Discouragement is a form of psychological resistance. Resistance not only drives Matthew Barney's creative zeal, he is zealously driven to create resistance. Barney contrives artistic projects that maximize the physical, cerebral, financial, and organizational demands he imposes upon himself. By escalating his artistic challenge, he continually tests his artistic resolve. But resistance does not come naturally to Barney. The facts that comprise his biography depict him as destiny's many-splendored child who has consistently met with success. No embellishment is required to provoke envy among his artistic competitors and amazement among admirers. His status as a winner commenced in high school, where as a star quarterback he earned a football scholarship to Yale. As a pre-med student at this prestigious institution, he demonstrated that he was an athlete who actually deserved the intellectual credentials that would be bestowed upon him at graduation. But even before he graduated, this smart, handsome athlete became a star beyond the walls of academe. He made a rapid ascent in the fashion world and was soon modeling for J. Crew. It must also be noted that Barney's amorous affair with the celebrated Icelandic singer and movie star Bjork fulfilled another marker of success—capturing the love of a pop idol.

Since he was a student, Barney has been accumulating signifiers of success within the art world. He was tagged a frontrunner even before most people his age had entered the professional race. By the time he turned thirty, he had been catapulted into the firmament of art stars. He had already been honored with traveling shows and an appearance on the cover of *Artforum*. Since then, his works have been featured in such coveted settings as Documenta IX and two Whitney Biennials. He was awarded the Europa 2000 Prize, the Aperto '93 at the XLV Venice Biennale, and the 1996 Hugo Boss Award. His career has been the subject of a *New York Times Magazine* feature article. At age 34, he is the youngest artist to ever be offered a full-scale retrospective exhibition at the Guggenheim Museum in New York, scheduled to open in Feburary 2003. For the most part, he attracts accolades like: "The artist, Matthew Barney, is at 28 possibly the hottest young conceptual/performance artist/sculptor in the history of modern art and definitely the hottest at this moment."[1] Likewise, he has been dubbed "the most crucial artist of his generation."[2] He has also come to epitomize the dazzle of "cathedral capitalism,"[3] a term used to denote the financial boom of the 1990s that boosted the price tags on artworks and allowed artists to finance the free reign of their expensive and expansive imaginations.

Matthew Barney, *Cremaster 4* (1994), production photograph. ©1994 Matthew Barney. Courtesy of Barbara Gladstone Gallery. Photograph: Michael James O'Brien.

But there exist many under-reported facts that undermine this glittery tale. One anecdote reports that when Barney was invited to be a guest lecturer at the Whitney Museum Studies Program, the students who eagerly assembled in anticipation of their meeting with a charismatic art celebrity were surprised to discover that the unassuming man arranging slides in the corner of the classroom was the famous Matthew Barney. Writer Katy Siegel was also impressed that Barney did not behave like a self-aggrandizing exhibitionist. She describes him as "elaborately nice, despite the fact that he is much better looking than you, much more successful, a much better artist with a much more interesting life (inner as well as outer, apparently)."[4] Critic Thyrza Nichols Goodeve, who has conducted extensive interviews with Barney over the last decade, portrays him as "controlled, sweet, funny, unpretentious, very polite." She concludes, "What's shocking is how unaffected he continues to be by his fame. He still acts like he's just a kid with his friends making stuff and having fun. But he is also canny and confident beyond belief."[5]

Price has long been the dominant indicator of success in the mainstream art world. Auction houses and sales reports reveal who's hot and who's not. This measure of success is based on the concept of input, or how much money an artist receives for his or her efforts. But in the 1990s, cost began to stake a competing claim against price as an indicator of an artist's importance. Barney epitomizes this shift from input to output, or how much money the artist spends on producing an artwork. The ability to create work that requires extravagant expenditure for production is an irrefutable sign of clout. But, as Barney demonstrates, output can also refer to the magnitude of the artist's ambition, vision, and inspiration.

Barney's personality may be modest, but his art is spectacular. The $1.7 million spent to produce just one of his films is proof of his budget-defying imagination and ambition. Although this sum would be considered paltry for a Hollywood blockbuster, it is exorbitant in the context of the art world and when considered in terms of cost-per-viewer. Barney's films are not mass distributed. They are shown to small audiences in art museums, galleries, and art cinemas. *Cremaster 2* cost $1.7 million to make; it was a film that required importing enough salt to construct a twenty-foot-high bull ring in the middle of the flooded flats in Utah. The money was also spent to decorate the bull ring with four huge fiberglass beehives and to import the Cowboy Days Ladies Flag Posse from Wyoming to parade within it. Barney's budget permitted him to elevate the standards of the finished product, to shoot seventeen minutes of film per minute of finished film to Hollywood's standard twelve. Yet hefty budget requirements have not interfered with his productivity. *Cremaster 2* is one film in a recently completed series of five equally lavish extravaganzas. In an audacious move, Barney announced his intentions by titling the first of the series *Cremaster 4* in 1994. It was followed by *Cremaster 1* in 1996, *Cremaster 5 in 1997*, *Cremaster 2* in 1999, and *Cremaster 3* in 2002. Through this strategy, Barney proclaimed the epic proportions of his artistic ambition and the comparable scale of his imagination before a single scene was ever shot.

Boundary-defying aspirations were already in evidence in Barney's first exhibition. His might, muscle, and vigor were the focus of his inaugural show in 1991 at the Barbara Gladstone Gallery in Manhattan. The space in which the show was presented was intended for exhibitions, but Barney changed the room's function. Instead of exhibiting evidence of the prowess he had already achieved, he used the exhibition opportunity to acquire more. Barney filled the gallery with weight-room paraphernalia: dumbbells, curl bars, decline benches, floor mats, protective pads. In private, when the gallery was closed, he performed excruciating exercise routines upon them. Videotapes of his activities were later shown to gallery visitors on overhead monitors. These art workouts became artworks. In a series titled

Drawing Restraint (1989–1993), Barney linked the building of a physique with the creation of a drawing by making the act strenuous. He climbed ramps while straining at the end of tethers, pushed blocked sleds used in football training, and shimmied up an elevator shaft, all forms of training that developed his capability to accomplish superhuman exploits through self-imposed resistance. In *Milehigh Threshold Flight with Anal Sadistic Warrior* (1991), Barney accomplished the impossible by clambering up gallery walls and across the ceiling aided only by a full-body harness and titanium ice screws. There was no opportunity to deceive the audience because, except for the harness, Barney was naked. Strength building enabled him to defy gravity and his human flaws. He aspires to the perfected status of a post-human.

Barney fixated on maximizing the energy production of his metabolism. His experience as a pre-med student and his athletic training taught him that maintaining peak physical conditioning depends on continually raising the level of difficulty of the workout—increasing the weight, lengthening the routines, increasing the speed. These early experiences implanted the no-pain-no-gain ethic and established a routine of continually increasing resistance. Barney applied this routine to all categories of human improvement, including his artistic practice. He transferred his physical fixations into art performances and expanded their meaning through the use of material substances that conveyed energy construction and strength-building. His athletic apparatuses, for example, were constructed out of high-energy biochemical substances. The weights were cast in sucrose. The exercise machines were coated with basic carbohydrates like glucose. The dumbbell was cast in tapioca. Because body implants and other surgical procedures can offer additional body enhancement, such materials as self-lubricating plastic, Teflon, titanium, stainless steel, and thermal gel packs also found their way into Barney's sculptures. They were accompanied by such surgical instruments as speculums, hemorrhoid distracters, and clamps used to retract the chest in open-heart surgery. All these athletic and medical interventions were employed to convey the means for body enhancement. They served as symbols for all forms of human enhancement.

In these early works, Barney established a measure of artistic success that depended upon maximizing the scale, quality, and quantity of the artistic activity he generated, and not the wealth, fame, and honor that he received. For Barney, art is a metabolic aid for releasing superhuman energy. The metaphor he uses to describe his goal is a "Hubris Pill". The word "hubris" denotes exaggerated pride or confidence. Barney removed the arrogant implications from the word by demonstrating that though his extraordinary successes might be beyond the realm of normalcy, they were not beyond the realm of possibility. From the beginning, Barney has earned his exalted stature as an artist through hard work. He describes the feeling he gets when he overcomes obstacles, reaches new plateaus of accomplishment, exceeds former capabilities. It feels like he has swallowed a hubris pill and is reveling in self-confidence. Barney describes it as "quivering on the threshold between hubris and some kind of real but repressed omnipotence."[6]

The task of honing a body into a machine capable of storing and expending prodigious amounts of energy is all consuming and self-absorbing. For Barney, it seems to prohibit him from seeking attention, an activity that would divert his concentration and deplete his precious store of energy. His staged athletic activities have never resembled performances. He seems oblivious of the camera and the eventual scrutiny of his actions by an audience, an awareness that could only siphon off his energy and thwart his attempts to achieve omnipotence. This might be why Barney is perceived as aloof, even by his admirers. Thyrza Nichols Goodeve notes that Barney "gives nothing of himself—guarded or just plain incapable of relating to people via a self the way the rest of us do."[7] The greatness to which he aspires supercedes the need for praise or reinforcement. Total retention of bodily energies also demands withdrawal from sexual relationships, a recurring theme in Barney's work. In the *Drawing Restraint* series, prosthetics restructured his body by either sealing his orifices or hiding his genitalia. Instead of depleting his sexual energies, he is thus able to retain and recirculate them. Interpersonal disconnection is made further manifest in the solo nature of Barney's athletic exploits. They occur without competitors. Barney's self-directed exercises are designed to achieve a hypertrophy of his own body. (Hypertrophy is the excessive development of a muscle or other organ.) Barney explains, "I wore a restraining device to make drawings. They were linked to my interest in how a muscle can grow under the resistance of a weight."[8] For Barney, the body and art are fields of parallel operations. Both are capable of being modified and redesigned. Both can be made to surpass previous limits. Hypertrophy through exertion can be expressed as a corporeal or aesthetic change. In one instance this exertion is physical and destroys existing muscle. In the other it is mental and destroys existing art conventions. The old muscle is replaced with superior tissue. The old artistic order is replaced with superior artistic accomplishment.

Barney's five films conjure an extravagant universe that is as distant from the otherworldly features of cyberspace as it is from the banal imperfections of Earth. Both of these familiar zones of experience are too ordinary. As the high priest of high-powered imagery, Barney makes films that have no truck with suburban standards. Instead, his architectural visions are inspired by the baroque splendor of a Budapest opera house, the extraordinary art deco ornamentation of the Chrysler building, and the grandeur of the World's Columbian Exposition of 1893. The landscapes his imagination invokes are always as grand as the salt flats in Utah and as emerald green as the terrain on the Isle of Man. Cars that are admitted into his world must be limos, customized Mustangs, or expensive motorcycles. Humans are overhauled into godly perfection from which sprout such supernatural appendages as horns, and from whom are removed such essential body parts as genitalia. Jeans and sneakers are banished in place of sumptuous gowns, futuristic suits, and Prada shoes. The assignments actors receive demand death-defying stunts like climbing up the proscenium of an opera house, digging through the ocean floor, and scaling the elevator shaft of a skyscraper.

Barney's stockpile of artistic devices is barely depleted by such sensational imagery. These optical and somatic wonders are applied to an array of themes in which the familiar becomes the springboard into fantastic realms. Picnics are attended by red-wigged fairies whose hairless bodies more closely resemble Arnold Schwarzenegger's than Tinker Bell's. Motorcycle races are run by leather-clad cyclists whose second skins disgorge large globular forms that resemble sets of auxiliary testicles; these self-propelled appendages ooze out of the racers' bodysuits and crawl along their torsos, legs, and backs. A drum solo becomes a mesmerizing event because it is accompanied by the drone of twenty thousand live bees. Barney has also imagined, and then staged, eighty smiling Idaho cheerleaders wearing bizarre costumes and waltzing on Astroturf beneath the hovering form of a blond-wigged deity in a huge blimp. The bigger-than-life historical characters that appear in his *Cremaster* films contribute their amazing life stories to Barney's mega vision. One example is Gary Gilmore, the famed double murderer who created a media sensation when he demanded to be executed. As a Mormon, Gilmore believed in "blood atonement." His execution by firing squad, he believed, would grant him eternal penance, assuring him immortality, a status that coincides with Barney's desire to transcend human limits, including mortality. He practiced for this role when he played the character of Gilmore in *Cremaster 2*.

In producing the *Cremaster* films, Barney made extravagant demands on his intelligence, his emotions, his obsessions, and his desires. They were subjected to the same strenuous weights he had earlier imposed upon his body. Each film exceeded its predecessor in splendor and complexity. This kept his audiences scurrying. The release of each film in the series produced a flurry of excitement and a new round of analysis. Critics, viewers, and curators attempted to link his themes backward to previously released films and forward to those they eagerly anticipated. Each release enriched the appreciation of the material that preceded it. Audience members became engaged in a strenuous mental workout. It was not until the series was complete, in 2002, that the arching chronicle emerged and all five films cohered. When placed in their chronological sequence, instead of in the order in which they were produced, the location of each film revealed a consistent, eastward pilgrimage. *Cremaster 1* is set in Idaho, where Barney spent his youth. The journey then proceeds to the Rocky Mountains, to New York, then on to the Isle of Man in the Irish Sea, concluding in *Cremaster 5* in Budapest.

Budapest is the birthplace of Harry Houdini, the legendary escape artist who contrived ever more difficult challenges, ever more death-defying feats. Houdini appears in the culminating *Cremaster 5* and serves as another connective tissue between the films. Barney perpetuates Houdini's legacy by summoning all the parts of the mind that are capable of being expanded—intellect, intuition, imagination, memory. With Houdini's help, Barney's *Cremaster* series becomes an allegory of the creative process. "I've begun to see the five parts … in terms of having an idea in 1, rejecting it in 2, experiencing a kind of narcissistic interlude in 3, panicking in 4, and resolving the idea in 5, which ultimately kills the thing."[9] Why is it killed? Barney explains, "After I understand something completely, I'm not interested in it anymore."[10] As long as the films present obstacles, they satisfy Barney's need for challenge. The same might be true for the audience. As long as the films remain obscure, they provide resistance to understanding. Though Barney uses spectacle to captivate the audience, spectacle produces a gasp and is easily forgotten; the viewers' immersion in Barney's work is prolonged by mental resistance. His films, photographs, and sculptures comprise a complex language of signs and symbols and references. They are workouts for the brain.

Barney's focus is on producing output, not acquiring input. Opportunities for extravagance are channeled away from himself and into the turbulent grandiloquence of his artworks. If artistic stature is measured according to the elegance of the artist's studio environment, then the warehouse where Barney and his crew work, a place "as glamorous as a sweatshop,"[11] proves the point. Yet the film sets constructed within these humble walls are extravagant. A description of one set explains the values of the filmmaker. "It is a recreation of the Chrysler Building's Cloud Club…. The walls are punctured by narrow triangular metal window frames. The carpets are pale green with inlaid cream-colored art deco patterned carpet panels. On either side of the room are art deco tables and chairs, and in the center of the room is the most unusual bar you've ever seen. The back of its sides is made of dark wood, attached to which are wood stools adorned with long sharp spears thrusting downward. Thin handcrafted inlaid wood panels flank the sides of the bar, and the back wall is covered with racks of empty glasses. The skin from the dark wood back of the bar peels up around a curved head made of two thirty-gallon drums of Freon-chilled Vaseline."[12] This elaborate construction originated as a napkin rendering by Barney. It was engineered and constructed by his crew.

On the set and in the studio, Barney claims exclusive rights of determination. This is significant because he relies on choreographers, animators, wardrobe fabricators, hair stylists, makeup designers, composers, editors, photographers, administrators, and fabricators. This extensive behind-the-scenes cast carries out his instructions. Few explanations are provided. Assignments are often fulfilled without knowledge of their role in Barney's invented universe,[13] for example, that the color green represents a hybrid sex because it is the mixture of blue, which Barney associates with males, and yellow, which represents females. Penetrations through space and the sealing of passages refer to bodily orifices, particularly those located in the pelvic region. Asexuality is associated with the wondrous event that takes place seven weeks after conception, the precise juncture at which the sex of the fetus is determined. This event holds particular fascination for Barney because it marks the moment when either outcome is possible. At this point in a fetus's development, the female reproductive organs form and move upward and the male reproductive organs form and move downward. Throughout the *Cremaster* films, movements in the upward direction refer to the ascended anatomy of females, while movements downward correspond to the descended anatomy of males. Upward and downward movement is also a component of the series title, the cremaster being the muscle in the male genitals that retracts the testicles in response to cold and fear. Thus, Barney camouflages his complex gendered scenarios with such elements as colors, patterns, numbers, heights, depths, textures, moistures, and temperatures. All carry thematic significance, but no image lingers long enough for contemplation. A mere eight seconds is the average length of time between cuts in some of his films. Decoding demands multiple viewings. Respected art critic Jerry Saltz reports that he has seen *Cremaster* 4 seventy-five times and that he discovers new meaning with each viewing.[14]

It is understandable that Barney is resented as well as praised—such expense, such effort placed in the service of one man's idiosyncrasies. Barney's works invite neither individualized responses nor physical participation. Initially they astound. Then they demand the prolonged process of deciphering the artist's meanings. Many question how he has financed his extravaganzas. In fact, Barney has devised a means to realize his ambitions without compromising his integrity. Funds to support his films are usually generated from gallery exhibitions and sales of the props from his movies. The marketing of these props has provoked the indignation of some critics who disdainfully compare the practice to the sales of memorabilia in Planet Hollywood theme park-like restaurants and to the commercial paraphernalia that surrounds Hollywood blockbusters. One such critic goes so far as to contest the status of Barney's work, stating, "It is not art. It is the expensive mold that produces and legitimizes brand-name tchotchkes. By having his gallery sell the props from his movies as 'artworks,' Barney gets to have relics which are legitimized by their pedigree. They're part of art historical moments. They are what is left over from those 'important' *Cremaster* movies, er, films, er, artworks … that just happened to have been displayed in movie theaters that sell popcorn and six-dollar Diet Cokes…. Anyone in Hollywood will tell you what it really is: Barney's 'artworks' are the Happy Meal movie tie-in. All collectors really end up with is a boring movie and Matthew Barney's rubble."[15]

Few collectors listen to such protestations. To many, Barney's cinematic relics carry the allure of fine art objects. In addition to these expensive sculptures, books with stills from each of his *Cremaster* films are sold to the mass public in museum shops and bookstores, and framed drawings and photographs are available to collectors with modest means. Barney has even contrived a means to sell films, an artistic medium not normally coveted as a collectible. Packaging them in elaborate cases, Barney markets them as limited edition laserdiscs/sculptures. Finally, his elaborate installations appeal to museums with large acquisitions budgets and large storage facilities. In an astute business move, he provides museums with exclusive deals for their gift shops in exchange for a time-share in his installations.

Peak value is maintained because Barney understands desire. Limited editions of his art objects, limited viewings of his films, and limited presentations of his installations prevent saturation of both the audience's capacity for engagement and the market's viability. The other limited commodity is Barney himself. Even if he is a star, he avoids behaving like a celebrity. Barney says, "Art needs to be defended. It's fragile. If a work is shown too many times, something gets stolen from it. And it is the same with an artist. So I try to protect myself and my work."[16] Hardly the words one might expect from an artist known for full throttle, high-gear art and a career already catapulted into the stratosphere. Barney's biography may resemble an ideal promoted by the media, pandered to by advertisers, and desired by the masses, but his experience is a different matter.

There are less glamorous and less reported components of his amazing narrative. Contrary to popular conception, Barney earned his way to fame and wealth. He grew up in Idaho with his father who was neither a Wall Street wizard, a media mogul, nor a CEO. When Matthew was young, Barney senior traded in his curbside sandwich truck for a cafeteria business. Then he worked for the catering service at Boise State University. It is also important to note that necessity drove Barney to become a model. He needed to earn tuition money once his football scholarship was discontinued. He has declined opportunities to model since he became a celebrated artist. He has never been attracted to the glamour of the fashion world. Barney enjoys redneck bars more than art openings. He defines success simply as the ability to make his work.

Thus, this essay returns to its original thesis—that concern for production not consumption, output not input, cost not price constitutes Barney's artistic definition of success. Here, as in his own works of art, the artist has the final word: "I used to think about a three-phase diagram: Situation, Condition, Production. Situation was a zone of pure drive, useless desire that needed direction, needed to be passed through a visceral disciplinary funnel, which was the second zone—condition. The third zone, production, was a kind of anal/oral production of form. It gets more interesting if production is bypassed: at that point the head goes into the ass, and the cycle flickers between situation and condition, between discipline and desire. If it goes back and forth enough times something that's really elusive can slip out—a form that has form, but isn't overdetermined."[17]

1. Vicki Woods, "Matthew Barney, Personality Parade", *Vogue*, January 1996, 160.

2. Michael Kimmelman, "The Importance of Matthew Barney," *The New York Times Magazine*, 10 October 1999, 65.

3. See Thomas Frank, *One Market Under God: Extreme Capitalism, Market Populism, and the End of Economic Democracy* (New York: Doubleday, 2000).

4. Katy Siegel, "Nurture Boy," *Artforum*, Summer 1999, 33.

5. ibid.

6. Thyrza Nichols Goodeve, "Travels in Hypertrophia," *Artforum*, May 1995, 68–69.

7. Goodeve, letter to author, n.d.

8. Goodeve, "Travels in Hypertrophia," 68.

9. Kimmelman, 69.

10. ibid., 67.

11. ibid., 68.

12. David Shapiro, "Coming Soon to the Guggenheim: A Visit to the Set of Matthew Barney's *Cremaster 3*," <http://wwwcolumbia.edu/cu/museo/barney/index.html>.

13. Kimmelman, 67.

14. Jerry Saltz, ed., *Matthew Barney Tony Oursler Jeff Wall* (Munich: Sammlung Goetz, 1996), 18.

15. Matt Gleason, "Matthew Barney's Rubble," <http://www.coagula.com/barney.html>.

16. Kimmelman, 67.

17. Goodeve, "Travels in Hypertrophia," 117.

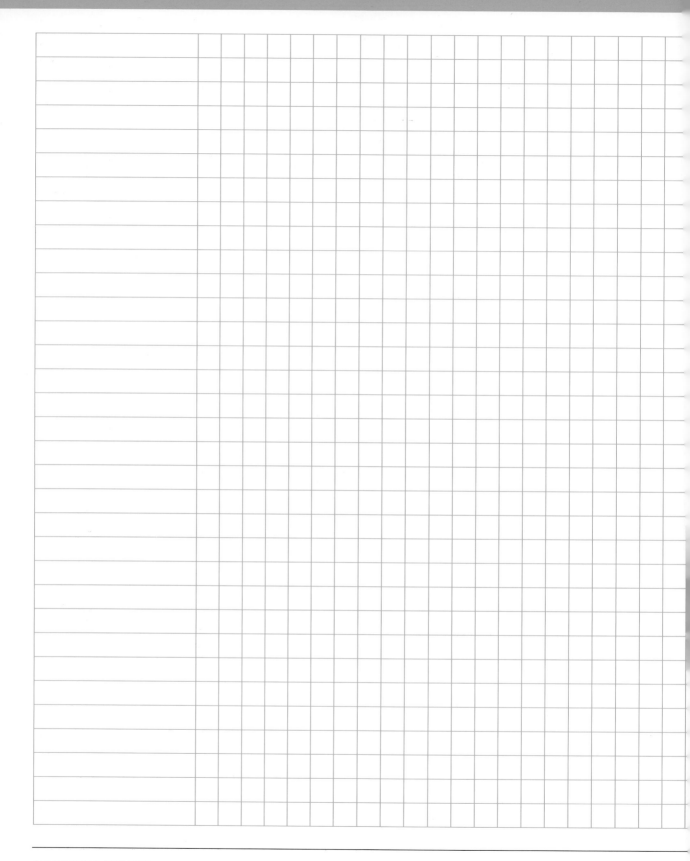

ETHAN ACRES

Acres, Ethan. *The Sermons of Reverend Ethan Acres*. Santa Monica, California: Art Issues Press and Smart Art Press, 2001.

———. "The Straight or Crooked Way: A Sermon by the Reverend Ethan Acres." *Art Issues*, January–February 1999.

———. "Virtual Heaven, A Sermon by the Reverend Ethan Acres." *Art Issues*, March–April 2001.

Drohojowska Philip, Hunter. "A Preacher's Art of Spreading the Word." *Los Angeles Times*, 8 June 1997.

Harvey, Doug. "Art for God's Sake: The Gospel according to Reverend Ethan Acres." *LA Weekly*, 28 May 1999.

Lloyd, Ann Wilson. "In a New Millennium, Religion Shows Its Face" *The New York Times*, 23 January, 2001.

McCormick, Carlo. "Holy Roller, Reverend Ethan Acres" *Paper*, December, 1999.

Mitchell, Charles Dee. "Rev. Ethan Acres." *Art in America*, December 1998.

Pagel, David. "Art Reviews: An Unorthodox Blend of Faith and Kitsch." *Los Angeles Times*, 20 June 1997.

Tager, Alisa. "Report from Las Vegas: Art on the Strip" *Art in America*, February, no.2 1997.

CHINA ADAMS

Adams, China. *Zyzzyva* 10, no. 4 winter 1994: Front and back covers.

Adams, Victoria. "*Premonition Scrolls Review*." *Artweek*, February, 2002.

Cooper, Bernard. "Art: The Uses of the Ghoulish." *Los Angeles Magazine*, February 2001.

Haden-Guest, Anthony. *True Colors*. New York: Atlantic Monthly Press, 1996.

Harvey, Doug. "Yuck!" *LA Weekly*, 1 September 2000.

Jiminez, Carlos. "China Adams." *Carta* (Madrid), February 2002.

Koplos, Janet. "China Adams at Ace." *Art in America*, July 1996.

Roth, Charlene. "China Adams at Ace." *Artweek*, February 1996.

MATTHEW BARNEY

Barney, Matthew. *Matthew Barney: Cremaster 1*. Basel: Kunsthalle Wein, Museum für Gegenwartskunst, 1997.

———. *Matthew Barney: Cremaster 2*. Minneapolis: Walker Art Center, 1999.

———. *Matthew Barney: Cremaster 3*. New York: Solomon R. Guggenheim Foundation, 2002.

———. *Matthew Barney: Cremaster 4*. Paris: Fondation Cartier; New York: Barbara Gladstone Gallery. Presentation of the film *Cremaster 4* by Artangel, London, 1995.

———. Matthew Barney: *Cremaster 5*. Frankfurt: Portikus Frankfurt; New York: Barbara Gladstone Gallery. Presentation of the film *Cremaster 5* by Portikus Frankfurt, 1997.

Bonami, Francesco. "Matthew Barney: The Artist as a Young Athlete." *Flash Art*, no. 162 January–February 1992.

Bryson, Norman. "Matthew Barney's Gonadotrophic Cavalcade." *Parkett*, no. 45 December 1995.

Carlisle, Isabel. "*Cremaster 5*." *Tate*, summer 1998

Frankel, David. "Engine" *2wice* vol. 5 no.2 2002.

Kertess, Klaus. *Matthew Barney: Drawing Restraint 7*. Ostfildern, Germany: Edition Cantz, 1996.

Kimmelman, Michael. "The Importance of Matthew Barney." *New York Times*, 10 October 1999.

Nichols Goodeve, Thyrza. "Travels in Hypertrophia." *Artforum*, May 1995.

Oneray, Michel. "Mannerist Variations on Matthew Barney." *Parkett*, no. 45 1995.

Pedrosa, Adriano. "Matthew Barney." *Poliester* 5, no. 17 winter 1997.

Poels, Jan-Willem "Master, Let Me Enter" *Frame Magazine*, November-December 2001.

Ritchie, Matthew. "Barney's *Cremaster 5*." *Flash Art*, no. 198 January–February 1998.

Saltz, Jerry. "The Next Sex." *Art in America*, October 1996.

Smith Roberta. "From a Fantasy Film, Luxury Transformed." *New York Times*, 14 November 1997.

———. "Matthew Barney's Objects and Actions." *New York Times*, 25 October 1991.

Spector, Nancy with Neville Wakefield. *Matthew Barney: The Cremaster Cycle*. New York: Guggenheim Museum Publications, 2002.

Wakefield, Neville. "Matthew Barney's Fornication With the Fabric of Space." *Parkett*, no. 39 1994.

Woods, Vicki, "Matthew Barney's Personality Parade." *Vogue*, vol. 186 #1, January 1996.

VANESSA BEECROFT

Benezra, Neal., Olga .M. Viso, and Arthur C. Danto. *Regarding Beauty: A View of the Late Twentieth Century*. Washington, D.C.: Smithsonian Hirshhorn Museum, 1999.

Bonami, Francesco. and Giacinto Di Pietrantonio, eds. *Primia Linea: The New Italian Art*. Trevi: Trevi Flash Art Museum, no. 3 1994.

Bourriaud, Nicolas, ed. *Traffic*. Bordeaux: CAPC Musée d'Art Contemporain 1996.

Bryson, Norman., Pier Luigi Tazzi, and Keith Sexton Seward. "Classic Cruelty, Parades, US Navy Seals." *Parkett*, no. 56 1999.

Celant, Germano, ed. *BV 97: Future, Present, Past*. Venice: La Biennale di Venezia, XLVII Esposizione Internazionale d'Arte, 1997.

Di Pietrantonio, Giacinto. "Vanessa Beecroft, Ouverture." *Flash Art*, no. 183 1995.

Elliot, David and Pier Luigi Tazzi, eds. *Wounds: Between Democracy and Redemption in Contemporary Art*. Stockholm: Moderna Musee, 1998.

Ghez, Susanne, ed. *Persona: The Renaissance Society at the University of Chicago*. Basel, Switzerland: Kunsthalle Basel, 1996.

Grosenick, Uta. *Women Artists*. Cologne. Taschen, 2001.

Hickey, David. *VB 08-86-Vanessa Beecroft Performances*. Ostfildern, Germany: Edition Cantz, 2000.

The Saatchi Gallery. *I Am A Camera*. London: Booth-Clibborn Editions, 2001.

Kontova, Helena, and Giancarlo Politi. "Arte: Vanessa Beecroft." *Intervista*, no. 14 July–August 1998.

SUGGESTED READINGS

Leffingwell, Edward. "Vanessa Beecroft Aboard the USS Intrepid." *Art in America*, October 2000.

Musée d'Art Contemporain de Montreal. *Metamorphosis and Clones*. Montreal: Musée d'Art Contemporain de Montreal, 2001.

Pallister, Kay, ed. *Vanessa Beecroft: VB 43*. New York: Gagosian Gallery, 2000.

Rosenblum, Robert. "Vanessa Beecroft." *Artforum*, December 2000.

XU BING

Abe, Stanley K. "No Questions, No Answers: China and *A Book from the Sky*." *boundary 2 25*, no. 3 fall 1998.

Berger, Patricia. "Pun Intended: A Response to Stanley Abe, *Reading the Sky*." In *Cross-Cultural Readings of Chineseness*, ed. Wen-hsin Yeh. Berkeley: Institute of East Asian Studies, University of California, 2000.

Bing, Xu. "To Frighten Heaven and Earth and Make the Spirits Cry." In *The Library of Babel*. Tokyo: ICC – NTT Inter communication Center, 1998.

Boardman, Andrew. "Xu Bing and the Door to the Infinite." In *Interzones*. Copenhagen: Kunstforeningen Copenhagen and Uppsala, Sweden: Uppsala Konstmuseum, 1996.

———. "Xu Bing's Square Words and the Fragility of Language." *Around Us, Inside Us*. Stockholm: Continents Boras Konsmuseum, 1997.

Cayley, John. Description of the *Book from the Sky*. London: Hanshan Tang Books, 1997.

Doran, Valerie C. "Xu Bing: A Logos for the Genuine Experience." *Orientations* 32, no. 8 October 2001.

Erickson, Britta. "Process and Meaning in the Art of Xu Bing." In *Three Installations by Xu Bing*. Madison: Elvehjem Museum of Art, University of Wisconsin-Madison, 1991.

———. *Words Without Meaning, Meaning Without Words: The Art of Xu Bing*. Seattle: University of Washington Press, 2001.

Gao, Minglu. "Meaninglessness and Confrontation in Xu Bing's Art." In *Fragmented Memory: Chinese Artists in Exile*. Columbus: Wexner Center for the Visual Arts, 1993.

Keough, Jeffrey. *Xu Bing: Language Lost*. Boston: Massachusetts College of Art, 1995.

Reuter, Laurel. "Into the Dark Sings the Nightingale: The Work of Xu Bing." In *Xu Bing Series Exhibition 1*. Grand Forks: North Dakota Museum of Art, 1992.

Weintraub, Linda. "Allegorical Persona." In *Animal.Anima.Animus.*, edited by Marketta Seppala, Jan-Pekka Vanhala, Linda Weintraub. Pori, Finland: Pori Art Museum, 1998.

Wu, Hung. "Counter Monument." In *Transience: Chinese Experimental Art at the End of the 20th Century*. Chicago: The Smart Gallery and the University of Chicago, 1999.

THOMAS JOSHUA COOPER

Collins, Tom. "Homage to Photographers Past: Thomas Joshua Cooper's Work Gives New Perspective to Views of the Rio Grande," *Venue North*. 12 January, 2001.

Cooper, Thomas Joshua. *Between Dark and Dark*. Edinburgh: Graeme Murray, 1985.

———. *Dreaming the Gokstadt*. Edinburgh: Graeme Murray, 1988.

———. *A Handful of Stones*. Norfolk: Coracle Press, Docking, 1994.

———. *Thomas Joshua Cooper: at the Serpentine*. Edinburgh: Graeme Murray, 1984.

Daniel-McElroy, Susan. *Thomas Joshua Cooper: To the Limit of the Visible*. Exhibition brochure. St. Ives, U.K.: Tate St. Ives, 2001.

Ferguson, Bruce, ed. *Longing and Belonging – From Faraway Nearby – Site Santa Fe*. Sante Fe, Site Santa Fe, 1995.

Gale, Iain. "Edge of Darkness." *Scotland on Sunday*, 30 November 1997.

Leffingwell, Edward. "Thomas Joshua Cooper at Sean Kelly." *Art in America*, October 1999.

Molder, Jorge, Ian Jeffrey, Peter Bunnell. *Simply Counting Waves*, Lisbon, Gulbenkian Foundation. Centre of Modern Art. 1995.

Mundt, Frank. "At the Edge of the World." *Katalog* 11, no. 3 fall 1999.

Wettendorff, Henning S. "Art is My Auto Pilot." *Katalog* 11, no. 3 fall 1999.

Yablonsky, Linda. "Smart Appreciation." *Time Out New York*. 4-11 November 1999.

BETSY DAMON

Bush Foundation. "Living Water: Combining Art & Science to Rejuvenate Communities and Restore Waterways." *Bush Foundation News*, autumn 2000.

Damon, Betsy. "Living Water Garden." *Hieronimusing* 1, no. 11 6 July 2001.

———. "The Living Water Garden of Chengdu, China." *Earthlight*, fall 2001.

Mavor, Anne H. "China's Living Water Garden." *YES! A Journal of Positive Futures*, winter 1999/2000.

Meyer, Mike. "A River Runs Through It: Chengdu's Living Water Garden." *Keepers of the Waters*. <http://www.keepersofthewaters.org>.

HUBERT DUPRAT

Assenmaker, Michel. "Hubert Duprat." *Forum*, no. 17, March-April 1993.

———. *Hubert Duprat*. Angoulême, France. FRAC Poitou-Charentes, 1992

Besson, Christian, *reConnaitre: Hubert Duprat Theatrum*. Paris: Musée departemental de Digne and Réunion des musées, 2002.

——— with Hubert Duprat. "Wonderful Caddis-Worm." *Leonardo* 31, no. 3 June 1998.

Fougere, Isabelle. "Hubert Duprat Et Les Trichopteres." *Recherches es Poietiques*, Valenciennes, Presses Universitaires de Valenciennes. Winter-Spring 1999-2000.

Frechuret, Maurice, Stephen Bann, Roland Recht. *Hubert Duprat* Musée Picasso, Mamco, and FRAC Limousin. Antibes: Musée Picasso; Genève: Mamco; and Limoges: FRAC Limousin, 1998.

Gourmelon, Mo. "Concrete Excess: The Art of Hubert Duprat", *Arts Magazine*, January 1992.

Koniger, Maribel, Francoise Chaloin, Ramon Tio Bellido, *Hubert Duprat*. Miraflores-Lima: Sale Arte
    Contemporaneo Luis Miro Quesada Garland, 2001.

Königer, Maribel. "Camera Obscura, Salon Bleu, Chambre Claire, Étui Doré." *Kunstforum*, no. 151 summer 2000.
    First published in El Guia, no. 6-7 February 1995.

Mousseigne, Alain, Ramon Tio Bellido. *Hubert Duprat*. Toulouse: Musée d'Art Moderne, 1985.

Paul, Frederic. "Hubert Duprat: La Bibliotheque de l'Instituteux." *Les Cahiers du Musée Nationale d'Arte Moderne
    Centre Georges Pompidou*, no. 72 summer 2000.

Rigou, Florence. "Hubert Duprat: Un Fantasme de Totalité." *Clinic* 19, no. 19, 1998.

NAN GOLDIN

Bracewell, Michael. "Landmarks in the Ascent of Nan." *The Independent*, 14 November 1999.

The Corcoran Gallery of Art and The National Hospice Foundation. *Hospice: A Photographic Inquiry*. Washington,
    D.C.: The Corcoran Gallery of Art; The National Hospice Foundation, 1996.

Costa, Guido. *Nan Goldin (Photographer)*. London: Phaidon Press, 2001.

Danto, Arthur C. "Nan Goldin's World." *The Nation*, 2 December 1996.

Garratt, Sheryl. "The Dark Room." *Life: The Observer Magazine*, 6 January 2002.

Goldin, Nan. *The Ballad of Sexual Dependency*. New York: Aperture, 1986.

———. *Couples and Loneliness*. Tokyo: Korinsha Press, 1998.

———. *I'll Be Your Mirror*. New York: Whitney Museum of American Art; Scalo, 1996.

———. *Nan Goldin: The Other Side* 1972-1992. Zurich: Scalo Verlag, 2000.

———. *Devil's Playground*. London: Phaidon Press, 2002.

———. *Nan Goldin*. Kempen, Dusseldorf, London, New York, Paris: Te Neues Publishing Group, 1999

——— with David Armstrong. *A Double Life*. New York: Scalo, 1994.

——— with Guido Costa. *Ten Years After*. New York: Scalo, 1998.

——— with Nobuyoshi Araki. *Tokyo Love*. Tokyo: Hon-Hon-Do, 1994.

——— with poems by Joachim Sartoruis. *Vakat*. Cologne: Walter König, 1993.

——— with text by Klaus Kertess. *Desire by Numbers*. San Francisco: Artspace, 1994.

Hughes, Robert J. "Goldin Years." *Wall Street Journal*, 12 May 2000.

Schjeldahl, Peter. "A Fine Rawness." *The New Yorker*, 16 November 1998.

GREGORY GREEN

Baring, Louise. "Mr. Cool." *British Vogue*, May 1996.

Brown, David, Robert Merril, ed. *Violent Persuasions: The Politics and Imagery of Terrorism*. Seattle: Bay Press, 1993.

Coulter, Alex. "Bombs for Sale." *P.O.V.*, September 1996.

Deitch, Jeffrey. *Irrational Concepts, Young Americans Catalogue*. January–March 1996.

Green, Gregory. "Gregory Green." *Documents* 4/5 spring 1994.

———. "Gregory Green Auto Interview." *Transcript: A Journal of Visual Culture* 3, no. 1 (fall 1997).

———, ed. *Manual !!: Gregory Green*. New York, Max Protetch and Feigen Incorporated, 1988.

Johnson, Ken. "Bombs 'R' Us." *Art in America*, July 1996.

Kuspit, Donald and Laurence A. Rickels. "Act Out Turn Off, Act Out Turn On." *Artforum*, April 1994.

Richard, Frances. "Art at the Edge of the Law." *Artforum*, October 2001.

Valdez, Sarah. "Outlaws in Art Land." *Art in America*, November 2001.

Weil, Benjamin. "After Terrorism." *Purple Prose*, fall 1994.

Zaya, Octavio. "From Terror to Non-Participation: A Conversation Between Gregory Green and Zaya." *Atlantico*,
    no. 14 fall 1996.

SCOTT GRIEGER

Cherix, Christophe, Lionel Bouler. "True, Older Generations: Scott Grieger Impersonations" *Documents Sur L'art*,
    #9, Summer 1996.

Drohojowska-Philip, Hunter. "This Time the Joke is On Us." *Los Angeles Times*, Sunday Calendar, 1 February 1998.

Grieger, Scott. *Impersonations*. Published by the artist, 1971.

———. *Mainstream Art*. Published by the artist, 1974.

Livingston, Jane. "Three Reconnoitered Artists." *Art in America*, May–June 1971.

Rubin, David S. *It's Only Rock 'n Roll*. Munich and New York: Prestel, 1995.

Walker, Perry. "Bengston, Grieger, Goode." *Art in America*, March–April 1973.

WENDA GU

Gu, Wenda. "Confucius Diary: A World-Wide Touring Art Performance." Wenda Gu Studio, May 1998.

Gustafson, Paula. "New China 1989-94/Here Not There." *The Georgia Straight*. Vancouver, April 20, 1995.

Heartney, Eleanor. *Wenda Gu: The Enigma of Blood (1988-1995)* Exhibition catalogue. New York: In-Khan Gallery, 1996.

Jingzhong, Fan. "Silence and Transcendence." *Meishu 7 (Fine Arts)*. Peking, July 1986.

Kee, Joan. "An Interview with Gu Wenda." *Asia Society: New Chinese Art*, July 1998.

Kember, Pamela. "Hairlooms." *Asian Art News*, September-October 1997.

Levin, Kim. "Splitting Hairs: Wenda Gu's Primal Projects and Material Misunderstandings," in *Wenda Gu: Dio e i Suoi
    Figli/God and Children: Italian Division of United Nations, 1993-2000*. Milan: Enrico Gariboldi/Arte Contemporanea, 1994.

SUGGESTED READINGS

Leung, Simon and Janet Kaplan. "Pseudo-Languages: A Conversation with Wenda Gu, Xu Bing, and Jonathan Hay." *Art Journal*, fall 1999.

Pelsers, Lisette. "Heart of Darkness." *Kunst and Museum Journal*. Netherlands 1, 1995.

Puy, Inma G. "Gu Wenda." In *Centre d'Art Santa Monica Catalogue*. Barcelona: Centre d'Art Santa Monica, 1995.

JAN HARRISON

Kolpan, Steven. "Beast of Eden." *Woodstock Times*, 25 May 1992.

Lauter, Estella. "Women as Mythmakers Revisited." *Quadrant, The Journal of Contemporary Jungian Thought* 23, no. 1 1990.

Pollak, Ann. "Myths for our Time." *Dialogue*, May 1989.

Schwindler, Gary J. "A Perilous Eden: Pastel Drawings by Jan Harrison." *Dialogue*, September 1988.

Weintraub, Linda. "Genus Fusion." In *Arcana Mundi: Jan Harrison, Selected Works, 1979-2000*. New York: Station Hill/Barrytown, Ltd, 2001.

KIM JONES

Blessing, Jennifer. "Acting Out: Learning from Los Angeles." *Parkett*, no. 53 1998.

Capasso, Angelo. *A.A. L'arte per l'arte*. Rome 2002 .

Centre Georges Pompidou. *Face `a l'Histoire, 1933-1996*. Paris: Centre Georges Pompidou; Flammarion, 1997.

Festa, Angelika. "Mudman in New York." *The Drama Review*, winter 1987.

Jones, Kim. *Rat Piece*. Published by the artist, 1990.

———. "Calendar (Portfolio)." *Grand Street 50* (fall 1994).

———. (Portfolio). *Columbia, A Journal of Literature and Art*, no. 33 (winter 2000).

———. "Kim Jones." In *Unwinding the Vietnam War: From War Into Peace* edited by Reese Williams. Seattle: Real Comet Press, 1987.

Loeffler, Carl E. and Darlene Tong, eds. *Performance Anthology: Source Book of California Performance Art*. San Francisco: Last Gasp Press and Contemporary Arts Press, 1989.

McEvilley, Thomas. *Art and Otherness: Crisis in Cultural Identity*. Kingston, New York: Documentext McPherson & Company, 1992.

Montano, Linda, *Performance Artists Talking in the Eighties*. University of California Press, 2000.

Parfrey, Adam, ed. *Apocalypse Culture*. New York: Amok Press, 1987.

Schimmel, Paul. *Out of Actions: Between Performance and the Object, 1949-1979*. Los Angeles: The Museum of Contemporary Art; London: Thames & Hudson, 1998.

Storr, Robert. *Mapping*. New York: Museum of Modern Art, 1994.

Varnedoe, Kirk, Paola Antonelli, and Joshua Siegel, eds. *Modern Contemporary Art at MoMA Since 1980*. New York: Museum of Modern Art, 2001.

Williams, Reese, ed. *Unwinding the Vietnam War*, the Real Comet Press, 1987.

Zweig, Janet, Nancy Princenthal, ed. *Chain 7: Memoir/Anti-Memoir*. Honolulu, New York, and Philadelphia: Chain, 2000.

ISAAC JULIEN

Corris, Michael. "Heavenly Bodies in Motion: Isaac Julien's Queer Trilogy." *artext*, no. 63 1998.

Cruz, Amanda, et al. *The Film Art of Isaac Julien*. Annandale-on-Hudson, New York: Center for Curatorial Studies, Bard College, 2001.

Enwezor, Okwui. "Towards a Critical Cinema: The Films of Isaac Julien." In *Isaac Julien*. Exhibition brochure. Kansas City: Grand Arts, 2000.

Fusco, Coco. "Sankofa & Black Audio Film Collective." In *Discourses: Conversations in Postmodern Art and Culture*, edited by R. Furguson, et al. Cambridge, Massachusetts: MIT Press; New York: New Museum of Contemporary Art, 1990.

———. "Visualizing Theory: An Interview with Isaac Julien." *NKA: Journal of Contemporary African Art* 6–7 summer-fall 1997.

Gilroy, Paul. "Climbing the Racial Mountain: A Conversation with Isaac Julien." In *Small Acts: Thoughts on the Politics of Black Cultures*. New York: Serpents Tail, 1993.

Grundmann, Roy. "Black Nationhood and the Rest in the West: An Interview with Isaac Julien." *Cineaste* 21, no. 1–2 1995.

hooks, bell. "Thinking Through Class: Paying Attention to *The Attendant*." In *Reel to Real: Race, Sex, and Class at the Movies*. New York: Routledge, 1996.

Julien, Isaac. "Black British Cinema—Diaspora Cinema." In *New Histories*, edited by Milena Kalinovska, et al. Boston: Institute of Contemporary Art, 1996.

———. "Burning Rubber's Perfume." In *Remote Control*, edited by June Givanni. London: British Film Institute, 1995.

——— with Colin Maccabe. *Diary of a Young Soul Rebel*. Bloomington: Indiana University Press, 1991.

Julien, Isaac and Kobena Mercer. "True Confessions: A Discourse on Images of Black Male Sexuality." In *Male Order: Unwrapping Masculinity*, edited by Chapman, Rowena & Jonathan Rutherford. London: Lawrence & Wishart, 1988.

Mercer, Kobena "Busy in the Ruins of a Wretched Phantasia." In *Mirage: Enigmas of Race, Difference and Desire*. London: inIVA, 1995.

——— with Chris Darke. *Isaac Julien*. United Kingdom: Ellipsis London, 2002.

Stam, Robert. "Permutations of the Fanonian Gaze: Isaac Julien's *Black Skin, White Mask*." *Black Renaissance/Renaissance Noire* 1, no. 2 summer–fall 1997.

WILLIAM KENTRIDGE

Benezra, Neal, Staci Boris, Dan Cameron, Lynne Cooke, and Ari Sitas. *William Kentridge*. Chicago: Museum of Contemporary Art; New York: New Museum of Contemporary Art and Harry N. Abrams, Inc., 2001.

Christov-Bakargiev, Carolyn. *William Kentridge*. Brussels: Palais des Beaux-Arts de Bruxelles, 1998.

———, Dan Cameron, and J.M. Coetzee. *William Kentridge*. London: Phaidon Press, 1999.

Doepel, Rory. *Ubu ±101: William Kentridge, Robert Hodgins, Deborah Bell*. Grahamstown, South Africa: Observatory Museum, Standard Bank National Festival of the Arts, 1997.

Enwezor, Okwui. "Truth and Responsibility: A Conversation with William Kentridge." *Parkett*, no. 54 1998-1999.

Godby, Michael. "William Kentridge: Four Animated Films." In *William Kentridge: Drawings for Projection*. Johannesburg: Goodman Gallery, 1992.

———. "William Kentridge's History of the Main Complaint: Narrative, Memory, Truth." In *Negotiating the Past: The Making of Memory in South Africa*, edited by Sarah Nuttal and Carli Coetzee. Cape Town: Oxford University Press, 1998.

———, Robert Hodgins, William Kentridge, and Deborah Bell. *Hogarth in Johannesburg*. Johannesburg: Witwatersrand University Press, 1990.

Kentridge, William with Hugh M. Davies. *Weighing...and Wanting*. New York: Distributed Art Publishers, 2001.

Krauss, Rosalind. "The Rock: William Kentridge's Drawings for Projection." *October*, no. 92 spring 2000.

Ollman, Leah. "William Kentridge: Ghosts and Erasures." *Art in America*, January 1999.

Williamson, Sue and Ashraf Jamal. *Art in South Africa: The Future Present*. Cape Town and Johannesburg: David Philip, 1996.

THOMAS KINKADE

Baker, Kenneth. "Thomas Kinkade: A Case Study in Kitsch." *San Francisco Chronicle*, 4 February 2001.

Balmer, Randall. "The Kinkade Crusade." *Christianity Today*, 4 December 2000.

della Cava, Marco R. "Thomas Kinkade: Profit of Light; Painter/QVC Regular Says He's Divinely Inspired to Mass-Produce Works and Expand His Empire." *USA Today*, 12 March 2002.

No author. "Despite Elitist Gripes, He's America's Most Popular Artist." *The Chronicle of Higher Education*, 22 February 2002.

Doherty, M. Stephen. "Thomas Kinkade Shares his Light." *American Artist*, October 2001.

King, John. "Kinkade Scenes Come to Life: New Gated Subdivision in Vallejo Patterns Itself on Painter's Art." *San Francisco Chronicle*, 9 September 2001.

Kinkade, Thomas. *The Home You Made for Me: Celebrating a Mother's Love*. Nashville: Thomas Nelson, 2000.

——— with Tama Fortner. *A Father's Memories to His Child*. Nashville: Thomas Nelson, 2000.

_____ with Wendy Jean Katz. *Thomas Kinkade: Masterworks of Light*. United Kingdom: Little, Brown & Company, 2000.

Leland, John. "Subdivided and Licensed, There's No Place Like Art." *New York Times*, 4 October 2001.

Orlean, Susan. "Art for Everybody." *The New Yorker*, 15 October 2001.

Winston, Kimberly. "Bibles and Sacred Texts: We Need Them Now." *Publishers Weekly*, 15 October 2001.

ALIX LAMBERT

XLV Biennale di Venezia. *Aperto '93*. Milan: Giancarlo Politi Editore, 1993.

Bovier, Lionel, Elein Fleiss, and Glenn O'Brien. *Male Pattern Baldness*. Geneva: Galerie Art & Public, 1994.

Cotter, Holland. "Alix Lambert." *New York Times*, 18 September 1998.

Dannatt, Adrian. "Art" *Swing*, vol. 1 no. 7, 1995.

Lambert, Alix. *Tattoos by Alix*. Newton, New Jersey: Abaton Book Company. Edition 250. N.d.

———. "Project for *Bomb*." *Bomb*, winter 1993.

———. "Russian Prisoners in Perm and Samara, a Project by Alix Lambert." *Open City*, 2000.

———. "Super Spectacular." *Artbyte*, vol.3 no.1 May 2000.

Mattison, Mike. "D-I-V-O-R-C-E", *Artpaper*, vol. 12 no. 7, 1993.

Schaffner, Ingrid. *The Return of the Cadavre Exquis*. New York: The Drawing Center, 1993.

Verzotti, Giorgio. "Alix Lambert." *Art & Text*, no. 48 May 1994.

EVE ANDRÉE LARAMÉE

Berressem, Hanjo and Uwe Schwagmeier, ed. *From Mercator Projection to Freudian Phantasm: The Myth of the Hllow Earth in Literature, Science and Culture*. Amsterdam/New York. Rodopi 2002.

Crary, Johathan and Barbara Maria Stafford, Jennifer Riddel, Jessica Riskin. *Eve Andree Laramee: A Permutational Unfolding*. Cambridge, MA: MIT List Center for Visual art, 1999.

Harrison, Helen A. "Works of Curious, Conflicting Directions: Yves Fissiault: Artist of the Cold War Era." *New York Times*, 13 April 1997, Long Island edition.

Heon, Laura and John Ackerman. *Unnatural Science*. North Adams, MA: Mass MoCA 2000.

Laramée, Eve Andrée. "No Vacancy." *Journal of Contemporary Art 5*, no. 1 spring 1992.

———. "Only Questions." In *Interaction: Artistic Practice in the Network*. New York: Eyebeam/D.A.P., 2001.

———. "A Permutational Unfolding." *New Observations*, winter 1998.

———. "Process and Natural Phenomena as Conceptual Points of Departure in Extended Format Sculpture." *Leonardo* 18, no. 1 1985.

———. "Secret History: Yves Fissiault, Artist of the Cold War Era." CD-ROM. Published in conjunction with *From Mercator Projection to Freudian Phantasm: The Myth of the Hollow Earth in Literature, Science, and Culture*, edited by Hanjo Berressem and Uwe Schwagmeier. Amsterdam and New York: Rodopi, 2001.

SUGGESTED READINGS

Laramée, Eve Andrée and Lewis DeSoto. "Wandering." In *Innerscapes: An Anthology of Artists' Writings*, edited by Maurizio Pelligrin. Trieste, Italy: Trieste Contemporanea, 1998.

Oliveria, Nicholas, Nicola Oxley, Michael Petry. *Installation Art*. Washington D.C. Smithsonian Institution Press, London: Thames & Hudson. 1994.

Watkin, Mil. *Eve Andree Laramee: Apparatus for the Distillation of Vague Inuitions*. St. Louis: Forum for Contemporary Art. 1998.

Wilson, Steve. *Information Arts: Intersections of Art, Science and Technology*. Cambridge, MA: MIT Press. 2002.

Yapelli, Tina. *Cellular Memories*. San Diego: San Diego State University, 1996.

JULIAN LAVERDIERE

Ebony, David. "Towers of Light for New York City." *Art in America*, 11 November 2001.

Goodman, Wendy. "Manhattan Project." *New York Magazine*, Home Design / The Art of Living, 9 April 2001.

Gullbring, Leo. "Art-vertising." *Form*, November 2001.

Heiss, Alanna. "Presente." *Connaissance Des Arts*, June 2001.

Henry, Max. "Julian LaVerdiere at Andrew Kreps." *Art in America*, May 2000.

Johnson, Ken. "Julian LaVerdiere at Andrew Kreps." *New York Times*, Art in Review, 3 December 1999.

Moshowitz, Boris. "Julian LaVerdiere, Controlling Your Dreams." *Flash Art*, no. 219 summer 2001.

Muschamp, Herbert. "In Lights at Ground Zero Steps Toward Illumination." *New York Times*, 12 March 2002.

Myoda, Paul. "Art Direction." *artext*, May 2001.

Plagens, Peter. "Art in The Fast Lane." *Newsweek*, 1 April 2000.

Tanguy, Sarah. "Reconstructing History: A Conversation with Julian LaVerdiere." *Sculpture*, December 2001.

Vincent, Steven. "The Marvelous Inventor." *Modern Painters*, winter 2002.

MARCIA LYONS

The American Academy in Rome Annual Exhibition. New York: Cambridge University Press, 1997.

Boulbina, Seloua Luste, "Interieurement sur la peau" *La Liberation* (January 2003).

Hafemann, Gottfried. *Folie*. Weisbaden, Germany: Kunstverein, 1995.

Knerr, Erika. "N2blak Marcia Lyons." *Zing Magazine*, fall 1999.

Lyons, Marcia. "Munging Bodies:www.marcialyons.com" Centerfold, *BOMB* Summer, `97

Smith, Roberta. "Marcia Lyons." *New York Times*, 18 December 1999.

Walsh, Susan. "Marcia Lyons." *Artcritical.com*. <http://www.artcritical.com/SWLyons.htm>, December 2001.

Weintraub, Linda. "Marcia Lyons" *Tema Celeste*, March/April 2003.

MARCO MAGGI

Camaño, María Julia. "El Arte de las Sensaciones Tenues." *El País*, 10 January 1999.

Caniglia, Julie. "Marco Maggi, 123 Watts." *Artforum*, March 2001.

Haber, Alicia. "Un Artista Uruguayo del Mundo." *El País*, 30 January 2000.

———. "Marco Maggi: In Praise of the Imperceptible." *ARCO Noticias*, no. 18 September 2000.

Hackman, Kate. "A Dynamic Universe, Sprung from One Mind." *Kansas City Star*, 20 April 2001.

Hobbs, Robert. "Displaying Data: Micro, Macro, Marco (Maggi)." <http://www.microwave.com>, March 2002.

MacAdam, Barbara A. "The Microwave." *ARTnews*, April 2001.

di Maggio, Nelson. "Marco Maggi: Dibujante." *La Republica*, 22 November 2001.

Phillips, Patricia. *Waiting to Surface*. New York: 123 Watts Gallery, 1999.

Scott, Sue. "Using Mundane Materials for Minimalist Installations." *Downtown Express*, 19 December–1 January 2001.

Self, Dana. *Global Myopia*. Brochure. Kansas City, Missouri: Kemper Museum of Contemporary Art, 1996.

Weintraub, Linda. *Unending Beginnings: The Graphic Work of Marco Maggi*. New York: 123 Watts Gallery, 1997.

Wolgamott, L. Kent. "A Touch of Tech." *Universal*, 20 May 2001

DANIEL JOSEPH MARTINEZ

Arts Festival of Atlanta. *Conversation at the Castle: Changing Audiences and Contemporary Art*. Cambridge, Massachusetts: MIT Press, 1998.

Brenson, Michael. "Experience, Complicity and Quality." *Sculpture* 17, no. 9 1998.

Fusco, Coco. "My Kind of Conversation: The Public Artworks of Daniel J. Martinez." *Atlantica*, no. 15 1996.

Goldman, Shifra M. *Dimensions of the Americas: Art and Social Change in Latin America and the United States*. Chicago: University of Chicago Press, 1994.

Martinez, Daniel J., et al. *The Things You See When You Don't Have a Grenade!* Santa Monica, California: Smart Art Press, 1996.

———. *Points of Entry: Three Rivers Arts Festival*. Pittsburgh: Three Rivers Arts Festival, 1997.

Meyers, Holly. "This Show is Not Just Kids' Stuff." *Los Angeles Times*, 19 December 2001.

Motes, Andre A. "Diseccion de un Cocktail-Bomba." *PUB Magazine*, no. 3 2000.

Noriega, Chon A. "On Museum Row: Aesthetics and the Politics of Exhibition." *Daedalus* 128, no. 3 summer 1999.

Olson, Marisa S., ed. "Daniel Joseph Martinez: Without Anesthesia or This Isn't A Nice Neighborhood." *Camerawork: A Journal of Photographic Arts* 29, no. 2 fall/winter 2002.

Sherlock, Maureen. "Unruly Publica: Conversation at the Castle." *New Art Examiner*, December 1995–January 1996.

Strauss, David Levi. *Between Dog and Man*. Brooklyn: Autonomedia, 1999.

Trend, David. *the killer in me is the killer in you*. Santa Monica, California: Smart Art Press, 1998.

Weems, Marianne. *Art Matters: How the Culture Wars Changed America*. New York: NYU Press, 1999.

Wilkinson, Samantha. . Newcastle, U.K.: Locus +, 1996.

ARNALDO MORALES

Barragan, Paco. *El Arte Que Viene (The Art to Come)*. Madrid: Subastas Siglo XXI, 2001.

———. "Los Ciberobjectos de Arnaldo Morales." *Lapiz*, Ano XIX, no. 163 2000.

Benitez, Marimar. "Neurotic Imperatives: Contemporary Art from Puerto Rico." *Art Journal*, winter 1998.

Cullen, Deborah. "Arnaldo Morales." In *Ambiguo: Proyecto de Interferencia Cultural, No. 7*. San Juan: Caldo de Siete Potencias, 2000.

Florez, Fernando Castro. "Review ARCO 2000/Afinidades Electivas: Arnaldo Morales." *ARCO Noticias*, no. 18 September 2000.

Gutierrez, Enrique Garcia. "Arnaldo Morales y sus Maquinas Prodigiosas." *El Nuevo Dia*, 19 February 1995.

Juhasz-Alvarado, Charles. "Jaque-te-jaque." *Alto Riesgo: Electrobjetos de Arnaldo Morales*. San Juan: Museo de Historia, Antropologia y Arte de la Universidad de Puerto Rico, 1996.

Lezama, Manuel Alvarez. "Call Arnaldo Morales Weird, Crazy—and Talented." *San Juan Star*, 7 November 1993.

Marxuach, Michelle, *Espacios en Transicion – Transicion en espacios*. San Juan: Museo De Arte De Puerto Rico, 1998.

Roulet, Laura. *Contemporary Puerto Rican Installation Art: The Guagua Aerea, The Trojan Horse and the Termite*. San Juan: Editorial de la Universidad de Puerto Rico, 2000.

Sirmans, Franklin, *Arnaldo Morales Animalitica*. Exhibition brochure. New York and San Juan: De Chiara/Stewart Gallery and Galeria Botello, 1999

MARIKO MORI

Apocalypse - Beauty and horror in Contemporary Art", London: Royal Academy of the Arts, 2000.

Paul D. Miller. *Across the Morphic Fields: The Art of Mariko Mori*. Boston: New Histories, ICA, 1996. http://www.djspooky.com/articles/acrossthemorph.html

Bryson, Norman. "Cute Futures: Mariko Mori's Techno Enlightenment", *Parkett* no. 54, 1998-1999.

Cohen, Michael. "Mariko Mori: Plastic Dreams in the Reality Bubble." *Flash Art*, no. 194 May–June 1996.

Hanru, Hou, Hans-Ulrich Obrist, Mohsen Mostafavi. *Cities on the Move: Urban Chaos and Global Change: East Asian Art, Architecture and Film Now*. London: Vienna: Secession and Bordeaux: Musee d'art contemporain de Bordeaux 2001.

Ikiro-Be Alive: Contemporary Art From Japan 1980 to the Present. Otterlo, Netherlands: Kroller-Muller Museum, 2001.

Heartney, Eleanor. "Mariko Mori, In Search of Paradise Lost", *Art Press*. April, 2000.

Made in Japan, Tokyo: Shiseido Gallery 1996.

Magnan, Kathleen F. "The Cyber Chic of Mariko Mori." *Art Asia Pacific* 3, no. 2 1996.

Mariko Mori. Le Magasin, Grenoble: Centre National d'Art Contemporain de Grenoble,1996

Morgan, Robert c. "Kitsch Today" *Art Press* no. 217, October 1996.

Molon, Dominic, et al., *Mariko Mori*. Chicago: Museum of Contemporary Art; London: Serpentine Gallery, 1998.

Mori, Mariko with Yasumasa Morimura, Luigi Ontani, Tony Oursler, Andres Serrano *Appearance*. Verona: Charta 2000.

——— with Germano Celant, Shin'Ichi Nakazawa. *Mariko Mori: Dream Temple*. Milan: Fondazione Prada, 1999.

Concentrations 30: Mariko Mori, Play with Me. Dallas: Dallas Museum of Art and Tokyo: Gallery Koyanagi, 1997.

Van Tuyl, Gijs with Dominic Molon. *Mariko Mori - Esoteric Cosmos*. Wolfsburg, Germany: Kunstmuseum Wolfsburg, Ostfildern, Germany: Edition Cantz, 1999.

SHIRIN NESHAT

Bastais, Helena. *Shirin Neshat, Women of Allah: Photographies, Films, Videos*. Paris: Maison Européenne de la Photographie, 1998.

Bonami, Francesco with Shirin Neshat and Octavio Zaya. *Shirin Neshat*. Torino, Italy: Marco Noire Editore, 1997.

Danto, Arthur C. "Pas de Deux, en Masse: Shirin Neshat's Rapture," *The Nation*, vol. 268, no. 24. June 28, 1999.

Gagnon, Paulette, Shoja Azari, Atom Egoyan,. *Shirin Neshat*. Montréal : Musée d'art contemporain de Montréal, 2001.

Goldberg, Roselee with Giorgio Verzotti. *Shirin Neshat*. Verona: Charta, 2002.

Hasegawa, Yuko ; Octavio Zaya. *Shirin Neshat*. Kanazawa: Kanazawa Contemporary Art Museum, 2001.

Hassan, Salah. *Genders and Nations: Reflections on Women in Revolution*. Ithaca, New York: Johnson Museum, Cornell University, 1998.

Melkonian, Neery. *Turbulent*. New York: Whitney Museum of American Art at Philip Morris, 1998.

——— and Selene Wendt. *Shirin Neshat*. Oslo: Henie Onstad Kunstsenter, 1999.

Milani, Farzaneh. *Shirin Neshat*. Verona: Charta, 2001.

Naficy, Hamid, Ruth Noack, Gerald Matt. *Shirin Neshat*. Wein: Kunsthalle Wien; London: Serpentine Gallery, 2000.

Neshat, Shirin with Sherri Geldin and Bill Horrigan. *Shirin Neshat: Two Installations*. Columbus, Ohio: Wexner Center for the Arts, 2001.

Olivia, Achille Bonito. *Disidentico: Maschile Femminile e Oltre*. Palermo, Italy: Panepinto Arte, 1998.

Rondeau, James. *Shirin Neshat, Rapture*. Paris: Galerie Jerome, 1999.

Wallach, Amei. "Shirin Neshat: Striking a Balance Between Western and Islamic Values," *The New York Times*, November 21, 1999, Arts & Leisure

Zaya, Octavio. *Echolot*. Kassel, Germany: Museum Fridericianum, 1998.

———. *Transatlantico*. Canary Islands, Spain: Centro Atlantico de Arte Moderno, 1998.

SUGGESTED READINGS

CHRIS OFILI

Barker, Godfrey. "Ofili on a Roll." *ARTnews*, December 1999.

Collings, Matthew. *Blimey! From Bohemia to Britpop: The London Artworld from Francis Bacon to Damien Hirst*. London: 21 Publishing, 1997.

Elliott, David. Foreword to *About Vision, New British Painting in the 1990's*. Oxford: Museum of Modern Art, 1996.

Frankel, David S. et al. *Carnegie International, 1999/2000*. Pittsburgh: Carnegie Museum of Art, 1999.

Halle, Howard. "Dung Deal." *Time Out New York*, no. 216 11 November 1999.

Hansen, Henning Steen, ed. *NowHere*. Humblebaek, Denmark: Louisiana Museum of Modern Art, 1996.

Macritchie, Lynn. "Ofili's Glittering Icons." *Art in America*, January 2000.

McFadden, Robert. "Madonna Painting is Defaced in a Disputed Brooklyn Show." *New York Times*, 17 December 1999.

Miller, Paul D. "Deep Shit: An Interview with Chris Ofili." *Parkett*, no. 58 2000.

Newsome, Rachel, "Afro Daze", *Dazed and Confused* no. 48, 1998.

Price, Dick. *Young British Art: The Saatchi Decade*. London: Booth-Clibborn Editions, 1999.

Schimmel, Paul. *Public Offerings*. London: The Museum of Contemporary Art; Thames & Hudson, 2001.

Shone, Richard, et al. *Sensation: Young British Artists from the Saatchi Collection*. London: The Royal Academy of Arts in association with Thames & Hudson, 1997.

Schumacher Rainald, editor. *The Mystery of Painting*. Munich: Sammlung Goetz, 2001.

Stallabrass, Julian. *High Art Lite*. London and New York: Verso, 2000.

Vogel, Carol. "Inside Art." *New York Times*, 21 January 2000.

Worsdale, Godfrey and Lisa Corrin, Kodwo Eshun. *Chris Ofili.*. Southampton City Art Gallery, London: Serpentine Gallery 1998.

TONY OURSLER

Ardenne, Paul. "Tony Ourlser's Cruel Theater." *Art Press*, November 1997.

Avrilla, Jean-Marc. *Tony Oursler*. Bordeaux, France: Musée d'Art Contemporain de Bordeaux, 1997.

Balkehol, Bernhard, ed. *Tony Oursler: My Drawings*. Kassel, Germany: Kasseler Kunstverein, 1996.

Bumpus, Judith. "Video's Puppet Master." *Contemporary Visual Arts*, no. 15 1997.

DeJong, Constance. "Diary of a Talking Head." *Juxtapoz*, July–August 1999.

——— with Tony Oursler and Stephen Vitiello. *Fantastic Prayers*. New York: Dia Center for the Arts, 1999.

Goldner, Martina, Eckhard Schneider, and Thyrza Nichols Goodeve. *Videotapes, Dummies, Drawings, Photographs, Viruses, Heads, Eyes, & CD-Rom*. Hannover, Germany: Kunstverein, 1998.

Janus, Elizabeth and Gloria Moure, eds. *Tony Oursler*. Barcelona: Ediciones Poligrafia, 2001.

———. *Tony Oursler: White Trash and Phobic*. Geneva: Centre d'Art Contemporain; Berlin: Kunst-werke, 1993.

Kimmelman, Michael. "A Sculptor of the Air with Video." *New York Times*, 27 April 2001.

Malsch, Friedemann and Elizabeth Janus, eds. *Tony Oursler: Dummies, Clouds, Organs, Flowers, Watercolors, Videotapes, Altars, Performances and Dolls*. Frankfurt: Portikus Frankfurt; Strasbourg: Les Musées de la Ville de Strasbourg; Geneva: Centre d'Art Contemporain; Eindhoven: Stedelijk Van Abbe Museum, 1995.

Oursler, Tony with Mike Kelley. *Poetics Project*. Danville, California: Waterton Press, 1999.

Richard, Frances. "Like Water." *Parkett*, no. 47 1996.

Rothschild, Deborah. *Introjection: Mid-Career Survey 1976-1999*. Williamstown, Massachusetts: Williams College Museum of Art, 1999.

Tony Oursler. Valencia, Spain: Institut Valencià D'Art Modern, 2001.

Tony Oursler: The Darkest Color Infinitely Amplified. New York: Whitney Museum of American Art, 2000.

Tony Oursler: The Influence Machine. London: Artangel, 2001.

Weiermair, Peter with Alice Rubini and Simona Lodi, eds. *Tony Oursler*. Verona: Charta, 1998.

CHARLES RAY

Barron, Stephanie et al. *Made in California: Art, Image, and Identity, 1900-2000*. Los Angeles:Los Angeles County Museum of Art 2000.

Bonami, Francesco, Jose Lebrero Sals. Artificial: *Figuracions contemporanies*. Barcelona: Museu d'Art Contemporani de Barcelona 1998.

———. "Charles Ray: A Telephone Conversation." *Flash Art*, vol. 25 no. 165 summer 1992.

Charles Ray. Newport, California: The Newport Harbor Art Museum, 1990.

Charles Ray. Essay by Bruce W. Ferguson. Malmo, Sweden: Rooseum – Center of Contemporary Art, 1994.

Charles Ray. Essays by Paul Schimmel and Lisa Phillips. Los Angeles: The Museum of Contemporary Art; Zurich: Scalo Verlag, 1998.

Drohojowska-Philip, Hunter. "Charles Ray's Way." *LA Weekly*, April 15 1983.

Estep, Jan "Going Both Ways: An Interview with Charles Ray" *New Art Examiner*, July/August 1999

Kertess, Klaus. "Some Bodies," *Parkett*, no. 37 1993.

Knight, Christopher. "Charles Ray's Still Lifes." *Parkett*, no. 37 1993.

Schimmel, Paul. *Helter Skelter: L.A. Art in the 1990s*. Los Angeles: The Museum of Contemporary Art, 1992.

Schjeldahl, Peter. "Ray's Tack." *Parkett*, no. 37 1993.

Stafford, Barbara "Seeing Double: A Meditation on Errant Perception" *Art Issues*, Summer 1999.

Storr, Robert. "Charles Ray: Ghosts and Dolls" *Art Press*, July/August 1998.

———. "All For One and One For All." *Parkett*, no. 37 1993.

Vergne, Philippe & Bernard Blisten. *Au-dela du spectacle*. Paris: Centre Pompidou 2001.
———, ed. *Let's Entertain: Life's Guilty Pleasures*. Minneapolis: Walker Art Center 2000.

PIPILOTTI RIST

Babias, Marius. "The Rist Risk Factor: When Dreams Twitch Like Dying Fish." *Parkett*, no. 48 1996.
Colombo, Paolo. "Shooting Divas" *Parkett*, no. 48 1996.
Gellatly, Andrew, and Heiser, Jorg, "Just Add Water", *Frieze*, Issue 48, September/ October, 1999.
Harris, Jane. "Psychedelic, Baby: An Interview with Pipilotti Rist." *Art Journal*, winter 2000.
Kimmelman, Michael. "Pipilotti Rist." *New York Times*, 21 April 2000.
Lubelski, Abraham, Cosimo Ricatto, "Pipilotti Rist, Sylvie Fleury, Sophie Calle and Shirin Neshat", *NY ARTS Magazine*, July/August, Vol. 5, No. 7, 2000.
Myers, Terry R. "Pipilotti Rist: Grist for the Mill." artext, no. 61 1998.
Rist, Pipilotti. *Pipilotti Rist: Apricots along the Streets*. Zurich: Scalo Verlag, 2001.
——— with Elizabeth Bronfen and Hans Ulrich Obrist. *Pipilotti Rist*. London: Phaidon Press, 2001.
——— with Peggy Phelan, Hans Ulrich Obrist, Elizabeth Bronfen, *Pipilotti Rist*, Contemporary Artists Series. London: Phaidon Press, 2001.
———. *I'm Not the Girl Who Misses Much*, artist book, Stuttgart, Oktagon 1994/1996
———. *Sip My Ocean*, Chicago, Museum of Contemporary Art, 1996.
———. *Wild Walls*, Stedelijk Museum, Amsterdam, catalogue no.792, September 1995.
———. *Remake of the Weekend* Nationalgalerie im Hamburger Bahnhof, Museum fur Gegenwart-Berlin Staatliche Museen zu Berlin. 1998.
Seabrook, John, "Nobrow Culture: Why It's Become So Hard To Know What You Like", *The New Yorker*, September 20, 1999.
Solomon, Deborah. "Visual Poetry in the Spirit of a Rock Video." *New York Times*, 17 May 1998.
Ursprung, Philip. "Pipilotti Rist's Flying Room." *Parkett*, no. 48 1996.

MATTHEW RITCHIE

Berman, Jennifer. "Matthew Ritchi", *Bomb Magazine*, Spring, 1997.
Cotter, Holland. "Matthew Ritchie." *New York Times*, 24 November 2000.
Galison, Peter and Caroline Jones. "Theories and the Dead." *Parkett*, no. 61 2001.
Hunt, David. "When Worlds Collide." *Time Out New York*, 16 November 2000.
Jones, Ronald. "Matthew Ritchie." *Frieze*, no. 58 2001.
Kane, Mitchell. *Tt (Double T):A Working Model to Develop a Hybrid Product*. Exhibition catalogue. October 1999.
Kastner, Jeffrey, "The Weather of Chance: Matthew Ritchie and the Butterfly Effect", *Art/Text*, May-July, 1998.
Marcus, Ben, "The Last You Need to Know About Radio", *Parkett* No. 61, 2001.
Princenthal, Nancy. "The Laws of Pandemonium" *Art in America*, May 2001.
Rabinowitz, Cay Sophie. "Not Two, Not Three, Not Even Four Dimensions." *Parkett*, no. 61 2001.
Ritchie, Matthew. "Mapping the Millennium." *The New York Times Magazine*, 16 September 1999.
———. "The New City." artext, no. 65 1999.
———. *Big Story Cleveland*. Cleveland: Cleveland Center for Contemporary Art, 1999.
Smith, Roberta. "Matthew Ritchie." *New York Times*, 13 November 1998.
Wilson-Goldie, Karen. "Matthew Ritchie's Matrix: An Artist Re-creates the World in Seven Steps." *Black Book*, summer 2000.

MICHAL ROVNER

Adams, Parveen. "Drive to the Border: Bordering the Drive." *Death Drive*: Contemporary Art and Psychoanalysis Conference at the Tate Gallery, London, 1998.
Conkelton, Sheryl. "New Photography 10." *MoMA*, fall 1994.
Drohojowska-Philip, Hunter. "From Dislocation, Artistic Direction." *Los Angeles Times*, 15 June 1997.
Hanhardt, John G. "Inside the Surface: The Art of Michal Rovner." *Bohen Foundation*, January 1996.
Madoff, Henry and Sylvia Wolf, *Michal Rovner*. Chicago: Chicago Art Institute 1993.
Michal Rovner: One Person Game Against Nature, Jerusalem: The Israel Museum 1994.
Morris, Frances. *Artnow 10: Michal Rovner*. London: Tate Gallery, 1997.
Morrissey, Simon. "Reviews: Michal Rovner at Montage Gallery and Stephen Friedman Gallery, London." *Creative Camera*, no. 337 (December 1995–January 1996).
Nahas, Dominique. "Overhang: Michal Rovner at the Whitney Biennial." *D'Art International* 3, no. 2 Fall 2000.
Nessel, Jen. "Ghostly Visions." *ARTnews*, summer 2000.
Rerych, Zdenek. "The Real Way of Existence: Interview with Michal Rovner." *Atelier Magazine*, April 1993.
Riddel, Jennifer L. "Reviews: Michal Rovner at Rhona Hoffman Gallery." *New Art Examiner*, November 1995.
Rovner, Michal. "Portfolio." *Creative Camera*, no. 321 (April–May 1993).
Wolf, Sylvia with Michael Rush. *Michal Rovner: The Space Between*. Göttingen: Steidl Gerhard Druckerei und Verlag, 2002.
———. *Michal Rovner*. Chicago: Art Institute of Chicago, 1994.

WILLIAM SCHADE

Hall, Carolyn. *Sewn and Stuffed Art*. Garden City, New York: Doubleday & Company, 1974.

SUGGESTED READINGS

Kettlewell, James K. and Linda Weintraub. *The Wild Wonderful World of William B. Schade Paintings, Drawings, Sculpture, Prints, Books*. Curated by Marijo Dougherty. Albany: University Art Museum, State University of New York, 1999.

Schade, William. *The Chicken Machine*. 30 min. program for public television. Albany: Albany Institute of History and Art, 1978.

SKIP SCHUCKMANN

Bryan, Robert. "Such Interesting People: Speaking with the Earth." *Ojai Valley News*, 12 August 1987.

No by-line. "Earth Artist Skip Schuckmann to Carve His Niche in New York." *Ojai Valley News*, 27 August 1988.

Kelly, David. "Ventura County; Art of the Earth; Culture: Iconoclastic Ojai Artist Has Carved a Name for Himself—and a Home, in an Overgrown Ravine." *Los Angeles Times*, 4 Dec 2001.

Michael, Kay. "Through the Looking Glass: Flood Buster Answers Call." *Ojai Valley News*, 28 August 1985.

Simpson, Paul. "Kivas As Living Structure: Sweathouses and Kivas." N.p., March 1992.

Stanley, Don. "Floodbusters: As California's Shangri-La Braces for Disaster from Winter Rains, Help Takes Many Forms." *The Sacramento*, 1985.

Stone, David. "Rock Garden a Work of Art: Ojai Stone Taking Shape." *Ventura County Star*, 15 February 1989.

LORNA SIMPSON

Brockington, Horace, "Logical Anonymity: Lorna Simpson, Steve McQueen, Stan Douglas", The *International Review of African American Art*. vol. 15 no.3, 1999.

Collins, Lisa Gail. *The Art of History: African American Women Artists Engage the Past*. Rutgers University Press, 2002.

Fusco, Coco. "Lorna Simpson." *Bomb*, fall 1997.

Golden, Thelma, Chrissie Iles, and Kellie Jones. *Lorna Simpson*. London: Phaidon Press, 2002.

Heartney, Eleanor. "Figuring Absence." *Art in America*, December 1995.

Henry, Lisa. *I'm Thinking of a Place*. Exhibition brochure. Los Angeles: UCLA Hammer Museum, 2001.

hooks, bell. "Lorna Simpson:Waterbearer." *Artforum*, September 1993.

Marquardt-Cherry, Janet "B(l)ack Talk: African American Women's Confrontational Art", *Exposure*, vol. 22, 2000.

Simpson, Lorna, Sarah J. Rogers, Lorna Simpson: Interior/Exterior, Full/Empty. Wexner Center for the Visual Arts. Ohio State University, 1998.

Simpson, Lorna and Sarah J. Rogers. *Lorna Simpson: For the Sake of the Viewer*. Chicago: Museum of Contemporary Art, 1997.

Villaseñor, Maria Christina. "Lorna Simpson 'Nine Props': An Interview and Art Porfolio." *Paris Review*, spring 1996.

Wilkes, Andres. "Lorna Simpson" *Aperture*. No. 133, Fall 1993.

Willis, Deborah, ed. *Lorna Simpson: Untitled* 54. San Francisco: The Friends of Photography, 1992.

Zaya, Octgavio. "Towards a Reconsideration of the Artistic Practice? (Art and Politics in the United States)", *Balcon*. vol. 8-9 1992.

RIRKRIT TIRAVANIJA

Berwick, Carly. "While Some Live for Art, Others Live in It." *New York Times*, 8 August 1999.

Cameron, Dan. "Food for Thought." *Frieze*, no. 17 1994.

Flood, Richard and Rochelle Steiner. "En Route." *Parkett*, no. 44 1995.

Gillick, Liam. "Forget about the Ball and Get on with the Game." *Parkett*, no. 44 1995.

Hainley, Bruce. "Where Are We Going: And What Are We Doing? Rirkrit Tiravanija's Art of Living." *Artforum*, February 1996.

Joyce, Julie. "Rirkrit Tiravanija and Lincoln Tobier." *Art/Text*, no. 67 November 1999–January 2000.

Knight, Christopher. "L.A. Map Makes the Invisible Plain." *Los Angeles Times*, Art Reviews, 23 July 1999.

Kraynak, Janet "Rirkrit Tiravanija's Liability", *Documents*, fall, 1998.

Melo, Alexandre,"Guess Who's Coming to Dinner", *Parkett* no. 44 1995..

Saltz, Jerry. "A Short History of Rirkrit Tiravanija" *Art in America*, February 1996.

Siegel, Katy. "Rirkrit Tiravanija." *Artforum*, October 1999.

Smith, Roberta. "The Gallery is the Message." *New York Times*, 4 October 1992.

Stange, Raimar. "Ein/raümen, in der Hamburgen Kunsthalle." *Das Kunstbulletin*, no. 12 (2000).

Tiravanija, Rirkrit. Interview. *Documents*, no. 5 February 1994.

———. *Untitled 1998 (On the Road With Jiew Jeaw Jieb Sri and Moo)*. Philadelphia: Philadelphia Museum of Art, 1998.

———. "Rirkrit Tiravanija Talks with Peter Fischli and David Weiss." *Artforum*, October 1996.

——— with Sherri Geldin. *Supermarket*. Columbus, Ohio: Wexner Center for the Arts, 1999.

——— with Udo Kittelmann. *Untitled 1996: Tomorrow Is Another Day*. Koln, Germany: Salon-Verlag, 1998.

VICTORIA VESNA

Lovejoy, Margot, Christiane Paul, and Victoria Vesna, eds. *Context Providers: Conditions of Meaning in Digital Arts*. Cambridge, Massachusetts: MIT Press, forthcoming 2002–03.

Vesna, Victoria. "Agents and Avatars or Information Personae?" *Swets & Zweilinger: Digital Creativity* 9 (January–February 2000).

———. "Another Day in Paradise and Virtual Concrete: Installation and Telepresence Works." *Leonardo* 31, no. 1 (1998).

———. "Avatars in Cyberspace: Marketing the Descent." In the proceedings of Ars Electronica 1997: "Fleshfactor: Informationsmaschine Mensch" conference. Vienna: Springer Verlag (reprint translation to German), 1997.

———. "Community of People with No Time: Shifts in Identity and Collaboration." In *First Person: New Media as Story, Performance, and Game*, edited by Noah Wardrip-Fruin and Pat Harrigan. Cambridge, Massachusetts: MIT Press, 2002.

———. "Third Culture: Being in Between." In *Art, Technology, Consciousness*, edited by Roy Ascott. United Kingdom: Intellect, 2000.

———. "Towards a Third Culture: Being in Between." *Leonardo* 34, no. 2 (2001).

———. "Tracing Bodies of Information Overflow." In *The Body Caught in the Intestines of the Computer & Beyond*, edited by Marina Grzinic. Budapest, New York, Cologne: Festival of Computer Arts, 2000.

———. "Under Reconstruction: Architectures of Bodies INCorporated." In *Veiled Histories: The Body, Place and Public Art*, edited by Anna Novakov. New York: Critical Press, 1997.

———, et al., ed. *Terminals*. Book/CD-ROM. University of California: ICA, January-February 1999.

———, et al., ed. "Database Aesthetics: Issues of Organization and Category in Online Art." *AI & Society: The Journal of Human-Centered Systems and Machine Intelligence*, February–March 2000.

GILLIAN WEARING

Bourriaud, Nicolas. *Traffic*. Bordeaux: CAPC Musée d'Art Contemporain, 1998.

Collings, Matthew, *Blimey! From Bohemia to Britpop: The London Artworld from Francis Bacon to Damien Hirst*, London, 21 pub. 1997.

DeSalvo, Donna, Russell Ferguson, Ben Judd, Gregor Muir, John Slyce. *Gillian Wearing*. London: Phaidon Press, 1999.

Lyttelton, Celia. "Gillian Wearing." *The Now Art Book*. Tokyo: Shiseido and Korinsha Press, 1996.

Molon, Dominic with Barry Schwabsky. *Gillian Wearing: Mass Observation*. London: Merrell Publishers, 2002.

Morgan, Stuart, Neville Wakefield, Richard Flood. *Brilliant New Art from London!*. Minneapolis: Walker Art Center, 1996.

Muir, Gregor. "Gillian Wearing: Say What You Want." In *ID: An International Survey on the Notion of Identity in Contemporary Art*. Eindhoven, The Netherlands: Van Abbemuseum, 1996.

Romano, Gianni "Rien a Signaler", *Rien à Signaler*. Geneva: Galerie Analix B & L Polla, catalogue. 1994.

Royoux, Jean-Christ "Gillian Wearing: Violent Emotions are the Heart of the Matter" *Sous Influence*, catalogue. Paris. Musee d'Art Moderne de la Ville de Paris, 2001.

Wearing, Gillian, *Gillian Wearing: A Woman Called Theresa*. Hydra, Greece: Ophiuchus Collection, The Hydra Workshop, 1999.

———. *Gillian Wearing: Signs that Say What You Want Them to Say and Not Signs that Say What Someone Else Wants You to Say*. London: Interim Art, 1997.

———. *Gillian Wearing, 26.9—16.11.1997*. Vienna: Wiener Secession, Vereinigung Bildender Kunstler, 1997.

YUKINORI YANAGI

Amano, Taro. *Japanese Art after 1945: Scream Against the Sky*. Kanagawa, Yokohama Museum of Art, 1994.

Deitch, Jeffrey. *Border Crawl*. Seoul: Kukje Gallery, 1995.

Dompierre, Louise, Yuko Hasegawa. *The Age of Anxiety* Toronto, The Power Plant Contemporary Art Gallery 1995

Farver, Jane. *The World Flag Ant Farm*, New York, Lehman College Art Gallery, 1991.

———. *Yukinori Yanagi: Project Article 9*. New York, Queens Museum of Art, 1995.

Gumpert, Lynn. "Yukinori Yanagi: The Emperor on the Carpet." *ARTnews*, November 1995.

Koplos, Janet. "Testing Taboos." *Art in America*, October 1995.

Munroe, Alexandra. *Scream Against the Sky*. New York: Guggenheim Museum Soho, 1994.

———. "Wandering Position" *Flash Art* (international), March-April, 1992.

Obigane, Akio and Osamu Fukunaga. *Asian Art Now*. Hiroshima: Hiroshima City Museum of Contemporary Art, 1994.

Rubin, David S. *Old Glory*. Cleveland: Cleveland Center for Contemporary Art, 1994.

Schacter, Kenny. "Yukinori Yanagi." *Poliester* 6, no. 18 spring 1997.

Yanagi, Yukinori, *Yukinori Yanagi: Fieed Work on Alcatraz*, San Francisco, Capp Street Project, 1996.

ACKNOWLEDGEMENTS

"Acknowledge" is a neutral word that simply means notice. It carries none of the heartfelt qualifiers earned by those whose names appear as contributors to this writing venture. Thus, the first requirement in composing these acknowledgements involves amending the word "acknowledge" by attaching indicators of what is being acknowledged—their dedication, their intelligence, and their encouragement. Although their names only appear in these acknowledgements, their input is apparent on every page.

Since these credits are being offered chronologically, the first acknowledgement is offered to the many students who seemed more confused than delighted by the amorphous character of contemporary art, and more overwhelmed than inspired by the unsystematic nature of becoming an artist. These students asked me to extend the concept of "making" art to include how to "make" a contribution to culture, how to "make" the public aware of their efforts, how to "make" a career, how to "make" a judicious choice in formulating an artistic mission. This book was inspired by their request for guidance.

The task of fulfilling this mandate has been a team effort led by the artists whose remarkable achievements constitute individual chapters in this book. The forty who made the final cut were selected because they had not only enriched the current art scene, but they seemed best qualified to serve as role models for future generations of artists. Like characters in a novel, these extraordinary artists guided my writing.

Chronologically, the next contributors were five bright and energetic Oberlin College students. The text for this book reflects our intergenerational, cooperative relationship. Ry Russo-Young, Lauren Harkrader, and Zoe Feigenbaum were art studio majors. Their student status made them ideal contributors to this book's explorations of artists' lifestyles and careers, issues they would soon be confronting as graduates. Their desire for this guidance propelled the interviews they conducted with many of the artists represented in this book. These distinguished artists seemed to welcome the opportunity to share their experience with three such hopeful prospects for the future. They reported their triumphs and confessed their frustrations. Most importantly, they offered heartfelt advice. The resulting verbal self-portraits satisfy one of the essential missions of this book—they offer a diversity of creative options for constructing a career and surviving as an artist.

Two art history students, Caitlin Poliak and Meghan Karsh, directed their aptitude for conducting rigorous research to the tasks of compiling a bibliography, checking facts, and confirming references. Gathering, formatting, organizing information required frequent contact with artists and their gallerists. The cooperation they received is evidence of their professionalism.

Although my name appears as the author, writing this book was not a solo affair. It was fortified by no less than seven editors representing four distinct editorial perspectives. A grant from the McGregor Foundation and the support of Oberlin College provided the opportunity for students to assess the work of their professor. Ry, Lauren, and Zoe reviewed the entire manuscript, offering comments from the studio-art angle. Caitlin and Meghan provided feedback that reflected an art history approach. Each of their red marks was given credence as a means to bridge the generation gap that separates us. I am grateful for the opportunity to switch roles with these bright and determined students. Such prepublication feedback will hopefully benefit postpublication readers. It should also be noted that the title for this book was inspired by a student suggestion. *In the Making* is a variant of Lauren Harkrader's suggestion, *Making It*.

The next round of edits was provided by Lori Waxman, Managing Editor of D.A.P. She contributed the vantage point of a recent graduate who is fully versed in the vanguard art scene. In order to comply with her recommendations, I augmented, deleted, explained, rearranged, and clarified. Lori was a worthy critic and a compatible partner in determining all phases of preparation of this book. Besides editing, she was the publisher's representative in picture selection, design, marketing, and so forth. The final review was conducted by Eugenia Bell, copy editor, and Jackie McCarthy, proofreader.

The D.A.P. imprint is not just evident in the D.A.P. logo, but in the manner in which the book was guided from inception to fruition. D.A.P. founder and director Sharon Gallagher continually sought ways to optimize the book's potential. The process of guiding this book into the public domain benefited not only from her prescience, but from the complementary talents of her employees. This team is represented by, among others, Cory Reynolds, marketing director, and Avery Lozada, vice-president and trade sales director, as well as graphic designer Steven Mosier/THING. I am grateful to them all for being diligent taskmasters who respected the unusual mission of this book.

This book is a product of the rare opportunity to enter academe with a mandate to experiment. Funded by the Henry Luce Foundation and directed by Terry Lautz, this program provides opportunities to professors to initiate innovative pedagogical programs in colleges and universities. It is a privilege to conduct such an experiment at Oberlin College. I am particularly indebted to the Chairman of the Art Department John Pearson. I'd also like to thank my colleagues at Oberlin for the encouragement they provided throughout the writing process.

This work is a culmination of interests that accumulated over decades spent in the midst of the encouraging family atmosphere created by my husband Andy, my children Paula, Alec, and Carolyn, with the recent addition of their mates Dave, Susie, and Ed. All contributed to the lively discussions around our dinner tables that helped clarify my professional mission and support the long procession toward its completion. Likewise, one friend in particular served as a valued sounding board. Skip Schuckmann permitted no statement to go unchallenged. I am grateful to them all.

—Linda Weintraub

ACKNOWLEDGEMENTS / COPYRIGHT

MAKING CONTEMPORARY ART:
How Today's Artists Think and Work

Editor: Lori Waxman
Design and typesetting: Steven Mosier/THING
Copyeditor: Eugenia Bell
Proofreader: Jackie McCarthy
Typeface: Fedra Sans Designed by Peter Bilak, http://www.typotheque.com
Printed by: Oceanic Graphic Printing, China

First published in the United Kingdom in 2003 by Thames & Hudson Ltd,
181A High Holborn, London WC1V 7QX

www.thamesandhudson.co.uk

British Library Cataloguing-in-Publication Data
A catalogue record for this book is available from the British Library

ISBN 0-500-284237